D0083679

VICTIMS OF CRIME

We dedicate this book to the millions of persons throughout the world who have been victimized by crime. We hope that the book sheds light on their experiences. We also hope that it inspires people to pursue the important work of helping crime victims and their loved ones rebuild their lives.

3rd Edition
Victims of Crime

ROBERT C. DAVIS
RAND Corporation

ARTHUR J. LURIGIO
Loyola University, Chicago, IL

SUSAN HERMAN
Pace University, New York City

EDITORS

SAGE Publications
Los Angeles ▪ London ▪ New Delhi ▪ Singapore

Copyright © 2007 by Sage Publications, Inc.

All rights reserved. No part of this book may be reproduced or utilized in any form or by any means, electronic or mechanical, including photocopying, recording, or by any information storage and retrieval system, without permission in writing from the publisher.

For information:

Sage Publications, Inc.
2455 Teller Road
Thousand Oaks, California 91320
E-mail: order@sagepub.com

Sage Publications Ltd.
1 Oliver's Yard
55 City Road
London EC1Y 1SP
United Kingdom

Sage Publications India Pvt. Ltd.
B-42, Panchsheel Enclave
Post Box 4109
New Delhi 110 017 India

Printed in the United States of America

Library of Congress Cataloging-in-Publication Data

Victims of crime / Robert C. Davis, Arthur J. Lurigio, Susan Herman [editors].—3rd ed.
    p. cm.
Includes bibliographical references and index.
ISBN-13: 978-1-4129-3656-9 (cloth)
ISBN-13: 978-1-4129-3657-6 (pbk.)

   1. Victims of crimes—United States. I. Davis, Robert C. (Robert Carl) II. Lurigio, Arthur J. III. Herman, Susan.

HV6250.3.U5V54 2007
362.880973—dc22

                        2006030622

This book is printed on acid-free paper.

08   09   10   11   10 9 8 7 6 5 4 3 2

Acquisitions Editor:	Jerry Westby
Editorial Assistant:	Kim Suarez
Production Editor:	Denise Santoyo
Copy Editor:	Mary L. Tederstrom
Typesetter:	C&M Digitals (P) Ltd.
Indexer:	Pam VanHuss
Cover Designer:	Candice Harman

Contents

Foreword

During my 20 years as a prosecutor, I learned to listen closely to victims. They had, after all, witnessed the crimes I was prosecuting. They knew what had happened to them, and I could seldom win a case without their help. Listening to their stories armed me with facts and also pulled me into their lives—forever changed by crime. I saw that for victims, even a quick conviction might never "close" the case.

I also learned that if I did my job well, I could help victims recover from the crimes that had disrupted their lives. If I took them seriously, treated them with respect, and made sure they could locate the right services, I could help victims regain the sense of control that crime steals from them. I watched victims—with the help of advocates, counselors, domestic violence networks, and a host of other experts—exercise their rights, grow in strength, and learn how to stay safe—while helping us win convictions. By trial and error, I was learning what victims can teach criminal justice professionals.

While I was learning how to work with victims, formal research on victimization was expanding dramatically. Researchers were discovering the psychological impact of crime—from posttraumatic stress disorder to a loss of balance and control. They were tracing the links between crimes—such as domestic violence and stalking or bullying and dating violence—and showing why crisis intervention services can help build cases

while rebuilding lives. They were showing why involving victims in the criminal justice system deepens their commitment to the process, helps law enforcement and prosecutors, and helps prevent future crime. In short, research has shown that the more we know about victimization, the more successfully we can prosecute crimes and help victims rebuild their lives.

Such research provides both inspiration and solid ground for the work of victim advocacy organizations, such as the National Center for Victims of Crime, where I now serve as executive director. We have learned from victims and other advocates—as well as from research—how crimes such as stalking can paralyze victims. We know that stalking, often linked to domestic violence, can lead to murder. We understand that laws must keep pace with the advances in technology—such as global positioning systems and spyware—that stalkers use to pursue their victims. And we know that communities must mobilize to protect victims, both before stalkers are convicted and after they leave prison. Only such comprehensive efforts can combat this disturbing crime.

We are also learning how financial crimes such as identity theft can devastate victims, robbing them of resources, homes, and financial security. Victims must complete a bewildering set of tasks to clear their names: notifying creditors and credit bureaus and even convincing law enforcement that they are who they say they are. Through both research and practice, we are grasping the urgent need to ease these burdens while finding better ways to solve these crimes.

No matter what we are seeking to achieve—better approaches to domestic violence, dating violence, elder abuse and exploitation, hate crimes, or terrorism—the exciting research in this volume will guide and light our way. This edition of *Victims of Crime* makes the latest research on victimization accessible to all readers and offers a promising roadmap for our field.

—Mary Lou Leary
Executive Director, National Center for Victims of Crime

Acknowledgments

W e would like to thank the following reviewers for their time in reviewing this current edition of the book:

Lynn Jones
Northern Arizona University

Joseph Carlson
University of Nebraska at Kearney

Laura Dugan
University of Maryland

Mitzy Mahoney
Sam Houston State University

Sue Cote
California State University, Sacramento

Catherine A. Gallagher
George Mason University

1

Introduction to *Victims of Crime*

The Interaction of Research and Practice

MARLENE A. YOUNG

SUSAN HERMAN

ROBERT C. DAVIS

ARTHUR J. LURIGIO

The real use of all knowledge is this, that we should dedicate it to the use and advantage of man.

Sir Francis Bacon

Perhaps no field has demonstrated the truth of the above comment more than the area of victimology and victim assistance. From the field's inception in the United States and in the rest of the world, theory and research have interacted closely in the study of crime victims and the establishment of programs and policies to assist victims and ensure that they are treated with dignity, compassion, and justice. In particular, three types of research have been significant in this interaction. The first documents the scope and nature of criminal victimization and is known as measurement research. The second examines the impact of victimization and has increasingly incorporated research from traumatology. The third centers on the role of victims in the criminal justice process.

MEASUREMENT RESEARCH

Beginning in 1972, the National Crime Victimization Survey (NCVS), conducted by the Bureau of the Census and the Bureau of Justice Statistics, has provided basic data on victimization rates, the demographic characteristics of victims, and the consequences of victimization. Although the survey has produced crude indicators of many aspects of victimization, NCVS data have focused critical attention on victims and their attributes. Early studies of victims and witnesses, such as Cannavale and Falcon (1976), helped develop victim and witness programs and heighten interest in the relationships among victims, law enforcement officers, prosecutors, judges, and members of the general public.

Over the past thirty years, numerous other victim surveys have broadened our knowledge about who is being victimized and how. Needs assessments are conducted in virtually all victim service programs and help service providers to better direct their efforts and resources. At the same time, researchers have recognized that victims should be involved in both the design and implementation of such surveys. "New" definitions of crimes or kinds of crime, such as bullying, hate or bias crime, identity theft, stalking, and cybercrime have recently been highlighted. In addition, the effects of crime on certain vulnerable populations, such as the elderly, teens, specific cultural minorities, or people with disabilities, are now being seriously studied. As Fattah (1991) noted, victimological surveys belong to the "most exciting developments in criminology."

RESEARCH ON THE TRAUMA OF VICTIMIZATION

Although many early victim assistance programs and victim advocates placed primary importance on more sensitive treatment for victims in the criminal justice system, their work quickly led them to the conclusion that better treatment went beyond simply changing laws or lending support during court proceedings. This observation was underscored by the fact that 80% of crimes never result in an arrest, and 90% of crimes are never prosecuted. Another question arose: What kind of assistance could be offered to all victims whether the criminal justice system was involved in their case or not? Research by Burgess on rape trauma syndrome and Walker on the battered woman syndrome encouraged investigators to examine more closely the traumatic effects of crime on psychological well-being and adjustment.

Crisis intervention services were incorporated into many programs and emphasized three elements: providing victims with a restored sense of safety and security, giving them an opportunity to tell their story of the event with appropriate reassurance and a validation of their emotional reactions, and helping them solve their immediate problems in the aftermath of the event. These lessons were learned by victim practitioners in their everyday work and affirmed by research from the mental health field. The lessons also led in 1980 to the reformulation of post-traumatic stress disorder (PTSD), as described in the third edition of the American Psychiatric Association's *Diagnostic and Statistical Manual of Mental Disorders* (*DSM*).

In the next twenty years, research exploded on two topics, the short-term psychological effects of crises and the long-term mental health impact of trauma. Many of those studies were clinical in nature. Many were also longitudinal studies of specific populations and in-depth interviews of victims, which refined the way practitioners deliver crisis intervention and other types of victim services. Research has taught providers that painful feelings can resurface with the recall of an event. Hence victim advocates argued that people interviewing victims in the health care or criminal justice systems should possess crisis intervention skills. Research also highlighted the need for long-term psychological services for crime victims.

The description of PTSD in the *DSM-IV* in 1994, which included the subjective perception of the person exposed to a traumatic event, resulted in two critical insights for victim assistance providers. The first confirmed what most practitioners were witnessing among their clients: Not all crime victims suffer a major aftershock from crime. Indeed, it is likely that most do not. Therefore it is important to reevaluate the essential elements of victim service programs. The lesson here was that the central feature of the impact of crime for most victims was a sense that they had lost control over their lives.

The second insight followed from the first. The more an intervener could do to help reestablish that sense of control, the more quickly victims could regain mastery over their lives. In many cases, this meant an emphasis on practical interventions, such as replacement or repair of property, emergency financial assistance, financial compensation or restitution, and helpful reassurance. Surveys of victim needs confirmed this insight. In other cases, this meant finding a positive way to get involved with their case or taking practical action to prevent being revictimized. Surveys not only suggested the therapeutic value that arose from victims' participation in various stages of the judicial system but also indicated the value of crime prevention activities forming an integral component of victim assistance. Research on repeat victimization has strengthened this view among practitioners.

ROLE OF VICTIMS IN THE CRIMINAL JUSTICE PROCESS

The growing body of research on victims, combined with the advocacy of a growing

victims field, created a new focus on victims within the criminal justice system. Several studies, beginning in the 1970s, found that victims are interested in information about their court cases and that the criminal justice system could benefit from treating victims more compassionately. In addition, many victims wanted their voices to be heard in the adjudication process. Both state and the federal governments enacted laws that accorded victims substantial rights to notification and participation. Thirty years later, victims across the country have the right to notice of critical stages in the criminal justice process, to speak or present written statements at sentencing or parole hearings, and to receive restitution.

THIS VOLUME

The tradition of victim research has encouraged efforts to improve the treatment of crime victims through concrete laws and policies and effective services. As information on the impact of victimization becomes more available and as the definition of crime and victimization expand to address issues of terrorism, genocide, transnational crime, human trafficking, and technological crime, research can continue to enrich our understanding of how we can best identify, respond to, and alleviate human suffering.

The contributions in this volume build on the traditions of measurement research, research on victim trauma, and research on the role of victims in the criminal justice process. Some contributions to this third edition of *Victims of Crime* update, expand, and provide a deeper understanding of topics that appeared in the earlier two editions. Other contributions present new topics, reflecting the dynamic changes that are always occurring in the field of victimization.

We divided the volume into two sections. Selections in the first part summarize research on the prevalence of various types and consequences of victimization. Finkelhor

elucidates the field of developmental victimology, which encourages a comprehensive
understanding of crimes against children and
adolescents. He describes the nature and
extent of victimization across the developmental span of young persons. Finkelhor crit-
icizes lifestyle and routine activities theories
as limited perspectives for exploring the victimization of children, and he presents developmental victimology as a comprehensive
framework for explaining the causes and
effects of victimization in childhood and
adolescence. He also suggests specific lines of
inquiry to expand our understanding of juvenile victims of crime.

O'Sullivan and Fry examine the prevalence
and emotional consequences of sexual
violence from infancy to adulthood. They
describe how service providers, trying to lend
assistance to victims, can unwittingly cause
them more distress. They discuss emerging
topics such as commercial child sexual
exploitation, sex trafficking, marital rape,
and rape in prisons. They conclude by summarizing promising new initiatives to support
the reporting of sexual assaults and facilitate
the prosecution of sex traffickers.

Buzawa's contribution on intimate partner
violence provides a comprehensive overview
of the problem. She examines the social,
legal, and research definitions of intimate
partner violence and discusses its prevalence
in the United States. In addition, Buzawa
explores the pernicious effects of intimate
partner violence on various subgroups of victims, which are defined along racial, ethnic,
and sociodemographic lines. As the author
notes, the consequences of intimate partner
violence include financial difficulties, psychological damage, physical injuries, and death.

Tjaden writes about stalking—a topic only
recently explored through extensive research
on both victims and perpetrators. Tjaden
reviews the development of legal responses to
stalking in America. She notes that all fifty
states and the federal government have

passed legislation that criminalizes stalking.
She also discusses research that demonstrates
stalking is more prevalent than previously
suspected and describes what we know about
how it affects victims.

McDevitt, Farrell, Rousseau, and Wolff
argue that, as a nation founded on tolerance
for group differences, hate crimes threaten
our core democratic principles. State and
federal legislation designed to measure the
prevalence of hate crime and to create additional penalties for such offenses have raised
public awareness about the problem. However,
as with financial crimes, there is a paucity of
rigorous scientific research on the prevalence
of crimes against different groups or the
effects of these crimes on individuals.

Thompson's chapter on the families of
homicide victims points out that, while there
is a vast amount of research on crime victims,
scanty attention has been given to the impact
of violence on secondary or indirect victims.
Thompson describes what we know about
the psychological, emotional, and behavioral
effects of homicide on families and how
social support, coping styles, and other
resources can help mitigate the ordeal of losing a loved one and dealing with the criminal
justice process.

Deem, Nerenberg, and Titus discuss one
of the categories of victims that has so far
received little attention—victims of financial
crimes—fraud, cybercrimes, and identity
theft. As the authors point out, victims of
financial crimes are critically underserved; in
fact, we have little information on the scope
of the problem. The authors argue that novel,
proactive approaches are needed to help
victims recover losses, hold perpetrators
accountable, alleviate the adverse consequences
of financial crimes, and prevent future victimization.

DiMaggio and Galea discuss the adverse
effects of natural and unnatural disasters,
focusing on the psychological harm caused
by terrorist attacks, especially September 11,

2001, and its impact on victims, rescuers, and direct witnesses involved in the tragedy. They explore, in depth, the correlates, symptoms, and treatment of PTSD and highlight a few of the methodological and research issues that complicate studies on the effects of terrorist acts and other traumatic events. They also examine the characteristics of disaster victims that promote recovery.

Heisler's chapter focuses on elder abuse, a problem that looms larger and results in greater costs to society as the American population ages. The chapter notes that elder abuse can assume several forms: physical harm, emotional damage, financial exploitation, neglect, and abandonment. The author presents brief case studies of each type. Her contribution also discusses the risk factors and indicators of elder abuse, relevant federal and state statutes, and promising programs to address its consequences.

Snowden and Lurigio focus on one particularly understudied and highly vulnerable group of crime victims: persons with mental illness. As they note, rates of victimization among the mentally ill are higher than those found in the general population. Among the mentally ill, the authors review investigations of the prevalence of criminal victimization, the likelihood of reporting crime, the correlates of victimization, and the adverse effects of crime. The chapter ends with a brief discussion of the limitations of research on this topic and the paucity of specialized programs for mentally ill crime victims.

Stein's chapter reviews survey research on peer-to-peer and other forms of sexual harassment in schools. Stein also explores the relationship between sexual harassment and bullying and analyzes the failure to consider the role of gender in our current discourse about bullying.

Daigle, Fisher, and Guthrie describe research on repeat victimization—the tendency for persons victimized once to be victimized again. Their chapter discusses the

prevalence of repeat victimization and what is known about the reasons why some persons suffer multiple victimizations. They also describe promising programs designed to reduce repeat victimizations for crimes as different as burglary and sexual assault.

To round out the first section, Alvazzi de Frate discusses the use of victimization surveys in countries in all parts of the world. Her chapter describes the growing reliance on international victim surveys, the importance of understanding the context of crime and the methodologies of each survey, and the many applications of this research.

The theme of the second section is on various ways to promote recovery from criminal victimization and a return to normal functioning. The section begins with Roberts and Green, who present an overview of the field of crisis intervention. They discuss crisis theory, innovations, and best practices in the field. They describe several crisis intervention models and show how an individual case might be handled using one of the models.

Davis describes the important role that family, friends, and neighbors play in helping victims readjust in the aftermath of crime. His chapter notes that, while help from professionals is necessary for some victim needs, many victim needs are both mundane and immediate, and it is here that those close to victims are in a position to lend assistance. The chapter also observes that, while research suggests that those who support victims often incur costs, they are overwhelmingly glad they helped and would do so again.

The next two chapters highlight different aspects of victim rights. Erez and Roberts discuss victim participatory rights and explore the continuing debate surrounding victims' claim to have a voice in criminal proceedings. They summarize important participatory reforms and consider arguments for and against victim participation in sentencing. They note that research has indicated that the right to participate in proceedings is important to many crime victims and—contrary to fears in the legal community—does not appear to affect court dispositions and sentences. Howley and Dorris trace the history of victim rights in America, documenting the wide array of participatory rights, the uneven implementation of these rights, and the difficulty of enforcing victim rights across the country.

Muscat and Walsh's chapter focuses on underserved populations of crime victims in the United States. Such victims consist of the homeless, ethnic and sexual minorities, persons with disabilities, and individuals who live in remote rural areas. For each category, the authors review the prevalence of victimization, the special needs of underserved victims, and barriers that they face when seeking resources. They also point to the pressing demand for additional, and more sensitive, services to meet the needs of underserved victims of crime.

This volume is designed to appeal to scholars, criminal justice practitioners, and government officials alike. For that matter, we hope it is of interest to anyone who wants to understand what we know about the experience of victims of crime. Our hope is that this compilation of research will not only inform the evolving field of victim assistance, but also serve as a catalyst for greater understanding of the needs and concerns of victims of crime throughout our criminal justice and social service systems.

REFERENCES

Cannavale, F. J., & Falcon, W. D. (Eds.). (1976). *Witness cooperation.* Lexington, MA: Lexington Books.

Fattah, E. A. (1991). *Understanding criminal victimization: An introduction to theoretical victimology.* Scarboro, Ontario: Prentice Hall Canada.

SECTION I

Crime and Its Impact

2

Developmental Victimology

The Comprehensive Study of Childhood Victimizations

DAVID FINKELHOR

In this chapter, I sketch the outlines of the field of developmental victimology. It is a field intended to help promote interest in and understanding of the broad range of victimizations that children suffer from and to suggest some specific lines of inquiry that such an interest should take. In promoting this holistic field, I contend that the problem of juvenile victimization can be addressed in many of the same comprehensive and conceptual ways that the field of juvenile delinquency has addressed the problem of juvenile offending.

The field of juvenile delinquency stands as a monument to social science, one of its most mature, theoretically and empirically developed domains. By contrast, despite substantial research on specific child victimization topics such as child abuse or child sexual assault, there is no similarly integrated and theoretically articulated interest that characterizes the field of juvenile victimization. In comparison to juvenile delinquency, juvenile victimization has much less theory about who gets victimized and why, much less solid data about the scope and nature of the problem, many fewer longitudinal and developmental studies that look at the "careers" of victimized children, and much less evaluation

Author's Note: The author wishes to thank Richard Ormrod and Stephanie Halter for their help with data analysis and computation and Kelly Foster for her help with preparing this manuscript.

For the purposes of compliance with Section 507 of PL 104–208 (the "Stevens Amendment"), readers are advised that 100% of the funds for this program are derived from federal sources (U.S. Department of Justice). The total amount of federal funding involved is $353,233.

to ascertain the effectiveness of policies and programs that respond to juvenile victims.

These deficiencies are ironic for a variety of reasons. For one thing, children are among the most highly victimized segments of the population (Hashima & Finkelhor, 1999). They suffer from high rates of the same crimes and violence adults do, and then they suffer from much victimization specific to childhood such as child abuse and neglect. Second, victimization has enormous consequences for children, derailing normal and healthy development trajectories. It can affect personality formation, have major mental health consequences, impact on academic performance, and also is strongly implicated in the development of delinquent and antisocial behavior (Margolin & Gordis, 2000). It is clear that because of several factors, such as children's special developmental vulnerability to victimization, its differential character during childhood, and the presence of specialized institutions to deal with it (such as child protection agencies), the victimization of children and youth deserves both more attention and specialized attention within the larger fields of criminology, justice studies, and even developmental psychology. This chapter addresses a variety of issues: how to define and categorize juvenile victimizations, what is known about the epidemiology of child victimization in broad terms, and how victimization changes across the developmental span of childhood.

DEFINITIONAL ISSUES

The interpersonal victimization of concern to developmental victimology is a special kind of negative life experience that stands apart from other life events. This victimization can be defined as harms that occur to individuals because of other *human actors* behaving in ways that *violate social norms*. The human agency and norm violation components give victimizations a special potential for traumatic impact. It is different from other stresses and traumas, such as accidents, illnesses, bereavements, and natural disasters. Even though we sometimes refer to "victims of hurricanes," "cancer victims," or "accident victims," the more general referent for the term *victimization* is interpersonal victimization. In interpersonal victimization, issues of malevolence, betrayal, injustice, and morality are much more present than is the case for accidents, diseases, and natural disasters. To a large extent, moreover, interpersonal victimizations engage a whole special set of institutions and social responses that are missing in other stresses and traumas: police, courts, agencies of social control, and other efforts to reestablish justice and mete out punishments.

Although this area is the traditional domain for the field of criminology, one reason why traditional criminology may not have fully explored its childhood dimensions is that child victimizations do not map neatly onto conventional crime categories. Although children do suffer from all the crimes that adults do, many violent and deviant behaviors by human actors that harm children are ambiguous in their status as crimes. The physical abuse of children, although technically criminal, is not frequently prosecuted and generally is handled by a different set of social control agencies from the police and criminal courts. Peer assaults, unless very serious or occurring among older children, are generally ignored by the official criminal justice system.

To encompass these complexities, I have proposed that the victimization of children be defined as including three categories: (1) conventional crimes in which children are victims (rape, robbery, assault), which I will call "crimes"; (2) acts that violate child welfare statutes, including some of the most serious and dangerous acts committed against children, such as abuse and neglect, but also some less frequently discussed topics such as the exploitation of child labor—which I will call "child maltreatment"; and (3) acts that would clearly be crimes if committed by adults against adults, but by convention, are not generally of concern to the criminal justice system when they occur among or against children. These would include sibling violence and assaults between preadolescent peers, and those that might be termed "noncriminal juvenile crime equivalents," which I will call "noncrimes."

Each of these categories is a complex domain, but each has its stereotypical forms, which sometimes help and at other times hinder thinking about the category. When the public thinks of crimes against children, what stands out are stranger abductions and extrafamily child molestations, situations of adults threatening children in which the proper domain of protective and retributive action is clearly the police, courts, and criminal justice system. When the public thinks of child maltreatment, they tend to think of parents abusing or neglecting parental responsibilities, and the appropriate domains of intervention are family courts, social work, and mental health remedies. The public also is aware that there is noncriminal violence against children, and they think of peer assaults, offenses that would be handled by parents or school authorities.

Different as their stereotypes may be, however, these are not neat and distinct categories; there is substantial overlap. Child maltreatment is sometimes treated as criminal, sometimes not (Figure 2.1). Child molesting, for example, is often considered as both a crime and a child welfare violation. The same act of peer assault that might result in an arrest in one jurisdiction may be treated as a "noncrime" for parents or school authorities to sort out in another jurisdiction. Moreover, there are normative shifts that are in progress (illustrated by arrows in Figure 2.1). Sibling sexual assaults once may have been viewed as neither crimes nor child maltreatment, but increasingly they are being handled by criminal justice and child welfare authorities. The

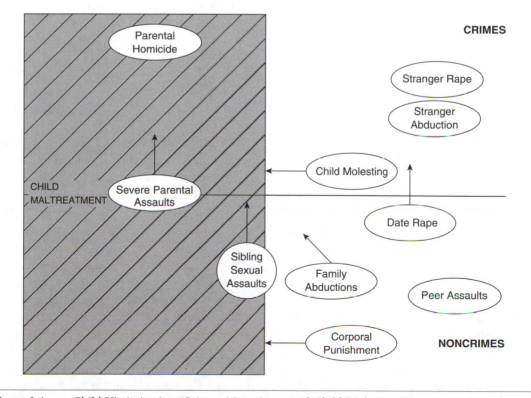

Figure 2.1 Child Victimization: Crimes, Noncrimes, and Child Maltreatment

abduction of children by family members is increasingly being viewed as both a crime and child maltreatment.

The category of "noncriminal juvenile crime equivalents" is one that often creates confusion or draws objections. Some might see it as a watering down of the concepts of "victim" or "crime" to include acts such as peer or sibling assault among children. But it is difficult to deny the functional equivalence, for example, between one adult hitting another, say, in a bar, and one child hitting another, say, on a playground. To study victimization in a developmental fashion, we must look at functionally equivalent acts across the life span, even if the social labels placed on the acts change as the participants get older. The cultural assumption is that these acts are less serious or less criminal when they occur at earlier ages. Whether and how these acts are different should really, however, be a matter of empirical investigation. When studied, violence between younger children has not been found to be less physically or psychologically injurious (Finkelhor, Turner, & Ormrod, in press). Understanding the basis for the social construction of victimization across the span of childhood should in fact be one of the key challenges for developmental victimology.

An even more problematic type of juvenile crime equivalent, however, is spanking and corporal punishment, which is a form of violence (defined as acts intended to cause physical pain) and would be considered an assault among adults. But corporal punishment is not just typically viewed as minor victimization but is actually viewed as salutary and educational by many segments of society. Because our definition of victimization requires the violation of social norms, forms of normatively accepted corporal punishment may not qualify. However, there are signs that a normative transformation is in progress regarding corporal punishment (Greven, 1990). A majority of states have banned all

its forms in schools, several Scandinavian countries have outlawed spanking even by parents, and the American Academy of Pediatrics has officially opposed spanking. Social scientists have begun to study it as a form of victimization with short- and long-term negative consequences (Strassberg, Dodge, Pettit, & Bates, 1994; Straus, 1994). Some have argued that it is the template on which other violent behavior gets built. Clearly, a developmental victimology needs to take account of corporal punishment, and spanking in particular, although it may deserve individualized theoretical and empirical treatment.

Another somewhat problematic category in developmental victimology concerns indirect victimizations, situations in which children witness or are closely affected by the crime victimization of a family member or friend. These include children who are first-hand witnesses to spouse abuse (Jaffe, Wolfe, & Wilson, 1990; Wolak & Finkelhor, 1998), who are deprived of a parent or sibling as a result of a homicide (Kilpatrick, 1990), or who are present but not injured in playground massacres or the public killing of a teacher (Nader, Pynoos, Fairbanks, & Frederick, 1990), all situations that have been studied by researchers. Although indirect victimization affects adults as well as children, the latter are particularly vulnerable to effects, due to their dependency on those being victimized. Because most of the acts creating indirect victimizations are crimes, these situations could be readily categorized in the "crime" category, but some, such as the witnessing of marital assault, also are treated as child welfare violations in which the child is seen as a direct, not indirect, victim.

A new domain in developmental victimology in recent years focuses on the topic of Internet victimization. Three kinds of diverse offenses have been subsumed under this rubric: (1) Internet sex crimes and solicitations for such crimes, (2) unwanted exposure to pornography, and (3) harassment and cyber-bullying (Wolak, Mitchell, & Finkelhor, 2006). When adults solicit underage youth for sexual activities or even online interactions, it falls in the category of conventional crime. But although youth receive an apparently large quantity of online sexual solicitations, it is difficult to assess how much of this is from adults and involves individuals who are aware of the underage character of their targets. The Internet has also created an enormous exposure of young people to inadvertent and unwanted sexual material, but although offensive to many youth and parents, it is not yet clearly defined as a crime or child welfare problem, in part because the harm element has not been clearly established. Harassment and cyber-bullying appear to be fairly straightforward extensions of conventional bullying behavior into the realm of electronic communication and are therefore the easiest to categorize. It is still early to fully understand how the development of a large electronic communications environment will alter the conception of or risk for victimization.

Another problematic category for developmental victimology is the one that includes mass victimizations, class victimizations, and institutional and policy victimizations. Warfare and generalized ethnic violence have great impact on children. Because the main agent of this impact is individual violent or hurtful acts perpetrated by individual people, this does not stray too far from the class of victimizations I am considering here. Children victimized by governmental or institutional policies, however, are in a different domain. Children deprived of rights or affected by budget cuts or land expropriations or environmental policies are often seen as victims of human agents, sometimes acting outside of established norms. However, these are victimizations that fall far enough outside the domain of the other interpersonal actions I am considering within this field that they need to be the subject of their own specialization.

An additional definitional complexity in the domain of developmental victimology is that, unlike in the domain of adult victimization, specific victimization categories have been much less clearly drawn. Thus, for example, child sexual assault, child sexual abuse, and child molestation are often thought of interchangeably, but these terms also can refer to very different portions of the problem of sexual offenses involving children. Thus child sexual abuse, when discussed in child welfare contexts, often means sexual offenses committed against children by caretakers and thus might not include sexual assaults by strangers or peers. Child molestation in colloquial terms is thought of as sexual offenses committed against children by adults and thus might exclude date rapes and sexual assaults by other juveniles. Child sexual assault is sometimes taken in its literal meaning to refer to violent and forceful sexual crimes against children and thus excludes nonassaultive sexual crimes against children. All this suggests that the field could benefit from a great deal of definitional refinement and organization.

DIFFERENTIAL CHARACTER OF CHILD VICTIMIZATION

The discussion of how child victimization should be defined highlights the fact that child victimization differs from adult victimization. Children, of course, suffer from all the victimizations that adults do—homicides, robberies, sexual assault, and even economic crimes such as extortion and fraud. But one salient difference is that children also suffer from offenses that are particular to their status. The main status characteristic of childhood is its condition of dependency, which is a function, at least in part, of social and psychological immaturity. The violation of this dependency status results in forms of victimization, such as physical neglect, that are not suffered by most adults (with the exception of those, such as the elderly and sick, who also become dependent).

The dependency of children creates what might be thought of as a spectrum of vulnerability. Interestingly, the victimization types that children suffer from can be arrayed on a continuum, according to the degree to which they involve violations of children's dependency status (Figure 2.2). At the one extreme is physical neglect, which has practically no meaning as victimization, except in the case of a person who is dependent and needs to be cared for by others. Thus it is a form of victimization that is created by children's dependent status and occurs primarily, if not exclusively, to children. Similarly, family abduction is a dependency-specific victimization, because it is the unlawful removal of a child from the person who is supposed to be caring for him or her. Other kinds of child victimization are a bit more ambiguous. Emotional abuse happens to both adults and children, but the sensitive psychological vulnerability of children in their dependent relationship to their caretakers is what makes society consider emotional abuse of children a form of victimization that warrants an institutional response. Therefore it is fair to say that emotional abuse is a dependency-related victimization as well.

At the other end of the continuum are forms of victimization that are defined largely without reference to dependency and that exist in very similar forms for both children and adults. Stranger abduction is prototypical in this instance, because both children and adults are taken against their will and imprisoned for ransom or sexual purposes. Homicide is similar: the dependency status of the victim does little to define the victimization. In some cases, to be sure, children's deaths result from extreme and willful cases of neglect, but there are parallel instances of adult deaths resulting from extreme and willful negligence.

One might think that most forms of child victimization are either dependency related or not. But in reality, there are forms of child victimization that actually should be located along the midsection of the dependency continuum. Sexual abuse falls here, for example, because it encompasses at least two different forms, one dependency related and one not. Some sexual abuse entails activities ordinarily acceptable between adults, such as consensual sexual intercourse, that are deemed victimizing in the case of children because of their immaturity and dependency. But other sexual abuse involves violence and coercion that would be victimizing even with a nondependent adult.

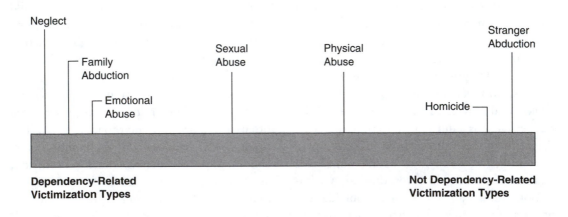

Figure 2.2   Dependence Continuum for Child Victimization Types

In the case of physical abuse, there also is some mixture of types. While most of the violent acts in the physical abuse category would be considered victimizing even between adults, some of them, such as the shaken baby syndrome, develop almost exclusively in a caretaking relationship in which there is an enormous differential in size and physical control. The dependency continuum is a useful concept in thinking about some of the unique features of children's victimizations. It also is helpful in generating some hypotheses about the expected correlates of different types of victimization at different ages.

SCOPE OF CHILD VICTIMIZATION

There is no single source for statistics on child victimizations. The National Crime Victimization Survey (NCVS), which is the ultimate authority on crime victimization in general, has two unfortunate deficiencies when it comes to child victimization. First, it does not gather information on victims younger than age 12. Second, it does not cover certain forms of child victimization such as child abuse, sexual abuse, and kidnapping that preoccupy public policy regarding children. But national estimates that compensate for these deficiencies of the NCVS are available from some other sources. Some of these various estimates are arrayed in Table 2.1.

Under some victimization categories, the estimates of several different studies have been listed, sometimes showing widely divergent rates. These differences stem from a variety of factors.

Some of the studies listed base their rates on cases known to authorities (NCANDS) or professionals (NIS-3). Such studies are certain to count fewer cases than studies that obtain information directly from youth and their families. While it misses many cases, the advantage of information from authorities and professionals, however, is that professional judgment is typically involved in assessing whether a real qualifying victimization (e.g., physical abuse) occurred.

Other discrepancies are more complicated to explain. For a variety of victimizations in Table 2.1, estimates are available from both the NCVS and the Developmental Victimization Survey (DVS; Finkelhor et al., 2005b), a study conducted by the author and colleagues. The NCVS is a highly rigorous survey conducted every year by the U.S. Bureau of the Census, that interviews nearly 10,000 youth ages 12 to 17. The DVS was a survey of both youth and caretakers regarding the experiences of 2,020 children from the ages of 2 to 17. The NCVS estimates are considerably lower than those from the DVS for every crime and also lower than many other survey estimates of specific forms of juvenile victimization (Wells & Rankin, 1995). This is generally attributed to several factors. The NCVS uses a complex definition for each crime it measures, and respondents need to endorse several sets of questions in specific ways in order to qualify. Second, the NCVS interviews respondents on several occasions over a period of three years to make sure that the incidents reported clearly fall within and not outside the exact one-year time period being investigated. Third, the NCVS survey clearly orients respondents to the topic of conventional "crime," so incidents that respondents might not think of as crimes (e.g., forced sex by a dating partner or being beaten by a parent) may not get reported. Fourth, the NCVS does not require that youth be interviewed confidentially, and young people may fail to disclose incidents they would not want their parents or family members to know about.

What this means is that the NCVS estimates are very conservative and count primarily incidents that would be considered conventional crimes in the narrow sense. The DVS estimates, by contrast, are probably inflated with minor incidents and incidents that some observers might dismiss as "not

Table 2.1   Rates and Incidence of Various Childhood Victimizations

	Age	Rate/1000[a]	No. Victimized	Year	Source[b]	Report Type	Notes
Assault, any physical	2–17	530	33,651,000	2002	DVS	Self/Caretaker report	
	12–17	(72.8)	(1,686,842)	1993–2003	NCVS	Self-report	
Sibling assault	2–17	355	22,481,000	2002	DVS	Self/Caretaker report	
Robbery	2–17	40	2,543,000	2002	DVS	Self/Caretaker report	Nonsibling
	12–17	7.8	(180,733)	1993–2003	NCVS	Self-report	
Theft	2–17	140	8,887,000	2002	DVS	Self/Caretaker report	Nonsibling
	12–15	2.1	(35,874)	2004	NCVS 2003	Self-report	
Sexual assault/Rape	2–17	32	2,053,000	2002	DVS	Self/Caretaker report	
	12–17	3.2	(74,147)	1993–2003	NCVS	Self-report	
Sexual abuse (sexual assault by known adult)	2–17	6	*	2002	DVS	Self/Caretaker report	
Sexual harassment	0–17	(1.2)	88,656	2002	NCANDS	Agency reports	
	0–17	4.5	300,200	1993	NIS-3	Agency reports	
	2–17	38	2,411,000	2002	DVS	Self/Caretaker report	
	8th–11th grade	(810)	(13,006,580)	2000	Hostile Hallways	Self-report	
Physical abuse	2–17	37	2,320,000	2002	DVS	Self/Caretaker report	
	0–17	(2.3)	166,920	2002	NCANDS	Agency reports	
	0–17	9.1	614,108	1993	NIS-3	Agency reports	
	0–17	49	(3,359,195)	1995	CTSPC-Gallup	Self-reports	
Neglect	2–17	14	909,000	2002	DVS	Self/Caretaker report	
	0–17	(7.7)	541,832	2002	NCANDS	Agency reports	Includes medical neglect
	0–17	(19.9)	(1,355,100)	1993	NIS-3	Agency reports	
	0–17	270	(18,509,850)	1995	CTSPC-Gallup	Self-reports	
Psychological/ Emotional abuse	2–17	103	6,498,000	2002	DVS	Self/Caretaker report	
Witnessing/ Domestic violence	0–17	(0.8)	58,022	2002	NCANDS	Agency reports	
	2–17	35	2,190,000	2002	DVS	Self/Caretaker report	
Family abductions (or custodial interference)	2–17	17	1,099,000	2002	DVS	Self/Caretaker report	
	0–17	(2.9)	203,900	1999	NISMART-2	Caretaker reports	

	Age	Rate/1000[a]	No. Victimized	Year	Source[b]	Report Type	Notes
Nonfamily abductions	0–17	(0.8)	58,200	1999	NISMART-2	Caretaker reports	Legal definition, includes stereotypical kidnappings
	0–17	(0.0016)	115	1999	NISMART-2	Law enforcement	Stereotypical kidnapping
Homicide	0–17	(0.02)	1,571	2002	SHR	Agency reports	
Bullying	6th–10th grade	(168.8)	(3,245,904)	1998	HBSC	Self-report	Moderate and frequent bullying
Teasing or emotional bullying	2–17	217	13,735,000	2002	DVS	Self/Caretaker report	
	0–17	614	42,092,770	1995	CTSPC-Gallup	Caretaker reports	
	2–17	249	15,745,000	2002	DVS	Self/Caretaker report	
Online victimization							
Sexual solicitations and approaches	10–17	130	3,220,000	2005	YISS-2	Self-reports	
Unwanted exposure to sexual material	10–17	340	8,430,000	2005	YISS-2	Self-reports	
Harassment	10–17	90	2,230,000	2005	YISS-2	Self-reports	
Corporal punishment	0–17	(147.6)	(29,887,672)	1999	PCAA	Caretaker reports	
	0–17	(171.7)	34,800,000	2002	ABC News Poll	Caretaker reports	Spanked or hit ever

a. Numbers given in parentheses did not appear in original source, but were derived from data presented therein.

b. Source acronyms: DVS, Developmental Victimization Survey (Finkelhor, Ormrod, Turner, & Hamby, 2005b); NCVS, National Crime Victimization Survey (Baum, 2005); NCVS 2003, National Crime Victimization Survey, 2003 (Catalano, 2004); NCANDS, National Child Abuse & Neglect Data System, 2002 (U.S. Department of Health and Human Services—Administration on Children Youth and Families, 2004); NIS-3, Third National Incidence Study of Child Abuse and Neglect, 1993 (Sedlak & Broadhurst, 1996); Hostile Hallways (Axelrod & Markow, 2001); NISMART-2, Second National Incidence Study of Missing, Abducted, Runaway and Thrownaway Children, 1999 (Hammer, Finkelhor, & Sedlak, 2002; Sedlak, Finkelhor, Hammer, & Schultz, 2002); SHR, Supplemental Homicide Reports (Fox, 2005); HBSC, Health Behaviour of School-aged Children (Nansel et al., 2001); CTSPC-Gallup (Straus, Hamby, Finkelhor, Moore, & Runyan, 1998); YISS-2, Second Youth Internet Safety Survey (Wolak et al., 2006); PCAA, Prevent Child Abuse America, (Daro, 1999); ABC News Poll (Crandall, 2002).

real crimes," such as sibling and peer assaults and disciplinary acts. Table 2.1 reveals an enormous quantity and variety of victimizations occurring to children and youth. Based on the DVS, over half of all children experienced a physical assault in the course of the previous year, much of it by siblings and peers. One fifth experienced physical bullying, and one fourth, emotional bullying. In addition, 1 in 7 experienced a theft, and 1 in 20 a robbery. The NCVS rates are typically only a fraction, in some cases a 10th or less of the DVS estimates, which suggests how far we may still be from a consensus about the epidemiology of child victimization. But even the NCVS estimates suggest that conventional crime victimization rates for youth are at least three to four times larger than what is known to police (Finkelhor & Ormrod, 2001) and two to three times the victimization rate for adults (Hashima & Finkelhor, 1999).

A TYPOLOGY OF CHILD VICTIMIZATION BY INCIDENCE

The estimates for various types of child victimization, in spite of their methodological limitations, definitional imprecision, and variability, nonetheless can be broken into three rough and broad categories according to their order of magnitude. First, there are the **pandemic** victimizations that appear to occur to a majority or near majority of children at some time in the course of growing up. These include, at a minimum, assault by siblings and theft, and probably also peer assault, vandalism, and robbery. Second, there is what might be called **acute** victimizations. These are less frequent and occur to a minority, although perhaps a sizeable minority, of children, but may be on average of a generally greater severity. Among these we would include physical abuse, neglect, and family abduction. Finally, there are the **extraordinary** victimizations that occur to only a very small number of children but that attract a great deal of attention. These include homicide, child abuse homicide, and nonfamily abduction.

Several observations follow from this typology. First, there has been much more public and professional attention paid to the extraordinary and acute victimizations compared to the pandemic ones. For example, sibling violence, the most frequent victimization, is conspicuous for how little it has been studied in proportion to how often it occurs. This neglect of pandemic victimizations needs to be rectified. For one thing, it fails to reflect the concerns of children themselves. In a survey of children, three times as many were concerned about the likelihood of their being beaten up by peers as were concerned about being sexually abused (Finkelhor & Dziuba-Leatherman, 1995). The pandemic victimizations deserve greater attention if only for the alarming frequency with which they occur and the influence they have on children's everyday existence. It is a rule of public health that threats to well-being that are minor or only have enduring consequences in a small number of cases can be very serious in their total effects if they occur frequently in a large population. So, peer assaults could potentially, on a population basis, be responsible for more mental health problems than child abuse.

Second, this typology can be useful in developing theory and methodology concerning child victimization. For example, different types of victimization may require different conceptual frameworks. Because they are nearly normative occurrences, the impact of pandemic victimizations may be very different from the extraordinary ones that children experience in relative isolation.

Finally, the typology helps illustrate the diversity and frequency of children's victimization. Although homicide and child abuse have been widely studied, they are notable for how inadequately they convey the variety and true extent of the other victimizations that children suffer. Almost all the figures in

Table 2.1 have been promoted in isolation at one time or another. When we view them together, we note that they are just part of a total environment of various victimization dangers in which children live.

Poly-Victims

With so many victimizations occurring to so many children, it is obvious that there must be considerable overlap. Ironically, though, the fragmentation of the field of child victimization has impeded inquiry into just how much overlap there is and why. Advocates and policymakers concerned about one form of child victimization or another, such as dating violence, have tended to present estimates and studies about their victims as though this was the primary or only victimization that such children suffered from. They could do this because studies of one kind of victimization rarely ask about other kinds. Some studies might inquire about multiple forms of child maltreatment, such as physical and sexual abuse. Other studies, like the NCVS, inquire about multiple forms of conventional crime, such as rape, robbery, and aggravated assault. But studies almost never ask about a very broad and comprehensive range of victimizations, including child maltreatment, conventional crime, and exposure to peer violence, for example.

It turns out that most juvenile victims experience multiple victimizations. To ascertain this, we have developed a questionnaire that asks about 34 different kinds of child victimization, the Juvenile Victimization Questionnaire. This questionnaire asks about victimizations in five broad domains: conventional crime, child maltreatment, peer and sibling, sexual victimization, and witnessing/indirect victimization. This questionnaire was utilized in a national survey of 2,020 American children ages 2 to 17. Some of the estimates from the survey, the Development or Victimization Survey, are listed in Table 2.1.

The survey found that victimization was a frequent occurrence with 71% of the children and youth experiencing at least one victimization in the last year. But more important, it found the experience of multiple victimizations very common as well. We defined multiple victimizations as having a different kind of victimization in a different episode over the course of a year. This meant that an assault and robbery on different occasions, even by the same perpetrator, would count as multiple victimizations, but two assaults by the same or even different perpetrators would not count as multiple victimizations. This conservative way of defining multiple victimization was adopted in light of findings that different kinds of victimization seem to be more harmful than repeated episodes of the same type (see Finkelhor et al., in press; Finkelhor, Ormrod, Turner, & Hamby, 2005a). Of the children with any victimization in the last year, two thirds had experienced two or more. The average number of victimizations for a victimized child was three in the last year, and the total ranged all the way up to 15. Obviously, children who had had one kind of victimization were at increased likelihood to have other victimizations as well. For example, if a child had been physically assaulted by a caretaker, he or she was 60% more likely than other children to also have been assaulted by a peer.

Children with multiple victimizations should be of particular professional concern. In other fields, it has been widely recognized that multiple intersecting adversities frequently have impacts far beyond those of individual stressful events. So, for example, clients with several psychiatric diagnoses (comorbidity) or who abuse different kinds of drugs (poly-drug users) have been found to pose particularly challenging problems. There is every reason to believe that this is also the case with child victims.

We have proposed to call this group of multiply victimized children "poly-victims."

(We prefer to the term "poly-victim" over "multiple victim" because the term "multiple victim" can mean a victimization in which there were several victims, a meaning that could be confused with what we were intending to designate—a victim who has had several victimizations.) We expected that research on poly-victims would show them to be particularly highly victimized, vulnerable, and distressed young people.

In fact, the DVS confirmed these predictions. We categorized as poly-victims the youth in our national survey who had experienced four or more victimizations over the course of the single year. Such youth comprised 31% of all victims and 22% of the full sample. But they were the youth with the most serious kinds of victimization. Forty percent of the poly-victims had had a victimization injury, 42% had experienced a form of maltreatment, and 25% had been victimized by a weapon-toting assailant. Although they were not that different from other youth in their demographic profile, they had considerably more other lifetime adversities, such as major illnesses, accidents, or other family problems. They were also clearly the most distressed youth. They were 5.8 times more likely than other youth to be angry, 20.2 times more likely to be depressed, and 10.3 times more likely to be anxious. In fact, most of the clinically distressed kids were also poly-victims. For example, 86% of the clinically depressed children also fit the criteria as poly-victims (Finkelhor et al., in press).

It appears increasingly that professionals should be looking for poly-victimization among children, not just one individual type of victimization, even a serious one. Our analyses have suggested that poly-victimization is most associated with mental health problems and bad outcomes and that poly-victims are the kids harboring the greatest amount of distress. The associations between distress and individual victimizations disappear when poly-victimization is taken into account (Finkelhor et al., in press). That is, children who experience a single kind of victimization, such as bullying or even child maltreatment, appear to be able to recover from it. But youth who experience victimization of multiple kinds from multiple sources are showing signs that they are locked in a pattern or trapped in a downward spiral that should be of the greatest concern to those trying to help.

As we come to understand poly-victims, it may change some of the assumptions that we have been used to making about victimization in general. Victimizations have in the past mostly been thought of as stressful or traumatic events. This is in part a legacy of the field's close connection to the literature on post-traumatic stress. The earliest victimization experiences to be studied in detail were sexual assaults, which were considered to be highly threatening individual episodes, happening to otherwise ordinary victims, who were overwhelmed by a short-term incident.

But as victimization research has expanded, we have come to understand that many victims are subjected to repeated episodes over a period of time, as with the child who is bullied again and again on the playground or emotionally and physically abused again and again by a parent. We are also now seeing that many children are subjected to a variety of different kinds of victimization, such as being beaten and sexually assaulted and robbed, over a relatively short period of time. This suggests that victimization for some children is more like a **condition** than an **event**. A condition is a much more stable and ongoing process, whereas an event is more time-limited. It is like the difference between failing a test and failing a course, or the difference between an acute medical condition such as appendicitis and a chronic one such as diabetes. One of the most important diagnostic challenges that face professionals concerned about child victimization is discerning those children for whom victimization has become a condition, rather than just an event. We should expect them to have different characteristics and a different prognosis.

Currently, most of what we know about poly-victims is that they experience a lot of victimization. They appear to be equally divided between boys and girls, and they appear to be somewhat more common among older youth, although there are certainly considerable numbers of poly-victims even at a very young age (Finkelhor et al., in press). Current evidence does not strongly suggest that they come from poor or minority backgrounds. Importantly, one feature that does seem to be associated with poly-victimization is living in a family that has been affected by divorce, separation, and/or remarriage. Obviously, we need considerably more study of these youth so that we can identify them and prevent or remediate their poly-victimization as a condition as early as possible.

DEVELOPMENTAL PROPOSITIONS

Childhood is such an extremely heterogeneous category—4-year-olds and 17-year-olds having little in common—that it can be inherently misleading to discuss child victimization in general without reference to age. We would expect the nature, quantity, and impact of victimization to vary across childhood with the different capabilities, activities, and environments that are characteristic of different stages of development. This is the key principle of developmental victimology.

Unfortunately, the general culture is already full of assumptions about development and victimization, many of them questionable and sometimes even contradictory. Some victimizations are presumed to be worse for younger children, others worse for older children—mostly based on stereotype, not evidence. We have already alluded to some of these assumptions. Peer violence is presumed to be more serious, injurious,

traumatizing, and crimelike as it occurs to older children, for example. That is, a teenager punched by another teen would be regarded as experiencing something much more serious than a five-year-old punched by another preschooler. Is there evidence for this? In fact, when we looked at these issues in a research study, we did **not** find less injury or psychological impact for younger children in instances of peer violence (Finkelhor et al., in press). Still, they are not entirely equivalent kinds of offenses if only because we have different mechanisms for responding to them—police might want to arrest the teenage assailant. But we probably should not assume until we can study the matter more that the acts are more dangerous or the consequences more serious simply because the participants are older.

In contrast to peer violence, the colloquial assumption about child molestation is that it is more serious for younger children. Some people make the naïve assumption that because children are at an earlier developmental stage, they may be vulnerable to more serious developmental disruption. For example, a child who has not yet been introduced to sex will be more affected by the molestation than one who has developed some ideas and concepts. But, here again, much of the available evidence casts doubt on the colloquial assumptions. Some studies have found sexual abuse and child molestation to have more consequences at younger ages, and others have found the opposite. One of the big problems is that victimizations that happen at an earlier age tend to go on for a longer period of time. It is clear that what developmental victimology needs is a rigorously empirical approach to developmental issues, one that does not accept facile developmental assumptions at their face value. Things are generally more complicated than most people, even experts, presume.

One good place to start an empirical developmental victimology is with propositions about how the types of victimization and types of perpetrators change over the course of childhood. The mix of victimization types is very likely to be different for younger children and older children. Based on one of the concepts introduced earlier, we would expect, for example, that victimizations stemming from the dependent status of children should be most common among the most dependent, hence, the youngest children. A corollary is that, as children get older, their victimization profile should come more and more to resemble that of adults.

We can examine such propositions in a crude way with the data that are available. In fact, we do know that some of the dependency-related victimizations are most concentrated in the under-12 age group. For example, physical neglect, the failure to take care of the needs of a dependent child, is heavily concentrated among younger children. Family abduction is also heavily concentrated among younger children. When children are no longer so dependent, they tend to make their own choices about which parent to live with, and abduction is no longer a feasible strategy for disgruntled parents. By contrast, victimizations that we grouped at the nondependency end of the continuum involve a greater percentage of teenagers. Homicide is a crime defined equivalently for minors and adults, and it is concentrated among teenagers (Figure 2.2).

Homicide is a particularly good crime for some additional insights about development and victimization, because fairly complete age data are available and because other efforts have been made to interpret the patterns (Christoffel, 1990; Christoffel, Anzinger, & Amari, 1983; Crittenden & Craig, 1990; Jason, 1983; Jason, Carpenter, & Tyler, 1983). Child homicide is also a complicated crime from a developmental point of view. It has a conspicuous bimodal frequency, with a high rate for the very youngest children, those under age 1, and another high rate for the oldest children ages 16 and 17 (Figure 2.3). But the two peaks represent very different phenomena. The homicides of young children are primarily committed by parents, by choking, smothering, and battering. In contrast, the homicides of older children are committed mostly by peers and acquaintances, primarily with firearms. Although the analysts do not agree entirely on the number and exact age span of the specific developmental categories for child homicides, a number of propositions are clear. There is a distinct group of neonaticides: children killed in the first day or few weeks of life. The proportion of female and rural perpetrators is unusually high in this group (Jason et al., 1983). Homicide at this age is generally considered to include many isolated parents dealing with unwanted children.

After the neonatal period, there follows a period through about age five during which homicides are still primarily committed by caretakers using "personal weapons," the criminologist's term for hands and feet, but the motives and circumstances are thought to be somewhat different from those pertaining to the neonatal period. These preschool victim homicides appear to be mostly cases of fatal child abuse that occur as a result of parents' attempts to control children or angry reactions to some of young children's aversive behavior—uncontrollable crying, hitting parents or siblings, soiling themselves, or getting dirty (Christoffel, 1990; Crittenden & Craig, 1990). Such children are frequently thrown against hard surfaces, struck hard with a blow to the head or belly, or smothered. Because of their small size and physical vulnerability, many children at this age die from acts of violence and force by adults that would not be fatal to an older child.

As children become school age, the rate of child homicide declines, and the nature of child homicide becomes somewhat different. Among school-age children, killings by parents and caretakers gradually decrease

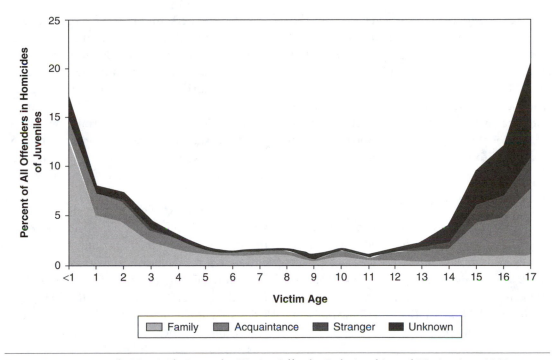

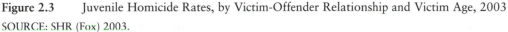

Figure 2.3   Juvenile Homicide Rates, by Victim-Offender Relationship and Victim Age, 2003
SOURCE: SHR (Fox) 2003.

and those by peers and acquaintances rise. There are more firearm deaths. Children get murdered by suicidal parents bent on destroying their whole families. Children this age are also sometimes killed in the child molestations that begin to increase in this period (although homicide is a rare accompaniment to child molesting). Some of the children in this age group die as innocent victims in robberies and arsons. There is a mixture of the kinds of homicides that affect younger children and also some of those that affect older children, but the overall rate is low, and it is one of the safest times in the life span in terms of homicide risk.

Then, at age 13, the homicide picture changes again, and rapidly. The rate for boys diverges sharply from that for girls. Acquaintances become the predominant killers. Gangs and drugs are heavily implicated for this group, and the rate for minority groups—African Americans, Hispanic

Americans, and Asian Americans—soars. The homicides for this group of youth look a lot like the homicides for young adults, although it is one of the few forms of victimization that they suffer at lower rates.

These patterns of homicide victimization suggest some interesting propositions relevant to developmental victimology. First, they suggest at least three somewhat different "ecological niches" in which victimization occurs: (1) a preschool, family-based, early development niche (with a possible neonatal subenvironment); (2) a middle childhood, somewhat protected, mixed school and family niche; and (3) an adolescent, risk-exposed, transition-into-adulthood niche. The types of homicide suffered by children are related to the nature of their dependency and to the level of their integration into the adult world. Among the things that may well change across childhood and across these niches are the victim-offender relationship, the locale where the homicide occurs, the nature of the weapons, the motives involved, and the contribution victims make to the crime in terms of risk taking and provocation. The homicide variations provide a good case for the importance and utility of a developmental perspective on child victimizations and a model of how such an approach could be applied to other types of victimization.

INTRAFAMILY VICTIMIZATION

Unlike many adults, children do not live alone; they live mostly in families. Moreover, their involvement in their families wanes as they get older. So a plausible principle of developmental victimology is that younger children have a greater proportion of their victimizations at the hands of intimates and correspondingly fewer at the hands of strangers. This is because they live more sheltered lives and spend more time in the home and around family.

Figure 2.4 indeed confirms this. Figure 2.4a shows data on crimes against children known to the police from the FBI's National Incident-Based Reporting System (NIBRS).

Family offenders are highest for the youngest age victims. But the percentage declines from near 70% to below 20% after age 12. At the same time, acquaintance victimizations rise during childhood until adolescence, where they plateau at about 70%. Stranger victimizations remain low throughout childhood but start to increase a bit after age 15. The patterns are very similar in data on victimizations reported in the DVS, shown in Figure 2.4b.

These trends are very consistent with what we know about children's social development. Social activities expand throughout childhood to include an increasingly large and more distant network of contacts. But, overall, children have fewer of the characteristics that might make them suitable targets for strangers, such as money and valuable possessions. In adolescence, they both acquire such valuables and begin to interact in even more public arenas so that increased victimization at the hands of strangers makes sense.

An additional possible principle is that the identity of perpetrators may vary according

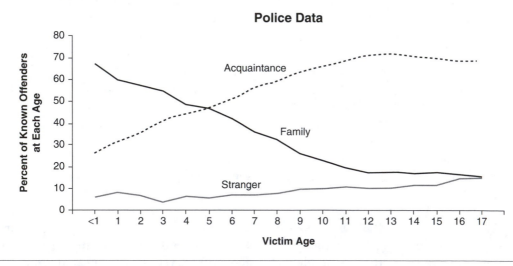

Figure 2.4a   Juvenile Victim Relationship to Offender by Victim Age: Police Data

SOURCE: Federal Bureau of Investigation (1997), National Incident-Based Reporting System (NIBRS; 12 states only), computer file. Tabulations undertaken by Crimes Against Children Research Center, Washington, D.C., U.S. Department of Justice, Federal Bureau of Investigation.

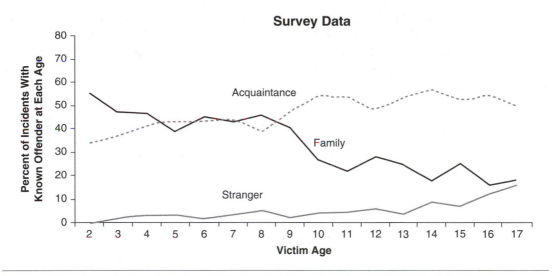

Figure 2.4b   Juvenile Relationship to Offender by Victim Age: Survey Data

SOURCE: Developmental Victimization Survey. All forms of victimization (Finkelhor et al., 2005b).

to the type of victimization and its place on the dependency continuum. Victimizations that are more dependency related should involve more perpetrators who are parents and family members. Available data suggests that this is true. Parents comprise 100% of the perpetrators of neglect (Sedlak, 1991)—the most dependency-related victimization—but only 28% of the perpetrators of homicide (Federal Bureau of Investigation, 1992). This pattern occurs because the responsibilities created by children's dependency status fall primarily on parents and family members. They are the main individuals in a position to violate those responsibilities in a way that would create victimization. Thus, when a sick child fails to get available medical attention, it is the parents who are charged with neglecting the child, even if the neighbors also did nothing.

Consistent with developmental patterns in victim–offender relationship and the dependency continuum, we would also expect that more of the victimizations of younger children would take place in the home and that victimizations would depart farther and farther from the home as children age

and move out into an ever-widening circle of social activity.

We would also expect that, as the homicide data shows, crimes against children involving firearms would increase along with development. In fact, one explanation for why teens are murdered less than young adults in spite of their equivalent or higher overall violent victimization rate could be that teens and their associates have less access to firearms than do young adults.

GENDER AND VICTIMIZATION

Developmental victimology needs to consider gender as well as age in its effort to map the patterns of victimization in childhood. In overall terms, many of the gender patterns seen among adults also apply among children. That is, boys overall suffer more victimization than girls, but girls suffer more sexual assaults. On the basis of the conventional crime statistics available from the NCVS and Uniform Crime Report, the ratio of boys to girls for homicide is 2.3 to 1; for assault, 1.7 to 1; and for robbery, 2 to 1. Girls suffer vastly more incidences of rape (8.1 to 1; Bureau of Justice Statistics,

1992; Federal Bureau of Investigation, 1992). But these ratios primarily pertain to the experience of adolescents, and they do not consider age variations, which add a considerable wrinkle to the pattern.

THE AGE CRIME CURVE

The life course patterns in crime and delinquency have been one of the most interesting threads for ongoing discussion and research in criminology. The empirical foundation for the discussion is the apparent observation that criminal behavior accelerates dramatically during the adolescent years to reach a peak in young adulthood and then falls off in later years. The dramatic rise from preadolescence to adulthood has been ascribed to a variety of factors. One argument is that it reflects a biosocially based status competition for mates that gets its start in adolescence (Kanazawa & Still, 2000). Others contend that crime rises in adolescence because at that stage young people begin to have adult aspirations but are excluded from the labor market (Greenberg, 1985; Grogger, 1998). Others point simply to the lax social controls that operate during adolescence and young adulthood—singlehood, no family responsibilities, and no commitment to employers. Does victimization risk have the same age pattern, accelerating during adolescence in the same dramatic fashion as delinquency? Official crime statistics would say yes, but more comprehensive self-report surveys suggest no.

Police data such as from NIBRS jurisdictions show that teens constitute three fourths of the juvenile crime victims, with risk escalating as youth age (Finkelhor & Ormrod, 2000). Only a few crimes, such as kidnapping, forcible sodomy, and incest, appear more evenly distributed across developmental stages. But the police data have serious limitations as valid testimony to the age curve for victimization. Many of the victimizations of younger children—assaults at the hands of peers, abuse at the hands of parents, neglect and other forms of child maltreatment—are forms of victimization that are considerably less likely to be defined as crimes or matters of police concern.

The age patterns in victimization rates are considerably different when the evidence comes from victims themselves and their family members, for example, from the DVS, which assessed victimizations from ages 2 through 17, using the same screening questions across all ages (Figure 2.5). Overall, victimization rose slightly but not precipitously for the adolescents.[1] The rise was largest for sexual victimizations and witnessing/indirect victimizations. There was no rise for assaults. Perhaps, most surprisingly, child maltreatment also rose with age. This might be the form of victimization that we would most expect to decline with age. In fact, some studies of child maltreatment known to professionals also show higher rates for older children. But it may be the case that the maltreatment of younger children is difficult to access, both in surveys (which almost of necessity must get this information from the caregivers themselves) and among cases known to professionals, who are less likely to have contact with younger children.

The absence of a steep increase in victimization is also apparent in the NCVS data. Rates of violent crime measured in the NCVS for 12- to 14-year-olds are as high as rates for 15- to 17-year-olds. Rape and aggravated assault are a bit higher for the older adolescents, but simple assault is actually more common for the younger youth. The steep increases noted in self-reported delinquency studies (Elliott, Huizinga, & Menard, 1989) are not apparent in the self-reported victimization studies.

Why does the self-report information contrast so starkly with the official police data? Studies clearly show that the younger the victims, the less likely it is that victimization will be reported to law enforcement (Finkelhor &

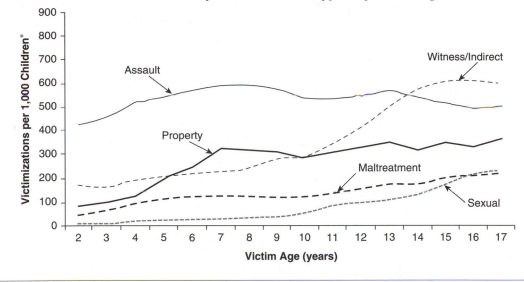

Figure 2.5 Major Victimization Types by Victim Age

NOTE: For purposes of generalization, data are shown as 3-year running averages.

Ormrod, 1999). The public and police do not want younger victims caught up in a judicial system. They are less apt to define juvenile victimizations as crimes. Families, schools, and child welfare officials lay claim to the arbitration of offenses against younger victims. Younger victims themselves have a harder time independently accessing police. So, in spite of police data, victimization does not accelerate in adolescence in the same way as delinquency.

THE LIFESTYLES AND ROUTINE ACTIVITIES THEORY OF CRIME VICTIMIZATION

Developmental victimology also needs to develop theories of victimization risk that take into account the specific context of childhood. This may mean altering some of the conventional approaches taken by victimology as it has been applied to adults. In victimology, in general, one conceptual framework has dominated the discussion: the closely related "lifestyle exposure" and "routine activities"

theories (Cohen, 1981; Garofalo, Siegel, & Laub, 1987; Gottfredson, 1986; Hindelang, Gottfredson, & Garofalo, 1978). Such theories, as they have been expounded in the past, highlight the fact that lifestyles and activities of different people put them in environments or situations in which they are more or less in contact with potential offenders and at risk of potential victimization.

Four central concepts have been used in these approaches to explain the connection between lifestyles and risk: proximity to crime, exposure to crime, target attractiveness, and guardianship (Miethe & Meier, 1994). Proximity to crime would mean living in high-crime areas. Exposure to crime would include things such as being out at night. Target attractiveness would be attributes that might entice offenders such as the ownership of desirable and portable possessions. Guardianship highlights that spending considerable time alone or apart from the family or other possibly protective individuals can create vulnerability. These concepts have proved useful in explaining why certain groups such as men, blacks, and single people have higher crime victimization rates. They have also been used to explain why rates of crime have increased over time in some places and in some periods, when, for example, fewer people began living in families, and people began acquiring more conspicuously valuable items.

When these concepts have been applied to some extent to the analysis of youth victimization, it has been primarily to point out how increased exposure and decreased guardianship heighten youth vulnerability. Young people are viewed in this theory as engaging in risky behaviors, such as staying out late, going to parties, and drinking, which compromise the guardianship provided by parents and adults and expose them to more possibilities for victimization (Jensen & Brownfield, 1986). Much of the research on youth victimization has particularly stressed its connection to delinquent activities (Lauritsen, Laub, & Sampson, 1992; Lauritsen, Sampson, & Laub, 1991). Delinquency is seen as a lifestyle that puts a person in close proximity to other offenders—aggressive or delinquent companions or rival gang members. Moreover, it also greatly reduces guardianship because delinquents tend to avoid conventional social environments and through their activities also largely forfeit their claims on the protection of police and other authorities (Sparks, 1982). Empirical research has confirmed that delinquents are indeed more prone to victimization than other youth (Lauritsen et al., 1992; Lauritsen et al., 1991).

CRITIQUE OF LIFESTYLE AND ROUTINE ACTIVITIES THEORY

The lifestyle theory perspective of youth victimization has ultimately been fairly narrow. For one thing, many youth get victimized without being involved in delinquency. Delinquent activities are primarily the domain of adolescents, particularly adolescent boys,

but even young children get assaulted, kidnapped, and sexually abused (Finkelhor & Dziuba-Leatherman, 1994) without any connection to delinquent behavior. For another thing, the lifestyle and routine activities theories were designed for and have always been best at explaining street crime such as stranger assaults and robberies. But much of youth victimization, especially of younger children, occurs at the hands of acquaintances and family members (Finkelhor & Dziuba-Leatherman, 1994).

These acquaintance and intrafamily victimizations are not as well suited to the lifestyle or routine activities concepts. For example, routine activities studies often operationalize *exposure to crime* as the amount of time routinely spent out at night or away from the family household. However, when trying to explain parental child abuse, such explanations collapse. It does not increase a child's risk of parental abuse to be away from their parents. In fact, it may actually reduce it.

Thus it is not surprising that theories developed to explain children's victimization by acquaintances and family members have virtually ignored lifestyle theory and have relied on other concepts besides exposure and guardianship. For example, in trying to account for who becomes the target of bullying, observers have noted that these tend to be children with "avoidant-insecure" attachment relationships with primary caregivers, who lack trust, have low self-confidence, have physical impairments, are socially isolated, and are physically weaker (Olweus, 1993; Smith, Bowers, Binney, & Cowie, 1993).

The literature on physical abuse also takes a very different tack from the lifestyles approach. This literature tends to equate victimization risk primarily with family and parental attributes, such as family stress, isolation, alcoholic and violence-prone caretakers, parents who have victimization histories and unrealistic expectations of their children (National Research Council,

1993), and youth characteristics such as oppositional behavior, difficult temperament, or impairments that are a burden or source of disappointment for caregivers (Berdie, Berdie, Wexler, & Fisher, 1983; Garbarino, 1989; Libby & Bybee, 1979; Schellenbach & Guerney, 1987). A still different victimization literature, the one on child sexual assault, notes even other risk factors: girls, children from stepparent families, children whose parents fight or are distant and punitive, reduced parental supervision, and emotional deprivation that make children and youth vulnerable to the offers of attention and affection that sexual predatory offenders sometimes use to draw children into sexual activities (Finkelhor, 1993; Finkelhor, 1994).

The concepts from these various literatures can, to a limited extent, be subsumed into the routine activities conceptual framework. Thus, for example, lack of supervision (considered a risk for sexual abuse) corresponds to the guardianship concept. Family social isolation (as a risk for parental physical abuse) also has an element of missing guardianship, but in this case the guardians are not the family members themselves, but members of a related social network. One might also consider characteristics such as having an impairment, being insecurely attached, being a female, or being emotionally deprived as features of "target attractiveness."

But target attractiveness, in the routine activities literature, has primarily been utilized in a very narrow sense, in reference to the value and portability of material objects that as a result of their lifestyle a person may own or carry (Hough, 1987; Miethe & Meier, 1994). It could be extended without too much distortion to refer to the value of a victim as an object of desire, such as for a sexual crime. But target attractiveness takes on a very different meaning in the case of violent victimizations, one in which the word *attraction* seems quite inappropriate. A child who is

beaten by a parent because the child's disability disappoints and frustrates a parent is an "attractive target" for parental anger in only a very ironic and convoluted way. Moreover, it is not necessarily true, as is often the case for property crime, that the offender is simply choosing among more attractive targets, deciding to burglarize the home with the fancier exterior. In the example of parental assault, if the child were not disabled, it is not clear that some other child would then suffer the abuse instead. Maybe, in this case, nobody would be abused.

But perhaps the biggest objection to trying to subsume these child victimization risk factors into routine activities theory is that none of these target attributes constitutes a "lifestyle." Nor do they necessarily increase risk through routine activities. Thus, femaleness, although it is a form of target attractiveness and does increase the risk for sexual abuse, is not a routine activity. Moreover, while maleness may put men at differential risk for physical assault because men engage in more unsupervised and risk-taking behavior (a lifestyle feature), femaleness does not put women at differential risk for sexual assault by virtue of anything they do. Femaleness itself is the risk attribute. Similarly, while emotional deprivation may change a person's routine activities, if a molester preys on such a child because she is needy, it is not the routine activities of the child that necessarily elevate the risk. The routine activities idea of target attractiveness does not seem broad enough.

A NEW CONCEPTUAL FRAMEWORK FOR THINKING ABOUT VICTIMIZATION

Thus, to explain the full range of victimizations among youth, the lifestyle or routine activities framework needs to be modified. Concepts such as guardianship, exposure, and proximity, when it comes to victimization by intimates, need to be seen not as aspects of routine activities or lifestyles but as environmental factors that expose or protect victims from victimization. Thus, when a child is placed at risk for sexual abuse because parents are fighting and inattentive, the lack of guardianship is an environmental condition conducive to victimization, not a problem of a lifestyle or routine activity for the child.

In addition to the environmental conditions highlighted by the lifestyle theory to explain the risks for youth victimization, more attention also needs to be given to the risk-increasing potential of individual characteristics and attributes, such as female gender or emotional deprivation. These personal characteristics of individuals would appear to increase vulnerability to victimization, independent of any routine activities, because these characteristics have some congruence with the needs, motives, or reactivities of offenders. That is, because certain offenders are drawn or react to certain types of victims or certain characteristics in victims, such victims are more vulnerable. This process might be called "target congruence," and it increases risk in one of three more specific ways, referred to here as *target vulnerability, target gratifiability,* or *target antagonism:*

1. In the case of target vulnerability, some victim characteristics increase risk because they compromise the potential victim's capacity to resist or deter victimization and thus make the victim an easier target for the offender. For youth victimization, the prototypical risk factors in the vulnerability category would be attributes such as physical weakness, emotional deprivation, or psychological problems.

2. In the case of target gratifiability, some victim characteristics increase risk because they are some quality, possession, skill, or attribute that an offender wants to obtain, use, have access to, or manipulate. The prototypical risk factor in the gratifiability category would be

female gender for the crime of sexual assault, but keeping in mind that for some sexual offenders, gratifiability focuses on prepubescent children or in some cases boys. Having valuable possessions, as in the routine activities notion of target attractiveness, would also fall into this category.

3. In the case of target antagonism, some characteristics increase risk by being qualities, possessions, skills, or attributes that arouse the anger, jealousy, or destructive impulses of the offender. Examples in this category would be ethnic characteristics or being gay or effeminate (for hate crimes), or being anxiously attached, a "mama's boy," etc. (as in the case of bully victims). In the case of parental assaults, characteristics such as being a burden due to disability or being disobedient would be other examples.

Although these target congruence concepts, and particularly the target gratifiability one, have similarities to the notion of target attractiveness, the word *attractiveness* and its stereotypical applications in the crime of sexual assault have victim-blaming connotations that should be avoided. The attractions implied in the concepts used here are specific to the predispositions, proclivities, and reactivities of the offender, hence the idea of congruence. Thus gratifiability means that the target fits what the offender is looking for, whether conventionally desirable or merely satisfying of an offender's idiosyncratic motive. Antagonism does not imply provocation in the conventional sense: without some predisposition, a crying baby does not provoke assault any more than does being the member of a minority.

It is important to note, as the examples also illustrate, that target congruence changes considerably from crime to crime, and from offender to offender. Thus a female may have more target gratifiability for a sexual assault, but a male may have more target antagonism for a gay-bashing. Characteristics that might increase target antagonism for parental assaults, such as disobedience, may have little if anything to do with risk for peer victimization. There may be some generalized target congruence characteristics, such as weakness, but even this may be a relatively insignificant factor in many victimizations.

These target congruence elements also clearly play a greater role in some offenses than others. In relatively impersonal street crimes or group victimizations (e.g., sniper attacks) and also in the case of family members who live with very violent individuals, offenders may not be choosing victims on the basis of any personal characteristic at all, only proximity. In other victimizations (e.g., attempts to assassinate the president, stalking crimes, or a parent maltreating a colicky baby) the congruence of the personal characteristics of the victim with the motives or reactivities of the offender provide a virtually complete explanation of victim choice.

These target congruence concepts seem to encompass most of the characteristics that have been cited in the literature on youth victimization outside the lifestyle theory domain, characteristics such as low self-esteem and disobedience. But they also seem quite relevant to the prediction of forms of victimization, such as street crime, which has been the primary focus of routine activities research.

RESEARCH NEEDS

The research needs in the field of developmental victimology are vast and urgent, given the size of the problem and the seriousness of its impact, and they range from studies of risk factors to studies of treatment efficacy to studies of criminal justice policy. But in the limited space of this discussion, we will mention only three important points.

First, if we are to take it seriously, we need much better statistics to document and analyze the scope, nature, and trends of child victimization. The National Crime Victimization Survey records crime victimizations only from age 12 and older. The Uniform Crime Reports in the past have made no age information available about crimes, with the exception of homicide (something that is changing under a new system, but the full national implementation of this system is still a long way off). The national data collection system about child abuse also has severe methodological limitations, restricting the way in which the information can be aggregated nationally or compared among states (Finkelhor & Wells, 2003). We need comprehensive yearly national and state figures on all officially reported crimes and forms of child abuse committed against children. These need to be supplemented by regular national studies to assess the vast quantity of unreported victimization, including family violence and child-to-child and indirect victimization. While there are methodological challenges in such efforts, studies such as the ones referenced in this chapter demonstrate that this is feasible.

Second, we need theory and research that cuts across and integrates the various forms of child victimization. A good example is the work on post-traumatic stress disorder in children, which has been applied to the effects of various victimizations: sexual abuse, stranger abduction, and the witnessing of homicide (Boney-McCoy & Finkelhor, 1995, 1996; Eth & Pynoos, 1985; Terr, 1990). Similar cross-cutting research could be done on other subjects, such as what makes children vulnerable to victimization or how responses by family members buffer or exacerbate the impact of victimization. To be truly synthesizing, this research needs to study the pandemic victimizations, not just the acute and extraordinary victimizations, which have been the main focus in the past.

Finally, the field needs a more developmental perspective on child victimization. This would begin with an understanding of the mix of victimization threats that face children of different ages. It would include the kind of factors that place children at risk and the strategies for victimization avoidance that are appropriate at different stages of development. It also would differentiate how children at different stages react to and cope with the challenges posed by victimization. It is ironic that until recently the problem of children as aggressors has had more attention in social science than has children as victims, reflecting perhaps the priorities of the adult world. It is encouraging that as the needs of children are more fully recognized, this balance is finally changing.

REFERENCES

Axelrod, A., & Markow, D. (2001). *Hostile hallways: Bullying, teasing, and sexual harassment in school.* Washington, DC: American Association of University Women Educational Foundation.

Baum, K. (2005). *Juvenile victimization and offending, 1993–2003* (Bureau of Justice Statistics Special Report No. NCJ209468). Washington, DC: Office of Justice Programs, U.S. Department of Justice.

Berdie, J., Berdie, M., Wexler, S., & Fisher, B. (1983). *An empirical study of families involved in adolescent maltreatment.* San Francisco: URSA Institute.

Boney-McCoy, S., & Finkelhor, D. (1995). Prior victimization: A risk factor for child sexual abuse and for PTSD-related symptomatology among sexually abused youth. *Child Abuse & Neglect, 19*(12), 1401–1421.

Boney-McCoy, S., & Finkelhor, D. (1996). Is youth victimization related to trauma symptoms and depression after controlling for prior symptoms and family relationships? A longitudinal, prospective study. *Journal of Consulting and Clinical Psychology, 64*(6), 1406–1416.

Bureau of Justice Statistics. (1992). *National crime survey.* Washington, DC: U.S. Department of Justice.

Catalano, S. M. (2004). *Criminal victimization, 2003* (BJS/NCVS Report No. NCJ 205455). Washington, DC: U.S. Department of Justice.

Christoffel, K. K. (1990). Violent death and injury in U.S. children and adolescents. *American Journal of Diseases of Children, 144*, 697–706.

Christoffel, K. K., Anzinger, N. K., & Amari, M. (1983). Homicide in childhood: Distinguishable pattern of risk related to developmental levels of victims. *The American Journal of Forensic Medicine and Pathology, 4*(2), 129–137.

Cohen, L. E. (1981). Modeling crime trends: A criminal opportunity perspective. *Journal of Research in Crime and Delinquency, 17*, 140–159.

Crandall, J. (2002). *Most say spanking's OK by parents but not by grade-school teachers.* ABC News and ICR International Communications Research. Retrieved February, 10, 2006, from http://abcnews.go.com/sections/us/DailyNews/spanking_p011021108.html.

Crittenden, P. A., & Craig, S. E. (1990). Developmental trends in the nature of child homicide. *Journal of Interpersonal Violence, 5*, 202–216.

Daro, D. (1999). *Public opinion and behaviors regarding child abuse prevention: 1999 survey.* Chicago: Prevent Child Abuse America.

Elliott, D. S., Huizinga, D., & Menard, S. (1989). *Multiple problem youth: Delinquency, substance use, and mental health problems.* New York: Springer-Verlag.

Eth, S., & Pynoos, R. S. (1985). *Post-Traumatic Stress Disorder in children: Progress in psychiatry.* Washington, DC: American Psychiatric Press.

Federal Bureau of Investigation. (1992). *Crime in the United States, 1991: Uniform crime reports.* Washington, DC: U.S. Department of Justice.

Finkelhor, D. (1993). Epidemiological factors in the clinical identification of child sexual abuse. *Child Abuse & Neglect, 17*, 67–70.

Finkelhor, D. (1994). Current information on the scope and nature of child sexual abuse. *The Future of Children, 4*(2), 31–53.

Finkelhor, D., & Dziuba-Leatherman, J. (1994). Victimization of children. *American Psychologist, 49*(3), 173–183.

Finkelhor, D., & Dziuba-Leatherman, J. (1995). Victimization prevention programs: A national survey of children's exposure and reactions. *Child Abuse & Neglect, 19*(2), 125–135.

Finkelhor, D., & Ormrod, R. K. (1999). *Reporting crimes against juveniles* (Juvenile Justice Bulletin No. NCJ178887). Washington, DC:

U.S. Department of Justice, Office of Juvenile Justice and Delinquency Prevention.

Finkelhor, D., & Ormrod, R. (2000). *Characteristics of crimes against juveniles* (Juvenile Justice Bulletin No. NCJ 179034). Washington, DC: U.S. Department of Justice, Office of Juvenile Justice and Delinquency Prevention.

Finkelhor, D., & Ormrod, R. K. (2001). *Child abuse reported to the police* (Juvenile Justice Bulletin No. NCJ187238). Washington, DC: U.S. Department of Justice, Office of Juvenile Justice and Delinquency Prevention.

Finkelhor, D., Ormrod, R. K., & Turner, H. A. (in press). Poly-victimization: A neglected component in child victimization trauma. *Child Abuse & Neglect.*

Finkelhor, D., Ormrod, R. K., Turner, H. A., & Hamby, S. L. (2005a). Measuring poly-victimization using the JVQ. *Child Abuse & Neglect, 29*(11), 1297–1312.

Finkelhor, D., Ormrod, R. K., Turner, H. A., & Hamby, S. L. (2005b). The victimization of children and youth: A comprehensive, national survey. *Child Maltreatment, 10*(1), 5–25.

Finkelhor, D., Turner, H. A., & Ormrod, R. K. (in press). Kid's stuff: The nature and impact of peer and sibling violence. *Child Abuse & Neglect.*

Finkelhor, D., & Wells, M. (2003). Improving national data systems about juvenile victimization. *Child Abuse & Neglect, 27*(1), 77–102.

Fox, J. A. (2005). Uniform Crime Reports [United States]: Supplementary Homicide Reports, 1976–2003 [Computer file] ICPSR04351-v1 (pp. 11–22). Ann Arbor, MI: Inter-University Consortium for Political and Social Research [producer and distributor].

Garbarino, J. (1989). Troubled youth, troubled families: The dynamics of adolescent maltreatment. In D. Cicchetti & V. Carlson (Eds.), *Child maltreatment: Theory and research of the causes and consequences of child abuse and neglect* (pp. 685–706). New York: Cambridge University Press.

Garofalo, J., Siegel, L., & Laub, J. (1987). School-related victimizations among adolescents: An analysis of National Crime Survey (NCS) narratives. *Journal of Quantitative Criminology, 3,* 321–338.

Gottfredson, M. R. (1986). Substantive contributions of victimization surveys. *Crime and Justice: An annual review of research, 7,* 251–287.

Greenberg, D. F. (1985). Age, crime, and social explanation. *American Journal of Sociology, 91,* 1–21.

Greven, P. (1990). *Spare the child: The religious roots of punishment and the psychological impact of physical abuse.* New York: Alfred A. Knopf.

Grogger, J. (1998). Market wages and youth crime. *Journal of Labor Economics, 16*(4), 756–791.

Hammer, H., Finkelhor, D., & Sedlak, A. J. (2002). *Children abducted by family members: National estimates and characteristics* (Juvenile Justice Bulletin No. NCJ196466). Washington, DC: U.S. Department of Justice, Office of Juvenile Justice and Delinquency Prevention.

Hashima, P., & Finkelhor, D. (1999). Violent victimization of youth versus adults in the National Crime Victimization Survey. *Journal of Interpersonal Violence, 14*(8), 799–820.

Hindelang, M. S., Gottfredson, M., & Garofalo, J. (1978). *Victims of personal crime.* Cambridge, MA: Ballinger.

Hough, M. (1987). Offenders' choice of targets: Findings from victim surveys. *Journal of Quantitative Criminology, 3,* 355–369.

Jaffe, P. G., Wolfe, D. A., & Wilson, S. K. (1990). *Children of battered women.* Newbury Park, CA: Sage Publications.

Jason, J. (1983). Child homicide spectrum. *American Journal of Diseases of Children, 137,* 578–581.

Jason, J., Carpenter, M. M., & Tyler, C. W. (1983). Underrecording of infant homicide in the United States. *American Journal of Public Health, 73*(2), 195–197.

Jensen, G. F., & Brownfield, D. (1986). Gender, lifestyles, and victimization: Beyond routine activity theory. *Violence and Victims, 1,* 85–99.

Kanazawa, S., & Still, M. C. (2000). Why men commit crimes (and why they desist). *Sociological Theory, 18,* 434–447.

Kilpatrick, D. G. (1990). *Violence as a precursor of women's substance abuse: The rest of the drugs-violence story.* Paper presented at the 98th Annual Convention of the American Psychological Association, Boston, MA.

Lauritsen, J. L., Laub, J. H., & Sampson, R. J. (1992). Conventional and delinquent activities: Implications for the prevention of violent victimization among adolescents. *Violence and Victims, 7*(2), 91–108.

Lauritsen, J. L., Sampson, R. J., & Laub, J. H. (1991). The link between offending and victimization among adolescents. *Criminology, 29,* 265–292.

Libby, P., & Bybee, R. (1979). The physical abuse of adolescents. *Journal of Social Issues, 35,* 101–126.

Margolin, G., & Gordis, E. B. (2000). The effects of family and community violence on children. *Annual Review of Psychology, 51,* 445–479.

Miethe, T. D., & Meier, R. F. (1994). *Crime and its social context: Toward an integrated theory of offenders, victims, and situations.* Albany: SUNY Press.

Nader, K., Pynoos, R., Fairbanks, L., & Frederick, C. (1990). Children's PTSD reactions one year after a sniper attack at their school. *American Journal of Psychiatry, 147,* 1526–1530.

Nansel, T. R., Overpeck, M., Pilla, R. S., Ruan, W. J., Simons-Morton, B., & Scheidt, P. C. (2001). Bullying behaviors among U.S. youth. *JAMA, 285*(16), 2094–2101.

National Research Council. (1993). *Understanding child abuse and neglect.* Washington, DC: National Academy Press.

Olweus, D. (1993). Bullies on the playground: The role of victimization. In C. H. Hart (Ed.), *Children of playgrounds: Research perspectives and applications* (pp. 85–128). Albany: SUNY Press.

Schellenbach, C. J., & Guerney, L. F. (1987). Identification of adolescent abuse and future intervention prospects. *Journal of Adolescence, 10*(1), 1–12.

Sedlak, A. J. (1991). *National incidence and prevalence of child abuse and neglect: 1988— Revised report.* Rockville, MD: Westat.

Sedlak, A. J., & Broadhurst, D. D. (1996). *Third national incidence study of child abuse and neglect.* Washington, DC: U.S. Department of Health and Human Services.

Sedlak, A. J., Finkelhor, D., Hammer, H., & Schultz, D. J. (2002). *National estimates of missing children: An overview* (Juvenile Justice Bulletin No. NCJ196466). Washington, DC: U.S. Department of Justice, Office of Juvenile Justice and Delinquency Prevention.

Smith, P. K., Bowers, L., Binney, V., & Cowie, H. (1993). Relationships of children involved in bully/victim problems at school. In S. Duck (Ed.), *Learning about relationships* (pp. 184–205). Newbury Park, CA: Sage Publications.

Sparks, R. F. (1982). Crime and delinquency issues: A monograph series. In R. G. Sparks (Ed.), *Research on victims of crime: Accomplishments, issues, and new directions.* Rockville, MD: National Institute of Mental Health, U.S. Department of Health and Human Services.

Strassberg, Z., Dodge, K. A., Pettit, G. S., & Bates, J. E. (1994). Spanking in the home and children's subsequent aggression toward kindergarten peers. *Development and Psychopathology, 6,* 445–461.

Straus, M. A. (1994). *Beating the devil out of them: Corporal punishment in American families.* New York: Lexington Books.

Straus, M. A., Hamby, S. L., Finkelhor, D., Moore, D., & Runyan, D. K. (1998). Identification of children maltreatment with the Parent–Child Conflict Tactics Scales: Development and psychometric properties data for a national sample of American parents. *Child Abuse & Neglect, 22*(4), 249–270.

Terr, L. (1990). *Too scared to cry.* New York: Harper/Collins.

U.S. Department of Health and Human Services—Administration on Children Youth and Families. (2004). *Child Maltreatment 2002: Reports from the states to the National Child Abuse & Neglect Data System.* Washington, DC: U.S. Government Printing Office.

Wells, L. E., & Rankin, J. H. (1995). Juvenile victimization: Convergent validation of alternative measurements. *Journal of Research in Crime, 32*(3), 287–307.

Wolak, J., & Finkelhor, D. (1998). Children exposed to partner violence. In J. L. Jasinski & L. M. Williams (Eds.), *Partner violence: A comprehensive review of 20 years of research.* Thousand Oaks, CA: Sage Publications.

Wolak, J., Mitchell, K. J., & Finkelhor, D. (2006). *Online victimization: 5 years later.* National Center for Missing and Exploited Children Bulletin. #07-06-025. Alexandria, VA.

NOTE

1. Figure 2.5 shows the percentage of each age cohort with any victimization or any specific type of victimization, but it does not show the total frequency of victimizations. However, taking into account victimization frequency—which is roughly the same at all ages—does not change the shape of the lines shown in Figure 2.5.

3

Sexual Assault Victimization Across the Life Span

Rates, Consequences, and Interventions for Different Populations

CHRIS S. O'SULLIVAN

DEBORAH FRY

Sexual violence represents a large public health problem across the globe. Sexual violence is defined as

> any sexual act, attempt to obtain a sexual act, unwanted sexual comments or advances, or acts to traffic, or [acts] otherwise directed, against a person's sexuality using coercion, by any person regardless of their relationship to the victim, in any setting, including but not limited to home and work. (WHO, 2002)

In one year alone in the United States, there were 209,880 victims aged 12 and older of rape, attempted rape, or sexual assault according to the National Crime Victimization Survey (NCVS; Catalano, 2005). Through a quasi-experimental design, however, Fisher, Cullen, and Turner (2000) found that the NCVS methodology leads to an undercount of sexual assaults. The National Violence Against Women Survey (NVAWS; Tjaden & Thoennes, 2000) found that 15% of U.S. women over the age of 17 reported having been raped.

Younger women are particularly vulnerable. A survey conducted with a randomly selected national sample of college women (Fisher et al., 2000) found a victimization rate of 28 rapes per 1,000 female students in just over six months. Because some women were victimized more than once in this period, the incidence was higher than the prevalence. Twenty-three percent were raped more than once. The study estimated that over the course of a college career (which now lasts an average of five years), between one fifth and one fourth of college women may experience completed or attempted rape. Internationally, up to one third of adolescent girls report that their first sexual experience was forced (WHO, 2002).

Childhood is also a time of high risk for sexual assault, especially for boys. The NVAWS found that 22% of female victims of sexual assault and 48% of male victims were under the age of 12 when they were first raped (Tjaden & Thoennes, 2006). (Note that the survey conducted from 1994 to 1996 is referred to as the National Violence Against Women Survey, but the sample included random samples of 8,000 women and 8,000 men.)

Contrary to the image of the rapist lurking in the shadows to surprise and victimize a solitary stranger, two thirds of the rapes of victims over the age of 12 were committed by someone known to the victim. A friend or acquaintance of the victim committed nearly half the rapes (Catalano, 2005). Men are more likely to be raped by strangers (29%) than women (17%; Tjaden & Thoennes, 2006). Attackers of college women are even more likely to be known to the victim: The National College Women Sexual Victimization Survey (Fisher et al., 2000) found that 90% of the offenders were known to their victims.

Rapes of women by male intimate partners are a global problem. In a 10-country study of violence against women, the World Health Organization (WHO) found that rates of sexual violence perpetrated by male partners ranged from a low of 6% in Japan to a high of 59% in Ethiopia (WHO, 2005). The WHO study provides one of the first cross-country examinations of patterns of partner violence. In most of the countries in the study, 30% to 56% of women who had experienced any violence by an intimate partner reported both physical and sexual violence (WHO, 2005). This pattern did not hold true for all sites, however: Across Thailand and in provincial Bangladesh and Ethiopia, a large proportion of women experienced sexual violence only.

This chapter will review research findings on sexual victimization of children, adolescents, and adults. It will cover the emerging topics of commercial sexual exploitation of children, sex trafficking, rape by intimate partners, and prison rape. It will conclude with recommendations for future research and new directions in practice.

SEXUAL VIOLENCE FROM INFANCY TO ADULTHOOD

Sexual Abuse of Children

Although the maximum age varies across definitions, child sexual abuse is generally defined as unwanted sexual activity with a child from birth to 14 years old, or sexual activity with a person 5 years or more older than the child. In 2000, the rate of substantiated sexual abuse for children under the age of 3 was 15.7 victims per thousand. Unlike other forms of child abuse, child sexual abuse is more often perpetrated against girls than boys. In a retrospective study, Finkelhor, Hotaling, Lewis, and Smith (1990) estimated that 27% of American women and 16% of men had been sexually abused as children; the median age of the children at the time of the abuse was between 9 and 10 years old. Girls are more at risk of sexual victimization than boys at any age, but the age of highest risk for boys is in childhood, whereas for girls it is more evenly distributed into young adulthood, although peaking in adolescence. In the NVAWS, among male respondents who had ever experienced rape or attempted rape, 71% were younger than 18 when they were first sexually assaulted, and 48% were younger than 12 years old.

Like adults, juveniles (birth to 17 years of age) are most often sexually assaulted by someone they know: acquaintances—such as family friends, neighbors, and baby-sitters—commit 59% of rapes of children. Juveniles, however, are more likely than adults to be assaulted by relatives: Family members commit 34% of child rapes (Snyder, 2000). Perpetrators are overwhelmingly male, whether the victim is a boy (86% male perpetrators) or a girl (94% male perpetrators). Children with disabilities (both physical and cognitive) are believed to be more vulnerable to sexual abuse.

Child sexual assault cases represent over one third of sexual assaults reported to law enforcement: According to the FBI's National Incident Based Reporting System, from 21 states from 1991 to 2000, 34% of sexual assault victims are younger than 12 years old, and 14% are younger than 6 years old. Still, sexual assaults of child victims can be difficult to substantiate. Children often do not disclose sexual abuse because they believe the situation is normal, blame themselves, are afraid of the consequences, and/or feel they will not be believed. These barriers to reporting are often reinforced by the perpetrator. Physical signs of sexual abuse may not be apparent, although when there is investigation, detection has improved.

Emotional and Physical Impact

Observable signs of sexual abuse in children include agitation, frightening dreams, and age inappropriate sexual behavior. Symptoms include depression to the point of suicidality, even in children as young as four years old; withdrawal; and traumatic stress (Boney-McCoy & Finkelhor, 1995). Boys who have been sexually violated are more likely than girls to act out with aggressive and cruel behavior. (Seventy-six percent of incarcerated male serial rapists claim to have been sexually abused as children.)

The psychological effects of childhood sexual abuse may be manifested in adolescence and early adulthood in the form of delinquency, multiple sexual partners, and suicide attempts. These effects persist into adulthood, including a higher rate of substance abuse, particularly alcohol abuse, and eating disorders; multiple consensual sexual partners with attendant risks of sexually transmitted diseases (STDs); depression; dissociation; problems forming relationships; and educational underachievement and underemployment. There is also a high risk for revictimization (see Daigle, Fisher, & Guthrie, in this volume). Survivors of childhood sexual abuse not only exhibit lasting psychopathology but also continue to seek psychological treatment.

Not only is child sexual abuse, especially incest, hidden within the family, but for many decades it was also hidden from awareness of professionals and the criminal justice system by Freudian theory, which attributed memories of incest to Oedipal longings. Several books altered that awareness, including Geoffrey Masson's questioning of the development of Freud's own views of the reality of these memories (1984), and research by Judith Herman (*Father-Daughter Incest*, 1981) and Diana Russell (*The Secret Trauma: Incest in the Lives of Girls and Women*, 1986). The trauma from incest and child sexual abuse was persuasively and influentially described in Judith Herman's *Trauma and Recovery* (1992b), which quickly became a classic for therapists. There is still much controversy surrounding the question of "recovered memories" of childhood sexual abuse, however.

Continuing research on child sexual abuse and trauma has been led by John Briere (cf. Briere & Runtz, 1990) and David Finkelhor, and Angela Browne has focused on lasting effects into adulthood, particularly among poor, homeless, and incarcerated women. Finkelhor and Browne developed the "traumogenic" model of childhood sexual abuse

(1985). According to this model, there are four dynamics that result from sexual abuse of young children: (1) traumatic sexualization (which may take two pathways: avoidance of sex and heightened interest in sex); (2) betrayal, because the perpetrator is usually a trusted adult; (3) powerlessness; and (4) stigmatization, which leads the child to feel different, damaged, and inherently bad. More severe abuse, as defined by sexual contact involving penetration (i.e., rape), greater use of force and threats, and injury, has been found to be associated with more symptoms. Other factors that increase the probability of traumatic stress symptoms and psychopathology include longer duration of the abuse or repeated assaults and a closer relationship with the perpetrator. Adults are more likely to be symptomatic if these characteristics pertained to their childhood abuse. Researchers at the University of Wisconsin, Yale, and in London have been investigating the environmental and genetic factors associated with "resilience": A minority of adults who experienced severe sexual abuse in childhood do not suffer from depression, drug addiction, and problems with trust. There appear to be both biological and social factors (e.g., the presence of a supportive adult) that are protective (Bazelon, 2006).

Sexual Victimization of Youth

Youth is generally defined as the age range from 10 to 24, with subcategories of adolescence, ranging from 10 to 19 years old, teenage years ranging from 13 to 19, and young adults from 20 to 24 years old (UN, 2006). Although there may be differing conceptualizations of this life stage, there is no dispute that sexual violence disproportionately affects women in these age ranges. The NCVS indicated that adolescent females ages 16–19 are four times more likely than the general population to experience sexual assault, rape, and attempted rape (Rennison, 2002).

Increasingly, studies have shown that many girls' first sexual encounter is forced. In a multicountry study in the Caribbean, nearly half of sexually active adolescent women reported that their first sexual encounter was forced (Halcón, Beuhring, & Blum, 2000). Likewise, in Lima, Peru, nearly 40% of young women reported forced sexual initiation as compared to only 11% of the young men (Caceres, Vanoss, & Hudes, 2000). Recent research has focused on sexual violence in young people's dating relationships. One study found that one in five female high school students reported experiencing physical and/or sexual violence from a dating partner (Silverman, Raj, Mucci, & Hathaway, 2001). The National Center for Juvenile Justice estimates that in two thirds of sexual assaults reported to law enforcement agencies in the United States, the victim was under the age of 18 at the time of the crime. These numbers are surprising given that reported violence is often just the tip of the iceberg. Sexual violence is often referred to as a "hidden crime" or "silent epidemic" because rape and sexual assault are so frequently not reported to the police and other authorities (Harner, 2003). Adolescents are particularly likely to hide a rape if they were intoxicated or engaged in other illegal or unapproved behavior. Fisher et al. (2000) noted that, of college women who described experiencing a sexual act that meets the legal definition of rape, fewer than 47% defined the experience as rape.

Sexual Violence Against Homeless Youth

Homeless youth are one of the most vulnerable populations (Ensign & Santelli, 1998). It is estimated that nearly 2 million youth are homeless in the United States (Rew, Taylor-SeeHafer, & Fitzgerald, 2001). Homeless youth include runaways, who have left their homes without permission; "throwaways," who have been forced to leave home; and "street-involved" youth, who spend most of their time on the street with peers and may have a home to which they can return (Rew et al., 2001). In addition to increasing risk of sexual victimization, homelessness is also a result of sexual violence. Abuse in the family is often pivotal in the decision to run away (Molnar, Shade, Kral, Booth, & Watters, 1998; Rew et al., 2001). Sexual minority youth (homosexual, bisexual, and transsexual) are particularly likely to be thrown out of their homes by their parents.

Rates of prior sexual abuse among homeless youth range from 32% to 60% (Noell, Rohde, Seeley, & Ochs, 2001; Rew et al., 2001; Tyler & Cauce, 2002). As with all sexual victimization of children, perpetrators were most likely to be nonfamily adults (58%) or a nonparent relative such as an older sibling or uncle (25%). Biological parents (10%), stepparents, and foster or adoptive parents (7%) were least likely to be the perpetrators of sexual abuse (Tyler, Whitbeck, Hoyt, & Cauce, 2004). Among homeless youth, girls experienced higher rates of sexual abuse than boys before leaving home, and sexual minority youth experienced higher rates of both physical and sexual abuse than heterosexual youth. A very high percentage (92%) of the homeless youth had told someone about experiencing sexual abuse.

After they leave home, sexual victimization of homeless youth remains higher than for their peers. Tyler and colleagues (2004) found that 23% of homeless girls and 11% of homeless boys had experienced sexual victimization at least once since being on the street. In part, this increased risk can be attributable to the higher rate of sexual assault of the previously victimized: Experiences of sexual abuse and combined physical and sexual abuse prior to becoming homeless were precursors to on-street rape (Ryan, Kilmer, Cauce, Watanabe, & Hoyt, 2000). In addition, there are risks in homelessness and the associated lifestyle. Several studies have found that approximately 25% of homeless youth engage in survival sex, that is, trading sex for food, shelter, or money, increasing their vulnerability to sexual assault (Greene, Ennett, & Ringwalt, 1999; Kipke, Simon, Montgomery, Unger, & Iversen, 1997; Kral, Molnar, Booth, & Waters, 1997). Females were most often victimized by male acquaintances (41%), then by male strangers (34%), and by male friends (23%). In contrast, homeless male youth reported being sexually victimized most often by strangers (56%), then by acquaintances (32%). Similar to females, 71% of the young men reported experiencing sexual victimization at the hands of other males (Tyler et al., 2004). Compared to other homeless youth, those who have been sexually abused report higher rates of suicide attempts, abuse of alcohol and drugs, and negative coping strategies (Cohen, Spirito, & Brown, 1996; Molnar et al., 1998; Rew et al., 2001; Rotheram-Borus, Mahler, Koopman, & Langabeer, 1996).

Sexual Victimization in Adulthood

The WHO Report on Violence and Health compiled several studies of the prevalence of sexual assault of adults across countries. The estimates range from less than 2% of the entire population in La Paz, Bolivia, and Beijing, China, to 5% or more in Tirana, Albania, and Rio de Janeiro, Brazil (WHO, 2002). In the United States, more than 300,000 women (0.3%) and more than 90,000 men (0.1%) reported being raped in the previous year. One in 6 women (17%) and 1 in 33 men (3%) reported experiencing an attempted or completed rape at some point during their lifetime: American Indian and Alaskan native women were more likely than other racial/ethnic groups to be raped. This finding is consistent with other research showing this group to experience more violent victimizations other than rape (Tjaden & Thoennes, 2000).

Nearly a third of the women and half as many men were injured during their most recent rape, but most of the injuries were minor—such as scratches, bruises, and welts. A third of the women and a fourth of the men sought mental health counseling in regard to the rape. About 1 in 5 of the women and 1 in 10 of the men raped in adulthood reported the rape to authorities. Counting all rapes these victims experienced since the age of 18, only 8% of the cases were prosecuted, 3% resulted in a conviction, and 2% of the perpetrators were incarcerated (Tjaden & Thoennes, 2000). As with sexual violence committed against children and adolescents, perpetrators of sexual assault of adults are usually known to the victim. Risk factors for rape in adulthood include prior victimization, alcohol abuse, and multiple sexual partners, including consensual sexual partners.

REVICTIMIZATION

"Revictimization" was originally used to refer to victim blaming, questioning of credibility, and other harsh treatment many survivors face from the criminal justice agents and health care providers when they attempt to report a rape. This treatment has been termed "the second rape" or secondary victimization. Of late, "revictimization" has come to refer more commonly to new incidents against someone who has already experienced sexual assault— usually being reassaulted by a different perpetrator or perpetrators. This use has grown because many studies have found that a survivor of sexual violence is more likely to be sexually revictimized than someone who has not been previously abused.

Secondary Victimization: Negative Interactions With Service Providers

Survivors of sexual violence often turn to a variety of services after an assault. They may seek medical care or counseling services, report the assault to the police, and/or work with prosecutors in a legal case. Often survivors

are treated poorly by the very systems set up to help them. Secondary victimization has been defined as the victim-blaming attitudes, behaviors, and practices engaged in by community service providers that result in additional trauma for rape survivors (Campbell & Raja, 1999). Examples include asking victims how they were dressed, questioning them about their sexual histories, asking if they were sexually turned on by the assault, or encouraging them not to prosecute (Campbell & Raja, 1999). Such treatment increases rape survivors' feelings of guilt, depression, and distrust and their reluctance to seek further help (Campbell, Wasco, Ahrens, Sefl, & Barnes, 2001).

A recent study by Rebecca Campbell (2005) compared victims' accounts of what happened during service delivery with those of doctors, nurses, and police officers. Police officers and doctors significantly underestimated the impact they were having on survivors. Victims reported more subsequent distress about their contacts with the medical and criminal justice systems than service providers thought they were experiencing.

Repeat Sexual Assault

Women who are raped are usually raped more than once: Among adults who report being raped in the previous year, women experienced 2.9 rapes, and men experienced 1.2 rapes. A study of women with disabilities found that 80% were sexually victimized more than once (Sobsey & Doe, 1991). Sexual abuse early in life has been particularly implicated in vulnerability to repeat sexual victimization, and there is a growing literature on this relationship, the risk factors and psychological correlates, and interventions. Perhaps the first study to uncover the correlation between childhood sexual abuse and rape in adulthood was a study of incest survivors conducted by Diana Russell (1986). In a retrospective study of 152 women who had experienced interfamilial sexual abuse (incest) before the age of 14, Russell found that 63% also experienced rape or attempted rape after the age of 14. More information on revictimization can be found in the chapter by Daigle, Fisher, and Guthrie (in this volume).

EMERGING TOPICS

Commercial Sexual Exploitation of Children

The commercial sexual exploitation of children (CSEC) involves sexual abuse primarily or entirely for financial benefit. The economic exchanges involved in the sexual exploitation may be either monetary or nonmonetary (e.g., for shelter, drugs, or trade for other sexual exploitation of children) but, in every case, provides the greatest benefits to the exploiter and a violation of the rights of the children involved (Hughes & Roche, 1999). Forms of CSEC include trafficking of children for sexual purposes, prostituting of children, sex tourism, the mail order bride trade, and pornography (Estes & Weiner, 2001; Hughes & Roche, 1999). Much sexual exploitation of children is domestic, but the Internet and globalization have expanded and exacerbated the problem.

According to the international nongovernmental organization (NGO) End Child Prostitution, Child Pornography and Trafficking of Children for Sexual Purposes (ECPAT), the U.S. Department of Justice estimates the number of children exploited through prostitution, pornography, and sex trafficking in the United States to be between 100,000 and 3 million. Some victims of prostitution are as young as 9 years old, and many are only 11 or 12, but the average age at which they are first commercially sexually exploited is 14. At least 25 to 30% of all those involved in commercial sexual exploitation are juveniles (ECPAT, 2006).

The theme of the UN-sponsored Second World Congress of Commercial Sexual Exploitation of Children was that CSEC is a global problem affecting rich and developed countries as well as poor and undeveloped countries (MOFA, 2001). The environmental factors contributing to CSEC include poverty, inequality, illiteracy, armed conflict, uncontrolled HIV/AIDS, and cultural values that do not regard child marriage or sex with children as a violation of human rights. Yet these factors are not fully explanatory: although child prostitution is most prevalent in countries with extreme poverty, hunger, and armed conflict, there are many poor countries where CSEC is not a major problem, and there are many developed countries where it is a significant problem. Additional contributing factors that may explain such discrepancies are discrimination against racial/ethnic groups and women and girls, criminality, and demand for children for sex (MOFA, 2001).

Child Pornography

Supreme Court chief justice Potter Stewart famously said in 1964 that it is difficult to define pornography, but "I know it when I see it." Child pornography is less subjective and ambiguous, defined simply as the "sexually explicit reproduction of a child's image." The United Nations Convention on the Rights of the Child, which has been ratified by a majority of member states, identifies child pornography as a violation of children's rights and requires nations to prevent the exploitative use of children in pornographic materials (USES, 1996).

ECPAT (2006) estimates that around 5 million images of child sexual abuse are in circulation on the Internet, featuring some 400,000 children. A recent case illustrates how the Internet has facilitated the globalization of CSEC. In 1998, an international law enforcement operation was targeted against a pedophile ring of 180 members that called itself "w0nderland." To become a member, one had to contribute new images of child pornography. Powerful gatekeeping and encryption devices protected the club. When police carried out their investigations, they found 750,000 pornographic images and 1,800 digitalized videos. A total of 1,236 exploited children were featured in these pictures and videos. Internationally, there were 107 arrests. The investigation found that the originator of "wonderland" was an American man living in New York.

"The Internet Porn Girl" and Masha's Law. Mike Zaglifa, a suburban Chicago police sergeant working undercover, began trading images with a pornographer that provided horrific images of child sexual abuse. Zaglifa gave his correspondent's IP address to the FBI, which traced the IP address to Matthew Mancuso, a wealthy, retired 46-year-old engineer living in a Pittsburgh suburb. Local police went to arrest Mancuso for purveying child pornography in 2003. They were surprised to find a little girl living with him: Masha was nearly 11 but the size of a 5-year-old because she had been malnourished by Mancuso to prevent her from growing and maturing. She immediately disclosed a history of abuse to the police. She was freed, adopted, and Mancuso was prosecuted. Meanwhile, the videos of Mancuso raping Masha were still on the Internet, and the Toronto police were concerned about the fate of the child. They conducted an international search to identify the child in the pornographic images and find her. Digitally removing her image, they released photographs to try to find out where the abuse was taking place: the location was identified as a Disney resort. By the time they finally tracked down the identity of the child in 2004, they learned that Masha had already been removed from her home with Mancuso and safely adopted by a woman.

Now 13, Masha testified before Congress in support of a bill sponsored by John Kerry and told her story. Masha was adopted from a Russian orphanage when she was 5 by Mancuso, a divorced father of two. The adoption agencies failed to investigate the cause of the alienation of his daughters: He had molested them until they reached puberty. When Mancuso took his new daughter home, he made her sleep in his bed and began molesting her; eventually he began to rape her and photograph her. The more than 200 pornographic images he distributed on the Internet were a hot commodity. Referring not only to the pornography but also to the fact that Mancuso found the adoption agencies and her picture on the Internet, Masha testified, "The Internet is everywhere in my story. You need to do something right away," and, because the pictures of her rapes are still being downloaded years after her abuser is in prison, "the abuse is still going on." She said she is more upset about the continued consumption of those images than about the physical abuse. The Kerry-Isakson bill triples the civil damages that child Internet porn victims can recover from $50,000 to at least $150,000 (the penalty for downloading songs off the internet) and allows victims to sue after they have turned 18 if pornographic images of them as children are still being distributed (Kerry, Isakson Push for Tougher Penalties, 2005; *Masha's Story,* 2006; Wikipedia, 2006).

Children can be harmed by pornography either through being forcibly exposed to it or by being filmed or photographed. Reviewing 1,202 prosecuted child sexual exploitation cases in the United States, Estes and Weiner (2001) found that 62% of the cases involved child pornography. These cases were split between those in which children were the subjects (370 cases) and those in which children were involuntarily exposed to child pornography (372 cases). The vast majority of these pornography cases were concentrated in three states: California (41%), Texas (31%), and New York (20%). As a side note, less than 5% of the children in pornographic images have been identified.

Child Prostitution

Child prostitution differs from child sexual abuse in that it involves commercial exploitation, although the coercive use of power and control is similar. Defining a child as a person younger than 18, an estimated 1 million children worldwide are forced into prostitution each year, and the total number of prostituted children could be as high as 10 million (Willis & Levy, 2002). A study conducted jointly by the Office of Juvenile Justice and Delinquency Prevention (OJJDP) and the National Center for Missing and Exploited Children found that physical, sexual, and psychological abuse are common in the families of female juvenile prostitutes (National Center for Missing and Exploited Children, 2002). For females, running away and childhood sexual victimization were two common pathways into prostitution (McClanahan, McClanahan, Abram, & Teplin, 1999).

Involvement in prostitution represents a range of negative health outcomes, including risk of sexual assault. Youth engaged in prostitution practice safer sex less frequently and have higher levels of drug use, including intravenous drugs, putting them at increased risk of contracting HIV and a wide range of STDs (Willis & Levy, 2002). In a study of 176 prostituted children in six countries by the Economic and Social Commission for Asia and the Pacific (ESCAP, 2000), HIV infection rates ranged from 5% in Vietnam to 17% in Thailand.

Prostituted children have very high levels of drug use, with three-fourths reporting that they abuse drugs or alcohol (Klain, 1999). A British study (Cusick, Martin, & Tiggey, 2003) found that chronic drug users—who were using crack cocaine, heroin, and non-prescription methadone—were least able to leave prostitution because they needed to support their drug habit. They were most likely to be supporting a pimp's or boyfriend's drug habit and not operating independently. Dependence on a pimp further constrained their options in regard to leaving prostitution, choice of customers, and their ability to retain earnings. All of the prostitutes who were drug dependent in the sample of 125 had begun engaging in commercial sex before the age of 18. Another study found that prostitutes are more likely to be raped and otherwise violently assaulted by customers if they are using crack or heroin (Kurtz, Surratt, Inciardi, & Kiley, 2004).

Sex Tourism

The United Nations (1996) defines child-sex tourism as "tourism organized with the primary purpose of facilitating . . . a commercial sexual relationship with a child." It is difficult to measure the exact number of victimized children. One estimate is that there are 1 million children in prostitution in Asia, the primary destination for child sex tourists (Klain, 1999). (However, the U.S. State Department estimates that 1 million children are sexually exploited annually around the globe.) In a sample collected by ECPAT of foreign tourists visiting Southeast Asia to have sex with children, tourists from the United States represented the largest group of customers (1996).

Sex Trafficking

Trafficking can involve crossing international or domestic borders—or, according to a U.S. State Department fact sheet (2005)—it may not even involve transporting a person from one locale to another. Trafficking of human beings into forced labor and prostitution is also called "modern day slavery." In other words, even if the person was not coerced or duped into crossing borders, they will be considered "trafficked" if the conditions under which they live resemble captivity or slavery. Under U.S. law, "severe forms of trafficking" include the recruitment, harboring, transportation, provision, or obtaining of a person for forced labor, resulting in debt bondage or slavery; a commercial sex act through the use of force, fraud, or coercion; or any commercial sex act if the person is under 18 years of age. The international NGO Coalition Against Trafficking in Women and Girls (CAT-W) instead draws on the 1949 UN resolution definition that considers all selling and buying of sex—all prostitution and other commerce in persons for sex—to constitute trafficking. Another term in use is "sexual slavery," defined as being forced to engage in prostitution when the victim is unable to escape the situation, whether through the use or threat of force, actual captivity, or threats against the family, or fraud and deception. Sex trafficking involves not only prostitution but also working in so-called gentleman's clubs, sex dancing, and forced participation in pornography.

NGOs working with trafficking victims find that about 50% have been trafficked into prostitution (DeWeese, 2004). The U.S. Department of Justice (DOJ) estimate of the proportion of sex trafficking is higher: According to the DOJ, of the 14,500–17,500 people trafficked into the United States each year, up to 70% are forced or coerced into commercial sex, including 23% girls and 10% boys under 18.

One successfully prosecuted case involved the Carreto family, which operated a prostitution ring recruiting poor and uneducated women from one town in Mexico. The traffickers smuggled them into the United States with false promises of marriage and work. Once in the United States, the women were moved around the country and forced into prostitution and servitude with a combination of threats, violence, and sexual abuse to keep them from fleeing or reaching out to authorities. The Carreto family kept their earnings.

Women are trafficked into prostitution in the United States not only from Mexico but also from Eastern Europe and Asia. In fact, the U.S. DOJ estimates that the largest number of trafficking victims into the United States come from East Asia and the Pacific (up to 7,000 annually). Sex trafficking is a global problem. For example, the director of a coalition of 25 Nigerian NGOs working on trafficking estimated that there are 50,000 Nigerian girls trafficked into prostitution in Italy, mostly from a single region of Nigeria where the parents do not consider the system to be trafficking (Musa, 2006). The U.S. DOJ estimates that trafficking provides up to $10 billion in profits for organized crime.

A problem in combating sex trafficking is the assumption that prostitution is usually freely chosen and offers a level of remuneration otherwise unavailable to those without skills, education, or legal status to work. The State Department counters this argument by citing a study by Farley that 89% of women in prostitution want to escape and other research documenting the frequent violence and abuse that prostitutes experience from customers and pimps (Farley, 2003). Traffickers may also use sexual assault to control women forced into labor: Women trafficked into domestic servitude are often raped as well.

Intimate Partner Violence and Marital Rape

Since the 1980s, there has been a surge in research on domestic violence, or violence inflicted by current or former intimate partners. More recently, the frequent reports of sexual abuse as a component of intimate partner violence have been receiving attention, although there remains much research to be done in this area. The related topic of marital rape has received attention since at least 1978, when Laura X founded the National Clearinghouse on Marital and Date Rape. In part, the interest in marital rape came from the legal community because of legal exemptions for husbands in rape statutes. In 1978, rape of a spouse was a crime in only four states; as of 1993, marital rape was a crime in all 50 states. In 30 states, however, there are exemptions if force is not used, even if the wife is incapacitated and unable to consent.

The topics of marital rape and rape as a component of intimate partner violence (IPV) are in some respects distinct, and some researchers have resisted collapsing the two topics, because then marital rape becomes subsumed under domestic violence and neglected, and because some men rape their partners but do not otherwise physically abuse them. At the same time, the accumulation of national data on IPV, as well as data on IPV in specific populations, and the increased sophistication of measurement of sexual assault within those studies, offers a rich source of information that has been inadequately utilized until recently.

For adult women, the highest risk of rape comes from an intimate partner. In reports from London, Guadalajara, Lima, and Zimbabwe, 23 to 25% of women reported having experienced rape or attempted rape by a partner in their lifetime (WHO, 2002). A Canadian study found that 30% of women who were raped in adulthood were assaulted by their intimate partners (Randall & Haskell, 1995). Mahoney, Williams, and West (2001) estimate that 7 million American women have been raped by intimate partners. In the United States, for 46% of women who have experienced rape or attempted rape, the perpetrator was a spouse or ex-spouse, a current or former cohabiting partner, a boyfriend or girlfriend, or—broadening the category beyond intimate partners—a date, with over half of these rapes committed by a current or former spouse or cohabiting partner (Tjaden & Thoennes, 2000). For men who have experienced rape or attempted rape, only 11% of the perpetrators fell into these categories.

Most of these intimate partner assaults of women occurred during the relationship (69%); 25% occurred both during the relationship and after the relationship ended (Tjaden & Thoennes, 2000).

Research indicates that batterers who also rape their partners are likely to be more violent and dangerous (Browne, 1987) and that rape as a component of IPV is more likely to include anal and oral intercourse than rape by acquaintances or strangers. Rape in an intimate relationship is also likely to be a repeated assault, up to 20 times or more. Financial dependence and dependence on the rapist for legal residency in the United States can make it difficult for victims of rape in marriage to escape the abuse (Russell, 1990). The NVAWS found that women were equally likely to report the rape if it was committed by an intimate partner as if it was committed by someone else. Interestingly, the police were actually more likely to refer the case for prosecution if the alleged offender was an intimate partner. However, the defendant was less likely to be prosecuted and convicted of rape if he was a former intimate partner (Tjaden & Thoennes, 2000).

Rape in Prisons

In 1973, Stephen Donaldson, a Quaker peace activist, was arrested for trespassing after a pray-in at the White House. In the course of Donaldson's two nights behind bars, he was gang-raped approximately 60 times by other inmates (Man & Cronan, 2002). Upon his release, Donaldson was one of the first survivors of prisoner rape to publicize his own abuse (Man & Cronan, 2002) and became president of Stop Prisoner Rape, a nonprofit organization that seeks to end sexual violence against men, women, and youth in all forms of detention (SPR, 2006). Donaldson died in 1996 of complications relating to AIDS, which he contracted through the rapes he experienced in prison (Man & Cronan, 2002).

It is common knowledge that men may be raped in prison—the popular media make frequent reference to the likelihood that young men without protection will be raped. Aside from the perspective of a few researchers and activists, however, this problem seemed not to be regarded as a crisis that required action on a national level until Human Rights Watch released a report in 2001. This study was the most comprehensive to date, including all 50 departments of corrections in the United States (Maruschak 2001). Only 23 departments reported collecting sexual assault statistics. Most of the correctional facilities denied that sexual violence was a problem. No statewide statistics were collected (Dumond 2003). Congress subsequently passed the Prison Rape Elimination Act in 2003, which mandates gathering national statistics about the problem, the development of guidelines for states about how to address it, creation of a review panel to hold annual hearings, and grants to states to combat the problem (SPR, 2003). The DOJ has issued grants to fund collection of data.

Men represent the vast majority of criminals sentenced to prison, and it has been assumed that sexual assault was primarily an issue among male prisoners. However, women in prison are also sexually assaulted. A study of incarcerated women in three midwestern prisons found rates of sexual coercion between 6% and 27% in the facilities (Struckman-Johnson & Struckman-Johnson, 2002). One fifth of the incidents were classifiable as rape. Half of the perpetrators were other female inmates, and half involved one or more staff. Sexual assault rates are similar for men in prison, ranging from 14% who reported sexual victimization in a study of a medium security prison (Wooden & Parker, 1982), to 21% who reported sexual pressure or assault in a study of 1,778 inmates in seven midwestern prisons (Struckman-Johnson & Struckman-Johnson, 2000).

Sexual assaults in prison differ from those outside prison in frequency and severity of assaults. Incarcerated victims are more often physically attacked during an assault than sexual assault victims outside of prison (Struckman-Johnson & Struckman-Johnson, 2000, 2002). Prisoners who have been sexually assaulted report an average of nine sexual assaults during their incarceration. Repeated abuse in prison results in feelings of helplessness and terror, trauma symptoms (Dumond, 2000, 1992; Herman, 1992a), and increased risk of suicide (Struckman-Johnson & Struckman-Johnson, 2002) and of contracting HIV (Maruschak, 2001). It is difficult for inmates to report sexual assaults because of repercussions, such as retaliation and further abuse (Dumond, 2000).

Prior Abuse

Extremely high rates of childhood physical and sexual abuse and sexual abuse in adulthood among incarcerated women suggest a causal relationship between abuse and criminality. There may be related factors such as leaving home at an early age, prostitution, substance abuse, and associating with delinquent youth and violent men that are significantly more frequent among child sexual abuse survivors. Browne, Miller, and Maguin (1999) examined abuse in the lives of female inmates in a maximum security setting in New York and found that 59% reported being sexually victimized in their childhood or adolescence. Similarly, in a recent study utilizing a random sample of 100 men incarcerated in a county jail, 59% reported some form of sexual abuse before the age of 15 (Johnson et al., 2005). In another study of 211 randomly selected male inmates, 40% met standard criteria for childhood sexual abuse, but almost 60% of those who met the criteria did not consider themselves to have been sexually abused (Fondacaro, Holt, & Powell, 1999).

RESEARCH, POLICY, AND PRACTICE DIRECTIONS

Following a public health model, which attempts first to understand the scope of the problem, we have a good idea of when, how, and by whom sexual violence is committed against girls and women and, to a lesser extent, against boys and men. We are also gaining solid information about the scope of sexual revictimization. More research needs to focus on hard-to-reach populations such as child prostitutes; children involved in pornography and sex tourism; homeless, runaway, and thrownaway youth; and adults and children forced into sex trafficking.

The second goal of the public health model is to determine the risk and protective factors associated with different forms of sexual violence. We have good understanding of the risk factors associated with acquaintance rape, sexual assault of homeless youth, and revictimization of sexual abuse survivors. We are beginning to understand the possible risk factors associated with prison rape and prostitution. However, more research is needed on the risk factors for childhood sexual abuse, commercial sexual exploitation of children, and sex trafficking. The research on protective factors and resilience need more attention from mainstream researchers and service providers. In the areas of sex trafficking and commercial sexual exploitation of children, the great problem is to understand and therefore address the demand factors.

The third cornerstone of the public health model is developing and testing prevention and avoidance strategies. This aspect is by far the weakest component of our knowledge of sexual victimization. Interventions have been developed to help young women avoid sexual assault, especially college students, and these interventions appear to be somewhat effective, but they have not been effective with the most vulnerable—survivors of childhood and adolescent sexual assault, with a single exception (Marx Calhoun, Wilson, & Meyerson, 2001). Prevention work with offenders and potential offenders has not found great success, either. A major problem in this regard, given that most sexual assaults are committed by acquaintances and go unreported, is that the great majority of offenders have not been identified and therefore cannot be targeted. Similarly, we have not learned how to reduce the demand for child pornography, child prostitution, and sex tourism, except by enhancing the criminal justice response.

In contrast, there are programs and policies in place to reduce child sexual victimization and to offer early intervention, however. The early interventions for child sexual abuse are critical because of the increased lifelong risk of revictimization among child sexual abuse survivors and the increased rate of perpetration of sexual assault and pedophilia among male child sexual abuse survivors (Lisak, Hopper, & Song, 1996). As Lisak et al. note, most men who have experienced childhood sexual abuse do not become perpetrators, but most perpetrators (70% in their sample of 126 survivors) were sexually abused. Emotional constriction and rigid gender roles were the primary predictors of which survivors would become offenders. There are also programs and policies in place to facilitate and support reporting of sexual assaults of adults and initiatives to address sex trafficking and facilitate prosecution of traffickers. Some of these more developed initiatives are described in the following segment.

Rape Crisis Programs

Rape crisis programs are the longest-standing community based interventions for sexual assault. They are included here because, despite their longevity, they have only recently been evaluated: There was an assumption that they were unquestionably good and helpful. Rape crisis programs have evolved and become institutionalized, from their roots in the 1970s when volunteer activists received training on the crisis response and were on call to come to the side of a rape victim wherever she was. As there were few women police officers when this movement was born, the police sometimes contacted the advocates to come talk to and comfort a rape victim. Now there are more than 1,200 rape crisis programs in the United States (Campbell, 2006). Volunteers still usually staff them and provide on-call crisis intervention, medical, and legal advocacy, but now there is usually an institutional sponsor, such as a battered women's agency or hospital-based crime victims counseling program. The advocates are called to hospitals when a patient reporting a sexual assault presents herself or himself to an emergency department.

In advocating on behalf of the survivors for service delivery and to prevent secondary victimization, advocates can easily run into conflict with service providers and especially with law enforcement. Detectives called to hospitals to investigate alleged sexual assaults sometimes view advocates as an impediment to investigation. A recent evaluation by Rebecca Campbell that interviewed victims and reviewed records, however, found that survivors who had the assistance of an advocate were more likely to have police reports taken and were less likely to be treated negatively by police officers (Campbell, 2006). Survivors accompanied by an advocate during their emergency department care received more medical services, including emergency contraception and sexually transmitted disease prophylaxis, and reported significantly fewer negative interpersonal interactions with medical personnel than survivors who did not have an advocate (Campbell, 2006). Furthermore, survivors reported less distress from their emergency department visit when they had an advocate present (Campbell, 2006).

Sexual Assault Forensic Examiner Programs

Sexual Assault Forensic Examiner, or SAFE, programs are a more recent innovation than rape crisis programs, but emanate from the same philosophy and have also become established throughout the United States and other countries. Victim advocates began to develop local, state, and national reforms to address victim-blaming attitudes and substandard care experienced by women and men when seeking medical attention for a sexual assault. SAFE programs—also called Sexual Assault Nurse Examiner (SANE) programs—provide specially trained forensic nurses and doctors who can provide 24-hour first response medical care and crisis intervention to sexual assault survivors in the hospital setting (Campbell, Patterson, & Lichty, 2005).

SAFEs are trained in forensic evidence collection to facilitate prosecution if survivors choose to report the crime, in legal issues that will facilitate use of medical records and expert testimony in prosecution, and in physical, biological, and psychological consequences of sexual assault. Only recently has the effectiveness of specially trained medical providers been evaluated. Preliminary evidence shows that SAFE programs are possibly effective in all five of these domains (Campbell et al., 2005); however, more rigorous studies are needed.

Child Advocacy Centers

When a child is sexually abused and there is interest in prosecuting the case, multiple agencies become involved, and each needs to conduct an interview and/or an exam with the child. The police are generally the first to become involved, followed by detectives from special victims units and prosecutors; child protective services must be brought in; then there are doctors who conduct a forensic exam, possibly using equipment specially designed for gynecological exams of infants and children; and psychologists, who may use dolls and drawings to find out what happened to the child.

A study conducted by Safe Horizon (Victim Services, 1994) found that sexually abused children had interviews about the abuse with eight different people on average and often had multiple interviews with each person. These interviews were conducted at many locations, including police precincts, hospitals, courts, and agency offices. Medical exams typically took place in emergency units and were often conducted by physicians with no special training in sexual exams of children. Child protective service agents tended to treat the parent who brought the child in as neglectful and, if the offender lived in the home, to place the child in foster care rather than having the police remove the offender, compounding the trauma. There was no immediate access to psychological treatment for the child.

To avoid multiple interviews with multiple strangers and to support the child and other family members, there has been a national movement to create child advocacy centers. A primary goal of the child advocacy center (CAC) is to reduce the number of interviews by videotaping sessions that can then be viewed by other professionals. A second objective is to colocate prosecutors, police, doctors, and counselors. Colocation allows different exams and interviews to be conducted at one location, requiring fewer appointments and less waiting, as well as better case coordination and information sharing. The third element is to provide a case manager who stays with the child throughout the process, providing a constant presence for the child and a resource for a nonoffending parent. CACs provide supportive counseling and support groups for the child victim as well as siblings and the nonoffending parent. The case manager can help the child become familiar with the courtroom to ease children's fears and confusion about testifying.

CACs can be expensive and difficult to set up, requiring a dedicated child-friendly space; trained staff from multiple agencies (police, prosecution, child protection, medical, and psychiatric) who can dedicate specific hours to the CAC weekly; and core staff who can provide counseling, advocacy, and case management. A national evaluation of CACs to determine whether they actually produce the intended benefits has been conducted by the University of New Hampshire's Center for Research on Children and Crime; unfortunately, results of this evaluation have not yet been made public at the time of this publication.

Combating Commercial Sexual Exploitation of Children

There are new federal initiatives in New York City and Atlanta sponsored by OJJDP, particularly focusing on prostitution of runaway and throwaway children. There are distinct barriers to working effectively with this older juvenile population. The first problem is that they are often treated as offenders rather than victims and are arrested for prostitution or loitering. If they are returned home, they often run away again or their homes are unsafe, and there are few facilities designed specifically for their needs. If they are treated as victims rather than offenders and are placed in group homes, foster care, or other nonsecure residences, they may also run away again. They may be loyal to their pimps who are often boyfriends.

New York City, a destination for runaway and thrownaway children from surrounding states, illustrates the obstacles and the programs. In the city, 150 children under 17 were arrested for prostitution in 2004 (Lowe, 2005). The center of trafficking and child prostitution is the borough of Queens, which is the focus of the CSEC initiative. From 2000 to 2004, 70 children under 17 were arrested for prostitution in Queens, and 35 pimps were prosecuted for prostituting children under 17. The initiative includes a residential facility for girls, psychological counseling, and medical treatment. The goal of the intervention is not only to save the children but also to free them from dominance of and dependence on their pimps so that they will cooperate with prosecution.

On the international level, 32 countries have adopted laws that allow them to prosecute sex tourism committed by citizens outside their own territory (ECPAT, 2006). In the United States, Congress passed the PROTECT Act (Prosecutorial Remedies and Other Tools to End the Exploitation of Children Today) in 2003, specifically to combat sex tourism and commercial sexual exploitation of children, as well as to strengthen federal statutes against child abuse, kidnapping, and torture. The PROTECT Act allows the United States to prosecute domestically Americans who travel outside the country for sex tourism and increases the penalties for sex tourism to 30 years in prison. It also supports programs in the State Department and the Department of Homeland Security to increase public awareness and facilitate prosecution.

Antitrafficking Legal Initiatives and Services

The U.S. DOJ, including the Office for Victims of Crime, and the Department of Health and Human Services fund programs to provide social services to victims of trafficking, with a major goal of ensuring that the victims are available and able to assist with prosecution of traffickers. Beginning in 2000, Congress enacted the Trafficking Victims Protection Act (TVPA), which creates stiff penalties for trafficking, allocates funding for the prosecution of trafficking cases and for protecting victims, and requires the State Department to issue an annual trafficking report. It also grants special legal status to trafficking victims from other countries through the T-visa, which allows trafficking victims to stay in the United States for three years and then apply for legal permanent status. In 2002, the president created a cabinet-level Interagency Task Force on trafficking headed by the State Department's Office to Monitor and Combat Trafficking in Persons.

Antitrafficking organizations have sprung up in the United States and in many other countries. Existing immigration, antislavery, and victim assistance programs have tailored their services for trafficking victims, most serving victims of all forms of trafficking, but some specializing in particular forms of exploitation, including sex trafficking. Like other trafficking victims, those who have escaped from sex trafficking usually need psychological treatment for trauma, housing, and a source of income. They also need support in testifying against their traffickers and legal assistance in applying for a T-visa. There are regional, national, and international coalitions of service providers. In the United States, these include the California-based organization Coalition to Abolish Slavery and Trafficking, the national Freedom Network, and the midwestern Heartland Alliance. CAT-W is an international coalition of organizations focusing solely on sex trafficking, with representation in Africa, the Philippines, and Asia. In Asia, member organizations have projects to rehabilitate girls and women forced into prostitution, providing them with education, training, and employment.

REFERENCES

Bazelon, E. (2006, April 30). A question of resilience. *The New York Times Magazine*, pp. 54–59.

Boney-McCoy, S., & Finkelhor, D. (1995). Psychosocial sequelae of violent victimization in a national youth sample. *Journal of Consulting and Clinical Psychology, 63*(5), 726–736.

Briere, J., & Runtz, M. (1990). Differential adult symptomatology associated with three types of child sexual abuse histories. *Child Abuse & Neglect, 14,* 357–364.

Browne, A. (1987). *When battered women kill.* New York: Free Press.

Browne, A., Miller, B., & Maguin, E. (1999). Prevalence and severity of lifetime physical and sexual victimization among incarcerated women. *International Journal of Law and Psychiatry, 22*(3), 301–323.

Caceres, C. F., Vanoss, M., & Hudes, E. S. (2000). Sexual coercion among youth and young adolescents in Lima, Peru. *Journal of Adolescent Health, 27,* 361–367.

Campbell, R. (2005). What really happened? A validation study of rape survivors' help-seeking experiences with legal and medical systems. *Violence and Victims, 20*(1), 55–68.

Campbell, R. (2006). Rape survivors' experiences with the legal and medical systems: Do rape victim advocates make a difference? *Violence Against Women, 12*(1), 30–45.

Campbell, R., Patterson, D., & Lichty, L. F. (2005). The effectiveness of Sexual Assault Nurse Examiner (SANE) programs: A review of psychological, medical, legal, and community outcomes. *Trauma, Violence & Abuse, 6*(4), 313–329.

Campbell, R., & Raja, S. (1999). The secondary victimization of rape victims: Insights from mental health professionals who treat survivors of violence. *Violence and Victims, 14,* 261–275.

Campbell, R., Wasco, S. M., Ahrens, C. E., Sefl, T., & Barnes, H. E. (2001). Preventing the "second rape": Rape survivors' experiences with community service providers. *Journal of Interpersonal Violence, 16,* 1239–1259.

Catalano, S. M. (2005). *Criminal victimization 2004.* National crime victimization survey (NCJ 210674). Washington, DC: Bureau of Justice Statistics.

Cohen, Y., Spirito, A., & Brown, L. K. (1996). Suicide and suicidal behavior. In R. J. Declemente, W. B. Hanson, & L. E. Ponton (Eds.), *Handbook of adolescent health risk behavior* (pp. 193–224). New York: Plenum Press.

Cusick, L., Martin, A., & Tiggey, M. (2003). *Vulnerability and involvement in drug use and sex work.* London: Great Britain Home Office Research Development and Statistics Directorate.

DeWeese, J. (2004, November 26). "Feds arrest six in Corona human trafficking ring." *Times-Ledger Newspapers.* Retrieved April 15, 2006, from http://safehorizon.org/page.php?page=in the newsdebil&rcid=72

Dumond, R. W. (1992). The sexual assault of male inmates in incarcerated settings. *International Journal of Sociology, 20,* 135–157.

Dumond, R. W. (2000). Inmate sexual assault: The plague which persists. *Prison Journal, 80,* 407–414.

Dumond, R. W. (2003). Confronting America's most ignored crime problem: The Prison Rape Elimination Act of 2003. *Journal of the American Academy of Psychiatry Law, 31,* 354–360.

Economic and Social Commission for Asia and the Pacific (ESCAP). (2000). *Sexually abused and sexually exploited children and youth in the greater Mekong subregion: A qualitative assessment of their health needs and available services.* Geneva, Switzerland: United Nations.

ECPAT. (1996). *The Paedo file. ECPAT Newsletter, 4*(4).

ECPAT. (2006). Commercial sexual exploitation of children in the United States. Retrieved January 10, 2006, from www.ecpat.net/eng/Ecpat_inter/projects/monitoring/online_database/index.asp

Ensign, J., & Santelli, J. (1998). Health status and service use: Comparison of adolescents at a school-based health clinic with homeless adolescents. *Archives of Pediatrics and Adolescent Medicine, 152*(1), 20–24.

Estes, R. J., & Weiner, N. A. (2001). The commercial sexual exploitation of children in the U.S., Canada and Mexico. Philadelphia: University of Pennsylvania. Retrieved March 2, 2006, from www.sp2.upenn.edu/%7Erestes/CSEC.htm

The Facts About Child Sex Tourism. (2005, April 14). Washington, DC: U.S. State Department, Department of Homeland Security.

Farley, M. (2003). Prostitution and trafficking in nine countries: An update on violence and posttraumatic stress disorder. *Journal of Trauma Practice, 2*(3/4), 33–74.

Finkelhor, D., & Browne, A. (1985). The traumatic impact of child sexual abuse: A conceptualization. *Journal of Orthopsychiatry, 55*(4), 530–541.

Finkelhor, D., Hotaling, G., Lewis, I. A., & Smith, C. (1990). Sexual abuse in a national survey of adult men and women: Prevalence, characteristics, and risk factors. *Child Abuse & Neglect, 14*(1), 19–28.

Fisher, B. S., Cullen, F. T., & Turner, M. G. (2000). *The sexual victimization of college women* (NCJ 182369). United States Department of Justice. Washington, DC: U.S. Government Printing Office.

Fondacaro, K. M., Holt, J. C., & Powell, T. A. (1999). Psychological impact of childhood sexual abuse on male inmates: The importance of perception. *Child Abuse and Neglect, 23*(4), 361–369.

Greene, J. M., Ennett, S. T., & Ringwalt, C. L. (1999). Prevalence and correlates of survival sex among runaway and homeless youth. *American Journal of Public Health, 89,* 1406–1409.

Halcón, L., Beuhring, T., & Blum, R. (2000). *A portrait of adolescent health in the Caribbean, 2000.* Minneapolis: University of Minnesota and the Pan American Health Association.

Harner, H. (2000, April). *Sexual violence and adolescents.* Applied Research Forum: National Online Resource Center on Violence Against Women. Available at www.vawnet.org/Sexual Violence/Research/VAWnetDocuments/AR_ Adolescent.pdf

Herman, J. L. (1981). *Father-daughter incest.* Boston: Harvard University Press.

Herman, J. L. (1992a). Complex PTSD: A syndrome in survivors of prolonged and repeated trauma. *Journal of Traumatic Stress, 5,* 377–391.

Herman, J. L. (1992b). *Trauma and recovery.* New York: Basic Books/HarperCollins.

Hughes, D., & Roche, C. (Eds.). (1999). *Making the harm visible: Global sexual exploitation of women and girls.* Kingston, RI: Coalition Against Trafficking in Women.

Johnson, R. J., Ross, M. W., Taylor, W. C., Williams, M. L., Carvajal, R. I., & Peters, R. J. (2005). A history of drug use and childhood sexual abuse among incarcerated males in a

county jail. *Substance Use and Misuse, 40*(2), 211–229.

Kerry, Isakson Push for Tougher Penalties for Child Internet Pornography. (2005, December 20). Press release. Congress of the United States, Washington, DC 20515.

Kipke, M. D., Simon, T. R., Montgomery, S. B., Unger, J. B., & Iversen, E. F. (1997). Homeless youth and their exposure to and involvement in violence while living on the streets. *Journal of Adolescent Health, 20,* 360–367.

Klain, E. J. (1999). *Prostitution of children and child-sex tourism: An analysis of domestic and international responses.* Alexandria, VA: Center for Missing and Exploited Children.

Kral, A. H., Molnar, B. E., Booth, R. E., & Waters, J. K. (1997). Prevalence of sexual risk behavior and substance use among runaway and homeless adolescents in San Francisco, Denver and New York City. *International Journal of STD & AIDS, 8,* 109–117.

Kurtz, S. P., Surratt, H. L., Inciardi, J. A., & Kiley, M. C. (2004). Sex work and "date" violence. *Violence Against Women, 10*(4), 357–385.

Lisak, D., Hopper, J., & Song, P. (1996). Factors in the cycle of violence: Gender rigidity and emotional constriction. *Journal of Traumatic Stress, 9,* 721–743.

Lowe, H. (2005, June 21). Operation guardian: Child prostitution project in Queens. *Newsday,* p. A7.

Mahoney, P., Williams, L. M., & West, C. M. (2001). Violence against women by intimate partner relationships. In C. Renzetti, J. Edleson, & R. Bergen (Eds.), *Sourcebook on violence against women* (pp. 143–178). Thousand Oaks, CA: Sage Publications.

Man, C. D., & Cronan, J. P. (2002). Forecasting sexual abuse in prison: The prison subculture of masculinity as a backdrop for "deliberate indifference." *Journal of Criminal Law and Criminology, 92*(127), 1–38.

Maruschak, L. M. (2001). HIV in prisons and jails, 1999 (NCJ 187456). Washington, DC: U.S. Department of Justice, Bureau of Justice Statistics.

Marx, B. P., Calhoun, K. S., Wilson, A. E., & Meyerson, L. A. (2001). Sexual revictimization prevention: An outcome evaluation. *Journal of Consulting and Clinical Psychology, 69*(1), 25–32.

Masha's story. (2006). Web site set up by Masha Allen's attorney, James R. Marsh. Retrieved May 5, 2006, from www.mashastory.info/

Masson, G. (1984). *The assault on truth: Freud's suppression of the seduction theory*. New York: Farrar, Straus, Giroux.

McClanahan, S. F., McClanahan, G. M., Abram, K. M., & Teplin, L. A. (1999). Pathways into prostitution among female jail detainees and their implications for mental health services. *Psychiatric Services, 50*, 1606–1613.

Ministry of Foreign Affairs of Japan (MOFA). (2001, December 17–20). *Report of the Second World Congress Against Commercial Sexual Exploitation of Children*. Yokohama, Japan.

Molnar, B. E., Shade, S. B., Kral, A. H., Booth, R. E., & Watters, J. K. (1998). Suicidal behavior and sexual/physical abuse among street youth. *Child Abuse & Neglect, 22*(3), 213–222.

Musa, J. N. (2006, February 7). 25 NGOs fight human trafficking. *Daily Trust (Ajuba)*. Retrieved May 9, 2006, from http://allafrica.com/stories/200602070363

National Center for Missing and Exploited Children. (2002). *Female juvenile prostitution: Problem and response* (2nd Ed.). Retrieved February 15, 2006, from www.missingkids.com/missingkids/servlet/ResourceServlet?LanguageCountry=en_US&PageId=750

Noell, J., Rohde, P., Seeley, J., & Ochs, L. (2001). Childhood sexual abuse, adolescent sexual coercion, and sexually transmitted infection acquisition among homeless female adolescents. *Child Abuse & Neglect, 25*(1), 137–148.

Randall, M., & Haskell, L. (1995). Sexual violence in women's lives: Findings from the Women's Safety Project, a community-based survey. *Violence Against Women, 1*(1), 6–31.

Rennison, C. (2002). *Criminal victimization, 2001: Changes 2000–01 with trends, 1993–2001*. National crime victimization survey (NCJ 194610). Washington, DC: Bureau of Justice Statistics.

Rew, L., Taylor-SeeHafer, M., & Fitzgerald, M. L. (2001). Sexual abuse, alcohol and other drug use, and suicidal behaviors in homeless adolescents. *Issues in Comprehensive Pediatric Nursing, 24*, 225–240.

Rotheram-Borus, M. J., Mahler, K. A., Koopman, C., & Langabeer, K. (1996). Sexual abuse history and associated multiple risk behavior in adolescent runaways. *American Journal of Orthopsychiatry, 66*, 390–400.

Russell, D. E. H. (1986). *The secret trauma: Incest in the lives of girls and women*. New York: Basic Books.

Russell, D. E. H. (1990). *Rape in marriage*. New York: Macmillan.

Ryan, K. D., Kilmer, R. P., Cauce, A. M., Watanabe, H., & Hoyt, D. R. (2000). Psychological consequences of child maltreatment in homeless adolescents: Untangling the unique effects of maltreatment and family environment. *Child Abuse & Neglect, 24*, 333–352.

Silverman, J. G., Raj, A., Mucci, L. A., & Hathaway, J. E. (2001). Dating violence against adolescent girls and associated substance use, unhealthy weight control, sexual risk behavior, pregnancy and suicidality. *JAMA, 286*(5), 572–579.

Snyder, H. N. (2000). Sexual assault of young children as reported to law enforcement: Victim, incident, and offender characteristics (NCJ 182990). Pittsburgh, PA: National Center for Juvenile Justice.

Sobsey, D., & Doe, T. (1991). Patterns of sexual abuse and assault. *Sexuality and Disability* [Special Issue]. *Sexual Exploitation of People with Disabilities, 9*, 243–259.

Stop Prisoner Rape (SPR). (2003). Press release: Prison Rape Elimination Act becomes federal law. Retrieved March 3, 2006, from www.spr.org/en/pressreleases/2003/0904.html

Stop Prisoner Rape (SPR). (2006). Stop prisoner rape: A brief history. Retrieved on March 3, 2006, from www.spr.org/en/spr_history.asp

Struckman-Johnson, C. J., & Struckman-Johnson, D. L. (2000). Sexual coercion rates in seven midwestern prison facilities for men. *Prison Journal, 80*, 379–390.

Struckman-Johnson, C. J., & Struckman-Johnson, D. L. (2002). Sexual coercion reported by women in three midwestern prisons. *Journal of Sex Research, 39*(3), 217–228.

Tjaden, P., & Thoennes, N. (2000). *Extent, nature, and consequences of intimate partner violence: Findings from the national violence against women survey* (NCJ 181867). Washington, DC: National Institute of Justice.

Tjaden, P., & Thoennes, N. (2006). *Extent, nature, and consequences of rape victimization: Findings from the national violence against women survey* (NCJ 210346). Washington, DC: National Institute of Justice.

Tyler, K. A., & Cauce, A. M. (2002). Perpetrators of early physical and sexual abuse among homeless and runaway adolescents. *Child Abuse & Neglect, 26,* 1261–1274.

Tyler, K. A., Whitbeck, L. B., Hoyt, D. R., & Cauce, A. M. (2004). Risk factors for sexual victimization among male and female homeless and runaway youth. *Journal of Interpersonal Violence, 19*(5), 503–520.

United Nations Economic and Social Council, Commission on Human Rights. (1996). *Report of the special rapporteur on the sale of children, child prostitution, and child pornography.* 52nd sess., agenda item 20. UN doc E/CN.4/1996/100. Retrieved March 20, 2006, from www.unhchr.ch/children/rapporteur.htm

United Nations. (2006). Youth at the United Nations: Frequently asked questions. Retrieved March 5, 2006, from www.un.org/esa/socdev/unyin/qanda.htm

United States Embassy Stockholm (USES). (1996, August 27–31). *Child pornography: An international perspective.* World Congress Against the Commercial Sexual Exploitation of Children, Stockholm, Sweden.

Victim Services. (1994, July). *Child sexual abuse public policy project and multidisciplinary response protocol: Executive summary.* New York: Victim Services (now Safe Horizon).

Wikipedia. (2006). Entry for *Masha Allen,* "Masha's Law." Retrieved May 6, 2006, from http://en.wikipedia.org/wiki/Masha_Allen

Willis, B. M., & Levy, B. S. (2002). Child prostitution: Global health burden, research needs and interventions. *Lancet, 359*(9315), 1417–1422.

Wooden, W. S., & Parker, J. (1982). *Men behind bars: Sexual exploitation in prison.* New York: Plenum.

World Health Organization. (2002). *World report on violence and health,* E. G. Krug, L. L. Dahlberg, J. A. Mercy, A. B. Zwi, & R. Lozano (Eds.). Geneva: World Health Organization.

World Health Organization. (2005). *Summary report: WHO multi-country study on women's health and domestic violence against women.* Geneva: World Health Organization.

Victims of Domestic Violence

EVE BUZAWA

The purpose of this chapter is to provide an overview of the key issues pertaining to victims of domestic violence. There has been a proliferation of research and general public awareness since domestic violence was recognized as a problem of national significance in the 1970s. The following discussion will highlight the inherent judgments implicit in how we define domestic violence, the strategies used to identify and measure it, and what we have learned about its victims. In addition, the chapter acknowledges some of the key questions raised that have not yet been fully answered. These include the differential impact of domestic violence on various subpopulations, the relationships between domestic violence and violence in other relationships, and how domestic violence is linked to other forms of violence that a victim may experience over a lifetime.

Fundamental controversies regarding the nature of domestic violence and its impact continue despite years of public attention, much research, and an active legislative response to this societal problem. The disagreements that began with basic questions—including those that ask how we define domestic violence and identify the "real" victims—continue and, although beyond the scope of this chapter, have led to perhaps the most important question: What do we do with this information about domestic violence victims?

WHAT IS DOMESTIC VIOLENCE?

What is meant by "domestic violence" and what is the proper definition of the term for the study of domestic violence? Different definitions of domestic violence have been the topic of considerable discussion among practitioners, researchers, policymakers, feminists, and victim advocates. There are societal definitions, legal definitions, and research definitions of domestic violence—all of which differ. However, they all involve two primary considerations. First, *what are the relationships considered in identifying cases of "domestic violence"?* What is not often acknowledged is the complexity of diverse relationships that this term encompasses, especially in the legal arena. Typically, people think of "domestic violence" as being interchangeable with, and limited to, "wife battering" or "spousal abuse" (e.g., an assault between intimate partners). In comparison, state statutes use definitions that typically cover a far broader range of relationships.

Although this chapter focuses on *intimate partner violence* or *traditional concepts of spouse abuse,* most state domestic violence statutes deal with a greater range of social issues. Thus, such statutes not only include acts committed between two adult, married or unmarried partners or ex-partners, but by their terms, also typically cover violence between parent(s) or caretakers(s) and dependent children, and violence committed by siblings and other family relationships. Such intrafamily violence can be severe, but its character, causes, and treatment differ markedly from the type of violence I discuss here. There are also overall patterns that distinguish partner violence from violence that occurs in these other relationships. Data on domestic violence suffers from being aggregated with these other problems, making suspect the conclusions drawn from such data on many critical variables, such as injury, criminal justice decision making, and revictimization. In addition, comparisons are made between states, despite differences in the types of relationships and acts that are statutorily covered.

When examining National Incident Based Reporting System data from nine states, Greenfield et al. (1998) found that only 53% of so-called domestic violence cases involved spouses, 4.9% involved ex-spouses, and 42% involved "other intimates." In this case,

"other intimates" were defined as current or past boyfriend or girlfriend relationships, common-law spouses, or partners in homosexual relationships. Of the 42% of intimate partner cases falling under the category of "other intimates," there is great room for interpretation. What type of relationship between a man and a woman constitutes a "boyfriend" or "girlfriend"? When classifying a call, do police routinely ask such couples if they have ever resided together or if they have been sexually intimate?

The second consideration is that *domestic violence encompasses many different acts and behaviors.* There are huge differences in how the legal system defines domestic violence and how practitioners, researchers, and many victim advocates define domestic violence. Unlike many felonies, such as murder, robbery, or burglary, there has always been disagreement about definitions of domestic violence. Many members of the public consider only physical abuse or sexual assault as qualifying. Controlling behaviors, including psychological, verbal, and economic abuse, are not included because they are seen as ambiguous and difficult to identify and perhaps not even worthy of criminal sanction. The significance of this problem can be seen in my later discussion of how much domestic violence there actually is, who commits these acts, and domestic violence's impact and consequences.

Certainly, the term *violence* encompasses a broad range of maltreatment. Generally included in statutes are (1) physical violence, including an assault or a homicide; (2) sexual violence; (3) threats of physical and/or sexual violence; (4) emotional or psychological abuse; and (5) stalking for the purpose of domestic violence. It is recognized that there has yet to be overall agreement regarding the harm caused by all such activities, and in all likelihood, a consensus may not be reached. Nonetheless, there are problems with aggregating what most people consider serious acts of violence with behaviors considered more ambiguous. If this becomes the definition of "domestic violence," many might dismiss as hyperbole any findings regarding the overall prevalence of violence.

Having stated that, regardless whether it is called "domestic violence," there is a growing trend toward recognizing the seriousness of "protoviolent" behavior, which often involves an attempt by abusive personalities to circumvent explicit statutes on domestic violence through "stalking." Stalking can be defined as the act of deliberately and repeatedly following or harassing another person in order to create fear in the victim or to coerce him or her to accede to the wishes of the stalker. Stalking is sometimes considered a separate phenomenon, but it is often closely related, and sometimes a precursor, to physical assaults and is therefore properly included in many domestic violence statutes. Although many in the general public consider this behavior as a mere nuisance or inconvenience, the reality of stalking, especially in the context of domestic violence, is far different and is potentially extremely dangerous.

One of the primary difficulties in defining partner violence arises from the confusion between patterns of behavior and violent acts. Our criminal justice system typically does not address patterns of behavior and can address only specific acts. Individuals are charged with an offense that must be proved "beyond a reasonable doubt" in a court of law, which inherently limits how our legal system defines domestic violence. In addition, there is confusion between violent acts and injuries. Many people incorrectly believe that the sole legal criterion for measuring a violent act is injury. However, physical contact is not required as an element of the crime in most statutes. Criminal law acknowledges differences in assault severity by distinguishing among simple assault, aggravated assault, and sexual assault, but researchers often use the umbrella term *assault* to measure the

wide range of behaviors, ranging from minor threats to serious violent behavior.

For estimation purposes, the United States Justice Department's Bureau of Justice Statistics adopted an inclusive definition of assault that acknowledges that an "assault" may range from a minor threat to nearly fatal incidents. State statutes regularly redefine what constitutes legal criteria for "attempts" and "acts." Most surveys take a much broader view of assault that go beyond a simple measure of injuries. Assault incidents may therefore range from face-to-face verbal threats to a serious attack resulting in extensive injuries. An even wider net can be cast in defining assault by arguing for the inclusion of behaviors, such as verbal aggression, harassment, or other behaviors that are emotionally distressing. This can, of course, be carried to the farcical. For example, some municipalities have considered an ordinance that would make a criminal assault exuding the odor of aftershave lotion or mouthwash in public eating establishments.

Definitions of domestic violence are largely dependent on descriptions by the police, assailants, victims, and witnesses and based in large part on societal values. Many people assume assaults are physical acts that result in injuries. However, physical contact is not the sole legal criterion for assault. For example, Uniform Crime Reports include "attempts" in its definition of aggravated assault. The wording used by the U.S. National Crime Victimization Survey (NCVS) is that "an assault ranges from minor threat to incidents which are nearly fatal" (Bureau of Justice Statistics, 2005).

INCIDENCE AND PREVALENCE OF INTIMATE PARTNER VIOLENCE

Researchers define domestic violence through a wide variety of instruments that the general public depends on to understand not only the incidence and prevalence of domestic violence but also its patterns and trends. Furthermore, there is wide variation in reported rates of intimate partner violence based on the type of survey used and, for some surveys, the year(s) it was administered. The NCVS, supported by the Bureau of Justice Statistics, is the most comprehensive source for data on victimization for individuals 12 years of age and older. Its sample draws on United States Census Bureau data and is address based. The same sample is used for three years and sampled seven times at six-month intervals. For 2000, the NCVS reported a prevalence rate of .43% for females and .08% males.

The "unofficial" data of the NCVS report rates of domestic violence higher than those in official reports. Police estimates are based on offenses known to the police, whereas the NCVS is based on self-reports of criminal victimizations. These are two very different conceptions of crime. The victimization rate is generally higher than the offense rate in police records for three primary reasons. First, there are times when a single incident of assault, known to police, involves two or more victims. Second, victimizations are based solely on victim accounts with no corroborating evidence, which is generally not the case in establishing the existence of a criminal offense. Third, some victimizations are not counted in police records because an incident is not even classified as one in which an assaultive offense has occurred.

In June 2005, NCVS data were used for the report *Family Violence Statistics: Including Statistics on Strangers and Acquaintances.* The report distinguished between violence involving spouses, including common-law spouses and ex-spouses, and those involving a child or stepchild or other family member. The report also included data that differentiated between family and nonfamily violence (Dunrose et al., 2005).

The study estimated that 5.4% of all violence between 1998 and 2002 was committed by one spouse against another. However, this report might be confusing to the general public because of its format. For example, the investigators are clear in identifying boyfriend, ex-boyfriend, girlfriend, ex-girlfriend, and homosexual partner as "nonfamily," but statutes and other researchers typically include these categories in definitions of domestic and intimate partner violence. The study also reported that the rate of family violence ranged from approximately 5.4 victims to 2.1 victims per 1,000 between the years 1993 and 2002.

The number of violent acts committed by a stranger is often reported as an indicator of the relative seriousness of intimate partner violence, compared with total violent acts. For example, in 2003, strangers committed 31.8% of violent acts against women, 9.8% were committed by "other relative," and 38.1% by a "friend or acquaintance." The percentage of violence crimes against women by an intimate partner was 18.7%, compared with 2.7% of men (Bureau of Justice Statistics, 2005).

The National Surveys of Family Violence (NSFV) relied on data generated by the conflict tactics scale (Straus, 1990) and its revision (Gelles, 1987) and reported overall physical violence rates of 12.1% for women and 11.6% for men, and 12.3% for women and 12.1% for men, in the late 1970s and mid-1980s, respectively. However, this study intended to examine how conflict and violence is expressed in families and has not been administered on a national basis since 1985.

The National Violence Against Women Survey (NVAWS) was a national telephone survey conducted from November 1995 to May 1996. The survey was an effort to improve on the NCVS by focusing specifically on violence against women (Tjaden & Thoennes, 2000). The study included only individuals 18 years and older and employed a methodology that differed from the one used in the NVAWS. Therefore the results are not directly comparable. Tjaden and

Thoennes reported a violence rate of 1.3% against women and .9% against men. However, unlike many other national surveys, they reported the prevalence of stalking as well. They estimated that 4.8% of women had been stalked by an intimate during their lifetime and that .5% of women (50,485) had been stalked by an intimate in the past 12 months. In comparison, they estimated that .6% men had been stalked by an intimate during their lifetime and that .2% (185,496) of the men had been stalked by an intimate in the past 12 months (Tjaden & Thoennes, 2000).

Studies have reported wide variation in domestic violence rates, which stem from differences in the age of the sample population, how they were selected, as well as other methodological issues. However, different findings reflect not only differences in methodology but also differences in the years that studies were conducted. For example, between 1993 and 2002, domestic violence rates fell by over 50%, paralleling a similar reduction in all violent offenses. Therefore, comparisons of the NVAWS data from 1995 with the more current NCVS data would have little utility. Moreover, it is premature to conclude that recent drops in domestic violence rates are related to proactive efforts to combat such offenses.

WHO ARE THE VICTIMS?

National-level, aggregate data on domestic violence often tend to mask major differences among specific groups in the population. These variations are now being identified, and their significance for practitioners and policymakers is being further explored. When domestic violence first became recognized as a national problem, researchers and advocates emphasized that it was equally prevalent among all groups of women. The fact that it was better known among victims of lower socioeconomic or racial minority status was attributed to its visibility in this group, compared with more affluent, white victims, who tend to keep such incidents hidden from the public eye. However, the differential impact of domestic violence is now widely acknowledged (Buzawa & Buzawa, 2003; Moore, 1997; Stanko, 2004).

Role of Gender

Although definitions of intimate partner violence are gender-neutral, women are at disproportionate risk for serious victimization. Their risks for intimate partner violence, sexual assault, and stalking are greater than those of men. They also are at greater risk for multiple types of victimization as well as recurrent violent victimization in relationships. In 2000, the NCVS reported that 20% of violence against women was committed by an intimate partner, compared with 3% of men (Rennison, 2001). In addition, although both men and women initiate violence, in most cases, violence initiated by women is far less severe and is often in response to actual or anticipated male violence. For example, the National Family Violence Survey (NFVS) found that the injury rate for women was six times higher than it was for men (3% and .5%, respectively). This survey also reported that 42% of women who were assaulted since the age of 18 were injured in their most recent assault; however, most of the injuries were relatively minor (Tjaden & Thoennes, 2000).

The NCVS found that approximately half of female domestic violence victims reported physical injury, compared with 32% of male victims. The rates of serious injury were similar (4% for men and 5% for women), but women are significantly more likely to incur minor injuries (more than 4 in 10 women, compared with fewer than 3 in 10 men; Rennison & Welchans, 2000). However, women initiate acts of domestic assault and these are not always the result of self-defense (Moore-Parmley, 2004). The historic reluctance of many victim advocates to hold women accountable for acts of violence could have contributed to the backlash expressed by many men's organizations. Data also suggest that lifetime domestic violence is experienced by a large percentage of lesbian and gay individuals, although there is considerable variation in the estimates of violent attacks that occur in these groups (Baum, 2002).

The NVAWS was the first study to include same-sex violence as part of a large-scale national survey. It reported that approximately 11% of women in a lesbian relationship reported being raped, physically assaulted, or stalked by their partner. Although a significant percentage, this number was less than the 30% of women who reported such violence when living with a man in a heterosexual relationship. In contrast, in male, same-sex couples, the rate of violence was approximately 15% against a partner, whereas women physically abused men in heterosexual relationships at a rate slightly less than 8%. Hence, while same-sex violence is clearly an underaddressed issue, this research suggests that men perpetrate more violence in both same-sex and heterosexual relationships, with the highest rates of male violence occurring in heterosexual relationships (Tjaden & Thoennes, 2000).

Racial Variations

Coker (2000) discussed how research simplifies the diverse experience of women in the United States. She observed that studies purporting to examine "women of color" have relied primarily on African American women and that research on White women in many studies has become the surrogate for all women. Even when such studies try to expand their generalizability, the results are sometimes difficult to interpret. For example, Coker (2000) noted that in one of the largest studies examining domestic violence rates among Latino women, the study included only women who spoke English.

African Americans. Data on intimate partner violence among African Americans, compared with the general population, vary considerably. In one of the earliest studies of African American victims, Straus and Gelles (1986) reported that the victims had four times the rate of partner violence, compared with Whites. More recently, Bent-Goodley (2001) observed that African Americans are more likely than other racial groups to sustain serious and lethal injuries from episodes of domestic violence. Hence, violent partners appear to victimize African Americans at rates significantly higher than any other group (Bent-Goodley, 2001; Rennison & Welchans, 2000).

NCVS data suggest that the comparative rates of domestic violence between African American and White women are similar for every age group, except the ages of 20 and 24; in this category, the rates were 29 per 1,000 for African American women, compared with 20 per 1,000 for White women (Rennison, 2001). The NVAWS reported higher rates of victimization rates for African American women, but found that when other sociodemographic and relationship variables were controlled, these differences disappeared. The NCVS data showed that the rate of intimate partner violence against African Americans is 2.5 times the rate of violence against women of other races (Rand & Rennison, 2004).

Each year between 1992 and 1996, an average of 12 per 1,000 African American women experienced violence by an intimate, compared with fewer than 8 per 1,000 White women (Greenfield et al., 1998). Rennison and Welchans (2000), who like Greenfield and colleagues used Bureau of Justice Statistics data, reported that African Americans "were victimized by intimate partners at significantly higher rates than persons of any other race between 1993 and 1998" (p. 4). It would be overly simplistic to state that this is due to some inherent features of the African American family. Instead, it appears that both environmental stress and family pathologies—including poverty, social dislocation, unemployment, and population density—all play a role in escalating the rates of violence (Bent-Goodley, 2001). The effects of poverty as well as other related factors are highlighted by the fact that these differences diminish (but are not totally absent) when other sociodemographic and relationship variables are controlled (Tjaden & Thoennes, 2000).

The effects of income inequality and differences in social structure might also encourage more domestic violence among African Americans. For example, M. P. Johnson (2001) found that unemployment was a significant predictor of violence. She suggested that some men might perceive employment as a critical component of their masculine identity and resort to violence in an effort to regain lost status. In addition, urban poverty differentially affects African American women, who are more likely than White women to live in neighborhoods with high rates of poverty overall. This is likely to have a disproportionate impact on the availability of services for African American victims of domestic violence (Coker, 2000).

Middle-class African American women are also more likely to experience domestic violence than White middle-class women. It has been suggested that the "lifestyle behaviors" or traditional cultural values that govern relationships are maintained even when social class changes (Bell & Mattis, 2000; Bent-Goodley, 2001). Employment may still be a factor in middle-class African American households. Specifically, research suggests that the discrepancy between employment and income places a woman at risk. When women earn more than men or have a higher employment status, many men feel psychologically threatened and use violence to reassert power in their relationship (Yllö & Straus, 1990). This may partially account for the higher rates of domestic violence among middle-class African American women, who may more often partner with men with lower status, or at least lower paying jobs, than they.

Domestic violence in the African American community can be viewed simply as maladaptive behavior in response to societal oppression, racism, and discrimination (Oliver, 1999; Williams, 1999). The experience of powerlessness, anger, and distrust of a dominant community might be responsible for increasing the potential for abuse between intimates of color (Bent-Goodley, 2001; Franklin, 2000). Franklin (2000) posed the intriguing hypothesis that American society has allowed African American men to become the "head" of the household and given him authority over African American women in tacit exchange for the men's avoidance of confrontations with the White power structure. A rationale for why domestic violence might have increased in the African American community during the 1960s and 1970s may be that minority women began to economically and politically challenge the position of African American men (West, 1999). The development of a strong African American political culture in the 1980s and 1990s meant that minority women—even those who knew of extensive domestic violence problems in their community—remained silent in order to support their community as a whole and challenge the stereotypes of African American men in society (Bent-Goodley, 2001).

Significant differences in intimate partner violence have also been reported among other racial groups; however, the data are inconsistent. The NVAWS found that American Indian/Alaska Native women reported significantly higher rates of intimate partner violence than women of other racial backgrounds, and Asian/Pacific Islander women and men reported significantly lower rates. The researchers noted that American Indian/Alaska Native women could have been more willing to report victimization to interviewers than are other victims (Tjaden & Thoennes, 2000). High rates of domestic violence in any racial or ethnic group are not inevitable. Rather, race may be a risk marker, increasing the likelihood of violence, compared with the population as a whole.

Ethnic Diversity. The victim-related needs of many groups of minority women have not been fully recognized, and such women have not been given the opportunity to receive culturally appropriate interventions and services. One of the goals of the Violence Against Women Act (VAWA) was to improve the availability and quality of such services. The country's increasing ethnic diversity demands a discussion of the *additional* challenges facing these groups of domestic violence victims.

Recent research has begun to address ethnic differences in victimizations and their implications for services. Although the NVAWS reported few differences in intimate partner physical violence and stalking between Hispanic and non-Hispanic women, they found significant differences in rape committed by a current or former partner. The researchers highlighted the significance of this finding because Hispanic women are less likely than other women to be sexually assaulted by a nonintimate or former nonintimate partner.

Overall rates of intimate partner violence among immigrant groups, as a defined population subset, are extremely difficult to determine for several reasons. Specifically, many surveys combine immigrants with persons born in the United States, but whose parents were immigrants. In addition, a national survey of criminal justice officials and leaders of six ethnic communities suggests that many recent immigrants fail to report crimes (Davis & Erez, 1998). In fact, 67% of the officials in the national survey believed that they were less likely to report crimes, compared with other victims, and only 12% thought they were as, or more, likely to report offenses to the police. Domestic violence victims were less likely to report their victimizations, making an overall appraisal of the rates of domestic violence in immigrant groups especially problematic. The reluctance to report may be a result of the increased criminalization of domestic assault. For example, many Latina, Asian, and African American women may be concerned about their abusers being arrested and brought into the criminal justice system.

There are many cultural differences and ideologies that can place women at greater risk of intimate partner violence. In Asian and Middle Eastern immigrant communities, role expectations for women are often rigid, and the right of men to physically "discipline" their wives may be considered culturally acceptable (Raj & Silverman, 2002). Research has suggested that these women are often more easily acculturated than their male partners and more willing (if not eager) to adopt American expectations for their behavior. The result of this conflict in role expectations increases the woman's risk of violence because of their partners' attempts to maintain the type of control that their culture has allowed them. Hence, intimate partner violence is more likely in relationships in which the partner holds their culturally traditional role expectations for women (Bui & Morash, 1999; Morash, Bui, & Santiago, 2000).

Many immigrant victims of domestic violence are socially isolated. They often do not have the traditional family supports available or may actually be isolated from contact by the offender (Abraham, 2000; Raj & Silverman, 2002). These victims may be less likely to receive emotional support because of cultural expectations (Raj & Silverman, 2002). They are also often deterred by their lack of familiarity with the legal system and fear that they will be deported, especially if they report their abuse. Many batterers deliberately fail to file the necessary immigration papers to legalize the victim's status (Teran, 1999). Research on Latina victims of domestic violence also reports the high levels of fear by undocumented women. These victims are often afraid that police involvement will lead to their deportation and to possible separation from children (Coker, 2000).

Given the long and ignominious history of White and Native American relations, it is not surprising that social problems, which are closely associated with widespread social disorganization, emerged shortly after tribal relocation. It is almost superfluous to comment on the miserable conditions in which Native Americans live on many reservations. The statistics pertaining to poverty levels, unemployment, infant mortality, and substance abuse—to name but a few of the social problems Native Americans on reservations face—clearly demonstrate the dire circumstances under which ancient cultures fight to survive.

American Indian and Alaska Native women report far higher rates of intimate partner violence than women of other racial backgrounds (Tjaden & Thoennes, 2000). However, most of the early studies attempting to measure the prevalence of intimate partner violence among Native American women were limited by small samples of research participants. A study of Native American women, conducted in western Oklahoma by Halinka-Malcoe and Duran (2004), reported that two-thirds of the women had been physically assaulted, one-half had been beaten, and one-fourth had been raped by a partner during their lifetime. However, the researchers also noted that there were variations within the Native American population; another study examining rates among Navajo women as well as the NVAWS survey reported rates that were considerably lower (Halinka-Malcoe and Duran, 2004).

THE IMPACT OF DOMESTIC VIOLENCE

Death and Physical Injury

Regardless of the methods used to measure incidents of domestic violence, it is clear that the high number of assaults have resulted in massive numbers of injured and dead victims. Each year, acts of domestic violence lead approximately 1.5 million women and 500,000 men to seek medical attention; more than half of the injuries require hospital visits or stays (National Clearing House on Domestic Violence, 1980; Straus, 1990). However, we also know that the number of incidents coming to the police's attention has grown considerably in recent years. Legislation, departmental policies, changing public values, and increased criminal justice personnel and resources have all contributed to an increase in assaults reported to and recorded by the police. As a result, we may also have a higher proportion of less serious or injurious assaults taking place (Blumstein, 2000). Therefore the actual *rate* of injury and serious of assaults might have decreased as a result. In addition, advances in emergency medical care have greatly reduced the fatalities resulting from domestic violence and thus decreased the homicide rate, because many of these incidents now result in only assaults (Harris, Thomas, Fisher, and Hirsch, 2002).

Domestic violence plays a major role in homicide. Approximately 30% of female victims of homicides are killed by an intimate partner (Rand & Rennison, 2004). Immigrant groups and racial minorities are more likely to be victims of such crimes (Bent-Goodley, 2001; Frye, Wilt, & Schonberg, 2000). Nonetheless, there has been a reduction in the actual numbers of domestic homicides of about 14%, overall, for men and women in the past 20 years, with a 67% decrease for men (from 1,357 to 388) and a 25% decrease for women (from 1,600 to 1,202; Fox and Zawitz, 2004). There are variations in injury and the use of medical care for domestic physical and sexual assaults. The NVAWS reported that 41.5% of the women who were physically assaulted and 36.2% of the women who were sexually assaulted by an intimate partner were injured. The survey also reported that nearly 15,000 of the rapes and 240,000 of the physical assaults resulted in emergency room visits (Tjaden & Thoennes, 2000).

Acute physical injury resulting from a domestic assault can lead to long-term problems with victims' physical health. These include chronic pain, sexually transmitted diseases, miscarriages, gastrointestinal disorders, genitourinary tract problems, and a variety of other disorders (Walker, Logan, Jordan, & Campbell, 2004). Many women receive medical treatment for their problems, but many others are denied access to health care for a variety of reasons, including lack of assistance, financial constraints, or prohibitions placed on them by their abuser.

Psychological Effects

Researchers and practitioners have observed that adjustment problems are correlated with disruptions in interpersonal relationships (Bruce, 1998; Walker et al., 2004). Intimate partner violence is a major stressor in relationships. Therefore the impact of domestic violence can extend beyond individual acts of physical violence and result in serious psychological harm.

The degree of psychological harm is not simply a function of the amount of force used or injuries sustained in an incident. Victims of violence are frequently emotionally traumatized. The battering syndrome is related to medical complaints, depression, low self-esteem, and a variety of other psychosocial problems (Campbell, Kub, Belknap, & Templin, 1997; Campbell & Soeken, 1999; Stark & Flitcraft, 1988; Zlotnick, Kohn, Peterson, & Pearlstein, 1998). It is also associated with the risk of rape, miscarriage, abortion, alcohol and drug abuse, attempted suicide, emotional well-being, and post-traumatic stress disorder (PTSD; Campbell & Soeken, 1999; Gore-Felton, Gill, Koopman, & Spiegel, 1999; Stark & Flitcraft, 1988; Stets & Straus, 1990).

The adverse psychological consequences of these problems are enormous. The rates of suicide of battered women are almost five times as high as they are in nonbattered populations (Stark, 1984). Furthermore, it appears that many of these problems begin *after* the abuse, not as a cluster of which abuse is merely one factor (Holtzworth-Munroe, Bates, Smytzler, & Sandin, 1997; Stark, 1984; Woods, 1999). The emotional toll of domestic violence is also greatly increased if a psychological assault is also part of the pattern of abuse. Researchers have reported that women often find psychological, verbal, and emotional abuse more harmful and of far greater duration than physical abuse alone (DeKeseredy & MacLeod, 1997).

Sexual assault, as a component of domestic violence, is also quite common, but it is less frequently reported, and there is a lack of empirical data on its prevalence or consequences. Although sexual assault occurs in isolation from physical and other forms of abuse, it is commonly seen in cases where there is also severe physical abuse (Gordon, 2000). This type of victimization can be particularly harmful for victims and can lead to chronic mental health problems (Foa & Riggs, 1994; Riggs, Kilpatrick, & Resnick, 1992).

The severity and extent of abuse is highly related to the expression of the symptoms of PTSD. Not only do high proportions of victims of sexual, physical, and psychological assault suffer from PTSD, but these individuals also constitute a significant proportion, overall, of the total number of people who experience the symptoms of this diagnosis.

Monetary Costs

Actual dollar figures have been calculated in an effort to better determine the effects of domestic violence on society. The Centers for Disease Control estimate that physical and mental health care costs for interpersonal violence are close to $4.1 billion. Researchers calculated an additional productivity cost of $858.6 million for days of employment and household chores lost as a result of intimate partner violence (CDC, 2003).

RISK MARKERS FOR VICTIMS

A number of situational, demographic, socio-economic, and relationship characteristics affect the likelihood of victimization. Simply looking at an entire population of victims without understanding the range of diversity within that population can blur efforts to understand these variations in risk. In addition, victims share characteristics and behaviors that are similar to those of nonvictims in the general population. The interaction among these characteristics and behaviors can identify people at risk. However, it is difficult, if not impossible, to conclusively establish causal relationships between predictor variables and victimization. We may never identify the definitive causes of domestic violence, because many interacting factors have differential effects on the individuals involved in such incidents. Instead, a body of research can help us better understand characteristics, behaviors, and relationships that increase the probability of battering or victimization. A comprehensive discussion of these factors is beyond the scope of this chapter. However, the following sections will highlight a few key factors.

Substance Abuse

Substance abuse has long been known to lower inhibitions to violence and is associated with offending behavior and risk for victimization (Anderson, 2002; Chermack, Booth, & Curran, 2006; Lipsey, Wilson, Cohen, & Derzon, 1997). Most researchers have reported that high numbers of domestic violence offenders use illegal drugs or consume excessive quantities of alcohol, at rates far beyond those found in the general population (Scott, Schafer, & Greenfield, 1999).

Alcohol and drug abuse are among the most important variables that predict female intimate violence (Kantor & Straus, 1989). In several studies that statistically controlled for sociodemographic variables, hostility, and marital satisfaction, the relationship of alcohol use to violence was still highly significant (H. Johnson, 2001; Kaufman Kantor & Straus, 1990).

Individuals who have a pattern of excessive alcohol use at one time, but not on a consistent basis ("binge drinking"), are far more likely to engage in domestic violence than individuals who engage in other patterns of sustained alcohol consumption (e.g., heavy drinkers). Specifically, the NFVS reported that domestic violence rates for "high moderate" drinkers were twice as high, and the rates for binge drinkers were three times as high as nondrinkers (Kaufman Kantor & Straus, 1990). The NVAWS estimated that binge drinkers are three to five times more likely to be violent against a female partner than those who do not drink (Tjaden & Thoennes, 2000).

The timing of the use of the alcohol and drugs appears to be closely related to the risk of assault. An in-depth study of the correlates of domestic violence in the city of Memphis reported an overwhelming association between substance abuse and domestic violence. This research reported that almost all offenders had used drugs or alcohol the day of the assault, two-thirds had used a dangerous combination of cocaine and alcohol, and nearly half of all assailants (45%) were reported by families as using drugs, alcohol, or both daily to the point of intoxication for the past month (Brookoff, 1997, p. 1). Another investigation found that 70% of the abusers, at the time of attack, were under the influence of drugs, alcohol, or both, with 32% using only drugs, 17% using only alcohol, and 22% using both (Roberts, 1988). A more recent study reported that male partners, entering domestic violence treatment, were eight times more likely to have used violence against their partner after drinking (Fals-Stewart, Golden, & Schumacher, 2003).

The use of alcohol and drugs appears to be even more common among those committing more serious acts of violence. For example, one study found that more than half of prison inmates convicted of violent crimes against intimates were drinking or using drugs at the time of the offense; the same study found that about 40% of intimate partner homicide offenders reportedly were drinking at the time of the incident (Greenfield et al., 1998).

Other studies maintain that the evidence to date provides inadequate empirical support for the conclusion that alcohol and drug use are causally related to domestic violence (M. P. Johnson, 2001; Kantor & Asdigian, 1997; Mears, Carlson, Holden, & Harris, 2001; Schafer, Caetano, & Cunradi, 2004; Schwartz & DeKeseredy, 1997; Testa, 2004). In fact, a Canadian study reported that if all attitudinal and behavioral measures that predict violence against women were controlled, the simple correlation with alcohol abuse would disappear (H. Johnson, 2001). In support of this position, it has been suggested that the relationship between alcohol and domestic abuse is indirect and a function of attitudes that support the use of intimate violence. Kaufman Kantor and Straus (1990) reported that rates of domestic abuse by men who supported the idea of hitting a partner, but who rarely consumed alcohol, had higher rates of actual violence than men who were heavy drinkers but did not approve of violence toward a partner. The highest rates of violence, however, were among men with attitudes supportive of violence against women and who were heavy drinkers, indicating that attitudes toward violence strongly mediated any effect that the consumption of alcohol might have on committing violent acts.

M. P. Johnson (2001) examined the role of alcohol abuse relative to male attitudes supporting domestic abuse and other sociodemographic variables. She reported that half of assaulted women said that their male attacker had been or usually was drinking at the time of assault. Furthermore, 29% of these women believed alcohol was the precipitating factor in the incident. Johnson's research did not find that alcohol and violence were causally related, however. In fact, when controlling for attitudes toward the acceptability of male dominance and violence toward women, alcohol abuse was not significantly related to violence. Nonetheless, most research reports that there is a fairly high correlation between alcohol abuse and the perpetration of domestic abuse Testa (2004).

The role of alcohol and drug use is also a risk marker for domestic violence victims. Research suggests that rates of substance abuse among women with victimization histories are higher than among women in the general population (Walker et. al., 2004). A number of studies have demonstrated that the use of alcohol and drugs by women could place them at increased risk for domestic violence (Breslau, Davis, Andreski, & Peterson, 1991; Kantor & Straus, 1989; Kessler & Zhao, 1999). Many victims use these substances before being attacked. According to their own reports or reports of family members, about 42% of victims used alcohol or drugs on the day of the assault; 15% had used cocaine. About half of those using cocaine said that their assailants had forced them to use it (Brookoff, 1997, pp. 1–2). Also significant is the increased risk for women's use of alcohol and drugs *after* abuse (Gilbert et al., 2000; Kilpatrick, Acierno, Renick, Saunders, & Best, 1997). Kilpatrick et al. (1997) reported that this relationship was significant even after controlling for a victim's substance abuse and assault history.

Victim's alcohol or drug use may not be a "cause" of domestic violence but merely a consequence; that is, it may simply be a reaction or a coping mechanism for abuse (Kantor & Asdigian, 1997). For example, one study reported that women's drinking was twice as likely to occur among victims than among perpetrators after the abusive incident (Barnett & Fagan, 1993). Such substance use could also increase the likelihood of revictimization, resulting in the continuance of substance abuse (Kilpatrick et al., 1997) and the creation of a pernicious feedback loop between violence and victim substance abuse. Binge drinking by either the offender or the victim seems to place victims at increased risk (Fals-Stewart, 2003; Kantor & Straus, 1989).

Substance and partner abuse might spring from a personality or physiological disorder, such as a chemical imbalance in the pleasure centers of the brain or elevated testosterone levels in males, which lead to the misuse of alcohol or illegal substances *and* the inability to control violent tendencies (Scott et al., 1999). Hence, although H. Johnson (2001) and others have not reported a causal relationship, the fact remains that the two phenomena are closely related. For this reason, the best we can say at this time is that substance abuse is highly correlated with intimate partner violence among both batterers and their victims. However, the reason for the correlation between alcohol and substance abuse and battering is unclear. The use of alternative methodologies, including laboratory analog designs, can improve our understanding of the linkages between substance use and violence (Testa, 2004).

The implications for treatment might be that offenders with substance abuse problems need help with long-standing issues of substance abuse as well as behavior modification therapy to address abusive tendencies. However, many court-ordered batterer treatment programs are simply inadequate, because they do not provide a sustained, two-pronged treatment approach or disqualify substance abuse offenders from treatment. Similarly, victims of violence could need substance abuse assistance to successfully avoid being revictimized.

The pernicious effects of substance abuse are not spread equally throughout the entire population. For a variety of reasons, African American, Latino, and Native American populations have been found to be at increased risk for heavy drinking, which dramatically increases the likelihood of domestic violence (Bachman, 1992; West, 1999). For example, one study reported that Latinas with partners who were binge drinkers were 10 times more likely to be assaulted than those with low to moderate drinking partners (Kaufman Kantor & Straus, 1990).

Poverty and Unemployment

Many battered women's activists and organizations, concerned with developing broad domestic violence policies, have noted that domestic violence crosses all economic boundaries (Moore, 1997; Schwanberg, Logan, & Macke, 2005). The observation that victims are drawn from all socioeconomic classes and ethnic groups has often been based on ideological beliefs and the desire to push universal policy changes rather than on empirical research rigorously examining the correlates of abuse.

Such studies rely on unrepresentative samples of middle- and upper-middle-class suburban White women. Many of these women have become spokespersons for battered women or were the focus of the press, perhaps because the media find their plight more newsworthy than that of more representative, abused women (i.e., those who are poor, minority, and disempowered). In contrast, most empirically based survey research consistently reports that although domestic violence is present in all social strata and ethnic groups, it is disproportionately concentrated in poor population subgroups (Kantor & Jasinski, 1998; Moore, 1997; Straus & Smith, 1990).

Women with less income have higher rates of victimization. For example, the NCVS data reported that women in households with incomes less than $7,500 reported a rate of nonlethal violence at a rate 10 times higher than those women who have an income of $75,000 or more. Women who are supported by welfare experience higher rates of abuse than women in a similarly low socio-economic bracket. One estimate reports that approximately one-third of women on welfare are current victims of abuse, while slightly more than half had been victims of abuse during their lifetime (Tolman & Raphael, 2000).

Domestic violence is often a barrier to employment (Moe & Bell, 2004). Batterers actively interfere with a victim at her place of employment; attempt to disable her vehicle or take money used for public transportation; threaten her, her children, or pets should she go to her place of employment; or even physically restrain or incapacitate her so that she is unable to leave her residence (Romero, Chavkin, Wise, & Smith, 2003). Economically disadvantaged women are also more likely than others to have a variety of physical and mental health problems, to have partners who oppose or interfere with school or employment, and to have more frequent periods of unemployment and welfare dependence (Walker, Logan, Jordan, & Campbell, 2004).

The link between domestic violence victimization and unemployment has not been established. A victim's participation in the labor force can increase her risk for abuse by threatening the batterer's position of symbolic or economic power (Kaukinen, 2004). Others argue that empowering her in her personal life and relationship with the batterer decreases a victim's risk. It also can create the means and support networks needed for independence (Gibson-Davis, Magnuson, Gennetian, & Duncan, 2005; Kaukinen, 2004). Finally, Melzer (2002) has argued that the relative difference between the batterer's income and social status, compared with the victim's, is critical in determining risk.

Childhood Experiences With Violence

Children in abusive families appear to be the most susceptible to the adverse effects of domestic violence. Large numbers of this especially vulnerable group regularly witness violence in the family. For example, Edelson (2001) reported that in a group of 114 battered women, 45% stated that their children entered situations in which abuse was occurring at least "occasionally," 18% responded that this occurred "frequently," and only 23% said that this "never" occurred. Even this startling data may underestimate the extent of child witnessing of adult violence, because another study reported that 77% of children whose parents said their children did not witness violence actually did (O'Brien, John, Margolin, & Erel, 1994). Despite the victim's or even the offender's attempts to hide acts of violence from the children, their witnessing of such acts clearly puts them at risk for becoming the "hidden victims" of domestic abuse (Fantuzzo & Mohr, 1999).

What impact does witnessing violence have on future victimization? Research has suggested that it might be a better predictor of future violence than even direct victimization (Hotaling & Sugarman, 1990; Widom & Maxfield, 2001). Could such an impact manifest itself in the context of general behavioral problems or a tendency to be a victim or a victimizer? These questions are important in the generation of theories of the long-term social and behavioral problems caused by violence and the intergenerational transfer of violence. Edleson (2001) noted that there are more than 100 studies on the impact of family violence. He reported that several studies found that "externalized" behaviors, such as aggression and antisocial behavior, were more common in children, especially boys, exposed to domestic violence; "internalized" behaviors, such as unusual fears and inhibitions, were also common, especially among girls.

Other studies have reported a variety of adverse effects on children who have witnessed domestic violence, including that, in general, they score lower on tests of social competency and higher on depression, anxiety, aggression, shyness, and school-related problems (Adamson & Thompson, 1998; Hotton, 2003). Another study indicated that children who witness violence score lower on tests of cognitive functioning (Rossman, 2001).

Research regarding the impact of childhood and adolescent exposure to violence is now emerging, but findings need further development. We lack sufficient data on the link between violence and subsequent victimization and offending. Many witnesses of early violence do not become victims or offenders as adults. Others become offenders, and still others become victims. A better grasp of how these behaviors evolve is needed. We also require more knowledge on how to intervene successfully with children and adolescents to decrease the likelihood of negative consequences. We know that we must intervene, but we lack an empirically based understanding of how best to provide assistance.

How are these events affected by the specific characteristics of the child such as age, personality, and other risk factors in his or her life, including poverty, parental substance abuse, and exposure to violence in other settings? These interactions are common and likely to be complex. For example, children exposed to parental violence are also far more likely to be physically abused and neglected, with estimates as high as 15 times the national average (Osofsky, 1999). They are also more likely to be at greater risk for exposure to sibling violence, violence in the schools, and street violence (Osofsky, 1999). To date, research cannot definitively identify the role of these and other factors in subsequent violence. In addition, a child's individual characteristics determine his or her resiliency and include traits such as intellectual development and interpersonal

skills. These protective factors are further linked to availability of outside support systems (Osofsky, 1999).

Victim-Offender Relationship

The relationship between a victim and offender influences the nature and severity of violence in a relationship. People who are unfamiliar with the dynamics of domestic violence often question the high numbers of women who stay with batterers. Nonetheless, the literature suggests that separation from an abusive partner often increases the risk of violence (Campbell & Boyd, 2003; Fleury, Sullivan, & Bybee, 2000).

The specific dynamics in relationships varies by the people involved and affects partners' expectations, levels of perceived and real stress, and degrees of conflict. For example, a partner may initiate the first act of violence in a particular relationship as a reaction to a partner's infidelity, substance use, or other "triggers." Unemployment or underemployment among men is a risk marker and depends on the parties involved. Thus the motivation for violence by an offender is not a constant across relationships.

Similarly, relationships in which the partners are cohabitants, rather than married, are at increased risk for domestic violence and homicides (Makepeace, 1997; Yllö, 1993; Yllö & Straus, 1990). This may disproportionately affect specific population groups, such as African Americans; there has been an increase in overall rates of cohabitation among all couples, but this increase is greater among African Americans than other groups (Bent-Goodley, 2001). Partners in cohabiting relationships could be more ambivalent about commitment and perceive less stability in the relationship, thereby increasing the likelihood of violence in cases of conflict (Makepeace, 1997). Another possibility is that these couples experience greater social isolation (Bent-Goodley, 2001).

Life Course Factors and Violence

The previous discussion addresses the evolving, but well-established, body of research examining a variety of factors associated with domestic violence. However, critics of this literature are concerned with attempts to "compartmentalize" our understanding of domestic violence by specific traits or factors. These typologies do not provide a more broad-based understanding of the range of violence a person might experience and the effects of witnessing family violence and abuse as a child. More recent attention has been placed on the co-occurrence of factors across relationships as well as patterns of violence over time. How do a victim's experience with violence and the outcome of a specific violent incident influence subsequent incidents both with the same offender and with different offenders and over her lifetime? Unfortunately, both the NFVS and the NVAWS are cross-sectional studies and cannot examine violence over time.

CONCLUSION

We have made considerable progress in addressing domestic violence in recent years. Many are concerned that our success in lowering domestic violence will lead to complacency and a reduction in funding for programs to prevent and treat the problem. Domestic violence is a multifaceted phenomenon, difficult to define, with a complicated causal structure and an apparent tendency to disproportionately affect the most vulnerable members of our population.

REFERENCES

Abraham, M. (2000). Isolation as a form of marital violence: The South Asian immigrant experience. *Journal of Social Distress and the Homeless, 9,* 221–236.

Adamson, J. L., & Thompson, R. A. (1998). Coping with inter-parental verbal conflict by children exposed to spouse abuse and children from nonviolent homes. *Journal of Family Violence, 13,* 213–232.

Anderson, K. L. (2002). Perpetrator or victim? Relationships between intimate partner violence and well being. *Journal of Marriage and the Family, 64,* 851–863.

Bachman, R. (1992). *Death and violence on the reservation: Homicide, family violence and suicide in American Indian populations.* Westport, CT: Auburn House.

Barnett, O. W., & Fagan, R. W. (1993). Alcohol use in male spouse abusers and their female partners. *Journal of Family Violence, 6,* 219–241.

Baum, R., with Moore, K. (2002). Lesbian, gay, bisexual and transgender domestic violence in 2001. Report of the National Coalition of Anti-Violence Programs, 1–70.

Bell, C. C., & Mattis, J. (2000). The importance of cultural competence in ministering to African American victims of domestic violence. *Violence Against Women, 6,* 515–532.

Bent-Goodley, T. (2001). Eradicating domestic violence in the African American community: A literature review and action agenda. *Trauma, Violence & Abuse: A Review Journal, 2,* 316–330.

Breslau, N., Davis, G. C., Andreski, P., & Peterson, E. (1991). Traumatic events and posttraumatic stress disorder in an urban population of young adults. *Archives of General Psychiatry, 48,* 216–222.

Brookoff, D. (1997). Drugs, alcohol and domestic violence in Memphis. National Institute of Justice Research Preview. Washington, DC: U.S. Department of Justice.

Bruce, M. (1998). Divorce and psychopathology. In B. Dohrenwend (Ed.), *Adversity, stress and psychopathology* (pp. 219–232). New York: Oxford University Press.

Bui, H. N., & Morash, M. (1999). Domestic violence in the Vietnamese immigrant community: An exploratory study. *Violence Against Women, 5,* 769–795.

Bureau of Justice Statistics. (2005, July). *Criminal victimization in the United States, 2003: Statistical tables.* Retrieved June 15, 2006, from .www.ojp.usdoj.gov/bjs/pub/pdf/cvus0302.pdf

Buzawa, E., & Buzawa, C. (2003). *Domestic violence: The criminal justice response.* Thousand Oaks, CA: Sage Publications.

Campbell, J., & Boyd, D. (2003). *Violence against women: Synthesis of research for health care professionals.* Washington, DC: U.S. Department of Justice, National Institute of Justice.

Campbell, J. C., Kub, J. E., Belknap, J., & Templin, T. (1997). Predictors of depression in battered women. *Violence Against Women, 3,* 271–293.

Campbell, J. C., & Soeken, K. L. (1999). Women's responses to battering over time. *Journal of Interpersonal Violence, 14,* 21–40.

Chermack, S. T., Booth, B. M., & Curran, G. M. (2006). Gender differences in correlates of recent physical assault among untreated rural and urban at-risk drinkers: Role of depression. *Violence and Victims, 21*(1), 67–80.

Coker, D. (2000). Shifting power for battered women: Law, material resources, and poor women of color. *U. C. Davis Law Review, 33,* 1009–1055.

Davis, R. C., & Erez, E. (1998). *Immigrant populations as victims: Toward a multicultural criminal justice system.* Research in brief. Washington, DC: National Institute of Justice.

DeKeseredy, W. S., & MacLeod, L. (1997). *Women abuse: A sociological story.* Toronto, Canada: Harcourt Brace.

Dunrose, M. R., Harlow, C. W., Langan, P. W., Motivans, M., Rantala, R. R., & Smith, E. L. (2005). *Family violence statistics: Including statistics on strangers and acquaintances* (NCJ 207846). Washington, DC: Department of Justice, Bureau of Justice Statistics.

Edleson, J. L. (2001). Studying the co-occurrence of child maltreatment and woman battering in families. In S. A. Graham-Bermann & J. L. Edleson (Eds.), *Domestic violence in the lives of children: The future of research, intervention and social policy* (pp. 91–110). Washington, DC: American Psychological Association.

Fals-Stewart, W. (2003). The occurrence of partner physical aggression on days of alcohol consumption: A longitudinal diary study. *Journal of Consulting and Clinical Psychology, 71,* 41–52.

Fals-Stewart, W., Golden, J., & Schumacher, J. A. (2003). Intimate partner violence and substance use: A longitudinal day-today-examination. *Addictive Behaviors, 28,* 1555–1574.

Fantuzzo, J. W., & Mohr, W. (1999). Prevalence and effects of child exposure to domestic violence. *The Future of Children, 9*(3), 21–32.

Fleury, R. E., Sullivan, C. M., & Bybee, D. I. (2000). When ending the relationship does not end the violence: Women's experience of violence by former partners. *Violence Against Women, 6,* 1363–1383.

Foa, E. B., & Riggs, D. (1994). Posttraumatic stress disorder and rape. In R. S. Pynoos (Ed.), *Posttraumatic stress disorder: A clinical review* (pp. 1333–1363). Lutherville, MD: Sidran.

Fox, J. A., & Zawitz, M. W. (2004). *Homicide trends in the United States: 2002 update.* Washington, DC: U.S. Department of Justice. Retrieved December 2005, from www.ojp.usdoj.gov/bjs/homicide/homtrnd.htm

Franklin, D. L. (2000). *What's love got to do with it: Understanding and healing the rift between Black men and women.* New York: Simon & Schuster.

Frye, V., Wilt, S., & Schonberg, D. (2000). *Female homicide in New York City, 1990–1997.* Retrieved from www.ci.Nyc.ny.us/html/doh/pdf/ip/female97.pdf

Gelles, R. (1987). *Family violence.* Newbury Park, CA: Sage Publications.

Gibson-Davis, C. M., Magnuson, K., Gennetian, L., & Duncan, G. (2005). Employment and the risk of domestic violence among low-income women. *Journal of Marriage and Family, 67,* 1149–1168.

Gilbert, L., El-Bassel, N., Rajah, V., Folena, A., Fontdevila, J., Frye, V., et al. (2000). The converging epidemics of mood-altering drug use, HIV, HCV, and partner violence: A conundrum for methadone maintenance treatment. *Mount Sinai Journal of Medicine, 67*(5 & 6), 452–463.

Gordon, M. (2000). Definitional issues in violence against women: Surveillance and research from a violence research perspective. *Violence Against Women, 6,* 747–826.

Gore-Felton, C., Gill, M., Koopman, C., & Spiegel, D. (1999). A review of acute stress reactions among victims of violence: Implications for early intervention. *Aggression and Violent Behavior, 4,* 203–206.

Greenfield, L. A., Rand, M. N. R., Craven, D., Flaus, P. A., Perkins, C. A., Ringel, C., et al. (1998). Violence by intimates: Analysis of data on crimes by current or former spouses, boyfriends, and girlfriends (NCJ-167237).

Washington, DC: U.S. Department of Justice, Bureau of Justice Statistics.

Halinka-Malcoe, L., & Duran, B. M. (2004). Intimate partner violence and injury in the lives of low-income Native American women. In B. S. Fisher (Ed.), *Violence against women and family violence: Developments in research, practice and policy* (NCJ 199703). Washington, DC: U.S. Department of Justice.

Harris, T., Fisher, G. A., & Hirsch, B. S. (2002). Murder and medicine: The lethality of criminal assault, 1960–1999. *Homicide Studies, 6*(2), 128–166.

Holtzworth-Munroe, A., Bates, L., Smytzler, N., & Sandin, E. (1997). A brief review of the research on husband violence: Part I. Maritally violent versus nonviolent men. *Aggression and Violent Behavior, 2*, 65–69.

Hotaling, G., & Sugarman, D. (1990). A risk marker analysis of assaulted wives. *Journal of Family Violence, 5*, 1–13.

Hotton, T. (2003). *Childhood aggression and exposure to violence in the home.* Ottawa, Canada: Canadian Centre for Justice Statistics.

Johnson, H. (2001). Contrasting views of the role of alcohol in cases of wife assault. *Journal of Interpersonal Violence, 16*, 54–72.

Johnson, M. P. (2001). Conflict and control: Images of symmetry and asymmetry in domestic violence. In A. Booth, A. C. Crouter, & M. Clements (Eds.), *Couples in conflict* (pp. 95–104). Mahwah, NJ: Lawrence Erlbaum Associates.

Kantor, G., & Jasinski, J. L. (1998). Dynamics and risk factors in partner violence. In J. L. Jasinski & L. Williams (Eds.), *Partner violence: A comprehensive review of 20 years of research* (pp. 1–43). Thousand Oaks, CA: Sage Publications.

Kantor, G., & Straus, M. A. (1989). Substance abuse as a precipitant of wife abuse victimizations. *American Journal of Drug and Alcohol Abuse, 15*, 173–189.

Kantor, G. K., & Asdigian, N. (1997). When women are under the influence. Does drinking or drug use by women provoke beating by men? *Recent Developments in Alcoholism, 13*, 315–336.

Kaufman Kantor, G., & Straus, M. A. (1990). Response of victims and the police to assaults on wives. In M. A. Straus & R. J. Gelles (Eds.), *Physical violence in American families: Risk factors and adaptations to violence in 8,145 families* (pp. 473–486). New Brunswick, NJ: Transaction.

Kaukinen, C. (2004). Status compatibility, physical violence, and emotional abuse in intimate relationships. *Journal of Marriage and Family, 66*, 452–472.

Kessler, R., & Zhao, S. (1999). The prevalence of mental illness. In A. Horwitz & T. Scheid (Eds.), *A handbook for the study of mental health* (pp. 58–78). New York: Cambridge University Press.

Kilpatrick, D., Acierno, R., Renick, H., Saunders, B., & Best, C. (1997). A two-year longitudinal analysis of the relationship between violent assault and substance use in women. *Journal of Consulting and Clinical Psychology, 65*(5), 834–847.

Lipsey, M. W., Wilson, D. B., Cohen, M. A., & Derzon, J. H. (1997). Is there a causal relationship between alcohol use and violence? A synthesis of evidence. In M. Galanter (Ed.), *Recent developments in alcoholism* (pp. 245–282). New York: Plenum.

Makepeace, J. (1997). Courtship violence as process: A developmental theory. In A. P. Cardarelli (Ed.), *Violence between intimate partners: Patterns, causes, and effects* (pp. 29–47). Boston: Allyn & Bacon.

Mears, D. P., Carlson, M. J., Holden, G., & Harris, S. D. (2001). Reducing domestic violence revictimization: The effects of individual and contextual factors and type of legal intervention. *Journal of Interpersonal Violence, 16*, 1260–1283.

Melzer, S. A. (2002). Gender, work, and intimate violence: Men's occupational violence spillover and compensatory violence. *Journal of Marriage and Family, 64*, 820–832.

Moe, A. M., & Bell, M. P. (2004). Abject economics: The effects of battering and violence on women's work and employability. *Violence Against Women, 10*, 29–55.

Moore, A. M. (1997). Intimate violence: Does socioeconomic status matter? In A. P. Cardarelli (Ed.), *Violence between intimate partners: Patterns, causes and effects* (pp. 90–100). Boston: Allyn & Bacon.

Moore-Parmley, A. M. (2004). Violence against women research post-VAWA: Where have we been, where are we going? *Violence Against Women, 10*(12), 1417–1430.

Morash, M., Bui, M., & Santiago, A. (2000). Gender specific ideology of domestic violence in Mexican origin families. *International Review of Victimology, 1,* 67–91.

National Clearing House on Domestic Violence. (1980). *Battered women: A national concern.* Rockville, MD: Author.

O'Brien, M., John, R. S., Margolin, G., & Erel, O. (1994). Reliability and diagnostic efficacy of parents' reports regarding children's exposure to marital aggression. *Violence and Victims, 9,* 45–62.

Oliver, W. (1999). *The violent social world of Black men.* San Francisco: Jossey-Bass.

Osofsky, J. (1999). The impact of violence on children. *Domestic Violence and Children, 9,* 33–49.

Raj, A., & Silverman, J. (2002): Violence against immigrant women: The roles of culture, context, and legal immigrant status no intimate partner violence. *Violence Against Women, 8,* 367–398.

Rand, M., & Rennison, C. (2004). How much violence against women is there? In B. Fisher (Ed.), *From violence against women and family violence: Developments in research, practice, and policy* (NCJ 199702). Washington, DC: U.S. Department of Justice.

Rennison, C. M. (2001, June). *Criminal victimization 2000: Changes 1999–2000 with trends 1993–2000.* Washington, DC: U.S. Department of Justice, Bureau of Justice Statistics.

Rennison, C. M., & Welchans, S. (2000). *Intimate partner violence.* Washington, DC: U.S. Department of Justice, Bureau of Justice Statistics.

Riggs, D. S., Kilpatrick, D. G., & Resnick, H. S. (1992). Long-term psychological distress associated with marital rape and aggravated assault: A comparison to other crime victims. *Journal of Family Violence, 7,* 283–296.

Roberts, A. R. (1988). Substance abuse among men who batter their mates. *Journal of Substance Abuse Treatment, 5,* 83–87.

Romero, D., Chavkin, W., Wise, P. H., & Smith, L. (2003). Low income mothers' experience with poor health, hardship, work and violence: Implications for policy. *Violence Against Women, 9,* 1231–1244.

Rossman, B. B. R. (2001). Longer term effects of children's exposure to domestic violence. In S. A. Graham-Bermann & J. L. Edelson (Eds.), *Domestic violence in the lives of children* (pp. 35–65). Washington, DC: American Psychological Association.

Schafer, J., Caetano, R., & Cunradi, C. B. (2004). A path model of risk factors for intimate partner violence among couples in the United States. *Journal of Interpersonal Violence, 19*(2), 127–142.

Schwanberg, J. E., Logan, T. K., & Macke, C. (2005). Intimate partner violence, employment, and the workplace: Consequences and future directions. *Trauma, Violence, & Abuse, 6*(4), 286–312.

Schwartz, M. D., & DeKeseredy, W. S. (1997). *Sexual assault on the college campus: The role of male peer support.* Thousand Oaks, CA: Sage Publications.

Scott, K., Schafer, J., & Greenfield, T. (1999). The role of alcohol in physical assault perpetration and victimization. *Journal of Studies on Alcohol, 60,* 528–536.

Stanko, B. (2004). A tribute to 10 years of knowledge. *Violence Against Women, 10*(12), 1395–1400.

Stark, E. (1984). *The battering syndrome: Social knowledge, social therapy, and the abuse of women.* Unpublished doctoral dissertation, State University of New York-Binghamton.

Stark, E., & Flitcraft, A. (1988). Violence among intimates: An epidemiological review. In V. B. Van Hasselt, R. L. Morrison, A. S. Bellack, & M. Hersen (Eds.), *Handbook of family violence* (pp. 293–317). New York: Plenum.

Stets, J. E., & Straus, M. A. (1990). Gender differences in reporting marital violence and its medical and psychological consequences. In M. A. Straus & R. J. Gelles (Eds.), *Physical violence in American families: Risk factors and adaptations to violence in 8,145 families* (pp. 151–166). New Brunswick, NJ: Transaction.

Straus, M. (1990). The National Family Violence Surveys. In M. A. Straus and R. J. Gelles (Eds.), *Physical violence in American families: Risk factors and adaptations to violence in 8,145 families* (pp. 3–26). New Brunswick, NJ: Transaction.

Straus, M., & Gelles, R. (1986). Social change and change in family violence from 1971 to 1985 as revealed by two national surveys. *Journal of Marriage and the Family, 489,* 465–479.

Straus, M., & Smith, C. (1990). Violence in Hispanic families in the United States: Incidence rates and structural interpretations. In M. Straus & R. Gelles (Eds.), *Physical violence in American families: Risk factors and adaptations in 8,145 families* (pp. 95–112). New Brunswick, NJ: Transaction.

Teran, L. J. (1999). Barriers to protection at home and abroad: Mexican victims of domestic violence and the violence against women act. *Boston University International Law Journal, 17,* 1–70.

Testa, M. (2004). The role of substance use in male-to-female physical and sexual violence: A brief review and recommendations for future research. *Journal of Interpersonal Violence, 19 (12),* 1494–1505.

Tjaden, P., & Thoennes, N. (2000). *Full report of the prevalence, incidence, and consequences of violence against women* (NCJ 183781). Washington, DC: U.S. Department of Justice.

Tolman, R., & Raphael, J. (2000). A review of research on welfare and domestic violence. *Journal of Social Issues, 56,* 655–682.

Tolman, R., & Rosen, D. (2001). Domestic violence in the lives of women receiving welfare. *Violence Against Women, 7,* 141–158.

Walker, R., Logan, T. K., Jordan, C. E., & Campbell, J. C. (2004). An integrative review of separation in the context of victimization: Consequences and implications for women. *Trauma, Violence, & Abuse, 5*(2), 143–193.

West, T. C. (1999). *Wounds of the spirit: Black women, violence, and resistance ethics.* New York: New York University Press.

Widom, C., & Maxfield, M. (2001, March). *Update on the cycle of violence.* Washington, DC: U.S. Department of Justice, National Institute of Justice.

Williams, O. J. (1999). Working in groups with African American males who batter. In R. Carrillo & J. Tello (Eds.), *Family violence and men of color: Healing the wounded male spirit* (pp. 74–94). New York: Springer.

Woods, S. J. (1999). Normative beliefs regarding the maintenance of intimate relationships among abused and nonabused women. *Journal of Interpersonal Violence, 14,* 479–491.

Yllö, K. A. (1993). Through a feminist lens: Gender, power and violence. In R. J. Gelles & D. R. Loseke (Eds.), *Current controversies on family violence* (pp. 47–62). Newbury Park, CA: Sage Publications.

Yllö, K. A., & Straus, M. A. (1990). Patriarchy and violence against wives: The impact of structural and normative factors. In M. A. Straus & R. J. Gelles (Eds.), *Physical violence in American families: Risk factors and adaptations to violence in 8,145 families* (pp. 473–486). New Brunswick, NJ: Transaction.

Zlotnick, C. K., Kohn, R., Peterson, J., & Pearlstein, T. (1998). Partner physical victimization in a national sample of American families. *Journal of Interpersonal Violence, 13,* 156–166.

5

Stalking in America

Laws, Research, and Recommendations

PATRICIA TJADEN

Stalking has existed throughout history, but it is only in the past 20 years that the term *stalking* has become a familiar part of our lexicon (Beatty, 2003). Indeed, 20 years ago, uttering the word *stalking* was more likely to conjure up images of women's hosiery than criminal conduct. This changed on July 18, 1989, when a young starlet named Rebecca Schaeffer was gunned down and killed in front of her apartment in Orange County, California, by an obsessed fan who had been following and harassing the young actress for several months (Dawsey & Malnic, 1989). Publicity surrounding Schaeffer's murder focused the nation's attention on the threat posed to celebrities by stalkers and galvanized the film industry to pressure the California legislature to pass a stalking law to protect movie stars (ABC, 1992; Axthelm, 1989; Bacon, 1990; Goleman, 1989; Toufexis, 1989).

Shortly after Schaeffer's murder, four other women in Orange County were stalked and murdered during a six-week time span, each by a former boyfriend or husband (Schaum & Parrish, 1995). Before their death, three of the four women had reported to the police they feared for their safety because of repeatedly being followed, harassed, and threatened by their ex-partners and had obtained a restraining order against their respective assailants. In each case, the restraining order proved ineffective (Schaum & Parrish, 1995).

Responding to pressure from the film industry and the wider community to pass a stalking law, state senator Edward Royce of Fullerton, California, and Judge John Watson of Orange County, California, drafted the nation's first stalking law (Beatty, 2003). Senate Bill 2184 was passed by the California legislature in 1990 and on January 1, 1991, became part of the California Penal Code 646.9 (Beatty, 2003).

News of the California law led to a flurry of stalking legislation around the country. In 1992, 29 states passed similar stalking legislation (Hunzeker, 1992). By 1993, legislators in all states and the District of Columbia had addressed stalking in their penal codes, either by creating the crime of stalking or by modifying existing harassment statutes to apply in stalking situations (Hunzeker, 1993). In 1996, Congress passed a federal law outlawing stalking within all federal jurisdictions and making it illegal for stalkers to cross state lines in pursuit of their victims (Federal Interstate Stalking Act, 1996). Thus, in just a few years, stalking went from being an activity for which there was no criminal sanction to one that was criminalized throughout the United States.

The rush to criminalize stalking was not without controversy. Immediately following passage of the first wave of stalking laws, there was a spate of law reviews questioning the constitutionality and effectiveness of specific state stalking statutes (e.g., Boychuk, 1994; Cormandy, 1994; Gilligan, 1992; Guy, 1993; Harmon, 1994; Lingg, 1993; Morin, 1993; Sohn, 1994; Thomas, 1993; Walker, 1993). One legal analyst described early stalking laws as a hodgepodge of flawed statutes that were unenforceable (Cormandy, 1994). Another argued that stalking laws violated the Constitution by blurring the line between criminal and innocent behavior and by infringing on First Amendment rights (Guy, 1993). Given this legal backdrop, it is not surprising that many of the newly enacted stalking statutes faced constitutional challenges as soon as they were enforced (Beatty, 2003). Indeed, one study found that in the 10 years following passage of the first stalking law, at least 134 stalking-related cases were challenged on constitutional grounds in 34 states, the District of Columbia, and at the federal level (Miller, 2001).

Adding to the controversy was the fact that stalking was criminalized before much was known about it. In 1994, Congress passed a law mandating the U.S. attorney general submit an annual report to Congress providing information concerning the incidence of stalking and domestic violence, and the effectiveness of antistalking efforts and measures (U.S. Department of Justice, 1996). At the time this law was passed, however, there was no empirical information on either the incidence of stalking or the effectiveness of stalking laws. Because stalking had only recently been criminalized, neither of the nation's two official crime measuring systems—the Federal Bureau of Investigation's Uniform Crime Reports (UCR) or the Bureau of Justice Statistics' National Crime Victimization Survey (NCVS)—had incorporated stalking in their data collection systems. And there had never been a comprehensive study of stalking in the general population. Instead, information about stalking was limited to media accounts of individual cases, usually those involving celebrities and politicians (e.g., Bacon, 1990; Meyer, 1992; Puente, 1992; Toufexis, 1989) and small, clinical samples of known stalkers (Dietz et al., 1991, Zona, Sharma, & Lane, 1993). Thus, when the nation's first stalking laws were passed, little was known about the dimension of the problem, the characteristics of stalkers and their victims, or the effectiveness of stalking laws.

Since passage of the nation's first stalking law in 1990, there has been an explosion of research on a wide range of stalking topics, including elements of state stalking statutes, stalking prevalence, characteristics of stalkers and their victims, the relationship between domestic violence and stalking, the effects of stalking on victims, and the implementation of stalking laws. The remainder of this chapter will examine this research, as well as issues related to cyberstalking. The chapter concludes with recommendations on how to improve research and policy with respect to stalking.

STATE STALKING STATUTES

Defining Stalking

Stalking has proved difficult for state legislators to define in ways that pass constitutional muster. This stems in part from the fact that stalking is not a common law crime[1] and must therefore be defined by statutes and by court decisions interpreting those statutes (Miller, 2001). Moreover, the term *stalking* refers to many different types of behaviors, criminal and noncriminal. For example, in common parlance, stalking means to seek and pursue game in order to kill it, such as a cat stalking a bird or a hunter stalking a deer (see any dictionary). It also has been used to describe obsessive courtship behavior, which historically, has been depicted in a humorous and innocuous manner in books, plays, and films. Recently, obsessive courtship behavior has been the focus of research by mental health professionals and behavioral scientists who are concerned with the serious psychological problems that may cause this behavior. In describing their research, these experts often use the terms *obsessional following* and *obsessive relational intrusion* interchangeably with *stalking,* even though the behaviors they are studying do not necessarily involve criminal behavior (Meloy, 1998; Spitzberg & Rhea, 1999). This has created some confusion with respect to the prevalence and characteristics of the crime of stalking. As the following discussion illustrates, from a legal perspective, stalking involves much more than predatory or obsessive behavior.

Model Stalking Code

To help states in their efforts to pass stalking laws, Congress in 1992 enacted a law charging the National Institute of Justice (NIJ) with drafting a model stalking code for states that would be both enforceable and effective.[2] The NIJ in turn commissioned the National Criminal Justice Association (NCJA) to develop, and aid states in implementing, such a code. The *Model Stalking Code* was delivered to Congress in October 1993 (National Criminal Justice Association, 1993). Since then, many states have amended their initial antistalking laws to bring them in line with recommendations and language outlined in the model code (National Conference of State Legislatures, 1995; Yee, 1994).

The *Model Stalking Code* specifically states:

> Any person who:
> (a) Purposely engages in a course of conduct directed at a specific person that would cause a reasonable person to fear bodily injury to himself or herself or a member of his or her immediate family or to fear death to himself or herself or a member of his or her immediate family, and
> (b) has knowledge or should have knowledge that the specific person will be placed in reasonable fear of bodily injury to himself or herself or a member of his or her immediate family or will be placed in reasonable fear of death of himself or herself or a member of his or her family; and
> (c) Whose acts induce fear in the specific person of bodily injury to himself or herself or a member of his or her immediate family, or induce fear in the specific person of the death of himself or herself or a member of his or her immediate family;
> is guilty of stalking. (National Criminal Justice Association, 1993, pp. 43–44)

The *Model Stalking Code* further defines course of conduct "as repeatedly maintaining a visual or physical proximity to a person, repeatedly conveying verbal or written threats or threats implied by conduct or a combination thereof directed at or toward a person," with repeated meaning "on two or more occasions" (National Criminal Justice Association, 1993, pp. 43–44).

Key Elements of State Stalking Statutes

Although they vary widely in language and specificity, most state statutes contain provisions that are similar to those contained in the *Model Stalking Code,* which, according to Beatty (2003, pp. 2–7), can be broken down into the following three elements:

A pattern of conduct directed at a specific person;

Conduct intended to place that person in fear for his or her safety; and

Conduct that actually places that person in fear for his or her safety.

Course of conduct is perhaps the most variously defined by state statutes. Some states specifically list the kinds of acts they are trying to proscribe (e.g., "lying in wait," "following," "pursuing," "placing someone under surveillance"), while others, acknowledging the ingenuity of stalkers, use language that focuses on the outcome of the criminal conduct rather than the conduct itself (e.g., "course of conduct that would cause a reasonable person fear"). Some states require that the alleged stalker engage in a course of conduct showing the crime was not an isolated event, while others specify how many acts (e.g., two or more) must occur before the conduct can be considered stalking.

The intent element of the crime of stalking is considered by many to be the most difficult element of the crime to prove (Beatty, 2003). All state stalking statutes require the prosecution to show that the stalking was intentional, that is, the stalker meant to perform the acts that constituted stalking (Miller, 2001). Some state statutes go further and require the prosecution to prove that the stalker intended to threaten the victim or cause fear. Court decisions in several states have reduced the prosecutorial burden of proving intent to threaten and cause fear by holding that the defendant's actions were such that he or she should have known that

his or her actions would be perceived as a threat or would provoke fear (Miller, 2001).

Initially, most state stalking statutes required that the stalker make a "credible threat" of violence against the victim. This requirement was problematic because it established two critical elements that had to be proven to secure a stalking conviction: the threat had to be explicitly communicated to the victim, and the stalker had to have the ability to carry out the threat (Beatty, 2003). Today, most states have adopted a broader standard, one allowing the threat to be explicit or implicit. Implicit threats differ from explicit threats in that they do not have to be conveyed in words, but may instead be inferred by the victim based on what the stalker says and does and taking into account any special knowledge the victim may have of the stalker (Beatty, 2003). To exclude oversensitive reactions from the law's reach, the threat must meet a reasonable person standard (Miller, 2001). Regardless if the threat is implicit or explicit, its execution does not have to be immediate but instead can occur in the indefinite future (Miller, 2001).

Fear is the fundamental justification for stalking laws and is therefore a very important element of the crime. The drafters of the *Model Stalking Code* made this very clear when they wrote, "Since stalking statutes criminalize what otherwise would be legitimate behavior, based upon the fact that the behavior induces fear, the level of fear in a stalking victim is a crucial element" (National Criminal Justice Association, 1993, p. 44). The *Model Stalking Code* does not require stalkers to make a credible threat—implicit or explicit—but it does require victims to feel a high level of fear (e.g., fear of bodily harm or death). In most state stalking statutes, the victim must actually feel fear as a result of the stalker's behavior or the behavior does not rise to the level of a crime. Thus, if a stalker follows a woman and she is unaware she is being followed, or if the stalker engaged in behaviors of which the woman is aware but does not become frightened, stalking has not occurred. Simply put, without fear there is no crime of stalking.

Constitutional Challenges to Stalking Statutes

As previously mentioned, constitutional challenges to state stalking statutes began almost as soon as the first stalking statute was prosecuted. Most of the challenges were based on two types of doctrines: "void for vagueness" and "overbreadth" (Beatty, 2003, pp. 2–13). The void for vagueness doctrine requires a penal statute to define the criminal offense with sufficient definiteness that ordinary people can understand what conduct is prohibited and to provide explicit standards to prohibit arbitrary and discriminatory enforcement (Guy, 1993). Over the years, the void for vagueness doctrine has been used to challenge specific language of state stalking statutes, including "pattern of conduct," "credible threat," "following," "willfully," and "maliciously." In general, the courts have rejected these challenges on the grounds that the language has meaning when viewed in context, or the words and phrases have dictionary definitions that are understood by ordinary persons (Beatty, 2003).

The overbreadth doctrine is based on the idea that a statute cannot be written so broadly that it criminalizes behavior that would otherwise be lawful. Civil libertarians argue that statutes that are overly broad might limit liberty because they discourage or intimidate individuals from engaging in what is otherwise constitutionally protected behavior (Guy, 1993). They also violate the Constitution because they may encourage selective enforcement of the law (Guy, 1993). Stalking defendants have used the overbreadth doctrine to argue that communications and interactions with victims constitute free speech and thus are protected. Courts have tended to reject overbreadth challenges in stalking cases because they concluded that the stalker's speech constituted a threat or harassment and was therefore not protected, or because the stalker's right to free speech was outweighed by the victim's right to privacy or right not to be harmed (Beatty, 2003, pp. 2–15).

Other stalking defendants have challenged specific state and federal stalking laws on issues pertaining to freedom of travel/movement, double jeopardy, and evidentiary and procedural matters pertaining to sufficiency of evidence, entrapment, jury instruction, ex post facto application, need for expert testimony to prove mental distress, and consolidation of acts of charges (Beatty, 2003, pp. 2–15). In general, the courts have rejected these arguments, either because the rights of the victim supersede those of the defendant or because the doctrine was applied too broadly (Beatty, 2003, pp. 2–15).

Examples of Court-Affirmed Stalking Cases

Following are descriptions of specific stalking incidents that were culled from court opinions affirming convictions in stalking cases (Miller, 2001, pp. 22–23):

- A woman who worked as a cashier in a store was grabbed by the hand by a customer when she tried to return his credit card. On several occasions he followed her throughout the store. He also repeatedly followed her during her drive home and on several occasions parked his car next to hers in the parking lot of the store. Once he stopped her father's car and talked to him.

- A woman was separated from her husband after eight years of marriage, and a divorce action had been initiated. The husband came by the woman's house and by the school she attended every day for two months. He also called her 40 to 80 times a day. Sometimes he questioned her about her activities and friends. He also appeared nude in her driveway, exposing himself to their two daughters.

• A woman dated a man for two to three years. After they broke up he threatened her with two screwdrivers while she was walking to a friend's house. He also entered her apartment while she was showering. He threatened to tear up her clothes and to throw a Molotov cocktail at her mother's house. Her apartment was vandalized and her clothes stolen. She woke up one afternoon to find the man beating on her. He then threatened to kill both her and her mother.

PREVALENCE, CHARACTERISTICS, AND EFFECTS OF STALKING

Stalking Prevalence

The first-ever national study of stalking prevalence in the United States was conducted by Tjaden and Thoennes (1998) using data from the National Violence Against Women Survey (NVAWS). The survey, which was funded jointly by the NIJ and the Centers for Disease Control and Prevention, consisted of telephone interviews with a representative sample of 8,000 U.S. women and 8,000 U.S. men 18 years of age an older. Respondents were queried about their experiences as victims of various forms of violence, including stalking. The survey employed a multiple measurement design that included direct questions about stalking victimization, as well as behaviorally specific screen questions with incident-specific follow-up questions.

Using a definition of stalking that is similar to the definition of stalking contained in the *Model Stalking Code* (see earlier discussion) that requires the victim to feel a high level of fear, Tjaden and Thoennes (1998, p. 3) found that 8% of female respondents and 2% of male respondents were stalked at some time in their lifetime. Extrapolating

these findings to U.S. census data, Tjaden and Thoennes estimated that 1 in 12 U.S. women (8.2 million) has been stalked at some time in her life, and 1 in 45 U.S. men (2.0 million) has been stalked at some time in his life. In addition, 1% of all women surveyed and 0.4% of all men surveyed were stalked in the 12 months preceding the survey. These estimates equate respectively to about 1 million women and 371,000 men who are stalked annually in the United States.

Tjaden and Thoennes (1998, p. 4) found that if a less stringent definition of stalking is used, one requiring victims to feel only a little frightened or somewhat frightened by their stalker, lifetime prevalence rates increase dramatically, from 8% to 12% for women and from 2% to 4% for men, while annual prevalence rates increase from 1% to 6% for women and from 0.4% to 1.5% for men. Tjaden, Thoennes, and Allison (2000) also found that stalking prevalence rates increased dramatically when respondents to the NVAWS were given the opportunity to self-define as stalking victims. Specifically, 12% of surveyed women and 6% of surveyed men replied affirmatively to the question "Have you ever been stalked?"

No nationwide study of the prevalence of stalking in the general population has been conducted since the NVAWS. However, a more recent study of stalking prevalence conducted by the Louisiana Office of Public Health (2000) found that 15% of Louisiana women interviewed were stalked at least once in their lifetime, or nearly twice the rate reported by the NVAWS. In addition, a telephone survey of a randomly selected, national sample of 4,446 women attending a two-to-four-year college or university during the fall of 1996 found that 13.1% of female students in the sample were stalked since the school year began (Fisher, Cullen, & Turner, 2000), while another study of stalking on colleges found that 10.5% of 861 women attending nine postsecondary institutions were stalked during the previous six months (Mustaine & Tewksbury, 1999). Extrapolating from the six-month estimates generated from the two college studies, it can be estimated that 21% to 26% of women attending postsecondary institutions are stalked each year. These figures are about 25 times greater than the NVAWS estimate that 1% of U.S. women 18 years of age and older are stalked each year.

There are a couple of possible reasons for the wide disparity in stalking victimization estimates generated by the NVAWS and the two college studies. First, the NVAWS used a more restrictive definition of stalking, one that required victims to feel a high level of fear as measured by their reporting that their stalkers' behavior made them feel very frightened and/or made them think they or someone close to them would be seriously injured or killed (Tjaden & Thoennes, 1998). In comparison, the college survey conducted by Fisher and colleagues (2000) used a definition that required victims only to experience repeated behaviors that would cause a reasonable person fear, whereas the college survey conducted by Mustaine and Tewksbury (1999) allowed victims to self-define stalking. Second, the NVAWS surveyed adult women of all ages, not just college age women, who are typically younger than women in the general population and therefore more at risk of violent victimization. Finally, as Fisher and colleagues note (2000, p. 27), "It is possible that the social domain of colleges places women in situations and in contact with a range of men that increase the chances of being stalked."

Characteristics of Stalkers and Victims

Based on data generated from the NVAWS, Tjaden and Thoennes (1998) found that stalkers are primarily men, and stalking victims are primarily women: Overall, 87% of the stalkers identified by the survey were

men, and 78% of the victims were women. Most of the victims (77% of the women and 64% of the men) knew their stalker. Tjaden and Thoennes (1998) also found that American Indian/Alaskan Native women were at greatest risk of being stalked at some time in their life, followed by mixed race women, white women, African American women, and Asian/Pacific Islander women.

Research suggests that stalking victims tend to be young adults. More than half (52%) of stalking victims identified by the NVAWS were between the ages of 18 and 29 (Tjaden & Thoennes, 1998). A study of 100 stalking victims in Australia found that most victims were in their mid to late thirties (Pathe & Mullen, 1997). Stalking victims appear to come from all walks of life. In her study of 145 stalking victims who volunteered to answer questions about their victimization, Hall (1998, pp. 150–152) found that 31% were professionals, 20% were managers, 16% were clerical or sales workers, 12% were students, 7% were technical workers, 3% were retired persons, and 3% were homemakers.[3]

There is some evidence that gay men are more likely to be stalked than heterosexual men: 8% of the men in the NVAWS sample who had ever lived with a man as a couple reported being stalked compared with 2% of the men who had never lived with a man as a couple (Tjaden & Thoennes, 1998).

Stalking and Violence in Intimate Relationships

Several studies have established a link between stalking and violence in intimate relationships. Information generated from the NVAWS indicates that women tend to be stalked by current or former intimate partners. Of all female stalking victims identified by the survey, 59% were stalked by a current or former spouse, cohabiting partner, date, or boyfriend; 4% were stalked by a relative other than a spouse; 19% were stalked by an acquaintance, such as a neighbor, coworker, or friend; and 23% were stalked by a stranger. (It should be noted that these percentages exceed 100 because some victims were stalked by more than one type of stalker.)

Meloy (1998) conducted a profile of known stalkers and found that stalkers who had been sexually intimate with their victims were most likely to be violent toward their victims. Tjaden & Thoennes (1998) found that 81% of the women in the NVAWS who were stalked by a current or former husband or cohabiting partner also were physically assaulted by that partner, while 31% were raped by that partner. Tjaden and Thoennes (1998) also found that ex-husbands/cohabiting partners who stalked their partners were significantly more likely than ex-husbands who did not stalk to have engaged in emotionally abusive (e.g., shouting or swearing) and controlling behavior (e.g., limiting contact with others, jealousy, possessiveness, denying access to family income) while the relationship was intact. Moracco, Runyan, and Butts (1998) found that nearly a quarter (23.4%) of femicide victims in North Carolina who were murdered by a current or former intimate partner had been stalked before the fatal incident. And McFarlane and colleagues (1999) found that 76% of partner femicide victims and 85% of attempted partner femicide victims in 10 cities were stalked by their assailant in the 12 months preceding the victimization. McFarlane and colleagues (1999) also found a statistically significant association between intimate partner physical assault and stalking for both femicide and attempted femicide victims. In a study of 1,785 domestic violence reports generated by the Colorado Springs Police Department, Tjaden and Thoennes (2000) found that one in six (16.5%) domestic violence cases reported to the police involved allegations of stalking. Finally, in a study of 144 battered women who had left their partners, Mechanic, Weaver, and

Resnick (2000) found that 13% to 29% (depending on the definition of stalking used) had been stalked in the six months immediately following separation.

Effects of Stalking on Victims

Research indicates that stalking victims suffer a variety of psychological and social consequences as a result of their victimization. Tjaden and Thoennes (1998, p. 11) found that 30% of female stalking victims and 20% of male stalking victims identified by the NVAWS sought mental health counseling as a direct result of their stalking victimization, while over a quarter (26%) of all stalking victims said their victimization caused them to lose time from work (on average, 11 days). Among those who lost time from work, 1 in 14 (7%) said they never returned to work. Compared to nonvictims, stalking victims were more likely to report that they were very concerned about their personal safety (42% vs. 24%) and about being stalked (30 vs. 10 percent). They also were nearly twice as likely as nonvictims to carry something to defend themselves (45% vs. 29%). In addition, many stalking victims reported engaging in some type of self-protective measure, such as enlisting the help of family and friends (18%), getting a gun (17%), moving out of town (11%), changing addresses (11%), avoiding their stalker (7%), and varying driving habits (5%).

Other studies have reported similar findings. The Louisiana stalking survey found that 36% of stalking victims moved from their household as a direct result of their victimization, while 11% purchased a gun (Louisiana Office of Public Health, 2000). In their stalking survey of college students, Mustaine and Tewksbury (1999) found that many stalking victims reported changes in their behavior, such as carrying mace and/or a pocketknife. In their study of 100 stalking victims in Australia, Pathe and Mullen (1997) found that 94% of victims reported making or experiencing major changes in their lifestyle and or daily activities, including relocating (40%), curtailing social activities (70%), decreasing or stopping altogether their attendance at work or school (50%), and changing their work location (34%). Many also reported symptoms of post-traumatic stress disorder, including chronic sleep disturbance (75%); excessive tiredness, weakness, or headaches (50%); nausea when going to places associated with the stalking (33%); reoccurring flashbacks to the stalking resulting in distress (55%); appetite disturbance (50%); increased alcohol or cigarette use (25%); and contemplating suicide (25%). The authors of the study concluded that there was not one stalking victim who did not experience some level of harm and that many victims experienced a profound deterioration of functioning.

IMPLEMENTATION OF STALKING LAWS

To date, little research has been conducted on the implementation of stalking laws or the experiences of stalking victims who have sought assistance from the justice system. The few studies that have been conducted in this area indicate that the laws are underutilized. For example, the NIJ twice conducted national surveys of police and prosecution agencies to determine what, if any, special efforts the agencies had undertaken to enforce antistalking laws (Miller, 2001). The first survey was conducted in 1998–1999 and consisted of mailed questionnaires to 204 police agencies and 222 prosecution agencies in jurisdictions with a population over 250,000. A replication of the first national survey was conducted in November 2000, at which time 169 police agencies and 183 prosecutor agencies were mailed questionnaires. (The sample sizes were smaller in the second survey because agencies who had indicated they had no responsibility for handling stalking cases in the first survey

were dropped from the sample.) In both surveys, agency representatives were queried about possible specialized units, training, and written policies and procedures they may have developed with respect to handling stalking cases.

Data from both surveys indicate a general lack of specialization and training among law enforcement and prosecution agencies with respect to enforcing stalking statutes. Only one police agency reported having a specialized stalking unit; instead, most police agencies assigned stalking cases to nonstalking specialist units, such as those dealing with domestic violence, sex crimes, or crimes against persons. Similarly, most prosecution agencies assigned stalking cases to a special unit that was responsible for prosecuting domestic violence and/or sex crimes. Data from both surveys show that only a small percentage of police agencies (13%) provided specialized stalking training to recruits that was independent of domestic violence training. And prosecutor training actually worsened over time, with the number of prosecutor offices reporting no stalking training increasing from 18% to 21% during the second survey. The study found that about half of all police and prosecution agencies had written policies and procedures for handling stalking cases; however, most of these were part of protocols for handling domestic violence cases. Given these findings, it is not surprising that the researchers concluded that much more needs to be done by law enforcement and prosecutors to implement state stalking statutes (Miller, 2001, p. 55).

Only one study has examined actual police and court case records to determine how stalking laws are implemented. Tjaden and Thoennes (2000) reviewed 1,785 domestic violence complaints generated by the Colorado Springs Police Department from April to September 1998 to determine how frequently stalking is alleged by a victim of domestic violence during the initial report to the police, and whether cases with stalking allegations are prosecuted under stalking statutes. Of the 1,785 domestic violence reports included in the sample, 1,731 (97%) had a victim narrative, a police narrative, or both, and therefore could be used to determine whether the victim or the police officer claimed that the suspect had stalked the victim. In 285 (16.5%) of these reports, there was evidence that the suspect stalked the victim. Crime reports with stalking allegations were significantly more likely to involve female victims and victims and suspects who were former, as opposed to current, intimate partners. Of the 285 reports with evidence that the suspect stalked the victim, only 1 resulted in the police officer formally charging the suspect with stalking (Tjaden & Thoennes, 2000, p. 12).

CYBERSTALKING

At the time the first wave of stalking laws was passed, relatively few persons used the Internet, and there was little concern about how stalkers might use the Internet to terrorize their victims. Since then, use of the Internet has grown exponentially, and with it concerns about cyberstalking. Generally speaking, cyberstalking refers to the use of any type of electronic means of communication, including electronic mail (e-mail), chat rooms, news groups, mail exploders, instant messaging, and community Web sites, to stalk another person (U.S. Department of Justice, 1999, p. 2). Examples of cyberstalking include repeatedly sending harassing and threatening e-mail messages, soliciting sex for minors through e-mail or online chat rooms and news groups, posting another person's photograph or private information on a highly accessible electronic bulletin board, and depicting a person as a prostitute or someone who enjoys kinky or sadomasochistic sex (U.S. Department of Justice, 1999). Specific incidents of cyberstalking include the following:

- A University of San Diego honors graduate student terrorized five fellow female students for more than a year by repeatedly sending them threatening e-mail messages, sometimes as many as five a day, because he thought they were laughing at him and causing others to ridicule him when in fact they didn't even know him (U.S. Department of Justice, 2001).
- A man in Texas posted a notice on the Web claiming that a nine-year-old girl was available for sex and providing her home phone number with instructions to call 24 hours a day (U.S. Department of Justice, 2001).
- A woman in Texas received numerous nasty e-mails and discovered that a photograph of a nude woman had been posted on the Internet along with her e-mail address after she got into an argument with a man during an online discussion about advertising (Snow, 1998).

At present there are no reliable estimates of the prevalence of cyberstalking. However, a growing body of anecdotal evidence suggests it is widespread. A 1991 report by the U.S. attorney general to the vice president estimates there may be "tens or even hundreds of thousands of victims of recent cyberstalking incidents in the United States" (U.S. Department of Justice, 1999). According to informal surveys conducted by the U.S. Department of Justice, approximately 20% of reports made to both the Los Angeles District Attorney's Office Threat Assessment Unit and the Manhattan Sex Crimes Unit involve unwanted e-mail or electronic communications (U.S. Department of Justice, 1999). The Computer Investigation and Technology Unit of the New York City Police Department estimates that about 40% of their cases involve electronic harassment and/or threats (U.S. Department of Justice, 1999). Researchers at the University of Cincinnati, who surveyed a nationally representative sample of college women about their experiences as victims of sexual assault and stalking, found that 25% of stalking victims had been stalked via their e-mail address (Fisher, 2001). A survey of 500 members of Systers, an electronic mailing list for women in computer science, found that 20% of respondents reported being the targets of sexual harassment via the Internet (Betts & Maglitta, 1995). And finally, in their study of online victimization of youth, aged 10–17, who regularly use the Internet, Finklehor, Mitchell, and Wolak (2000) found that 20% had received a sexual solicitation over the Internet in the past year, about a quarter of which induced fear or distress in the victim.

Because specific stalking provisions do not typically mention specific means for communicating threats or harassing targets, cyberstalking—which simply refers to stalking using electronic means of communication—should be covered under most existent stalking statutes (Beatty, 2003, pp. 2–20). Nonetheless, some states have amended their laws in recent years to make it clear that stalking statutes apply to communications by all electronic means, while some have passed amendments to specifically address cyberstalking (Beatty, 2003, pp. 2–20). At least one state (Georgia) has made it a crime to electronically publish personal information about the victim for the purpose of inducing other parties to harass the victims (Beatty, 2003, pp. 2–20).

Cyberstalking presents unique challenges to law enforcement. Anecdotal evidence suggests that the majority of law enforcement agencies nationwide have no experience investigating or prosecuting cyberstalking cases (U.S. Department of Justice, 2001). This is due, in part, to the fact that most police officers have not been trained to recognize the seriousness of cyberstalking. According to CyberAngels (2000), an online stalking victim advocacy group, many victims who report their cyberstalking to the police say the police did not take the online harassment seriously until it became offline harassment. In addition, many law enforcement agencies lack personnel who have expertise in computers or Internet use.

Lack of coordination between law enforcement and Internet service providers also hampers the investigation and prosecution of cyberstalking cases. Historically, contact between Internet service providers and law enforcement has been sporadic and episodic (U.S. Department of Justice, 1999). In addition, law enforcement agencies are typically unfamiliar with the types of online behaviors Internet service providers prohibit or the procedures and policies they use to follow-up user complaints. Many experts believe that better coordination is needed between law enforcement and Internet service providers before serious inroads can be made in controlling cyberstalking (U.S. Department of Justice, 2001).

Finally, jurisdictional issues hamper law enforcement responses to cyberstalking. Perpetrators of cyberstalking often reside in different cities or states than their victims, making it difficult for local law enforcement agencies to investigate allegations of cyberstalking without first obtaining cooperation from other law enforcement agencies. Moreover, because some instances of cyberstalking cross national borders, consideration must be given to how nations can work together to target cases of international cyberstalking.

CONCLUSIONS AND RECOMMENDATIONS

In their groundbreaking book *Sex, Crime, and the Law,* MacNamara and Sagarin (1977) note that changes in the law usually occur slowly and unevenly, emerging first in one jurisdiction or geographic region and only gradually moving to another. Clearly, this was not the case with respect to changes in laws governing stalking behavior. The speed with which stalking was criminalized is unprecedented in the history of American jurisprudence and shows just how quickly the legal landscape can change once public opinion is

aroused. But enacting laws to proscribe stalking is only the first step toward combating this
serious social problem. Unless measures are
developed to ensure that stalking laws are
implemented, the passage of stalking laws will
prove to be an empty promise. As Beatty
(2003, p. 22) notes, "The passage of stalking
legislation is about promises made—their
implementation is about promises kept."

An important measure needed to be taken
to ensure stalking laws are implemented is
increased training of law enforcement officers and prosecutors about what constitutes
the crime of stalking. Research indicates that
nearly 20 years after the passage of the
nation's first stalking law, misconceptions
about the legal definition of stalking are still
quite common among criminal justice professionals. In his report on stalking laws and
implementation practices, Miller (2001) cites
several statements made by criminal justice
professionals that clearly misinterpret the
definition of stalking: For example, a prosecutor stated that following a victim without
her knowledge constituted stalking, a police
officer stated that stalkers had to act on their
threats before the crime of stalking had
occurred, and a STOP Grants administrator
stated that the use of date rape drugs constituted stalking. Obviously, none of these
statements accurately describes the *crime* of
stalking.

Given the lack of understanding that exists
about legal definitions of stalking, it is imperative that law enforcement officers and prosecutors receive specialized training on the
specific elements of stalking statutes in their
respective states, as well as training on how to
identify and investigate stalking cases. This
will undoubtedly increase the amount of stalking known to the police as well as police
awareness of the pervasiveness and seriousness
of stalking. One study found that 16.5% (one
in six cases) of domestic violence crime reports
generated by a police department in Colorado
during a five-month time span contained

evidence that the suspect stalked the victim
(Tjaden & Thoennes, 2000). Because this estimate represents stalking allegations that were
made spontaneously by the victim and not
in response to systematic questioning by the
police officer, it probably underestimates the
true amount of stalking that occurred. Thus
training police officers to ask specific questions about possible stalking victimization
while investigating reports of domestic violence will probably increase the amount of
stalking known to the police. Hopefully, it also
will increase police awareness of the link
between stalking and intimate partner violence
perpetrated against women by their male partners and the need to take stalking seriously.

In addition to learning about specific elements of their state stalking statutes, prosecutors need more training on how to meet
specific requirements of the laws, such as
proving how a pattern of conduct shows
intent to cause victim fear and whether the
victim experienced the level of fear required
(e.g., fear of bodily harm). Hopefully, as
prosecutors gain more experience (and success) prosecuting stalking cases, they will feel
more vested in stalking laws and therefore
more willing to put the necessary effort into
prosecuting them.

Research has shown that stalking is more
prevalent than previously suspected. Before
any scientific studies were conducted on the
prevalence of stalking, information on stalking prevalence was limited to unscientific
estimates provided by forensic and mental
health professionals based on their work with
known stalkers. The most frequently cited
"guesstimate" of stalking prevalence was
made by forensic psychiatrist, Park Dietz,
who, when pressed by a reporter to do so,
guessed that 5% of U.S. women had been
stalked at some time in their life, while
200,000 U.S. women are stalked each year
(Puente, 1992). Given the lack of official estimates on stalking prevalence, these figures
quickly became part of the stalking literature

and were quoted extensively by reporters, government officials, legal scholars, and researchers. However, victimization surveys conducted since then indicate that stalking prevalence is much higher than previously thought, especially among college populations.

Given the high rate of stalking uncovered by these surveys, as well as scientific evidence on the deleterious effects of stalking on victims, it is inexplicable that stalking has yet to be included in either of the nation's two official crime measurement systems. Proposals to include stalking in the Federal Bureau of Investigation's Uniform Crime Reporting system have been proffered and if implemented would provide data on the number of stalking cases reported to the police nationwide, as well as the number of stalking reports cleared by arrest. To date, however, stalking is not included in the UCR. Similarly, a stalking component has been developed for the Department of Justice's National Crime Victimization Survey and is scheduled to be implemented in the near future. There is, however, no plan to field a stalking supplement on a regular basis. Thus it is unlikely that official statistics on either the prevalence of stalking victimization or the number of stalking reports made to the police will be available in any systematic fashion in the near future. Without these statistics, it will be difficult to gauge whether any inroads have been made on implementing stalking laws or preventing stalking crimes. It is therefore imperative that stalking be included in these two measurement systems as soon as possible.

Finally, cyberstalking is a problem that will only increase in frequency and complexity, as electronic communications technologies become more complex and widespread. As such, it is important that research be conducted on the extent and nature of stalking perpetrated via the Internet and other electronic communication devices. It also is important that law enforcement and prosecution agencies hire personnel that understand these technologies. Finally, it is essential that our laws keep up with cyberstalking. Where necessary, state laws should be amended to include stalking through electronic communications, federal laws should continue to target interstate cyberstalking, and consideration must continually be given to how nations can work together to target cases of international cyberstalking.

REFERENCES

ABC. (1992, January 10). *Agenda: Little protection for the victims of stalking* [Television broadcast]. New York, ABC.

Axthelm. P. (1989, July 31). An innocent life, a heartbreaking death. *People, 60.*

Bacon, D. (1990, February 12). When fans turn into fanatics, nervous celebs call for help from security expert Gavin de Becker. *People,* p. 106.

Beatty, D. (2003). Stalking legislation in the United States. In M. Brewster (Ed.), *Stalking: Psychology, risk factors, interventions, and law* (pp. 1–55). Kingston, NJ: Civic Research Institute.

Betts, M., & Maglitta, J. (1995, February). ISP policies target e-mail harassment. *Computerworld,* 12.

Boychuk, K. M. (1994). Are stalking laws unconstitutionally vague or overbroad? *Northwestern University Law Review, 88,* 2, 769–802.

Cormandy, C. (1994, September). Deadly mistakes. *American Bar Association Journal, 80,* 68–71.

CyberAngels. (2000). How prevalent is cyberstalking? Retrieved January 2000, from www.cyberangels.org/stalking/defining.html

Dawsey, D., & Malnic, E. (1989, July 19). Actress Rebecca Schaeffer fatally shot at apartment. *Los Angeles Times,* p. 1.

Dietz, P. E, Matthews, D. B., Martell, D. A., Stewart, T. M., Hrouda, D. R., & Warren, J. I. (1991). Threatening and otherwise inappropriate letters to members of the United States Congress. *Journal of Forensic Sciences, 36*(5), 1445–1468.

Federal Interstate Stalking Act, 18 U.S.C. § 2261A (1996).

Finklehor, D., Mitchell, K., & Wolak, J. (2000). *Online victimization: A report on the nation's youth*. Alexandria, VA: National Center for Missing and Exploited Children.

Fisher, B. S. (2001). Being pursued and pursuing: Stalking victimization in a national study of college women: The extent, nature, and impact of stalking on college campuses. In J. A. Davis (Ed.), *Stalking crimes and victim protection: Prevention, intervention, threat assessment, and case management* (pp. 207–238). Boca Raton, FL: CRC Press.

Fisher, B. S., Cullen, F. T., & Turner, M. G. (2000). *The sexual victimization of college women*. Washington, DC: U.S. Department of Justice, Bureau of Justice Statistics.

Gilligan, M. (1992). Stalking the stalker: Developing new laws to thwart those who terrorize others. *Georgia Law Review, 27*, 285–342.

Goleman, D. (1989, October 31). Dangerous delusions: When fans are a threat. *New York Times*, p. C6.

Guy, R. A., Jr. (1993). Nature and constitutionality of stalking laws. *Vanderbilt Law Review, 46*(4), 991–1029.

Hall, D. M. (1998). The victims of stalking. In J. R. Meloy (Ed.), *The psychology of stalking: Clinical and forensic perspectives* (pp. 113–137). San Diego, CA: Academic Press.

Harmon, B. K. (1994). Illinois' newly amended stalking law: Are all the problems solved? *Southern Illinois University Law Journal, 19*, 165–198.

Hunzeker, D. (1992, October 17). Stalking laws. *State legislative report*. Denver, CO: National Conference of State Legislatures.

Hunzeker, D. (1993, November 5). *Stalking legislation update*. Denver, CO: National Conference of State Legislatures.

Lingg, R. A. (1993). Stopping stalkers: A critical examination of anti-stalking legislation. *Saint John's Law Review, 67*(2), 347–381.

Louisiana Office of Public Health. (2000). Prevalence and health consequences of stalking—Louisiana, 1998–1999. *Morbidity and Mortality Weekly Report*. Atlanta, GA: Centers for Disease Control and Prevention.

MacNamara, D. E., & Sagarin, E. (1977). *Sex, crime, and the law*. New York: Free Press.

McFarlane, J. M., Campbell, J. C., Wilt, S., Sachs, C., Ulrich, Y., & Xu, X. (1999, November). Stalking and intimate partner femicide. *Homicide Studies, 3*(4), 300–316.

Mechanic, M. B., Weaver, T., & Resnick, P. (2000). Intimate partner violence and stalking behavior: Exploration of patterns and correlations in a sample of acutely battered women. *Violence and Victims, 15*, 5.

Meloy, J. R. (Ed.). (1998). *The psychology of stalking: Clinical and forensic perspectives*. San Diego, CA: Academic Press.

Meyer, J. (1992, June 25). Man held in stalking of pop singer Janet Jackson. *Los Angeles Times*, p. 1.

Miller, N. (2001). *Stalking laws and implementation practices: A national review for policy makers and practitioners*. Washington, DC: National Institute of Justice.

Moracco, K., Runyan, C. W., & Butts, J. D. (1998). Femicide in North Carolina, 1991–1993: A statewide study of patterns and precursors. *Homicide Studies, 2*, 422–446.

Morin, K. S. (1993). The phenomenon of stalking: Do existing state statutes provide adequate protection? *San Diego Justice Journal, 1*(1), 123–162.

Mustaine, E. E., & Tewksbury, R. (1999). A routine activity theory explanation of women's stalking victimization. *Violence Against Women, 5*(1), 43–62.

National Conference of State Legislatures. (1995, August 14). *Report: Stalking enactments*. Denver, CO.

National Criminal Justice Association. (1993, October). *Project to develop a model anti-stalking code for states*. Washington, DC: U.S. Department of Justice, National Institute of Justice.

Oran, D. (1983). *Oran's dictionary of the law*. St. Paul, MN: West.

Pathe, M., & Mullen, P. E. (1997, January). The impact of stalkers on their victims. *British Journal of Psychiatry, 170*, 12–17.

Puente, M. (1992, July 21). Legislators tackling the terror of stalking: But some experts say measures are vague. *USA Today*, p. 9A.

Schaum, M., & Parrish, K. (1995). *Stalked: Breaking the silence on the crime of stalking in America*. New York: Pocket Books.

Snow, R. L. (1998). *Stopping a stalker: A cop's guide to making the system work for you.* New York: Plenum Press.

Sohn, E. (1994). Antistalking statutes: Do they actually protect victims? *Criminal Law Bulletin, 30*(3), 203–241.

Spitzberg, B., & Rhea, J. (1999). Obsessive relational intrusion and sexual coercion victimization. *Journal of Interpersonal Violence, 14,* 33–47.

Thomas, K. R. (1993). How to stop the stalker: State antistalking laws. *Criminal Law Bulletin, 29*(2), 124–136.

Tjaden, P., & Thoennes, N. (1998, April). *Stalking in America: Findings from the National Violence Against Women Survey.* Washington, DC: National Institute of Justice.

Tjaden, P., & Thoennes, N. (2000). The role of stalking in domestic violence crime reports generated by the Colorado Springs Police Department. *Violence and Victims, 15*(4), 427–441.

Tjaden, P., Thoennes, N., & Allison, C. (2000). Comparing stalking victimization from legal and victim perspectives. *Violence and Victims, 15*(1), 7–22.

Toufexis, A. (1989, July 31). Fatal obsession with the stars. *Time,* 43.

U.S. Department of Justice. (1996, April). *Stalking and antistalking legislation: Annual report to Congress under the Violence Against Women Act.* Washington, DC: National Institute of Justice.

U.S. Department of Justice. (1999, August). *Cyberstalking: A new challenge for law enforcement and industry: A report from the attorney general to the vice president.* Washington, DC: U.S. Department of Justice.

Walker, J. M. (1993). Anti-stalking legislation: Does it protect the victim without violating the rights of the accused? *Denver University of Law Review, 71*(2), 273–302.

Yee, A. (1994, October 10). *Stalking: Legislative update.* Denver, CO: National Conference of State Legislatures.

Zona, M. A., Sharma, K. K., & Lane, J. (1993). A comparative study of erotomanic and obsessional subjects in a forensic sample. *Journal of Forensic Sciences, 38*(4), 894–903.

NOTES

1. Common law crimes are based on judge-made law (as opposed to legislative law) and have their origins in England (Oran, 1983, p. 88).

2. The model code was mandated in P.L. 102–395, the U.S. Department of Commerce, Justice, and State, the Judiciary, and Related Agencies Appropriations Act for Fiscal Year 1993. The directive to develop model antistalking legislation is contained in Section 109(b).

3. Percentages exceed 100 due to rounding.

6

Hate Crimes

Characteristics of Incidents, Victims, and Offenders

JACK McDEVITT

AMY FARRELL

DANIELLE ROUSSEAU

RUSSELL WOLFF

Late one June night in 1988 in Jasper, Texas, James Byrd Jr. left a family party. He had a few too many drinks at the party, and because he had a predisposition to seizures and other health issues, he had no car, so he decided to walk home. When a pickup stopped to offer him a ride, it was a relief. In the truck were three White men, Bill King, Russell Brewer, and Shawn Berry, who were small-time criminals and White supremacists looking for a victim. Earlier in the week, King had discussed with Brewer the idea of starting a Jasper chapter of the Confederate Knights of America, the KKK hate group he and Brewer had joined while in prison. After drafting a constitution, bylaws, and membership applications, King wanted a dramatic incident to publicize the cause and attract members.

James Byrd accepted their offer of a ride and climbed into the truck.

Around 3:00 A.M., the men pulled Byrd from the truck. King stomped him with his boot and spray-painted his face black. They then tied Byrd's ankles with a heavy logging chain and connected him to the back of the truck. Byrd was alive and conscious for more than two miles over dirt and concrete roads as the men dragged him behind the truck. His ankles, elbows, and buttocks were ground to the bone as he tried desperately to keep his head and shoulders above the road. Eventually his struggle ended when his body hit the edge of a concrete culvert that decapitated him.

The men never got the chance to establish their Jasper chapter. King and Brewer were convicted of capital murder and sentenced to death, while Shawn Berry received a life sentence after testifying against his friends.

Though the chilling torture and murder of James Byrd Jr. is not typical of hate crimes, this horrific crime highlights aspects of what makes hate crimes different from other offenses. Byrd was targeted because he was a Black man, not for any other reason; any Black man walking down that road would have done. Hate crime victims are viewed by their attackers as interchangeable, attacked simply because they are perceived to be members of a particular race, religion, or other target group, not because of anything the victim may have done. As often occurs in hate crimes, the offense was committed by multiple offenders. This contributes to a third element more often seen in hate crimes—the excessive brutality of the attack. Hate crimes often involve unusually brutal attacks on victims who are innocent.

The terms *hate crime* and *bias crime*, coined during the 1980s, refer to behavior prohibited by law in which the perpetrator's actions are motivated by bias against a particular group. Acts of violence motivated by bigotry and hatred have occurred throughout history, including major acts of genocide such as the Holocaust during World War II, the "ethnic cleansing" we see across the globe, as well as acts of personal violence targeted at members of specific groups such as the killing of James Byrd Jr. described previously. Despite this lengthy history, it is only during the last three decades that this behavior has been defined as a hate crime and constructed as a social problem that requires additional public policy and legislation.

The term *bias* more accurately reflects a preconceived prejudice toward members of a group characterized by certain attributes, whereas *hate* suggests a more personalized anger associated with a particular individual. However, in light of the fact that *hate* has become more popularly associated with the crime we are considering here, we will continue to use that term throughout this chapter. In addition, although bias, prejudice, and bigotry can influence a wide variety of behavior, this chapter focuses on those *criminal behaviors* that are motivated primarily by hatred or discrimination toward a particular group.

Responses to hate crime have varied across the United States. Federal and state legislation have been passed over the past two decades calling for law enforcement to report incidents involving hate crimes and criminalizing certain types of hate-motivated actions. Hate crime laws differ significantly by state, although most statutes share a few broad commonalities. They traditionally provide for state action, contain a subjective standard to interpret the intent of the offender, and specify a list of protected status characteristics (e.g., race, religion, ethnicity, sexual orientation, disability, etc.; Jenness, 2001). The Federal Bureau of Investigation (FBI) defines hate crimes on the federal level as "criminal offenses that are motivated, in whole or in part, by the offender's hatred toward a race, religion, sexual orientation, ethnicity/national origin, or disability, and committed against persons, property, or society" (FBI, 1999). The Anti-Defamation League (ADL) also employs a law-based standard, defining hate crime as "a criminal act against a person or property in which the perpetrator chooses the victim because of the victim's real or perceived race, religion, national origin, ethnicity, sexual orientation, disability or gender" (ADL, 2001).

HATE CRIME REPORTING AND STATISTICS

Over the last two decades significant efforts have been made to enhance the quality of information about the existence and prevalence of hate crimes in the United States. With the passage of the Hate Crime Statistics Act

(HCSA) in 1990, the attorney general charged the FBI to establish the first national hate crime data collection and reporting program. Utilizing the FBI's existing Uniform Crime Reporting (UCR) program, local, county, and state law enforcement agencies began to submit information about hate crime incidents to the FBI. Incorporating the new hate crime data collection effort into the UCR program was a critical decision, as the UCR program has been an accepted method of national data collection for more than 70 years. Today more than 17,000 local, county, and state law enforcement agencies participate in the UCR program. Despite these advantages, hate crime data collection and reporting have remained challenges for many agencies.

The number of agencies participating in the national hate crime data collection program has grown considerably since the program's initial years. In 1991, 2,771 law enforcement agencies participated in the national data collection program by submitting statistics on the number of hate-motivated crimes that come to the attention of their agency; by 2004, that number had grown to nearly 13,000 agencies (Figure 6.1). Even with this remarkable growth, still only three-fourths of those agencies that participated in the general UCR program also participated in the national bias crime data collection program. As a result, the national statistics on hate crime are missing information from many police agencies across the country.

Despite the growth in the total number of agencies participating in the hate crime reporting program, many major cities report no hate crimes or surprisingly low numbers of hate crimes. Today nearly 85% of participating agencies report no hate crimes, according to the most recent FBI report. While reporting zero hate crimes may accurately reflect the number of hate crimes in many jurisdictions, scholars suggest that some agencies, particularly in larger, more diverse communities, are not fully and accurately collecting information on and

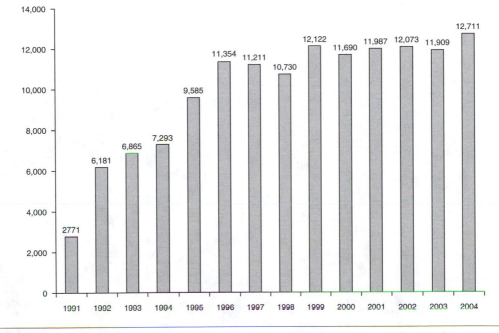

Figure 6.1   Number of Agencies Participating, National Bias Crime Data Collection Program, 1991–2004

SOURCE: Federal Bureau of Investigation, *Hate crime statistics reports* (1991–2004). Washington, DC: U.S. Department of Justice.

reporting hate crimes (McDevitt et al., 2003). For example, in 2004, three states reported fewer than five hate crimes for the entire state: Mississippi (2), Wyoming (2), and Alabama (3). Similarly, a number of major cities reported surprisingly low numbers of hate crimes, such as Detroit, Michigan (0), Indianapolis, Indiana (0), Milwaukee, Wisconsin (2), Nashville, Tennessee (5), New Orleans, Louisiana (6), and Houston, Texas (14; FBI, 2005b).

Though limited to those crimes that are reported to the police, national hate crime statistics provide a critical measure of the prevalence and distribution of hate crimes throughout the county. Between 1995 and 2004, the FBI reports that the total number of hate-motivated crimes reported in the national statistics remained relatively constant, ranging from a low of 7,459 (2002) to highs of 9,792 (1999) and 9,721 (2001; Figure 6.2).

The relatively stable level of reported hate crime is more troubling when compared to other national estimates of violent and property crime (including the FBI's UCR program), which have reported dramatic decreases in all types of crimes over the same period (FBI, 2005a).

Of the 7,642 hate-motivated incidents reported in 2004, most of these crimes were motivated by race. A little more than half (52%) of all hate crimes were motivated by the race of the victim. The remaining incidents were motivated by religion (18%), sexual orientation (16%), ethnicity/national origin (13%), and disability (1%; Figure 6.3).

While race has been the overwhelming motivation for hate crime over the past 10 years, the proportion of reported hate crimes based on religion or ethnicity/national origin has increased throughout this 10-year period (Figure 6.4). Some suggest that this increase

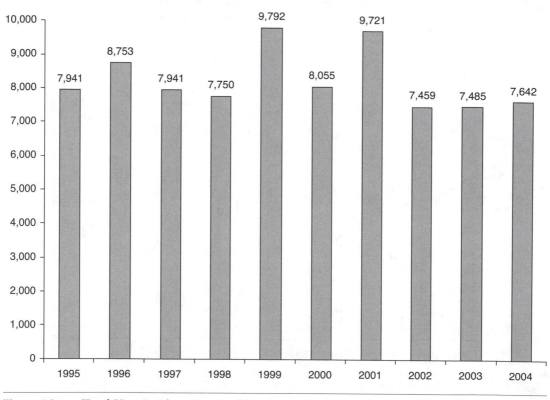

Figure 6.2   Total Hate Incidents Reported by Year, 1995–2004

SOURCE: Federal Bureau of Investigation, *Hate crime statistics reports* (1995–2004). Washington, DC: U.S. Department of Justice.

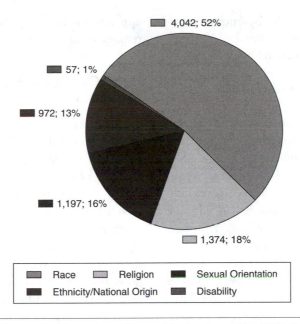

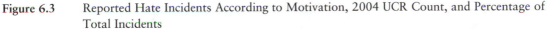

Figure 6.3   Reported Hate Incidents According to Motivation, 2004 UCR Count, and Percentage of
Total Incidents

SOURCE: Federal Bureau of Investigation. (2005). *Hate crime statistics, 2004*. Washington, DC: U.S. Department of
Justice.

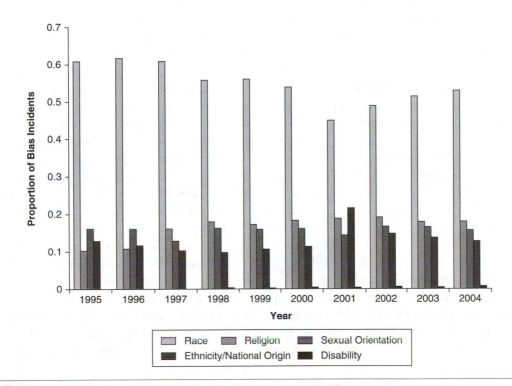

Figure 6.4   Proportion of Hate Incidents Motivation Reported by Year, 1995–2004

SOURCE: Federal Bureau of Investigation, *Hate crime statistics reports* (1995–2004). Washington, DC: U.S.
Department of Justice.

may be related to anti-Arab sentiment following the events of September 11, 2001.

In addition to information about the type of victim, the national hate crime statistics provide useful information about the type of underlying crime that has been reported. In 2004, 34% of all hate crime victimizations involved destruction of property or vandalism, 20% involved actions intended to intimidate the victim, 18% were simple assaults, and 11% were aggravated assaults (FBI, 2005b).[1] These figures indicate that in 2004 almost one half of all hate crimes reported nationally involved attempts to intimidate or physically harm the victim.

In addition to the collection of national statistics on hate-motivated crime by the FBI, a program that is voluntary, 24 states have adopted mandatory hate crime reporting programs (ADL, 2005b). Some data are also generated by national advocacy organizations, such as the ADL and the Southern Poverty Law Center, and state human rights commissions. The statistics gathered from these sources are in many cases different than those reported in the national hate crime statistics due to inconsistencies in reporting practices and definitions of hate crime. Most importantly, the national hate crime statistics report only those incidents that are known to the police. Many victims may not report a hate-motivated crime to the police but will provide information to an advocacy group that tracks such incidents. Particular groups, such as gay men, lesbians, and people of color, may be more likely to resist reporting hate-motivated incidents to the police based on historically negative interactions with law enforcement. In all hate crimes, victims are less likely to report the crime than in similar non-hate-motivated crimes. The reason for this is that the victim carries the cause of their victimization around with them; there is nothing they can do to change their race or ethnicity, so they remain vulnerable to future attacks in all areas of their life, work, socializing, and most importantly when they are at home. This apparent vulnerability causes many victims to remain silent.

HATE CRIME LEGISLATION AND POLICY

Laws and policies addressing hate crime as a distinctive subset of criminality are fairly recent in the United States. Popular understanding of the concept of a hate crime did not arise until the late 1970s. Nonetheless, since then the construction of hate crime as a unique crime typology has had a significant effect on legislation, as well as law enforcement procedure. Legislative responses to hate crimes have primarily established an additional category of offense specifying that an existing criminal act was committed out of hatred or permitted a sentencing enhancement for existing criminal offenses that can be shown to have been committed based in part on hatred toward a particular group. It is important to note that these statutes do not criminalize thoughts, beliefs, or legal forms of expression.

The agenda for hate crime legislation was shaped by social movements, legislatures, courts, and law enforcement agencies at the local, state, and national levels. This agenda was born of an integration of several seemingly disparate social movements, including Black civil rights, the women's movement, the gay and lesbian movement, the disability movement, and the crime victims' movement (Jenness, 2001). Many different victim groups galvanized around the violence that was directed at them simply because of who they were. Initially, the goal of these social movements was to make the public aware of the existence and extent of hate-motivated violence, fundamentally through publicizing statistical information and advocating for hate crime legislation (Jenness & Grattet, 2001). The cause was advanced through efforts of civil rights groups, advocacy groups, victims' rights groups, and private monitoring organizations including the Southern Poverty Law Center and the ADL.

Stakeholders seeking legislation stressed initially the importance of documenting the prevalence of hate crimes and raising awareness through data gathering and reporting. Subsequently, the 1990s witnessed the introduction of four fundamental pieces of federal hate crime legislation. The first victory for hate crime advocates came in 1990, when the Hate Crime Statistics Act (HCSA) was signed into law by President George H. W. Bush. The law required that the U.S. attorney general collect data and publish a summary annually describing the incidence of hate crime in the nation. This data gathering responsibility was delegated to the FBI, who then developed the National Hate Crime Data Collection Program (Cogan, 2002; Levin, 2002; Nolan, Akiyama, & Berhanu, 2002).

Once data were being recorded about the prevalence of hate-motivated crime, advocates sought enhanced penalties for acts of hate-motivated violence. In 1994, the Hate Crime Sentencing Enhancement Act (HCSEA) was passed. This statute increased sentence penalties in federal cases with proof of victim targeting based on race, color, religion, national origin, ethnicity, gender, disability, or sexual orientation (Cogan, 2002; Levin, 2002). In 1994, the Violence Against Women Act was passed allowing for punishment and compensation in relation to federal crimes motivated by gender, promoting the inclusion of gender in the definition of hate crime in a number of states (Jenness & Grattet, 2001).

The Hate Crimes Prevention Act was introduced in 1998, and in subsequent years, in an attempt to expand the jurisdiction of federal officials to investigate and prosecute hate-motivated crimes, broadening both protection and circumstances of protection. This piece of federal legislation has yet to pass Congress.

Following the institutionalization of federal hate crime laws, a majority of states have enacted legislation specifically addressing crimes motivated by hate. State laws vary, but the main principles include prohibiting specific behavior, establishing a unique intimidation offense, or providing for increased sentences in crimes with hate motivation. In addition to allowing various types of responses to hate-motivated crime, states differ significantly in what constitutes requisite prejudice and what crimes specifically qualify under legislation. Currently, 45 states, as well as Washington, D.C., have provisions based on race, religion, and ethnicity; 32 on sexual orientation; 27 on gender; and 32 on disability. Five states also include political affiliation, 11 include transgender identity, and 13 include age as statuses protected under the law. To date, Wyoming has no hate crime legislation (ADL, 2005b). In addition, some states have enacted legislation requiring data collection, mandating law enforcement training, prohibiting paramilitary training, and providing for compensation to victims (ADL, 2005b; Jenness, 2001).

Concerns regarding the constitutionality of hate crime have been addressed by the Supreme Court on multiple occasions. *R.A.V. v. City of St. Paul* (1992) represented a free speech challenge to the establishment of hate crime legislation. In *R.A.V.*, a teenaged skinhead was prosecuted for burning a cross in the yard of a neighborhood Black family. The appeal challenged an ordinance prohibiting the placement of any anger or resentment arousing symbol or object on personal or private property when such action targeted the status of "race, color, creed, religion, or gender" (St. Paul Bias-Motivated Crime Ordinance, 1990). The Court found the local ordinance unconstitutional, arguing that it punished speech, not action, and went beyond the bounds of permissible state regulation.

Wisconsin v. Mitchell (1993) addressed the issue of the legality of penalty enhancements in hate crime legislation. The accused, a Black male named Todd Mitchell, was charged and faced enhanced sentencing after encouraging and participating in the beating of a White youth. The incident resulted from a discussion of a scene from the film *Mississippi Burning* in which a White supremacist beats a Black youth who is praying. Although the accused claimed violation of First Amendment rights, upon review, the Supreme Court, in a unanimous decision, held that the state statute was not in violation of the accused's First Amendment rights. Further, the court held that the First Amendment does not prohibit use of speech as evidence in establishing motive or intent.

Despite the establishment and ongoing clarification of hate crime legislation, such legislation still faces both procedural and theoretical challenges. The constitutional validity of penalty enhancements for hate crimes was again called into question before the Supreme Court in the case of *Apprendi v. New Jersey* (2000), where the court determined that judicial decisions to increase a sentence beyond the maximum prescribed by law must be proved before a jury beyond a reasonable doubt. Here, the state's procedures for enhancing penalties for hate crime were questioned, not the substantive validity of sentence enhancements in cases of hate motivation.

On a theoretical level, some scholars question the usefulness of keeping hate crime as a distinct criminal category. For example, Jacobs and Potter (1997) raise concerns regarding the definition of hate crime and its conceptualization as a unique construct, describing the potential for subjectivity and bias. They argue that hate crime laws have the capacity to generate conflict and social strain by further politicizing crime along lines of racial or ethnic identity and difference. Despite such opposition, however, categorizing offenses as hate crimes has proven to be a useful tool for identifying and addressing this unique phenomenon.

UNIQUENESS OF HATE CRIME VICTIMS

Central to the idea of maintaining separate categories and penalties for hate crimes is the notion that these crimes impact their victims in unique ways. Perpetrators of hate crimes specifically target victims on the basis of identity characteristics (e.g., race, ethnicity, religion, etc.). Accordingly, it is important to understand the unique effects of such crime on the victim and others identifying with the victim's targeted group.

Research suggests that the effects of hate crimes are in fact unique and may produce a more serious emotional, psychological, and behavioral impact on victims when compared to similar crimes lacking a hate motivation. Victims of hate crime often experience unusual levels of fear of the perpetrator or perpetrators and may demonstrate behavioral changes, including avoidance of high-risk situations or desire for retaliation. In addition, hate crime victims possess an increased risk for experiencing symptoms of depression or post-traumatic stress disorder (PTSD; Barnes & Ephross, 1994; Herek, Gillis, & Cogan, 1999; Herek, Gillis, Cogan, & Glunt, 1997). In determining how to effectively assist victims of hate crime, empirical examination of the nature of victimization and its unique characteristics becomes crucial.

Methodologies and Methodological Issues in Studying Hate Crime Impact

As Herek and Berrill (1990) point out, there are three principal means of attempting to study hate crime perpetration. First, criminal victimization records and statistics obtained by law enforcement agencies (e.g., FBI UCR data) may be examined. Second, researchers can study self-report data from samples of perpetrators, including those who are convicted or admitted perpetrators as well as individuals at risk for becoming perpetrators. Finally, victims can be sampled and asked about their personal experiences.

In attempting to sample the population of hate crime victims, a questionnaire or survey format is most frequently implemented, and the majority of studies conducted to date have been cross-sectional self-report measures. Though generally efficient and cost effective, these self-report methods face several limitations. First, survey design can be hindered by the difficulty of determining an accurate definition of hate crime. Further, self-report measures must rely on the victim's perception of a perpetrator's motivation. With such measures, validity can be threatened due to limitations in memory or complexities resulting from question interpretation. (Herek et al., 1997; Shively, 2005).

Impacts of Hate Crime on Victims

Although weaknesses in current research do exist, there is evidence suggesting the presence of unique emotional, psychological, and behavioral consequences for victims of hate crime. Barnes and Ephross (1994) conducted focus groups based on a sample of victims obtained through human rights and social service agencies as well as police departments. Victims provided narrative responses to the presentation of open-ended questions and, in addition, completed questionnaires addressing demographic characteristics and emotional responses to victimization. Results indicate that physical assaults, verbal assaults, and mail or telephone threats were the most common form of hate crime committed. The most prevalent emotion expressed by victims was anger toward the perpetrator. One third of participants reported behavioral changes including both avoidance and preparation for retaliation. The authors found that, unlike victims of other crimes, hate crime victims did not demonstrate a lowered sense of self-esteem (Barnes & Ephross, 1994).

Research examining the effects of hate crimes against lesbians, gays, and bisexual adults supports the existence of higher levels of psychological distress in victims of hate crime assaults. According to a study conducted in Sacramento, California, by Herek et al. (1997), more than half of the respondents had, as an adult, experienced at least one hate crime or attempted hate crime related to sexual orientation. Approximately one fifth of respondents had specifically experienced an assault related to sexual orientation. In this study, self-administered questionnaire data were obtained from a convenience sample of 147 gay, lesbian, and bisexual respondents, with 45 respondents additionally completing a follow-up interview. Assault survivors indicated more anxiety and anger, as well as increased symptoms of depression and PTSD. The hate crime victims were less willing to believe in the general benevolence of people and rated their own risk for future victimization higher than other individuals in the sample.

Herek et al. (1999) compared psychological distress in the victims of sexual-orientation-related hate crimes with victims of non-hate crime and nonvictims. The study is based on a targeted sample of 2,259 gay, lesbian, and bisexual respondents obtained from the Sacramento, California, area. Data were obtained by means of a self-report questionnaire examining victimization experiences, psychological well-being, and victimization-related beliefs, with results indicating that hate crimes appear to have a more serious impact on the victims than do other forms of crime. Greater distress seems to be present based on the fact that the negative symptomology and vulnerability of hate crime victims was directly connected with the victim's identity. Again, analysis supports the findings that hate crime survivors experienced less belief in the benevolence of people, more fear of future crime, and greater perceived vulnerability.

A study conducted by McDevitt, Balboni, Garcis, and Gu (2001) found differences in victims' psychological reactions to being assaulted, depending on whether the attack was hate motivated or not. The study examined data in relation to hate-motivated assault victims and a comparison group of non-hate-motivated assault victims. Study participants completed self-administered questionnaires based on the Horowitz Impact of Events scale. Results of the survey demonstrate that victims of hate crimes experienced increased fear and indicated a greater likelihood of experiencing intrusive thoughts, even controlling for the type and severity of crime. Effects experienced by victims of hate crime were more intense and lasted longer than those of the non-hate victims in the sample.

Overall, the victimization that occurs as result of hate crimes is unique in the fact that it is twofold in nature and targets core identity issues. Like any crime, hate crime victims experience an initial or primary assault. However, hate crime victims may also experience a secondary form of victimization that can include stigmatization and even denial of resources based on their status. Like other victims of crime, victims of hate crime may ask "why me," question their perception of the world as a meaningful place, and even question their own worth. However, unlike other victims, the responses experienced by victims of hate-motivated crimes may result in an increased feeling of stigmatization or an increased feeling of future vulnerability (Berrill & Herek, 1990; Garnets, Herek, & Levy, 1990).

As a result of the fear and trauma associated with the crime, many victims are afraid to report crimes of hate. For example, Herek et al. (1999) found that victims targeted on the basis of sexual orientation were significantly less likely to report crime to the police. Victims of hate crime may fear revictimization, retaliation, or having their privacy compromised. Many victims lack trust in law enforcement and other officials; they believe that authorities will not take their victimization seriously and will thus fail to bring perpetrators to justice. Gay and lesbian victims may specifically fear being "outted" as a result of reporting a hate crime. "Outting" refers to a process where external groups identify a person as gay, lesbian, bisexual, or transgender when that

person desires to keep that information private. Other groups, such as immigrants, may believe they will not be understood, either culturally or because of language barriers. Resident and illegal aliens may fear deportation in the process of reporting. Finally, victims may simply want to avoid the humiliation and retraumatization of having to recount the event (Berrill & Herek, 1990; Bureau of Justice Assistance, 1999; Garnets et al., 1990).

It has also been noted by law enforcement officials and advocates that hate crime offenders do not specialize or target one particular group. Individuals who attack victims because of one characteristic (e.g., race) do not embrace others whom they also view as different (e.g., gay men). While hate crime offenders may not specialize, it is the case that many victim groups experience unique consequences as a result of their victimization.

Race

Race has long been one of the difficult issues facing American society, so it is not surprising that crimes motivated by racial hatred are the most common category of hate crimes reported to the police (Figure 6.4). According to 2004 hate crime data as collected by the UCR program of the FBI, more than half (52%) of all hate incidents are racially motivated. When incidents of ethnicity- and nationality-based hatred are included, the figure rises to 65 percent (FBI, 2005b). Furthermore, along with ethnicity and religion, race represents one of the original and most consistently protected statuses under hate crime legalization and initiatives. However, there currently exists little research that examines in depth the effects of hate crime on victims of racially motivated violence.

Research has begun to examine the effect of racially motivated hate speech. Although much hate speech does not rise to the level of criminality, research in this area highlights attitudes and reactions that may help to predict victims' responses to more severe victimization. Boeckmann and Liew (2002) found evidence to suggest that hate speech targeted at group characteristics is perceived as being unique in comparison to offenses targeted at individual characteristics. Racially and ethnically targeted hate speech were found to justify increased support for punishment as well as to elicit a stronger emotional response in participants. Nielsen (2002) found that racist hate speech is common. In a survey of three communities, half of all people of color experienced racial remarks "every day" or "often," while less than 5% of White participants experienced similar remarks. The experience of racial hate speech by non-Whites led to a variety of emotional responses, including fear and anger; however, few participants responded to the crime by reporting to the police, retaliating, or telling others about the incident, opting instead to simply ignore the incident or leave the situation.

Consistent with studies of hate crime in general, a defining characteristic of racially motivated hate crime appears to be the potential vulnerability expressed by victims. In a study of Black and White college students, Craig (1999) examined reactions to portrayals of hate-motivated assault, general assault, and nonviolent control scenes. Black participants rated the likelihood that they would find themselves in a situation such as the hate-motivated assault significantly higher than White participants did. In addition, Blacks were more likely than White participants to express suggestions that the victim of the hate crime should seek revenge (Craig, 1999).

It is important to recognize the continued existence of racism and the role social belief systems play in the occurrence of hate crimes. In a qualitative study of the responses of White students to the occurrence of a campus-based hate crime, participants indicated they should not personally be held liable, because of their being White, for radicalized

hatred targeted toward other racial groups (Jackson & Heckman, 2002). However, the role of race relations in hate-motivated crime goes beyond the extreme racist beliefs of a few. According to Perry (2002),

> Racially motivated violence is not an aberration associated with a lunatic or extremist fringe. It is a normative means of asserting racial identity relative to the victimized other; it is a natural extension—or enactment—of the racism that allocates privilege along racial lines. (p. 89)

Hate crime, and racialized violence in particular, targets core identity issues. Accordingly, it is important to understand the greater social and cultural context within which such crimes occur. This understanding can facilitate more effective assistance to victims of crime targeted on the basis of their race.

Religion

In 2004, according to federal hate crime statistics, 18% of hate crime incidents were motivated by hatred of religious affiliation. Of such religiously motivated incidents, 69% were anti-Jewish, 11% anti-Islamic, approximately 4% anti-Catholic, approximately 3% anti-Protestant, approximately 3% against multiple religions, and less than 1% anti-Agnostic or anti-Atheist.

From the earliest versions of hate crime legislation, religion has been included as a protected status, largely a result of the work of social advocacy organizations, particularly of the ADL. Representing one of the most long-standing anti-hate violence groups, the ADL has been documenting and publishing data on anti-Semitic and other forms of hate violence since 1979 (Jenness & Grattet, 2001). Currently, the vast majority of states have laws addressing crimes motivated by religious hatred, and 21 states and Washington, D.C., have legislation specifically criminalizing interference with religious worship (ADL, 2005b). According to audit results of the ADL, anti-Semitic incidents have reached the highest level in almost a decade, with high numbers of incidents occurring in schools and on college campuses (ADL, 2005a). One aspect of antireligious hate crimes is the location of the acts of criminal violence. A majority of antireligious hate crimes are targeted at property such as synagogues, churches, mosques, or cemeteries. It has been suggested that because it may be hard to identify potential victims as members of a particular religion, it is relatively easy to attack a symbol of that religion such as a mosque, synagogue, or church (Levin & McDevitt, 1993).

Hate crimes perpetrated against Arabs and/or Muslims have increased dramatically following the events of September 11, 2001. Hate crimes motivated by anti-Islamic sentiment increased from 34 in 2000 to 546 in 2001—a 1,554% increase during this time period. Hate crimes based on national origin (other than Hispanic) increased from 429 in 2000 to 1,752 in 2001—a 308% increase. While such crimes have decreased sharply since 2002, the number of anti-Islamic hate crimes remains much higher than the pre-September 11, 2001, levels. Analysis indicates that anti-Arab or anti-Islamic hate crimes increased sharply and dramatically in response to global events.

Gay, Lesbian, Bisexual, and Transgender

There were 1,197 hate crime incidents targeting sexual orientation reported to law enforcement agencies in 2004, representing 16% of total hate crime incidents reported (FBI, 2005b). According to the ADL, 31 states and the District of Columbia have hate crime laws that specifically include sexual orientation as a protected status, and 16 of those (50%) collect data relating to antihomosexual hate crime (ADL, 2005b). The majority (62%) of incidents targeting sexual orientation that were reported by law enforcement to

the FBI were anti-male homosexual, 14% were anti-female homosexual, 20% were anti-homosexual, 3% were antiheterosexual, and 1% were anti-bisexual in nature. Of the 1,406 offenses involved in these incidents, 28% were for intimidation; 26% were simple assaults; 25% were destruction, damage, or vandalism; and 15% were aggravated assaults (FBI, 2005b).

Research suggests that hate-motivated crimes present opportunities for a varied and severe set of consequences for members of the gay, lesbian, bisexual, and transgender (GLBT) community. Hate crime survivors had higher levels of depression, anxiety, anger, and post-traumatic stress symptoms than victims of non-hate crimes and nonvictims (Herek et al., 1997; Herek et al., 1999). In addition, although many hate crimes were committed by only one perpetrator, hate crimes against gay individuals were more likely than non-hate crimes to involve two or more offenders (Herek, Cogan, & Gillis, 2002), increasing the likelihood of serious injury. Research has also shown that violent hate-motivated attacks against gay males are often more excessive and brutal than those against other groups (see Willis, 2004).

Perhaps more than for members of other groups, identity issues can be very complex for GLBT individuals, making victimization potentially more severe and complicated. Because antigay sentiment is still relatively acceptable in American society—we can see it from church pulpits, in statewide elections, and in a wide variety of media outlets—an individual identifying him or herself as gay may alienate even the people closest to him or her. Despite this, hiding one's identity produces negative consequences and can make it more difficult to weather "heterosexism." Research has shown that those persons who are committed to their gay identity and do not try to hide it from others typically experience stronger psychological adjustment (see Garnets, Herek, & Levy, 2003). Ironically, those who do identify themselves publicly as gay are increasingly likely to be victimized (Herek et al., 1997). Thus embracing a gay identity may act simultaneously as a psychological buffer as well as a risk factor.

Several important methodological issues in antihomosexual hate crime research need to be addressed in order to more accurately assess the effects of victimization. More work needs to be done on accurately locating GLBT individuals and obtaining victimization data from those populations. This is even more vital to the study of bisexual and transgender populations, as well as GLBT individuals of racial and ethnic minorities, all of whom do not typically appear in research in large enough numbers.

Last, the reluctance to report hate crime victimization is an essential factor to understand in working with victims of antihomosexual hate crime. For example, Herek et al. (1999) found that victims targeted on the basis of sexual orientation were significantly less likely to report crime to the police. Victims may fear the insensitive or hostile response by police, as well as being "outted" as a result of reporting a hate crime (Kuehnle & Sullivan, 2003).

Disability

A group that has, until recently, often been ignored in the development and implementation of hate crime policy and legislation is that of disabled individuals. Hate crimes targeting disabled individuals are now legally proscribed in 31 states and in Washington, D.C. (ADL, 2005b). Disabled individuals represent one of the largest minority populations in the United States, and victimization against the disabled is both prevalent and seemingly on the rise. Furthermore, this group is often disregarded in social, legal, and policy arenas. Both data collection efforts as well as law enforcement training procedures have infrequently addressed the disabled population, and there have been no appellate cases dealing with the inclusion of disability in hate crime legislation (Grattet & Jenness, 2001). Violence experienced by disabled individuals is often perpetrated in private and thus may be more veiled than other forms of group targeted violence.

According to FBI data, reported incidents of disability-targeted crime account for less than 1% of all reported hate crime, however, the actual occurrence is almost certainly much higher. Another important difference to recognize is the fact that, unlike other hate crimes in which the perpetrator is generally a stranger or a group of strangers (Berk, 1990; Downey & Stage, 1999; Levin & McDevitt, 1993), the perpetrators of crime against disabled individuals are often known to the victim and many times may be a person on whom the disabled individual must depend (Waxman, 1991). Accordingly, attempts to assist this population must pay particular attention to the group's uniqueness as well as to the fact that disabled victims represent a population that has often been overlooked and often only peripherally linked to hate crime initiatives.

Gender

Like sexual orientation, gender is often a controversial status category in discussions of hate crime. Gender was not included as a protected category under the original HCSA; it was added as a protected category in the HCSEA of 1994, but it is largely overlooked. According to McPhail (2002), "The inclusion [of gender] remains more symbolic than realized as it is rarely invoked and remains controversial" (p. 130). Despite passage of the HCSEA, the FBI still does not collect data on gender. In addition, only 27 states and the District of Columbia have statutory provisions addressing hate crimes committed out of gender hatred (ADL, 2005b), and some of those laws are ineffective. For example, to prove a hate crime motivated by gender, some statutes require that the perpetrator must verbally denigrate women as a class, and in other states at least two restraining orders must have been filed against the perpetrator by two different women for hate crime charges to be filed (McPhail, 2002).

One of the main arguments used by opponents of gender's inclusion as a protected category is that crimes against women are typically committed by people known to the women, ostensibly violating the interchangeability criterion of hate crime. However, hate crimes do not require that the offender and victim be complete strangers, only that the offense be committed at least in part because of the victim's actual or perceived membership of a group. For gender-motivated hate crimes, the challenge is identifying when acts of violence against women are motivated by specific hatred of women as a class or are more broadly caused by existing power differences between men and women commonly found throughout American society.

HATE CRIME OFFENDERS

As discussed previously, hate crime offenses differ significantly in their defining characteristics from other crimes not motivated by hatred. For example, the FBI has identified as an indicator of hate or bias crimes that these offenses tend to be excessively brutal where often the force used is far beyond what is necessary to subdue a victim. Furthermore, hate crimes are generally perpetrated on strangers in acts that can often appear to be random, senseless, or irrational. As discussed in previous sections, victims are selected based on their group affiliation, not personal attributes. Finally, hate crimes are perpetrated by multiple offenders more often than is the case in non-hate crimes (Levin & McDevitt, 2002).

Hate crime perpetrators may be somewhat distinct in comparison to other criminals. For example, in a study of undergraduate

perceptions of hate crime victims and perpetrators, participants viewed perpetrators of hate-motivated crime as being more culpable than perpetrators of non-hate crime (Rayburn, Mendoza, & Davidson, 2003). Further, in a survey of law enforcement, the majority of hate crime investigators indicated that they viewed hate-motivated incidents as more serious than similar crimes not motivated by hatred (McDevitt et al., 2000).

Typologies have been established to characterize the distinctive motivation of hate crime perpetrators. Building on an earlier typology conceptualization (Levin & McDevitt, 1993), McDevitt, Levin, and Bennett (2002) propose a theory characterizing four unique hate crime perpetrator motivations: thrill, defensive, retaliatory, and mission. In a review of 169 hate crime cases investigated by the Boston Police Department, thrill was found most frequently to be the motivation, distinguishing well over half of all hate incidents. Thrill crimes are characterized by a desire for excitement and may be typified by an immature desire for power. Thrill offenses are often perpetrated by groups of teenage or young adult offenders, with offenses occurring on the victim's "turf." In comparison to other perpetrators, there is often less of a commitment to hatred in such offenders (McDevitt et al., 2002). In many of these cases, young men looking for excitement or thrills decide to attack someone who they perceive as different. Based on messages they have received from our culture, these young criminals do not think anyone will care if they attack a member of one of these target groups.

Defensive hate crimes represent the next most common type. These crimes are committed when perpetrators target victims under the perception that the perpetrator is protecting valuable resources or defending threats to his or her neighborhood. As with thrill offenses, defensive crimes are often perpetrated by groups of teenagers or young adults, but in contrast, most defensive hate crimes occur in the offender's neighborhood, not the victim's. It is the offender's "turf" being defended. A common example of defensive hate crimes involves harassment suffered by a Black family who moves into an all-White neighborhood (McDevitt et al., 2002).

The third most common hate crime motivation is that of retaliation. Retaliatory offenses occur in reaction to a perceived hate crime. Here, it is not important whether in fact an assault occurred, only that the offender believes it took place. Retaliatory offenders are likely to act out individually, often seeking out a victim to target in the victim's own territory.

Finally, the least common, but potentially most critical motivation for hate crime offenders, is that of mission offenders. Mission offenders perceive themselves to be crusaders whose lives are completely committed to hatred and bigotry. Mission offenders may operate in groups (in affiliation with an organized hate group) or alone (such as in the example of Timothy McVeigh; McDevitt et al., 2002).

Franklin (2000) also proposes perpetrator typologies in examination of hate crimes perpetrated against gay and lesbian victims. Franklin defines four factors, including peer dynamics, antigay ideology, thrill-seeking, and self-defense. Peer dynamic motivation is characterized by a desire to be closer to friends, to live up to expectations, and to demonstrate toughness or heterosexuality. Antigay ideology is comprised of negative attitudes toward homosexuals, including expression of religious and moral values. Thrill-seeking refers to acts similar to those described in McDevitt et al. (2002), which are committed out of a desire for excitement or fun. Motivations of self-defense are based on the perceived need to respond to a fight initiated by one or more homosexuals.

Overall, typologies categorize perpetrator motivation and can assist law enforcement and other agencies to better detect hate-motivated crime when it occurs. In fact, the FBI incorporates the McDevitt et al. (2002) typology in its agent-training curriculum. These typologies also provide guidance for more empirically based research addressing the etiology of hate crimes and intricacies that may exist among diverse perpetrators. Ultimately, a better understanding of motivation for hate crime will lead to stronger policy and prevention strategies.

CONCLUSIONS

Hate crime is a challenge facing communities and law enforcement both internationally and in the United States. As a nation founded on tolerance for group difference, criminal acts motivated by hatred toward particular groups threaten our core democratic principles. State and federal legislation designed to help measure the prevalence of hate crime and create additional penalties for crimes motivated by hatred toward a particular group have helped raise public awareness about the problem of hate-motivated crime. Through these efforts we have learned a great deal about the hate crimes that are reported to the police; however, much more work needs to be done to understand how hate crimes affect individual victims and groups.

Several strategies for dealing with hate crime have been suggested in the literature (ADL, 2005a; Levin & McDevitt, 2002). These strategies include strong legislation making it clear that any hate-motivated violence will be met with significant criminal sanctions, training for law enforcement in how to identify and respond to acts of hate-motivated violence, and, most important, community reaction to each and every incident that supports the victims and sends a message to the offenders that hate-motivated violence will never be tolerated in our community.

REFERENCES

Anti-Defamation League. (2001). *How children learn and unlearn prejudice: Responding to hate-motivated behavior in schools.* Retrieved March 24, 2006, from www.adl.org/ctboh/Responding1.asp

Anti-Defamation League. (2005a). *ADL audit: Anti-Semitic incidents at highest level in nine years.* Retrieved March 24, 2006, from www.adl.org/PresRele/ASUS_12/4671_12.htm

Anti-Defamation League. (2005b). *Anti Defamation League state hate crime statutory provisions.* Retrieved March 24, 2006, from www.adl.org/learn/hate_crime_laws/state_hate_crime_statutory_provisions_chart.pdf

Apprendi v. New Jersey, 530 U.S. 466 (2000).

Barnes, A., & Ephross, P. H. (1994). The impact of hate violence on victims: Emotional and behavioral responses to attacks. *Social Work, 39*(3), 247–251.

Berk, R. A. (1990). Thinking about hate-motivated crime. *Journal of Interpersonal Violence, 5*(3), 334–349.

Berrill, K., & Herek, G. M. (1990). Primary and secondary victimization in anti-gay hate crimes: Official response and public policy. *Journal of Interpersonal Violence, 5*(3), 401–413.

Boeckmann, R. J., & Liew, J. (2002). Hate speech: Asian American students' justice judgments and psychological responses. *Journal of Social Issues, 58*(2), 363–381.

Bureau of Justice Assistance. (1999). *A policymaker's guide to hate crimes.* Washington, DC: U.S. Department of Justice.

Cogan, J. C. (2002). Hate crime as a crime category worthy of policy attention. *American Behavioral Scientist, 46*(1), 173–185.

Craig, K. M. (1999). Retaliation, fear, or rage: An investigation of African American and White reactions to racist hate crimes. *Journal of Interpersonal Violence, 14*(2), 138–151.

Downey, J. P., & Stage, F. K. (1999). Hate crimes and violence on college and university campuses. *Journal of College Student Development, 40*(1), 3–9.

Federal Bureau of Investigation. (1999). *Hate crime data collection guidelines: Uniform crime reporting,* Washington, DC: U.S. Department of Justice.

Federal Bureau of Investigation. (2005a). *Crime in the United States, 2004.* Washington, DC: U.S. Department of Justice.

Federal Bureau of Investigation. (2005b). *Hate crime statistics, 2004.* Washington, DC: U.S. Department of Justice.

Franklin, K. (2000). Antigay behaviors among young adults: Prevalence, patterns, and motivators in a noncriminal population. *Journal of Interpersonal Violence, 15*(4), 339–362.

Garnets, L., Herek, G. M., & Levy, B. (1990). Violence and victimization of lesbians and gay men: Mental health consequences. *Journal of Interpersonal Violence, 5*(3), 366–383.

Garnets, L. D., Herek, G. M., & Levy, B. (2003). Violence and victimization of lesbians and gay men: Mental health consequences. In L. D. Garnets & D. C. Kimmel (Eds.), *Psychological perspectives on lesbian, gay, and bisexual experiences* (2nd ed., pp. 188–206). New York: Columbia University Press.

Grattet, R., & Jenness, V. (2001). Examining the boundaries of hate crime law: Disabilities and the "dilemma of difference." *Journal of Criminal Law and Criminology, 91*(3), 653–698.

Herek, G. M., & Berrill, K. T. (1990). Documenting the victimization of lesbians and gay men. *Journal of Interpersonal Violence, 5*(3), 301–315.

Herek, G. M., Cogan, J. C., & Gillis, J. R. (2002). Victim experiences in hate crimes based on sexual orientation. *Journal of Social Issues, 58*(2), 319–339.

Herek, G. M., Gillis, J. R., & Cogan, J. C. (1999). Psychological sequelae of hate-crime victimization among lesbians, gay, and bisexual adults. *Journal of Counseling and Clinical Psychology, 67*(6), 945–951.

Herek, G. M., Gillis, J. R., Cogan, J. C., & Glunt, E. K. (1997). Hate crime victimization among lesbian, gay, and bisexual adults: Prevalence, psychological correlates and methodological issues. *Journal of Interpersonal Violence, 12*(2), 195–215.

Jackson, R. L., II, & Heckman, S. M. (2002). Perceptions of White identity and White liability: An analysis of White student responses to a college campus racial hate crime. *Journal of Communication, 52*(2), 434–450.

Jacobs, J. B., & Potter, K. A. (1997). Hate crimes: A critical perspective. *Crime and Justice, 22,* 1–50.

Jenness, V. (2001). The hate crime canon and beyond: A critical assessment. *Law and Critique, 12*(3), 279–308.

Jenness, V., & Grattet, R. (2001). *Making hate a crime: From social movement to law enforcement.* New York: Russell Sage Foundation.

Kuehnle, K., & Sullivan, A. (2003). Gay and lesbian victimization: Reporting factors in domestic violence and bias incidents. *Criminal Justice and Behavior, 30*(1), 85–96.

Levin, B. (2002). From slavery to hate crime laws: The emergence of race and status-based protection in American criminal law. *Journal of Social Issues, 58*(2), 227–245.

Levin, J., & McDevitt, J. (1993). *Hate crimes: The rising tide of bigotry and bloodshed.* New York: Plenum.

Levin, J., & McDevitt, J. (2002). *Hate crime revisited: America's war on those who are different.* Boulder, CO: Westview Press.

McDevitt, J., Balboni, J., Garcia, L., & Gu, J. (2001). Consequences for victims: A comparison of bias and non bias motivated assaults. *American Behavioral Scientist, 45*(4), 697–713.

McDevitt, J., Balboni, J. M., Bennett, S., Weiss, J. C., Orchowsky, S., & Walbolt, L. (2000). *Improving the quality and accuracy of bias crime statistics nationally: An assessment of the first ten years of bias crime data collection.* Washington, DC: U.S. Department of Justice, Bureau of Justice Statistics.

McDevitt, J., Cronin, S., Balboni, J., Farrell, A., Nolan, J., & Weiss, J. (2003). *Bridging the information disconnect in bias crime reporting.* Washington, DC: U.S. Department of Justice, Bureau of Justice Statistics.

McDevitt, J., Levin, J., & Bennett, S. (2002). Hate crime offenders: An expanded typology. *Journal of Social Issues, 58*(2), 303–317.

McPhail, B. A. (2002). Gender-bias hate crimes: A review. *Trauma, Violence, & Abuse, 3*(2), 125–143.

Nielsen, L. B. (2002). Subtle, pervasive, harmful: Racist and sexist remarks in public as hate speech. *Journal of Social Issues, 58*(2), 265–280.

Nolan, J. J., III, Akiyama, Y., & Berhanu, S. (2002). The Hate Crime Statistics Act of 1990: Developing a method for measuring the occurrence of hate violence. *American Behavioral Scientist, 46*(1), 136–153.

Perry, B. (2002). Defending the color line: Racially and ethnically motivated hate crime. *American Behavioral Scientist, 46*(1), 72–92.

R.A.V. v. City of St. Paul, Minnesota, 505 U.S. 377 (1992).

Rayburn, N. R., Mendoza, M., & Davidson, G. C. (2003). Bystanders' perceptions of perpetrators and victims of hate crime: An investigation using the person perception paradigm. *Journal of Interpersonal Violence, 18*(9), 1055–1074.

Shively, M. (2005, June). *Study of literature and legislation on hate crime in America.* Publication of U.S. Department of Justice, National Institute of Justice.

St. Paul Bias-Motivated Crime Ordinance, St. Paul, Minn., Legis. Code § 292.02 (1990).

Waxman, B. F. (1991). Hatred: The unacknowledged dimension in violence against disabled people. *Sexuality and Disability, 9*(3), 185–199.

Willis, D. G. (2004). Hate crimes against gay males: An overview. *Issues in Mental Health Nursing, 25*(2), 115–132.

Wisconsin v. Mitchell, 505 U.S. 476 (1993).

NOTE

1. The remaining 7% of crimes were made up of 2% robbery, 2% burglary, 2% larceny-theft, 1% arson, and less than 1% homicide, rape, and other crimes combined (percentages are rounded).

7

Homicide Survivors

A Summary of the Research

MARTIE P. THOMPSON

On November 10, 1992, I saw my son at school, and at 3:30 I was leaving. We hugged. He said, "Mama, I love you." I said I love you too and I'll see you tonight. I was going to my second job. . . . Later that evening, I called my grandmother's house where he was, and we talked. He was cooking French fries. About 9:00, security came and told me someone wanted to see me upstairs. It was my uncle, and the feeling I got—I knew something was wrong. He said, "Gwen, you've got to come home." The first thing I asked was "where's Mike?" He said "Mike is at home . . . we need you at home." I could see tears in his eyes. My grandmother had just had heart bypass surgery so I thought maybe she was sick. So I got in his truck and he said "Gwen, Mike's dead." It was like I didn't hear what he said. It was like I was in shock. It was like I could hear him calling me way off. I tried to get out of the truck—if I could have just run—run all the way to where I had to go, I would have felt better. He started shaking me and said, "Gwen, Mike is dead." I could hear myself screaming, just screaming. And I thought "Wow—my world is going to come to an end." He couldn't drive fast enough. He was running red lights. When we got to my grandmother's house, I saw all these people I knew. It was like they were waiting to see what I would do. And it was like all I wanted was to see and to hear was Mike. So I went upstairs and I didn't see Mike. And people were like "Honey, it's going to be okay." And I was thinking, "What's going to be okay, what's wrong with these folks?" So I said "where is Mike?" And they said, "he's really dead." And I said "not Mike." So I ran out of the house and I went on the hill where they said he was killed. And I said "Mike!" I was just calling him. Whenever I called my son, he would always answer. I don't care how far we were, if he was a long way from me, when I started calling him, he would come running—"here I come, Mama." So that's what I was looking for. And so the paramedics came and they say I was in shock. . . . I told them I wanted to see him.

So we went to the morgue and some guy rolled him out. And he was just laying there. I mean, he was just there, and the guy said I couldn't touch him. I felt that if I could touch him I could bring breath back into his body. He had on his jacket, his lunch card. . . . I just saw and hugged this child at 3:00 today, just talked to him at 7:00 this evening. And I just could not believe it.

—From author's interview with a homicide survivor

There is a vast amount of research literature on crime victims, in terms of both its prevalence and its consequences. Little attention, however, has been given to the consequences of violence on secondary or indirect victims, such as family members of homicide victims. In this chapter, I first provide a discussion of the prevalence of homicide and estimates of the number of people who have lost a family member to homicide (i.e., homicide survivors). Second, I discuss the effects of loss of a family member to homicide, including psychological, behavioral, and cognitive consequences. Third, I focus on factors that affect family members' recovery, such as social support and coping resources. Fourth, I focus on family members' interactions with the criminal justice system and how these interactions can impact the recovery process. Last, I present information on mental health services for homicide survivors.

PREVALENCE

In 2002, homicide was the 14th leading cause of death in the United States, resulting in an estimated 17,368 fatalities (CDC, 2003). Violent death rates are about twice as high in low- to mid-income level countries (32.1 per 100,000) than in high-income level countries (14.4 per 100,000) such as the United States (Krug, Dahlberg, Mercy, Zwi, & Lozano, 2002). However, the homicide rate in the United States is twice as high as the rates found in other high-income countries (Mercy, Dahlberg, & Krug, 2003).

Homicide rates vary significantly by different demographic groups. Homicide was the forth leading cause of death for children ages 1 to 14, and the second leading cause of death for 15- to 24-year-olds. Homicide is more common among males (13th leading cause of death) than females (not in top 20 leading causes of death). The most pronounced demographic differences in homicide rates are between Blacks and Whites. Whereas homicide was the 20th leading cause of death for Whites, it was the 6th cause of death for Blacks in 2002. Among black males ages 15 to 34, homicide was the leading cause of death (CDC, 2003).

These data underscore the prevalence of homicide in the United States and reflect the vast number of people who are the family members of these victims. It is difficult to estimate the number of family members or "survivors" of these homicide victims. Using a national probability sample, researchers estimate that 5 million U.S. adults have lost an immediate family member to criminal or vehicular homicide, and 16 million have lost an immediate family member, other relative, or close friend to homicide (Amick-McMullan, Kilpatrick, & Resnick, 1991).

RESEARCH ON REACTIONS TO LOSS OF A FAMILY MEMBER TO HOMICIDE

The death of a family member is almost always a stressful event. The loss of a family member to homicide is even more traumatic for a variety of reasons. First, it is almost always sudden. Second, it is a violent event, and the bereaved family members know that their loved ones suffered when they died. Third, there are often feelings of guilt associated with loss of a family member to homicide, as bereaved family members may feel they could have done something to prevent the death. Fourth, because of the nature of the death, the criminal justice system becomes involved. Family members may be questioned about the deceased and about various circumstances of the victim's life, such as their acquaintances and their lifestyle patterns. Fifth, there is stigma associated with murder, as many people may blame the victim's lifestyle for the murder.

Every study that has been conducted with homicide survivors indicates that they experience many types of posttrauma symptoms that manifest themselves psychologically, behaviorally, and cognitively (Amick-McMullan et al., 1991; Bard, Arnone, & Nemiroff, 1980; Thompson, Norris, & Ruback, 1998). The opening story at the beginning of this chapter provides a look into how a survivor of homicide is impacted from the tragedy of loss to murder. The psychological, behavioral, and cognitive reactions to loss of a family member to homicide are discussed next.

Psychological Consequences

High levels of psychological distress, including post-traumatic stress disorder (PTSD), depression, and anxiety have been found among family members of homicide victims. For example, in a nationally representative sample of U.S. adults, 19% of those who lost an immediate family member to homicide had PTSD at some time during their lives, and 5% had current PTSD (Amick-McMullan et al., 1991). To place homicide survivors' distress in context, it is worth comparing their distress levels to those of victims of direct crime (e.g., rape victims) as well as family members who have lost a loved one to death other than homicide. One study indicated that homicide survivors had significantly higher PTSD symptoms than did rape victims or individuals who lost a significant other to a nonhomicide death (Amick-McMullan, Kilpatrick, & Veronen, 1989). In a second study, 150 family members of homicide victims were identified through the medical examiner's office. The number of

years elapsing between interviewing respondents and the death of their loved ones ranged from 1½ to 5 years (M = 3). These homicide survivors were compared to a group of 108 demographically similar individuals who had experienced another type of traumatic event (e.g., robbery, physical assault, sexual assault) within the past 5 years (Thompson, Norris, et al., 1998). Homicide survivors reported significantly higher PTSD symptoms than the other trauma group. A third study found that parents whose children had been murdered reported higher levels of PTSD than parents whose children had died accidentally (Applebaum & Burns, 1991). It is interesting to note that both homicide and accidental deaths are sudden, so the differences in PTSD were due to aspects of the homicide other than its suddenness.

More studies are needed that focus on the trajectory of survivors' distress over time. A prospective study by Murphy, Braun, Cain, Johnson, and Beaton (1999) provides important information on homicide survivors because it was longitudinal and sampled parents whose children died by different modes. A sample of 173 parents of children who died by homicide, suicide, or accidental death was identified from official death records in six counties in the northeastern United States. The sample was assessed at one-, two-, and five-year follow-up periods. At four months postdeath, twice as many parents who had lost a child to homicide met diagnostic criteria for PTSD compared to parents who lost a child to suicide or accidental death (Murphy, Braun, et al., 1999). Mothers (41%) were more likely than fathers (14%) to report PTSD symptoms. Reexperiencing symptoms were the most common symptoms reported by mothers (87%) and fathers (67%). PTSD symptoms declined by the two-year follow-up period for women only; 21% of mothers and 14% of fathers still met diagnostic criteria for PTSD two years later (Murphy, Braun, et al., 1999). At the five-year follow-up period, mothers (28%)

continued to show higher levels of PTSD than did fathers (13%), but mode of death did not predict PTSD status anymore (Murphy, Johnson, Chong, & Beaton, 2003; Murphy, Johnson, & Lohan, 2002). These data suggest that it may take several years to cope with the homicide of a loved one.

Homicide survivors also evidence other types of psychological distress in addition to PTSD. In the study described earlier that compared the distress levels of 150 family members of homicide victims with other trauma victims, homicide survivors reported significantly more distress than adults from the general population (Thompson, Norris, et al., 1998). Twenty-six percent of the homicide survivors scored in the clinically significant range on depression, anxiety, hostility, or somatization, compared to only 3% of the no trauma group (see Table 7.1). Of note, hostility was the only symptom on which homicide survivors differed significantly from violent crime victims.

Data from Murphy's prospective study with parents who lost children to homicide, suicide, or accidental death also indicate elevated rates of distress at four months postdeath across various types of symptoms. Compared to a general population sample of adult women, mothers who lost children were significantly more likely to score in the clinical range for depression (3.5 times more likely), anxiety (3.8 times more likely), somatization (2.1 times more likely), and hostility (2.5 times more likely). Similarly, bereaved males were more likely than a normative sample of men to score in the clinical range for depression (4.3 times more likely), anxiety (3.0 times more likely), somatization (1.8 times more likely), and hostility (2.5 times more likely). Although these symptoms significantly declined by two years postdeath, they were still significantly higher than those found in the normative samples (Murphy, Gupta, et al., 1999). It should be pointed out, however, that this sample

Table 7.1 Sample Means and Standard Deviations on Distress Measures of Homicide Victims Compared to Published Norms (Thompson, Norris, et al., 1998)

	Homicide Survivors (N = 150)	Nonpatient Adults (N = 341)	Psychiatric Outpatients (N = 576)	Violent Crime Victims (N = 175)
Depression				
M	.91[ab]	.28	1.80	.91
SD	.76	.46	1.08	.88
Anxiety				
M	.87[ab]	.35	1.70	.93
SD	.80	.45	1.00	.81
Somatization				
M	.78[a]	.29	.83	.62
SD	.82	.40	.79	.73
Hostility				
M	.50[abc]	.35	1.16	.85
SD	.53	.42	.93	.73

NOTE: BSI norms for nonpatient and outpatient adults were taken from Derogatis and Spencer (1982); those for violent crime victims were taken from Norris and Kaniasty (1994).

a. Homicide sample significantly different from nonpatient adults ($p < .05$).

b. Homicide sample significantly different from psychiatric outpatients ($p < .05$).

c. Homicide sample significantly different from recent violent crime victims ($p < .05$).

included parents who lost their children to suicide and accidental death in addition to homicide. Given the finding reported earlier that loss of a child to homicide was related to a greater likelihood of PTSD than loss of a child to other types of death, these data may actually underestimate the increased psychological distress experienced by homicide survivors.

Behavioral Consequences

How a family member reacts to losing a loved one to homicide is not limited to psychological difficulties. Research indicates that family members of homicide victims also can experience negative behavioral consequences, such as suicidal behaviors, avoidant behavior, and alcohol and drug use. Murphy compared parents who lost a child to homicide, suicide, and accidental death on the likelihood of suicidal ideation. Whereas 19% of the parents whose children had been murdered expressed suicidal ideation, 7% of parents whose children died by suicide and 14% of parents whose children died accidentally reported suicidal ideation. Not surprisingly, parents who reported suicidal ideation were more likely than their nonsuicidal counterparts to score higher on other indicators of psychological distress, such as depression and PTSD, and report lower acceptance of their children's deaths (Murphy, Tapper, Johnson, & Lohan, 2003).

Another negative behavioral consequence to loss of a family member to homicide is the avoidance of things that serve as reminders of the homicide or the deceased (Burgess, 1975). For example, one respondent in a study conducted with 200 parents who had lost a child to murder was quoted as saying, "I stay at home all the time now. I'm scared to death to go for a walk in my own neighborhood" (Rinear, 1988). In another study, a woman who had lost a brother to an unsolved homicide said that she was afraid to let people walk behind her (Burgess, 1975). In the Murphy, Gupta, et al. (1999) study, psychological distress significantly declined over time for 8 of the 10 distress indicators assessed (e.g., depression, anxiety). However, social alienation and interpersonal sensitivity did not improve over time, suggesting that survivors might be avoiding social contacts and situations, particularly those that remind them of the homicide, and thus becoming isolated and detached.

Although no study could be located that assessed if homicide survivors had elevated rates of substance use, research indicates that bereaved individuals in general are at increased risk for elevated consumption of alcohol (Clayton, 1990; Umberson & Chen, 1994). In a large cohort study that followed 1.5 million 35- to 84-year-old adults for five years, those who experienced the death of a spouse were at increased risk of dying from alcohol-related causes (Martikainen & Valkonen, 1996). Thus it is likely that homicide survivors may also be at risk for substance use related problems.

Cognitive Consequences

Research with crime victims indicates that one of the more insidious and common consequences of being violently victimized is the undermining of certain cognitive schemas or assumptions that people hold about themselves, the world, and their relationship to it (Frieze, Hymer, & Greenberg, 1987; McCann, Sakheim, & Abrahamson, 1988; Norris & Kaniasty, 1991). Researchers have focused on different schemas and have referred to them by different names. These schemas include assumptions about the world as safe, meaningful, and predictable. Research suggests that the shattering of these assumptions contributes to the psychological distress associated with victimization (Norris & Kaniasty, 1991; Taylor, 1983).

The importance of cognitive schemas also applies to coping with the loss of a family member to homicide. Homicide survivors evidence negative consequences in several cognitive domains following the murder, including feelings of fear and vulnerability, lack of perceived control, and loss of meaning. Because homicide is typically the result of intentional maliciousness on the part of one person toward another, family members of the victim are likely to experience feelings of fear and vulnerability. In some cases, survivors may literally fear for their lives if a suspect has not been apprehended. For example, in a study with 200 parents who had lost a child to homicide, a quarter of the parents reported fears about their safety and the safety of their surviving children and other family members (Rinear, 1988). One respondent interviewed was quoted as saying, "I am much more concerned about the safety and life of my remaining daughter. Before, I never thought anything like this could happen to us. . . . We're still scared that what happened once might happen again."

Losing someone to homicide also can undermine one's faith in the world as meaningful and predictable. Murder is an event that few would expect to happen to them and can shatter one's sense of control over one's life and the world. The story at the beginning of this chapter illustrates how a survivor's sense of the world as predictable and understandable can be shattered upon learning of the loss of a family member to homicide. In general, homicide survivors who are able to restore their perceptions of the world as meaningful and predictable are able to combat their sense of helplessness and cope better than those who cannot restore this perception. Interestingly, in a study with parents whose children died in a fatal bus crash, the search for factual information about the crash was unrelated to psychological symptomatology in the first three years following the death, but was related to poorer psychological adjustment after that. Those parents who continued to feel the need for information showed poorer adjustment than parents who felt adequately informed (Winje, 1998). Although this sample was comprised of parents who lost their children to a nonhomicide death, it indicates that the need to find meaning in the event is a critical aspect of posttrauma recovery.

The importance of finding meaning also was supported in the prospective study by Murphy, Johnson, et al. (2003). Murphy asked parents at each data collection point (4, 12, 24, and 60 months after the child's death), "How have you searched for meaning in your child's death as well as your own life?" Parents who reported responses that indicated finding a new appreciation of what really matters were considered successful in finding meaning. Parents who were able to find some meaning in their child's death reported significantly less psychological distress, higher marital satisfaction, and better physical health than parents who did not find meaning. One year after the deaths of their children, only 12% of the parents found any meaning in their child's death, but by five years postdeath, 57% had found meaning.

One way survivors may attempt to restore their sense of the world as predictable and controllable is to find someone or something to blame for the murder of their loved ones. In that way, the event can be explained and the world can still be perceived as fair. Targets of blame for the murder may include the perpetrator, the criminal justice system, society at-large, and sometimes even the victim or the survivors (Burgess, 1975; Rinear, 1988). In a study with parents of murdered children, parents reported a high amount of self-blame for the murder (Rinear, 1988). For example, one parent was cited as saying, "I helped him to buy the Corvette that attracted the murderers to him." Another parent was quoted as saying, "I should have insisted that he wear a bulletproof vest since there was danger in one of the neighborhoods where he delivered papers." Although these statements may not sound rational, they exemplify the self-blame that survivors often experience.

FACTORS THAT AFFECT FAMILY MEMBERS' RECOVERY

Although loss of a family member to homicide invariably has negative consequences on survivors' well-being, the pattern of recovery is not the same for everyone. Other factors may moderate or mediate the effects of the homicide on survivor's recovery. Factors that have been studied in relation to homicide survivors are discussed in the following sections.

Relationship to Victim. One factor that has been shown to be associated with survivors' psychological reactions to the homicide is their relationship to the victim—in terms of both type of relationship as well as quality of relationship. For example, in the study with 150 adult family members of homicide victims described earlier, mothers who lost a child to homicide scored significantly higher on psychological distress variables than did other types of relatives (Thompson, Norris, et al., 1998). This finding was replicated in Murphy's prospective study with parents whose children died by homicide, suicide, or accident; mothers had higher PTSD levels than fathers at both one year and five years after their child's death (Murphy, Johnson, et al., 2003). Research also indicates that family members who lived with the victim and reported being very close to the victim had the highest rates of posttraumatic stress symptoms and depression and lower self-reported esteem (Thompson, Norris, et al., 1998).

Social Support. Research indicates that crime victims who report high levels of social support cope better than crime victims without adequate support (Ruback & Thompson, 2001). Unfortunately, although social support is beneficial to survivor's recovery, it is often hard to obtain. Many people do not know how to respond effectively. This could be due to several reasons (Wortman, Battle, & Lemkau, 1997). Others may feel that survivors have more control over their symptoms and should be coping with their loss in a timely manner. Their abilities to provide support also may be impeded by their own feelings of vulnerability that the homicide incites. In order to offset their own fears that this could happen to their loved one too, they may attribute the homicide to a nonrandom cause, such as the victim's living a dangerous lifestyle, rather than a random cause, such as the victim's being in the wrong place at the wrong time. The need to believe in a just world can make it difficult for others to provide adequate emotional support to survivors.

Secondary Stressors. Another factor that can affect recovery is the precipitation of secondary stressors. Homicide can set into motion a series of other life events and stressors, and these stressors can exacerbate survivors' distress. These events that occur after the homicide have been referred to as secondary stressors. In a study comparing children who lost a parent to homicide, children who lost a parent to natural death, and a nonbereaved control group, secondary stressors were integral to understanding the psychological consequences of parental death (Thompson, Kaslow, Price, Williams, & Kingree, 1998). Bereaved children experienced more bereavement-related stressors (people at school acted uncomfortable around child after parent's death; child's relatives told him/her to act differently than he/she did before parent's death) and general stressors (e.g., family moved to new house) than did the children who had not lost a parent to death. The more stressors experienced, the greater the children's psychological distress. The increase in secondary stressors accounted for bereaved youth's higher distress scores, especially among those who had lost a parent to homicide. In other words, high levels of psychological distress levels among homicide survivors were partly due to the changes in their lives that were set in motion by their parents' deaths.

Coping Style. Another factor that can affect recovery is coping style. As with all traumatic events, people use different coping styles, and these coping activities are associated with how well a victim or survivor adjusts to trauma. Among bereaved parents, including parents who lost a child to homicide, repressive and affective styles of coping have been found to be related to PTSD, but in divergent ways. Repressive coping (e.g., denial, substance use) was related to higher levels of PTSD, whereas effective coping (e.g., seeking social support, acceptance) was related to lower levels of PTSD. However, coping styles were only important in predicting PTSD in the first year after the death, but not five years later (Murphy, Johnson, et al., 2003).

Resources. Homicide does not strike randomly. Certain subgroups of the population are more likely to be killed than other subgroups. People with fewer economic resources are at greater risk for being murdered than people of higher socioeconomic status (Cohen, Farley, & Mason, 2003; Hsieh & Pugh, 1993). Because homicide victims are more likely to have few economic resources, their surviving family members also are likely to have few economic resources. This lack of resources is likely to compound the effects of loss of a family member to homicide. According to the conservation of resources theory (Hobfoll, 1988), a trauma, such as homicide, can cause a rapid loss of resources, including loss of objects (e.g., housing), conditions (e.g., job, marriage), personal resources (e.g., self-esteem), and energies (e.g., time, knowledge). People who lack resources before a traumatic event are more susceptible to post-trauma psychological problems than people who have a reservoir of resources before the trauma. The concept of loss spiral has been used to describe how initial loss can provoke future loss, particularly when pretrauma resources are limited (Hobfoll & Lilly, 1993). Although there are no data on whether homicide survivors with few economic resources are at greater risk for maladjustment than survivors with more resources, the conservation of resources theory would suggest that this is the case.

INVOLVEMENT WITH THE CRIMINAL JUSTICE SYSTEM

Homicide is a crime that most always is investigated by law enforcement agencies. Consequently, homicide survivors must interact with criminal justice system personnel and navigate the criminal justice system while coping with their bereavement. Unfortunately, this involvement with the justice system can exacerbate many of the negative consequences precipitated by the homicide (Thompson, Norris, & Ruback, 1996). In the words of a man whose mother was one of the 168 people killed in the Oklahoma City bombing, "The last year or so, we have been able to kind of put it out of our minds because of all of the other things going on. But with the trial starting up again, it kind of brings it all back. . . . It reopens the scab" (Atlanta Journal/Constitution, 1997). In the words of another homicide survivor, "You never bury a loved one who's been murdered, because the justice system keeps digging them up" (Schlosser, 1997).

Many times, homicide survivors have their views of the criminal justice system challenged and violated. Before the murder of their loved one, many survivors likely held fairly benevolent or neutral views of the criminal justice system and perceived its function as one in which justice was meted out. However, when these expectations are violated, the survivors can feel vulnerable, helpless, and angry. According to one homicide survivor who wrote a book about her own and other survivors' experiences, "Murder is a crime against the state, not the survivor. . . . Homicide survivors have to contend with light sentences, the crime never being solved, or the murder presented to the grand jury and not prosecuted, as well as the release of the perpetrator" (Bucholz, 2002, p. 115).

The quality of contacts after a homicide is critical for successful coping. When family members are treated sensitively by justice system personnel, they can start to trust in society again. However, if they have unsatisfactory experiences with the justice process, they are likely to have pessimistic and cynical attitudes regarding justice (Frieze et al., 1987; Greenberg, Ruback, & Westcott, 1983). For example, in the Oklahoma City bombing case against Terry Nichols, family members and relatives of bombing victims were disappointed and angry that the jury did not convict Nichols of first-degree murder charges and did not sentence him to the death penalty. They were also distraught over comments made by the jury forewoman, who announced to reporters that the case against Nichols was circumstantial. Family members likely felt that the justice process did not do "justice" for their loved ones who were killed, thereby exacerbating their distress over their loved ones' murders.

It is important that the justice system provides homicide survivors with information about the murder in order to help attenuate their high levels of distress. If family members are not informed about the investigation and prosecution of the homicide (e.g., if the offenders have been caught, plans for the cases, and when court cases will be heard), they will experience what is referred to as the "second injury to victims" (Symonds, 1980). When a police officer does not take the time to explain to family members what happened to their loved one, family members are likely to feel ignored and unimportant. When a defense attorney paints a portrait of their loved one as having brought about the crime, family members are likely to be hurt and angered. When a plea bargain takes place without their knowledge, family members are likely to feel devalued. One woman whose son was murdered was so distraught over the lack of information and action provided by the police that she started looking for the killers herself.

"I was down there every weekend . . . doing my own investigation. . . . Every time I went down there, I hoped that someone would shoot me. I wasn't fearful. My only child, all I had in my life, was gone" (McDonald, 1995).

In one study, 80% of homicide survivors reported feeling that the justice system should provide them with legal assistance and information on the status of the case, but only 33% reported that they had received this service (Amick-McMullan et al., 1989). Over 80% also believed that the system should provide an advocate, yet only 27% reported that they were adequately served in this area. Eighty percent also believed that the courts should provide personal protection for family members, while only 10% reported receiving this service. In this study, those who reported the most psychological distress were the least satisfied with the criminal justice system. The feelings of dissatisfaction and frustration with the criminal justice process are illustrated by the words of a woman who lost her husband to murder: "I would love to be able to put this in the past and go on, but the laws of our justice system don't allow me to do that. Regardless of how many years go by, I have to relive this every time he (the murderer) is up for parole" (Ogelsby, 1997).

INTERVENTIONS WITH HOMICIDE SURVIVORS

Even though homicide survivors have a high need for mental health services, little research has been conducted on their use of mental health services. Estimates of the percentage of violent crime victims in general who seek professional mental health services indicate that only about 23% sought professional mental health services within the first few months of the incident, and only 22% of those who received services thought the services were "very helpful" (Norris, Kaniasty, & Scheer, 1990). In another study with victims with some involvement with the criminal justice system, rates of service use varied by type of crime: 50% of sexual assault victims, 22% of physical assault victims, and 16% of homicide survivors had used mental health services (Freedy, Resnick, Kilpatrick, Dansky, & Tidwell, 1994).

A recent review of mental health service utilization among people who experienced traumatic events, including violent crime, identified several factors that were important in predicting mental health service use after a traumatic event (Gavrilovic, Schutzwohl, Fazel, & Priebe, 2005). The authors applied a behavioral model of health service use to mental health service use and examined how predisposing, enabling, and need factors were related to service use. Predisposing factors include characteristics of the individual, most typically demographic factors such as age, sex, and race. Enabling factors include characteristics that allow for an individual to seek mental health services, such as transportation, employment, insurance, and knowledge of the availability of services. Need factors include the individual's degree of psychological distress. Using data from 24 published studies, the researchers found that predisposing factors inconsistently predicted use of mental health services. For example, some studies found that younger age, unemployment, and being married predicted treatment seeking, whereas other studies found that older age, employment, and being separated or divorced predicted treatment seeking. Enabling factors that significantly predicted treatment seeking were insurance benefits and compensation. The effects of income were inconsistent. Several need factors were associated with treatment seeking. Most notably among these were psychological symptoms, with higher levels of distress predictive of a higher likelihood of seeking services. Other factors associated with treatment seeking among trauma victims were the occurrence of other stressful life events,

previous use of services, and social support. Other researchers also have found that higher depressive symptoms and more severe crimes are associated with an increased likelihood of seeking mental health services. Among a subset of violent crime victims, predictors of mental health service utilization included urban residence, high social support, internal locus of control, and prior crime experience (Norris et al., 1990).

Although little research has focused on the use of professional mental health services among homicide survivors, several articles have been published on other types of support services for homicide survivors. Salloum and Vincent (1999) presented information on community-based support groups they conducted with adolescent homicide survivors. The general goals of their intervention were to educate adolescent homicide survivors about the nature of trauma and grief, facilitate the expression of trauma-related thoughts and feeling, and reduce PTSD symptoms. They provided recommendations for implementing the intervention, as well as a synopsis of the content of their group sessions. In terms of facilitating successful implementation, they recommend the following: (1) offering support groups in community-based settings, such as schools; (2) educating the administration and teachers about traumatic loss from homicide and explaining the purpose of the group; (3) securing consistent and private space for the group; (4) consulting with administrators when scheduling the groups to ensure that they coincide with the school schedule (e.g., do not fall on holidays); (5) screening to ensure that the group includes only adolescents who have lost a family member to homicide; (6) keeping the group to an optimum size (a maximum of 8 to 10); (7) obtaining written informed consent from youth's guardian for them to participate; and (8) matching the facilitator's ethnicity to the ethnicity of the group.

The content of their intervention sessions is briefly provided below.

Session 1   Explain purpose of group, explain time frame of group, discuss importance of confidentiality, introductions

Session 2   Administer measure of PTSD symptoms, educate about normal reactions, discuss what happened and relationship to the person that died. Worksheets (e.g., a favorite memory) can be used to facilitate discussions

Session 3   Discuss group goals, discuss grieving process

Session 4   Recognize types of losses, find creative ways to cope

Session 5   Identify traumatic reactions (e.g., avoidance of people or places that remind them of homicide), discuss ways to reduce negative reactions, discuss safety issues, teach relaxation techniques

Session 6   Discuss ways to cope during special occasions (e.g., holidays)

Session 7   Discuss feelings of revenge and teach anger management techniques

Session 8   Discuss support, spirituality

Session 9   Review progress toward goals, readminister PTSD symptoms measure; discuss future goals

Session 10   Recognize progress, distribute certificates

Salloum, Avery, and McClain (2001) have evaluated the intervention and reported favorable results. Forty-five African American youth ages 11 to 19 participated in the 10-week intervention. The community-based intervention was conducted at four different public schools in New Orleans. After participating in the group, adolescents experienced significant decreases in PTSD symptoms (assessed at Sessions 2 and 9), particularly in the areas of reexperiencing and avoidance symptoms of PTSD. More than half (58%) of the youth had PTSD symptom scores in the clinical range at the beginning of the intervention. At postintervention, 22% had PTSD scores in the clinical range. However, because there was no control group of bereaved children who did not receive the intervention, it is not possible to know if the decreases in PTSD were due to the intervention or to the passage of time.

In another study specifically with homicide survivors, Rynearson (1995) contacted family members of homicide victims in the Seattle area within three months of the murder. Among the families they were able to contact (75%), 22% agreed to participate in a survey on trauma. Families were then offered supportive intervention services. Because only a portion of families accepted the intervention services, it was possible to compare family members who accepted services (62%) to those who did not seek services (38%). Comparisons revealed that homicide survivors who desired treatment were younger, less religious, less likely to be married, more likely to have had prior therapy, and more likely to have a childhood history of physical and sexual abuse. Results also showed that homicide survivors who desired intervention services reported higher levels of grief, posttraumatic stress, and dissociation symptoms than their counterparts who did not want services.

Another study on service use patterns of homicide survivors in Tennessee used case records from the homicide response program of the county government Victims Assistance Center to gather data on the relationship of the victim to the survivor and the degree of service utilization for counseling, court advocacy, and case management during the four months following the homicide. Survivors were more likely to utilize all three forms of services during the initial eight weeks after the homicide than in the following eight weeks. Further, intrafamilial homicide survivors utilized services more frequently than extrafamilial homicide survivors during the initial eight weeks (Horne, 2003).

SUMMARY AND SUGGESTIONS FOR FUTURE RESEARCH

Because homicide is a leading cause of death in the United States, many people have experienced this tragic loss. One national study indicated that approximately 5 million U.S. adults have lost an immediate family member to criminal or vehicular homicide, and another 11 million have lost another relative or close friend to homicide (Amick-McMullan et al., 1991). Losing a family member to homicide can have negative affective, behavioral, and cognitive consequences. These reactions can include PTSD, depression, suicidal behavior, substance use, and schema shifts regarding fear, control, and meaning. As with a direct experience with crime, losing a family member to murder can negatively affect the indirect victim in multiple ways. However, people who lose a family member to homicide do not all react the same way. Other factors, such as survivors' relationships to the victims, the quality of their social support, and their coping strategies, impact their psychological, behavioral, and cognitive reactions.

The criminal justice system and mental health services also influence reactions of survivors. Because death by homicide, unlike death by natural causes, necessitates the justice system's involvement, it is important to understand how this involvement affects survivors' reactions. Unfortunately, the justice system can exacerbate many of the negative consequences precipitated by the homicide. Survivors' views of the criminal justice system are often violated, and survivors can feel helpless and angry. The quality of contacts after a homicide is critical for successful coping. Regarding mental health services, one study

estimated that 16% of homicide survivors sought mental health services after the crime (Freedy et al., 1994).

Among homicide survivors, predictors of seeking services include being related to the perpetrator, less elapsed time since the homicide (Horne, 2003), being younger and unmarried, being less religious, having a childhood history of abuse, and having higher levels of grief, posttraumatic stress, and dissociation symptoms (Rynearson, 1995). One community-based intervention specifically for homicide survivors indicated that the intervention was effective in reducing PTSD (Salloum et al., 2001).

There are many methodological difficulties inherent in studying family members of homicide victims. One of these difficulties is the inability to use optimal research designs such as randomization to experimental or control group. Obviously, it is not possible to randomly assign people to experience loss of a family member to homicide. However, future research should incorporate nonrandomized control groups into study designs. This would allow for comparing homicide survivors to demographically similar people who have not experienced loss to homicide, thereby enabling researchers to disentangle the psychological consequences due to the homicide from the effects due to other confounding factors, such as limited economic resources. Research on interventions with homicide survivors should try to randomly assign participants into control and intervention groups. Without a control group, it is not possible to determine if improvements in mental health functioning are due to the passage of time or to the intervention. Another suggestion for future research is to utilize longitudinal designs. The studies by Murphy and colleagues on parents who lost a child to death number among the few studies to examine distress levels longitudinally (Murphy, Braun, et al., 1999; Murphy, Gupta, et al., 1999). This work has shed light on the trajectories of parent's distress levels over time. A third suggestion for future research is to examine moderators when studying post-loss consequences. For example, future research should investigate the role of economic resources in coping with loss to homicide. Are survivors with few resources at greater risk for maladjustment compared to their wealthier counterparts? Not all survivors experience a loss to homicide in the same way. It is important for researchers to identify factors that help to buffer the negative consequences of loss to homicide. In this way, clinicians can be alerted as to what factors may predispose some survivors to have poorer outcomes and some survivors to be resilient. Interventions then can be designed that bolster those factors that buffer against the negative effects of loss of a family member to homicide.

REFERENCES

Amick-McMullan, A., Kilpatrick, D., & Resnick, H. (1991). Homicide as a risk factor for PTSD among surviving family members. *Behavior Modification, 15*, 545–559.

Amick-McMullan, A., Kilpatrick, D., & Veronen, L. (1989). Family survivors of homicide victims: A behavioral analysis. *Behavior Therapist, 12*, 75–79.

Applebaum, D. R., & Burns, G. L. (1991). Unexpected childhood death: Posttraumatic stress disorder in surviving siblings and parents. *Journal of Clinical Child Psychology, 20*, 114–120.

Bard, M., Arnone, H., & Nemiroff, D. (1980). Contextual influences on the post-traumatic stress adaptation of homicide survivor-victims. In C. Figley (Ed.), *Trauma and its Wake: Vol. 2. Traumatic stress theory, research, and intervention* (pp. 292–304). New York: Brunner/Mazel.

Bucholz, J. (2002). *Homicide survivors: Misunderstood grievers.* Amityville, NY: Baywood.

Burgess, A. (1975). Family reactions to homicide. *American Journal of Orthopsychiatry, 45*, 391–398.

Centers for Disease Control and Prevention. (2003). Web-Based Injury Statistics Query and Reporting System (WISQARS). National Center for Injury Prevention and Control, Centers for Disease Control and Prevention (producer). Retrieved February 5, 2006, from www.cdc.gov/ncipc/wisqars

Clayton, P. J. (1990). Bereavement and depression. *Journal of Clinical Psychiatry, 51*(Suppl.), 34–40.

Cohen, D. A., Farley, T. A., & Mason, K. (2003). Why is poverty unhealthy: Social and physical mediators. *Social Science and Medicine, 57*, 1631–1641.

Derogatis, L., & Spencer, P. (1982). *The Brief Symptom Inventory (BSI): Administration, scoring, and procedures manual-1.* Baltimore, MD: Author.

Freedy, J. R., Resnick, H. S., Kilpatrick, D. G., Dansky, B. S., & Tidwell, R. P. (1994). The psychological adjustment of recent crime victims in the criminal justice system. *Journal of Interpersonal Violence, 9*, 450–468.

Frieze, I., Hymer, S., & Greenberg, M. (1987). Describing the crime victim: Psychological reactions to victimization. *Professional Psychology: Research and Practice, 18*, 299–315.

Gavrilovic, J. J., Schutzwohl, M., Fazel, M., & Priebe, S. (2005). Who seeks treatment after a traumatic event and who does not? A review of findings on mental health service utilization. *Journal of Traumatic Stress, 18*, 595–605.

Greenberg, M., Ruback, R. B., & Westcott, D. (1983). Seeking help from the police: The victim's perspective. In A. Nadler, J. Fisher, & B. DePaulo (Eds.), *New directions in helping: Vol. 3. Applied perspectives on help-seeking, and -receiving* (pp. 71–103). New York: Academic Press.

Hobfoll, S. (1988). *The ecology of stress.* New York: Hemisphere.

Hobfoll, S., & Lilly, R. (1993). Resource conservation as a strategy for community psychology. *Journal of Community Psychology, 21*, 128–148.

Horne, C. (2003). Families of homicide victims: Service utilization patterns of extra- and intrafamilial homicide survivors. *Journal of Family Violence, 18*, 75–82.

Hsieh, C., & Pugh, M. D. (1993). Poverty, income inequality, and violent crime: A meta-analysis of recent aggregate data. *Criminal Justice Review, 18,* 182–202.

Krug, E., Dahlberg, L. L., Mercy, J. A., Zwi, A. R., & Lozano, R. (2002). *World report on violence and health.* Geneva, Switzerland: World Health Organization.

Martikainen, P., & Valkonen, T. (1996). Mortality after the death of a spouse: Rates and causes of death in a large Finnish cohort. *American Journal of Public Health, 86,* 1087–1093.

McCann, L., Sakheim, D., & Abrahamson, D. (1988). Trauma and victimization: A model of psychological adaptation. *Counseling Psychologist, 16,* 531–594.

McDonald, R. R. (1995, March 20). Son's slaying haunts mom. *Atlanta Journal & Constitution,* p. B2.

Mercy, J. A., Dahlberg, L. L., & Krug, E. (2003). Violence and health: The United States in a global perspective. *American Journal of Public Health, 92,* 256–261.

Murphy, S. A., Braun, T., Cain, K., Johnson, L. C., & Beaton, R. D. (1999). PTSD among bereaved parents following the violent deaths of their 12–28-year old children: A longitudinal prospective analysis. *Journal of Traumatic Stress, 12,* 273–291.

Murphy, S. A., Gupta, A. D., Cain, K. C., Johnson, L. C., Lohan, J., Wu, L., et al. (1999). Changes in parents' mental distress after the violent death of an adolescent or young adult child: A longitudinal prospective analysis. *Death Studies, 23,* 129–159.

Murphy, S. A., Johnson, L. C., Chong, I., & Beaton, R. D. (2003). The prevalence of PTSD following the violent death of a child and predictors of change 5 years later. *Journal of Traumatic Stress, 16,* 17–25.

Murphy, S. A., Johnson, L. C., & Lohan, J. (2002). The aftermath of the violent death of a child: An integration of the assessments of parents' mental distress and PTSD during the first 5 years of bereavement. *Journal of Loss and Trauma, 7,* 203–222.

Murphy, S. A., Tapper, V. J., Johnson, L. C., & Lohan, J. (2003). Suicide ideation among parents bereaved by the violent deaths of their children. *Issues in Mental Health Nursing, 24,* 5–25.

Norris, F. H., & Kaniasty, K. (1991). The psychological experience of crime: A test of the mediating role of beliefs in explaining the distress of victims. *Journal of Social and Clinical Psychology, 10,* 239–261.

Norris, F., & Kaniasty, K. (1994). Psychological distress following criminal victimization in the general population: Cross-sectional, longitudinal, and prospective analyses. *Journal of Consulting and Clinical Psychology, 62,* 111–123.

Norris, F. H., Kaniasty, K., & Scheer, D. (1990). Use of mental health services among victim of crime: Frequency, correlates, and subsequent recovery. *Journal of Consulting and Clinical Psychology, 58,* 538–547.

Ogelsby, C. (1997, April 18). Widow protests parole of mall killer. *Atlanta Journal & Constitution,* p. F8.

Rinear, E. (1988). Psychosocial aspects of parental response patterns to the death of a child by homicide. *Journal of Traumatic Stress, 1,* 305–322.

Ruback, R. B., & Thompson, M. P. (2001). *Social and psychological consequences of violent victimization.* Newbury Park, CA: Sage.

Rynearson, E. K. (1995). Bereavement after homicide: A comparison of treatment seekers and refusers. *British Journal of Psychiatry, 166,* 507–510.

Salloum, A., Avery, L., & McClain, R. P. (2001). Group psychotherapy for adolescent survivors of homicide victims: A pilot study. *Journal of the American Academy of Child and Adolescent Psychiatry, 40,* 1261–1267.

Salloum, A., & Vincent, N. J. (1999). Community-based groups for inner-city adolescent survivors of homicide victims. *Journal of Child and Adolescent Group Therapy, 9,* 27–45.

Schlosser, E. (1997, September). A grief like no other. *Atlantic Monthly,* pp. 37–76.

Symonds, M. (1980). The "second injury" to victims. In L. Kivens (Ed.), *Evaluation and change: Services for survivors* (pp. 36–38). Minneapolis, MN: Medical Research Foundation.

Taylor, S. (1983). Adjustment to threatening events: A theory of cognitive adaptation. *American Psychologist, 38,* 1161–1173.

Thompson, M. P., Kaslow, N. J., Price, A., Williams, K., & Kingree, J. B. (1998). The role of secondary stressors in the parental death—Child distress relation. *Journal of Abnormal Child Psychology, 26,* 357–366.

Thompson, M. P., Norris, F., & Ruback, B. (1996). System influences on posthomicide beliefs and distress. *American Journal of Community Psychology, 24,* 787–812.

Thompson, M. P., Norris. F., & Ruback, B. (1998). Comparative distress levels of inner-city family members of homicide victims. *Journal of Traumatic Stress, 11,* 223–242.

Umberson, D., & Chen, M. D. (1994). Effects of a parent's death on adult children: Relationship salience and reaction to loss. *American Sociological Review, 59,* 152–168.

Winje, D. (1998). Cognitive coping: The psychological significance of knowing what happened in the traumatic event. *Journal of Traumatic Stress, 11,* 627–643.

Wortman, C. B., Battle, E. S., & Lemkau, J. P. (1997). Coming to terms with the sudden, traumatic death of a spouse or child. In A. Lurigio, W. Skogan, & R. Davis (Eds.), *Victims of crime* (2nd ed., pp. 108–133). Newbury Park, CA: Sage.

8

Victims of Financial Crime

DEBBIE DEEM

LISA NERENBERG

RICHARD TITUS

At the zoo, there always seem to be more visitors around the lions and tigers than around the wildebeest and antelope. That predators are intrinsically more interesting than prey may help explain why criminology has been more intrigued with offenders than with victims and has paid more attention to violent crime and criminals. For decades, crime victims were all but ignored by researchers, criminal justice professionals, and policymakers.

In recent years, there has been a dramatic reversal of this situation, with public officials and a grassroots victims' rights movement focusing unprecedented attention on the physical injuries, financial losses, and suffering caused by violent crimes. The victims' movement has spawned significant policy reforms, with victim-rights legislation and assistance programs developed across the nation. This heightened attention has not, however, included victims of financial crimes, whose needs have scarcely been addressed by investigators and policymakers.

The field of financial crime lacks agreed-upon definitions. Moreover, controversies and competition regarding definitions go into matters that are beyond the scope of this chapter. In the age of computers and global interconnectedness, definitions of financial crime will quickly obsolesce anyway as services or software features yield new vulnerabilities just waiting to be discovered by cybercriminals, who can be based anywhere

Author Note: The information, views, and opinions provided by author Debbie Deem do not express the official policy of the FBI or U.S. Department of Justice.

in the world. In general, the types of crime that will be discussed here include traditional forms of fraud, such as telemarketing and investment fraud, as well as emerging trends, which include cybercrimes, identity theft, and elder financial abuse. This discussion focuses on individual victims as opposed to small businesses and corporations, government agencies, and nonprofit organizations, which may also be victims. It further discusses the challenges that financial crimes in the new global environment pose to law enforcement and victim advocates. While strategies for addressing crimes such as burglary have changed little in the last generation, today's advice for achieving safety on the Internet may seem quaint a month from now.

FRAUD

Fraud, the use of deliberately deceptive practices to gain unlawful or unfair advantage, occurs within an American context of truth stretching in merchandising and politics. Thus there is a continuum ranging from cases of consumer misinterpretation of information, to consumer dissatisfaction with products or services, to high-pressure salesmanship, to outright theft. There may be interaction between the criminal and the victim, with the criminal using strategies to get the victim to carry out facilitating acts (Davis, Taylor, & Titus, 1997; Titus, 2001). Victims may or may not be aware that they are being victimized. For example, a person on the Web may unknowingly install "malware" that will allow theft of assets, a bank employee's laptop containing customer information may be stolen, or personal information from business or government sources may be obtained from sites on the Web.

"Mass marketing" crimes are crimes in which perpetrators use technology to target and defraud many people, often from distant locations, including other countries. They include fraudulent telemarketing and Internet crimes such as "phishing." Phishing is when one receives an e-mail that appears to be from a reliable source, such as a bank, the Department of Homeland Security, Federal Deposit Insurance Corporation, Federal Bureau of Investigation (FBI), Internet Crime Complaint Center, Internal Revenue Service (IRS), or other government agencies and legitimate businesses, which purports to be about something that will engage the recipient's interest (e.g., an e-mail from the IRS concerning a problem with the individual's filing or tax refund). The individual is asked to divulge personal information, which can then be used for credit card fraud, identity theft, and Nigerian or "419" scams (named after the relevant section of the Nigerian criminal code; Internet Crime Complaint Center, 2005a, 2005b, 2005c, 2005d, 2006; U.S. Department of Justice, 2004). Advance fee schemes are when victims are told that they have won sweepstakes or contests but have to pay "advances" on their supposed winnings to cover insurance, taxes, and other "fees." Victims may be convinced to make payments several times, sometimes losing hundreds of thousands of dollars.

In "affinity frauds," con artists are or claim to be members of the same ethnic, religious, career, professional, or civic group as their victims. In a world of increasing complexity, many people feel the need for a shorthand way of knowing whom to trust. This is especially true when it comes to investing money. Unfamiliar with how financial markets work or how to research investments and salespersons, many people fall prey to this type of fraud. "You can trust me," says the scamster, "because I'm like you. We share the same background and interests, and I can help you make money" (North American Securities Administrators Association, 2005). Recent immigrants, minority communities, and religious groups have been particularly hard hit by affinity-based investment crimes.

Information on fraud victimization comes mainly from crimes reported to authorities or complaint lines. Little of the available data is derived from methodologically sound research (FTC, 2004). Reporting rates are low; in one study of previously identified victims, up to half failed to report the incidents to interviewers (AARP, 2003). Those who do report may not be representative of all victims or of the general population. Because many victims do not know they have been victimized and because of the difficulties with distinguishing criminal from noncriminal conduct, the issue of respondent over/under-reporting is perhaps more salient in this form of research than that which focuses on other crimes.

The FBI's Uniform Crime Report (UCR), the most widely cited source of aggregate criminal statistics, provides a nationwide view of crime based on information submitted by city, county, and state law enforcement agencies. Because the UCR is based on arrest information, it is not an ideal indicator, as fewer than half of all criminal incidents are reported to the police or lead to arrest.

Some UCR reporting jurisdictions, comprising 17% of the U.S. population, also participate in the National Incident-Based Reporting System (NIBRS), in which responding police officers ask questions about financial crime. A study by the National Institute of Justice[1] study found that 239,184 incidents involving fraud, forgery, or embezzlement were available for analysis. The distribution of offenses for younger and older victims was quite similar, which runs counter to conventional wisdom that suggests that elders are more vulnerable, but is consistent with most research on the subject. Older victims had higher dollar losses than younger victims, however, and there was some evidence that risk increases among the members of the population older than 70 years of age.

In a nationally representative telephone survey of 1,246 people aged 18 and older, respondents were asked if they had been victims of 21 specific types of fraud (there was also an "other" category) or if attempts had been made to victimize them within the previous 12 months (Titus, Heinzelmann, & Boyle, 1995). Nearly a third (31%) reported one or more fraud attempts, of which 48% were successful. Across crime types, there was wide variation in the percentage of attempts that resulted in victimization. A substantial proportion of individuals are repeat victims, with 8% reporting a past victimization or attempted victimization for five or more of the fraud categories. The average amount of money and property loss incurred was $216; the overall loss range for victims was from $0 to $65,000. The elderly were slightly less likely to have been victimized.

A 1992 survey of telemarketing fraud found that one in three Americans reported having been cheated out of money through various deceptive means (Bass & Hoeffler, 1992). In a 1995 survey of Delaware and Pennsylvania residents, 17% of those surveyed reported that they had been victims of fraud at least once during their lives (Princeton Survey Research Associates, 1995). Individuals over the age of 50 were least likely to have succumbed to potentially fraudulent sales techniques. In a survey conducted among Montana AARP members aged 50 and over, 33% reported being victims of auto-related or telephone service fraud, 24% of credit card fraud, and roughly one in five (20%) of insurance, home repair, and charity frauds (AARP, 2003).

In a national survey of 2,500 randomly selected adults conducted by the Federal Trade Commission (FTC, 2004), unauthorized change in long distance telephone service was reported by 6.5% respondents, and one or more other frauds were reported by 11.2%. Victims first learned of the fraudulent offers most often by print media (33%), followed by telemarketing (17%), and the Internet/e-mail (14%). Ethnic minorities were victimized more often, as were persons who expected their incomes to significantly increase or decrease, and those who felt they had more debt than they could comfortably handle. Consumers aged 65 and older faced no greater victimization risk than younger consumers. Dollars lost varied widely across types of fraud and also within specific fraud types. Median losses to credit repair frauds were three times higher.

In 1994, Shichor surveyed 152 randomly selected victims of approximately 9,000 identified victims of an oil and gas partnership scam. The amount of money stolen was estimated at approximately $217 million dollars (Shichor, Doocy, & Geis, 1996). Most of the victims were between the ages of 52 and 63 years old, well educated, and male. The losses were significant, with 17% losing between $30,000 and $74,999, and 18% losing more than $75,000.

Telemarketers are relentless in their pursuit of victims. A 1995 AARP survey of 745 victims of telemarketing fraud found that respondents were "besieged by telemarketers," with 42% reporting that they had received 20 or more calls from telemarketers during the past six months, 82% receiving one or more attempts within the past six months, and 46% receiving calls within the past week (AARP, 1996). Fraud victims are added to "mooch" lists that are exchanged and sold among con artists for "reload" schemes (the same or similar scams) and "recovery" schemes (offers to assist victims recover their losses).

EMERGING TRENDS IN FINANCIAL CRIME

Cybercrimes

While the smooth-talking con artist will always be with us, crimes associated with use of the computer and the Internet is a growing threat. Willie Sutton today would be wrong; the money now is in cyberspace, not banks. And so are the people. Approximately 60% of U.S. teens have created online content (Pew Internet and American Life Project, 2005c), and 68% of

American adults use the Internet (Pew Internet and American Life Project, 2005a). For seniors age 65 and over, this figure is 22%, a number that jumped by 47% between 2000 and 2004 (Pew Internet and American Life Project, 2004). Teens are more likely than adults to share passwords, download files, click on "free" offers, include too much personal information on their blogs, utilize sites like MySpace.com, and engage in other high-risk behavior that may have financial crime consequences, not only for them but for other household members (Earthlink, 2005).

Reports to the National Fraud Information Center reveal that in 2005 the top ten Internet scams and mean amounts lost were as follows: auctions (42%, $1,155), nonauction sales (30%, $2,528), "419" Nigerian letter scams (8%, $6,937), fake checks (6%, $4,361), lotteries (4%, $2,919), phishing (2%, $612), advance fee loans (1%, $1,426), information/adult services (1%, $504), work-at-home (1%, $1,785), and Internet access services (1%, $1,262) (National Fraud Information Center, 2005). Among crimes reported in 2005 to the FBI-National White Collar Crime Center's Internet Crime Complaint Center (2005b), the top ten complaint categories were auction fraud (62.7%), nondelivery of cash or merchandise (15.7%), check/debit card fraud (2.6%), investment fraud (1.5%), confidence fraud (1.4%), and ID theft, financial instrument fraud, and child pornography (all less than 1.0%). The median reported loss was $424.00. Males lost $1.86 to every female loss of $1.00. Those over the age of 50 reported the highest losses, and those under 20, the lowest. Although few victims report the extent of their losses, the available information suggests wide variations by type of crime (FTC, 2004; Titus et al., 1995). For some crimes, there were very few losses reported, but the amounts were very high. For example, although Nigerian letter scams accounted for just 2.7% of cases reported, the average loss was $5,000.00. The average loss for auction fraud, which accounted for 41.0% of cases, was $385.00. Three-fourths (75%) of offenders were male, and 71% were from the United States (8% were Nigerian, 4% were from the United Kingdom, and 3% were Canadian). Only in California were more than 20% of offenders and complainants residents of the same state.

Computer users are also besieged by scamsters. A survey of Internet users revealed that almost one in four received phishing-type e-mails every month; 70% thought they might be legitimate. Almost three-quarters (74%) used their computers for sensitive transactions (Pew Internet and American Life Project, 2005b).

Individuals, families, and businesses may believe that they are protected, and aren't. A survey conducted by the National Cyber Security Alliance (2005) found that 81% of the homes contacted were missing one of three vital elements of personal computer security: updated virus software, spyware protection, and/or a firewall. New technologies and gaps in protecting such new technologies remain an important way cyber criminals steal information.

Identity Theft

Identity theft has become one of the fastest-growing crimes in the United States and Canada. It occurs by (1) theft of payment cards and documents from purses or wallets, trash, or mailboxes; (2) at ATMs; (3) credit card "skimming"; (4) phishing; (5) theft from company or government databases; (6) theft via devices such as "skimmers"; and other such means (U.S. Department of Justice, 2003). Theft of personal information was used for the following types of fraud: credit card fraud (32%), phone or utilities (21%), bank (17%), employment-related (11%), government documents/benefits (8%), other (19%), and attempted (8%; AARP, 2004).

Estimates of the extent of the problem vary widely. Preliminary data from the National Crime Victimization Survey (NCVS),

an ongoing national survey of victims, offenders, and crime, which includes criminal events that go unreported to the police, indicate that in 2004, 3% of U.S. households experienced one or more incidents of identity theft (BJS, 2006). Younger, metropolitan, and upper income households were overrepresented among victims. Another national survey of 4,057 U.S. adults (FTC, 2005a) found that 1.5% had been ID theft victims in the past year, and 12.7% had been victims in the past five years. Victims on average reported to police 25% of the time; this rate rose to 43% with the most serious types of ID theft. Finally, a higher ID theft victimization rate of 20% was reported in a Chubb Group survey of 1,850 Americans (Chubb Group, 2005). A similar rate of 18% resulted from an Experian-Gallup (2005) survey. These higher rates may perhaps result from what appear to be more inclusive definitions and reporting periods in the Chubb and Experian surveys.

In addition to financial losses, victims of identity theft may devote weeks, months, or years to recover assets or repair damage. According to the Identity Theft Resource Center (2005), the mean is 330 hours, with a range of 3 to 5,840 hours.

Despite the common perception that identity theft is a "high tech" crime committed by strangers, recent studies show that it is most frequently committed by family members, acquaintances, and employees (Javelin Strategy and Research, 2005).

Financial Abuse and Exploitation of the Elderly

Elder financial abuse, which is also referred to as elder financial exploitation, material abuse or exploitation, fiduciary abuse, and financial mistreatment is believed by many experts to be on the rise (Rabiner, O'Keeffe, & Brown, 2004). A defining feature of elder financial abuse is the fact that most perpetrators are family members, caregivers, friends, acquaintances, or predators who have gained the trust and confidence of their victims. In addition, age-related impairments, including diminished physical and cognitive functioning, contribute to elders' risk, reduce the likelihood that the abuse will be reported or discovered, and create special challenges for law enforcement and other helping professionals (Hafemeister, 2003; Nerenberg, 1999; Rabiner et al., 2004).

Elder financial abuse includes a broad range of conduct, some of which is criminal and some of which is not. Common examples include:

1. Misusing legal documents (e.g., getting an older person to sign a deed, will, or power of attorney through deception, coercion, or undue influence)

2. Using an elders' property or possessions without permission or promising lifelong care in exchange for money or property and not following through on promises

3. Forging an older person's signature

4. Using deception to gain victims' confidence (referred to as confidence crimes, or "cons")

5. Using trickery, false pretenses, or dishonest acts or statements for financial gain

6. Using deceptive romantic overtures to gain access to older peoples' assets ("sweetheart scams") (Hafemeister, 2003; Nerenberg, 1999; Rabiner et al., 2004)

Although the prevalence of financial abuse in the United States is not known, experts believe that it is significantly underreported (Rabiner et al., 2004). What is known about the extent of the problem comes primarily from a national incidence study conducted by the National Center on Elder Abuse in 1996 (1998) and surveys of state agencies charged with investigating and responding to reports of abuse under elder abuse reporting laws (most states require professionals and others

to report elder abuse to adult protective service [APS] programs for investigation).

The National Elder Abuse Incidence Study (NEAIS) drew from two sources of information: reports from APS agencies and reports from "sentinels," specially trained individuals who work in law enforcement agencies, health care facilities, social service agencies, and financial institutions. The NEAIS revealed that 449,924 persons aged 60 and over experienced physical, sexual, emotional, or financial abuse; abandonment; or neglect in 1996. Of these, 70,942 (16%) were reported to and substantiated by APS agencies, and the remaining 378,982 (84%) were identified by sentinels. Financial/material exploitation accounted for 21,427 of the cases.

Those at heightened risk for elder financial abuse (by persons known to them) include the very old, women, and minorities (National Center on Elder Abuse, 1998). Nearly half (48%) of substantiated APS financial abuse reports and 25.3% of sentinel reports involved victims 80 years of age or older, even though members of this age group comprised only 19% of the total elderly population. Women were the victims in 63% of the cases reported to APS, and 91.8% of cases identified by "sentinels" (the percentage of women in the elder population was 57.6%). African American elders accounted for 15.4% of cases reported in 1996, although they represented only 8.3 % of the population (National Center on Elder Abuse, 1998).

The National Center on Elder Abuse has, since 1986, collected information on elder abuse cases reported to state APS programs. In 2004, the most recent year for which information is available, APS programs in 29 states investigated a total of 192,243 reports of abuse against persons aged 60 and older. Of these, 18.5% were for financial exploitation. Of the 88,455 cases of all forms of abuse that were substantiated, 13.8% were for financial abuse (Teaster, Dugar, Mendiondo, Abner, & Cecil, 2006).

Elders with physical or cognitive impairments are at heightened risk for certain forms of elder exploitation, with impairment contributing to risk in several ways (Blunt, 1993; Choi, Kulick, & Mayer, 1999). Elders with impaired mobility, vision, or memory are likely to depend on others to help them manage their finances, run errands, or transact business. These caregivers, who include family members, personal care attendants, friendly visitors, and meal service providers, have access to victims' homes and property and can exert significant control and influence. They can isolate elders, withhold care to gain compliance, and undermine others' efforts to help. Further heightening risk is a severe shortage of in-home helpers, which has resulted in more seniors hiring "independent providers" directly from newspaper ads or referral services as opposed to agency-employed workers who are screened, supervised, and monitored. Elders with dementia are at risk for being tricked or coerced or may be exploited by persons who have been appointed to manage their finances including guardians, representative payees, or money managers.

In addition to heightening elders' risk, disabilities may prevent victims from getting help. Frail individuals are likely to decline, become incapacitated, or even die during the course of protracted legal proceedings, and it is not uncommon for cases to continue for many years, particularly when defendants must be extradited. Abusers may assume that frail victims will not survive long enough to follow through on legal interventions or that they will not make convincing witnesses if they are unable to recall details or explain the impact of crimes.

Elder financial abuse cases pose special challenges to victim advocates, law enforcement, and other helping professionals. Perhaps foremost among these are assessing elderly victims' mental capacity and determining whether or not they have been unduly influenced. Determining whether financial abuse has occurred often involves assessing whether elders with diminished mental capacity are capable of executing financial transactions or giving informed consent, often at an earlier point in time. For example, financial abuse frequently involves the transfer of assets through instruments such as wills and powers of attorney, transactions that are improper or illegal if the older person lacks the mental capacity to understand the nature of the agreements (Naimark, 2001). For a transaction to be legal, the person making it must be provided with information about the transaction and have sufficient mental capacity to understand and "appreciate" it. The consent must be voluntary and free from coercion; merely being passive does not amount to consent.

Assessing mental capacity is complex. A person's mental capacity may fluctuate and is affected by such variables as the time of day, nutritional status, and stress. In addition, mental capacity is made up of many mental skills and abilities such as memory, abstract thinking, and reasoning. The skills that are needed depend on the decisions in question. For example, a person who is capable of deciding whom he or she wants to leave his or her assets to may be incapable of weighing the benefits of a reverse annuity mortgage. Professionals have little guidance when assessing capacity for many of the decisions commonly questioned in abuse cases, and the standards of capacity that are needed for certain transactions are better understood than for others. For example, there is general agreement about testamentary capacity, or the degree of capacity necessary to make a will, but less agreement about the level of capacity needed for other common contractual agreements, such as giving gifts or getting married (Nerenberg, 1999).

One's ability to make decisions may also be impaired by psychological manipulation or control exerted by others. Undue influence is the concerted, deliberate effort to assume control over another person's decision making through psychological control and manipulation (Nievod, 1993). It involves the use of power and control to exploit the trust, dependency, and fear of others, a process that typically occurs over time. Abusers play on emotional vulnerability and dependence by endearing themselves to victims to get them to comply with their demands, gain their trust, and foster dependency. Whereas victims of coercion typically feel pressured to do what they are told, victims of undue influence may not even be aware that they are being manipulated. They may even defend or collude with perpetrators.

Elders at risk for undue influence include persons with cognitive impairment; who are socially isolated; who are undergoing major life transitions; and who have recently lost spouses, friends, homes, or independence (Quinn, 2002). Depression, stress, serious health problems, and medications that reduce cognitive status may also contribute to risk. Although these factors increase susceptibility, it is the manipulation, coercion, compulsion, or restraint that occurs as the result of a relationship that constitutes undue influence.

Abusers use a variety of tactics to unduly influence others (Naimark, 2001; Nerenberg, 1996; Nievod, 1993; Quinn, 2002). They may isolate the older person by discouraging or preventing visits, phone calls, and letters, and then convince the elder that he or she has been abandoned by others. Creating a "siege mentality" is convincing someone that others, such as friends, family members, caregivers, or service providers have malevolent motives and cannot be trusted. The abuser may foster dependency by withholding assistive devices, failing to provide food or medical care, or preventing the elder from receiving support or assistance that would enhance independence. The manipulator may intentionally foster a sense of powerlessness so that the elder loses confidence in his or her abilities. Another common technique is discouraging or preventing victims from seeking advice

from others prior to signing documents such as powers of attorney or deeds.

Although undue influence is difficult to prove, courts are increasingly coming to recognize it. In determining whether or not someone has been unduly influenced, courts and other entities may further consider whether transactions are fair, reasonable, or commensurate with the relationship between the parties. For example, the sale of a home to a caregiver at a price significantly below market value or the gifting of an expensive car to a "friend" whom the person has just met may suggest undue influence. In criminal law, undue influence can be exercised on incompetent as well as competent victims to establish many kinds of theft and fraud (Myers, 2005).

Elders as Victims of Mass Identity Theft and Marketing Fraud

As noted earlier, the research on fraud suggests that elders are no more likely than other adults to become victims. However, the number of elders affected is significant, and elders are more likely to experience certain types of fraud. The impact to elders may also be extremely profound, and many encounter formidable obstacles to getting help.

Of the 9.3 million victims of identity theft in 2004, nearly 10% were elderly (Javelin Strategy and Research, 2005). According to Linda Foley, executive director of the Identity Theft Resource Center, certain elders are at heightened risk (Foley, 2002). For example, perpetrators may steal the identities of recently deceased persons, whom they identify through death announcements, creating problems for surviving partners. Some hospitals and nursing homes use patients' Social Security numbers as identification (with some even printing numbers on patients' wristbands). Elders who rely on others for help and have in-home helpers are particularly vulnerable to this type of crime, because these helpers have access to identifying information. Many elders have, in fact, been advised to keep identifying information together in readily accessible places or to carry it with them in case of emergency. Finally, people with diminished strength and mobility are more susceptible than others to muggers, who may use stolen wallets to create financial profiles.

According to the FTC, nearly 4 million people age 65 or older were victims of consumer fraud in 2003 (FTC, 2004). Those aged 50 and older reported $152,000,000 in fraud losses. Unlike victims of "traditional" elder financial abuse, who are likely to be isolated and suffer from impairments, elderly victims of consumer fraud are relatively well educated and well informed, with extensive networks of family and friends. Victims, however, appear to be less able than other seniors to differentiate fraudulent from legitimate pitches and to end conversations with telemarketers, even when they believe offers are fraudulent (AARP, 1996, 2003).

IMPACT OF FINANCIAL CRIME ON VICTIMS

Few studies have explored the short- and long-term impact of financial crimes and abuse on victims (Hafemeister, 2003). Law enforcement officers, victim service providers, and others who work with victims of financial crime, however, have described devastating consequences (Deem, 2000). Financial consequences include the loss of homes, life savings, pensions, children's college funds, and inheritances. Some victims have gone into debt, declared bankruptcy, had bank accounts frozen or closed so that they can no longer pay bills and conduct business, been pursued by collection agencies, been sued, or even charged criminally for unknowingly depositing and drawing on counterfeit checks.

Financial crimes can also significantly affect victims' physical, mental, social, and spiritual well-being. Mental health consequences

associated with financial crime include depression, anger, substance abuse, and suicide. The long-term social effects include divorce, estrangement from families, dependence on others, withdrawal from daily life, cessation of activities that victims found enjoyable or meaningful in the past, and even placement in long-term care facilities. Physical effects that have been reported include the inability to sleep or eat, weight loss or gain, high blood pressure, strokes, heart attacks, and declining health (Deem, 2000).

Financial crime may also affect victims emotionally and spiritually. Some victims report that they have lost trust in others or in their own ability to make judgments. Some experience a deep sense of betrayal from their abusers, their families, or the civil and criminal justice systems. Some have lost their faith in God or their religion, or their will to live.

> The sense of personal betrayal, of abused trust, was an almost universal theme . . . and yet unlike many other victims, they are not treated as are most other crime victims: there is ambivalent sympathy for them. If they were denied the opportunity to pursue their grievances through the criminal justice system, this would contribute to their sense of alienation and self-blame. (Levi, 2001, p. 345)

Health care fraud, such as unnecessary medical procedures or surgeries, and crimes involving adulterated medications or treatment may be particularly devastating, impacting hundreds of individuals as demonstrated by the following case. This case is also an example of why the historic continuum of seeing violent versus nonviolent crime as opposing ends no longer fits many crimes, as this crime can be classified as both violent and nonviolent.

> In February 2002, Kansas City pharmacist Robert Courtney pleaded guilty in federal court to twenty counts of charges based on product tampering causing serious bodily injury and adulterating chemotherapy

drugs, involving 34 patients within a short time. During later debriefings by the FBI, he admitted that he had started diluting drugs as early as 1992, and perhaps earlier. He listed over sixty drugs that he sold to patients, most of which were to treat cancer, AIDS and multiple sclerosis. Officials estimate approximately 4,200 patients received diluted drugs intravenously or through injections. (FBI Kansas City Mo. Press Release, April 22, 2002)

The district court judge noted both the life-threatening bodily injury and the extreme psychological injury suffered by elderly victims, one of whom wrote the following in a victim impact statement to the court: "When I was diagnosed with cancer, I discovered I had to fight an emotional battle as well as a physical one. During this time, I tried to accept that I had a very dangerous set of cells invading my body. Early last fall, I discovered I had another force invading my body. This was one I hadn't counted on. I had to face the reality that someone had purposely diluted the drugs going through my body. I have no idea how it affected my disease, but I felt violated—I felt raped" (*U.S. v. Robert Ray Courtney*, 2004, p. 9). Robert Courtney was sentenced to a maximum thirty-year sentence and ordered to pay $10.4 million dollars in restitution.

A 2004 report on the impact of identity theft also likened the emotional impact to that felt by victims of violent crimes, including rape, violent assault, and repeated battering, with some reporting that they felt dirty, defiled, ashamed, embarrassed, and undeserving of assistance (Identity Theft Resource Center, 2005). Others reported a strain or split with a significant other or spouse and being unsupported by family members. The crime may also have long-term effects, whether it occurs to one victim or to many victims. For example, in 2005, Philip Cummings was sentenced to 14 years in federal prison for his role in stealing financial information of more than 30,000 victims, the largest case of identity

theft prosecuted in the United States as of 2005. He was a company "insider" who had access to and downloaded credit histories that he provided to others who manufactured fraudulent credit cards used to make purchases in the names of victims. Victims reported devastating consequences from the theft, including purchases of homes, boats, and loans fraudulently obtained in their name. The prosecutor, James B. Comey, stated: "With a few keystrokes, these men essentially picked the pockets of tens of thousands of Americans and, in the process, took their identities, stole their money and swiped their security" (U.S. Department of Justice, 2002).

A study of investment fraud revealed that victims are likely to suffer from major depressions, with a few experiencing suicidal ideation (Ganzini, McFarland, & Bloom, 1990). The authors also report "a persistence of symptoms of depression, which may be the result of a domino effect whereby the initial financial loss resulted in subsequent catastrophes such as loss of home or difficulty paying debts and taxes" (Ganzini et al., 1990).

In a 2005 study, victims of a Canadian real estate fraud reported extreme or major harm to their emotional well-being, their current financial situation, and their retirement security (Boyd, Malm, & Kinney, 2005). Almost 30% reported extreme or major harm to friendships and marital relationships. According to the authors, their findings "raise important questions about the extent to which both current criminal and civil penalties for investment fraud adequately reflect the harms imposed by this conduct" (Boyd et al., 2005).

The impact of financial exploitation on elders can be particularly severe, as replacing lost assets is generally not a viable option for retired individuals or individuals with physical or mental disabilities (Coker & Little, 1997; Deem, 2000). The depletion of assets may result in elders becoming dependent upon family members or public assistance. Elders with severe impairments may face legal action, including guardianship, or have their families pressure or force them to agree to have their financial affairs taken over by others. In ruling on an advance fee scheme that targeted the elderly, the Honorable Daniel B. Sparr, of the U.S. District Court for the District of Colorado, stated

> The defendant targeted elderly, infirm people, people who obviously did not understand or appreciate their rights or what he was attempting to do. . . . I have seen every conceivable kind of case in this Court and in twenty years on the bench this is probably as despicable an offense in its way as any that I have seen. . . . I have had before me seventeen first-degree murder cases, and in many respects this offense is more touching or more serious, the conduct of this man, his effect on these people, the fact that they are so, so defenseless to this kind of activity. At least when somebody is accosted in a barroom fight they have a chance to fight back. These people never had that chance. (United States v. Benjamin Alex Smith and Elizabeth Marjorie Roberson, Criminal Action #95-CR-448, D. Colo, 1996, as cited in FTC, 1997, p. 1)

Elders are among the groups targeted for mortgage fraud, which, according to the FBI, is a "pervasive and growing" problem, based in large part on the collusion of mortgage or real estate insiders (FBI, 2005). A report by the Consumer Law Center titled "Dreams Foreclosed: The Rampant Theft of Americans' Homes Through Equity-Stripping Foreclosure 'Rescue Scams'" describes how one fraudulent real estate broker "seemed to prey on very vulnerable victims, those on the edge. . . . Some had suffered severe medical catastrophes, some could not read or speak English and others were elderly with limited understanding of these complicated transactions" (Tripoli & Renuart, 2005).

A single mass marketing crime can affect hundreds or even thousands of victims. For example, in 2004, Iowa attorney general Tom

Miller served a search warrant on a postal mail drop involving over 12,000 pieces of mail that were responses to fraudulent solicitations (bait letters) from a list broker. Each included a $10 to $20 "registration fee" for "prize" winnings that did not exist mailed in by unsuspecting victims (Iowa Attorney General Press Release, 2004). This payment of $20 in response to a fraudulent solicitation could be the initial step in targeting a financial crime victim until all life savings and assets, such as home and credit, are destroyed. Because perpetrators engage in "information trafficking," the selling or trading of victim information to other mass marketing criminals, victims are likely to be targeted repeatedly by others predators.

The direct victims are not the only ones who suffer the consequences of financial crimes. Spouses and other family members may be deprived of assets, and heirs may be deprived of legacies. Bogus charity scams may deprive legitimate charities of needed support. One victim of mass marketing fraud reported,

> The charge a Canadian-based telemarketer made to my account caused about 50 checks to be returned because of non-sufficient funds. The bank charged me $875 in overdraft charges and hired a debt collector to collect the money from me and my husband. The debt collection service threatened to call the sheriff on us. One of the recipients of a check that bounced threatened to report me to the District Attorney's Office if I did not pay it back by a specific date. Another merchant reported me to the postal inspectors for $2000 in lost money, non-sufficient check fees and merchant fees. We could not afford to pay for my husband's cancer medicine. I felt as if I were going through a nervous breakdown. (FTC, 2005b)

Factors that influence the impact that financial crimes will have on victims include the amount of assets stolen, whether the exploitation was a single act or a series of acts, victims' ability to remain financially solvent, and the degree of trust victims had in their perpetrators. Finally, the impact is influenced by how victims are treated. Their ability to recover emotionally and financially depends on the amount of support they receive from family and friends, the response of criminal and civil justice systems, and social services. How victims perceive these sources of support, their willingness to use community resources, and their success in locating them are also important factors. Victims' needs, and the legal and social service systems' response to them, are described in the next section.

VICTIM SERVICES

Historically, victims of financial crimes have not had access to most publicly administered victim service programs. Both public and private nonprofit services developed for victims in the 1980s and early 1990s were designed for victims of violent crimes. Many programs were required by their funding sources, agency mandates, or even state victim rights laws to focus their activities on violent crime victims. Whereas well-organized activist groups advocated for rights and services to victims of violence, there were few comparable efforts on behalf of victims of financial crimes. Jane Kusic, an early financial crime victim advocate who wrote *White Collar Crime 101: Prevention Handbook* in 1989, after her own victimization, was a notable exception.

In 1998, the Office for Victims of Crime, after canvassing extensively and interviewing scores of victim advocates and victims over a three-year time period, published *New Directions From the Field: Victim Rights and Services for the 21st Century*. This otherwise seminal and groundbreaking text challenged the field of victim advocacy on the future of crime victim assistance but did not even include financial crime as a focus or major recommendation for ensuring victim services for this underserved group in the future. It

was a very unfortunate missed opportunity to recognize the disparity in services and to address the unmet needs of these victims—their lack of rights and services and their lack of access to the criminal justice process and to promising programs then in existence.

Fortunately, government recognition of the unmet needs of financial crime victims is slowly improving. In 1984, Congress passed the Victims of Crime Act (VOCA), which provides funding for hundreds of government and nonprofit programs that until recently could serve only victims of violent crimes. The source of these funds, which are administered by the Office for Victims of Crime, Department of Justice, are federal criminal fines, federal forfeited bail bonds, and federal court assessments owed by federally convicted criminal offenders. It is widely acknowledged that most VOCA funding comes from fines collected from "white collar" offenders and businesses committing financial crime.

VOCA program funding allotted to the states include both compensation and victim assistance programs. State crime victim compensation programs, which are administered by each state, usually out of system-based county victim services programs, compensate crime victims for counseling, funeral expenses, medical bills, and other expenses. States establish their own eligibility requirements but must follow federal regulations to receive federal VOCA funds. State crime victim assistance programs support community-based victim assistance programs such as domestic violence comprehensive centers and sexual assault programs.

Recent changes to VOCA federal regulations allow funds to now also be used for financial crime victims. The Office for Victims of Crime (OVC) Web site lists the types of services for financial crime victims that states can authorize under VOCA funding as an underserved victim category. They include direct services for (1) immediate health and safety, (2) mental health assistance and support groups, (3) respite care and services for victims with disabilities, (4) credit counseling and advocacy or other special services, (5) restitution advocacy, (6) public presentations, and (7) the use of advanced technologies. The funds can also be used for training programs and publications (OVC, 2004).

Although the changes to VOCA regulations are an important milestone, violent crime victims remain the priority in most states, with few electing to support victim assistance and compensation programs for financial crime victims. According to information requested and compiled by the National Center for Victims of Crime in 2004 (personal communication), only six states had modified their state laws or procedures to allow VOCA compensation funds, VOCA assistance funds, or both, to be used for services to financial crime victims. As of 2005, these states were reported to include Arizona, Idaho, Iowa, Pennsylvania, South Carolina, and West Virginia. The number of system-based victim service providers that serve both violent and financial crime victims is not known.

Victims of financial crimes may be ineligible for other services as well. Those referred to APS may be ineligible unless they meet narrowly defined eligibility criteria. For example, some APS programs only assist victims of "traditional" elder financial exploitation involving caretakers or family members, but not victims of mass marketing, mortgage, health care, Internet, or investment scams. Some only serve victims who are considered "vulnerable" or "dependent" as a result of physical or cognitive impairment, even if they were victims of financial exploitation or undue influence.

A shortage of experienced professionals further reduces the likelihood that victims will receive the help they need. Few licensed counselors or other mental health providers specialize in financial crime victimization, and few are covered under crime victim compensation that could provide free counseling,

as is available for violent crime victims. Another critical unmet need is for practitioners with expertise in financial counseling who can assist victims recover assets, repair credit, and so on.

Some victims turn to ministers, rabbis, priests, or other religious leaders for help. Of those who do, many report that they did not receive knowledgeable assistance or constructive support. Even worse, according to the North American Securities Administrators Association, affinity fraud by faith leaders is increasingly being reported.

Prosecutions, Restitution, and Civil Remedies

Experts agree that victims of financial crimes fail to report for the same reasons as violent crime victims. They may have made reports in the past that were not responded to or made calls that were not returned, resulting in cynicism or hopelessness. Victims may keep crimes secret because they are ashamed to tell their families or friends or because they have been told to do so by perpetrators. Victims may be fearful of publicity or of others knowing. Some have been threatened with retaliation. For those who still hope that their perpetrators will pay them what they are owed, the act of reporting permanently dashes these hopes. In "the perfect financial crime," victims do not even know that financial transactions were crimes. This is often the case in charity scams.

Even when they report to law enforcement, few victims of financial crimes see their cases result in successful prosecutions or convictions. Many victims report that law enforcement officials refused to take reports or simply filed a complaint with no investigation, citing lack of resources, jurisdiction, criminal options, leads, or because the losses did not meet minimum thresholds (even in cases where there are multiple victims whose collective loss would meet the threshold).

Cases are also less likely to be investigated when perpetrators do not live in the same areas as their victims, which is often the case, or when victims are viewed as stupid, greedy, or naïve. Police may accept reports for the purpose of collecting information only, with no follow-up. This may even include failing to enter the complaint in national databases such as the FTC's Consumer Sentinel.

Perhaps the term *nonviolent crime* when used to differentiate a violent crime from that of a financial crime may make it easier to justify disparate treatment of both victims and perpetrators of financial crime in comparison to those of violent crime. When the definition of a criminal behavior is defined by what it isn't, for example, when the term *"nonviolent" crime* is used, it is apparent that language can also be used to diminish victims and treat the crimes and the criminals less seriously.

The lines between criminal conduct and "civil matters" may also be unclear, preventing law enforcement personnel from accepting reports or resulting in referrals to the civil system (Rabiner et al., 2004). There may be a lack of clarity with respect to investigative jurisdiction, as financial crimes may be handled by a variety of agencies, including local police, state regulatory agencies, Medicaid fraud and control units, the FBI, the FTC, the Securities and Exchange Commission, U.S. postal inspectors, the Secret Service, IRS, or others (Nerenberg, 1999).

The passage of the Crime Victim Rights Act of 2004 specifically provided for certain victims' rights, including notice of the status of the case and the right to speak and attend court hearings. Under the definition of a federal victim, the statute did not discriminate between violent crime victims and financial crime victims. The act applied the rights to all victims of federal crime (even requiring the approval of the court in approving alternative notification processes in large number or multiple victim cases). Increasingly, the types of cases testing the limits and extent of this

new law are occurring in cases involving victims of financial crime. In *W. Patrick Kenna v. U.S. District Court for the Central District of California* (2006), the 9th Circuit Court of Appeals found that a district judge court had erred in refusing the right of a financial crime victim to provide an oral victim impact statement. The district court judge was ordered to do the sentencing over—with the victims' participation. This financial crime case is widely cited as very significant in advocating the rights of crime victims in the criminal courts.

Even when their perpetrators are convicted, few victims receive restitution. Restitution orders have limited enforceability because many perpetrators do not have sufficient funds to make repayments or hide assets and income to avoid paying, and few government resources and laws focus on the collection of restitution. Although in the past there were few meaningful efforts to improve this situation, states are increasingly looking at new ways to hold convicted offenders accountable (Office for Victims of Crime, 2002).

In January 2005, the U.S. General Accounting Office (GAO) released *Criminal Debt: Court Ordered Restitution Amounts Far Exceed Likely Collections for the Crime Victims in Selected Financial Fraud Cases,* which reviewed several federal financial crime cases in which offenders had been released from prison several years earlier. The report revealed that only 7% of the ordered restitution had been paid, despite the fact that the defendants had reported significant wealth or assets prior to their judgments. The GAO made recommendations for ways to better enforce restitution, which included encouraging prosecutors to place more pressure on offenders to pay off all restitution and fines prior to sentencing as part of plea agreements. They also recommended that asset forfeiture measures be taken earlier in investigations and prior to sentencing (GAO, 2005). Both measures could be more widely implemented at the state and federal levels.

Other legal services that may be needed by victims include assistance creating or revoking powers of attorney, suing for civil recoveries, annulling bogus marriages or adoptions, handling guardianships or problems with guardians, managing creditors, or disputing fraudulent information appearing on bank, credit, or other financial accounts. The need for these services far exceeds the current supply, and most legal aid programs are not funded to provide them. Few private attorneys will help when there is no readily available perpetrator or "deep pocket." Many victims cannot pay as a result of the crimes they've experienced. Although restitution can be enforced with civil judgments, the process for doing so in most states and federally is likely to be expensive and cumbersome, and information about the process is often not readily available.

RESOURCES TO ASSIST FINANCIAL CRIME VICTIMS

Fortunately, a few system-based victim service providers are beginning to address some of these needs. This may in part be credited to the attention that identity theft, with its large number of victims, has garnered and the activism it has generated. The Internet has also increased access to the growing body of knowledge about financial crimes. Many of the resources that are now available are national in scope. Government agencies are using the Internet to share advice, provide information on recent scams, post press releases, and even take online complaints on financial crimes.

The FTC has a toll-free number and online complaint process that provides preliminary advice for victims of identity theft and consumer fraud. Complaints that are filed are shared with local, federal, and international law enforcement agencies through the Consumer Sentinel database. Law enforcement members are encouraged to include their own complaints to give others information and leads on additional victims and perpetrators. The FTC also has a site to assist in reporting cyber or computer crime as well as identity theft. The FTC is collaborating with other countries in its antifraud efforts by sharing information on transborder crimes, all of which is entered in the Consumer Sentinel database. In addition, victims are increasingly using the Internet to post information on the status of criminal and civil proceedings, for restitution advocacy, or to provide support, locate additional victims, and post warnings about a fraud or for help in locating a perpetrator.

State, county, and city governments are also using Web sites to provide information and guidance in preventing or reporting financial crime to consumer protection organizations, local police departments, state attorneys general, and local district attorneys' offices. Under federal and some state laws, financial crime victims are included in regulations that require victim notification about the status of investigations or prosecutions and victim assistance in accessing resources and services. With some cases involving thousands of financial crime victims on a single case, this will present an increasing challenge in meeting victim needs. Increasingly, victim assistance programs, law enforcement, prosecutors, and corrections officials are using the Internet, or sending notification via e-mail instead of by letter, to post information about cases, offer suggestions for mitigating future risk, and maintain contact with victims as ways to begin to address this requirement. The Attorney General of Arizona Victim Services Web page is an example of a model demonstrating the ways in which the Internet can be used to provide information, support, court information, and criminal justice system access to victims in large scale, multiple victim financial crime cases (see www.azag.gov/victims_rights/).

Nonprofit organizations, including the Identity Theft Resource Center, the Privacy Rights Clearinghouse, AARP, and the National Consumer League, are also offering help online. The Better Business Bureau and the National Association of Securities Dealers (NASD) are examples of agencies that provide online information about complaints against businesses or individuals. Victims' sites have also emerged, providing information and support to victims of particular schemes or certain types of crimes.

Victim service providers at the local and federal levels, legal aid groups, APS programs, consumer protection groups, and others have come to recognize the benefits of collaboration. State consumer protection agencies, legal aid groups, and others share reports, collaborate on multidisciplinary teams, sponsor fraud fairs, and share resource lists. Several examples are described in the following section.

PROMISING PRACTICES

Communities across the country have demonstrated remarkable ingenuity and creativity in developing responses to financial crime and abuse. The following programs and statutes serve as examples:

- Temple University's Institute on Protective Services (Philadelphia) operates a multi-county pilot project in which financial investigators are placed within protective services programs to provide training and consultation to workers. One county hired a retired FBI agent and another hired an accountant/insurance fraud investigator. The units have also developed partnerships with law enforcement to conduct in-depth, collaborative investigations.
- Several communities have started Financial Abuse Specialist Teams (FASTs), which are groups of professionals who meet routinely to review complex cases of elder financial abuse. Members typically include representatives from law enforcement, bank personnel, legal aide providers, public guardians, daily money managers, APS, case managers, and others.
- The Identity Theft Verification Passport program of the Ohio Attorney General's office helps identity theft victims demonstrate to law enforcement and creditors that their identities have been stolen, correct their credit histories, and identify fraudulent criminal charges. Once police have taken reports, victims' identification is verified and they file PASSPORT applications. Photographs, signatures, and fingerprints are added to a secured Web site, and victims are issued with PASSPORT cards.
- Clergy Against Senior Exploitation (CASE), a program of the Denver District Attorney's office, works with faith-based partners, law enforcement, and prosecutors to collaborate with local clergy in developing programs on elder financial exploitation. A community advocate and representatives from the Denver District Attorney's Economic Crime Unit Victim Assistance Program helps individuals who have been victimized navigate the legal and social services system. They work closely with local faith leaders in educating the community, including monthly fraud alerts, for use in newsletters and community bulletins that can be used by faith leaders in the Denver area on such topics as foreclosure scams, identity theft, and telemarketing crime.

DISCUSSION AND RECOMMENDATIONS

New forms of financial crime are appearing almost daily, propelled by the Internet and the internationalization of crimes and criminals. Although these new forms of fraud victimization surpass traditional NCVS crimes such as burglary in frequency and dollar losses (FTC, 2004; Titus et al., 1995), their victims remain critically underserved. Clearly, new, proactive approaches are needed to help them recover losses, hold perpetrators accountable, mitigate the damage, and prevent future victimization.

A primary barrier is the lack of information about financial crime victims and the number of victims and a better means to document and include all victims on the basis of each fraud committed, their service needs, and the effectiveness of various interventions and services on which to base policy and practice. The existing research is based on ad hoc samples reported to authorities and complaint lines, which do not provide an accurate picture of the full extent of the problem. Data on losses, which is needed to make comparisons with other crimes, varies widely depending on how extreme losses reported by victims of certain forms of fraud are treated (FTC, 2004; Titus et al., 1995). Significant differences also exist among the various forms of financial crime in terms of frequency of attempts, the percentage of attempts that are successful, and losses. These factors need to be considered in crafting solutions and prioritizing resources. Also needed are studies on the long-term impact of serious financial crime on victims and communities. In particular, victim assistance providers, policy and funding directors, researchers, public and private program developers, and others need information on victims' immediate and long-term needs that are drawn from nationally representative samples and collected on an ongoing basis.

Funding to assist victims of elder abuse and exploitation is slowly becoming available to local county victim assistance programs and others. While this is a welcome first step, much still remains to be done. Services needed by victims of financial crime include those traditionally offered to other victims, such as information about the criminal justice system, their rights, the status reports of their cases, court accompaniment, compensation, restitution, shelters, support groups, and other assistance. In addition, these victims have special needs. For example, crisis intervention with victims of financial crime may include securing assets that are still in jeopardy, mitigating the risk of further harm, finding legal resources, intervening with creditors and banks, and assisting victims to change phone numbers or request credit reports and address discrepancies or fraudulent activity, and understanding their risk of revictimization and steps that can be taken to reduce that risk. Later, victims may need additional help managing crime-related debt, applying for public benefits programs, getting fraudulent credit cards and bank account debits cleared up, repairing their credit, filing for bankruptcy, or addressing foreclosure actions. Special services may also be needed for victims with diminished mental capacity. Victims and those at risk may, for example, need mental health assessments to determine whether they are capable of meeting their own basic needs, managing their finances, making decisions about services, offering testimony, and protecting themselves against crime and abuse. Those with impairments may benefit from services such as daily money management or surrogate decision makers. Limited English-speaking victims and those with limited language or financial literacy may need special services and interventions.

Because past fraud victimization raises the risk for future victimization, special attention should be focused on "repeat" or "chronic victims." Successful programs can serve as models. For example, law enforcement in the United Kingdom provides special police services and counseling to repeat victims, recognizing that if con artists spotlight fraud victims for special attention, law enforcement should do the same (Forrester et al., 1990).

Extending victim rights and services to all victims of crime and effectively meeting the needs of the large number of victims affected by some financial crimes are among the most challenging problems facing criminal justice and victim service providers. Advanced technologies will be needed to identify and assist the hundreds or thousands of victims around the United States and other countries.

Requiring businesses to assume a greater role is one avenue that warrants consideration.

The speed at which hackers discover vulnera-bilities in new software suggests that busi-nesses could be called upon to do the same prior to releasing new products. Other prac-tices that could be reexamined include allow-ing businesses to mass mail preapproved credit cards for which they assume no responsibility. The ease with which criminals can obtain personal information such as Social Security numbers and mothers' maiden names on various Internet search services also warrants reevaluation.

The complexity, diversity, and repetitive nature of financial crimes require a compre-hensive and well-coordinated response. Victims' need for mental health counseling, emergency financial assistance or loans, legal assistance, financial or creditor counseling, identity theft repair, restitution advocacy, and education on prevention may best be met by comprehensive service systems. One-stop centers for victims of financial crimes, which provide education, legal assistance, mental health services, restitution and public benefits advocacy, and social services, may be a pro-mising approach.

REFERENCES

AARP. (1996). *Telemarketing fraud and older Americans: An AARP survey.* Washington, DC: Author.

AARP. (2003). *Off the hook: Reducing participa-tion in telemarketing fraud.* Washington, DC: Author.

AARP. (2004). *Identity theft: An update on the experience of older complainants.* Washington, DC: Author.

Bass, R., & Hoeffler, L. (1992). *Telephone-based fraud: A survey of the American public.* New York: Louis Harris and Associate.

Baum, K. (2006). *Identity theft, 2004.* Retrieved May 20, 2006, from www.ojp.usdoj.gov/bjs/pub/pdf/it04.pdf

Blunt, A. (1993). Financial exploitation of the inca-pacitated: Investigation and remedies. *Journal of Elder Abuse & Neglect, 5*(1), 19–32.

Boyd, N., Malm, A., & Kinney, B. (2005). *Eron mortgage study, final report March 31, 2005.* Retrieved May 14, 2006, from www.bcsc.bc.ca/uploadedFiles/Eron_Research_Study.pdf

Bureau of Justice Statistics (BJS). (2006). *Report: 3.6 million U.S. households learned they were identity theft victims during a six-month period in 2004.* Washington, DC: Bureau of Justice Statistics.

Choi, N. G., Kulick, D. B., & Mayer, J. B. (1999). Financial exploitation of elders: Analysis of risk factors based on county adult protective services data. *Journal of Elder Abuse & Neglect, 10*(3/4), 39–62.

Chubb Group. (2005). One in five Americans has been a victim of identity theft. Retrieved May 20, 2006, from www.chubb.com/corporate/chubb3875.html

Coker, J., & Little, B. (1997). Investing in the future: Protecting the elderly from financial abuse. *FBI Law Enforcement Bulletin, 66*(12), 1–5.

Crime Victim Rights Act (CVRA), 18 U.S. Code §3771 (2004).

Davis, R., Taylor, B. G., & Titus, R. M. (1997). Victims as agents: Implications for victim ser-vices and crime prevention. In R. Davis, A. Lurigio, & W. Skogan (Eds.), *Victims of crime* (pp. 167–179). Thousand Oaks, CA: Sage Publications.

Deem, D. L. (2000). Notes from the field: Observations in working with the forgotten victims of personal financial crimes. *Journal of Elder Abuse & Neglect, 12*(2), 33–48.

Dessin, C. L. (2000). Financial abuse of the elderly. *Idaho Law Review, 36,* 203–226.

Earthlink. (2005). *Online teen shoppers may miss fraud signs.* Dallas, TX: Author.

Experian-Gallup. (2005). *Experian-Gallup Personal Credit Index shows 18 percent of consumers report being victims of identity theft.* Costa Mesa, CA: Author.

Federal Bureau of Investigation. (2004). Kansas City FBI division press release: List of drugs Courtney claims to have diluted, April 22, 2002. Retrieved October 13, 2004, from http://kansascity.fbi.gov/kcmostate042202.htm

Federal Bureau of Investigation. (2005). *Financial crimes report to the public: Mortgage fraud.* Retrieved August 25, 2005, from www.fbi

.gov/publications/financial/fcs_report052005/fcs_report052005.htm#d1

Federal Trade Commission. (1997). *Fighting consumer fraud: The challenge and the campaign.* Retrieved May 13, 2006, from www.ftc.gov/reports/Fraud/

Federal Trade Commission. (2004). *Consumer fraud in the United States.* Retrieved February 13, 2006, from www.ftc.gov/reports/consumerfraud/040805confraudrpt.pdf

Federal Trade Commission. (2005a). *Identity theft: Facts and figures.* Retrieved May 21, 2006, from www.ncjrs.gov/spotlight/identity_theft/facts.html

Federal Trade Commission. (2005b). *The U.S. Safe Web Act: Protecting consumers from spam, spyware, and fraud. A legislative recommendation to Congress.*

Foley, L. (2002). *Identity theft and legislative solutions.* Retrieved February 13, 2006, from www.idtheftcenter.org/s1742.shtml

Forrester, D. (1990). *The Kirkholt burglary prevention project.* Crime prevention unit paper no. 23. London: Home Office.

Ganzini, L., McFarland, B., & Bloom, J. (1990). Victims of fraud: Comparing victims of white collar and violent crime. *Bulletin of the American Academy of Psychiatric Law, 18*(1), 55–63.

General Accounting Office. (2005, January). *Criminal debt: Court ordered restitution amounts far exceed likely collections for the crime victims in selected financial fraud cases.* GAO Highlights of Report. GAO-05–80. Retrieved May 27, 2005, from www.gao.gov/cgi-bin/getrpt?GAO-05–80

Hafemeister, T. L. (2003). Financial abuse of the elderly in domestic settings. In R. J. Bonnie & R. B. Wallace (Eds.), *Elder mistreatment: Abuse, neglect and exploitation in an aging America.* Washington, DC: National Academies Press.

Identity Theft Resource Center. (2005). *The Identity Theft Resource Center (ITRC) releases its second identity theft victimization study—Identity theft: The aftermath, 2004.* San Diego, CA: Author.

Internet Crime Complaint Center (2005a). *E-mail disguised as the Internal Revenue Service (IRS) phishing for personal information.* Washington, DC. Author.

Internet Crime Complaint Center. (2005b). *Fraudulent FBI e-mail alert.* Washington, DC: Author.

Internet Crime Complaint Center. (2005c). *IC3 internet crime report.* Washington, DC: Author.

Internet Crime Complaint Center. (2005d). *A new e-mail titled "Refund Notice" purporting to provide information to recipients regarding the status of their IRS tax refunds.* Washington, DC: Author.

Internet Crime Complaint Center. (2006). *Fraudulent IC3 e-mail alert!* Washington, DC: Author.

Iowa Attorney General Press Release. (2004, April 30). Alleged nationwide scheme preying on the elderly must stay out of Iowa—And take Iowans off prospect lists. Retrieved February 19, 2006, from www.state.ia.us/government/ag/latest_news/releases/apr_2004/Panas_consent.html

Javelin Strategy and Research. (2005). *The 2005 identity fraud survey report.* Retrieved July 18, 2005, from www.javelinstrategy.com/reports/documents/2005_Javelin_Strategy_Research_Identity_Fraud_Survey_Complimentary_Report.pdf

Kusic, Jane. (1989). *White collar crime 101: Prevention handbook.* Vienna, VA: Author.

Levi, M. (2001). Transnational white collar crime: Some explorations of victimization impact. In H. Pontell & D. Shichor (Eds.), *Contemporary issues in crime and criminal justice: Essays in honor of Gilbert Geis* (pp. 341–358). Upper Saddle River, NJ: Prentice Hall.

Myers, J. E. B. (2005). *Myers on evidence in child, domestic, and elder abuse.* New York: Aspen.

Naimark, D. (2001). Financial exploitation of the elderly: The evaluation of mental capacity and undue influence. *American Journal of Forensic Psychiatry, 22*(3), 5–19.

National Center on Elder Abuse. (1998). *The national elder abuse incidence study.* Washington, DC: Author.

National Cyber Security Alliance. (2005). One in four computer users hit by phishing attempts each month, according to major in-home computer safety study. Retrieved May 13, 2005, from www.staysafeonline.info/news/press_dec07_2005html

National Fraud Information Center. (2005). *Telemarketing scams, January–December 2005.* Washington, DC: Author.

Nerenberg, L. (1996). Hornswoggled? An interview with Margaret Singer on undue influence. *Nexus: A publication for affiliates of the National Committee for the Prevention of Elder Abuse.* Retrieved September 8, 2006, from www.preventelderabuse.org/nexus/singer.html

Nerenberg, L. (1999). Forgotten victims of elder financial crime and abuse: A report and recommendations. Retrieved December 14. 2005, from www.elderabusecenter.org/pdf/publication/fvefca.pdf

Nievod, A. (1993). Undue influence in contract and probate law. *Cultic Studies Journal, 10*(1), 1–33.

North American Securities Administrators Association (NASAA). (2005). *Affinity fraud: Beware of swindlers who claim loyalty to your group.* Retrieved May 12, 2005, from www.nasaa.org/Investor_Education/Investor_Alerts___Tips/1679.cfm

Office for Victims of Crime. (1998). New directions from the field: Victim rights and services for the 21st century (NCJ 170600). Washington, DC: U.S. Department of Justice.

Office for Victims of Crime. (2002). *Making restitution work.* Legal Series no. 5. Retrieved December 28, 2005, from www.ojp.usdoj.gov/ovc/publications/bulletins/legalseries/bulletin5/ncj189193.pdf

Office for Victims of Crime. (2004) *Providing services to victims of fraud: Resources for victim witness coordinators.* Appendix A. *How Victims of Crime Act (VOCA) funds may be used to assist victims of financial fraud.* Retrieved April 24, 2005, from www.ojp.usdoj.gov/ovc/publications/infores/fraud/psvf/appenda.htm

Pew Internet and American Life Project. (2004). *Older Americans and the Internet.* Chicago: Author.

Pew Internet and American Life Project. (2005a). *Digital divisions: There are clear differences among those with broadband connections, dial-up connections, and no connections at all to the internet.* Chicago: Author.

Pew Internet and American Life Project. (2005b). *Spam and phishing: Email users get more spam, but the harmful impact of unsolicited messages is diminishing for them. More than a third of email users have gotten phishing solicitations.* Chicago: Author.

Pew Internet and American Life Project. (2005c). *Survey: One in five teens have own blogs.* Chicago: Author.

Princeton Survey Research Associates. (1995, March). *Consumer rights and technology survey: Pennsylvania and Delaware markets.* Princeton, NJ: Author.

Quinn, M. J. (2002). Undue influence and elder abuse: Recognition and intervention strategies. *Geriatric Nursing, 23*(1), 11–16.

Rabiner, D. J., O'Keeffe, J., & Brown, D. (2004). A conceptual framework of financial exploitation of older persons. *Journal of Elder Abuse & Neglect, 16*(2), 53–73.

Shichor, D., Doocy, J., & Geis, G. (1996). Anger, disappointment and disgust: Reactions of victims of a telephone investment scam. In C. Sumner, M. Israel, M. O'Connell, & R. Sarre (Eds.), *International victimology: Selected papers from the 8th International Symposium.* Proceedings of a symposium held August 21–26, 1994. Canberra: Australian Institute of Criminology, 1996. Available at www.aic.gov.au/publications/proceedings/27/shichor.pdf

Teaster, P. B. (2002). Abuse of adults age 60+: The 2004 survey of adult protective services. Retrieved September 8, 2006, from www.nasua.org/pdf/2-14-06%20FINAL%2060+REPORT.pdf#search=%2213.8%25%20were%20for%20financial%20abuse%20(Teaster%22

Teaster, P. B., Dugar, T. A., Mendiondo, M. S., Abner, E. L., & Cecil, K. A. (2006). *The 2004 Survey of State Adult Protective Services: Abuse of adults 60 years of age and older.* Retrieved October 3, 2006, from www.elderabusecenter.org/pdf/2-14-06%20FINAL%2060+REPORT.pdf

Titus, R., & Gover, A. (2001). Personal fraud: The victims and the scams. In G. Farrell and K. Pease (Eds.), *Repeat victimization: Crime prevention studies* (Vol. 12). Monsey, NY: Criminal Justice Press.

Titus, R., Heinzelmann, F., & Boyle, J. (1995). Victimization of persons by fraud. *Crime and Delinquency, 41*(1), 54–72.

Titus, R. M. (2001). Personal fraud and its victims. In Neal Shover & John P. Wright (Eds.), *Crimes of privilege* (pp. 57–66). New York: Oxford University Press.

Tripoli, S., & Renuart, E. (2005). *Dreams foreclosed: The rampant theft of Americans' homes through equity-stripping foreclosure "rescue scams": National Consumer Law Center.* Retrieved August 18, 2005, from www.consumerlaw.org/news/ForeclosureReportFinal.pdf

U.S. Department of Justice. (2002, November 25). U.S. Attorney's Office, Southern District of New York. *U.S. announces what is believed to be the largest identity theft case in American history: Losses are in the millions.* Retrieved May 13, 2006, from www.justice.gov/criminal/cybercrime/cummingsIndict.htm

U.S. Department of Justice. (2003). *Public advisory: Special report for consumers on identity theft.* Washington, DC: Author.

U.S. Department of Justice, Criminal Division. (2004). *Special report on "phishing."* Washington, DC: Author.

U.S. v. Robert Ray Courtney, U.S. Court of Appeals, Opinion Number 02-4083 (8th Cir. 2004).

W. Patrick Kenna v. U.S. District Court for the Central District of California, Opinion Number 05-73467 (9th Cir. Ct. App. 2006).

NOTE

1. National Institute of Justice, unpublished report.

9

The Mental Health and Behavioral Consequences of Terrorism

CHARLES DiMAGGIO

SANDRO GALEA

he behavioral consequences of terrorist incidents have received considerable recent attention, much of it driven by the 1995 Oklahoma City bombings and the attacks of September 11, 2001, in the United States. In this chapter we will review the available evidence about the mental health and behavioral consequences of terrorism, consider methodological and research issues that challenge the field, and discuss the evidence for specific prevention and treatment efforts aimed at mitigating the mental health and behavioral consequences of terrorism.

Terrorism is psychological warfare, and behavioral disturbance is the primary intent of terrorists (Alexander, 2005). As Lenin stated, "The object of terrorism is to terrorize," and as long ago as the 4th century B.C.E.

Sun Tzu advised, "Kill one to terrorize ten thousand" (Beare, Burrows, & Merrett, 1978). The more incomprehensible the event, the greater the potential mental health effects. Human intent, as seen in terrorist incidents, may be associated with the greatest risk of behavioral disturbance (Norris, Friedman, & Watson, 2002).

Definitions of terrorism vary (Butler, Panzer, & Goldfrank, 2003). According to the United States Department of State, terrorism is "premeditated, politically motivated violence perpetrated against non-combatant targets by sub-national groups or clandestine agents usually intended to influence an audience" (Atran, 2003). A broader definition, proposed by public health practitioners, states that it is "the intentional use of violence—real or threatened—against one or more non-combatants and/or those services essential for or protective of their health, resulting in adverse health effects in those immediately affected and their community, ranging from a loss of well-being or security to injury, illness, or death" (Arnold & Birnbaum, 2003).

Neither definition captures the sense of chilling brutality associated with what is commonly accepted as terrorism. Perhaps closer to the mark is an evocative description of terrorist violence in Northern Ireland: "One atrocity provoked another, equally inhumane and gruesome, and the whole 20-year history has been pockmarked by some particular incidents of quite indescribable cruelty as man has visited his inhumanity upon his fellow man in some utterly barbaric ways" (Curran, 1988). It is notable that, prior to 1964, Northern Ireland was "one of the most peaceful societies in Europe," with only one murder reported in Belfast between 1960 and 1964 (Curran, 1988).

The intended consequences of terrorist acts extend beyond those immediately affected.

Exposure may be defined in terms of physical proximity to incidents, level of threat, and personal loss or injury to family or friends (Herman, Felton, & Susser, 2002). For example, 2,795 people were killed at the World Trade Center as a result of the September 11, 2001, terrorist attacks; an additional 7,467 persons were injured. The two groups together had 17,642 family members. A total of 17,859 were exposed to the attack as were 32,361 employees and their 87,383 family members (Herman et al., 2002). All told, 164,710 persons were directly exposed to this terrorist attack. For every individual killed, an additional 59 persons were traumatized (Figure 9.1). An additional 4,800,000 residents of the surrounding 10 counties, in ways large and small, coped with the events of that day. It should be no surprise, then, that 20% of New York City residents living below Canal Street, in proximity to the events, met the criteria for post-traumatic stress disorder (PTSD) at some point in the two-month period following September 11, 2001 (Galea et al., 2002). Analogously, the 467 terrorist deaths

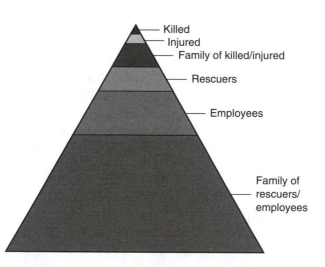

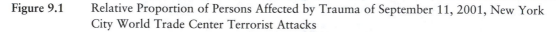

Figure 9.1   Relative Proportion of Persons Affected by Trauma of September 11, 2001, New York City World Trade Center Terrorist Attacks

in Northern Ireland in 1972 directly or indirectly affected an additional 27,000 people, or 18 per 1,000 of the population (Curran, 1988). The 472 deaths attributed to the intifada in Israel in the 19 months between 2000 and 2003, affected 4 persons per 1,000 of the population (Bleich, Gelkopf, & Solomon, 2003).

POSTTRAUMATIC STRESS DISORDER

PTSD is likely the most prevalent and debilitating consequence of disasters, in general, and terrorism, in particular (Galea, Nandi, & Vlahov, 2005). There is an emerging consensus in the literature both that PTSD is a likely outcome of terrorism incidents, and that PTSD after such events is frequently accompanied by other behavioral and health disturbances (Galea et al., 2005). Although the behavioral consequences of terrorist incidents have received considerable recent attention—much of it driven by the Oklahoma City bombings and the attacks of September 11, 2001, in the United States—most of the information on disaster-related PTSD comes from the general disaster literature. Of the 160 studies included in a recent meta-analysis of postdisaster psychiatric disturbance, only 8 specifically addressed terrorism (Norris, Friedman, Watson, et al., 2002).

First described in the 1980s and included in the *Diagnostic and Statistical Manual, Third Edition* (*DSM–III*), the diagnosis of PTSD arose largely in response to the experiences of war veterans (APA, 1982). To qualify for a diagnosis, an individual required at least one eligible traumatic event (a "criterion A" stressor), a symptom of reexperiencing the trauma (intrusion), a numbing or blunting of affect (avoidance), and at least two symptoms of hypervigilance and startling (arousal). The diagnostic criteria underwent revision in the *DSM–III–R* (APA, 1987), when the requirement of at least one month's duration was added and again, and in *DSM–IV* (APA, 1994), when the individual's perception of the event was added to the criteria.

The work impairment associated with PTSD is as great or greater than it is in major depressive disorder, and PTSD is associated with increased rates of medical utilization (Lovejoy, Diefenbach, Licht, & Tolin, 2003). The general population rate of PTSD has been estimated between 5.4% (Lovejoy et al., 2003) and 7.8% (Kessler, Sonnega, Bromet, Hughes, & Nelson, 1995). Left untreated, PTSD is thought to last between 36 to 64 months, but can persist for as long as a decade; time to remission can be reduced by half with treatment (Lovejoy et al., 2003; North, 2002). Over the course of a lifetime, one half of the general population will meet a "Criteria A" stressor at some point; about one third of these individuals will develop PTSD (North, 2002).

Reports of the prevalence of PTSD among victims of manmade disasters vary greatly. Rates are highest for victims and survivors, from 25% of individuals exposed to a 1991 Killeen, Texas, mass shooting up to 75% of individuals in a 1988 oil rig fire. Prevalence rates among rescuers vary from 5% to 40%. Approximately 13% of Oklahoma City firefighters met criteria for PTSD several months later. Nearly half of the Australian firefighters involved in battling a bush fire in 1993 had PTSD at some point in the first two years following the incident. The prevalence of PTSD in the general population after a disaster is lower. Between 7% and 11% of New York City residents met criteria for PTSD after September 11, 2001, and 9% of Alaskans were reported to have PTSD after the Exxon Valdez incident (Galea et al., 2005).

In the first weeks following the September 11, 2001, terrorist attacks, 1 in 10 New York area residents met the criteria for PTSD (Marshall & Galea, 2004). There were estimates that 520,000 people in New York City (NYC) and the surrounding areas would experience symptoms of PTSD and that 129,000 would seek treatment (Herman et al., 2002). Nearly 8% of NYC residents reported using mental health services in the 30-day period five months after September 11 (Boscarino et al., 2004). A year later, NYC residents continued to be "very concerned" about future terrorist attacks (Boscarino, Figley, & Adams, 2003).

Although the number of studies that has considered PTSD after terrorism specifically is limited, one review of the topic suggested that in the year following terrorist incidents, the prevalence of PTSD in directly affected populations varies between 12% and 16% and that this prevalence can be expected to decline 25% over the course of that year (DiMaggio & Galea, 2006). In contrast, some researchers have found evidence of persistently elevated prevalence of psychological distress many months after and at long distances from the events of September 11, 2001 (Silver, Holman, McIntosh, Poulin, & Gil-Rivas, 2002). There is also evidence of resilience in the face of terrorism (Lovejoy et al., 2003; Satel, 2003). Among U.S. military veterans, there was no significant increase in the utilization of mental health services for the treatment of PTSD in the NYC area (Rosenheck & Fontana, 2003b), and among a national sample of veterans with a preexisting diagnosis of PTSD, there was, in fact, evidence of less severe symptoms on admission after September 11, 2001, than before (Rosenheck & Fontana, 2003a).

CORRELATES OF PTSD

Gender and prior psychiatric diagnoses are strongly associated with subsequent PTSD and may be useful triage factors for outreach or treatment, particularly when taken together with such variables as direct exposure to events as either a survivor or rescuer.

In one review, 94% of these studies that looked at gender found that being female was associated with an increased risk of postdisaster behavioral health disturbance (Norris, Friedman, & Watson, 2002), with women reported as being twice as likely to develop PTSD (North, 2002). Marriage and parenthood are also associated with increased risk (Norris, Friedman, Watson, et al., 2002). Taken together, these associations point to the potential common mediating factor of an imbalance of resources or the stress of caring for others and being obligated to provide more resources than are received (Norris, Friedman, & Watson, 2002).

Although minority status and lower socioeconomic status are associated with increased risk of postdisaster behavioral diagnoses, this is likely attributable, at least in part, to increased risk of exposure (Norris, Friedman, Watson, et al., 2002). For example, after the events of the September 11, 2001, terrorist attacks, NYC residents of lower socioeconomic status were 2.5 times more likely to develop PTSD (Galea et al., 2002), and there were reports of increased alcohol and tobacco use among drug users, although there was no change in heroin or cocaine use (Factor et al., 2002).

Particularly relevant to acts of terrorism, human intent underlying a disaster has been associated with increased risk of behavioral disturbances, compared with natural disaster (Norris, Friedman, & Watson, 2002). Kidnappings and torture are associated with the highest rates of PTSD, and flooding is associated with the lowest (North, 2002). Severe behavioral effects are also seen in which there is extreme and intensive property damage, serious and ongoing financial problems, or a high prevalence of trauma and death (Norris, Friedman, & Watson, 2002). In NYC after the September 11, 2001, terrorist attacks, those who lived closest to the World Trade Center area had a three times greater risk of developing PTSD (Galea et al., 2002). Deaths are not necessary for there to be behavioral health effects (Norris, Friedman, Watson, et al., 2002); for example, 43% of residents near the Exxon Valdez disaster had psychiatric impairments.

Loss of psychosocial resources, such as family, friends, and jobs as well as relocation and disruption of neighborhood patterns may be key mediators of postterrorism behavioral disturbances, and preexisting psychiatric conditions predispose individuals to postdisaster PTSD (Norris, Friedman, Watson, et al., 2002). Although associations with media exposure have been reported, many of these studies are cross-sectional, and the direction of the association is unclear.

Risk for developing postterrorism PTSD varies by age, with an increase during school age, followed by a second, more prominent increase during middle age (Norris, Friedman, Watson, et al., 2002). In a study of PTSD among 7,000 children seven weeks after the bombing in Oklahoma City, physical, interpersonal, and TV exposure accounted for 12% of variance, and peri-traumatic response alone accounted for 25%. The authors concluded that a child's subjective response to trauma is a key predictor of PTSD and should be included in the diagnostic criteria for PTSD in children (Pfefferbaum, Doughty, et al., 2002).

Studies of children most often report symptoms rather than diagnoses, which may account, in part, for such high rates as the reported 95% of children who had symptoms of PTSD after the Armenian earthquakes (Galea et al., 2005). In one study of the psychological sequelae of the September 11, 2001, terrorist attacks, there was a 46% increase in the diagnosis of PTSD in children in the following months, compared with the previous months. The increase for adults was 12%. Notably, there was no increase in the diagnosis of depression or substance abuse (Hoge, Pavlin, & Milliken, 2002).

Violence, such as terrorism, is associated with the highest level of mental health disturbances in children, but the relative impact of different kinds of exposures varies (Herman et al., 2002). Kuwaiti children were relatively unaffected by interpersonal exposure during the Gulf War, but those whose friends were killed in a non-war-related bus crash were (Pfefferbaum, Doughty, et al., 2002). Half of the children exposed to Hurricane Andrew were reported to have a new onset behavioral disorder; 33% had PTDS, and 56% of children in high-impact areas were impaired two months after the event (Norris, Friedman, Watson, et al., 2002).

OTHER POSTDISASTER BEHAVIOR

Other postterrorism behavioral disturbances are reported to varying degrees. There were a reported 99 hate crimes against Middle Easterners in the United States in the month following the September 11, 2001, terrorist attacks, compared with 93 such crimes in all of 2001 and 12 in 2000 (Swahn et al., 2003). Some of this increase may be attributed to increased surveillance. There was no increase in divorces following the Oklahoma City bombing (Nakonezny, Reddick, & Rodgers, 2004). Postterrorism alcohol use among military veterans with a preexisting diagnosis of PTSD has been shown to increase, but has not been demonstrated among civilians (Pfefferbaum, Vinekar, et al., 2002).

There are reports from war zones that patients with depressive disorders, obsessive-compulsive disorders, and phobias may show symptomatic improvement as a result of a traumatic experience (Curran, 1988). According to one researcher, citing the British experience during the Long Blitzkrieg of World War II and the U.S. experience during the race riots of the 1960s, "Civil disorder can paradoxically have a beneficial psychological effect possibly through collective forces including increasing social cohesion" (Curran, 1988). Another researcher noted a 50% decline in the suicide rate as well as a decrease in stress-related "lichen planus" in Northern Ireland between 1969 and 1975, which is regarded as evidence of resiliency (Beare et al., 1978). Yet another investigator cites the nationwide decline, in the United States, in chronic fatigue syndrome following the September 11, 2001, terrorist attacks (Heim, Bierl, Nisenbaum, Wagner, & Reeves, 2004). According to this line of reasoning, some individuals will invariably develop psychiatric illness after being subjected to or witnessing trauma, but many in the general population may actually improve psychologically: "The general population (of Northern Ireland) . . . is largely unaffected from the psychiatric point of view . . . [and] whilst the victims of violence do suffer emotional reactions . . . those reactions are often comparatively short-lived" (Curran, 1988). However, much of the evidence about the behavioral consequences of terrorism and mass violence is unclear, such as the conflicting reports on the effect of the September 11 terrorist attacks on suicide rates (De Lange & Neeleman, 2004; Salib, 2003), and resilience in the face of terror must be balanced against the growing literature on medically unexplained symptoms and physical diagnoses following terrorism and disasters.

Medically unexplained symptoms are "physical symptoms that provoke care seeking but have no clinically determined pathogenesis" (Clauw et al., 2003). Research suggests that at least one third of the symptoms in both clinical and population-based studies are medically unexplained (Clauw et al., 2003). At times, these constellations of symptoms are characterized as physical and, at other times, as primarily psychological. This may have more to do with the background, training, and prior assumptions of the investigators than with the illness itself (Clauw et al., 2003). However, it is rare to have a truly new disease; similar constellations of symptoms are given new names based on the event from which they arose

(Clauw et al., 2003). Such syndromes have followed vaccination programs for U.S. and U.K. military personnel and have been a prominent feature of Gulf War syndrome among U.S. troops. Other instances include Canadian troops concerned about exposure to "red soil" in Croatia, a so-called Balkan War syndrome attributed to exposure to depleted uranium, a "mystery syndrome" after a jetliner crashed into a populated area of Amsterdam, and "jungle fever" among Dutch peacekeepers in Cambodia in the 1980s (Peterson, Nicolas, McGraw, Engler, & Blackman, 2002).

The noninjury physical diagnoses reported following disasters have often been cardiac in nature. There was a greater than threefold increase in myocardial infarctions in Japan following the Honshin Awerjuu earthquake (Qureshi, Merla, Steinberg, & Rozanski, 2003). This was attributed to increased hematocrit, fibrinogen, and other coagulation factors, with the elderly perhaps most at risk (Qureshi et al., 2003). In animal models, acute stress decreases the arrhythmia threshold by up to 40%. This effect has been shown to be interrupted by the administration of beta blockers (Qureshi et al., 2003).

METHODOLOGICAL AND RESEARCH ISSUES

Although the field of postdisaster research is burgeoning, there remain many questions, as suggested by the review discussed earlier, and substantial methodological challenges that need to be overcome in future research. Approximately two thirds of disaster-related behavioral studies are cross-sectional (Norris, Friedman, Watson, et al., 2002). Such studies are likely to pick up more long-standing cases of disease and may explain, at least in part, reports of extended chronicity (North, McCutcheon, Spitznagel, & Smith, 2002). Studies that have attempted a longitudinal approach, although often based on two data points, have demonstrated rapid declines in PTSD prevalence over time (Norris, Friedman, Watson, et al., 2002). Most of these latter studies are prospective, although retrospective approaches, such as interrupted time series analyses, may yield informative results as well (Nakonezny et al., 2004).

The majority of postdisaster studies are individual level rather than ecologic. The observations of cross-community differences in responses to terrorist events, such as the September 11, 2001, terrorist attacks, suggest that ecologic studies may play an important role in assessing the determinants of population mental and behavioral heath after disasters and terrorism (Silver, 2004). Postterrorism studies are likely to detect other non-disaster-related chronic conditions. For example, approximately half of the Oklahoma City firefighters in one sample met lifetime criteria for alcohol abuse or dependency (North, Tivis, et al., 2002). The vast majority (90%) of the one sample of children studied after the 1998 U.S. embassy bombing in Kenya were deemed exposed to other crimes or human-caused violence (Pfefferbaum, North, et al., 2003). This complicates the task of assessing the health problems that were caused by exposure to the disaster or terrorist attack. The exposure under study may also be confounded by other events that occurred during the same time period. For example, the 2001 attacks on the World Trade Center were quickly followed by both anthrax-laced mail attacks and a passenger jet crash.

Resource utilization may be particularly difficult to measure during times of crisis. Fear of violence may cause people to stay home, decreasing hospitalization numbers (Beare et al, 1978). Psychiatric admission rates may not capture successful outpatient treatments, and there may be changes in available services over time. Some psychiatric conditions may be overshadowed by physical complaints (Curran, 1988).

PTSD continues to be a focus of research attention after disasters and terrorism, perhaps to the detriment of other behavioral disorders. In one review of all postdisaster behavioral research, 68% of studies addressed PTSD, 36% included major depressive disorder, and 20% included generalized anxiety (Norris, Friedman, Watson, et al., 2002). Behavioral diagnoses such as alcohol abuse and somatic disorders are not commonly studied (Norris, Friedman, Watson, et al., 2002). But changes in diagnostic and screening instruments for PTSD over time (APA, 1982, 1987, 1994) and the myriad screening instruments available for assessing PTSD (Blake et al, 1995; Blanchard, Jones-Alexander, Buckley, & Forneris, 1996; Breslau, Davis, Peterson, & Schultz, 1997; Horowitz, Wilner, & Alvarez, 1979; Lindal & Stefansson, 1993) make comparisons difficult even within the same geographic region. The number of studies conducted worldwide bear little resemblance to the overall risk of disaster and terrorism. Figure 9.2 shows the number of postterrorism behavioral health studies conducted since 1980, compared with the number of reported terrorist incidents in the region (Significant Terrorist Incidents, 2004).

PREVENTION, TREATMENT, AND RESILIENCE

Ascribing suicide terrorism to individual characteristics may be misattributing the primary causes of terrorism (Attran, 2003). Psychopathology, poverty, and lack of education also are not reliable indicators of whom may become a terrorist: "Suicide terrorists have no appreciable psychopathology and are at least as educated and economically well off as their surrounding populations" (Attran, 2003). In fact, there may be a slight positive correlation with education, and although relative economic loss may be a factor, there is no real association with poverty. The only distinguishing characteristics of suicide bombers are that they tend to be single, male, and religious (Attran, 2003). This, then, suggests that preemptive screening and identification of persons who might

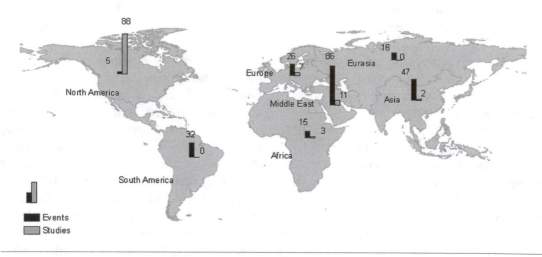

Figure 9.2   Comparison of Proportion of Postterrorism Behavioral Health Studies (Grey) to Proportion of Reported Terrorist Incidents (Black) Since 1980 by Region of the World

SOURCE: Reprinted from DiMaggio and Galea (2006).

become terrorists may be impossible. It has been argued that interventions are needed at the community (ecologic) level. An effective approach may be to target moderates within a community and address issues of discontent so as to encourage the communities themselves to abandon support for terrorist activities (Attran, 2003). Although this is intuitively appealing, the scant data on the evolution of terrorism make it difficult to muster the empirical evidence to support such sweeping recommendations. Therefore our relatively limited armamentarium of empirically validated measures to prevent terrorism suggests that it is incumbent on policymakers to consider ways to mitigate the potential consequences of terrorism and not simply focus on preventing terrorism.

Primary prevention of behavioral health effects among first responders may be feasible in the form of training as well as control of the postterrorist environment. The mental health effects of disasters on recovery workers can be mitigated by training and experience (Norris, Friedman, Watson, et al., 2002). Training must be tailored to the type of likely exposure. Firefighters and other first responders are exposed to personal risk, medical workers must confront death and horror, and counselors risk vicarious trauma (Norris, Friedman, & Watson, 2002). Rescuers with realistic expectations of what to expect may experience fewer behavioral breakdowns (Clauw et al., 2003). It has been shown that soldiers with higher rank and esprit de corps exhibit fewer behavioral problems during times of war and that isolated support troops sometimes have higher rates of illness than frontline forces (Clauw et al., 2003). Cultivating a culture of collegiality and common purpose may also control postdisaster pathology.

Individual pre-event screening among the civilian population may look for individuals at risk of developing behavioral symptoms and offer early treatment. Once identified, interventions may include cognitive-behavioral therapy (Clauw et al., 2003). However, studies about the predictive power of screening instruments and the cost-effectiveness of individual versus community-level interventions are limited.

Secondary prevention, in the forms of early identification and quick intervention is also possible. The onset of PTSD is fairly early after an incident, so interventions should start early with triage to identify those most at risk due to preexisting psychiatric disease and other risk factors such as proximity to the event (North, 2002). There is little evidence to endorse any particular treatment approach. While there have been no randomized clinical trials of postdisaster behavioral interventions (Peterson et al, 2002), there is no evidence that critical stress debriefing is effective (Clauw et al., 2003; Peterson et al., 2002), although identifying high-risk individuals and providing several sessions of cognitive-behavioral therapy can prevent PTSD (Clauw et al., 2003). There have been few studies of the effects of drug regiments (Norris, Friedman, & Watson, 2002). Interventional trials with drugs that have an acceptable safety profile, such as beta blockers, may be warranted.

Because most individuals experiencing medically unexplained symptoms will get better spontaneously (Clauw et al., 2003), public health messages reminding people that most symptoms will resolve may be helpful. Efforts should be directed at symptom management and not at the establishment of a hard diagnosis (Clauw et al., 2003). It is important, however, on both the individual and community levels to avoid trivializing people's concerns.

Perceptions of self-efficacy may be a key to resilience. "What matters, apparently, is not so much how people actually cope, but rather how they perceive their capacities to cope and control outcomes" (Norris, Friedman, Watson, et al., 2002). Resilience may reside as much in the community as in the individual. Resource dynamics "undoubtedly account for the overall resilience many, if not most, people show in the face of-even quite serious stress" (Norris, Friedman, & Watson, 2002). Collective interventions should replace valued resources as quickly as possible, emphasize self-empowerment, and reinforce indigenous networks. If relocation is necessary, people should be kept in natural groups and be encouraged to return to normal activities as soon as possible (Norris, Friedman, & Watson, 2002).

Community and neighborhood interventions such as public education, capacity building, and a return to normalcy probably should receive higher priority than individual interventions (Norris, Friedman, & Watson, 2002). Disasters are characterized by a loss of community services just at the time they are most needed (Norris, Friedman, & Watson, 2002). Social support can be defined as both the perceived support and the goods and services that are actually delivered. Interventions thought to be effective "improve community cohesion[,] . . . provide appropriate direction and high quality leadership[,] . . . and build a sense of individual responsibility and control" (Clauw et al., 2003).

TERRORIST-RELATED PHYSICAL INJURY

Despite concern over chemical, radiological, and biological attacks, the majority of direct terrorist-related physical injury to date has been the result of direct trauma. While many terror-related injuries tend to be of greater severity than non-terror-related injuries and are characterized by penetrating wounds and the consequences of explosions, there are often a large proportion of persons with minor injuries.

An Israeli review of a pediatric population found that 54% of 138 children injured due to terrorist activity had the highest injury severity score (25+), compared with 3% of 8,363 non-terror-injured children. The terrorist-related injuries were significantly more likely to require a higher degree of critical care, more likely to involve penetrating injuries to the torso or open head wounds, and more likely to involve internal injuries (Aharonson-Daniel, Waisman, Dannon, & Peleg, 2003). In Bologna, Italy, in 1980, 73 of 291 casualties died at the scene of the terrorist bomb explosion.

Morbidity was characterized by primary blast injuries such as so-called blast lung and flash burns as well as secondary injuries such as concussions, lacerations, and factures (Brismar & Bergenwald, 1982).

Terrorist-related injuries are more likely to involve gunshot wounds and explosives than non-terrorist-related injuries. In a one-year period between 1993 and 1994, one Israeli hospital reported treating 220 terrorist-related injuries. While more than half the patients (54%) were injured by thrown projectiles and stones, a fourth (25%) had been shot, and 10 patients (4.5%) were injured by explosives (Emile & Hashmonai, 1998).

These kinds of injuries are labor and resource intensive and exact a great toll on healthcare systems. During a 15-month period between 2000 and 2001, 2.4% (561) of all trauma admissions to nine acute-care Israeli hospitals were for terrorist-related injuries. Three fourths of patients were in their twenties and male. Forty eight percent of injuries were due to explosions, and 47% due to gunshot wounds. The authors concluded that the severity of injuries required a greater level of critical care from that seen in non-terrorist-related injuries and imposed a significant burden on the Israeli health care system (Peleg, Aharonson-Daniel, Michael, & Shapira, 2003).

Researchers have attempted to pool terrorist-related injuries to describe overall patterns. One such study combined 3,357 casualties from 220 worldwide terrorist incidents and found an immediate fatality rate of 13%. Nearly one third of survivors were hospitalized, of whom, 1.4% died. The authors concluded that discriminating triage could decrease overall survival (Frykberg & Tepas, 1988). A meta-analysis of 29 terrorist bombings concluded that most of the 903 deaths among the 8,634 casualties were immediate and untreatable. Penetrating soft-tissue injuries (41% to 86%) predominated, followed by pulmonary injuries (1% to 21% of survivors) depending on the environment (closed or open space) in which the bombing occurred (Arnold, Halpern, Tsai, & Smithline, 2004).

Many injuries are immediately fatal, but the majority of survivors will suffer less significant trauma. During a four-and-a-half-year period from 1975 to 1979, one Jerusalem hospital reported 272 terrorist-related hospital admissions, the majority of which (87%) were graded as "light" according to a commonly used "injury severity score." Only 10% of injuries were considered severe (Adler, Golan, Golan, Yitzhaki, & Ben-Hur, 1983). A 1978 British study of 1,532 consecutive terrorist bombing victims found only nine deaths in hospital (Hadden, Rutherford, & Merrett, 1978). More recent events have borne out this experience. For example, 759 persons sustained injuries after the 1995 Oklahoma City bombing: 167 persons died, 83 survivors were hospitalized. Survivors' injuries were characterized by soft-tissue trauma, such as lacerations and sprains (Mallonee et al., 1996). Following the events of September 11, 2001, in NYC, two nearby hospitals treated approximately 900 patients, of whom 85% were "walking wounded" sustaining ocular injuries and lacerations. A total of 135 patients were admitted to hospital, of whom 18 required surgery (Cushman, Pachter, & Beaton, 2003). Of the 970 recorded injuries to rescue and nonrescue workers on that day in New York, 49% involved inhalation injuries followed by ocular injuries (26%) and minor soft-tissue trauma, such as sprains and contusions (14%) and lacerations (14%; Rapid Assessment, 2002).

Injury research and control in general deserves greater attention and resources. Although injury is the number one killer of 1- to 34-year-olds in the United States (Rivara, Grossman, & Cummings, 1997) and results in more potential years of life lost than cancer and cardiovascular disease combined (Meyer, 1998), for every dollar spent on cancer research, the federal government spends about 11 cents for injury research (Robertson, 1998).

Despite its seemingly random nature, injuries, including those due to terrorism, are far from chance events and can be fitted to predictive models. Once adequately described, there is every reason to expect that terrorist-related injuries are at the very least amenable to secondary and tertiary public health interventions.

Many questions remain to be answered (CDC, 2005). What are the types, prevalence, and incidence of fatal and nonfatal injuries? What are the demographic characteristics, including race, ethnicity, and socioeconomic status, of affected individuals? What are the best means of transport, and what are the most effective treatments? What resources will be needed and how will they affect surge response? This kind of information is crucial for medical and public health professionals and community planners and policy makers to prepare for the possibility of terrorist incidents.

CONCLUSIONS

Effective postterrorist public health interventions require the recognition that behavioral consequences are, in fact, the intent of terrorists. The behavioral consequences of terrorist incidents have received considerable recent attention, much of it driven by the Oklahoma City bombings and the attacks of September 11, 2001, in the United States. PTSD is the most commonly studied psychopathology after disasters. Survivors of terrorist incidents consistently suffer the highest rates of PTSD; rescuers and first responders are at next highest risk. Prevalence estimates of disorders, such as PTSD, may mask great variability, depending on who is being studied, who is conducting the study, and where the event occurred.

It appears that terrorism-related behavioral diagnoses, such as PTSD, apply also to victims of natural disasters. The accumulated evidence on interventions following natural disasters is likely to be appropriate for the postterrorist environment. The presence of previous psychiatric diagnoses is strongly associated with subsequent PTSD and may be a useful triage factor, particularly when taken into consideration with such factors as female gender and direct exposure to events as either a survivor or rescuer. These associations are consistent among study types and environments and are important variables to consider when developing triage, outreach, and treatment programs.

Although most people in the general population can be expected to recover spontaneously within several months to a year from natural and unnatural disasters, there are potential population-level interventions to perhaps facilitate and speed the process. These include recognition of honest appraisals of behavioral health effects in community health announcements; preserving, as much as possible, community, family, and social networks; and returning individuals to normal activities as soon as feasible. Finally, some individuals such as survivors, rescuers, and those with a psychiatric history are at increased risk of conditions, such as PTSD, and may require individual interventions. These persons should be identified and referred for treatment. The physical injuries associated with terrorism are characterized by immediately fatal and severe injuries in those most directly exposed to the event, and a greater number of minor injuries for those more peripherally exposed. However, many questions remain to be answered about how best to utilize health care resources in response to terrorism.

REFERENCES

Adler, J., Golan, E., Golan, J., Yitzhaki, M., & Ben-Hur, N. (1983). Terrorist bombing experience during 1975–79: Casualties admitted to the Shaare Zedek Medical Center. *Israel Journal of Medical Sciences, 19*(2), 189–193.

Aharonson-Daniel, L., Waisman, Y., Dannon, Y. L., & Peleg, K. (2003). Members of the Israel Trauma G: Epidemiology of terror-related versus non-terror-related traumatic injury in children. *Pediatrics, 112*(4), e280.

Alexander, D. (2005, May 18). *Psychological aspects of terrorism*. Paper presented at 14th World Congress on Disaster and Emergency Medicine, Edinburgh, Scotland.

American Psychiatric Association. (1982). *Desk reference to the diagnostic criteria from DSM–III*. Washington, DC: Author.

American Psychiatric Association. (1987). *Diagnostic and statistical manual of mental disorders* (3rd ed., rev.). Washington, DC: Author.

American Psychiatric Association. (1994). *Diagnostic and statistical manual of mental disorders* (4th ed.). Washington, DC: Author.

Arnold, J. L., & Birnbaum, M. L. (2003, April–June). A proposed universal medical and public health definition of terrorism. *Prehospital and Disaster Medicine, 18*(2), 47–52.

Arnold, J. L., Halpern, P., Tsai, M. C., & Smithline, H. (2004). Mass casualty terrorist bombings: A comparison of outcomes by bombing type. *Annals of Emergency Medicine, 43*(2), 263–273.

Atran, S. (2003, March 7). Genesis of suicide terrorism. *Science, 299*, 1534–1539.

Beare, J. M., Burrows, D., & Merrett, J. D. (1978). The effects of mental and physical stress on the incidence of skin disorders. *British Journal of Dermatology, 98*(5), 553–558.

Blake, D. D., Weathers, F. W., Nagy, L. M., Kaloupek, D. G., Gusman, F. D., Charney, D. S., et al. (1995, January). The development of a Clinician-Administered PTSD Scale. *Journal of Traumatic Stress, 8*, 75–90.

Blanchard, E. B., Jones-Alexander, J., Buckley, T. C., & Forneris, C. A. (1996, August). Psychometric properties of the PTSD Checklist (PCL). *Behaviour Research and Therapy, 34*, 669–673.

Bleich, A., Gelkopf, M., & Solomon, Z. (2003). Exposure to terrorism, stress-related mental health symptoms, and coping behaviors among a nationally representative sample in Israel. *JAMA, 290*(5), 612–620.

Boscarino, J. A., Figley, C. R., & Adams, R. E. (2003). Fear of terrorism in New York after the September 11 terrorist attacks: Implications for emergency mental health and preparedness. *International Journal of Emergency Mental Health, 5*(4), 199–209.

Boscarino, J. A., Galea, S., Adams, R. E., Ahern, J., Resnick, H., & Vlahov, D. (2004, March). Mental health service and medication use in New York City after the September 11, 2001, terrorist attack. *Psychiatric Services, 55*, 274–283.

Breslau, N., Davis, G. C., Peterson, E. L., & Schultz, L. (1997, January). Psychiatric sequelae of posttraumatic stress disorder in women. *Archives of General Psychiatry, 54*, 81–87.

Brismar, B., & Bergenwald, L. (1982). The terrorist bomb explosion in Bologna, Italy, 1980: An analysis of the effects and injuries sustained. *Journal of Trauma-Injury Infection & Critical Care, 22*(3), 216–220.

Butler, A. S., Panzer, A. M., & Goldfrank, L. R. (2003). Preparing for the psychological consequences of terrorism a public health strategy. Washington, DC: National Academies Press. Retrieved January 20, 2006, from http://site.ebrary.com/lib/yale/Doc?id=10046858

Centers for Disease Control (CDC). (n.d). Mass trauma preparedness and response. Retrieved November 14, 2005, from www.cdc.gov/masstrauma/research/possible_studies/medical_clinical/rapid_assessment.htm

Clauw, D. J., Engel, C. C., Jr., Aronowitz, R., Jones, E., Kipen, H. M., Kroenke, K., et al. (2003, October). Unexplained symptoms after terrorism and war: An expert consensus statement. *Journal of Occupational and Environmental Medicine, 45*, 1040–1048.

Curran, P. S. (1988, October). Psychiatric aspects of terrorist violence: Northern Ireland, 1969–1987. *British Journal of Psychiatry, 153*, 470–475.

Cushman, J. G., Pachter, H. L., & Beaton, H. L. (2003, January). Two New York City hospitals' surgical response to the September 11, 2001, terrorist attack in New York City. *Journal of Trauma, 54*, 147–154; discussion 147–154.

De Lange, A. W., & Neeleman, J. (2004, Winter). The effect of the September 11 terrorist attacks on suicide and deliberate self-harm: A time trend study. *Suicide and Life-Threatening Behavior, 34*, 439–447.

DiMaggio, C., & Galea, S. (2006). The behavioral consequences of terrorism: A meta-analysis. *Academic Emergency Medicine, 13*, 559–566.

Emile, H., & Hashmonai, D. (1998). Victims of the Palestinian uprising (Intifada): A retrospective review of 220 cases. *Journal of Emergency Medicine, 16*(3), 389–394.

Factor, S. H., Wu ,Y., Monserrate, J., Edwards, V., Cuevas, Y., Del Vechio, S., et al. (2002, September). Drug use frequency among street-recruited heroin and cocaine users in Harlem and the Bronx before and after September 11, 2001. *Journal of Urban Health, 79,* 404–408.

Frykberg, E. R., & Tepas, J. J., III. (1988). Terrorist bombings: Lessons learned from Belfast to Beirut. *Annals of Surgery, 208*(5), 569–576.

Galea, S., Nandi, A., & Vlahov, D. (2005, July 1). The epidemiology of post-traumatic stress disorder after disasters. *Epidemiologic Reviews, 27,* 78–91.

Galea, S., Resnick, H., Ahern, J., Gold, J., Bucuvelas, M., Kilpatrick, D., et al. (2002, September). Posttraumatic stress disorder in Manhattan, New York City, after the September 11th terrorist attacks. *Journal of Urban Health, 79,* 340–353.

Hadden, W. A., Rutherford, W. H., & Merrett, J. D. (1978). The injuries of terrorist bombing: A study of 1532 consecutive patients. *British Journal of Surgery, 65*(8), 525–531.

Heim, C., Bierl, C., Nisenbaum, R., Wagner D., & Reeves, W. C. (2004, September–October). Regional prevalence of fatiguing illnesses in the United States before and after the terrorist attacks of September 11, 2001. *Psychosomatic Medicine, 66,* 672–678.

Herman, D., Felton, C., & Susser, E. (2002, September). Mental health needs in New York State following the September 11th attacks. *Journal of Urban Health, 79,* 322–331.

Hoge, C. W., Pavlin, J. A., & Milliken, C. S. (2002, August 8). Psychological sequelae of September 11. *New England Journal of Medicine, 347,* 443–445.

Horowitz, M., Wilner, N., & Alvarez, W. (1979, May). Impact of event scale: A measure of subjective stress. *Psychosomatic Medicine, 41,* 209–218.

Kessler, R. C., Sonnega, A., Bromet, E., Hughes, M., & Nelson, C. B. (1995, December 1). Posttraumatic stress disorder in the National Comorbidity Survey. *Archives of General Psychiatry, 52,* 1048–1060.

Lindal, E., & Stefansson, J. G. (1993, July). The lifetime prevalence of anxiety disorders in Iceland as estimated by the U.S. National Institute of Mental Health Diagnostic Interview Schedule. *Acta Psychiatrica Scandinavica, 88,* 29–34.

Lovejoy, D. W., Diefenbach, G. J., Licht, D. J., & Tolin, D. F. (2003). Tracking levels of psychiatric distress associated with the terrorist events of September 11, 2001: A review of the literature. *Journal of Insurance Medicine, 35*(2), 114–124.

Mallonee, S., Shariat, S., Stennies, G., Waxweiler, R., Hogan, D., & Jordan, F. (1996). Physical injuries and fatalities resulting from the Oklahoma City bombing. *JAMA, 276*(5), 382–387.

Marshall, R. D., & Galea, S. (2004). Science for the community: Assessing mental health after 9/ 11. *Journal of Clinical Psychiatry, 65*(Suppl. 1), 37–43.

Meyer, A. A. (1998, January). Death and disability from injury: A global challenge. *Journal of Trauma, 44,* 1–12.

Nakonezny, P. A., Reddick, R., & Rodgers, J. L. (2004, February). Did divorces decline after the Oklahoma City bombing? *Journal of Marriage & Family, 66,* 90–100.

Norris, F. H., Friedman, M. J., & Watson, P. J. (2002, Fall). 60,000 disaster victims speak: Part II. Summary and implications of the disaster mental health research. *Psychiatry, 65,* 240–260.

Norris, F. H., Friedman, M. J., Watson, P. J., Byrne, C. M., Diaz, E., & Kaniasty, K. (2002, Fall). 60,000 disaster victims speak: Part I. An empirical review of the empirical literature, 1981–2001. *Psychiatry, 65,* 207–239.

North, C. S. (2002, March). Psychiatric effects of disasters and terrorism: Empirical basis from study of the Oklahoma City bombing. Paper presented at American Psychopathological Association, Fear and anxiety: The benefits of translational research. Retrieved September 14, 2006, from http://ajp.psychiatryonline.org/cgi/content/full/162/1/200

North, C. S., McCutcheon, V., Spitznagel, E. L., & Smith, E. M. (2002, September). Three-year follow-up of survivors of a mass shooting episode. *Journal of Urban Health, 79,* 383–391.

North, C. S., Tivis, L., McMillen, J. C., Pfefferbaun, B., Spitznagel, E. L., Cox, J., et al. (2002, May). Psychiatric disorders in rescue workers after the Oklahoma City bombing. *American Journal of Psychiatry, 159,* 857–859.

Peleg, K., Aharonson-Daniel, L., Michael, M., & Shapira, S. C. (2003). Israel Trauma G: Patterns of injury in hospitalized terrorist victims. *American Journal of Emergency Medicine, 21*(4), 258–262.

Peterson, A. L., Nicolas, M. G., McGraw, K., Englert, D., & Blackman, L. R. (2002, September). Psychological intervention with mortuary workers after the September 11 attack: The Dover Behavioral Health Consultant model. *Military Medicine, 167*(Suppl. 9), 83–86.

Pfefferbaum, B., Doughty, D. E., Reddy, C., Patel, N., Gurwitch, R. H., Nixon, S. J. et al. (2002, September). Exposure and peritraumatic response as predictors of posttraumatic stress in children following the 1995 Oklahoma City bombing. *Journal of Urban Health, 79,* 354–363.

Pfefferbaum, B., North, C. S., Doughty, D. E., Gurwitch, R. H., Fullerton, C. S., & Kyula, J. (2003, April). Posttraumatic stress and functional impairment in Kenyan children following the 1998 American embassy bombing. *American Journal of Orthopsychiatry, 73,* 133–140.

Pfefferbaum, B., Vinekar, S. S., Trautman, R. P., Lensgraf, S. J., Reddy, C., Patel, N., et al. (2002, June). The effect of loss and trauma on substance use behavior in individuals seeking support services after the 1995 Oklahoma City bombing. *Annals of Clinical Psychiatry, 14*(2), 89–95.

Qureshi, E. A., Merla, V., Steinberg, J., & Rozanski, A. (2003, January). Terrorism and the heart: Implications for arrhythmogenesis and coronary artery disease. *Cardiac Electrophysiology Review, 7,* 80–84.

Rapid assessment of injuries among survivors of the terrorist attack on the World Trade Center—New York City, September 2001. (2002, January 11). *Morbidity and Morality Weekly Report, 51,* 1–5.

Rivara, F. P., Grossman, D. C., & Cummings, P. (1997, August 21). Injury prevention: First of two parts. *New England Journal of Medicine, 337,* 543–548.

Robertson, L. S. (1998). *Injury epidemiology: Research and control strategies* (2nd ed.). New York: Oxford University Press.

Rosenheck, R. A., & Fontana, A. (2003a). Post-September 11 admission symptoms and treatment response among veterans with post-traumatic stress disorder. *Psychiatric Services, 54*(12), 1610–1617.

Rosenheck, R., & Fontana, A. (2003b). Use of mental health services by veterans with PTSD after the terrorist attacks of September 11. *American Journal of Psychiatry, 160*(9), 1684–1690.

Salib, E. (2003, September). Effect of 11 September 2001 on suicide and homicide in England and Wales. *British Journal of Psychiatry, 183,* 207–212.

Satel, S. (2003, December). The mental health crisis that wasn't. *Psychiatric Services, 54,* 1571.

Significant terrorist incidents, 1961–2003: A brief chronology. (2004). Retrieved August 16, 2005, from www.state.gov/r/pa/ho/pubs/fs/5902.htm

Silver, R. (2004, Spring). Conducting research after the 9/11 terrorist attacks: Challenges and results. *Families, Systems, & Health, 22,* 47–51.

Silver, R. C., Holman, E. A., McIntosh, D. N., Poulin, M., & Gil-Rivas, V. (2002, September 11). Nationwide longitudinal study of psychological responses to September 11. *JAMA, 288,* 1235–1244.

Swahn, M. H., Mahendra, R. R., Paulozzi, L. J., Winston, R. L., Shelley, G. A., Taliano, J., et al. (2003). Violent attacks on Middle Easterners in the United States during the month following the September 11, 2001 terrorist attacks. *Injury Prevention, 9*(2), 187–189.

10

Elder Abuse

CANDACE J. HEISLER

"Elder abuse represents an unbroken saga in the relations between adults and their elders" (Reinharz, 1986). While the term *elder abuse* has been coined recently, it is a new name for an old problem. Examples of it have been found in Greek mythology, English literature, and law for centuries. Typical of these is Oedipus and the murder of his father, King Lear's mistreatment at the hands of two of his daughters, and Jonathan Swift's *Gulliver's Travels*. In the early seventeenth century, Sir Francis Bacon reported the case of Mr. and Mrs. Death, in which a younger woman won over and married a man of 80, then abused and neglected him and threatened to harm anyone he might summon for help (Bacon, 1617). In 1975, an article in the *British Medical Journal* (Burston, 1975) described "granny battering." In twenty-first-century America, the once-hidden problem of elder abuse, neglect, and exploitation has begun to surface and is being recognized as a legal, social, medical, and complex societal problem.

This chapter describes elder abuse, its definitions and forms, incidence and prevalence, risk factors, characteristics of victims and perpetrators, and indicators and markers. To understand the context in which it occurs, demographic patterns, theories about causes, costs, and the congressional response are described. Finally, the problem from the victim's perspective, including impact, obstacles and barriers, reporting laws, challenges, and promising practices are highlighted.

DEFINITIONS AND FORMS OF ELDER ABUSE

Elder abuse is generally understood to mean an act or a failure to act when there is a duty to act that causes physical, economic, and psychological harm or violation of human rights to an elderly person. It includes all types of mistreatment and abuse against an older person. Some acts of elder abuse are criminal, others are not (Wolf, 2000), and they occur in domestic community settings and facilities.

The National Center on Elder Abuse (NCEA) has identified seven forms of abuse. They are defined as follows:

Form of Abuse	Definition
Physical abuse	The use of physical force that may result in bodily injury, physical pain, or impairment
Sexual abuse	Nonconsensual sexual contact of any kind with an elderly person
Emotional/psychological abuse	The infliction of anguish, pain, or distress through verbal or nonverbal acts
Financial/material exploitation	Illegal or improper use of an elder's funds, property, or assets
Neglect	Refusal or failure to fulfill any part of a person's obligations or duties to an elderly person
Abandonment	The desertion of an elderly person by an individual who has physical custody of the elder, or desertion by a person who has assumed responsibility for providing care to the elder
Self-neglect	Behaviors of an elderly person that threaten the elder's health or safety

SOURCE: NCEA, 2001.

Physical abuse includes subsets of domestic violence, homicide, and homicide-suicide, in addition to acts of assault and battery where there is no intimate relationship between the parties. Sexual assault includes forcible and nonconsensual conduct, as well as acts with an elder who is so cognitively impaired that he or she is legally unable to give consent. It also includes acts of sexual assault accompanied by homicide. Neglect by a caregiver may include abandonment, as well as denying a frail elder necessary food, clothing, shelter, medical care, and assistance. Financial abuse includes acts where the victim is unable to give consent or where the consent has resulted from deceit, coercion, manipulation, subterfuge, duress, or the use or threatened use of violence. Psychological/emotional abuse includes criminal and noncriminal acts that cause distress, anguish, fear, or humiliation. Examples of criminal acts are criminal threats, stalking, vandalism, and pet abuse.

Self-neglect is not criminal conduct, as there is no third-party perpetrator. However, self-neglect is the most frequent form of abuse reported to Adult Protective Services (APS; Teaster, 2003; Teaster et al., 2006). The origin of cases of self-neglect should be investigated. A previously independent and high-functioning older adult could lose interest in personal care and his or her living environment and become hopeless and depressed as a result of criminal victimization (Dyer, 2006).

The line between self-neglect and "lifestyle choice" is capacity, that is, the elder's ability to provide for personal needs and to understand, process information, and make reasoned choices. If a person has capacity, he or she is entitled to make choices, whether they appear wise or foolish. When a person loses the ability to make such decisions about his or her life and lifestyle, protective services and various legal remedies, including the court appointment of a surrogate decision maker may be employed to protect the elder even against his or her own desires.

Most self-neglecting elders are isolated and live in poor conditions. Most have difficulty caring for themselves. Many have medical or mental illnesses (Brandl et al., 2007). Bozinovski found an overlap between self-neglecting and previous family violence victimization, relationship failures, abandonment by family members, betrayal, poor relationship with parents, and family estrangement (Bozinovski, 1995; Brandl et al., 2007, p. 50).

In most elder abuse cases, multiple forms coexist. For example, neglect or psychological, emotional, or physical abuse may be employed to exploit an elder financially. ("Give me the money or I will break your arm . . . not feed you . . . abandon you, and you will die alone in a nursing home.") Those investigating elder abuse should explore all forms and should always consider whether financial abuse is present or not, no matter what the nature of the initial report (Brandl et al., 2007).

There is no single statutory definition of "elderly." Federal law defines older individuals as persons aged 60 and older (42 USC 35 Subchapter I, §3002[38]). State laws use a variety of ages. For example, California uses age 65 for elder abuse but 70 for procedures to memorialize testimony and for trial-setting priorities (California Penal Code §§368[g]; 1335–1345; 1048). Some states do not use the term *elderly*, but instead focus on all adults aged 18 and above who have physical or cognitive disabilities or other conditions and cannot protect their legal rights or provide for their basic needs.

With the exception of self-neglect, these broad definitions may or may not parallel criminal definitions. Some states include abandonment within statutes dealing with neglect. Some states have enacted specific elder abuse crimes that may include many forms of abuse. For example, in California, Penal Code Section 368 criminalizes willful infliction of physical pain or mental suffering; causing or permitting an elder to suffer; causing or permitting the person or health of an elder to be injured; causing or permitting an elder to be placed in a situation in which his or her person or health is endangered; financial abuse through theft, embezzlement, forgery, fraud, or identity theft; and false imprisonment by the use of violence, menace, deceit, or fraud. Some states provide for sentencing enhancements that are added to basic sentencing terms or that direct the court to order a greater penalty when the victim is elderly or vulnerable. Other states have no special statutes, and criminal violations, such as assault or battery, larceny, rape, or robbery, are punishable under general criminal statutes. Some state

reporting laws use the same definitions in their protective services and criminal statutes, though most states do not.

Recognizing the limitations and inconsistencies in definitions of elder abuse, a recent study panel attempted to define abusive conduct to help facilitate advances in knowledge (Bonnie & Wallace, 2003). The panel adopted a definition of *elder mistreatment* to include "intentional actions that cause harm or create serious risk of harm, whether or not intended, to a vulnerable elder by a caregiver or other person who stands in a position of trust to the elder, or failure by a caregiver to satisfy the elder's basic needs or to protect the elder from harm." A trust relationship is defined as "a care-giving relationship or other familial, social, or professional relationship where a person bears or has assumed responsibility for protecting the interests of the older person or where expectations of care or protection arise by law or social convention" (Bonnie & Wallace, 2003, p. 39). This definition excludes self-neglect and stranger victimization of elders. The panel felt that predatory stranger-elder victimization is criminal conduct but not a component of the distinct category of elder mistreatment, which is uniquely characterized by the special relationship between the parties. In this chapter, self-neglect will not be discussed further, as there is no "crime victim." Similarly, this chapter will focus on crimes against persons in trusted relationships, so stranger crimes generally are not discussed.

THE GRAYING OF AMERICA

The importance of understanding and addressing elder abuse is underscored as the United States ages. The United States is a rapidly aging nation, with more people over the age of 65 than ever before. The trend will continue for the first half of the twenty-first century as the "baby boomers" age. The proportion of those aged 65 and older has increased steadily since 1950. Between 1950 and 2000, the total

U.S. population increased by 87%; the population aged 65 and older increased by 188% (Bonnie & Wallace, 2003). In the decade spanning 1993 to 2003, the elder population increased 9.5%, to 35.9 million. About 2 million people celebrated their 65th birthday in 2003 (Administration on Aging, 2004).

The fastest growing elder population are those aged 85 and above. During the 50-year period between 1950 and 2000, the number of those 85 years and older increased by 635% (Bonnie & Wallace, 2003). The total number of those 85 and older is 38.5 times larger than it was in 1900 (Administration on Aging, 2004). By 2030, this age group will number about 9.6 million (Administration on Aging, 2004). By 2050, it is estimated that the population will be seven times the size it was in 1980 (Gorbien, 2005). In 2003, there were more than 50,000 persons aged 100 or older. This is a 36% increase since 1990 (Administration on Aging, 2004).

The aging trend will continue. In 2003, persons 65 and older constituted 12.8% of the population. By 2030, this will rise to 20%, numbering more than 71.5 million people (Administration on Aging, 2004; Gorbien, 2005). By 2030, there will be proportionally more elderly persons than those younger than 18 (22% vs. 21%).

Most elderly live in just nine states: California, Florida, New York, Texas, Pennsylvania, Ohio, Michigan, Illinois, and New Jersey. California has more than 3.8 million, Florida has more than 2.9 million, New York and Texas each have more than 2 million, and the remaining states have at least 1 million elders (Administration on Aging, 2004). Several states have seen enormous increases in the number of elderly residents, including Nevada (60.5%), Alaska (50.3%), and Arizona (32.4%; Administration on Aging, 2004).

As persons age, the number who have significant physical and/or cognitive disability grows (Administration on Aging, 2004), increasing their need for assistance with personal care, financial management, and other activities. For example, although only 5% of the elderly reside in nursing homes at any given time, the need for nursing home care increases with age. Persons 85 and older are disproportionately overrepresented in nursing home populations (Hawes, 2003). As persons age and become more ill and frail, their risk of elder abuse increases (Burgess, Dowdell, & Prentky, 2000; Gorbien & Eisenstein, 2005).

INCIDENCE AND PREVALENCE

The precise number of elder abuse cases is unknown. Several studies have attempted to quantify its incidence and prevalence. A landmark study of more than 2,000 seniors aged 65 and older who lived in the Boston area found a prevalence rate of elder abuse of 3.2%. This study did not consider financial exploitation (Pillemer & Finkelhor, 1988). A Canadian study that also studied financial abuse found a prevalence rate of 4%. The largest category (2.5%) was victims of financial abuse (Podnieks, 1992). Other international studies found abuse rates of between 5% and 5.6% (Wolf, 2000).

A recent study of findings from the National Violence Against Women Survey found that 6.9% of women aged 60 and older, or 1 in 15, had been victims of sexual assault in their lifetimes. This is considered to be an underestimation, as prior studies of sexual assault, marital rape, and stalking had found that elder victims were less likely than younger women to define themselves as victims of such conduct (Tjaden & Thoennes, 2006).

Although the exact numbers of elder abuse cases are unknown, studies show there has been an increase in the number of reported cases. Between 1986 and 1996, reports of elder abuse increased by 150%, from 117,000 to 293,000, at a time when the elder population increased by 10% (National

Center on Elder Abuse, 1998). The study of National Elder Abuse Incidence was conducted in 20 counties in 15 states using "sentinel agencies." It reviewed data over a two-month period in 1996 and estimated that at least 500,000 incidents of elder abuse occur annually. It also found that only 20% of cases are reported. This study has been widely criticized for the small data set and the fact that it did not reach significant segments of the elder population (Cook-Daniels, 1999). Data from APS programs across the country, the District of Columbia, and Guam were collected for the year 2000. APS agencies received 472,813 reports (Teaster, 2003). Most recently, data from APS programs were again collected in 2004. That study found a 19.7% increase in reports between 2000 and 2004 (from 472,813 to 565,747; Teaster et al., 2006). With all studies relying on APS data, it is important to acknowledge that many programs do not serve persons who are elderly and without disabilities. As a result, the numbers of APS cases are below the actual incidence of elder abuse.

COSTS OF ELDER ABUSE

Costs associated with elder abuse include health and medical; community services; civil and criminal justice; institutional settings and care; labor; prevention, education, and research; business; taxes; and pain, suffering, and other intangibles, including decreased quality of life, loss of independence, and increased stress (Spencer, 1999). The following table describes these costs:

Category of Cost	Explanation
Health and medical	• Hospitalization • Outpatient medical care • Ambulance/medical transport • Mental health services • Case management • Post-mortem investigations by coroners and medical examiners • Protocol development • Substance-abuse programs and services
Community services	• Adult Protective Services • Legal advocacy • Guardianship/conservatorship • Long Term Care Ombudsman program • Shelter programs • Support groups • Housing services • Money-management services • Volunteer services
Criminal and civil justice	• Providing civil and criminal courts (including special courts or calendars for elderly victims) • Law enforcement • Prosecution • Victim assistance • Victim compensation • Interpreters • Legal services • Corrections, including probation and parole

(Continued)

(Continued)

Category of Cost	Explanation
Institutional settings and care	• Adequate staffing levels • Care costs • Legal costs associated with lawsuits regarding quality of care • Criminal records (background) checks • Training staff to identify and respond to suspected abuse
Labor	• Including premature retirement due to abuse • Worker's compensation • Less staff time for equally pressing matters • Frequent turnover
Prevention, education, and research	• Organizing and supporting conferences • Development of training materials • Retraining staff
Business	• Forensic audits • Increased insurance claims • Defending lawsuits • Lost productivity from abused older workers
Taxes	• Loss of government revenue • Support victims who are indigent as a result of their victimization
Intangibles	• Pain and suffering • Decreased quality of life • Diminished independence • Loss of life • Stress

Estimates of more direct costs of elder abuse are difficult to determine. It is estimated that Medicare fraud and related health care crimes, including overbilling for services that were not needed and billing for services not performed, annually cost the U.S. government about $40 billion and the state of Florida alone $1.6 billion (De Pommereau, 2003; Rosoff, Pontell, & Tillman, 2003). Financial exploitation, including thefts and scams, costs elderly victims approximately $40 billion dollars each year (Johnson, 2004; Tighe, 1994). Medical fraud, including offers of "miracle cures" and useless medical treatment, costs approximately $25 billion a year (Rosoff et al., 2003). Direct medical costs of elder abuse and neglect are estimated to be approximately $5.3 billion (Mouton et al., 2004).

It is also useful to consider the costs of child abuse and domestic violence. Annually the cost of child abuse is estimated to be $94 billion— $24 billion in direct costs and $69 billion in indirect costs (Fromm, 2001). Domestic violence costs are estimated to be $5.8 billion: $4.1 in medical and mental health care and $1.8 billion in lost productivity and earnings (Centers for Disease Control and Prevention, 2003). These are relevant numbers, as the health consequences of abuse and neglect in older persons are more severe, numerous, and costly than in younger victims. Furthermore, elder abuse and neglect increase the rate of disease and mental health problems and the need for hospitalization, placement in a care facility, use of community care services, and medication and rehabilitative care. It may also increase an elder's need to use programs and funds for indigent persons, as victimization may have "wiped out" that person's life savings.

THEORIES ABOUT
CAUSES OF ELDER ABUSE

Early theories of elder abuse focused on caregiver stress. That is, as persons age and they become more frail, it becomes harder to meet their needs. Caregivers try to meet these increasing needs while balancing other aspects of their lives. The competing demands cause stress, which results in abuse and neglect. According to this theory, a victim's dependence on the caregiver is the "cause" of the stress. Subsequent research has questioned the validity of this theory, because of a lack of proof that increased dependence or caregiver stress increases the risk of elder abuse (Bonnie & Wallace, 2003; Wolf, 2000).

Another theory is that persons who were abused as children or witnessed abuse in their childhood are likely to abuse their aging relatives. While this is true for child abuse and domestic violence, there is no evidence that this "intergenerational transmission" of violence applies to elder abuse (Bonnie & Wallace, 2003). Other theories to explain why abuse occurs have focused on the offender's pathologies, including mental health, alcoholism, and substance abuse; a power imbalance between the offender and elder victim; and societal marginalization of elder persons (Wolf, 2000). In reality, no single model explains why elder abuse occurs. Instead, an "ecological model" that looks at individual, interpersonal, and societal factors may be a more balanced explanation. Such an approach considers the abuser's dependence on the elder; the quality of the relationship between the elder and abuser; the abuser's emotional, psychological, and substance abuse problems; and the victim's lack of external social supports (Wolf, 2000).

CONGRESSIONAL
RESPONSE TO ELDER ABUSE

Congressional recognition of elder abuse began in the United States Congress in the 1950s, with legislation providing matching funds to states to establish protective services (Wolf, 2003). Beginning in the early 1960s, U.S. senator Frank Moss conducted hearings that led to the creation of a 12-volume report regarding abuse in facilities, "Nursing Home Care in the United States: Failure in Public Policy." Two decades later, Congress created committees on aging. In 1981, the House Select Committee on Aging estimated that 1.1 million elderly people were victims of elder abuse annually in the United States and found that only one in six cases was reported. The committee recommended that states enact laws modeled on child abuse laws and designate agencies to handle cases. It also urged Congress to support these efforts by creating a funding stream for the states (U.S. House of Representatives, 1981). In 1985, the same committee issued a follow-up report, "Elder Abuse: A Decade of Shame." The committee found that one in five cases was reported, compared to one in six in 1981, and that states spent an average of $22.14 per child for child protection and only $2.91 per elder for elder abuse protection (Anonymous, 2002). Five years later, the committee issued its report, "Elder Abuse: A Decade of Shame and Inaction" (U.S. House of Representatives, 1990). It found that elder abuse was not isolated conduct but instead is "a full-scale national problem which exists with a frequency that few have dared to imagine. In fact, abuse of the elderly by their loved ones and caretakers exists with a frequency and rate only slightly less than child abuse." It concluded that about 5% of the elderly, some 1.5 million people, were victims of elder abuse each year (U.S. House of Representatives, 1990). It found that only one in eight incidents was reported to officials, and funding was disproportionate to that for child abuse (Koenig & DeGuerre, 2005). In fact, funding for child abuse was $45.03 per child, and corresponding funding for elder abuse was $3.80 per elder (Anonymous, 2002). The 1990 report echoed its 1981 recommendations that the federal government better assist states in addressing elder abuse. Since 1990, there have been numerous congressional hearings on issues related to elder abuse and neglect in domestic and institutional settings (Anonymous, 2002).

The reality is that elder abuse continues to be less recognized and funded than child abuse and domestic violence. "The federal government spends $153.5 million on programs directly addressing issues of elder abuse. In sharp contrast, the federal government spends $520 million dollars on programs combating violence against women, and $6.7 billion dollars on child abuse prevention efforts. Of the $153.5 million spent directly on elder abuse prevention, $143.34 million is spent through the Department of Health and Human Services, with the remaining $10.16 million being spent on Department of Justice programs" (Anonymous, 2002, p. 16). Currently there are no federally funded programs specifically for the protection of elder abuse victims (Reed, 2005).

The Older Americans Act, Title VII, Vulnerable Elder Rights Protection program, is administered by the U.S. Department of Health and Human Services, Administration on Aging. Title VII provides funding for the Long Term Ombudsman program, public education, legal assistance program development at the state level, and the National Center on Elder Abuse (Reed, 2005). Other responses largely have been left to the individual states.

RISK FACTORS FOR ELDER ABUSE

A variety of risk factors associated with various types of elder abuse have been identified. Although their presence may not prove abuse has occurred, identification of risk factors will assist in identifying and proving or substantiating suspicion.

Risk Factor	Explanation
Functional and cognitive decline	• Impaired ability to care for themselves (Dyer, Connolly, & McFeeley, 2003) • Decreased ability to defend self or escape (Bonnie & Wallace, 2003) • Uncertain if victim frailty is itself a risk factor for abuse (Bonnie & Wallace, 2003)
Poor social functioning in the community	• Conflict with family members • Historically poor relationship between caregiver and care recipient • Social isolation • Psychiatric illness
Abuser's dependence on victim	• For financial support (Bonnie & Wallace, 2003; Gorbien & Eisenstein, 2005)
Alcohol and drug abuse	• Especially for physical abuse • High incidence of alcohol abuse
Advanced age	• Increasing probability of debilitating physical condition and cognitive decline requiring assistance from others (Gorbien & Eisenstein, 2005)
Living arrangements	• Those elders living alone are at lowest risk of abuse (Bonnie & Wallace, 2003) • Shared living arrangements increase the risk of abuse (Bonnie & Wallace, 2003)

Risk Factor	Explanation
Social isolation	• Isolation due to deterioration of social network • Accompanied by lack of social supports (Lachs & Pillemer, 1995) • Often present in domestic violence situations • Illegal conduct is hidden from public scrutiny (Bonnie & Wallace, 2003)
Dementia	• Higher rate of violence by caregiver than when no dementia • May also be correlated to violence and disruptive behaviors by care recipients (Bonnie & Wallace, 2003)
Caregiver mental illness	• Strong predictors of abuse • Physical abusers more likely to have depression than neglectors (Bonnie & Wallace, 2003)
Hostility	• More hostility found in persons providing care to Alzheimer's Disease patients (Bonnie & Wallace, 2003)

CHARACTERISTICS OF VICTIMS AND PERPETRATORS

Most victims of elder abuse are female. Women are more likely than men to be victims of physical, sexual, financial, and psychological/emotional forms of abuse and neglect. Men are more likely to be abandoned (NCEA, 1998). There is no single profile of victims. Victims fall along a continuum of physical and cognitive abilities. Elder abuse occurs throughout society and respects no cultural, religious, ethnic, socioeconomic, gender, or other boundaries. It occurs in gay and lesbian relationships, just as it does among heterosexual parties.

Many victims of physical abuse do not have cognitive or physical disabilities. Conversely, victims of elder sexual abuse committed by persons in trusted relationships most often have significant limitations. Victims of neglect do have significant disabilities, and that may be the reason they require a caregiver.

Victims of financial abuse tend to be female, over 80 years of age, and live alone (NCEA, 1998). Some are lonely and grieving. Many previously have not handled financial matters and are unsophisticated in money management and conducting certain financial transactions, such as wire transfers and electronic banking, and are unwilling to disclose financial matters. Many are unaware of the current value of assets acquired years or decades earlier, including their homes (Hafemeister, 2003). Physical and mental difficulties may diminish their ability to understand financial transactions or pay bills.

Most perpetrators are family members (NCEA, 1998). Studies of cases reported to APS have identified adult children as the most frequent abusers (32.6%), followed by other family members (21.5%). Over 75% (75.1%) of abusers were under the age of 60 (Teaster, 2003; Teaster et al., 2006). Interestingly, studies of domestic violence programs have identified spouses as the most frequent abusers (Brandl & Cook-Daniels, 2002).

Perpetrators of most forms of abuse are male (Gorbien & Eisenstein, 2005). In physical abuse cases, men are usually the abusers (53%). In neglect, women are the perpetrators slightly more often than males (NCEA, 1998; Teaster et al., 2006). This is not surprising, as most caregiving is provided by women. Elder sexual assault victims are overwhelmingly female and perpetrators male (Holt, 1993; Ramsey-Klawsnik, 1991, 1993). Nearly all perpetrators of elder homicide-suicide are male (Cohen, 1998). Financial abusers, in particular, are generally male and comparatively younger than most of those who inflict other forms of abuse (45.1% were 40 or younger in financial abuse, while 27.4% were 40 or younger in all other forms of abuse).

Offenders generally fall into two categories: The first comprises dysfunctional persons, who abuse drugs or alcohol, have psychosocial difficulties, or are stressed caregivers. They are opportunistic offenders. The second category comprises predatory individuals who seek out likely targets, establish a relationship of control, and then obtain assets by deceit, intimidation, and other psychological tactics (Treuth, 2000). "In a typical sequence, the victim is identified as impaired and vulnerable; the victim's trust is then secured by being friendly, helpful, and providing assistance; the victim is made passive and comfortable, and then isolated; and finally the perpetrator takes possession of assets by employing psychological abuse" (Hafemeister, 2003, pp. 401–402).

INDICATORS AND MARKERS OF ELDER ABUSE

There are a number of indicators that suggest elder abuse may have occurred or is occurring. The presence of these indicators should increase suspicion and trigger inquiry.

Physical Abuse

Examples:

Mrs. G., who lived independently in her home with her 46-year-old unemployed son, was struck repeatedly in the face and pushed down and kicked when the son became upset with her.

Mr. and Mrs. R. have been married for 58 years. He became angry when she challenged him for buying a pressure cooker. He threatened to kill her and struck her in an area where she had recently had surgery.

Mr. B. learned he was ill and would have to move to a nursing home. He believed his wife would not survive alone in their home without him, so he shot and killed her and himself.

Indicators of Physical Abuse

Injuries	• Injuries, particularly those in different stages of healing • Repeated "accidental" injuries • Patterned injuries in the shape of the object which caused them • Bilateral injuries (in two planes of the body, such as the left hip and right cheek) • Wraparound bruises (suggestive of being grabbed around the full circumference of an arm, leg, or torso and pulled upward or restrained) • Injuries on the outside of arms, inside of legs, scalp, around the throat, face, or behind the ears • Burn marks • Multiple skin tears
Medical issues	• Unexplained or untreated injuries • Implausible explanations for injuries • Delay in seeking of treatment • Missed appointments • Frequent changes of doctors • Hospital or physician visits with vague complaints such as anxiety, headaches, digestive problems

Medication	• Over- or under-medicating, or mismedicating • Failure to fill required prescriptions
Restraints	• Signs of restraint or confinement, such as bindings or locks on the outside of an elder's bedroom door or refrigerator
Miscellaneous	• Forced feeding

Identifying physical abuse may be difficult, as older adults may have medical conditions or use medications that make bruising more common. Poor balance may result in falling. Brittle or thinning bones may make them more prone to fractures. Diseases may result in wasting or failure to thrive and resemble abuse or neglect. In elder abuse, there are no "gold standard" injuries that prove abuse has occurred (Dyer et al., 2003). Instead, the location, extent, appearance, severity, and number of injuries are significant. Injuries to the head and neck; fractures of the head, spine, or trunk; and internal injuries suggest abuse (Bonnie & Wallace, 2003, p. 119). A recent study has also shown that bruises do not progress in a predictable order so they should not be "aged" by their color (Dyer et al., 2003; Mosqueda, Burnight, & Liao, 2005).

Domestic violence occurs across the lifespan. While most studies find that it occurs at a lower rate than in younger couples, at least one study has found a similar rate across the lifespan (Fisher & Regan, 2006; Jasinski & Dietz, 2003; Straka & Montminy, 2006). While it includes intimate partner violence, it also includes abuse in trusted and ongoing relationships. Although most perpetrators of domestic violence are spouses and intimate cohabitants, other family members and, occasionally, caregivers may perpetrate domestic violence. It is considered domestic violence because of the dynamics of power and control that characterize it (Brandl, 2000; Brandl & Cook-Daniels, 2002).

Homicide of the elderly is relatively uncommon (Flynn, 2000). This may be due, in part, to poor identification and detection; lack of law enforcement training on elder abuse; the fact that indicators may be subtle and masked by existing medical conditions; and the expectation that older people die. All help explain why some homicides are not detected. Older perpetrators usually kill family members with a firearm (Flynn, 2000; Goetting, 1992). Particular attention should be paid when disengagement, poor health, isolation, depression, and alcohol abuse are present (Flynn, 2000). Strangulation and suffocation account for an unusually high percentage of elder homicides, many of which are not identified as homicides. Strangulation and suffocation may leave no exterior bruising; injuries are often internal and are discovered only during autopsy (McClane, Strack, & Hawley, 2001). Homicide-suicide must also be considered. Research over the past two decades has found that the incidence of homicide-suicide is higher in the population aged 55 and above than in the population under age 55 (Malphurs & Cohen, 2001). Of the cases studied, the overwhelming majority involves intimate partners, with older men being the perpetrators (Cohen, 1998, 2000). About 25% to 30% of cases involve couples with histories of domestic violence. All involve an overvalued attachment of the perpetrator to the victim and a desire to maintain the relationship when threatened with separation or dissolution. A high incidence of untreated and undetected psychiatric problems, especially depression, is usually present (Cohen, 1998, 2000).

Sexual Abuse

Examples:

Ms. R. is demented and lives with her caregiver son in her home. He shares her bed and he fondles her under her nightgown. During a medical appointment, the nurse observes pinch marks and bruises on Ms. R.'s breasts.

Mr. B. regularly visits his wife at her nursing home. She is unable to talk. Mr. B. often checks her out at lunchtime. One day, while bathing Mrs. B., staff observe that she has a vaginal discharge. They question Mr. B. who remarks that he can make love to his wife whenever he wants.

An elderly woman is found in her home sexually assaulted and strangled. An investigation leads to the identification of a 20-year-old man who lives nearby. When arrested he has several items of the victim's jewelry in his possession.

Indicators of Sexual Abuse

Medical findings	• Bleeding in genital areas • Difficulty walking or sitting • Bruises to outer arms, chest, or inside thighs • Bite marks • Sexually transmitted diseases • HIV infection • Trauma to breasts, genitalia, or mouth • Prolapsed uterus
Unusual relationships	• Inappropriate (enmeshed) relationships between elder and abuser • Shared bedroom and sleeping arrangements • Mental illness
Nature of disclosure	• Coded disclosures (hints or clues about what has occurred, such as an elderly woman calling a rape crisis line to ask if she could be pregnant or have a venereal disease)

Elder victims who have been sexually abused by family members are often demented and dependent on others for care and the management of their assets (Holt, 1993; Ramsey-Klawsnik, 1991). Sexual abuse is often part of a pattern of multifaceted, intimate partner abuse (domestic violence; Ramsey-Klawsnik, 2003). When victims reside in care facilities, the personnel, other residents, or visitors may sexually assault them. It appears that some people seek employment in these facilities for easy access to victims who are unable to report abuse, or if they do, are unlikely to be believed (Burgess, Dowdell, & Brown, 2000; Heisler, 2001a). Because of decreased levels of estrogen, less lubrication of the tissue, and thinning genital tissue, elderly victims of sexual assault are at high risk of genital trauma (Brown, Streubert, & Burgess, 2004).

Stranger Sexual Assault and Sexual Assault Homicide

Occasionally, strangers target elderly women living independently in the community as victims of sexual abuse. In such cases, excessive violence is employed, far more than that needed to overcome resistance and take control of the victim (Groth, 1979; Groth, Burgess, & Holmstrom, 1977; Ramin, Satin, Stone, & Wendel, 1992). Suspects are often armed and commit robbery and theft during the attack. Some abusers murder their victims in the course of these rapes. In a study of 125 elderly victims of sexual assault, 16 had been murdered. Strangulation was present in most of these homicides. Seventy-five percent of all the study's victims were attacked without warning and were physically incapacitated by overwhelming and injurious force. Over one third suffered head trauma (Brown et al., 2004).

Safarik and colleagues studied homicides of elderly sexual assault victims and found excessive violence and injury; sexual assault accompanied by burglary or robbery; the use by the perpetrator of hands, fists, and feet rather than firearms; and a suspect who was not known to the victim and lived within six blocks of the victim (nearly a third lived within the same block as the victim). Only about one fifth of the suspects had a criminal history involving sexual offenses. Victims were considerably older than the perpetrator and were most often strangled to death in their homes (Safarik, Jarvis, & Nussbaum, 2002).

Neglect

Examples:

Mr. A. was found dead in his home, covered with multiple infected pressure ulcers that had never been treated. His son was living in his home and cashing his retirement checks. The man had been bedridden for months and was demented.

A man was found wandering at a shopping mall. He could not state his name, where he lived, or who had left him.

Mrs. F. has arthritis and cannot walk on her own. Her husband is supposed to care for her. He leaves her in bed, has moved the phone out of reach, and on two occasions has left her lying on the floor for hours following a fall.

Indicators of Neglect

Appearance of victim	• Unclean, unkempt appearance • Poor nail care • Poor skin hygiene • Dirty clothing • Odors • Underweight • Clothing not appropriate for conditions
Medical findings	• Pressure ulcers, especially if untreated • Over- or under-medicating, or mismedicating • Poor dental care • Malnourishment or dehydration • Unexplained weight loss ("Failure to thrive") • "Wolfing" food • Mentally confused
Environmental features	• Lack of appropriate food, water • Aids not present • Unable to reach a telephone or summon help • Lack of adequate heating or cooling for conditions • Home, yard in disrepair • Odors • Pest infestations

In cases of neglect, identification of a legal caregiver is a critical issue. Legal definitions vary from state to state. In some states caregivers are limited to those who are paid to provide care. In others a caregiver may be paid or unpaid; may be a person who assumes care for a person who requires it; or is in a relationship, such as a spouse, in which a duty of care is imposed for the duration of the relationship. There are some states where adult children have a legal duty to care for an aging parent; there are others in which there is no such duty (Moskowitz, 2001; *People v. Heitzman*, 1994).

Victims of caregiver neglect have significant physical and mental impairments and, as a result, are dependent on others for care. They are often unable to describe their victimization and, because of their condition, may be easily isolated so that the neglect is not detected. Differentiation of neglect from disease processes can be difficult and require medical assessment. Pressure ulcers, also called bedsores and decubitus ulcers, can develop even with proper care in a person who has limited mobility or is bedridden. They develop over bony areas which are in contact with surfaces such as a bed, wheelchair, or floor. Once they develop, they require medical care to manage and heal.

Financial Exploitation

Examples:

An elderly man who lived alone was befriended by a young woman at a local restaurant. Within a few weeks they were married, and her name was added to the man's accounts. Shortly afterward, she had transferred all of his money into a new, separate account in her name only. She then abandoned him.

A woman gave her son her power of attorney when she entered hospital for surgery. Upon her release, she learned he had put her house up for sale and had bought himself a new sports car and paid for an expensive vacation with her funds.

Mr. L., a longtime friend of Mrs. P., convinced her she was unable to live alone, and then moved into her home. He cut her off from friends and family, told her children she did not want to see them, convinced her that her children did not care about her and only wanted her money, and that he was her only friend. He disconnected the television and broke her reading glasses so she could not read the newspaper. He then got her to agree to sign over her home to him in return for his promise of lifelong care.

Indicators of Financial Exploitation

Environmental	• Missing items • Unopened mail • Utilities turned off when elder should have funds to pay for service • Lack of amenities when elder should be able to afford them or has previously been able to afford them • Absence of food or other necessities • Necessary home repairs not made when elder should be able to afford them
Responses by others	• Elder denied necessary services or aids because abuser refuses to pay for them (with the elder's money) • Suspect has strong interest in cost of things, not the elder's needs • Promises of lifelong care
Financial matters	• Unusual amount of banking or ATM activity, especially if elder is homebound • Newly executed legal documents, especially if the elder is confused or was rushed to sign them • Loans and gifts made to suspect • Signatures on checks and other documents that do not look like elder's signature, or when the elder is unable to write • New signers on checks, credit cards • Unpaid bills, rent, taxes, insurance • Suspect holds power of attorney for elder • Caregiver has no visible means of support

Changes in household	• Mail redirected to a new address
	• Elder has "new best friend"
	• Changes in spending patterns of elder and/or suspect
	• Prescriptions for medications needed by elder not filled
	• Missing items
	• New will, trust, or power of attorney (Hafemeiser, 2003)

Financial abuse often underlies other forms of abuse. The abuser may threaten or neglect an older person in order to get control of the assets. She or he may hasten an elder's death to get the property sooner, or before it is dissipated by the costs of long-term care. It is worth examining the financial picture in all types of elder abuse and to keep an index of suspicion that it may be present.

Financial exploitation usually involves a series of acts rather than a single moment in time. One of the challenges of identifying it is to find the complete paper trail and locate all the missing property. This task can be daunting when the perpetrator has taken over management of the finances, redirected statements and other mail to new addresses, established new bank and credit card accounts, set up joint accounts with the elder, or used the elder's credit and good name to commit identity theft.

A person with legal authority to handle an elder's assets may exploit him or her financially. In the past, when the perpetrator was the victim's attorney-in-fact through a power of attorney, misuse and exploitation of the elder's assets were considered civil disputes. Criminal prosecution was not considered, and powers of attorney began to be known as "licenses to steal." More recently, some cases of misappropriation have been prosecuted successfully, especially when the power of attorney limited gift giving and personal loans to the attorney-in-fact.

Allegations of financial abuse are often defended as consensual gifts or loans from the victim. Consent requires that the person making the transaction be fully informed about it, that person must possess sufficient mental capacity to understand and "appreciate" the information, and that the person freely and voluntarily agree to the transaction. The person must be able to reason logically, use judgment, understand the consequences of proposed actions, relate connected events to one another, select among alternatives, and be aware of steps to achieve goals (Naimark, 2001).

Even if a person has the ability to give consent and appears to have done so, financial abuse may be accomplished through brainwashing-like tactics called undue influence, the "concerted, deliberate effort to assume control over another person's decision-making" using psychological control and manipulation (Nerenberg, 2000, p. 56). Undue influence occurs when people use their role and power to deceptively exploit the trust, dependency, and fear of others and get them to do what they otherwise would not have done (Hafemeister, 2003; Quinn, 2001; Singer, 1992). Some of the tactics are similar to the power and control dynamics of domestic violence, stalking, and some grooming techniques employed by child molesters (Brandl, Heisler, & Stiegel, 2006).

Perpetrators use a variety of tactics, including restricting or denying food or medicine to make the victim weak and compliant; poisoning existing relationships; promoting indispensability; restricting access; deceptively manipulating the elder; and reinterpreting events (Turkat, 2003). While victims of coercion typically feel pressured to comply, victims of undue influence may be unaware that they are being manipulated and "willingly" comply.

Psychological/Emotional Abuse

Examples:

A caregiver constantly belittled her elderly aunt, S. R., calling her demeaning names and threatening to place her in a nursing home. S. R. became withdrawn, quiet, and depressed.

A younger neighbor, with a criminal history of burglary, continuously watched his elderly neighbor and made sexually explicit comments to her that she found unwelcome and disturbing. He broke into her home and stole underwear. He left her unwanted gifts and love notes.

Mr. G. likes to taunt his wife by cleaning his gun and pointing it at her cat. He says he hates the animal and thinks her pet would be a great target.

Indicators of Psychological/Emotional Abuse

Threats	• Threats to punish • Threats to abandon or put in a nursing home • Threats to injure or kill the victim or others • Threat to commit suicide
Treatment	• Verbal harassment • Demean and belittle • Constant criticism • Treat like an infant • Give the "silent treatment" • Berate and ridicule personal values
Environmental	• Darken the residence, cut out sunlight • Remove clocks and calendars • Refuse to provide news and information • Deny companionship
Harm to pets and property	• Pet abuse • Damage items the victim values

Generally, psychological abuse is considered noncriminal. In reality, certain acts that cause emotional pain, anguish, and suffering are crimes. Examples include animal abuse, stalking, criminal threats, and vandalism. In addition, psychological abuse may be employed to facilitate other forms of abuse. For example, threats to abandon or place in a nursing home may be made to keep a victim from reporting physical abuse or financial exploitation. Behaviors that cut a victim off from sources of information and that employ constant belittling may be part of the campaign of financial exploitation through the use of undue influence. Pet abuse and related threats to harm pets are used to keep a victim of domestic violence from leaving the batterer. Psychological abuse can undermine self-esteem and make the victim feel hopeless.

Victim and Suspect Behavioral Indicators

Victim	*Suspect*
Withdrawn	
Isolated	Isolates the elder; tries to cut off outsider contact with the elder
Disoriented	
Agitated	
Fearful	
Passive and resigned	

Victim	Suspect
Depressed	Depressed
Nonresponsive or hesitant to speak openly; defers to suspect when questioned	Always present when anyone talks with the elder; verbal domination of the elder; speaks for elder
Embarrassed and ashamed	
Wary and distrustful of others	Exaggerated protectiveness, concern, or defensiveness about the elder
Sleep disturbances or sleeplessness	
Denies that anything has occurred or that help is desired	Lacks understanding of the elder's needs and abilities; unwilling to accept own caregiving limitations and to plan and carry out a viable care plan
Coded disclosures	
Inexplicable changes in behaviors	
Fear reactions when touched or bathed	
Self-destructive behaviors	
	Unusual interest in the elder's financial affairs and the amount of money spent on the elder's care; feels that too much money is spent on the elder
	Caregiver disappears or abandons elder
Marries suspect	Marries elder
Implausible explanations of events	Implausible explanations of events

IMPACT OF ELDER ABUSE ON ITS VICTIMS

The consequences of elder abuse are profound. Research over a 13-year period disclosed that one result of elder abuse victimization is earlier morbidity, that is, the victims die sooner than they otherwise would have (Lachs, Williams, O'Brien, Pillemer, & Charlson, 1998). This may be due to the trauma of recovering from injuries, but it also reflects the emotional and psychological toll elder abuse exacts.

The medical impact can be devastating. "The quality of life can be jeopardized in the forms of declining functional abilities, progressive dependency, a sense of helplessness, social isolation, and a cycle of worsening stress and psychological decline. . . . It can induce fractures, depression, dementia, malnutrition, and death. It was found that the risk of death for elder abuse and neglect victims is three times higher than for nonvictims" (Dong, 2005, p. 293).

Financial exploitation can cause financial ruin. In fact, its impact can be as profound as violent crime (Deem, 2000) or physical abuse (Dessin, 2000). Older persons have little or no ability to rebuild financial assets or recoup losses. They may be dependent on their lifetime savings to support them for the rest of their lives. The result may be a loss of independence and security, dependency on family members for support, or reliance on public assistance and social welfare programs, with a significant reduction in quality of life. In addition, the psychological impact may include loss of trust in others and their own ability to manage financial matters; fearfulness of additional victimization; isolation from, and conflict with, family members; depression; hopelessness; and suicide (Hafemeister, 2003).

Obstacles and Barriers for Older Victims

Elder abuse victims face obstacles and barriers that younger victims do not. Some acts, such as domestic violence or sexual assault by a spouse, may not be perceived as illegal. Remedies such as divorce, separation, obtaining a restraining order, or entering a shelter may not be acceptable due to personal, cultural, religious, or community values.

Similar values may dictate that the victim's needs are secondary to those of children and spouse. As a result, victims may be unwilling to report, discuss, or accept help. They may decline help or financial assistance because of views that acceptance is disgraceful or a sign of weakness (Heisler, 2001a).

In addition, not every culture or ethnicity defines or identifies the same acts as abusive or improper. What is perceived as abusive in one community may not be in another. What is seen as theft in one culture may be sharing of communal resources in another. Some cultures may not impose a duty to care for older family members in need, while others may take the opposite view. Some communities may be willing to obtain help from outsiders, whereas in others, help should be obtained only from family members and entities within the culture (Lachs & Pillemer, 2004; Moon, 2000; Moon & Williams, 1993; Simpson, 2005).

Because some victims live alone, it may be difficult to report or summon help. If the victim relies on others for transportation, his or her driver may be their attacker. Abusers may prevent victims from obtaining medical treatment (Dong, 2005). Reporting or pursuing help may well mean the loss of their only transportation to programs, medical appointments, and social activities. Many fear that if they tell family members, those relatives may use the victimization to monitor their activities, decrease their independence, relocate them against their will,

or place them in a nursing facility. Victims fear if they report abuse there will be additional mistreatment. Abusers may threaten more assaults, destroy property, harm pets, or kill the victim, relatives, or themselves (Dong, 2005).

Older victims, like younger crime victims, often suffer emotional injuries, including post-traumatic stress syndrome, shock, embarrassment, denial, and disbelief. Many blame themselves and their needs for what happened (Dong, 2005).

If the abuser is someone they know and love, the elderly victim may feel ashamed or betrayed and may feel the need to protect a family member. They may believe that the outcome of reporting will be worse than the abuse that has occurred. The outcome may well be depression, helplessness, hopelessness, and ultimately premature death or suicide.

If the victim has suffered economic losses, he or she may no longer have resources to pay for necessary services and care. He or she may be unable to afford to remain in his or her home, pay medical premiums, or afford medications. The victim may even have lost his or her home in the course of the victimization.

If the victim lives in a facility he or she may not report because of cognitive or physical impairment. If the victim does report, family members and staff may discount the relevant information. If there are no independent witnesses, it is likely the case will never be reported to, or investigated by, law enforcement. Family members may not seek action for fear that the victim will be discharged from that facility and left without a suitable place to live.

Reporting Laws

Every state and the District of Columbia have enacted elder protection legislation. Legislation is typically modeled after child-abuse statutes and usually includes provisions for coordination of services for eligible persons and the creation of authority to act and protect persons who are in danger (Koenig & DeGuerre, 2005). Mandatory reporting has sparked considerable debate, with opponents arguing that such statutes are paternalistic and interfere with the individual's right to self-determination, that is, the right to make personal decisions, even if they may be perceived as unwise or imprudent, violate confidentiality in the doctor-patient relationship, and discourage elders from reporting incidents of abuse on their own behalf (Moskowitz, 1998). Advocates of mandatory reporting argue that it increases awareness of elder abuse by professionals who may be the only source of contact with an isolated elder, increases the number of reported incidents, is a cost-effective response to a historical failure to respond to such matters, and is critical to identifying and lessening the incidence and prevalence of abuse (Koenig & DeGuerre, 2005). A total of 44 states have enacted mandatory reporting of suspected abuse by designated persons. Voluntary reporting by others is also permitted. The remaining six—Colorado, South Dakota, North Dakota, New York, New Jersey, and Wisconsin—authorize voluntary reporting (Dyer, Heisler, Hill, & Kim, 2005; see also NCEA Web site for "Laws Related to Elder Abuse" at www.elderabusecenter.org).

In mandatory reporting states, there is considerable variation regarding who and what must be reported. In some states everyone is a mandatory reporter. In others, health care, social services, and law enforcement are mandatory reporters (Koenig & DeGuerre, 2005). Some states, such as California, require the reporting of abuse involving persons who are "elderly." Others require reporting when the person meets a state's definition of "vulnerable, dependent, disabled, infirm or incapacitated."

In mandatory reporting states, physical abuse and neglect are universally included; financial abuse is frequently included. Self-neglect and psychological or emotional abuse

may not be included as mandatory reporting categories (Koenig & DeGuerre, 2005). Sexual assault and isolation may be separately categorized or included within physical abuse. Categories may include criminal and noncriminal acts, and definitions may use the same terms as found in criminal statutes but not include the same elements. Some states, such as South Carolina and California, use the same definitions in their protective services laws as in their criminal statutes (Thomas & Heisler, 1999). Only 10 states have statutory definitions of self-neglect. These are Alaska, Colorado, Louisiana, Maryland, New Hampshire, New York, Utah, Washington, D.C., Wisconsin, and Wyoming (National Center on Elder Abuse, 2006). Statutes include mandatory timelines for reporting and general immunity from arrest and civil liability for reporting in good faith. Failure to report when mandated to do so is subject to criminal or civil penalties. (A guide to reporting laws by state is located at www.elderabusecenter.org/default.cfm?p=statelaws.cfm)

In most states APS is the first responder to reports of abuse, neglect, and the exploitation of vulnerable adults. APS provides or offers services to older people and people with disabilities who are in danger of being mistreated or neglected, are unable to protect themselves, and have no one to assist them (see www.elderabusecenter.org/default.cfm?p=statelaws.cfm).

Most APS programs serve vulnerable adults (i.e., persons who are being mistreated or are in danger of mistreatment, and who because of age and/or disability are unable to protect themselves) regardless of age, others serve only the elderly, and others serve persons aged 18 to 59 who have disabilities that prevent them from protecting themselves (Teaster et al., 2006). APS interventions include receiving reports of abuse, neglect, or exploitation; investigating those reports; assessing risk; developing and implementing case plans; monitoring services; and evaluating the impact of intervention. APS may provide or arrange for medical, social, economic, legal, housing, law enforcement, or other protective emergency or supportive services (NAAPSA, 2001). Guiding principles of APS include advocating for the client's right to autonomy, preserving the rights of clients who have the capacity to make their own decisions (self-determination), selecting the least restrictive alternative among service alternatives, and preserving the family unit when possible (Dyer et al., 2005).

In some states and situations reports of abuse in facilities are reported to the Long-Term Care Ombudsman program as well as various licensing and regulatory agencies. In some states, the Ombudsman program conducts nursing investigations, and regulatory agencies may undertake parallel licensing and monitoring; if abuse occurs in other types of facilities, such as state hospitals, licensing and regulatory agencies may have sole authority to investigate.

Challenges to Addressing Elder Abuse

Elder abuse is a pervasive and serious crime and a social problem. Finding solutions has been complicated by several issues. These include a lack of awareness and federal leadership, an inadequate knowledge base, inconsistent practices, and an array of issues related to reporting abuse. Elder abuse awareness has been described as being today where child abuse was in the 1960s (Lachs, 2000). Individuals, communities, and governments are beginning to respond, but efforts have been inconsistent, localized, and often underfunded, either temporarily or continuously. To date, not a single federal employee is exclusively dedicated to elder abuse, neglect, and exploitation issues (Breaux, 2002). While there have been congressional hearings and reports for more than four decades, funding is inconsistent, and there is

no overarching federal elder abuse legislation (Anonymous, 2002).

Two elder justice acts have been introduced, but neither has been enacted. A third, Senate Bill 2010, was introduced in late 2005 but to date has not been enacted. If passed it would provide a direct funding stream of $300 million annually for seven years for APS separate from the Social Services Block Grant; establish federal offices of elder justice in the U.S. Department of Justice and the Department of Health and Human Services; create an advisory board to develop a multidisciplinary strategic plan to address elder abuse; establish an elder justice resource center to collect information and data and fund projects to improve data collection; create a long-term care consumer clearinghouse; develop training for Ombudsman staff, provide technical assistance, and support demonstration projects and research; develop dementia training for nursing assistants; distribute grants to the nursing home industry to improve staffing levels through training, recruitment, and retention, and increased training for managers; fund a study to evaluate the value of a national nurse's aide registry; require national background checks for employees at demonstration projects; oversee safe-haven and legal-advocacy grants; fund centers of excellence and forensic centers; and study model state laws.

To address the lack of medical knowledge, medical forensic research for distinguishing abuse and neglect from aging and disease processes and identifying critical locations and types of injuries associated with abuse is needed (Heisler, 2001b). With such information, increased identification of elder abuse is likely.

Inconsistent practices affect detection of, and response to, elder abuse. For example, inconsistent definitions may result in one agency conducting an investigation while another identifies the conduct as nonabusive. Because some protective services programs only serve those who have significant impairments, while others serve all abused elders, service delivery is inconsistent. In some states, abuse in nursing homes is investigated by protective services programs, usually APS; in other states, the Long-Term Care Ombudsman program is mandated to investigate (Anonymous, 2002). Differing rules and limitations may greatly affect the type of investigation and the legal propriety of reporting findings to law enforcement.

Problems associated with reporting abuse include variation in who is a mandated reporter, what must be reported, and the responses to reports. If a person with dementia makes a report, it may well be discounted. Health professionals, while often mandated to report, rarely do so (Otto, 2000). There are few consequences for failing to do so.

Promising Practices

In response to the various barriers and obstacles already described, numerous promising practices are underway at national, state, and local levels. Some focus on addressing systemic responses; others seek to assist individual victims of elder abuse and neglect.

Federal Responses

The most far-reaching federal response is the Elder Justice Act of 2005. If passed, it would have provided consistent funding for protective services and support the identification and implementation of effective practices. In addition, the Department of Justice has convened round-table meetings of national experts in forensics to identify knowledge gaps and develop recommendations for the development of a forensic research agenda. The department has also led a national Nursing Home Initiative, which has resulted in the creation of state working groups. The groups include participation of law enforcement, regulatory, protective services, and prosecution

representatives at state and federal levels. Each team has identified critical issues relevant to its jurisdiction related to nursing home care (Anonymous, 2002).

The Department of Justice Office for Violence Against Women has provided grant funding for the development of training curricula on elder abuse, domestic violence, stalking, and sexual assault for law enforcement, prosecutors, and court officials. The Office for Victims of Crime has funded the development of law enforcement curricula on elder abuse and provided some funding for the development of specialized victim advocacy for elder crime victims.

In December 2001, the Administration on Aging, part of the Department of Health and Human Services, and the Office for Victims of Crime jointly funded the first National Policy Summit on Elder Abuse. National experts in elder abuse from a variety of fields and disciplines attended the summit. The summit identified 10 recommendations for protecting America's most vulnerable elders. These are to support the passage of a National Elder Abuse act; mount a national education and awareness effort; improve the legal landscape by strengthening elder abuse laws; develop and implement a national elder abuse training curriculum; ensure that age-appropriate, specialized mental health services are available and accessible; commission a General Accounting Office study (to analyze the effectiveness of federal programs in combating elder abuse); increase awareness within the justice system; establish a national elder abuse research and program innovation institute; invest in a national resource center on APS; and seek a presidential executive order (calling on federal agencies and governors to evaluate the extent to which current policies assist elder abuse victims). More information on the National Policy Summit on Elder Abuse is available at www.elderabusecenter.org/pdf/whatnew/proceedings.pdf. As a result of federal funding, the American Prosecutor's Research Institute (APRI) has developed several publications on the prosecution response to elder abuse. Information on APRI publications on elder abuse is available at www.ndaa-apri.org/publications/apri/wwc_publications.html. Criminal investigations, arrests, and prosecutions regarding elder abuse, previously infrequent, are much more common. The criminal justice system's ability to protect victims and hold offenders accountable in appropriate cases has become more of a reality and less of the rare possibility it was a decade ago (Heisler, 1991).

State Responses

This section will highlight some of the trends of multijurisdictional response. For a state-by-state review of promising practices, please refer to the National Center on Elder Abuse Web site at www.elderabusecenter.org, then selecting "Promising Practices."

Several states have developed specialized statutes criminalizing elder abuse and/or adding sentencing enhancements for crimes committed against elders (Heisler & Stiegel, 2002; Stiegel, 1995). States have also enacted civil statutes that create special civil causes of action or add monetary penalties when elders are targeted in civil cases (Stiegel, 2000). In some states, persons who commit elder abuse are precluded from inheriting from their victims (Quinn & Heisler, 2002). In many states, expedited procedures to obtain the testimony of elderly victims have been created so that critical testimony can be memorialized early. In addition, criminal and civil cases with elderly victims often are given trial-setting preferences so they can proceed more quickly (Quinn & Heisler, 2002).

Increasing awareness of elder abuse and developing responses to it led the National Sheriff's Association, the International Association of Chiefs of Police, and the American Association of Retired Persons (AARP) to form

TRIAD, signifying the three groups that partner at the community level to keep seniors safe—seniors, law enforcement, and providers. Local TRIAD programs have been established in many states. These link elders and local law enforcement together to raise awareness about elder abuse and to respond to it (Heisler & Stiegel, 2002). More information is available at www.nationaltriad.org.

Beginning in Massachusetts and Oregon, bank-reporting projects were created to educate bank officials in recognizing indicators of elder financial abuse and reporting suspected instances. Other communities have adopted these programs (Heisler & Stiegel, 2002).

Jurisdictions have recognized the value of specialized law enforcement and prosecution units to handle elder abuse victims and their cases. Elder service officers (ESO) have been trained to take case reports and interview elderly victims. ESO units operate in Chicago, Louisiana, and parts of Florida. Many have received specialized elder abuse training (Heisler & Stiegel, 2002). For example, in Louisiana in 2004, every ESO completed an advanced three-day intensive elder abuse course, in addition to their other training. In many places, specialized investigative units have been created in law enforcement and prosecution agencies, and such officers and investigators may work as a team with the local prosecutor. Some agencies have specially trained victim advocates to assist elderly crime victims. Some work within law enforcement agencies; others are part of the victim-witness program.

Many agencies provide elder abuse training to their members. In California and South Carolina, for example, every line officer and supervisor must complete a course on elder abuse (Heisler & Stiegel, 2002). In many states, various groups or professionals, such as APS, victim advocates, prosecutors, health care professionals, and aging services staff have received training on elder abuse for a number of years. Increasingly, these trainings are multidisciplinary in nature. In Florida, the Rural Victimization Project has developed a training manual for Meals on Wheels and other Elder Services staff on elder domestic violence (Maxwell & O'Rourke, 1999).

One of the most important initiatives in addressing elder abuse has been the development of teams. "Elder abuse and neglect cases often pose multiple, complex issues that may be social, medical, ethical, legal, and financial in nature, and which require expertise beyond that available from any single discipline" (Dyer et al., 2005, p. 430). Teams form to benefit from the varied experience, knowledge, training, and resources available to its members. Teams may manage cases, develop intervention plans, identify and investigate criminal conduct, investigate facilities, or identify and address systemic service gaps. They may be based in a medical center, criminal justice agency, APS agency, or community-based organization.

Elder abuse medical management teams began in Massachusetts at Beth Israel Hospital in response to a 1980 law. In 1998, Mount Sinai Hospital in New York began its team. Subsequently, teams have formed in Minnesota, New Jersey, California, and Texas (Dyer et al., 2005). Two of the most well-known teams are located at the Baylor College of Medicine in Houston (TEAM) and the University of California at Irvine (VAST). TEAM and VAST members include those from medical staff, law enforcement, APS, and others. They review medically complex cases to develop a case plan. Law enforcement provides safety for members making home visits as part of their case assessment. They also follow up if criminal conduct is suspected.

Law enforcement teams take several forms. Some are local code enforcement teams, which investigate problem locations that appear to be public nuisances. Members may include law enforcement, local humane and public health officials, fire marshals, city attorneys or county counsel, and public health and APS staff. At the state level, California and Florida have developed programs to conduct unannounced inspections of problematic nursing facilities. Teams of local and state law enforcement officials, licensing and regulatory agents, code enforcement officers, fire marshals, and agencies that fund care for the elderly and low-income recipients make unannounced checks. Their goals are to identify problems, leverage improvements, and, when necessary, seek court supervision or closure of substandard facilities.

Other law enforcement teams may focus on rapid response to elder abuse calls in which APS and law enforcement may jointly respond to alleged financial abuse cases. In Delaware and Utah, APS hired law enforcement officers to train their workers and made joint house calls (Heisler & Stiegel, 2002). A third type team, most often used in domestic violence cases, is composed of law enforcement officers and a victim advocate who respond together; the officer or deputy investigates and builds a criminal case, while the advocate attends to the victim's needs.

Another example of a type of team is the Fiduciary Abuse Specialist Team (FAST). Originally established in Los Angeles in 1993, teams now exist throughout California, in Oregon, and elsewhere (Dyer et al., 2005). These teams may be convened by APS or another community agency and bring together law enforcement, mental health, and other health care practitioners, prosecutors, and experts from financial institutions to consider financial exploitation referrals, to determine if criminal conduct is present, to help review evidence, and to meet victims' needs (Brandl et al., 2007; Nerenberg, 2003). One program in Oregon has recruited retired experts in financial transactions to review and analyze transactions and assist law enforcement and prosecutors in case development.

Community-based multidisciplinary teams may conduct case reviews to assist agencies in developing service plans in especially complex cases or may provide community education and awareness campaigns and training. The San Francisco Consortium on Elder Abuse Prevention provides case reviews and has more than 50 participating agencies and organizations. Law enforcement and prosecution historically have participated in reviews of criminal matters. The Maricopa County (Arizona) Elder Abuse Prevention Alliance is another example. Its team provides community education; has developed a community response plan; developed partnerships between law enforcement, service providers, and elderly residents; created an Elder Watch program; closed service gaps; advocated legislative changes; and developed a law enforcement certified program to train law enforcement personnel and dispatchers (Maricopa Area Agency on Aging, 2002).

A recent innovation is the elder abuse fatality review team. Drawing from child abuse and domestic violence death review teams, these teams focus on elder deaths to identify criminal conduct and to identify systemic failures that may help prevent future deaths (Stiegel, 2005). Teams now operate in eight states: Maine, California, Arizona, Arkansas, Montana, Texas, Kentucky, and Michigan. In addition, in San Diego, a Medical Examiner-Adult Protective Services Response Team (MERT) ensures that elder death cases referred to the medical examiner are cross-checked with APS files to identify any with prior abuse investigations.

These programs and initiatives show that increasing attention is being given to elder abuse and its victims. However, these systemic responses are not the only efforts to stop abuse, protect victims, and make restitution to them. At the individual victim level, new approaches are also being developed.

Domestic violence and sexual assault programs have begun to serve older victims, with services tailored to their needs. Safety planning instruments have been designed (see e.g.,

National Clearinghouse on Abuse in Later Life at www.ncall.us, "Resources."). Elder shelters now exist in approximately 20 locations. There are more than 100 programs across the country focusing on elder abuse in later life and 34 support groups for older abused women (National Clearinghouse on Abuse in Later Life, 2003a, 2003b). Free cellular telephone programs for elder victims are available in many communities. Transitional housing for up to two years for elders escaping abuse is becoming available. In Maricopa County, Arizona, for example, the DOVES program provides emergency and transitional housing in a safe and supportive environment, living supplies, crisis counseling, case management for residents, support groups, assistance with job searches when appropriate, skills development, and assistance in applying for public benefits (Freeland, 2002).

CONCLUSION

Elder abuse is a complex phenomenon that causes untold suffering and pain. It strips victims of their dignity, independence, and self-worth. Because of its emotional, physical, and financial impact, it often brings on premature death. It is committed by those older people most trust— their families and friends, caregivers, and advisors. It has no easy solutions, but with greater societal awareness, increased options, and improved responses, there is hope that the promise of "the golden years" can be realized. Once locked in the shadows, its victims invisible, elder abuse has begun to be recognized for what it is—a critical social, legal, and medical problem that can no longer be hidden.

REFERENCES

Administration on Aging. (2004). A profile of older Americans: 2004. Washington, DC: U.S. Department of Health and Human Services.
Anonymous. (2002). Protecting older Americans: A history of federal action on elder abuse,

neglect, and exploitation. *Journal of Elder Abuse & Neglect, 14*(2/3), 9–85.

Bacon, F. (1617). *Reports, 33,* 34.

Bonnie, R. J., & Wallace, R. B. (Eds.). (2003). Panel to Review Risk and Prevalence of Elder Abuse and Neglect. Committee on National Statistics and Committee on Law and Justice, Division of Behavioral and Social Sciences and Education National Research Council. *Elder mistreatment: Abuse, neglect, and exploitation in an aging America.* Washington, DC: National Academies Press.

Bozinovski, S. D. (1995). Self-neglect among the elderly: Maintaining continuity of self. Unpublished doctoral dissertation. University of Denver, Colorado.

Brandl, B. (2000). Power and control: Understanding domestic abuse in later life. *Generations, 24*(11), 39–45.

Brandl, B., & Cook-Daniels, L. (2002, December). *Domestic violence in later life.* Retrieved May 3, 2005, from www.vawnet.org/Domestic Violence/Research/VAWnetDocs/AR_later-life.php

Brandl, B., Dyer, C. B., Heisler, C. J., Otto, J. M., Stiegel, L. A., & Thomas, R. W. (2007). *Elder abuse detection and intervention: A collaborative approach.* New York: Springer.

Brandl, B., Heisler, C., & Stiegel, L. (2006). The parallels between undue influence, domestic violence, stalking, and sexual assault. *Journal of Elder Abuse & Neglect, 17*(3), 37–52.

Breaux, J. (2002). Senator Breaux's elder justice proposal of 2002 executive summary. *Journal of Elder Abuse & Neglect, 14*(2/3), 33–36.

Brown, K., Streubert, G. E., & Burgess, A. W. (2004, August). Abuse. *Nurse Practitioner, 29*(8), 23–31.

Burgess, A., Dowdell, E., & Brown, K. (2000). The elderly rape victim: Stereotypes, perpetrators, and implications for practice. *Journal of Emergency Nursing, 26*(5), 516–518.

Burgess, A., Dowdell, E., & Prentky, R. (2000). Sexual assault of nursing home residents. *Journal of Psychosocial Nursing, 38*(6), 10–18.

Burston, G. R. (1975). Granny battering. *British Medical Journal, 3,* 592.

Centers for Disease Control and Prevention. (2003). *Costs of intimate partner violence against women in the United States.* Atlanta, GA: National Center for Injury Prevention and Control.

Cohen, D. (1998). Homicide-suicide in older persons. *American Journal of Psychiatry, 155,* 390–396.

Cohen, D. (2000). An update on homicide-suicide in older persons: 1995–2000. *Journal of Mental Health and Aging, 6*(3), 195–197.

Cook-Daniels, L. (1999, May/June). Interpreting the National Elder Abuse Incidence Study. *Victimization of the Elderly and Disabled, 2*(1), 1–2, 14–15.

Deem, D. (2000). Notes from the field: Observations in working with the forgotten victims of personal financial crimes. *Journal of Elder Abuse & Neglect, 12*(2), 33–48.

De Pommereau, I. (2003). Florida fraud squads protect seniors from Medicare scams. *Christian Science Monitor, 90*(33), 3. Cited in Payne, B. K. (2005). *Crime and elder abuse: An integrated perspective.* Springfield, IL: Charles C. Thomas.

Dessin, D. L. (2000). Financial abuse of the elderly. *Idaho Law Review, 36,* 203–226.

Dong, X. (2005). Medical implications of elder abuse and neglect (M. J. Gorbien, Ed.). *Clinics in geriatric medicine, 21*(2), 293–313.

Dyer, C. B. (2006). Self-neglect can be hazardous to your health. Unpublished manuscript.

Dyer, C. B., Connolly, M. T., & McFeeley, P. (2003). The clinical and medical forensics of elder abuse and neglect. In R. J. Bonnie & R. B. Wallace (Eds.), *Elder mistreatment: Abuse neglect and exploitation in an aging America* (pp. 339–381). Washington, DC: National Academies Press.

Dyer, C. B., Heisler, C. J., Hill, C. A., & Kim, L. C. (2005). Community approaches to elder abuse. *Clinics in Geriatric Medicine, 21*(2), 429–447.

Fisher, B. S., & Regan, S. L. (2006). The extent and frequency of abuse in the lives of older women and their relationship with health outcomes. *Gerontologist, 46*(2), 200–209.

Flynn, E. E. (2000). Elders as perpetrators. In M. B. Rothman, B. D. Dunlop, & P. Entzel (Eds.), *Elders, crime, and the criminal justice system* (pp. 43–83). New York: Springer.

Freeland, K. (2002). DOVES program. In *Elder Abuse and Late Life Domestic Violence* (pp. 36–38). Maricopa Area Agency on Aging, Region One.

Fromm, S. (2001). *Total estimated cost of child abuse and neglect in the United States: Statistical evidence.* Report by Prevent Child Abuse America. Retrieved October 8, 2006, from www.member.preventchildabuse.org/site/DocServer/cost_analysis.pdf?docID=144

Goetting, A. (1992). Patterns of homicide among the elderly. *Violence and Victims, 7,* 203–215.

Gorbien, M. (2005). Preface. *Clinics in Geriatric Medicine, 21*(2), 279.

Gorbien, M. J., & Eisenstein, A. R. (2005). Elder abuse and neglect: An overview. *Clinics in Geriatric Medicine, 21*(2), 279–292.

Groth, A. N. (1979). *Men who rape: The psychology of the offender.* New York: Plenum Press.

Groth, A. N., Burgess, A. W., & Holmstrom, L. L. (1977). Rape: Power, anger, and sexuality. *American Journal of Psychiatry, 134*(11), 1239–1243.

Hafemeister, T. L. (2003). Financial abuse of the elderly in domestic settings. In R. J. Bonnie & R. B. Wallace (Eds.), Panel to Review Risk and Prevalence of Elder Abuse and Neglect, Committee on National Statistics and Committee on Law and Justice, Division of Behavioral and Social Sciences and Education National Research Council. *Elder mistreatment: Abuse, neglect, and exploitation in an aging America* (pp. 382–445). Washington, DC: National Academies Press.

Hawes, C. (2003). Elder abuse in residential long-term care settings: What is known and what information is needed? In R. J. Bonnie & R. B. Wallace (Eds.), Panel to Review Risk and Prevalence of Elder Abuse and Neglect, Committee on National Statistics and Committee on Law and Justice, Division of Behavioral and Social Sciences and Education National Research Council. *Elder mistreatment: Abuse, neglect, and exploitation in an aging America* (pp. 446–500). Washington, DC: National Academies Press.

Heisler, C. J. (1991). The role of the criminal justice system in elder abuse cases. *Journal of Elder Abuse & Neglect, 3*(1), 5–33.

Heisler, C. J. (2001a). Elder sexual assault. In California District Attorney's Association, *Investigation and prosecution of sexual assault* (Chap. 9). Sacramento, CA: California District Attorney's Association.

Heisler, C. J. (2001b, May 25). Panel on Elder Abuse and Neglect. Medical Forensic Roundtable discussion, Washington, DC.

Heisler, C. J., & Stiegel, L. A. (2002). Enhancing the justice system's response to elder abuse: Discussions and recommendations of the "improving prosecution" working group of the National Policy Summit on Elder Abuse. *Journal of Elder Abuse & Neglect, 14*(4), 31–54.

Holt, M. G. (1993). Elder sexual assault in Britain: Preliminary findings. *Journal of Elder Abuse & Neglect, 5*(2), 63–71.

Jasinski, J. L., & Dietz, T. (2003). Domestic violence and stalking among older adults: An assessment of risk markers. *Journal of Elder Abuse & Neglect, 15*(1), 3–18.

Johnson, K. D. (2004). *Financial crimes against the elderly.* Office of Community Oriented Policing Services, U.S. Department of Justice, Problem-Oriented Guides for Police Problem-Specific Guides Series, Guide No. 20. Retrieved October 9, 2006, from www.cops.usdoj.gov/mime/open.pdf?Item=963

Koenig, R. J., & DeGuerre, C. R. (2005, May). The legal and government response to domestic elder abuse. *Clinics in Geriatric Medicine, 21*(2), 383–398.

Lachs, M. (2000). Selected clinical and forensic issues in elder abuse. U.S. Department of Justice Elder Justice Roundtable Discussion, Washington DC.

Lachs, M. S., & Pillemer, K. (1995). "Abuse and Neglect of Elderly Persons. *The New England Journal of Medicine, 332*(7), 437–443.

Lachs, M. S., & Pillemer, K. A. (2004). Elder abuse. *Lancet, 364,* 1192–1263.

Lachs, M. S., Williams, C. S., O'Brien, S., Pillemer, K. A., & Charlson, M. E. (1998). The mortality of elder mistreatment. *Journal of the American Medical Association, 280,* 428–432.

Malphurs, J. E., & Cohen, D. (2001). A state-wide case control study of spousal homicide-suicide in older persons. *American Journal of Geriatric Psychiatry, 9*(1), 49–57.

Maricopa Area Agency on Aging & Maricopa Elder Abuse Prevention Alliance. (2002). *Elder abuse and late life domestic violence.* Phoenix, AZ: Author.

Maxwell, M. S., & O'Rourke, K. S. (1999). *Domestic violence in later life: A competency-based training manual for Meals on Wheels volunteers & other elder services staff.* Tallahassee: Florida State University, Rural Victimization Project, Institute for Family Violence Studies.

McClane, G. E., Strack, G. B., & Hawley, D. (2001). A review of 300 attempted strangulation cases: Part 2. Clinical evaluation of the surviving victim. *Journal of Emergency Medicine, 21*(3), 311–315.

Moon, A. (2000). Perceptions of elder abuse among various cultural groups: Similarities and differences. *Generations, 24*(2), 75–80.

Moon, A., & Williams, O. (1993). Perceptions of elder abuse and help-seeking patterns among African-American, Caucasian American, and Korean-American elderly women. *Gerontologist, 33*(3), 386–395.

Moskowitz, S. (1998). Saving Granny from the wolf: Elder abuse and neglect—The legal framework. *Connecticut Law Review, 31,* 77–201.

Moskowitz, S. (2001). Filial responsibility statutes: Legal and policy considerations. *Journal of Law and Policy, 9*(3), 709–736.

Mosqueda, L., Burnight, K., & Liao, S. (2005). The life cycle of bruises in older adults. *Journal of the American Geriatrics Society, 53,* 1339–1343.

Mouton, C. P., Rodabough, R. J., Rovi, S. L. D., Hunt, J. L., Talamantes, M. A., Brzyski, R. G., et al. (2004). Prevalence and a 3-year incidence of abuse among postmenopausal women. *American Journal of Public Health, 94,* 605–612.

Naimark, D. (2001). Financial exploitation of the elderly: The evaluation of mental capacity and undue influence. *American Journal of Forensic Psychiatry, 22*(3), 5–19.

National Association of Adult Protective Services Administrators (NAAPSA). (2001, May). Position paper on self-neglect.

National Center on Elder Abuse. (1998). *National elder abuse incidence study.* Washington, DC: Author. Retrieved October 8, 2006, from www.elderabusecenter.org/basic/

National Center on Elder Abuse. (2001). *The basics: What is elder abuse? What are the major types of elder abuse?* Retrieved February 15, 2006, from www.elderabusecenter.org/basic/

National Center on Elder Abuse. (2006). Laws related to elder abuse—State laws: Citations. Retrieved October 8, 2006, from www.elderabusecenter.org/pdf/publication/APS%20Statutes%20Citations.pdf

National Clearinghouse on Abuse in Later Life. (2003a). *Golden voices: Support groups for older abused women.* Madison, WI: Author.

National Clearinghouse on Abuse in Later Life. (2003b). *National domestic abuse in later life resource directory.* Madison, WI: Author.

Nerenberg, L. (2000). Forgotten victims of financial crime and abuse: Facing the challenge. *Journal of Elder Abuse ands Neglect, 12*(2), 49–73.

Nerenberg, L. (2003). *Multidisciplinary elder abuse prevention teams: A new generation.* Washington, DC: National Center on Elder Abuse.

Otto, J. (2000). *Detecting and diagnosing elder abuse and neglect (Forensic MARKERS).* Washington, DC: U.S. Department of Justice Elder Justice Roundtable Discussion.

People v. Heitzman, 9 Cal. 4th 189, 37 Cal. Rptr. 2d 236, 886 P. 2d 1229 (1994).

Pillemer, K. A., & Finkelhor, D. (1988). The prevalence of elder abuse: A random sample survey. *Gerontologist, 28*(1), 51–57.

Podnieks, E. (1992). National survey on abuse of the elderly in Canada. *Journal of Elder Abuse & Neglect, 4*(1/2), 5–58.

Quinn, M. J. (2001). Friendly persuasion, good salesmanship, or undue influence. *Elder Advisor,* 49–56.

Quinn, M. J., & Heisler, C. J. (2002). The legal response to elder abuse and neglect. *Journal of Elder Abuse & Neglect, 14*(1), 61–77.

Ramin, S. M., Satin, A. J., Stone, I. C., & Wendel, G. D. (1992). Sexual assault in post-menopausal women. *Obstetrics and Gynecology, 80*(5), 860–864.

Ramsey-Klawsnik, H. (1991). Elder sexual abuse: Preliminary findings. *Journal of Elder Abuse & Neglect 3*(3), 73–90.

Ramsey-Klawsnik, H. (1993). Questions and answers: Elder sexual abuse. *Illness, Crisis and Loss, 2*(4), 92–96.

Ramsey-Klawsnik, H. (2003). Sexual abuse within the family. *Journal of Elder Abuse & Neglect, 15*(1), 43–58.

Reed, K. (May, 2005). When elders lose their cents: Financial abuse of the elderly. *Clinics in Geriatric Medicine, 21*(2), 365–382.

Reinharz, S. (1986). Loving and hating one's elders: Twin themes in legend and literature. In K. A. Pillemer & R. S. Wolf (Eds.), *Elder abuse: Conflict in the family* (pp. 25–48). Dover, MA: Auburn House.

Rosoff, S. M., Pontell, H. N., & Tillman, R. (2003). *Profit without honor: White collar crime and the looting of America.* Upper Saddle River, NJ: Prentice Hall. Cited in Payne, B. K. (2005). *Crime and elder abuse: An integrated perspective.* Springfield, IL: Charles C. Thomas.

Safarik, M. E., Jarvis, J. P., & Nussbaum, K. E. (2002, May). Sexual homicide of elderly females. *Journal of Interpersonal Violence, 17*(5), 500–525.

Simpson, A. R. (2005). Cultural issues and elder mistreatment (M. J. Gorbien, Ed.). *Clinics in Geriatric Medicine, 21*(2), 355–364.

Singer, M. T. (1992). Undue influence and written documents: Psychological aspects. *Journal of Questioned Document Examination, 1*(1), 4–13.

Spencer, C. (1999). *Exploring the social and economic costs of abuse in later life.* Unpublished report.

Stiegel, L. (1995). *Recommended guidelines for state courts handling cases involving elder abuse.* Washington, DC: American Bar Association, Commission on Legal Problems of the Elderly.

Stiegel, L. A. (2000). The changing role of the courts in elder abuse cases. *Generations, 24*(2), 59–64.

Stiegel, L. (2005). *Promising practices in the development of elder abuse fatality review teams: A replication manual.* Washington, DC: American Bar Association.

Straka, S. M., & Montminy, L. (2006, March). Responding to the needs of older women experiencing domestic violence. *Violence Against Women, 12*(3), 251–267.

Teaster, P. B. (2003). *A response to the abuse of vulnerable adults: The 2000 survey of state adult protective services.* Washington, DC: National Center on Elder Abuse. Retrieved October 8, 2006, from www.elderabusecenter. org/pdf/research/apsreport030703.pdf

Teaster, P. B., Otto, J. M., Dugar, T. D., Mendiondo, M. S., Abner, E. L., & Cecil, K. A. (2006). *The 2004 survey of state adult protective services: Abuse of adults 60 years of age and older.* Report to the National Center on Elder Abuse, Administration on Aging, Washington, DC.

Thomas, R. W., & Heisler, C. J. (1999, Fall). Law enforcement and adult protective services: Critical collaboration in elder maltreatment. *Victim Advocate, 13*–15.

Tighe, T. (1994, January 30). Swindlers zero in on elderly. *St. Louis Post-Dispatch,* p. 1D. Cited in Payne, B. K. (2005). *Crime and elder abuse: An integrated perspective.* Springfield, IL: Charles C. Thomas.

Tjaden, P., & Thoennes, N. (2006, January). *Extent, nature, and consequences of rape victimization: Findings from the National Violence Against Women Survey.* Retrieved February 2, 2006, from www.ojp.usdoj.gov/nij

Treuth, M. J. (2000). Exposing financial exploitation of impaired elderly persons. *American Journal of Geriatric Psychiatry, 8*(2), 104–111.

Turkat, I. D. (2003, January/February). *Psychological aspects of undue influence: Probate and property.* American Bar Association. Retrieved February 25, 2005, from www.elderabusecenter.org/enews/nceae news050228.cfm

United States House of Representatives, Select Subcommittee on Aging. (1981). *Elder abuse: An examination of a hidden problem.* 97th Congress, 1st Sess.

United States House of Representatives, Subcommittee on Health and Long-Term Care of the Select Subcommittee on Aging. (1990). *Elder abuse: A decade of shame and inaction: A report by the chairman of the Subcommittee on Health and Long-Term Care of the Select Subcommittee on Aging.* U.S. House of Representatives. 101st Congress, 2nd Sess.

Wolf, R. S. (2000, Summer). The nature and scope of elder abuse. *Generations, 29*(14), 6–12.

Wolf, R. S. (2003). Elder abuse and neglect: History and concepts. In R. J. Bonnie & R. B. Wallace (Eds.), *Elder mistreatment: Abuse neglect and exploitation in an aging America* (pp. 238–248). Washington, DC: National Academies Press.

11

The Mentally Ill as Victims of Crime

JESSICA SNOWDEN

ARTHUR J. LURIGIO

Few studies have been conducted on the mentally ill as victims of crime. Rather than viewing them as potential targets of crime, most researchers have studied persons with mental illness as perpetrators of violent crime or as a danger to themselves or others. The mentally ill often underreport their victimization experiences, and when they do report the incidents, they are often disbelieved. The handful of studies of the mentally ill as victims of crime, which we examine in this chapter, has demonstrated that individuals with mental illness are particularly vulnerable to victimization (Marley & Buila, 2001). Studies have shown that people with serious mental illness are at a substantial risk for criminal victimization. As stated in a recent report by the Consensus Project (2005), persons with mental illness are 24 times more likely to be victims of rape, 9 times more likely to be victims of any violent crime, and 7 times more likely to be victims of any crime, compared with individuals in the general population. These rates are alarmingly high and must be attended to more closely by researchers, policymakers, and advocates.

The need to study the criminal victimization of the mentally ill is critical for four basic reasons. First, as we noted earlier, studies indicate that persons with mental illness are victimized at very high rates and are substantially more likely to be victimized than individuals without mental illness (cf. Goodman et al., 2001; Marley & Buila, 1999, 2001). Second, individuals with mental illness are more likely to experience multiple or repeated victimizations, which renders them more susceptible to trauma and other painful reactions (Marley & Buila, 2001). Third, crime victims with mental illness have to cope not only with the symptoms of their disease but also with the emotional and physical consequences of victimization and the fear of future victimization; this fear can limit their participation in social interactions and psychiatric programs. Fourth, research on the victimization of the mentally ill can help identify specific risk factors for victimization, which can improve the assessment, monitoring, and treatment of crime victims with mental illness (Goodman et al., 2001).

This chapter presents an overview of crime victims with mental illness and is divided into four major sections. The first section reviews research on the criminal victimization of the mentally ill. Although not exhaustive, the review includes a wide range of studies, including samples of persons staying in hospitals, group homes, and the community. In this chapter, the term *mental illness* refers to serious, persistent, and life-altering brain diseases, such as major depression, schizophrenia, and bipolar disorder.

All studies cited here have found that the rates of criminal victimization among the mentally ill are higher than the rates in the general population. For illustrative purposes, we compare the victimization rates of the mentally ill with persons in the general population—but only for those few studies that actually have made such comparisons. We also draw on self-reported victimization data in the United States that estimate the prevalence of victimization (Catalano, 2003). We realize that such data can provide only a very crude statistical base rate and were collected in a time frame that differs from those of the reviewed studies; however, we cite the victimization data to set a context from which to understand the exceptionally high proportions of the mentally ill who are crime victims.

The second section focuses on the reporting of crime among mentally ill victims. We discuss the few studies that have explored the reliability of crime reporting within this population and the variables that can affect the likelihood and accuracy of such victimization reports. The third section describes the correlates of victimization and explores why persons with mental illness are vulnerable to

victimization and why some with mental illness are more likely to become crime victims than others. The fourth section reports the results of studies on the adverse impact of victimization on the mentally ill.

PREVALENCE OF VICTIMIZATION

In one of the earliest investigations of the prevalence of criminal victimization among the mentally ill, Lehman and Linn (1984) studied individuals who were discharged from a psychiatric hospital to a group home. They found that 33% reported being robbed or assaulted in the past year since their discharge. Specifically, 15% were robbed, 8% were victims of other violent crimes, and 10% were both robbed and assaulted.

In a study of psychiatric inpatients, Jacobson and Richardson (1987) found that 81% reported a history of physical or sexual assault. More than two thirds of these inpatients reported physical abuse as an adult, and 21% reported sexual abuse as an adult. In Jacobson and Richardson's (1987) sample, women with mental illness were found to be more likely than men to be victims of adult sexual abuse, and men with mental illness were more likely than women to be victims of nonsexual assault. Many of the psychiatric inpatients were victimized before being hospitalized, which suggests either that their recent victimization increased symptom severity or that symptom severity increased their risk for victimization.

In a study of outpatients and inpatients with mental illness, Jacobson (1989) found that 42% of outpatients and 63% of inpatients reported physical abuse as adults, and 32% of outpatients and 21% of inpatients reported sexual abuse as adults. A lower proportion of outpatients experienced physical assault as adults, and a higher proportion experienced sexual assault as children. Hence, sexual assault among persons with mental illness tended to occur in childhood, and physical assault tended to occur in adulthood. No men in the study reported being sexually assaulted as an adult. Given the results of other investigations, which show that the rate of sexual abuse among men with mental illness is also high, the men in this study were probably underreporting their sexual abuse experiences (e.g., Lam & Rosenheck, 1998).

Hiday, Swartz, Swanson, Borum, and Wagner (1999) found that 8% of individuals with mental illness had been victims of violent crimes in the past four months, which was more than twice the rate for the general population. In addition, 22% of individuals with mental illness reported being victims of nonviolent crimes, and 3% reported being victims of both violent and nonviolent crimes in the prior four months. The overall victimization rate of individuals with mental illness was 27% for the past four months, which was significantly higher than the rate of 2.3% for individuals without mental illness (Catalano, 2003).

Silver (2002) reported that psychiatric patients were victimized at more than two times the rate of individuals in the general population. Specifically, 15% of patients reported being a victim of violence during the previous ten weeks, compared with 7% of individuals in the general population. In another study of a community-based sample of individuals with mental illness, 38% reported being a victim of a crime during the previous three years; 91% of these individuals were victims of violent crimes. These victimization rates were 65% to 130% higher than those found in the general public (Brekke, Prindle, Woo Bae, & Long, 2001).

Women with mental illness are particularly vulnerable to criminal victimization, and homeless women with severe mental illness are even more so (Mowbrary, Oyserman, Saunders, & Rueda-Riedle, 1998). Homeless women with severe mental illness report high rates of sexual and physical abuse. In one study, nearly 90% of homeless women with severe mental illness reported being physically assaulted, and 76% reported being sexually assaulted as adults. With respect to the prevalence of recent victimizations, another study of the homeless mentally ill found that 20% reported physical assault, and 15% reported sexual assault in the prior month (Goodman, Johnson, Dutton, & Harris, 1997).

Lam and Rosenheck (1998) studied the recent victimization of homeless men and women with mental illness. They found that in the previous two months, 13% of the entire sample reported being a victim of robbery, 29% reported property theft, 18% reported hostile threats with a weapon, 16% reported physical assault, and 6% reported sexual assault. Lam and Rosenheck (1998) also found that mentally ill women were significantly more likely than mentally ill men overall to report being victimized. Moreover, women were more likely than men to be sexually assaulted and beaten with a fist, club, or heavy object. No differences were found among homeless men and women with mental illness in terms of prevalence rates of robbery, property theft, and threats with a weapon. Among a sample of homeless men in New York City, Padgett and Struening (1992) found that those with symptoms of psychosis were significantly more likely than those with no such symptoms to have been beaten, robbed, threatened with a weapon, or injured as the result of criminal victimization.

Goodman and colleagues (2001) studied the victimization of people with severe mental illness—the majority of whom were diagnosed with schizophrenia. In the past year, 22% of the women reported being sexually assaulted, and 26% reported being physically assaulted. These rates were significantly higher than those for women in the general population. In addition, 8% of men reported being sexually assaulted in the past year, and 34% reported being physically assaulted. Similar to those for women, these rates were significantly higher than for men in the general population, where only .1% reported sexual assault and only 3% reported physical assault in the past year (Catalano, 2003).

When the participants in the Goodman et al. study (2001) were asked about their victimization experiences in adulthood, 80% of both women and men reported some type of assault. Nearly 60% of the women and 25% of the men reported sexual assault. Approximately three fourths of the women and 79% of the men reported physical assault. The vast majority (87%) of men and women with mental illness reported being a victim of crime at some point in their lives. In their lifetimes, 68% of women reported being sexually assaulted and 82% reported being physically assaulted; among men, 40% reported being sexually assaulted and 86% reported being physically assaulted. Friedman and Harrison (1984) found that half the women in their study who had been hospitalized for schizophrenia reported that they had been raped one or more times as adults.

According to Marley and Buila (2001), among those individuals with severe mental illness in their study—most diagnosed with bipolar disorder or schizophrenia—28% of the women and 5% of the men reported being forced to engage in unwanted sexual activity. Women were significantly more likely to have been raped or threatened with rape, whereas men were significantly more likely to have been the victims of robbery or attempted robbery. In addition, 44% of the women and 30% of the men reported being coerced to give property away (Marley & Buila, 2001). These rates are much higher than those for individuals in the general population, for whom the rates of rape and property theft were .08% and 16%, respectively (Catalano, 2003).

The disproportionate criminal victimization of the mentally ill has been found in studies outside the United States. For example, Walsh and colleagues (2003) researched victimization among persons with mental illness in

England. Their study showed that 16% of patients reported a violent victimization in the past year. Similar to other investigations, Walsh and colleagues concluded that victimization rates are much higher for individuals with mental illness than for people in the general population. Using the Social Register as the source for their data, researchers in Denmark found that men with schizophrenia, similar to men with alcohol use disorders, were at significant risk of being murdered. The researchers speculated that the risk was attributable to where the mentally ill men lived (mostly in high-crime areas), their hostile and paranoid behaviors toward others, and their general lack of awareness of the dangers in their surrounding environment (Hiroeh, Appleby, Mortensen, & Dunn, 2001).

Although many of the subjects in the preceding studies were asked about the details of their victimization experiences, most provided no information about whether their victimization occurred before or after the onset of mental illness. In one of the few studies that examined the temporal ordering of the onset of mental illness and victimization, Jenkins, Bell, Taylor, and Walker (1989) found that in general women with mental illness who had been sexually assaulted reported that the crime occurred after the onset of their mental illness. Men also reported that physical and sexual assault occurred after the onset of their mental illness. A large majority of the persons in this sample reported being physically assaulted as an adult. These findings suggest that mental illness renders individuals more vulnerable to criminal victimization.

Marley and Buila (1999) identified the most common violent crimes experienced by women and men with mental illness. Among women, 17% reported being raped by a known perpetrator, 12% reported adult sexual abuse by a known perpetrator, 10% reported rape by an unknown perpetrator,

7% reported childhood sexual abuse by a known perpetrator, and 6% reported unwanted sexual activity. Among men, 15% reported sustaining injury from an aggravated assault, 13% were injured during a robbery, 11% were robbed without being injured, 9% were assaulted with a minor injury, and 9% reported childhood physical abuse by a known perpetrator.

Researchers have studied the perpetrators of crimes against individuals with mental illness. Among victims who were recently admitted as inpatients to a psychiatric hospital and who identified their perpetrators, 63% reported that their partners and 46% reported that their family members had physically assaulted them (Cascardi, Mueser, DeGirolomo, & Murrin, 1996). In the general population, 25% of women and 3% of men reported that their partners were the perpetrators of physical assault, and 2% of men and 10% of women reported that their family members were the perpetrators of physical assault (Catalano, 2003).

Among women with schizophrenia, 32% reported being raped by a friend and 5% reported being raped by a service provider. Of the 27% of women who reported adult sexual abuse, 27% identified the perpetrator as a police officer (Marley & Buila, 2001). Women with mental illness reported that strangers were responsible for 53% of their physical assaults and 57% of their sexual assaults, and their partners were responsible for committing nearly all of the remaining assaults of both types. In the general population, 32% of women reported that strangers accounted for physical assaults, and 30% accounted for sexual assaults, while partners accounted for 25% of physical and 12% of sexual assaults (Goodman et al., 1997). In short, studies indicate that individuals with mental illness are at greater risk than others for criminal victimization at the hands of strangers, family members, and intimate partners.

REPORTING OF VICTIMIZATION

The reports of victimization by the mentally ill are often considered unreliable. Goodman and colleagues (1999) conducted repeated interviews with individuals with severe mental illness to determine the consistency of victimization reports. When asked about the past year, 50% of individuals with severe mental illness reported being physically abused, 33% reported sexual coercion, and 33% reported being injured by someone else. The researchers found that the consistency of reports for abuse was high and that the reliability for men dropped only slightly with respect to incidents of sexual coercion (Goodman et al., 1999). The data suggest that reports by individuals with mental illness are generally reliable.

Even though research shows that individuals with mental illness are generally reliable, they are often disbelieved or discredited when they report being victimized (Mowbrary et al., 1998). Therefore it is somewhat surprising that 47% of women and 57% of men with mental illness reported their victimization to police (Marley & Buila, 1999). When asked about reporting victimization to the police, 60% of individuals in the general population reported robbery, 38% of victims reported rape, 59% reported assault, and 38% reported property crime (Catalano, 2003).

The relationship of the victim to the perpetrator of the crime can affect the willingness of victims to report the crime. Individuals with mental illness who were victimized by their family members, relatives, service providers, or police officers were less likely to report the crime to the police or anyone else. Women who knew the perpetrator were less likely to report the crime to the police, but were more likely to report the crime to others. Specifically, individuals with mental illness were more likely to report their victimization to family members, if they were married, lived in their own home or apartment, had a higher level of income, were diagnosed with bipolar disorder, had no history of substance abuse, or had fewer previous victimizations.

Some of the same factors associated with the reporting of violent crime were also related to the experiences of the victims. For individuals who reported their victimization, a positive response from the police was significantly more likely if the victims had higher levels of education, fewer previous victimizations, were married, lived in their own home, had higher incomes, were diagnosed with bipolar disorder, and had no substance use disorder. Those who lived in a group home, had a history of substance abuse, and were diagnosed with schizophrenia were more likely to have negative responses when reporting victimization, such as being disbelieved and further emotionally traumatized by police (Marley & Buila, 1999).

THE CORRELATES OF VICTIMIZATION

Why indeed are mentally ill persons more likely to be victimized? Understanding the factors associated with crimes against individuals with mental illness is critical to the development of prevention and intervention strategies to protect these individuals from victimization and its adverse consequences. Hiday and colleagues (1999) found that individuals with severe mental illness are "easy targets" of crime because of their cognitive and emotional deficits. They tend to be isolated and unemployed, live in unstable environments, and have problems with alcohol and drug use. The judgment of individuals with co-occurring substance use and mental illness is often highly impaired. Furthermore, individuals with mental illness can often misinterpret people's motives (Sells, Rowe, Fisk, & Davidson, 2003).

Homeless women with serious mental illness are especially vulnerable because of a dearth of emotional, material, and social resources (Goodman et al., 1997). Women with mental illness are highly susceptible to partners' attempts to control and intimidate them (Mowbrary et al., 1998). Researchers have found similar risk factors for men with severe mental illness. For both women and men, having access to more social support, developing a higher level of functioning, and experiencing fewer substance use problems lowered the risk for being victimized (Goodman et al., 2001).

Hiday, Swartz, Swanson, Borum, & Wagner (2002) studied individuals with mental illness ordered to outpatient commitment—at a 12-month follow-up—and compared these patients with those who were given no outpatient commitment order. Among the individuals with outpatient commitment orders, 51% reported no victimization, 33% reported being victimized at least once in the past year, and 27% reported criminal victimizations that had occurred more than one year previously. Of those who were victimized in the prior year, 10% were victims of violent crime, three times higher than the national rate of 3%, and 29% reported nonviolent victimization (Catalano, 2003). Persons who were ordered to outpatient commitment were two times less likely to be victimized than those who were released without outpatient commitment. In addition, the longer the individuals stayed in outpatient treatment, the lower their risk of victimization (Hiday et al., 2002). These findings suggest that treatment and other services might help decrease the rates of victimization among the mentally ill. According to Hiday et al.,

> Medication adherence can be expected to reduce symptoms of severe mental illness and thus reduce victimization. Psychotic symptoms and bizarre behavior can lead to tense and conflictual situations, which, in turn, may result in a patient's victimization—either because others become violent toward the patient or because the patient lashes out

physically and others react with stronger violence. By facilitating adherence and ensuring more consistent follow-up, outpatient commitment may lead to reduced symptoms, better functioning in social relationships, and improved judgment. In turn, these changes should lessen a person's vulnerability to abuse by others and lower the probability of becoming involved in dangerous situations where victimization is more likely. (2002, p. 1408)

Another factor that increases the risk for victimization among individuals with mental illness is a history of involvement with the law (Lam & Rosenheck, 1998; Lehman & Linn, 1984; Walsh et al., 2003). Only one study reported that previous violent behavior or arrests were unrelated to victimization among the mentally ill (Hiday et al., 2002). Silver (2002) found that recent violence toward others to be significantly related to victimization. Therefore, some individuals with mental illness who are victims of violence can also be perpetrators of violence.

Previous episodes of criminal victimization can predict future episodes of victimization. For example, Hiday and colleagues (2002) found that individuals who were victimized in the past were two times more likely to be victimized in the future. Similarly, Goodman and colleagues (2001) found that childhood physical and sexual abuse as well as recent assaults predicted future victimization. Thus studies show that individuals with mental illness who have already been victimized are at an even higher risk for future victimization.

Substance abuse is another factor that can increase the risk of victimization (Gearson, Bellack, & Brown, 2003; Goodman et al., 2001; Lam & Rosenheck, 1998; Marley & Buila, 2001; Sells et al., 2003; Silver, 2002; Walsh et al., 2003). Hiday and colleagues (2002) found that individuals with mental illness and substance use disorders are three times more likely to be victimized than individuals without co-occurring disorders.

Consequently, providing integrated treatment for such disorders can lessen or even prevent the risk of victimization (Silver, 2002). Although most studies have found that both drug and alcohol use increased the risk for victimization, Walsh and colleagues (2003) found that drug, but not alcohol, use increased the risk of victimization among persons with mental illness.

Mixed results have been found regarding the relationship between diagnosis and symptoms and the likelihood of criminal victimization. Both Goodman and colleagues (2001) and Walsh and colleagues (2003) found that the more severe and untreated the symptoms were, the greater the risk for criminal victimization. In addition, having a comorbid Axis I and personality disorder (Hiday et al., 2002; Walsh et al., 2003) or having symptoms of paranoia have been found to increase the risk for victimization (Hiday et al., 2002). A few studies have reported that a diagnosis of schizophrenia is related to a higher risk for victimization (Darvez-Bornoz, Lemperiere, Degiovanni, & Grillard, 1995; Gearson et al., 2003; Marley & Buila, 2001). However, Goodman and colleagues (2001) found no relationship between specific diagnosis and victimization. Similarly, Hiday and colleagues (1999) found no relationship between victimization and clinical variables such as primary diagnosis, global functioning, and hospital admissions.

The relationship between demographic variables and the risk for victimization is also unclear. Researchers generally agree that violent crimes occur more often among young, single people (Goodman et al., 2001; Hiday et al., 1999; Lehman & Linn, 1984; Silver, 2002; Walsh et al., 2003). Age at first psychiatric hospitalization, which is positively correlated with symptom severity, is negatively correlated with the risk for victimization (Goodman et al., 2001); in other words, the younger persons are at first admission, the more likely it will be for them to be victims of crime.

Researchers are unsure about how other demographic factors affect victimization risk among persons with mental illness. Specifically, Walsh and colleagues (2003) found that men were more likely to be victimized, whereas studies by Marley and Buila (2001) and Mowbrary and colleagues (1998) found that women were at higher risk. Both Silver (2002) and Hiday and colleagues (1999) found African Americans to be at a greater risk for victimization; however, Goodman and colleagues (1997, 2001) found no relationship between race and risk. Similarly, Hiday and colleagues (1999) found no relationship between demographic characteristics and victimization risk. Future research is needed to elucidate the relationship between demographic variables and victimization among the mentally ill.

The social network of individuals with mental illness can affect their likelihood of victimization. Individuals who are victimized tend to have less contact with their families (Lehman & Linn, 1984; Walsh et al., 2003). Conflicts in interpersonal relationships are another significant predictor of victimization, and individuals with mental illness are more likely to have turbulent social relationships (Silver, 2002). Helping individuals with mental illness form supportive, healthy relationships might reduce their chances of victimization.

As we discussed earlier, homelessness has been found to be a significant predictor of victimization (Goodman et al., 2001; Hiday et al., 1999, 2002). Individuals who are homeless and also have mental illness are two times more likely to be victims of nonviolent crimes and more than three times more likely to be victims of violent crimes (Hiday et al., 1999). Sells and colleagues (2003) proposed two hypotheses to explain why homeless individuals with mental illness are at an increased risk. First, homelessness is related to lower levels of functioning and greater exposure to dangerous situations. (Conversely, the person might have been victimized by a member of the household, which led to the homelessness.) Second, substance abuse increases the risk for victimization, and many homeless shelters require individuals to be substance free. Therefore, homeless individuals with mental illness and substance use problems are especially vulnerable to victimization.

THE ADVERSE IMPACT OF VICTIMIZATION

In addition to estimating victimization rates among the mentally ill, Walsh and colleagues (2003) gathered information about perceived levels of safety. Of individuals who had been victimized, 40% were concerned about their personal safety, and 44% were concerned about the safety of their neighborhoods. Crime victims who were mentally ill were more likely to report fear about their personal and neighborhood safety, compared with both nonvictims and those individuals without mental illness.

Marley and Buila (2001) studied the crimes that women and men with mental illness viewed as most traumatic. The most traumatic crimes reported by women with mental illness were rape by a known perpetrator (experienced by 17% of the sample), adult sexual abuse by a known perpetrator (12%), rape by an unknown perpetrator (10%), childhood sexual abuse by a known perpetrator (7%), and unwanted sexual activity (6%). For men, the most traumatic crimes were aggravated assault with injury (15%), robbery with injury (13%), robbery without injury (11percent), simple assault with minor injury (9%), and childhood physical abuse by a known perpetrator (9%). Women were more likely than men to report that their most traumatic crime occurred more than once. An understanding of how individuals with mental illness view their criminal victimization experiences can further explicate the impact of crime on their lives.

Mentally ill crime victims report higher levels of depression and anxiety, lower levels of self-control, and higher overall psychopathology (Lehman & Linn, 1984). The sequelae of victimization must be considered when formulating treatment plans for these victims. Individuals with mental illness who have been victimized are more likely to be in outpatient treatment; however, the relationship between treatment and victimization is unclear. Are these individuals being seen because their psychopathology is more severe, or are they being treated because of the victimization (Hiday et al., 2002)?

Marley and Buila (2001) suggested that individuals with mental illness already have feelings of isolation. Being victimized leads to more isolation and loneliness, conditions that further diminish an individual's functioning. In addition, people with mental illness who were violently victimized were significantly more likely to meet the criteria for a comorbid personality disorder and to report severe psychopathology, homelessness, substance misuse, and previous violent victimizations (Walsh et al., 2003). In another study, 33% of male and 41% of female crime victims met the criteria for post-traumatic stress disorder in addition to their primary psychiatric diagnosis (Goodman et al., 1999).

Different types of victimization have different effects on crime victims with mental illness. For example, mentally ill victims of violent crime reported significantly lower levels of satisfaction with their lives than did victims of theft, and victims of theft were less satisfied with their lives than were nonvictims (Lehman & Linn, 1984). These findings indicate that individuals with mental illness who are victimized, especially those who are violently victimized, experience a diminution in their quality of life.

The frequency of victimization also plays a role in the effects of crime on the mentally ill. Women with mental illness who reported frequent abuse also reported more symptoms than did women who reported less frequent abuse. In addition, the recency of abuse has an effect on the well-being of victims. Individuals who had experienced sexual or physical abuse in the past month reported higher levels of anxiety, depression, hostility, somatization, post-traumatic stress disorder, and dissociation than did individuals who had not been recently victimized (Goodman et al., 1997). In summary, the frequency, timing, and type of victimization are all related to the effects of criminal victimization on the mentally ill.

LIMITATIONS OF RESEARCH

Research on the victimization of individuals with mental illness has limitations. As we noted earlier in the chapter, many studies examine lifetime victimization, a factor that makes it difficult to determine when the onset of the mental illness actually occurred relative to the victimization. In other words, is mental illness causing victimization, or is victimization causing mental illness, or both? Did the victimization precede or follow the mental illness (Mowbrary et al., 1998)? Reports of victimization in research and references to victimization in patient charts are quite disparate. Only 9% of instances of previous victimization were discovered in patients' treatment records; conversely, 90% of physical assaults were not discovered during treatment (Jacobson, Koehler, & Jones-Brown, 1987). Professionals who work with the mentally ill should be continually aware of the high rates of victimization in this population.

Researchers are only just beginning to study the victimization of the mentally ill. Of the studies reviewed in this chapter, prevalence rates for victimization varied between 15% and 35% for recent occurrences and up to 80% for lifetime occurrences. These data indicate that individuals with mental illness are victimized at high rates. Most of this research has focused on the prevalence of victimization. Studies of risk and protective factors for victimization are critical to the development of prevention and intervention programs. Similarly, increasing the knowledge of service providers regarding victimization can also serve to increase treatment options for mentally ill victims of crime. Simply put, more research is needed to help improve the safety and quality of life for these afflicted individuals.

REFERENCES

Brekke, J. S., Prindle, C., Woo Bae, S., & Long, J. D. (2001). Risk for individuals with schizophrenia who are living in the community. *Psychiatric Services, 52,* 1358–1366.

Cascardi, M., Mueser, K., DeGirolomo, J., & Murrin, M. (1996). Physical aggression against psychiatric inpatients by family members and partners: A descriptive study. *Psychiatric Services, 47,* 531–533.

Catalano, S. (2003). *National Crime Victimization Survey.* Washington, DC: U.S. Department of Justice, Bureau of Justice Statistics. Retrieved May 15, 2006, from www.ojp.usdoj.gov/bjc/cvictgen.htm

Consensus Project. (2005). *Fact sheet: Criminal victimization of people with mental illness.* Retrieved May 15, 2006, from www.consensusproject.org

Darvez-Bornoz, J. M., Lemperiere, T., Degiovanni, A., & Grillard, P. (1995). Sexual victimization in women with schizophrenia and bipolar disorder. *Social Psychiatry and Psychiatric Epidemiology, 30,* 78–84.

Friedman, S., & Harrison, G. (1984). Sexual histories, attitudes, and behavior of schizophrenic and "normal" women. *Archives of Sexual Behavior, 13,* 555–567.

Gearson, J. S., Bellack, A. S., & Brown, C. H. (2003). Sexual and physical abuse in women with schizophrenia: Prevalence and risk factors. *Schizophrenia Research, 60,* 38–42.

Goodman, L., Johnson, M., Dutton, M., & Harris, M. (1997). Prevalence and impact of sexual and physical abuse in women with severe mental illness. In M. Harris & C. Landis (Eds.), *Sexual abuse in the lives of women diagnosed with serious mental illness: New directions in therapeutic interventions* (Vol. 2, pp. 277–299). Amsterdam, Netherlands: Harwood Academic.

Goodman, L., Salyers, M., Mueser, K., Rosenberg, S. D., Swartz, M., Essock, S., et al. (2001). Recent victimization in women and men with severe mental illness: Prevalence and correlates. *Journal of Traumatic Stress, 14,* 615–632.

Goodman, L., Thompson, K., Weinfurt, K., Corl, S., Acker, P., Mueser, K., et al. (1999). Reliability of reports of violent victimization and posttraumatic stress disorder among men and women with serious mental illness. *Journal of Traumatic Stress, 12,* 587–599.

Hiday, V. A., Swartz, M. S., Swanson, J. W., Borum, R., & Wagner, H. R. (1999). Criminal victimization of person with severe mental illness. *Psychiatric Services, 50,* 62–68.

Hiday, V. A., Swartz, M. S., Swanson, J. W., Borum, R., Wagner, H. R. (2002). Impact of outpatient commitment on victimization of people with severe mental illness. *American Journal of Psychiatry, 15,* 1403–1411.

Hiroeh, U., Appleby, L., Mortensen, P. B., & Dunn, G. (2001). Death by homicide, suicide, and other unnatural causes in people with mental illness: A population-based study. *Lancet, 358,* 2110–2112.

Jacobson, A. (1989). Physical and sexual assault histories among psychiatric outpatients. *American Journal of Psychiatry, 146,* 755–758.

Jacobson, A., Koehler, J., & Jones-Brown, C. (1987). The failure of routine assessment to detect histories of assault experiences by psychiatric patients. *Hospital and Community Psychiatry, 38,* 386–389.

Jacobson, A., & Richardson, B. (1987). Assault experiences of 100 psychiatric inpatients: Evidence for the need for routine inquiry. *American Journal of Psychiatry, 144,* 908–913.

Jenkins, E., Bell, C., Taylor, J., & Walker, L. (1989). Circumstances of sexual and physical victimization of black psychiatric outpatients. *Journal of the National Medical Association, 81,* 246–252.

Lam, J., & Rosenheck, R. (1998). The effect of victimization on clinical outcomes of homeless persons with serious mental illness. *Psychiatric Services, 49,* 678–683.

Lehman, A., & Linn, L. (1984). Crimes against discharged mental patients in board-and-care homes. *American Journal of Psychiatry, 141,* 271–274.

Marley, J., & Buila, S. (1999). When violence happens to people with mental illness: Disclosing victimization. *American Journal of Orthopsychiatry, 69,* 398–402.

Marley, J., & Buila, S. (2001). Crimes against people with mental illness: Types, perpetrators, and influencing factors. *Social Work, 46,* 115–124.

Mowbrary, C., Oyserman, D., Saunders, D., & Rueda-Riedle, A. (1998). Women with severe mental disorders: Issues and service needs. In B. Levin & A. Blanch (Eds.), *Women's mental health services: A public health perspective* (pp. 175–200). Thousand Oaks, CA: Sage Publications.

Padgett, D. K., & Struening, E. L. (1992). Victimization and traumatic injuries among the homeless: Associations with alcohol, drug, and mental problems. *American Journal of Orthopsychiatry, 62,* 525–534.

Sells, D. J., Rowe, M., Fisk, D., & Davidson, L. (2003). Violent victimization of person with co-occurring psychiatric and substance use disorders. *Psychiatric Services, 54,* 1253–1257.

Silver, E. (2002). Mental disorder and violent victimization: The mediating role of involvement in conflicted social relationships. *Criminology, 40,* 191–211.

Walsh, E., Moran, P., Scott, C., McKenzie, K., Burns, T., Creed, F., et al. (2003). Prevalence of violent victimization in severe mental illness. *British Journal of Psychiatry, 183,* 233–238.

12

Gender-Based Violence in Schools

NAN STEIN

Being harassed makes me angry and I feel degraded. I'm always on my guard trying to prevent what may happen next. (13-year-old African American girl, from Texas, as quoted in Stein, Marshall, & Tropp, 1993, p. 22)

I grow angry, sad and I had wanted to get back at him. . . . I was very speechless and quiet for sometime. I felt like crying but I kept it inside and I didn't say anything to anyone. (12-year-old Chinese American girl, New York City, as quoted in Stein, Marshall, & Tropp, 1993, p. 23)

My place was in the art room. For my next class after art, I had to go up to the third floor to English, past the landing where the rednecks hung out. They tripped me. I never did anything to them. It was always, "faggot," "queer." I got pushed down the flight of stairs. . . . It got so I didn't go to the locker room or the bathroom. I stopped using my locker. My lock started disappearing and reappearing on other people's lockers. (Matt P., New Hampshire, as quoted in Human Rights Watch, 2001)

NOTE: The author has previously addressed the issues discussed in this chapter in "Bullying and Harassment in a Post-Columbine World," in Kathy Kendall-Tackett & Sarah Giacomoni (Eds.), *Child Victimization,* Civic Research Institute (2005); in "A Rising Pandemic of Sexual Violence in Elementary and Secondary Schools: Locating a Secret Problem," in *Duke Journal of Gender Law & Policy,* 12 (2005, Spring): 33–52; and in "Bullying, Harassment and Violence Among Students," in Barbara Bank (Ed.), *Gender and Education: An Encyclopedia* (in press).

Student-to-student gender-based harassment and violence have become common and normalized behaviors in our nation's schools, sometimes performed in public seemingly with impunity. Students report behavior perpetrated by their peers, during the school day on school grounds, that sometimes rises to the magnitude of criminal assault or grounds for a Title IX lawsuit in federal civil court against the school district (Stein, 1981, 1992, 1995, 1999, 2005b).

DEFINITION AND LAWS

Sexual harassment, a form of sex discrimination made illegal by the federal Civil Rights in Education Law Title IX passed by Congress in 1972, has been defined by the federal courts as unwanted and unwelcome behavior of a sexual nature that interferes with one's right to receive an equal educational opportunity (Federal Title IX, 1972). The behavior can range from spreading sexual rumors, writing/drawing graffiti, grabbing body parts, pulling at clothing (bra snapping, pulling down pants, skirt flipping) to sexual assault and rape. Some of these sexually harassing behaviors clearly are criminal, which places both the perpetrator as well as the school district into the realm of liability—the alleged perpetrator might be charged under criminal law while the school district could be sued under federal civil rights law as failing to provide an educational environment that provides equal educational opportunity (U.S. Department of Education, 1997).

Yet, despite legal decisions for more than two decades from the federal courts, including the U.S. Supreme Court (*Davis v. Monroe*, 1999), notwithstanding the fact that national scientific surveys repeatedly have shown that students face a daily onslaught of sexual/gender harassment that interferes with their rights to receive an equal educational opportunity (AAUW, 1993, 2001; Harris Interactive & GLSEN, 2005; Human Rights Watch, 2001) and irrespective of laws at both the federal and state levels that require attention and compliance from school officials, our nation's schools are riddled with examples of conduct that qualifies as gender-based harassment or violence.

The Davis case, which involved a fifth-grade girl, LaShonda Davis, from Macon, Georgia, in the Monroe County School District, began in 1994 and lasted for nearly five years traveling through every level of the federal court system. LaShonda was repeatedly sexually harassed by a male classmate who is only known by his initials, G. F. He repeatedly attempted to touch LaShonda's breasts and genital area, rubbed against her in a sexual manner, constantly asked her for sex, and in one instance, put a doorstop in his pants to simulate an erection and then came at her in a sexually suggestive manner (Brake, 1999). LaShonda told him to stop and reported his conduct to her teachers, who failed to take any action, not even to move their seats, which were in close proximity to each other. Her parents also complained about the sexual harassment to teachers and principal alike. After four months of enduring this behavior and her grades falling, her parents found a suicide note, went to the police, and filed a criminal complaint against the boy and his family. He later pled guilty to sexual misconduct and his family moved away (Brake, 1999).

In addition, the Davis family initiated a Title IX federal civil rights lawsuit against the Monroe County School District. Represented by the National Women's Law Center, a feminist legal advocacy group in Washington, D.C., the case was argued in the U.S. Supreme Court and resulted in a 5-to-4 decision announced on May 24, 1999 (*Davis v. Monroe*). In the majority opinion written by Justice Sandra Day O'Connor, the Court ruled that schools are liable for student-to-student sexual harassment if they knew about the harassment but failed to take any action.

Lawsuits initiated by gay and lesbian students against their school districts have also garnered attention to the illegal sexual harassment they have endured at the hands of their peers (Pogash, 2004; Quinn, 2002; Walsh, 2003). In particular, the legal victories in federal courts in cases in California and Nevada have set new standards for ensuring a safe learning environment for students. In the case of six middle school students who sued the Morgan Hill Unified School District in Morgan Hill, California, for the harassment that they endured for years, the 9th Circuit Court of Appeals unanimously ruled that if a school district knows that antigay harassment is taking place, it must take meaningful steps to end it and to protect the students (*Flores v. Morgan Hill Unified School District,* 2003). The settlement requires that the school district implement comprehensive training programs for administrators, staff, and students (ACLU, 2006). In addition, in Washoe, Nevada, Derek Henkle won his case for suffering harassment during his years at three Reno, Nevada, high schools. His case resulted in a $451,000 settlement that requires the school district to implement training and explicit antiharassment protections for students (Quinn, 2002).

SURVEY RESEARCH ON PEER HARASSMENT

Survey research has continued to point out the tenacity of sexual harassment and gender-based violence in schools (AAUW, 1993, 2001; Stein, 1981; Stein et al., 1993). A national sample in 2001 of 2,064 students in Grades 8–11 found sexual harassment to be widespread in schools, with 83% of the girls and 79% of the boys indicating that they had ever been sexually harassed. For purposes of this survey, sexual harassment was defined as "unwanted and unwelcome sexual behavior that interferes with your life. Sexual harassment is not behaviors

that you like or want (for example wanted kissing, touching, or flirting)" (AAUW, 2001). Students were given 14 examples of harassment that ranged from sexual comments, jokes, gestures, or looks to touching, grabbing, or pinching you in a sexual way, or pulling your clothing off or down. Thirty percent of the girls and 24% of the boys reported that they were sexually harassed often. Nearly half of all students who experience sexual harassment felt very or somewhat upset afterward, pointing to the negative impact that sexual harassment has on the emotional and educational lives of students (AAUW, 2001). As compared to the 1993 American Association of University Women (AAUW) survey on sexual harassment among 8th to 11th graders, the results from 2001 showed an increase in both awareness about and incidents of sexual harassment, yet students in 2001 had come to accept sexual harassment as a fact of life in schools (AAUW, 2001, pp. 4, 32). The greatest change in the eight-year period was in students' awareness of their schools' policies and materials to address sexual harassment (AAUW, 2001, p. 15).

Educational personnel are also responsible for some of the sexual harassment, sometimes as perpetrators and other times as spectators (AAUW, 2001, p. 5). According to the 2001 AAUW survey, 38% of the students reported being sexually harassed by teachers and other school employees (AAUW, 2001). It is also the case that school personnel can turn away or ignore incidents of sexual harassment when it happens in front of them or when reports are brought to their attention (Stein, 1995, 1999; Stein et al., 1993).

Surveys of gay, lesbian, bisexual, and transgender (GLBT) students are equally alarming. In the 2001 Human Rights Watch study, interviews with 140 gay, lesbian, and bisexual students, along with 130 school and youth service personnel in seven states, showed daily human rights abuses of the students by their peers, and in some cases, by some of their teachers and administrators.

A larger survey in 2005 conducted online with 3,450 students aged 13 to 18 and with 1,011 secondary school teachers (Harris Interactive & GLSEN, 2005) revealed a school climate that includes verbal and physical harassment because of perceived or actual appearance, gender, sexual orientation, gender expressions, race/ethnicity, disability, or religion (Harris Interactive & GLSEN, 2005, p. 3). One third of teens report that students are harassed due to perceived or actual sexual orientation. Because of their sexual orientation, two thirds of GLBT students have been verbally harassed, 16% have been physically harassed, and 8% have been physically assaulted (Harris Interactive & GLSEN, 2005, p. 4). Results from educators showed that 53% of them acknowledged that bullying and harassment of students was a serious problem at their schools (Harris Interactive & GLSEN, 2005, p. 8). In this survey, the terms, *bullying, harassment*, and even *assault* were often used interchangeably and were never defined or distinguished.

SCHOOL VIOLENCE— SHOOTINGS ECLIPSE OTHER FORMS OF GENDER VIOLENCE

One month prior to the *Davis* decision in the U.S. Supreme Court, the nation was confronted by the horrors of school shootings, this time at Columbine High School, in Littleton, Colorado (April 1999), where 12 students were killed along with one teacher and the two shooters committed suicide. Within a short period of time, multiple reports appeared on the topic of "school violence," with many urging that school administrators take measures that would purportedly make schools safer than before by passing state laws on bullying, and/or suspending and expelling more and more students under the "one strike, you're out" rules of zero tolerance (National Research Council and Institute of Medicine, 2003; Vossekuil, Fein, Reddy, Borum, &

Modzeleski, 2002). What got lost in this surge of reports and frenzy to reduce school violence, while at the same time elevating a rather expansive notion of bullying in schools, is the role that gender plays in school safety and violence. This contributes to the disproportionate focus on the most extreme, rare forms of violence, while the more insidious threats to safety are largely ignored (Kimmel, 2001; Lesko, 2000; Perlstein, 1998; Stein, 1995, 1999; Stein, Tolman, Porche, & Spencer, 2002). In general, the school shootings were widely reported in a gender-neutral way, when in fact the majority of these tragedies were perpetrated by White middle-class boys who were upset about either a breakup or rejection by a girl (e.g., Jonesboro, Arkansas; Pearl, Mississippi) or who did not meet traditional expectations and norms of masculinity (e.g., Columbine, in Littleton, Colorado) and were thus persecuted by their peers (National Research Council and Institute of Medicine, 2003; Perlstein, 1998; Vossekuil et al., 2002).

The current framework of bullying degenders harassment and removes it from the discourse of rights by placing it into a more psychological, pathologizing realm. Antibullying laws largely do not hold school administrators liable in the same ways to resolve the problems that Title IX federal law requires, but instead put the onus on solving the problem on the victim. Within this framework, sometimes egregious behaviors are framed as bullying when in fact they may constitute illegal sexual or gender harassment or even criminal hazing or assault (Stein, 2003, 2005a, 2005b).

THE RESEARCH ARENA— HARASSMENT OR BULLYING?

In the United States the discourse around bullying is a relatively new phenomenon, in large part imported from the Europeans and the research conducted there since the 1970s (e.g., Ahmad & Smith, 1994; Olweus, 1993).

Prior to the emphasis on bullying as a new trend for U.S. educators and researchers, redress of injustices and wrongs were addressed through civil and constitutional rights (Whalen & Whalen, 1985). The discourse of bullying, however, may eclipse the rights discourse (Stein, 2003).

A typical example of the conflation of bullying and harassment can be found in the April 24, 2001, issue of the *Journal of the American Medical Association* (*JAMA;* Nansel et al., 2001). This study of nearly 16,000 6th to 10th graders from public and private schools came from a larger sample of those who had filled out a World Health Organization (WHO) instrument administered in 1998 in 30 countries. To be applicable, the original instrument had to use questions, definitions, and terms that would make sense in all of the 30 participating countries, from France to Indonesia. Thus behaviors that legally could be sexual harassment or assault in the United States were framed as bullying for purposes of this survey—for example, being hit, slapped, or pushed; spreading rumors; or making sexual comments.

In the United States, the results showed that nearly 30% of the sample reported moderate or frequent involvement in bullying, either as the bully (13%), one who was bullied (10.6%), or both (6.3%). Males were more likely than females to be both perpetrators and targets of bullying.

The term *sexual harassment* was never raised—not by the researchers or in the accompanying article in *JAMA* written by public health researchers Drs. Spivak and Prothrow-Stith (2001). These sixth through tenth graders were asked to identify behavior as bullying without acknowledging the realities of sexual or racial harassment, behaviors that in fact may be criminal conduct or could be covered by sexual harassment or other civil rights in education laws.

Research into bullying that takes a socioecological approach may offer the most honest assessment of the continuum of bullying behaviors from childhood through adolescence, rather than looking solely at the most egregious forms of bullying. The socioecological approach explores how bullying is associated with individual, familial, and environment factors. Espelage and colleagues (Bosworth, Espelage, & Simon, 1999; Espelage, Bosworth, & Simon, 2000; Espelage & Holt, 2001; Espelage, Mebane, & Adams, 2004; Holt & Espelage, 2005; Mayberry & Espelage, in press) have successfully raised awareness about the importance of studying low-level aggression such as bullying, have challenged widely held beliefs about how to define and categorize adolescents as bullies, and have identified areas of prevention and intervention based on strong empirical support.

Interestingly, the effectiveness of bullying training has been challenged by results from a study on sexual coercion in Australia, which is part of a six-country study that found that antibullying policies are not effective in reducing or eliminating sexual harassment (Australia Broadcasting Corporation, 2004; K. Rigby, personal correspondence, September 4, 2004). In a study of approximately 200 14-year-old students who attended four schools in Adelaide, South Australia, that all had antibullying policies, a substantial minority said they would ignore sexual harassment if they saw it happening, and a smaller minority (boys) thought they would support the boy aggressor (Rigby & Johnson, 2004). Some 37% estimated that sexual harassment happened on a weekly basis at school with bystanders present, while somewhat higher estimates were obtained in some other countries in the study (Rigby & Johnson, 2004; K. Rigby, personal correspondence, September 4, 2004). Among the Australian students, 14% indicated that they would report it to a teacher (Rigby & Johnson, 2004).

In the absence of similar studies in the United States, this sobering data from Australia points to the ineffectiveness of antibullying policies in changing or challenging the culture of sexual harassment in schools.

The failure to consider the role of gender is endemic to much of the bullying research. Researchers of bullying, for the most part, have failed to consider the ways in which adolescent boys (and adult men) police each other with rigid and conventional notions of masculinity and the imposition of compulsive heterosexuality. Not to factor in or even recognize these potent elements is to deny a central and operating feature in boy culture, namely the maniacally driven, tireless efforts to define oneself as "not gay." Researchers such as Joe Pleck (1981), R. W. Connell (1987, 1995), Michael Kimmel (1987, 1996, 2001; Kimmel with Aronson, 2000), and Michael Messner (1990) have written about this phenomenon and its consequences for several decades, yet most bullying researchers have failed to draw upon their findings.

LOCATING VIOLENCE IN TEEN RELATIONSHIPS

Teen dating violence, a form of gendered violence, is a well-documented phenomenon. Results from two questions asked on the Youth Risk Behavior Survey (YRBS), a comprehensive survey about general behavior of teens from the U.S. Department of Health and Human Services, the Centers for Disease Control and Prevention, that ask about physical and sexual violence in teen dating relationships unfortunately provides troubling data about the creeping normality of teen dating violence (Centers for Disease Control and Prevention, 1992–2000). The first question is "During the last 12 months, did your boyfriend or girlfriend ever hit, slap or physically hurt you on purpose?" and the second question asks about forced sexual violence in a dating relationship: "Have you ever been physically forced to have sexual intercourse when you did not want to?"

Data from both versions of the YRBS (the state-by-state versions, and the national version, with its sample of 13,000 students

between the ages of 14 and 18 years old) have revealed that in some states up to 20% of girls experience violence from a dating partner—some of that as physical violence and some as sexual violence (Silverman, Raj, Mucci, & Hathaway, 2001). A recent analysis of the national 2001 data from 6,864 female students in Grades 9 through 12 found that 9.8% of all girls reported being intentionally physically hurt by a date in the previous year, and 17.7% of sexually active girls reported the same abuse (Silverman, Raj, & Clements, 2004). By 2003, the results for the United States overall showed that 11.9% of females experienced forced sexual intercourse, compared to 6.1% of males (Silverman et al., 2004).

Analyses from two states illustrate the rise in teen dating violence. In Massachusetts, teenage girls experience a more violent reality than their counterparts in other parts of the United States. In the 1999 survey, up to 18% of females reported experiencing either physical violence or sexual violence (Silverman et al., 2001). In Idaho, a more socially and religiously conservative state than Massachusetts, the report shows a safer picture, but 10% of students still reported physical violence from a dating partner in 2001 (7.6% females, 11.8% boys; Centers for Disease Control and Prevention, 1992–2000). The 2001 responses from Idaho also showed that 7.8% of students reported being forced to have sexual intercourse (10.5% females, and 5.2% males). Data from the 2003 survey, however, shows a rise in dating violence, even in Idaho, where one in nine students have been physically hit by a dating partner (12.1% of the females and 10.4% of the males), while one in seven has experienced sexual violence (14% of the females and 6% of the male students report that they have been physically forced to have sexual intercourse).

However, prevalence data on sexual violence in elementary and middle schools have not been consistently collected, disaggregated, or reported. Researchers lack a complete picture about the violence that children younger than 12 years old experience, whether that violence happens at home, in the streets, in public spaces, or at school. This lack of information may lie largely with the resistance of the parents who will not permit researchers to ask these sorts of questions to children younger than 12 years old.

CONCLUSION

In an era when school administrators are afraid of being sued for civil rights/harassment violations, as a consequence of the May 1999 decision of the Supreme Court in the *Davis* case, naming the illegal behaviors as "bullying" serves to deflect the school's legal responsibility for the creation of a safe and equitable learning environment onto an individual or group of individuals as the culprit(s) liable for the illegal conduct.

Yet school administrators have been quick to embrace the antibullying movement and to abandon the antiharassment focus. If behaviors are labeled "bullying," administrators and their school districts hope to escape being sued in federal court because there are no federal laws encompassing bullying, as it is not tied to civil rights. Conversely, harassment and discrimination based on race, disability, gender/sex, religion, or national origin are civil rights violations, and rigorous standards of proof must be met. Subsuming serious violations under the bullying umbrella means that schools avoid the liability they would face if sued successfully in federal court for a civil rights violation. It may also mean that students who have been bullied lose their rights to redress if they cannot get their grievances heard in federal court.

Think back to the *Davis* case that was discussed earlier in this chapter. It is very unlikely that if the behaviors that LaShonda had been subjected to were identified as bullying that her complaint would have ever been heard in a federal court, let alone in the U.S. Supreme Court. As it was, the conduct that was inflicted upon her, both the behavior by the male classmate and the treatment that she received from the school personnel, were framed as civil rights violations. To have viewed this conduct as bullying would have relegated her case to the principal's office, a place where she had not received justice or redress prior to filing a federal lawsuit or a criminal complaint.

This chapter has covered the realms of research, legal rights, state and federal laws, and shifting paradigms. Laws and policies don't happen in a vacuum—they are passed, implemented, ignored, transformed, challenged, used, misinterpreted, and reinterpreted—and not necessarily in that order. Laws and policies aren't static; they are used and lived by people. The existence and saliency of gender-based violence seems to be one for which acknowledgment is often lacking despite the rising problem of gender-based violence in our schools.

Further research into gender violence is needed in a variety of realms. First, we need to know the relationship between the victim and victimizer/harasser: Do they know each other? Were they once dating or romantically involved? Are they total strangers? Or are they somewhat familiar to each other as classmates? Having information on the sorts of relationships that exist between victim and victimizer/harasser will illuminate the sorts of interventions that might be created to prevent the gender violence before it starts or before it escalates.

In addition, we need to collect data from younger children; it is not sufficient to only collect information from high school students. As students date (i.e., affiliate) at younger and younger ages, we need to interrupt negative patterns that might develop, thus necessitating the acquisition of information at younger ages. Typically, it is not researchers who hesitate to collect this data, but rather it is the parents of these children who restrict researchers from having access to students. We need to alleviate the parental fears and collect this vital information on precursors to dating relationship.

Moreover, the right sorts of questions need to be asked on surveys, ones that get to the heart of the matter of sexual/gender violence in schools. We need to stay vigilant so that surveys do not cluster questions that merge acts of "physical" violence with incidents of "sexual" violence, but rather formulate discrete questions. To combine sexual/gender violence under the larger rubric of "physical violence" would render sexual/gender violence as invisible or as some minor category when compared to physical violence.

We also need longitudinal studies that gather the right kind of statistical information as well as qualitative information that can only be collected by focus groups, individual interviews, and a variety of ethnographic methods. Such deep research projects require a lot of ongoing financial support.

Furthermore, we need research that looks at the effectiveness of a variety of interventions. Before claims can be made about the efficacy of various curricular approaches or even systemic interventions, nonbiased, full-scale evaluations must be done by outside researchers rather than by those who developed or have a stake in the particular intervention or curriculum. Moreover, the results of such evaluations need to be published in peer-reviewed journals so that other scholars and researchers may look over the findings, the methods, and the implications. It's not enough for the evaluation to reside in a drawer or to stay isolated—it needs to be put into the light of day, into the scrutiny of others.

Finally, we need to remember that the whole point of conducting surveys, acquiring data, and doing evaluations is to put these sources of information into action—to create new school policies and/or new social/public policies. The point is to create a whole society, from the schools to the streets and public places, and from the home to the workplace, that is safe, just, and fair.

REFERENCES

Ahmad, Y., & Smith, P. K. (1994). Bullying in schools and the issue of sex differences. In J. Archer (Ed.), *Male VIOLENCE* (pp. 70–83). New York: Routledge.

American Association of University Women Foundation. (1993). *Hostile hallways: The AAUW survey on sexual harassment in America's schools.* Washington, DC: Author.

American Association of University Women Foundation and Harris Interactive. (2001). *Hostile hallways II: Bullying, teasing and sexual harassment in school.* Washington, DC: Harris Interactive.

American Civil Liberties Union. (2006). "Case background: Flores v. Morgan Hill Unified School District." Retrieved June 2, 2006, from www.aclu.org/lgbt/youth11947

Australian Broadcasting Corporation Online. (2004, June 18). Anti-bullying policies failing to cut school harassment. Retrieved September 2, 2004, from www.abc.net.au/pm/content/2004/s1135441.htm

Bosworth, K., Espelage, D. L., & Simon, T. (1999). Factors associated with bullying behavior in middle school students. *Journal of Early Adolescence, 19,* 341–362.

Brake, D. (1999).The cruelest of the gender police: Student-to-student sexual harassment and anti-gay peer harassment under Title IX. *Georgetown Journal of Gender and Law, 1,* 37, 39–40.

Centers for Disease Control and Prevention. (1992–2002). *Youth risk behavior surveillance: United States, 1991–2001.* CDC Surveillance Summaries. U.S. Department of Health and Human Services. Atlanta, GA: Centers for Disease Control. Retrieved June 2, 2006, from www.cdc.gov/HealthyYouth/yrbs

Connell, R. W. (1987). *Gender and power: Society, the person and sexual politics.* Cambridge, UK: Polity Press.

Connell, R. W. (1995). *Masculinities*. Berkeley: University of California Press.

Davis v. Monroe County Bd. of Education, 526 U.S. 629 (1999).

Espelage, D. L., Bosworth, K., & Simon, T. (2000). Examining the social environment of middle school students who bully. *Journal of Counseling and Development, 78*, 326–333.

Espelage, D. L., & Holt, M. (2001). Bullying and victimization during early adolescence: Peer influences and psychosocial correlates. *Journal of Emotional Abuse, 2*, 123–142.

Espelage, D. L., Mebane, S., & Adams, R. (2004). Empathy, caring, and bullying: Toward an understanding of complex associations. In D. L. Espelage & S. M. Swearer (Eds.), *Bullying in American schools: A social ecological perspective on prevention and intervention* (pp. 37–61). Mahwah, NJ: Lawrence Erlbaum Associates.

Flores v. Morgan Hill Unified School District, 324 F. 3rd, 1130 (9th Cir. 2003).

Harris Interactive & GLSEN. (2005). *From teasing to torment: School climate in America, A survey of students and teachers*. New York: GLSEN.

Holt, M. K., & Espelage, D. L. (2005). Social support as a moderator between dating violence victimization and depression/anxiety among African-American and Caucasian adolescents. *School Psychology Review, 34*(3), 309–328.

Human Rights Watch. (2001, June). *Hatred in the hallways: Violence and discrimination against lesbian, gay, bisexual, and transgender students in US Schools*. New York: Human Rights Watch.

Kimmel, M. (1987). *Changing men: New directions in research on men and masculinity*. Newbury Park, CA: Sage Publications.

Kimmel, M. (1996). *Manhood in America: A cultural history*. New York: Free Press.

Kimmel, M. (2001, March 8). Snips and snails . . . and violent urges. *Newsday*, pp. A41, A44.

Kimmel, M., with Aronson, A. (2000). *The gendered society reader*. New York: Oxford University Press.

Lesko, N. (2000). *Masculinities at school*. Thousand Oaks, CA: Sage Publications.

Mayberry, M., & Espelage, D. L. (in press). Associations among empathy, social competence, and subtypes of aggression in early adolescents. *Journal of Youth and Adolescence*.

Messner, M. A. (1990). Boyhood, organized sports and the construction of masculinities. *Journal of Contemporary Ethnography, 18*(4), 416–444.

Nansel, T. R., Overpeck, M., Pilla, R. S., Ruan, W. J., Simons-Morton, B., & Scheidt, P. (2001). Bullying behavior among US youth: Prevalence and association with psychosocial adjustment. *JAMA, 285*(16), 2094–2100.

National Research Council and Institute of Medicine. (2003). *Deadly lessons: Understanding lethal school violence*. Washington, DC: National Academy Press.

Olweus, D. (1993). *Bullying at school*. Cambridge, MA: Blackwell.

Perlstein, D. (1998). Saying the unsaid: Girl killing and the curriculum. *Journal of Curriculum and Supervision, 14*(1), 88–104.

Pleck, J. (1981). *The myth of masculinity*. Cambridge, MA: MIT Press.

Pogash, C. (2004, January 7). California school district settles harassment suit by gay students. *New York Times*, p. A17.

Quinn, A. (2002, August 29). Nevada school district to pay student in gay-bashing case. *Boston Globe*, p. A4.

Rigby, K., & Johnson, B. (2004). Students as bystanders to sexual coercion. *Youth Studies Australia, 23*(2), 11.

Silverman, J. G., Raj, A., & Clements, K. (2004). Dating violence and associated sexual risk and pregnancy among adolescent girls in the United States. *Pediatrics, 114*(2), 220–225.

Silverman, J. G., Raj, A., Mucci, L. A., & Hathaway, J. E. (2001). Dating violence against adolescent girls and associated substance use, unhealthy weight control, sexual risk behavior, pregnancy, and suicidality. *JAMA, 286*(5), 572–579.

Spivak, H., & Prothrow-Stith, D. (2001). The need to address bullying: An important component of violence prevention. *JAMA, 285*(16), 2131–2132.

Stein, N. (1981). *Sexual harassment of high school students: Preliminary research results*. Boston: MA: Massachusetts Department of Education, unpublished manuscript.

Stein, N. (1992). *Secrets in public: Sexual harassment in public (and private) schools*. (Working

Paper No. 256). Wellesley, MA: Wellesley College Center for Research on Women.

Stein, N. (1995). Sexual harassment in K–12 schools: The public performance of gendered violence. *Harvard Educational Review, Special Issue: Violence and Youth, 65*(2), 145–162.

Stein, N. (1999). *Classrooms and courtrooms: Facing sexual harassment in K–12 schools.* New York: Teacher's College Press.

Stein, N. (2003). Bullying or harassment? The missing discourse of rights in an era of zero tolerance. *Arizona Law Review, 45*(3), 783–799.

Stein, N. 2005a. Bullying and harassment in a post-Columbine world. In K. Kendall-Tackett & S. Giacomoni (Eds.), *Child victimization* (pp. 16-1–16-16). Kingston, NJ: Civic Research Institute.

Stein, N. (2005b, Spring). A rising pandemic of sexual violence in elementary and secondary schools: Locating a secret problem. *Duke Journal of Gender Law and Policy, 12*, 33–52.

Stein, N., Marshall, N., & Tropp, L. (1993). *Secrets in public: Sexual harassment in our schools. A report on the results of a Seventeen magazine survey.* Wellesley, MA: Wellesley College Center for Research on Women.

Stein, N., Tolman, D., Porche, M., & Spencer, R. (2002). Gender safety: A new concept for safer and more equitable schools. *Journal of School Safety, 1*(2), 35–50.

Title IX of the Education Amendments of 1972, 20 U.S. C. § 1681, § 1687 (1972).

U.S. Department of Education, Office for Civil Rights. (1997, March 13). *Sexual harassment guidance: Harassment of students by school employees, other students, or third parties.* Notice (62 Federal Register 12034–12051).

Vossekuil, B., Fein, R., Reddy, M., Borum, R., & Modzeleski, W. (2002). *Final report and findings of the Safe School Initiative: Implications for the prevention of school attacks in the United States.* U.S. Department of Education, Office of Elementary and Secondary Education, Safe and Drug-Free Schools Program and U.S. Secret Service, National Threat Assessment Center, Washington, DC.

Walsh, M. (2003, April 16). Administrators not immune in suit over alleged taunts. *Education Week, 22*(31), 4.

Whalen, C., & Whalen, B. (1985). *The longest debate: A legislative history of the 1964 Civil Rights Act.* Washington, DC: Seven Locks Press.

13

The Reoccurrence of Victimization

What Researchers Know About Its Terminology,
Characteristics, Causes, and Prevention

LEAH E. DAIGLE

BONNIE S. FISHER

PAMELA GUTHRIE

The reoccurrence of victimization against individuals, households, and businesses continues to attract scholarly pursuits. The accumulated work of these researchers prompted Skogan's observation that "the most important criminological insight of the decade has been the discovery in a very systematic fashion of repeat multiple victimization" (Brady, 1996, p. 3).

From a practical and policy perspective, reoccurring victimization is also appealing for several reasons. Skogan yet again noted, "Repetitive victimizations are important for policy purposes because they are predictable from past reported crime, they typically involve offenders who are immediately identifiable, intervention is possible, and they add disproportionately to the overall crime count" (1990, pp. 259–60). The criminal justice, criminology, and victimology communities are using what is known about reoccurring victimization to allocate crime control and prevention resources (Farrell & Pease, 2006; Weisel, 2005).

This chapter provides an overview of the theoretical developments and findings from the emergent field of the reoccurrence of victimization. In the first section, the two terms commonly used to describe reoccurring victimization—*repeat victimization* and *revictimization*—are distinguished from each other. A discussion of the extent of repeat property, personal, and sexual revictimization provides the background to the time course (amount of time between incidents) and crime-switch patterns (type of crime that happens after a preceding one) of repeat victimization. Next, the research that has examined the correlates of repeat victimization and revictimization is summarized and provides the backdrop for the discussion of the two leading theoretical explanations for repeat victimization; event dependence and risk heterogeneity. And last, results from prevention programs that specifically target the reduction of repeat victimization and revictimization are summarized, and future research areas are identified.

TERMINOLOGY AND DEFINITIONS USED TO DESCRIBE THE REOCCURRENCE OF VICTIMIZATION

Researchers have not been consistent in their use of terminology to label the reoccurrence of victimization. Among the terms they have used to describe this phenomenon are repeat/ repetitive victimization and revictimization.

Researchers have referred to a person, household, or business as the target of repeat victimization (see Farrell, 1995). A *repeat victim* experienced two or more of the *same type* of victimization within a short time frame (e.g., a few days, weeks, or months or within a year). To illustrate, consider the case of a young female college student named Sally[1] enrolled in her sophomore year. The fall semester seemed to be going well for her until, in November, she was raped by an intimate partner in living quarters on campus. She suffered a black eye during the attack. Later in the same month, Sally was again the victim of a completed rape. This incident also occurred in campus living quarters; however, the perpetrator, although someone known to Sally, was not someone with whom she had an intimate relationship. Given Sally's experience of two completed rapes, she would be considered a repeat victim.

Another term commonly used is *revictimization* (see Classen, Pales, & Aggarwa, 2005). Used most often in sexual abuse, victimization, and intimate partner violence research, revictimization refers to the experience of *more than one type of violent victimization episode,* usually in the *same violence category, over a relatively long period of time.* In thinking about how revictimization can move across developmental periods, consider the case of Jenny,[2] a young woman who was repeatedly sexually abused and raped by a family friend during her childhood. At the age of 16, Jenny was raped after drinking alcohol on a date with a man she met through friends. She became pregnant as a result of the rape, decided to raise her child alone, and stopped drinking, believing that sobriety would reduce her risk of revictimization. However, at the age of 19, she attended a coworker's party and fell asleep on the couch (she had not been drinking) and woke up to find a man she worked with but did not know well taking her pants off. Jenny told him a few times to stop but he did not. She does not remember much of the rape itself.

The cases of Sally and Jenny illustrate the nature of the two differences between repeat victimization and revictimization: the length of time period between incidents and the crime category that the victim experienced. Unlike for repeat victimization, revictimization typically occurred during two different developmental time periods, usually childhood, adolescence, or adulthood. Revictimization also differs from repeat victimization in that a person can experience different types of crime victimization, so long as the incidents are from the same crime category, such as child abuse and intimate partner violence. Also, researchers have used the term *revictimization* only in reference to a person being the target. The term *repeat victimization* has been used to refer not only to a person being the target but also property being the target, such as burglary (Farrell &

Pease, 2006) and theft (Osborn & Tseloni, 1998). To more fully understand another dimension of experiencing more than one incident, we now turn to a discussion of the extent to which targets are victimized more than once.

THE EXTENT OF BEING VICTIMIZED MORE THAN ONCE

Researchers have generated two distinctive growing bodies of research: repeat victimization and sexual revictimization. Each has focused on estimating the extent to which targets are victimized more than once. A summary of the results from this research follows.

The Extent of Repeat Victimization

Results from several national-level victimization surveys have revealed that most households or individuals are not victimized annually. For example, results from the National Violence Against Women Study (NVAWS) showed that 2.1% of the women and 3.5% of men were either raped or physically assaulted in the previous 12 months (Tjaden & Thoennes, 2000, 2006). In this same vein, average annual rates from the 2002–2003 National Crime Victimization Survey (NVCS) showed that 3% of households were burglarized (Catalano, 2004).

What these results mask is that a substantial proportion of households and individuals who are victimized experienced more than one incident. Much research has reported that households and individuals are at risk of experiencing not just one, but repeated incidents. Property and violence research in the United States using the General Social Survey (Gabor & Mata, 2004), the National Youth Survey (NYS; Lauritsen & Davis Quinet, 1995), NVAWS (Tjaden & Thoennes, 2000, 2006), and the National Crime Survey (NCS) and NCVS (Farrell, Tseloni, & Pease, 2005), and abroad using the International Crime

Victimization Survey in 17 countries (Farrell & Bouloukous, 2001), the British Crime Survey (BCS) in Wales and England (Nicholas, Povey, Walker, & Kershaw, 2005) and the National Crime and Safety Survey in Australia (Mukherjee & Carcach, 1998) all illustrate this point. For example, in the 2004/2005 and 2003/2004 BSC surveys, 14% and 16% of the burglary victims, respectively, were victimized two or more times within the same year (Nicholas et al., 2005). In the United States, the NVAWS reported that women who were raped in the previous 12-month period averaged 2.9 rapes, whereas men averaged fewer, at 1.2 rapes (Tjaden & Thoennes, 2006). Rates are even higher when the perpetrator is an intimate partner. Females averaged 4.5 rapes by the same intimate partner, and female physical assault victims averaged 6.9 assaults by the same partner. Men averaged slightly fewer, at 4.4 intimate partner physical assaults by the same partner (Tjaden & Thoennes, 2000). Nearly 60% of the assaulted youths in Lauritsen and Davis Quinet's (1995) research were repeat victims. Similarly, 61% of their robbery victims were robbed twice or more.

Proportions of Incidents Experienced by Repeat Property and Personal Victims

Not only do a substantial proportion of crime victims experience more than one incident, but a growing body of research shows that repeat targets also experience a disproportionate amount of all crime victimizations. As shown in Table 13.1, there are a range of studies conducted in the United States and England that show the skewed distribution of repeat property victimizations.

For example, analyzing 10 years of BCS data, Pease (1998), reported that 6% of the respondents experienced 68% of all of the property thefts. Studies of residential burglary, including the 1997 BCS results, also evince

Table 13.1 The Distribution of Reoccurring Property Victimizations

Number of Times Victimized	British Crime Survey[a] (1982–1992) Property		British Crime Survey (1997)[b] Residential Burglary		Beenleigh, Australia Police Incident Management System (June, 1995–November, 1996)[c] Residential Break and Enter		National Youth Survey (Wave 1, 1977)[d] Larceny		Vandalism		University Students in East Midlands, UK (2003)[e] Property	
	Respondents %	Incidents %	Respondents %	Incidents %	Respondents %	Incidents %	Respondents %	Incidents %	Respondents %	Incidents %	Respondents %	Incidents %
0	84	0	95	0	91.6	0.0	50.3	0.0	74.2	0.0	73	0
1	10	32	5	60	7.0	68.1	20.6	15.8	12.5	18.5	18	44
2	3	17	1	19	1.1	20.8	13.5	20.8	7.3	21.6	7	33
3	1	10	<1*	21	0.2	5.7	6.2	14.4	2.7	11.8	3*	23
4	2*	41			0.1	1.6	3.4	10.6	1.3	7.6		
5 or more					0.1	3.8	5.9	38.5	2.0	40.5		

NOTE: Total percentage for each type of crime does not add up to 100 or may be slightly more than 100 due to rounding.

* This was highest count category reported.

a. Pease (1998), Table 1. Property crimes include burglary, criminal damage, theft and attempted theft, and nonvehicle property theft.

b. Budd (1999), Table 3.3.

c. Townsley, Homel, & Chaseling (2000).

d. Lauritsen & Davis Quinet (1995), Table 1.

e. Barberet, Fisher, & Taylor (2004), Table S.2. Property crimes include burglary, criminal damage, theft, and attempted theft.

this pattern in which a small proportion of victims experience a large proportion of all victimization incidents (see Weisel, Clarke, & Stedman, 1999). A similar highly skewed distribution can also be seen in police data of residential break and enter in Australia.

Among young persons, this repeat pattern is also evident. Barberet and her colleagues (2004) examined victimization for university students in East Midlands, United Kingdom. They reported that 10% of the property victims experienced 56% of all of the property victimization incidents. Similar results were reported by Lauritsen and Davis Quinet (1995) using data from the NYS. They found that 27% of the youths experienced 84% of all the larcenies, and 13% of them experienced 82% of all acts of vandalisms. Taken together, what these results show is that regardless of the data used and the type of property crime examined, repeat victims experience a disproportionate amount of all property victimizations.

Table 13.2 shows a similar pattern to the one exhibited in the distribution of repeat property victimizations. The distribution of repeat personal victimizations are generated from the BCS, England, the NYS, and three studies, including two national level ones, of college students. Regardless of the population from which the sample was drawn—general population, youths, or college students—these studies revealed what has become a consistent pattern: a small percentage of respondents reported experiencing more than one personal victimization. Those who did experience more than one, however, experienced a disproportionate amount of the personal victimization incidents.

Highlighting this finding are the results from Pease's (1998) BCS work, which indicates that 3% of the respondents reported experiencing 78% of the personal crime victimization incidents. Work with college student samples conducted by Barberet et al. (2004) and Daigle et al. (2006) also find similar results. To

illustrate, less than 1% of the more than 4,000 college women surveyed in the National College Women Violent Victimization Study experienced more than one violent incident. Despite this small percentage of repeat victims, they experienced over 28% of all violent incidents, a percentage that is notably disproportionate to the percentage they constitute in the sample.

Other research has examined the distribution of repeat victimizations for younger persons. Lauritsen and Davis Quinet (1995) found that for assaults, 18% of the youth reported experiencing almost 90% of the assault victimizations. Slightly more than 14% of those surveyed reported experiencing 86% of the robbery incidents. Notably, although most young people included in the NYS do not report experiencing any assaults or robberies, a small proportion report experiencing almost all of these particular types of crimes.

Researchers have also begun to examine repeat sexual victimization. Using data collected from the National College Women Sexual Victimization Study (NCWSV) on rape, sexual coercion, sexual contact with force, sexual contact without force, and threats, Daigle and her colleagues (2006) find that college women not only are at risk of experiencing one sexual victimization in an academic year, but that they also are at risk of experiencing more than one of these incidents. Although only 7% of women reported that at least two different sexual victimizations occurred, these women experienced 72% of all sexual victimization incidents.

Considered together, this discussion on the likelihood and distribution of repeat victimization can generate two main conclusions. First, repeat victimization is a real phenomenon, with many households and individuals experiencing more than one victimization in a relatively short period of time. Second, although most individuals do not experience any crime victimization, there is a portion of individuals and households that experience a

Table 13.2 The Distribution of Reoccurring Personal Victimizations

Number of Times Victimized	British Crime Survey[a] (1982–1992) Personal		National Youth Survey (Wave 1, 1977)[b] Assault		Robbery		National College Women Violent Victimization Study (1997)[c] Violence		National College Women Sexual Victimization Study (1997)[d] Sexual		University Students in East Midlands, UK (2003)[e] Personal	
	Respondents %	Incidents %	Respondents %	Incidents %	Respondents %	Incidents %	Respondents %	Incidents %	Respondents %	Incidents %	Respondents %	Incidents %
0	92	0	68.9	0.0	75.4	0.0	95.13	0.0	84.46	0.0	91	0
1	5	25	12.9	10.4	9.7	14.2	4.17	72.27	8.19	27.62	6	46
2	1	12	8.2	13.2	6.8	19.8	.56	19.53	4.03	27.16	2	28
3	1	7	2.9	6.9	3.3	14.2	.14*	8.20	3.33*	45.22	1*	26
4	1*	59	2.0	6.4	1.4	8.1						
5 or more			5.2	63.2	3.4	43.6						

NOTE: Total percentage for each type of crime does not add up to 100 or may be slightly more than 100 due to rounding.

* This was the highest count category reported.

a. Pease (1998), Table 1. Personal crimes include assaults, sexual offences, robbery, and theft from a person.

b. Lauritsen & Davis Quinet (1995), Table 1.

c, d. Daigle, Fisher, & Cullen (2006), Table 1. Violence includes robbery and simple and aggravated assault. Sexual victimization includes rape, sexual coercion, unwanted sexual contact with or without force, and threat of sexual victimizations (see Fisher et al., 2000).

e. Barberet et al. (2004), Table S.2. Personal crimes include assaults, sexual offences, robbery, and theft from a person.

disproportionate share of all victimization experiences. Perhaps what is most striking is that these patterns are found for victims of property as well as personal crimes using different sources of data and methodological approaches.

The Extent of Sexual Revictimizaton

Victims of sexual assault have the highest revictimization rate of any group apart from domestic violence, with one study indicating that these women are 35 times more likely to be sexually victimized than women with no history of sexual abuse (Canadian Urban Victimization Survey, 1988; National Board for Crime Prevention, 1994). A high risk of revictimization for those sexually abused in childhood, adolescence, and adulthood has been established in a multitude of studies across various populations (e.g., college, clinical, military recruits, and community samples for reviews; see Breitenbecher, 1999; Classen et al., 2005; Roodman & Clum, 2001). Indeed, a meta-analysis by Roodman and Clum (2001) found a moderate effect size (.59) for revictimization and noted that between 15% and 79% of women sexually abused in childhood were raped as adults.

The prevalence of revictimization is high, although estimates vary, and holds consistent using the most inclusive samples. Using a nationally representative sample of adults with childhood sexual abuse (CSA), Desai, Arias, Thompson, and Basile (2002) found that women with CSA were 6 times more likely to be sexually victimized by a current intimate partner, 11 times more likely if they experienced physical abuse in addition to CSA, and held an even greater risk for sexual victimization by a nonintimate partner. Similarly, an epidemiological study of 3,131 adults by Sorenson, Stein, Siegel, Golding, and Burnam (1987) found that of the 447 participants who reported sexual abuse, 67% experienced more than one sexual assault. Among community samples, it has been estimated that CSA doubles or triples the risk of adult sexual victimization (Fleming, Mullen, Sibthorpe, & Bammer, 1999; Wyatt, Guthrie, & Notgrass, 1992). Randall and Haskell (1995) reported that in a community sample of women with CSA, 62.4% were revictimized.

Changes in Risk From One Developmental Time Period to Another

Although research clearly establishes a correlation between a history of sexual abuse and risk of revictimization, this relationship changes over time and developmental life stages. An abundance of research focuses on the link between CSA and revictimization in adulthood, and the findings here are remarkably consistent (for a review, see Classen et al., 2005). For example, Russell (1986) found that of women with CSA before the age of 14, a full 63% experienced rape or attempted rape as opposed to only 35% of the non-CSA sample, indicating a rate of victimization nearly twice that for women without a history of sexual abuse. In the NVAWS, 18% of women raped before the age of 18 were also raped as adults, an estimate that does not include other types of sexual victimization or attempted rape (Tjaden & Thoennes, 2006).

Other researchers, however, have tied the severity of childhood sexual abuse to the risk of revictimization in adulthood. Coid et al. (2001) reported that whereas women who experienced unwanted intercourse were two to three times more likely to be sexually assaulted or raped after age 16, women who experienced sexual abuse other than intercourse were three to four times more likely to be sexually assaulted after age 16, even after controlling for demographic factors.

Other research has focused on risks between CSA and sexual victimization in adolescence and revictimization in late adolescence or young adulthood. Humphrey and White (2000) examined the incoming freshman classes at two different universities and found that prior to entering college, 13% of the women experienced rape before the age of 14. These women were 14 times more likely than other women to be raped within their first year at college. In a prospective, longitudinal study, Noll, Horowitz, Bonanno, Trickett, and Putnam (2003) studied CSA victims between the ages of 6 and 16 (mean age at baseline = 11 years) who reported sexual abuse at the age of 14 or younger. Participants were assessed three times over a seven-year period, and those with a history of CSA were twice as likely to be sexually assaulted or raped than their matched counterparts. Even across adjacent developmental periods, revictimization remains a significant risk for sexual assault victims.

While the majority of research on revictimization focuses on experiences across life stages, such as from childhood/adolescence to adulthood, there are some studies that examine revictimization within the same developmental period. Regardless of the life stage being examined, the risk of revictimization remains a constant. Boney-McCoy and Finkelhor (1995) found that in a random sample of 2,000 kids between the ages of 10 and 16, within the last year, 7.6% were sexually victimized, and those with a prior history of CSA were 11.7 times more likely to experience a repeat victimization. The authors established that these results were not likely attributed to the repeated assaults of one perpetrator. Similarly, using a national probability sample of adolescent women in grades 7 through 12 drawn from the National Longitudinal Study of Adolescent Health, Raghavan, Bogart, Elliott, Vestal, & Schuster (2004) reported that of the 7% of women raped at the first wave, 8% had experienced a repeat victimization by the second wave. As this study only examined rape (defined as forced intercourse), other types of sexual victimizations were not documented. Small and Kerns (1993), however, found that in a sample of 1,149 adolescents, 20% reported an unwanted sexual experience within the last year (one third of which involved rape), which was predicted by a history of sexual victimization. Whether looking at more inclusive types of abuse (sexual victimization) or more stringent criteria (rape), research clearly indicates that revictimization does occur within the same developmental trajectory.

REPEAT VICTIMIZATION: WHAT DOES IT LOOK LIKE?

The Time Course of Repeat Victimization

Two distinct patterns have begun to emerge from the time course of repeat property and personal victimization research. First, if a second incident is going to occur, it is likely to occur relatively quickly after the first incident. Second, there is a period of heightened risk immediately following the occurrence of the prior incident that decreases over time.

As shown in Table 13.3, residential burglary follows a time course such that repeats are most likely to occur within a month of the initial burglary episode. Analyzing police crime data in Canada, Polvi et al. (1991) found that half of the second residential burglaries that occurred happened within seven days of the first burglary. Similar to this finding, work examining police data in cities within the United States also shows that the time immediately following an incident appears to hold the greatest risk for a repeat incident (Farrell, Sousa, & Weisel, 2002). For example, Robinson's (1998) examination of police call data in Tallahassee, Florida, revealed that 25% of the repeat burglary incidents occurred within a week, and slightly more than half occurred within a month.

The time course of repeat victimization also shows that the risk of being victimized a subsequent time drops over time. That is, the relationship fits an exponential negative slope. In Canada, Polvi and her colleagues

Table 13.3 Sources of Information on Time Course of Repeat Victimization by Type of Crime

Type of Crime	Location and Source of Data (Dates)	Unit of Time	Repeats by Unit of Time	Reference
Property				
Residential burglary	Saskatoon, Canada, Police Crime Data (1984–1987)	Days	Within one month, half of second victimizations occurred within seven days of first burglary.	Polvi, Looman, Humphries, and Pease (1991)
		Months	Risk of being burgled a second time was 12.42 times more likely within a one-month period. Risk dropped to 2.41 times as likely following this month-long period. Average 1.27 times over the 7–11 month period.	
Residential burglary	Tallahassee, Florida, Police Crime Data (1992–1994)	Weeks Months	25% within a week 51% within a month	Robinson (1998)
Violence				
Simple assault	United States, Self-report victimization survey (since school began in the Fall 1996–Spring 1997)	Months	31% within same month, 23% within one month, 23% within two months, 4% within three months	Daigle et al. (2006)
Domestic violence	United Kingdom, Call for service to police (1989–1991)	Days	After a first incident, 35% of households call for a second incident within five weeks of first; after second incident, 45% call for a third incident within five weeks.	Farrell, Clarke, and Pease (1993, as cited in Farrell & Pease, 2006)
Racial attacks	East End London, Bengali and Somali tenants living in an estate (September 1990–February 1991)	Weeks	37 incidents happened within one week, 30 within 2 weeks, 20 within 3 weeks, 5 within 4 weeks, and then steady until weeks 14–17, where number of incidents declined.[a]	Sampson and Phillips (1992)
Sexual				
Rape	United States, Self-report victimization survey (since school began in the Fall 1996–Spring 1997)	Months	48% within same month, 12% within one month, 18% within two months	Daigle et al. (2006)

a. These estimates were extrapolated from a graph presented in Figure 13.1.

reported that "a dwelling was 12.42 times more likely to be burgled a second time within a one-month period. This risk of a second burglary dropped dramatically after the passage of a month, resulting in a residence being 2.41 times likely to be burgled again following this month-long period" (Polvi, Looman, Humphries, & Pease, 1990, p. 10).

At least four different types of repeat personal crimes have been evaluated in terms of their time course: simple assault, domestic violence, racial attacks, and sexual victimization. For each of them, the time course of repeat victimization has a downward exponential fit. Reporting results from two national level studies of college women, Daigle and her colleagues (2006) show that over half (54%) of repeat simple assault incidents occurred within a month of the initial incident. Repeat domestic violence and racial attacks have also been shown to frequently reoccur in the time period immediately following a first episode (Farrell, 1995; Sampson & Phillips, 1992). To illustrate, 35% of households called the police for a second domestic violence event within five weeks of the first (Farrell, et al., 1993, as cited in Farrell & Pease, 2006). Similar results have been found with repeat sexual victimization, in that subsequent incidents of sexual victimization tended to occur within one month of the first incident (Daigle et al., 2006).

Several of these research endeavors have also shown that this elevated risk of repeat victimization decreases over time. In their study of racial attacks in London, Sampson and Phillips (1992) found that the risk of repeat racial attacks was most pronounced in the weeks immediately following the first attack, but that this risk declined around 14 to 17 weeks. This decrease in risk over time was also found in research on simple assault and sexual victimization.

Figure 13.1 depicts the months between incidents for rape and simple assault for a sample of college women.

As shown, the largest percentage of repeat incidents occurs within the same month and the month immediately following the first incident. Moreover, the percentage of the occurrence of repeat incidents decreases over time, with about 48% of the repeat rapes happening within the same month, but only 21% of rape incidents occurring three months or more after the initial rape.

Taken together, the results presented in Table 13.3 and Figure 13.1 show that there is a time course of repeat victimization that is similar across property, personal, and sexual crimes. This time course indicates that the greatest risk of repeat victimization is in the time immediately following the incident—usually within the same month or the next month. In addition, the accumulated research depicts a period of heightened risk that wanes as time passes.

Crime-Switch Patterns and Victim Proneness

After a crime victimization incident has occurred, what type of victimization is most likely to follow? To address this question, using data from the NCS, Reiss (1980) constructed crime-switch matrices that depict both the number and percentage of personal and property victimization incidents that are followed by the same type of incident (e.g., an assault as the first incident and an assault as the second incident), thus indicating victim proneness (see also Feinberg, 1980). In addition, the matrices show the number and percentage of incidents that are followed by a different type of incident (e.g., an assault as the first incident and a rape as the second incident), thus indicating crime switching. Overall, Reiss's (1980) results show that for repeat victims, the most likely next type of crime victimization is by the same type of crime. This proneness pattern was evident for people who experienced personal larceny, burglary, household larceny, and assault. For rape, however, crime switching appears to occur. For example, the most

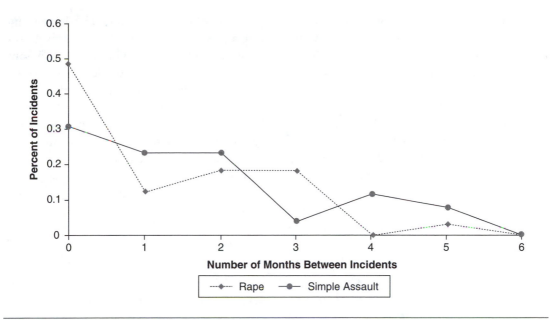

Figure 13.1   Time Course of Rape and Simple Assault Incidents

commonly occurring crimes that followed a rape were personal larcenies and assaults.

Such findings regarding rape not being likely to occur after a rape were not supported by Daigle et al. (2006). Using data from the NCWSV, they found that there is a significant relationship between the type of incident that occurs first in a pair and the type of incident that follows. For each type of sexual victimization, most of the incidents were followed by the same specific type of sexual victimization. Over 30% of the rape incidents were followed by a rape, and over half of the sexual contact without force incidents were followed by a sexual contact without force incident.

CORRELATES AND CAUSES OF REPEAT VICTIMIZATION

Correlates of Repeat Victimization: Neighborhood and Household Characteristics

The neighborhood in which people reside may increase their risks of experiencing more

than one victimization. In particular, living in areas that are vulnerable may place a person living within those areas at risk. For example, living in an urban area is a risk factor for repeat victimization, probably because urban areas typically have higher crime rates than nonurban areas (Tseloni, 2000; Wittebrood & Nieuwbeerta, 2000). Furthermore, persons who live in areas with a high concentration of single-parent households are also more likely to be victimized more than once than are other persons (Osborn, Ellingworth, Hope, & Trickett, 1996). Neighborhood disorder is also related to an increase in the number of assault, larceny, and vandalism victimizations experienced by youth (Lauritsen & Davis Quinet, 1995) and repeat property victimization for adults (Outlaw, Ruback, & Britt, 2002).

Several studies have shown that the number of property crime victimizations experienced is related to household characteristics (Mukherjee & Carcach, 1998; Osborn, et al., 1996; Osborn & Tseloni, 1998; Tseloni, 2000). For example, research using the NCVS has shown that living in a low-income household, having children in the family, owning four or more cars, participating in neighborhood watch, and having installed security devices in the home are all related to an increase in the number of personal victimizations experienced (Tseloni, 2000). Similar to this finding, in their study of property crime victimizations using the BCS, Osborn and Tseloni (1998) found that the age of the head of household, having two or more adults in the household, the number of children in the household, and having more than one car were all positively related to the number of crime victimizations. Another important household attribute that is related to repeat victimization is length of residence. The shorter the length of residence in a particular house, the greater the chances are of experiencing repeat victimization, both personal (Mukherjee & Carcach, 1998) and property (Osborn & Tseloni, 1998; Tseloni, 2000). Still other research has examined whether a residence is owned or if persons are renting their accommodations. The main finding from this avenue of inquiry is that living in rented accommodations increases the risk of experiencing more than one victimization (Mukherjee & Carcach, 1998; Osborn et al., 1996; Osborn & Tseloni, 1998). Lack of guardianship of a home has also been identified as a risk factor for repeat victimization (Mukherjee & Carcach, 1998; Outlaw et al., 2002).

Correlates of Repeat Victimization: Incident-Level Characteristics

At the onset of a victimization, two elements—the victim-offender relationship and the use of alcohol and/or drugs—are fixed. Generally, the repeat victimization literature suggests that the victim-offender relationship is related to repeat victimization in that repeat victimizations are more likely than nonrepeat victimizations to involve people known to the victim (Hindelang, Gottfredson, & Garafalo, 1978; Nicholas et al., 2005).

Illustrative of this point, Hindelang and colleagues (1978) found that victimizations of repeat victims were more likely to involve offenders who were not strangers to the victim than were victimizations of one-time victims (41% vs. 18%). This pattern emerged for several different types of violence: rape, aggravated assault, and simple assault. One study on repeat sexual victimization found that single unwanted sexual contact with force incidents were more likely to involve someone known and less likely to involve an intimate partner than were repeat incidents (Daigle et al., 2006).

Alcohol consumption has also been considered an important factor in repeat victimization incidents; however, the research is mixed regarding its relevance. Lasley and Rosenbaum (1988) found that the likelihood of experiencing more than one personal victimization increased with alcohol use, with 41% of the high-level drinkers also being multiple crime victims. Other research investigating the link between alcohol use and repeat sexual victimization has not supported this finding (Daigle et al., 2006; Ellis, Atkeson, & Calhoun, 1982; Gidycz, Hanson, & Layman, 1995).

The last set of characteristics examined is those that occur following the incident. To date, only one study has investigated whether single and repeat incidents differ in terms of reporting, both to authorities and to other people. This study, using the NCWSV, found that for none of the five types of sexual victimization studied were one-time victimizations more likely to be reported to authorities or to someone else than were repeat incidents (Daigle et al., 2006).

Correlates of Repeat Victimization: Individual Characteristics

Within the investigation of characteristics of individuals related to being victimized repeatedly, research has centered on two sets of characteristics that may differentiate repeat victims from single victims. The first set includes personal attributes such as demographic characteristics and individual-level factors, while the second set includes lifestyle characteristics. It appears that young persons are more likely to be repeatedly victimized than older individuals (Gabor & Mata, 2004; Lauritsen & Davis Quinet, 1995; Mukherjee & Carcach, 1998; Outlaw et al., 2002; Tseloni, 2000; Wittebrood & Nieuwbeerta, 2000) and that males are at greater risk of being repeatedly victimized than are females (Lauritsen & Davis Quinet, 1995; Mukherjee & Carcach, 1998), except for in cases of repeat sexual offenses (Wittebrood & Nieuwbeerta, 2000). Marital status has also been found to be related to repeat victimization, with single (Lasley & Rosenbaum, 1988), separated (Mukherjee & Carcach, 1998), and divorced (Tseloni, 2000) individuals having the greatest risk. Generally, individuals with low socioeconomic status are more likely than individuals from high socioeconomic status to be repeat victims of personal crimes (Lauritsen & Davis Quinet, 1995), while repeat property crimes have been shown in the research to be more likely to occur to persons with greater income (Lauritsen & Davis Quinet, 1995; Outlaw et al., 2002). Employment status also is related to repeat victimization, with persons who are unemployed (without a job, students) being at a greater risk than persons who are employed (Mukherjee & Carcach, 1998).

Lifestyle characteristics have also been used to differentiate repeat victims from single victims. The frequency that people go out in the evenings has been shown to be related to repeat victimization, with persons who more frequently spend time away from home at night being more likely than those who do not spend many nights away from home to be repeat victims (Lasley & Rosenbaum, 1988; Tseloni, 2000). In their study using the 1982 BCS, Lasley and Rosenbaum (1988) found

that three out of seven persons who spend either Friday or Saturday night out were repeatedly victimized. A large percentage of repeat victims were found by Mukherjee and Carcach (1998) to frequently use public transport after 6 P.M. and/or go out for entertainment at night. Some research suggests, however, that time away from home is a risk factor for victimization in general and that it does not distinguish between repeat and single victims (Outlaw et al., 2002).

Others have examined risky lifestyle as a possible correlate of repeat victimization. For example, Lauritsen and Davis Quinet (1995) found that among a national sample of youth, time spent with delinquent peers was related to the number of assaults experienced, while prior involvement in delinquency was related to more assault, robbery, larceny, and vandalism victimizations. Multiple victimization was predicted by participation in dangerous activities in Outlaw et al.'s (2002) study of Seattle adults, and frequency of offending increased risk of victimization for individuals in Wittebrood and Nieuwbeerta's (2000) study of individuals in the Netherlands.

Correlates of Sexual Revictimization

A large body of research has documented the negative effects of sexual abuse, only one of which is the increased risk for revictimization. Sexual trauma has been linked to a number of psychological problems such as depression, post-traumatic stress disorder (PTSD), substance abuse, anxiety, sexual dysfunction, and difficulties in interpersonal relationships (for reviews, see Briere & Runtz, 1986; Goodman, Koss, & Russo, 1993; Noll, 2005). However, since few studies control for the presence of prior sexual assaults and are retrospective in nature, we cannot be sure which abusive experience is most reflective of maladjustment, and causal relationships are difficult to identify (Maker, Kemmelmeier, &

Peterson, 2001). Nonetheless, it is clear that there are some differences in situational and psychological variables among women who are revictimized as opposed to those with a single victimization.

Numerous studies have documented a link between alcohol use and sexual assault, and some of this research has been extended to revictimization. Raghavan et al. (2004) found that alcohol use within the last year predicted revictimization in a probability sample of adolescent women, Siegel and Williams (2003) found a relationship between alcohol use and adult revictimization for CSA survivors, and Messman-Moore and Long (2000) found that women with CSA were more likely to experience unwanted sexual contact while using drugs or alcohol than other women. However, other research has found alcohol to be a risk factor for sexual assault independent of CSA (Merrill et al., 1999; Messman & Long, 2002). While there appears to be some type of relationship between alcohol-related factors (use, diagnosis, etc.) and sexual assault, the role of alcohol in revictimization remains unclear (see Messman-Moore & Long, 2003).

Sexual behaviors have also received attention as risk factors for revictimization. Several studies have made connections between childhood sexual abuse and more promiscuous behavior, such as having sex at a younger age, having a higher number of sexual partners, having sex more often with casual acquaintances, or engaging in prostitution (Rodriguez, Ryan, Vande Kemp, & Foy, 1997; Simons & Whitbeck, 1991). The focus on sexual behaviors is important because research has shown that a higher than average number of sexual partners increases the risk of sexual victimization (Gidycz et al., 1995).

Other research has focused on psychological and cognitive factors such as attributions, PTSD and related symptoms, dissociation, self-esteem, and communication skills. A large body of research has documented that women who are revictimized suffer from higher levels of distress and more PTSD symptoms than women with one episode of victimization (Banyard, Williams, & Siegel, 2001; Gibson & Leitenberg, 2001; Murphy et al.; 1988), although some studies have been unable to replicate this finding (Classen et al., 2002; Sorenson, Siegel, Golding, & Stein, 1991). Symptoms of PTSD may play some role in revictimization by reducing a woman's ability to recognize danger and take action in threatening situations (Casey & Norius, 2005; Sandberg, Matorin, & Lynn, 1999). Arata (2000) found PTSD to be mediator of revictimization, and Wilson, Calhoun, and Bernat (1999) found that PTSD symptoms reduced latency among revictimized women in recognizing risk while listening to an audiotape of a date rape situation. Meadows, Jaycox, Webb, and Foa (1996) also found that women who had been repeatedly raped had lower levels of risk recognition yet higher levels of dissociation. Indeed, once the authors controlled for dissociation, there was no difference in risk recognition between revictimized women and those with a single sexual assault. Last, empirical results on the role of self-esteem and self-blame in revictimization have been mixed. While some studies have found such a relationship (Kellogg & Hoffman, 1997), the majority have been unable to establish any correlation (Marhoefer-Dvorak, Resick, Hutter, & Girelli, 1988; Wyatt et al., 1992).

TWO EXPLANATIONS OF REPEAT VICTIMIZATION: EVENT DEPENDENCE AND RISK HETEROGENEITY

Based on the finding that victimization at one point in time is a risk factor for victimization later in time, it is believed that this initial victimization may increase the likelihood of a subsequent victimization incident. This assertion is at the heart of the event dependence (or "boost"; see Pease, 1998) argument for explaining repeat victimization. According to the event dependence argument, a successful victimization somehow makes a target—albeit a person, place, or household—more vulnerable for future victimization.

In testing the event dependence explanation for repeat victimization, most research has found that there is a strong effect between past victimization and subsequent victimization for both property and personal crime victimization. For example, using the BCS, Osborn and Tseloni (1998) found that prior victimization (car theft, burglary, assault) was a strong, positive predictor of the number of property crimes experienced in a model including all crimes and in separate models for burglary and theft.

Others have argued that past victimization is not the only predictor of future victimization and that characteristics of individuals, beyond just being a previous victim, place them at risk of repeat victimization. This argument, known as risk heterogeneity (or the "flag" explanation; see Pease, 1998), centers on the idea that some individuals are more vulnerable for victimization at one point in time, and the characteristics that make them vulnerable do not change over time. As a result, if a person is at risk of being victimized at one point in time, they are at risk of subsequently being a victim because of their attractiveness or vulnerability as compared to others. As indicated in the previous section, lifestyle, household, and personal characteristics all may contribute to a person's risk of being repeatedly victimized, thus supporting the notion of risk heterogeneity.

Despite the statistical sophistication that has been employed in repeat victimization research, there is still uncertainty regarding what "truly" causes repeat victimization. Research supports that event dependence and risk heterogeneity both contribute to a person's risk. From the extant work there is unexplained heterogeneity as well. What

unexplained heterogeneity refers to is that even when controlling for various risk factors and past victimization, there is still differences in the risk for repeat victimization across individuals that is left unexplained (Osborn & Tseloni, 1998; Tseloni, 2000). More advanced theorizing and more rigorous measures are needed to tease out what these unexplained forces are that place individuals at risk of experiencing not just one victimization, but repeated victimizations.

PREVENTING VICTIMIZATION FROM REOCCURRING

The majority of repeat victimization prevention programs have focused on reducing residential burglary, with recent attention being given to programs that address the reoccurrence of domestic violence and sexual victimization.

Repeat Burglary Prevention Programs

Most of the research that has examined preventing repeat burglary has been conducted in the United Kingdom, although prevention efforts have also occurred in Australia and the United States. Generally, these programs have focused on preventing residential burglary by upgrading security, target hardening, instituting neighborhood watches, and distributing information to households who have been burgled or that are at a high risk for experiencing a burglary (for a review, see Farrell & Pease, 2006). Several of these programmatic efforts have been shown to reduce the occurrence of repeat burglary victimization (Budz, Pegnall, & Townsley, 2001; Forrester, Frenzz, O'Connell, & Pease, 1990; Henderson, 2002; Tilley, 1993). For example, the first prevention program specifically targeting the reduction of repeat burglary, the Kirkholt burglary prevention program, resulted in the incidence of repeat burglary falling to zero after six months of the program (Forrester et al., 1990). Furthermore, overall burglary was less likely to occur at households that instituted upgraded security measures, while households without these security changes did not experience a decrease in burglary incidence. This program's success is likely attributable to the high implementation rates, with 68% of the burgled households receiving security upgrades and almost all of those households participating in a mini-neighborhood watch program.

Although many programs implemented in the United Kingdom and Australia met their objective in reducing burglary rates, strategies in the United States have been strikingly less successful (for exception, see Bennett & Durie, 1999). In their review of repeat residential burglary prevention programs conducted in three cities—Baltimore, Dallas, and San Diego—Weisel and colleagues (1999) found that there was no reduction in repeat burglary rates in any of the three cities, and in two of the cities, there was an increase in the amount of burglary relative to the control group.

The tactics employed in these programs to address reducing repeat burglary probably influenced effectiveness. Each program centered on the police providing information and advice to people who had their homes burglarized, though little or no money was provided to the officers to actually assist people in implementing prevention tactics. What can be gleaned from this research, then, on reducing repeat burglary is the necessity of fully implementing program components so that a true measure of their effectiveness can be produced. Although not discussed in detail here, there are other reasons that more and better prevention programs are not currently in place. For example, prevention programs require a coordinated effort from multiple agencies, such as the police and community groups, which is oftentimes difficult to establish. Furthermore, it is difficult to truly know how much crime is prevented, because a crime that does not occur is almost impossible to identify (Pease & Laycock, 1996).

Preventing the Reoccurrence of Sexual Victimization

Given the increased risk of sexual revictimization, researchers have identified risk factors and developed interventions designed to reduce the likelihood of future victimization. A number of studies have tied situational factors, such as alcohol use, isolated locations, and multiple sexual partners, and individual characteristics, such as being less assertive, PTSD, dissociation, and lower risk recognition, to revictimization and repeat victimization (for reviews, see Breitenbecher, 2001; Classen et al., 2005; Messman-Moore & Long, 2003;). Based on this research, interventions that target these risk factors have been developed for college students, but only a small number have been empirically evaluated. The results of these evaluations are mixed, with some finding increases in knowledge about sexual assault or improvements in psychological functioning, but only two to date (Gidycz et al., 2001; Marx, Calhoun, Wilson, & Meyerson, 2001) have been shown to lower any rates of the reoccurrence of sexual victimization.

One of the first such interventions, developed by Hanson and Gidycz (1993), used a single session to address rape myths, prevalence of sexual assault on college campuses, sexual communication, and behavioral risk factors. While the intervention was successful in reducing sexual assault among women without a prior history of sexual abuse at the nine-week follow up, it was not effective in reducing incidence of revictimization. In 1998, Breitenbecher and Gidycz tested a revised version of their intervention, this time with a special focus on the heightened risk of women with a history of sexual abuse while reinforcing that victims are not responsible for their assaults. In this study, however, the program was ineffective in reducing incidents of sexual assault among all women, regardless of their history. Gidycz et al. (2001), using the intervention from previous studies, which was now extended to two 2-hour sessions, found some success in reducing sexual victimization during the follow-up period. At the two-month follow up, there was no difference in revictimization between the experimental and control groups, but at the six-month follow-up, women who were "moderately" victimized again at the two-month period were significantly less likely to experience repeat victimization at the six-month period if they received the intervention.

Marx et al. (2001) delivered an expanded version of Gidycz and colleagues' intervention to a group of college women with a history of sexual victimization. Their intervention also addressed risk recognition skills, including how to identify danger cues in social interactions. At the two-month follow up, women in the experimental group were significantly less likely to be raped than women in the control condition. The intervention did not reduce overall rates of revictimization, but in addition to the reduction in the likelihood of rape, women showed increased self-efficacy and psychological functioning in comparison to control subjects.

Researchers at the Vera Institute of Justice (Davis, O'Sullivan, Guthrie & Ross, 2006) adapted the intervention by Marx et al. for an urban sample, using victimization profiles gathered from 33 in-depth interviews with revictimized women living in New York City and Seattle. However, at the six-month follow-up, Davis et al. found no significant differences between the control and experimental groups on revictimization, sexual assault knowledge, attributions for their assault, self-efficacy, and improvements in psychological functioning. While creating effective prevention programs for sexual revictimization is a challenging task that often requires multiple pilots and program revisions, the work of Marx et al. (2001) illustrates that it is possible to reduce revictimization, at least in the short term, through a brief intervention.

DIRECTIONS FOR FUTURE RESEARCH AND IMPLICATIONS FOR PREVENTION

The area of reoccurring victimization is ripe for more research whose results would inform the development of crime prevention efforts. Future researchers should be mindful of the various issues presented in this chapter. First and foremost, the terminology used should be chosen with care and used in accordance with standard definitions. Doing so will lead to a better understanding of the extant research and enable valid comparisons across research studies. Second, the correlates and causes of repeat and multiple victimization and revictimization need more theoretical development and empirical testing. Finally, crime prevention programs should be designed with the specific intent of reducing the occurrence of reoccurring victimization. Because repeat victims experience a disproportionate amount of all victimizations, if effective interventions could be designed and implemented, crime prevention could be maximized. Once the extent and nature of repeat victimization and revictimization are more thoroughly understood and evaluations of programs are published, preventions programs can be both better implemented and tailored to the casual mechanisms of both types of reoccurring victimization.

REFERENCES

Arata, C. M. (2000). From child victim to adult victim: A model for predicting sexual assault. *Child Maltreatment, 5,* 28–38.

Banyard, V. L., Williams, L. M., & Siegel, J. A. (2001). The long-term mental health consequences of child sexual abuse: An exploratory study of the impact of multiple traumas in a sample of women. *Journal of Traumatic Stress, 14*, 697–715.

Barberet, B., Fisher, B. S., & Taylor, H. (2004). *University student safety in the East Midlands.* London: Home Office.

Bennett, T., & Durie, L. (1999). *Preventing residential burglary in Cambridge: From crime audits to targeted strategies.* Police Research Series, Paper 109. London: Home Office, Police and Reducing Crime Unit.

Boney-McCoy, S., & Finkelhor, D. (1995). Prior victimization: A risk factor for child abuse and for PTSD-related symptomology among sexually abused youth. *Child Abuse and Neglect, 19*, 1401–1421.

Brady, T. V. (1996). *Measuring what matters: Part 1. Measures of fear, crime, and disorder.* Washington, DC: U.S. Department of Justice, National Institute of Justice.

Breitenbecher, K. H. (2001). Sexual revictimization among women: A review of the literature focusing on empirical investigations. *Aggression and Violent Behavior, 6*, 415–432.

Breitenbecher, K. H., & Gidycz, C. A. (1998). An empirical evaluation of a program designed to reduce the risk of multiple sexual victimization. *Journal of Interpersonal Violence, 13*, 472–488.

Breitenbecher, K. H., & Scarce, M. (1999). A longitudinal evaluation of the effectiveness of a sexual assault education program. *Journal of Interpersonal Violence, 14*(5), 459–478.

Briere, J., & Runtz, M. R. (1986). Suicidal thoughts and behaviors in former sexual abuse victims. *Canadian Journal of Behavioral Science, 18*, 413–423.

Budd, T. (1999). *Burglary of domestic dwellings: Findings from the British Crime Survey.* London: Home Office.

Budz, D., Pegnall, N., & Townsley, M. (2001). *Lightning strikes twice: Preventing repeat home burglary.* Queensland, Australia: Criminal Justice Commission.

Canadian Urban Victimization Survey. (1988). Bulletin No. 10. *Multiple victimization.* Ottawa: Ministry of the Solicitor General.

Casey, E. A., & Norius, P. S. (2005). Trauma exposure and sexual revictimization risk. *Violence Against Women, 11*, 505–530.

Catalano, S. M. (2004). *Criminal victimization, 2003.* NCJ 210674. Washington, DC: U.S. Department of Justice, Office of Justice Programs.

Classen, C., Nevo, R., Koopman, C., Nevill-Manning, K., Gore-Felton, C., Rose, D., et al. (2002). Recent stressful life events, sexual revictimization and their relationship with traumatic stress symptoms among women sexually abused in childhood. *Journal of Interpersonal Violence, 17*, 1274–1290.

Classen, C., Pales, O. G., & Aggarwa, R. (2005). Sexual revictimization: A review of the empirical literature. *Trauma, Violence, & Abuse, 6*(2), 103–129.

Coid, J., Petruckevitch, A., Feder, G., Chung, W., Richardson, J., & Moorey, S. (2001). Relation between childhood sexual and physical abuse and risk of revictimisation in women: A cross-sectional survey. *Lancet, 358*, 450–454.

Daigle, L. E., Fisher, B. S., & Cullen, F. T. (2006). *The extent and nature of repeat victimization against college women: Results from two national level studies.* Unpublished manuscript.

Davis, R., O'Sullivan, C., Guthrie, P., & Ross, T. (2006). *Reducing repeat sexual revictimization: A field test with an urban sample.* New York: Vera Institute of Justice.

Desai, S., Arias, I., Thompson, M. P., & Basile, K. C. (2002). Childhood victimization and subsequent adult revictimization assessed in a nationally representative sample of women and men. *Violence and Victims, 17*(6), 639–653.

Ellis, E. M., Atkeson, B. M., & Calhoun, K. S. (1982). An examination of differences between multiple- and single-incident victims of sexual assault. *Journal of Abnormal Psychology, 91*, 221–224.

Farrell, G. (1992). Multiple victimization: Its extent and significance. *International Review of Victimology, 2*, 85–102.

Farrell, G. (1995). Preventing repeat victimization. In M. Tonry & D. P. Farrington (Eds.), *Crime and justice: A review of research* (pp. 469–534). Chicago: University of Chicago Press.

Farrell, G., & Bouloukos, A. C. (2001). International overview: A cross-national comparison of rates of repeat victimization. In G. Farrell and K. Pease (Eds.), *Repeat victimization.* Crime

Prevention Studies, Vol. 12 (pp. 5–25). Monsey, NY: Criminal Justice Press.

Farrell, G., & Pease, K. (2006). Preventing repeat residential burglary. In B. C. Welsh & D. P. Farrington (Eds.), *Preventing crime: What works for children, offenders, victims, and places* (pp. 161–178). Dordrecht: Springer.

Farrell, G., Sousa, W., & Weisel, D. (2002). The time-window effect in the measurement of repeat victimization: A methodology for its examination, and an empirical study. In N. Tilley (Ed.), *Analysis for crime prevention.* Crime Prevention Studies, Vol. 13 (pp. 15–27). Monsey, NY: Criminal Justice Press.

Farrell, G., Tseloni, A., & Pease, K. (2005). Repeat victimization in the ICVS and the NCVS. *Crime Prevention and Community Safety, 7,* 7–18.

Fienberg, S. (1980). Statistical modeling in the analysis of repeat victimization. In S. Fienberg & A. Reiss (Eds.), *Indicators of crime and criminal justice: Quantitative studies* (pp. 54–58). Washington, DC: U.S. Department of Justice.

Fisher, B. S., Cullen, F. T., & Turner, M. G. (2000). *The sexual victimization of college women.* Washington, DC: U.S. Department of Justice, National Institute of Justice and Bureau of Justice Statistics.

Fleming, J., Mullen, P. E., Sibthorpe, B., & Bammer, G. (1999). The long-term impact of childhood sexual abuse in Australian women. *Child Abuse and Neglect, 23,* 145–159.

Forrester, D., Frenzz, S., O'Connell, M., & Pease, K. (1990). *The Kirkholt "Burglary Prevention Project": Phase II.* Crime Prevention Unit Paper 23. London: Her Majesty's Stationery Office.

Gabor, T., & Mata, G. (2004). Victimization and repeat victimization over the life span: A predictive study and implications for policy. *International Review of Victimology, 10,* 193–221.

Gibson, L. E., & Leitenberg, H. (2001). The impact of child sexual abuse and stigma on methods of coping with sexual assault among undergraduate women. *Child Abuse and Neglect, 25,* 1343–1361.

Gidycz, C. A., Hanson, K., & Layman, J. L. (1995). A prospective analysis of the relationships among sexual assault experiences: An extension of previous findings. *Psychology of Women Quarterly, 19,* 5–29.

Gidycz, C. A., Lynn, J. L., Rich, C. L., Marioni, N. L., Loh, C., Blackwell, L. M., et al. (2001). The evaluation of a sexual assault risk reduction program: A multisite investigation. *Journal of Consulting and Clinical Psychology, 69,* 1073–1078.

Goodman, L. A., Koss, M. P., & Russo, N. F. (1993). Violence against women: Physical and mental health effects. *Applied and Preventive Psychology, 2,* 79–89.

Hanson, K. A., & Gidycz, C. A. (1993). Evaluation of a sexual assault prevention program. *Journal of Consulting and Clinical Psychology, 61,* 1046–1052.

Henderson, M. (2002). *Preventing repeat residential burglary: A meta-evaluation of two Australian demonstration projects.* National Circuit, Barton Act 2600. Australia: Commonwealth Attorney-General's Office.

Hindelang, M., Gottfredson, M., & Garafalo, J. (1978). *Victims of personal crime: An empirical foundation for a theory of personal victimization.* Cambridge, MA: Ballinger.

Humphrey, J. A., & White, J. W. (2000) Women's vulnerability to sexual assault from adolescence to young adulthood. *Journal of Adolescent Health, 27*(6), 419–424.

Kellogg, N. D., & Hoffman, T. J. (1997). Child sexual revictimization by multiple perpetrators. *Child Abuse and Neglect, 21,* 953–964.

Lasley, J. R., & Rosenbaum, J. L. (1988). Routine activities and multiple personal victimization. *Sociology and Social Research, 73,* 47–50.

Lauritsen, J., & Davis Quinet, K. F. (1995). Repeat victimization among adolescents and young adults. *Journal of Quantitative Criminology, 11,* 143–166.

Maker, A. H., Kemmelmeier, M., & Peterson, C. (2001). Child sexual abuse, peer sexual abuse, and sexual assault in adulthood: A multi-risk model of revictimization. *Journal of Traumatic Stress, 14*(2), 351–368.

Marhoefer-Dvorak, S., Resick, P. A., Hutter, C. K., & Girelli, S. A. (1988). Single-versus multiple-incident rape victims: A comparison of psychological reactions to rape. *Journal of Interpersonal Violence, 3,* 145–160.

Marx, B. P., Calhoun, K. S., Wilson, A. E., & Meyerson, L. A. (2001). Sexual revictimization prevention: An outcome evaluation. *Journal of Consulting and Clinical Psychology, 69*(1), 25–32.

Meadows, E. A., Jaycox, L. H., Webb, S., & Foa, E. B. (1996, November). Risk recognition in narratives of rape experiences. In S. Orsillo & L. Roemer (Chairs), *The use of narrative methodologies to explore cognitive and emotional dimensions among women with posttraumatic stress disorder.* Symposium conducted at the 30th annual meeting of the Association for Advancement of Behavior Therapy, New York.

Merrill, L. L., Newell, C. E., Thomsen, C. J., Gold, S. R., Milner, J. S., Koss, M. P., et al. (1999). Childhood abuse and sexual revictimization in a female navy recruit sample. *Journal of Traumatic Stress, 12*(2), 211–225.

Messman, T. L., & Long, P. J. (2002). Alcohol and substance abuse disorders as predictors of child to adult sexual revictimization in a sample of community women. *Violence and Victims, 17,* 319–340.

Messman, T. L., & Long, P. J. (2003). The role of childhood sexual abuse sequelae in the sexual revictimization of women: An empirical and theoretical reformulation. *Clinical Psychology Review, 23,* 537–571.

Messman-Moore, T. L., & Long, P. J. (2000). Child sexual abuse and its relationship to revictimization in the form of adult sexual abuse, adult physical abuse, and adult psychological maltreatment. *Journal of Interpersonal Violence, 15*(5), 489–502.

Mukherjee, S., & Carcach, C. (1998). *Repeat victimization in Australia.* Australian Institute of Criminology Research and Public Policy Series No. 15. Griffith: Australian Institute of Criminology.

Murphy, S. M., Kilpatrick, D. G., Amick-McMullan, A., Veronen, L. J., Paduhovich, J., Best, C. L., et al. (1988). Current psychological functioning of child sexual assault survivors: A community study. *Journal of Interpersonal Violence, 3,* 55–79.

National Board for Crime Prevention. (1994). *Wise after the event: Tackling repeat victimization.* London: Home Office.

Nicholas, S., Povey, D., Walker, A., & Kershaw, C. (2005). *Crime in England and Wales 2004/2005.* London: Home Office.

Noll, J. G. (2005). Does childhood sexual abuse set in motion a cycle of violence against women? What we need to know and what we need to learn. *Journal of Interpersonal Violence, 20*(4), 455–462.

Noll, J. G., Horowitz, L. A., Bonanno, G. A., Trickett, P. K., & Putnam, F. W. (2003). Revictimization and self-harm in females who experienced childhood sexual abuse: Results from a prospective study. *Journal of Interpersonal Violence, 18*(12), 1452–1471.

Osborn, D. R., Ellingworth, D., Hope, T., & Trickett, A. (1996). Are repeatedly victimized households different? *Journal of Quantitative Criminology, 12,* 223–245.

Osborn, D. R., & Tseloni, A. (1998). The distribution of household property crimes. *Journal of Quantitative Criminology, 14,* 307–330.

Outlaw, M. S., Ruback, R. B., & Britt, C. (2002). Repeat and multiple victimizations: The role of individual and contextual factors. *Violence and Victims, 17,* 187–204.

Pease, K. (1998). *Repeat victimization: Taking stock.* Crime Detection and Prevention Series Paper 90. London: Home Office.

Pease, K., & Laycock, G. (1996). *Revictimization: Reducing the heat on hot victims.* Washington, DC: U.S. Department of Justice.

Polvi, N., Looman, T., Humphries, C., & Pease, K. (1990). Repeat break-and-enter victimization: Time course and crime prevention opportunity. *Journal of Police Science and Administration, 17,* 8–11.

Polvi, N., Looman, T., Humphries, C., & Pease, K. (1991). The time course of repeat burglary victimization. *British Journal of Criminology, 31,* 411–414.

Raghavan, R., Bogart, L. M., Elliott, M. N., Vestal, K. D., & Schuster, M. A. (2004). Sexual victimization among a national probability sample of adolescent women. *Perspectives on Sexual and Reproductive Health, 36*(6), 225–232.

Randall, M., & Haskell, L. (1995). Sexual violence in women's lives: Findings from the Women's Safety Project, a community-based survey. *Violence Against Women, 1,* 6–31.

Reiss, A. (1980). Victim proneness in repeat victimization by type of crime. In S. Fienberg & S. A. Reiss (Eds.), *Indicators of crime and criminal justice: Quantitative studies* (pp. 41–53). Washington, DC: U.S. Department of Justice.

Robinson, M. B. (1998). Burglary revictimization: The time period of heightened risk. *British Journal of Criminology, 38,* 78–87.

Rodriguez, N., Ryan, S. W., Vande Kemp, H., & Foy, D. W. (1997). Post-traumatic stress disorder in adult female survivors of child sexual abuse: A comparison study. *Journal of Consulting and Clinical Psychology, 65*(1), 53–59.

Roodman, A. A., & Clum, G. A. (2001). Revictimization rates and method variance: A meta-analysis. *Clinical Psychology Review, 21*(2), 183–204.

Russell, D. (1986). *The secret trauma: Incest in the lives of girls and women.* New York: Basic Books.

Sampson, A., & Phillips, C. (1992). *Multiple victimization: Racial attacks on an East London estate.* Police Research Group Crime Prevention Unit Series: Paper No. 36. London: Home Office Police Department.

Sandberg, D. A., Matorin, A. L., & Lynn, S. J. (1999). Dissociation, posttraumatic symptomatology, and sexual revictimization: A prospective examination of mediator and moderator effects. *Journal of Traumatic Stress, 12,* 127–138.

Siegel, J. A., & Williams, L. M. (2003). Risk factors for sexual victimization of women: Results from a prospective study. *Violence Against Women, 9*(8), 902–930.

Simons, R. L., & Whitbeck, L. B. (1991). Sexual abuse as a precursor to prostitution and revictimization among adolescent and adult homeless women. *Journal of Family Issues, 12,* 361–379.

Skogan, W. G. (1990). The National Crime Survey redesign. *The Public Opinion Quarterly, 54,* 256–272.

Small, S. A., & Kerns, D. (1993). Unwanted sexual activity among peers during early and middle adolescence: Incidence and risk factors. *Journal of Marriage and the Family, 55,* 941–952.

Sorenson, S. B., Siegel, J. M., Golding, J. M., & Stein, J. A. (1991). Repeated sexual victimization. *Violence and Victims, 6,* 299–308.

Sorenson, S. B., Stein, J. A., Siegel, J. M., Golding, J. M., & Burnam, M. A. (1987). The prevalence of adult sexual assault: The Los Angeles Epidemiologic Catchment Area Project. *American Journal of Epidemiology, 126,* 1154–1164.

Tilley, N. (1993). *After Kirkhold: Theory, method and results of replication evaluations.* Police Research Group, Crime Prevention Unit Series Paper 47. London: Home Office.

Tjaden, P., & Thoennes, N. (2000). *Extent, nature, and consequences of intimate partner violence: Findings from the national violence against women survey.* Washington, DC: National Institute of Justice and the Centers for Disease Control and Prevention.

Tjaden, P., & Thoennes, N. (2006). *Extent, nature, and consequences of rape victimization: Findings from the National Violence Against Women Survey.* Washington, DC: National Institute of Justice and the Centers for Disease Control and Prevention.

Townsley, M., Homel, R., & Chaseling, J. (2000). Repeat burglary victimization: Spatial and temporal patterns. *Australian and New Zealand Journal of Criminology, 33,* 37–63.

Tseloni, A. (2000). Personal criminal victimization in the United States: Fixed and random effects of individual and household characteristics. *Journal of Quantitative Criminology, 16,* 415–442.

Weisel, D. L. (2005). *Analyzing repeat victimization: Problem-oriented guides for police problem-solving tool.* Series Guide No. 4. Washington, DC: U.S. Department of Justice, Office of Community Oriented Policing Services.

Weisel, D. L., Clarke, R. V., & Stedman, J. R. (1999). *Hot dots in hot spots: Examining repeat victimization for residential burglary in three cities, final report.* Washington, DC: U.S. Department of Justice.

Wilson, A. E., Calhoun, K. S., & Bernat, J. A. (1999). Risk recognition and trauma-related symptoms among sexually revictimized women. *Journal of Consulting and Clinical Psychology, 67,* 705–710.

Wittebrood, K., & Nieuwbeerta, P. (2000). Criminal victimization during one's life course: The effects of previous victimization and patterns of routine activities. *Journal of Research in Crime and Delinquency, 37,* 91–122.

Wyatt, G. E., Guthrie, D., & Notgrass, C. M. (1992). Differential effects of women's child

sexual abuse and subsequent sexual revictimization. *Journal of Consulting and Clinical
Psychology, 60,* 167–173.

NOTE

1. Sally is not the real name of the woman
depicted in this example. The description,
however, does convey events that did in fact occur
to a female respondent in the National College
Women Sexual Victimization Study (Fisher,
Cullen, & Turner, 2000).

2. Jenny is not the real name of the woman
depicted in this example. The description is based on
Jenny's discussion with a rape crisis counselor while
receiving care at a New York City hospital in 2004.

14

Victimization

An International Perspective

ANNA ALVAZZI DEL FRATE

Over the past few decades, the focus on victims of crime and the advent of victim surveys have facilitated a broader understanding of the crime problem as well as a better assessment of its burden on citizens at the international level. While in the past only police and criminal justice data were used to measure crime, it is now widely acknowledged that such information alone is not sufficient and should be integrated with victim surveys results. Surveys of victims of crime are a more comparable tool to assess risks across countries and world regions. The International Crime Victim Survey (ICVS) represents the major research project in this respect, with more than 80 participating countries since 1989. International surveys are also addressing women victims of crime and violence (World Health Organization [WHO] multicountry study and the International Violence Against Women Survey [IVAWS]) as well as measuring the impact of crime and corruption on businesses. More and more countries regularly carry out victim surveys. Researchers, policymakers, and practitioners, as well as international organizations addressing crime as an impediment to development, governance, and rule of law, make an extensive use of their comparative results.

MEASURING/COMPARING VICTIMIZATION AT THE CROSS-NATIONAL LEVEL

Crime affects all parts of the world, although with different intensity and trends. However, "crime" is too broad a concept to reflect the

Author's Note: The opinions expressed in this paper are solely those of the author and do not necessarily reflect the views of the United Nations.

entire scope of behaviors that may be considered "criminal" across the world, which range from the most threatening transnational crimes to incidents such as assault, robbery, and theft, which many people may have personally experienced.

In his report "In Larger Freedom: Towards Development, Security and Human Rights For All," the secretary-general of the United Nations identified civil violence among the major threats to peace and security in the twenty-first century, together with international war and conflict, organized crime, terrorism, and weapons of mass destruction. A crime-free environment is fundamental for human security: "We will not enjoy development without security, we will not enjoy security without development, and we will not enjoy either without respect for human rights" (United Nations, 2005).

Assessing the burden of crime and violence is of great importance for any preventive action to take place. Two main sources of information are generally used for this purpose: police records of reported crime and surveys of the victims of crime. The two sources capture different dimensions of the problem and therefore should complement each other.

For many years the only available quantitative information on crime was that relevant to crimes recorded by the police. Such statistics obviously reflect the efficiency of law enforcement and the criminal justice system in the process of recording and are limited to the portion of crimes being discovered by the police or reported by victims or witnesses. If these data are used for benchmarking purposes at the international level, it is likely that the countries with the most efficient policing and the most advanced technologies will rank higher than others. Furthermore, countries where victims are more confident in approaching the police are likely to capture higher numbers of incidents.

International collections of administrative crime statistics are maintained by the United Nations Office on Drugs and Crime (UNODC)[1] and Interpol.[2] Data on police recorded crime cover the main types of crime, which occur in most societies. For comparative purposes, these collections provide broad descriptions of the most frequent categories. Reporting government agencies respond according to such descriptions, where possible adjusting data that are originally collected on the basis of national criminal codes. This process of transformation from national to international statistics is likely to be easier in the countries where data collection is more accurate and more details about the incidents are known. In general, it is considered easier to compare across countries data on serious crime, notably intentional homicide. However, even homicide rates may contain different information in different countries. International comparison of crime statistics encounters enormous difficulties due to different judicial systems, definitions, criminal codes and procedures, translation of concepts into different languages, and efficiency of the system in responding to reports or complaints from citizens.

When dealing with "conventional" categories of crime, or "volume" crime, it should be taken into account that most of these crimes are recorded by the police only as a consequence of reports received from victims and citizens. Patterns of reporting crime to the relevant authorities vary depending on many variables. At the level of the individual, several reasons for nonreporting have been identified, including those related to the profile of the victim, fear of revenge from the part of the offender, as well as practical obstacles between the victim and the police (distance of the police station, language problems, unwillingness of victims to approach the police, and—in some extreme cases—the police being the offenders). Patterns of reporting also vary across countries; thus the extent of the "dark figure" (the estimated number of unreported cases) is likely to be different in different countries. In some cases the presence of alternative mechanisms for dispute resolution, such as justice of the peace or traditional leaders, may divert victims from formally approaching the police. Recent studies have shown a correlation between reporting and income, thus suggesting that reporting levels may vary not only across countries and cultures, but also over time due to the changes in the economic situation of a given society, with unemployed victims much less likely to report property crimes compared to individuals who are employed (MacDonald, 2001).

It is therefore clear that any measure of the burden of crime should take into account the context in which crime occurs. Surveys on population (victim surveys) may provide information on crime, crime victims and their attitudes toward the police, reporting patterns and reasons for not reporting, fear of crime, and crime prevention measures.

Victim surveys started in the 1960s and their diffusion was relatively rapid in developed countries, becoming more focused and regular, while their presence in the developing world was scarce.

Four decades after, several countries are regularly collecting information through victim surveys (e.g., the National Crime Victimization Survey in the United States, the British Crime Survey, the Dutch Victim Survey, Canada's National Survey on Criminal Victimization, etc.) and have already developed considerable longitudinal series. Some other countries have started carrying out victim surveys only in the recent past.[3] In the developing world, victim surveys are still considered expensive and very much depend on funding from donors. Nevertheless, their importance and potential are now fully appreciated all over the world.

Different societies, however, experience crime in different ways, thus the structure and content of national victim surveys reflect the issues that are perceived as crucial in each country. For example, violence may occur in diverse contexts, juvenile gangs may be more or less active and organized, and the availability and use of weapons may largely differ from country to country. The same applies to property crime. While burglary may affect citizens in affluent societies by depriving them of cash, jewelry, hi-tech equipment, art objects, and furniture, burglary in developing countries may entail theft of basic household items such as crockery, cutlery, and linen. Even though the monetary loss may be small, the impact on the victim is significant. In many developing countries where cattle are a vital resource, theft of livestock is perceived by victims as one of the most serious victimization experiences.

National victim surveys differ from each other not only in context, but also in the methodology adopted. Different objectives, sample size, questionnaires, and interview techniques may be used. Taking everything into account, it is not advisable to carry out straightforward comparisons among national victim surveys. In order to compare experiences of crime among citizens from different countries it is necessary to apply some standardization: This includes objectives, methodology, and data collection instrument.

THE INTERNATIONAL CRIME VICTIM SURVEY

A first proposal to organize an international victimization survey was launched by the Organisation for Economic Co-operation and Development (OECD) in the 1970s. Pilot studies were carried out in the United States, the Netherlands, and Finland. Further to a meeting of the Standing Conference of Local and Regional Authorities of the Council of Europe held in 1987 in Barcelona, a working group was created and started developing the survey methodology and questionnaire.[4] Finally, in 1989, a group of European researchers was able to start an international standardized survey on crime, called at the time the International Crime Survey. It consisted of national surveys in 16 countries and a city survey in Surabaya, Indonesia (Van Dijk, Mayhew, & Killias, 1990). Findings revealed the great potential of the tool, especially for the countries where, for a number of reasons, it was more difficult to collect official statistics. Its application in developing countries started in 1992 with the involvement of the United Nations (initially, the United Nations Interregional Crime and Justice Research Institute (UNICRI), based in Turin, Italy, and recently the Vienna-based UNODC). Since then the ICVS has represented a very important instrument in expanding knowledge on victimization across the world.[5]

The ICVS shares with national crime/victim surveys the objective of measuring crime beyond the information provided by police statistics. One of the most important features of the ICVS is the opportunity for respondents to explain reasons for non-reporting of crimes in different countries, thus providing useful information to understand crime experiences in different contexts in order to supplement administrative data.

FINDINGS OF THE ICVS IN DIFFERENT WORLD REGIONS: WHAT IS THE SAME AND WHAT IS DIFFERENT IN DIFFERENT CONTEXTS

Five rounds of the ICVS have been done in 1989, 1992, 1996, 2000, and 2004–2005.[6] The questionnaire has basically remained unchanged over time: It includes sections on experiences of victimization at the household and personal levels, for each of which a standard definition is provided.[7] Furthermore, the questionnaire explores whether victims reported crimes to the police and, if they did not, what were the reasons. Fear of crime is measured through general questions on feelings of personal safety and one question on the likelihood of burglary during the next

12 months. Questions dealing with attitudes toward the police refer to both overall perceptions of police performance in controlling and preventing crime and specific experience of victims further to reporting crimes. Finally, the questionnaire deals with crime prevention measures and ownership of firearms.

Between 1,500 and 2,000 households are interviewed in each country/city either by telephone (CATI) or face-to-face and asked about incidents that occurred over the past five years but with a particular focus on the past calendar year.

The ICVS database contains a wealth of information on crime experienced by citizens from approximately 80 countries, including surveys done in many cities in Africa, Asia, and Latin America. More than 300,000 individual cases are contained in the international database,[8] which provides a unique source of information.

On average, approximately 30% of interviewed citizens suffered at least one form of victimization over the year preceding the interview. Overall, victimization levels around 27% were observed in five out of seven regions of the world (Western Europe, Eastern-Central Europe, North America, Australia, and Asia), while in Africa and Latin America much higher levels of victimization were observed (35% and 46%, respectively).

Many of the crimes experienced by citizens are not reported to the relevant authorities. Different patterns of reporting to the police were observed in the various regions, as presented in Figure 14.2. Crimes are more frequently reported to the police in Western Europe, North America, and Australia than in the other regions, thus showing an opposite trend with respect to the frequency of victimization.

In practice, in the regions where more crime occurs, the police get to know very little about it. By contrast, there may be an overestimate in police recorded crime in many countries where the occurrence of crime is comparatively low but citizens have

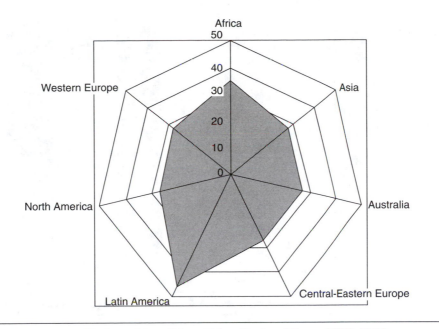

Figure 14.1   Percentage Victims of Any Crime. Urban Regional Rates, ICVS, 2000

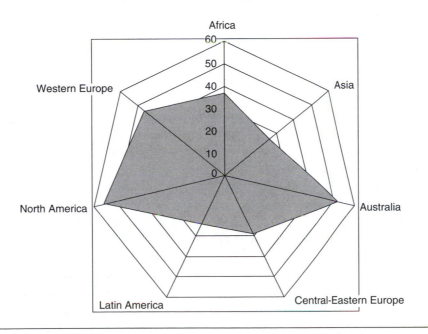

Figure 14.2   Average Percentage of Crimes Reported by Victims to the Police, by Region. ICVS, 2000

more confidence in and easier access to the police.

Figure 14.3 shows that the "dark figure," that is, the percentage of crimes that are not captured by the statistics, is minimal for theft of car and much bigger for other types of crime. Theft of car is generally reported to the police because of car registration and for insurance reasons. Data show that on average 90% of car thefts were indeed reported to the police, thus representing a comparable benchmark for reporting rates of other

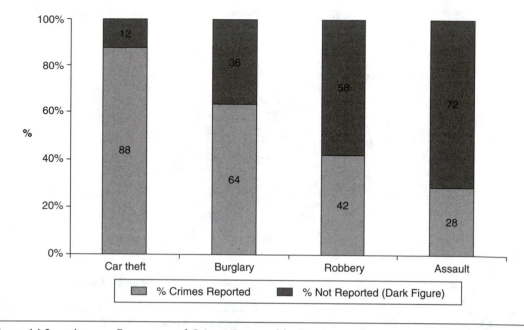

Figure 14.3   Average Percentage of Crimes Reported by Victims to the Police, by Type of Crime. ICVS, 2000

crimes. Burglary is the second most frequently reported crime, especially in Western Europe, North America, and Australia where reporting rates for burglary are only slightly lower than those observed for car theft. In these regions more than 80% of victims of burglary reported to the police. Much lower rates were observed in other regions (the lowest in Asia, with approximately 40%).

Robbery and assault were the least reported types of crime, especially in the developing regions. On average, only 42% of victims of robbery and 28% of victims of assault reported to the police. Robbery was frequently reported in Western Europe (67%), but much less in the remaining regions, with a minimum in Latin America, where only one victim of robbery out of five reported. More than half of the Latin American victims of robbery who did not report to the police said they did not because "the police would not do anything," and approximately 25% said that they feared or disliked the police.

In the case of assault, on average, only one of every four victims turned to the police. Only in three regions (North America, Australia, and Western Europe) did more than one third of victims of assault turn to the police. In the remaining regions, reporting rates for assault remained very low, with a minimum of 15% in Africa.

In some countries the (in)efficiency of the police in responding to crime may be at the basis of low reporting. If efficiency improves, a trust relationship with citizens may be established, and thus more crime may end up being reported. This may indeed generate higher numbers in police data of recorded crime. For this reason, it is advisable to keep consistency between data sources in analyzing trends and making comparisons in order to avoid mixing police data with victim surveys results. Nevertheless, the assessment of the extent of crime needs to take into account and integrate the two sources.

Figure 14.4 shows an example of the information provided by two different data

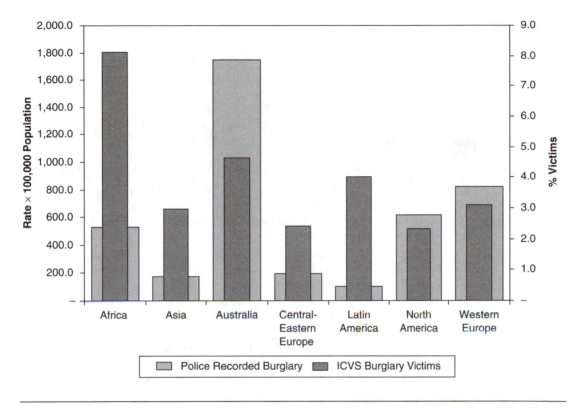

Figure 14.4   Percentage of Victims of Burglary and Rate of Burglaries per 100,000 Population, by Regions. ICVS, 2000, and UN Crime Trends Survey, 2001–2002

sources, the ICVS and the UN Survey on Crime Trends (police recorded data), regarding burglary. The comparison across regions based on police data (the light-shaded bars) shows that burglaries recorded in Australia were highest. On the contrary, burglary victimization rates (the dark-shaded bars) show that African citizens were those most frequently victims of burglary. If police records only were taken into account, it may appear that burglary in Africa is much less frequent than in Western Europe, the Americas, or Oceania.

FEELINGS OF SAFETY

Questions on feelings of safety are generally included in victim surveys. The ICVS addresses the issue of perceived vulnerability to street crime through the following question: "How

safe do you feel walking alone in your area after dark? Do you feel very safe, fairly safe, a bit unsafe, or very unsafe?" Figure 14.5 shows the urban regional rates.

The regional rates of feelings of being unsafe on the streets are highest in Latin America, Africa, and Central-Eastern Europe. The distribution roughly matches that of regional victimization rates for contact crimes (such as assaults/threats and robberies). Previous analyses at the country level have, however, shown that this measure of street safety is not consistently related to levels of contact crime. One implication of the lack of such relationship is that fear of street crime is culturally mediated and may be influenced by national media presentations of violent crime.

General feelings of (un)safety may not be directly related to crime experience and may

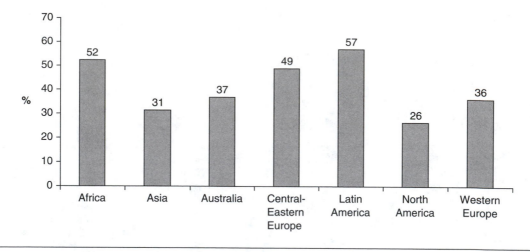

Figure 14.5 Percentage Feeling a Bit or Very Unsafe While Alone After Dark in Their Area. Urban regional rates, ICVS, 1996–2000

not represent actual fear of crime. Research has demonstrated that at the individual level feelings of unsafety are related to age and gender, with the elderly and women showing much higher levels of fear and concern (Van Kesteren, Mayhew, & Nieuwbeerta, 2000). Such levels of concern do not necessarily match actual risks of victimization which tend to be higher among young males.

Feelings of safety and public perception of crime may also be influenced by external variables, for example, the pattern of television viewing. Research findings suggest that television broadcasts that include fictional or factual treatment of crime stimulate the perception that violent crime is more frequent than in reality (Pfeiffer, Windzio, & Kleimann, 2005). However, this may not apply to all countries and cultures, since a study carried out among 700 citizens of Trinidad in 2000 indicated no relationship between media consumption and fear of crime (Chadee & Ditton, 2005).

Victimization rates may to some extent influence the perceived likelihood of burglary. Figure 14.6 shows a similar pattern between burglary rates and perceived risk of burglary over the next 12 months. However,

citizens of Central-Eastern Europe were those showing the highest concern about risk of being victimized, while ranking second lowest in actual burglary rate among the observed regions.

VICTIM SURVEYS AND ACCESS TO JUSTICE

A fundamental right of victims is to seek justice from state institutions. The police generally represent the first contact between victims and the criminal justice system when crimes are reported. However, many crimes are not reported. According to the ICVS results, this may happen not only because crimes were not considered serious enough to be reported but also because victims perceived that the police either could or would do nothing about them. Many victims in developing countries did not report because of fear of the police.

A section of the ICVS deals with the overall assessment of police performance. Responses are given by all respondents, whether or not they had been victimized. Results in Figure 14.7 confirm that residents of Latin America, East Europe, and Africa show a poor appreciation of police efforts in

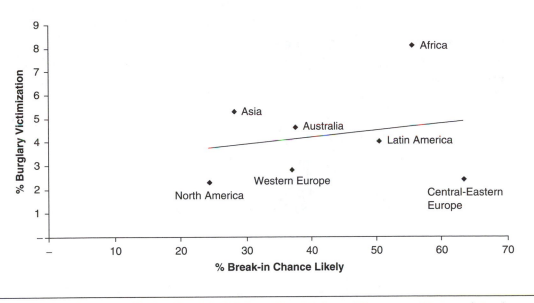

Figure 14.6   Percentage Feeling Break-in Likely or Very Likely and Percentage Victims of Burglary. Urban regional rates, ICVS, 1996–2000

preventing and controlling local crime. The percentage of respondents satisfied with the job that the police were doing was much lower in these regions. In many developing countries as well as in many of the new democracies in Europe, the public is still not perceiving the police as a service to citizens but rather as a distant and almost inaccessible agency, certainly not one to turn to for help and assistance. The interpretation of these data suggests that much remains to be done in order to promote a service approach to policing which would enable victims to get fair treatment.

The following question was asked: "Taking everything into account, how good do you think the police in your area are at controlling crime? Do you think they do a very good job, a fairly good job, a fairly poor job, or a very poor job?" The chart shows percentages for "very good" and "fairly good" answers.

Among the victims who reported to the police, fewer than half were satisfied with the way their case was dealt with. Figure 14.8 shows that those least satisfied were the respondents from Latin America, Asia,

and Africa. Within Europe satisfaction was lowest in Central-Eastern Europe. Only in Western Europe, North America, and Australia did more than 50% of victims who reported to the police positively evaluate the treatment received.

The perception of the police about their own performance may not match that of citizens. As an example, a survey conducted in Mozambique (UNICRI, 2003) addressed a similar question to a sample of police officers.[9] While most citizens were dissatisfied about the reaction of the police to their reports, officers were almost unanimous in thinking that they were providing a good service to citizens. There was a wide discrepancy between the perceptions of citizens (the "users" or "clients" of police services) and those in charge of responding to crime victims, to assist them in getting into the criminal justice system.

In many parts of the world police agencies fail to meet the expectations of citizens reporting crime. As presented in Figure 14.9, the most common reason for dissatisfaction was that the police "did not do enough"

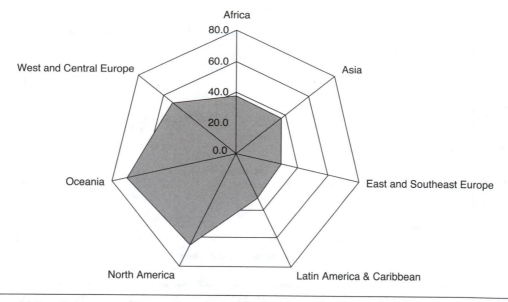

Figure 14.7   Percentage of Respondents Satisfied With the Police in Controlling Crime, by Regions. ICVS, 2000

SOURCE: ICVS, 2000 (UNODC elaboration).

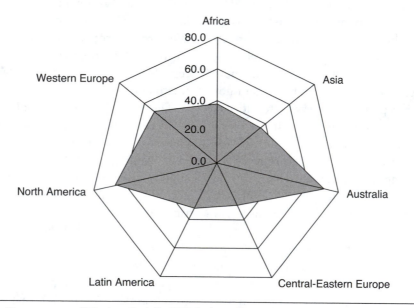

Figure 14.8   Percentages of Victims Satisfied With the Police After Reporting Serious Crimes, by Regions. ICVS, 2000

(31%). About a quarter said that they "did not recover the goods" or "did not find the offender," while according to 21%, the police "were not interested." Victims of property crimes from developing countries more often gave as reason for their dissatisfaction that their property was not returned. Thirteen percent of victims were unhappy that the police had not kept them sufficiently informed. Finally, 11% said the police did

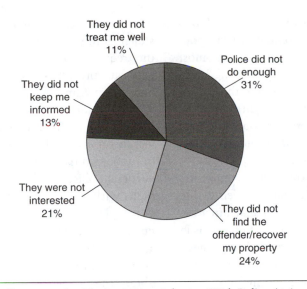

They did not treat me well 11%

Police did not do enough 31%

They did not keep me informed 13%

They were not interested 21%

They did not find the offender/recover my property 24%

Figure 14.9 Overall Reasons for Victims' Dissatisfaction With Police Action Upon Reporting. ICVS, 2000

not treat them well, either being impolite or incorrect. This reason was given most often by victims of violence against women, especially by those from Latin America.

This indicates that at least one 1 of 10 victims who reported crime, by his or her own admission, was also a victim of "secondary victimization."[10] As a consequence, victims may feel abandoned by institutions, lose confidence in the criminal justice system, resort to self-defense, and seek revenge against the offender. This situation in which the victim is isolated from the surrounding context represents a fracture in the social fabric that, if not addressed as a matter of urgency, may generate further damage in the victim's family and community.

REGIONAL SURVEYS WITH VICTIMIZATION MODULES

Instead of dedicated/specialized victim surveys, some multiscope household surveys include a victimization module. This is the case in several countries that regularly repeat multiscope surveys and rotate modules on various issues at different points in time. A similar approach has been adopted by the regional surveys called "barometers," which address a number of social issues through international surveys carried out in geopolitical regions such as Europe, Latin America, and Africa.

The *Eurobarometer*[11] is a program of cross-national comparative surveys conducted on behalf of the European Commission twice a year. It is designed to monitor social and political attitudes and includes separate supplementary surveys on special issues. The *Latinobarometro*[12] is a survey equivalent to the *Eurobarometer* conducted since 1995. The *Afrobarometer*[13] has been conducted since 1998.

Most crime issues covered by the regional barometers are dealt with through attitudinal questions rather than measuring direct experience of victimization. This is possibly due to the small size of the sample. As an example, a question of the *Latinobarometro* asked respondents if they knew someone who had been a victim of crime in the past 12 months (thus aiming at capturing a broader response than the direct victimization experience questions). Indeed, 41% of respondents in the region said that was the case.

One recurrent question in the *Eurobarometer* and *Latinobarometro* asks respondents what they think are the two most important issues their country is facing at the moment. In 2005, crime was the third most important issue, after unemployment and the economic situation for the Europeans, while for the Latin American citizens, it ranked second after unemployment.

Common survey modules on victimization to be used in different countries, even within the same region, require particular attention in the translation of concepts and questions in the different cultural contexts and languages.

The *Afrobarometer* regularly deals with conflict and crime. The topic includes questions on feelings of safety and experience with crime and violence. In the surveys conducted in 15 African countries in 2002–2003, respondents were asked the following question: "Over the past year, how often (if ever) have you or anyone in your family had something stolen from your house?" Figure 14.10 shows the frequency of responses for the two aggregate categories "Once or twice/Several times" and "Many times/Always."

The results of these surveys are not directly comparable with those of specialized victim surveys and may produce either over- or underestimates of the problems. In this particular case, burglary rates appear very high with respect to those captured by other victim surveys in the same region. Furthermore, due to the need to save time and costs, this question aims at concentrating as much information as possible and tries to obtain the *incidence* of burglary (how many incidents) without having first dealt with the *prevalence* (how many persons have been victims at all).

It is however important to observe that victimization is considered by these surveys

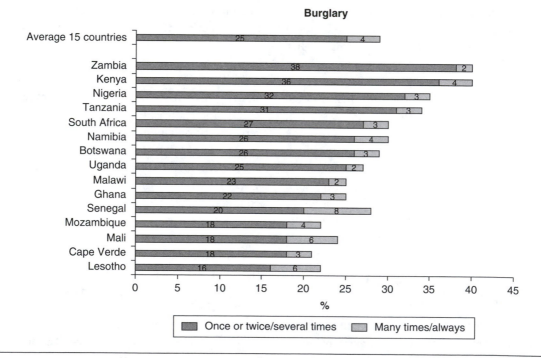

Figure 14.10   Percentage of Respondents Having Had Something Stolen Over the Previous Year
SOURCE: Afrobarometer, 2004 (UNODC elaboration).

among the key issues to be measured while assessing the overall socioeconomic situation in the region.

SPECIAL INTERNATIONAL SURVEYS

Violence Against Women: The International Violence Against Women Survey and the WHO Multicountry Study on Domestic Violence

Violence against women occurs in various forms and crosses economic and cultural boundaries. It affects women in countries around the world, regardless of class, religion, language, or region of the world. The United Nations Declaration on the Elimination of Violence Against Women, proclaimed by General Assembly Resolution 48/104 of December 20, 1993, at Article 1, defines violence against women as

> any act of gender-based violence that results in, or is likely to result in, physical, sexual or psychological harm or suffering to women, including threats of such acts, coercion or arbitrary deprivations of liberty, whether occurring in public or private life. (United Nations, 1993)

General population victimization surveys may not be the best instrument to capture the extent and characteristics of violence against women. National studies on violence against women such as those carried out in Canada and the Netherlands in the early 1990s and in Finland in 1997 started developing specialized methodologies for obtaining the best results in interviewing women, who may be particularly reluctant to talk to outsiders about violent incidents. These episodes are actually largely underreported, be it to the police or to interviewers. Researchers developed training curricula to prepare the interviewers to deal with particularly sensitive issues.

The same principle to design and conduct a specialized survey on violence against women was applied at the international level with the IVAWS. Coordinated by the European Institute on Crime Prevention and Control, affiliated with the United Nations (HEUNI), the IVAWS is supported by input from UNODC, UNICRI, and Statistics Canada. The IVAWS started in the early 2000s and has so far involved nine countries in which data have been collected (Australia, Costa Rica, Czech Republic, Denmark, Hong Kong Special Administrative Region (SAR) of China, Mozambique, Philippines, Poland, and Switzerland). The project aims are dealing with the issue of violence against women from a criminal justice perspective, providing victims the opportunity to disclose their feelings, needs, and attitudes, and promoting fair treatment of victims within the criminal justice system (Aromaa, 2004).

These objectives may be seen as complementary to those of the WHO, which launched a multicountry study on domestic violence. The study deals with physical and sexual violence by husbands and partners and its effects on the health and well-being of women around the world.[14] Women from rural and urban areas were interviewed in 10 countries: Bangladesh, Brazil, Ethiopia, Japan, Namibia, Peru, Samoa, Serbia and Montenegro, Thailand, and the United Republic of Tanzania (WHO, 2005).

Both surveys cover different time frames: one year (last year), five years (last five years), and lifetime (after the age of 15, "ever") reference periods. The IVAWS questionnaire has a focus on male violence against women since the age of 15 (respondents should be aged 16 or older). It deals with physical, sexual, and psychological violence committed by any man (husband, boyfriend, relative, acquaintance, stranger). Acts of violence included in the IVAWS are detailed in the following table.

IVAWS	*WHO Multicountry Study*
Physical abuse	
Any physical force without the woman's consent, for example, slapping, punching, pushing, choking, and beating by any man, including marital partners Dowry-related assaults	A current or former partner having slapped her, or thrown something at her that could hurt her; pushed or shoved her; hit her with a fist or something else that could hurt; kicked, dragged, or beaten her up; choked or burnt her on purpose; threatened her with, or actually used, a gun, knife, or other weapon against her
Sexual abuse	
Grabbing or assault of the sexual parts of a woman's body, oral or anal rape, incest, rape within marriage Forced prostitution	Being physically forced to have sexual intercourse against her will Having sexual intercourse because she was afraid of what her partner might do Being forced to do something sexual she found degrading or humiliating

Details about the woman's experiences and their consequences are collected through an elaborated series of sets of questions dealing with different types of incidents involving different types of threats and psychological, physical, and sexual violence perpetrated by any man. For each incident, the questionnaire probes the characteristics of the offender and his relationship to the victim, as well as details of the context in which it happened (when, where, how, and how many times it happened).

International comparative results of the IVAWS have not been released yet. However, reports from four countries (Australia, Czech Republic, Denmark, and Switzerland) have already been published,[15] and thus comparable data from these countries can be analyzed. Figure 14.11a shows the results as to lifetime prevalence of violence.

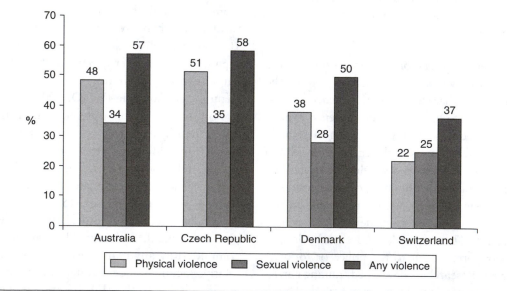

Figure 14.11a   Percentage of Women Respondents Who Were Victims of Physical, Sexual, and Any Violence Over Lifetime

SOURCE: IVAWS, 2003–2005.

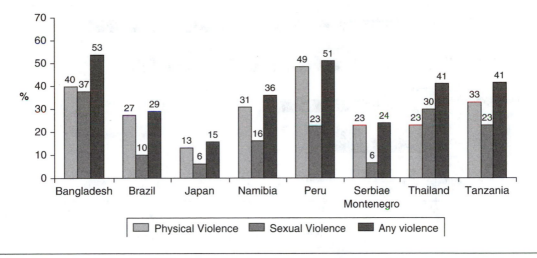

Figure 14.11b   Percentage of Women Respondents Who Were Victims of Physical, Sexual, and Any Violence Over Lifetime, Urban Rates

SOURCE: WHO multicountry study (2005).

It appears that the risks for women in Australia and Czech Republic were highest. Very similar percentages were observed in these two countries, where more than half of the respondents had experienced any type of violence since the age of 15. Risks were slightly lower in Denmark and lowest in Switzerland. However, the difference among the countries was smallest for sexual violence, which was suffered by 34% of Australian women, 35% of Czech women, 28% of Danish women, and 25% of Swiss women. Interestingly, Switzerland was the only country among the four in which women were more frequently victims of sexual violence than physical violence.

Figure 14.11b shows the results from the comparable questions of the WHO study. It appears that similar patterns can be observed in most countries. These data do not mean much if they are not put in context and read against the information that emerges and is known outside the domestic environment. Most women do not report their experiences. The ICVS found that, on average and depending on the seriousness of the offences, sexual incidents were reported to the police in a measure of one out of three rapes and one out of five sexual assaults.

The IVAWS and the WHO study confirmed these assessments.

The WHO study highlights the suffered physical injuries as a direct result of violence and points to the health consequence of these incidents. Women victims are likely to suffer multiple victimization that generates a situation of prolonged stress. They can easily get sick and become psychologically weak, even cultivate suicidal thoughts. The WHO also uses the results of its study to warn about the damage to women's sexual and reproductive health and the increased risk of sexually transmitted infections, including HIV. These acts of violence are a violation of women's human rights and no country is immune to them. The IVAWS' developers considered other acts of violence, such as dowry-related murder, honour killings, female infanticide, child marriage and trafficking of women, although no less important issues, outside the boundaries of the survey.

Businesses as Victims of Crime

Victim surveys traditionally focus on households and individuals. However, the economic consequences of victimization of

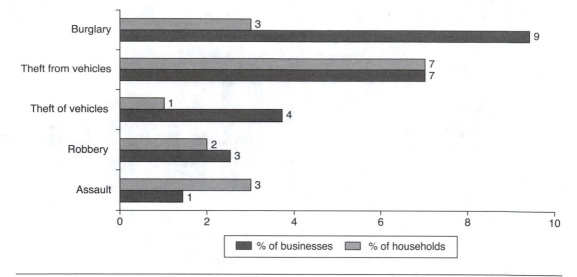

Figure 14.12   One-Year Prevalence of Victimization by Type of Conventional Crime, ICBS and ICVS, Nine Central-Eastern European Cities

the business sector may have an impact on the entire community. Thus the importance of devoting attention to the assessment of the extent and causes of crime against businesses.

Many surveys have looked at the experiences of victimization of businesses. Research in several European countries has demonstrated that they are likely to become victims of crime, including theft, robbery, assault, extortion, corruption, and fraud, more frequently than households.

At the international level, the first International Commercial Crime Survey (ICCS) was launched in 1994 as a parallel to the ICVS. A standardized questionnaire targeting businesses as respondents was drafted, and eight countries participated in the fieldwork (Van Dijk & Terlouw, 1996). A number of comparable surveys followed in Australia, South Africa, Finland, Estonia, Latvia, and Lithuania (Alvazzi del Frate, 2004b). The ICCS questionnaire mostly focused on experiences of victimization, information on perceptions, and attitudes toward several aspects of everyday business. Questions dealt with experiences of crime,

safety in the area, pollution issues, security devices and costs involved in physical measures for crime prevention, attitudes toward the police and private policing. In 2000, the ICCS was revised in order to capture more of the corruption/extortion issues and businesses' perceptions in this respect. A new name was used (International Crime Business Survey—ICBS) for the round of surveys that took place in nine Central-Eastern European cities in 2000.[16]

Figure 14.12 shows that property-related conventional crime such as burglary, theft of vehicles, and robbery is experienced by businesses more frequently than households. Furthermore, many businesses experienced other types of theft. For example, 13% experienced theft committed by outsiders, 9% gave accounts of theft by customers, and 5% experienced theft by employees.

Businesses are also frequently at risk of other types of crime, as shown in Figure 14.13. The importance of measuring the extent of actual experience of corruption, rather than only perceptions, has become clear over the years, thus transforming

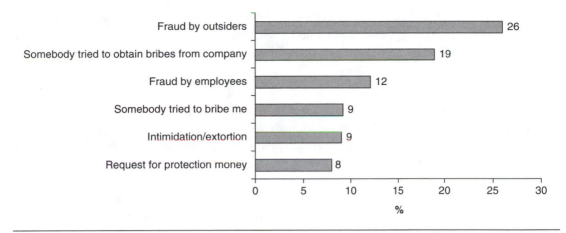

Figure 14.13 One-Year Prevalence of Businesses Victims of Fraud, Corruption, Intimidation, Extortion, and Requests for Protection Money, ICBS, Nine Central-Eastern European Cities

ordinary business surveys into victim surveys aiming at assessing the social and economic costs of corruption and bribery. More than a quarter of the interviewed companies had been victimized by fraud committed by someone not related, while 12% were victims of fraud by employees. One out of five companies had to face bribery requests, while 9% were offered bribes. Businesses may be exposed to bribery/corruption not only in dealing with the public sector, for example, in obtaining licenses from municipal authorities or clearing goods with customs, but also within the private sector.

FUTURE RESEARCH NEEDS

As previous examples have shown, victim surveys have become an indispensable research tool and a building block of knowledge on crime. This applies at the national and international levels. In some countries, victim surveys are the main source of information on the crime situation, while in others they are still at the pilot phase. A considerable amount of research is currently devoted to further development of victim surveys in developing countries, as a priority to enhance their capacity to collect and analyze data on trends in crime. Victim surveys will provide baseline and benchmark information for more effective and targeted assistance. This implies a policy use of victim survey findings, which considers the results in view of the development of relevant strategies for crime prevention, victim support, and policing.

Among the current initiatives, a number of main trends can be identified:

1. *Internationally comparable surveys.* There is an increasing demand for internationally comparable data. Traditionally, crime and criminal justice statistics suffer from little international comparability due to the different legal systems and definitions. The ICVS has been successful at supporting dedicated research specifically aimed at international comparisons. However, many countries are now developing their own national surveys with an eye to international comparability. This does not mean the end of the ICVS, but a development in the direction of more national ownership of survey methodology, process, and analysis of the results. In this context, it would be desirable that *victim surveys become an integral part of the work of national statistical offices.*[17] In some countries where it may not be possible to conduct full-fledged victim

surveys, there may be the possibility of including victimization modules in general household surveys, such as multiscope surveys or even the census.

2. The United Nations Economic Commission for Europe (UNECE) and the UNODC have produced an inventory of victim surveys in the ECE region[18] and started developing a *Manual for Conducting Victimization Surveys* with the objective of helping countries to design their own national victimization surveys considering the experience accumulated in the region. The manual will also provide a short core module to be included in national surveys to ensure international comparability for a limited set of victimization experiences.

3. *Surveys on important vulnerable parts of the population,* such as women, children, minorities, and the elderly. It may be difficult to obtain information on risks of vulnerable groups. Some of the challenges include designing appropriate samples to produce reliable statistics, reaching vulnerable groups, defining minorities, applying relevant ethical safeguards to protect the privacy of respondents, and providing adequate training to interviewers. Research on these groups should be multidisciplinary and take into account—depending on the case—victimological, sociological, political, educational, and medical aspects. An international victimization survey of migrants and minorities (including the Roma) is planned to be carried out by the European Monitoring Centre on Racism and Xenophobia (EUMC) in 2006.

4. Research is developing on how to address victimization issues within *multipurpose household surveys* and *regional surveys* (such as the *Eurobarometer*). This includes which type of crimes and definitions should be covered in view of developing a short set of questions (possibly comparable at the international level). Inserting victimization questions into a social survey with many different objectives may generate the need for specific training of interviewers to capture information on sensitive issues.

5. Research should also look at *interviewing methods*. Although telephone interviewing (Computer Assisted Telephone Interviewing—CATI) may be the most popular method in industrialized countries, in some countries an increasing number of people do not have a fixed telephone line and only own mobile phones. CATI sampling is becoming more complicated. Furthermore, telephone surveys may not be applicable in developing countries, where the (paper-and-pencil) face-to-face method is still prevalent. The face-to-face method is also preferred by some of the main victim surveys in countries such as the United States and the United Kingdom. A variation of the face-to-face method is the Computer Assisted Personal Interviewing (CAPI) used, for example, in the British Crime Survey. If the mode of data collection has an influence on the prevalence rates, research should focus on the choice of the appropriate method for each survey.

REFERENCES

Afrobarometer. (2004, March). Afrobarometer round 2: Compendium of comparative results from a 15-country survey. Working Paper No. 34.

Alvazzi del Frate, A. (2004a). Counting crime in Europe: Survey trends, 1996–2000. In *Crime and crime control in an integrating Europe* (pp. 61–72). Helsinki: HEUNI.

Alvazzi del Frate, A. (2004b). The International Crime Business Survey: Findings from nine Central-European countries. *European Journal on Criminal Policy and Research, 10,* 137–161.

Alvazzi del Frate, A. (2004c). The voice of crime victims: Establishing the true level of correctional crime. *Forum on Crime and Society, Volume III.* UNODC.

Alvazzi del Frate, A., Hatalak, O., & Zvekic, U. (Eds.). (2000). *Surveying crime: A global perspective.* Rome: ISTAT/UNICRI.

Alvazzi del Frate, A., Zvekic, U., & van Dijk, J. J. M. (Eds.). (1993). *Understanding crime: Experiences of crime and crime control.* Publication No. 49. Rome: UNICRI.

Aromaa, K. (2004). The International Violence Against Women Survey, European Institute for Crime Prevention and Control, Affiliated with the United nations (HEUNI), paper at the Joint UNECE/UNODC Meeting on Crime Statistics, Geneva, November 3–5, 2004.

Balvig, F., & Kyvsgaard, B. (2006). Vold of overgreb mod kvinder Dansk rapport vedrørende deltagelse i International Violence Against Women Survey (IVAWS). Copenhagen: University of Copenhagen/Ministry of Justice, Research Unit.

Chadee, D., & Ditton, J. (2005). Fear of crime and the media: Assessing the lack of relationship. *Crime Media Culture, 1,* 322–332.

European Forum for Victim Services. (1998). Statement of principles on the social rights of victims of crime. Retrieved October 9, 2006, from www.euvictimservices.org/about_the_forum.asp?policies

Killias, M., Simonin, M., & De Puy, J. (2005). *Violence experienced by women in Switzerland over their lifespan.* Results of the International Violence Against Women Survey (IVAWS). Bern: Stämpfli Verlag.

MacDonald, Z. (2001, Winter). Revisiting the dark figure. *British Journal of Criminology, 41*(1) 127–149.

Mouzos, J., & Makkai, T. (2004). *Women's experiences of male violence.* Findings from the Australian Component of the International Violence Against Women Survey (IVAWS). Canberra. Australian Institute of Criminology. Research and Public Policy Series No. 56.

Nieuwbeerta, P. (Ed.). (2002). *Crime victimisation in comparative perspective: Results from the International Crime Victim Survey, 1989–2000.* The Hague: Boom Juridische uitgevers.

Pikalkova, S. (Ed.). (2004). International Violence Against Women Survey: Czech Republic/2003. *Sociological Research on Domestic Violence, 2.*

Pfeiffer, C., Windzio, M., & Kleimann, M. (2005). Media use and its impacts on crime perception, sentencing attitudes and crime policy. *European Journal of Criminology, 2,* 259–285.

United Nations. (1993). *Declaration on the elimination of violence against women.* A/RES/48/104.

United Nations. (2003). *Manual for the development of a system of crime and criminal justice statistics.* United Nations publications, Sales No. E.03.XVII.6. New York: Author.

United Nations. (2005). Report of the secretary general. *In larger freedom: Towards development, security and human rights for all.* UN doc. A/59/2005.

United Nations Interregional Crime and Justice Research Institute. (2003). *Strategic plan of the police of the Republic of Mozambique: Results of surveys on victimization and police performance.* Turin, UNICRI.

Van Dijk, J. J. M., Mayhew, P., & Killias, M. (1990). *Experiences of crime across the world.* Deventer: Kluwer.

Van Dijk, J. J. M., & Terlouw, G. J. (1996). An international perspective of the business community as victims of fraud and crime. *Security Journal, 7*(3), 157–167.

Van Kesteren, J., Mayhew, P., & Nieuwbeerta, P. (2000). *Criminal victimisation in seventeen industrialised countries: Key findings from the 2000 International Crime Victims Survey.* The Hague: Research and Documentation Centre, Ministry of Justice.

World Health Organization. (2005). *WHO Multi-country Study on women's health and domestic violence against women: Initial results on prevalence, health outcomes and women's responses.* C. Garcia Moreno, H. Jansen, M. Ellsberg, L. Heise, & C. Watts (authors). Retrieved September 21, 2006, from www.who.int/gender/violence/who_multicountry_study/en/

NOTES

1. Since 1976, the United Nations Survey of Crime Trends and Operations of Criminal Justice Systems (UN Crime Trends Survey [CTS]) provides information on recorded crimes from responding member states. Government agencies in each responding country provide official data adjusted to standard definitions of crimes, including homicide, assault, rape, robbery, theft, burglary, fraud, corruption, and drug-related crimes.

In each country information is collected from the police, prosecution, courts, and prisons and is accompanied by explanatory notes. UNODC warns against direct benchmarking and makes raw data available on the Internet (www.unodc.org/unodc/crime_cicp_surveys.html). Efforts are currently being made in order to enhance quality checks of the data, in view of enhancing secondary analysis.

2. Since 1950, Interpol has compiled crime statistics from a large number of countries. Until recently, statistics used to be electronically available to the public on the Internet. Interpol has recently changed its publication policy, and data are only available to authorized police users. The data collection form includes broad categories of crime departing from legal definitions envisaged by criminal codes. Interpol warns that such statistics are not meant for international comparisons because of different definitions, reporting, and recording methods. Despite the major difficulties and gaps, Interpol statistics represent a valuable source of information and are very frequently mentioned in comparative literature.

3. For example, Italy in 1998, South Africa in 1998 and so on.

4. The working group that coordinated the first international survey was composed of J. J. M. van Dijk, P. Mayhew, and M. Killias (1990, pp. 3–4).

5. Results of the ICVS at the global level are presented in Alvazzi del Frate, Zvekic, and van Dijk (1993); Alvazzi del Frate, Hatalak, Zvekic (2000); Nieuwbeerta (2002); and Alvazzi del Frate (2004c).

6. Results of the 2004–2005 ICVS have not been released at the time of writing.

7. Theft of car, theft from car/of parts of car, car vandalism, burglary, attempted burglary, robbery, theft of personal property, sexual offences, assault/threat, consumer fraud (cheating), and corruption/bribery. The questionnaire is available for download at www.unicri.it/icvs

8. The database containing data from the first four international surveys (1989–2002) can be downloaded from the UNICRI Web site at www.unicri.it/icvs

9. The question for the police officers was the following: "What is your opinion of the way the police deal with citizens who report crime? Do you think it is very good, pretty good, rather bad, or very bad?"

10. "Secondary victimisation involves a lack of understanding of the suffering of victims which can leave them feeling both isolated and insecure, losing faith in the help available from their communities and the professional agencies. The experience of secondary victimisation intensifies the immediate consequences of crime by prolonging or aggravating the victim's trauma; attitudes, behaviour, acts or omissions can leave victims feeling alienated from society as a whole" (European Forum for Victim Services, 1998).

11. http://ec.europa.eu/public_opinion/index_en.htm

12. www.latinobarometro.org/

13. www.afrobarometer.org/

14. The study was carried out in collaboration with the London School of Hygiene and Tropical Medicine, the non-profit international organization PATH, and national research institutions and women's organizations in the participating countries.

15. Australia (Mouzos & Makkai, 2004), Czech Republic (Pikalkova, 2004), Denmark (Balvig & Kyvsgaard, 2006), and Switzerland (Killias, Simonin, De Puy, 2005)

16. Bucharest (Romania), Budapest (Hungary), Kiev (Ukraine), Minsk (Belarus), Moscow (Russia), Sofia (Bulgaria), Tirana (Albania), Vilnius (Lithuania), and Zagreb (Croatia).

17. The United Nations *Manual for the Development of a System of Crime and Criminal Justice Statistics* (United Nations, 2003) indicates victimization surveys as the primary vehicle for collecting information on citizens' direct contact with crime and the criminal justice system.

18. The UNECE counts 55 member states in Europe and beyond. See www.unece.org

SECTION II

Responses to Victims

15

Crisis Intervention With Victims of Violent Crimes

ALBERT R. ROBERTS

DIANE GREEN

Recognition of the psychological, traumatic, and mental health impact of violent crimes has increased dramatically in recent years throughout the world. We live in an era in which violent crime victims—domestic violence, rape, armed robbery, aggravated assault, violence in schools and the workplace, terrorist bombings, bioterrorism threats, sniper or drive-by shootings, and attempted murder—result in millions of situational and acute crisis episodes for children, youth, adults, and families. Every single day, throughout the world, millions of people are struck by potentially crisis-inducing violent victimizations that they are not able to resolve on their own. They need immediate help from mental health professionals, crisis intervention workers, victim advocates, and/or their families.

Many people have existing resources, inner strengths and social supports to rely on in the aftermath of a victimization. However, many more crime victims are poor, physically ill, or suffering from mental disorders which makes them considerably more vulnerable to short-term crisis and long-term PTSD in the aftermath of serious crimes. For example, mental health problems are considerably worsened when a crime victim has a pre-existing serious mental illness (e.g. schizophrenia, bipolar disorder I and II, schizo-affective disorder, personality disorder, obsessive compulsive disorder, and/or major depression). The prevalence of mental health problems in American society is mind-boggling. Over 42,000 thousand adults are diagnosed with affective disorders (bipolar, major depression, dysthymia) each day of the year. Over 55,000 adults are diagnosed with anxiety disorders such as phobias, panic disorders and obsessive compulsive disorders each day of the year. (Roberts, 2005)

In the early part of the 21st century the Federal Bureau of Investigation (FBI) reported a significant increase in threats of terrorism throughout the nation, particularly chemical, biological, radiological, and nuclear terrorism. The homicide rate in the United States is the highest of all countries except for Colombia and South Africa. Cybercrime and cyberstalking are costing millions of dollars in computer and network damages to businesses and fear and physiological trauma to millions of cyberstalking victims. Domestic violence is prevalent throughout the United States, with an estimated 8.7 million cases annually. More specifically, every nine seconds somewhere in the United States a woman is assaulted by her intimate partner or former partner (Roberts & Roberts, 2005).

All of these situations, events, and crimes can produce acute crisis episodes and posttraumatic stress disorder (PTSD). Therefore it is critical for all mental health and criminal justice professionals to provide early responses in the form of crisis intervention and trauma treatment.

A crisis-oriented or traumatic event can change people's lives forever. Crisis intervention can lead to early resolution of acute stress disorders or crisis episodes, while providing a turning point so that the individual is strengthened by the experience. Crisis and traumatic events can provide a danger or warning signal, or a challenge or opportunity to sharply reduce emotional pain and vulnerability. The ultimate goal of crisis intervention is to bolster current coping methods or help the individual to reestablish coping and problem-solving abilities while helping individuals to take concrete steps toward managing their feelings and developing concrete steps toward an action plan. Crisis intervention can reinforce strengths and protective factors for individuals who feel somewhat overwhelmed by a traumatic event; in addition, it aims to reduce lethality and potentially harmful situations and provides referral linkages to community agencies. Each person's perceptions and perspective in the aftermath of a violent crime is

a critical factor in determining whether or not an incident will escalate into an acute crisis episode. Specifically, two people could experience the same potentially crisis-inducing event, and one will cope in a positive way and experience a minimum of stress, while the other person may fall apart and become dysfunctional due to inadequate coping skills and a lack of crisis counseling (Roberts, 2005).

Throughout the United States, Canada, Australia, and England crisis counselors, victim advocates, clinical social workers, psychiatric nurses, psychologists, and emergency services personnel are working collaboratively to provide a new vision and clinical insights into crisis intervention and crisis response teams. Crisis intervention has become the most widely used time-limited treatment modality in the world. As a result of the crisis intervention and critical incident stress management movement, millions of persons in crisis situations have been helped in a cost-efficient and timely manner (Roberts, 2005). However, many victim advocates throughout the United States and Canada are receiving only minimal training in crisis intervention and time-limited treatment modalities. This chapter examines innovations, best practices, and the application of Roberts's Seven-Stage Crisis Intervention Model (R-SSCIM) with crime victims.

Previous research indicates that crime victims have been shown to suffer from a variety of psychological and emotional problems (Green, Streeter, & Pomeroy, 2005; McCann, Sakheim, & Abrahamson, 1988). Depression, anger, complicated grief, crime-related PTSD, and anxiety have been identified as possible common consequences for victims of violent crime (Breslau, Davis, Andreski, & Peterson, 1991; Freedy, Resick, Kilpatrick, Dansky, & Tidwell, 1994; Gray & Acierno, 2002; Resnick & Kilpatrick, 1994). Confusion remains about the experience of victims and the severity and clinical significance of the recovery process reported by clinicians and victims. The sudden and unanticipated criminal act is a catalyst to the trauma and grief that is experienced, and psychological consequences of crime are not limited to a few days or weeks after the crime. Evidence is mounting that criminal victimization can be an extremely stressful event, leaving many victims with significant levels of psychological distress (Atkeson, Calhoun, Resick, & Ellis, 1982; Brewin, Andrews, & Rose, 2003; Kilpatrick et al., 1995; Pico-Alfonso, 2005; Wohlfarth, Winkel, & Van Den Brink, 2002). The presence of such distress implies that many victims would benefit from professional mental health services (Norris, Kaniasty, & Scheer, 1990). The needs and stresses confronting victims of crime are complex and often overwhelming. Social, cultural, and economic conditions have significant and measurable effects on violence in the United States. One result is a growing awareness of the demands of services needed by victims of crime, including social work services. Social workers should develop treatment interventions for victims of crime that discourage feelings of helplessness and encourage feelings of confidence and hopefulness. Social work interventions that incorporate the crisis intervention and critical incident stress management from a strengths perspective could provide victims with a sense of empowerment, reduce fear and anger, and engage victims in the recovery process (Green & Pomeroy, in press).

CRISIS THEORY

Crisis theory has its roots in grief theory, stress theory, psychodynamic theory, and learning theory. Crisis theory and crisis intervention practice was not formally elaborated until the 1940s, primarily by community psychiatrists Erich Lindemann and Gerald Caplan at Massachusetts General Hospital and Harvard Medical School (Roberts, 1991, 2005). Lindemann and Caplan mentioned that a hazardous event produces a crisis, that the second stage is characterized by an increased level of tension and disruption, that the third stage is failed coping and problem-solving attempts, and that the final stage can be a mental collapse or breakdown—full-blown crisis state. In order to understand the basis of crisis intervention, crisis theory must be defined. A crisis has been defined as "a specific set of temporary circumstances that result in a state of upset and disequilibrium" (Wallace, 1998, p. 132). Theory has been defined as "a set of interrelated constructs (concepts), definitions and propositions that present a systematic view of phenomena by specifying relations among variables, with the purpose of explaining and predicting phenomena" (Kerlinger, 1986, p. 9).

Turner (1996) states the following with regard to using theory in practice intervention:

> When the practitioner looks at theory, the goal is to develop and refine an intellectual structure by which the complex array of facts encountered in practice can be understood, so that the nature of the intervention can be deduced and the effects of such intervention predicated. The clinician's principal interest is in the utility of the theory: What can it tell me about the situation that will permit me to act differently? (p. 4)

From this perspective, crisis theory offers a framework to understand a victim's response to crime. The basic assumption of crisis theory asserts that when a crisis occurs, people respond with a fairly predictable physical and emotional pattern. The intensity and manifestation of this pattern may vary from individual to individual. The initial physical response includes the inability to move accompanied by emotional responses of numbness, denial, and disbelief. This stage typically ends rapidly and results in a fight or flight response. In preparation for danger, the body accelerates heartbeat, adrenaline begins pumping into the system, and emotions begin to burst forth including fear, anger, rage, confusion, and so on. After some time, the exhausted body rests, and the minds begins the process of emotional restructuring (Turner, 1996).

The emotional state of the victim of a crime can escalate into an acute crisis episode following the crime event, based on his or her perceptions and cognitions. The initial state of the violent crime victim is frequently a state of shock, confusion, and disequilibrium. In addition to the disequilibrium experienced, loss is often the result of a crisis event. People live their lives on certain assumptions, which provide a grounding to help them make sense of the world around them. When a crime occurs, these assumptions may be shattered. These losses may include the loss of a sense of control, loss of trust in a higher being, lose of a sense of fairness, loss of security, guilt, and a sense of helplessness. A victim whose family member has been murdered may feel responsible for not protecting the victims, may question his or her faith, and may have lost the feeling of safety in his or her own home. The critical response to the crisis is affected by their appraisal of the losses, which results in certain coping responses that in turn either impede or assist in the recovery process (Green & Pomeroy, in press). The coping strategy is expected to influence the emotion of the victims. Individuals may attempt to gain their equilibrium by problem solving, seeking direct information, and taking direct action, often returning a sense of control. From this perspective, victims may emerge from a crisis with new coping skills, stronger social support, and stronger well-being. Early psychological intervention can reduce the harmful psychological and emotional effects of crime victimization. Identifying those individuals most at risk for higher levels of distress and lower levels of well-being will guide practitioners' clinical interventions (Green et al., 2005). While some practitioners assume that people have relatively stable preferences for coping styles, the implication from Green et al. emphasizes that people's

choice among alternative coping processes is based on their appraisal of the situation and that these choices are tantamount to understanding the critical need of treatment immediately following the crime event into the positive adaptation of the recovery process. Crisis intervention may help victims gain a sense of control in daily activities and understand reactions such as depression, anger, and anxiety, which may enhance their coping. Educating social workers and counselors about coping tasks and disentangling the recovery process will enable practitioners to assess and treat victims of crime.

If victims are to recover from the victimization event, it is crucial that they are provided with the proper support during the initial impact. Every victim's experience is different, and therefore the recovery process is unique to the individual. If victims have difficulty rebuilding or finding new equilibrium, they may suffer from long-term crisis and trauma reactions or PTSD. Victims who suffer from long-term crisis reaction can be thrown back into the initial crisis reaction when "triggers" to the event occur, such as the one-month or one-year anniversary after the crime. The treatment of PTSD has three principal components: (1) processing and coming to terms with the horrifying, overwhelming experience; (2) controlling and mastering physiological and biological stress reactions; and (3) reestablishing secure social connections and interpersonal efficacy. Crisis intervention and multicomponent critical incident stress management are approaches utilized to reduce the severity of a victim's crisis. As stated earlier in this chapter, "crisis" encounters involve a myriad of intense and turbulent emotions. While there is no way to predict which victims will experience crisis, when the crisis onset will occur, or how severe the intensity or duration, the sooner crisis intervention is offered, the better. There is a conviction among practitioners that on-scene crisis intervention, when the victim is in the early stages of distress, may prove to potentially prevent or reduce the crisis symptoms of the victim (NOVA, 2001). Federal authorities immediately recognized the Oklahoma City bombing's traumatic impact on surviving victims, family members, rescue workers, allied professionals, and the community at-large. By the end of the first day, April 19, 1995, the federal Office of Victims of Crime (OVC) placed a nine-member crisis intervention team on the ground in Oklahoma City to work with victims and people responding to the disaster.

It is imperative that crisis workers have a step-by-step crisis assessment and intervention model in mind in order to guide them in rapidly responding to the mental health needs of crime victims. A comprehensive and structured model allows the relatively new as well as the experienced crisis clinician to be mindful of maintaining the fine line that allows for a response that is active and directive enough but does not take problem ownership away from the client. In addition, a crisis intervention model is like a blueprint or roadmap that can suggest steps for how the crisis worker can intentionally meet the client where he or she is at, assess level of risk, mobilize a client support system and community resources, and move strategically to stabilize the individual and improve social functioning. The R-SSCIM (Roberts, 1991, 2005) identifies and discusses seven critical stages through which clients typically pass on the road to crisis stabilization, resolution, and mastery.

CRISIS INTERVENTION

Guidelines for practice need to be rooted in theoretical foundations of transactional intrapersonal coping theory coupled with crisis theory. Practitioners need to be aware that the theoretical underpinning from which they practice and recognize that recovery from criminal victimization is not congruent with "normal" change. Clinicians cognizant of incremental changes with victims will continually

assess the progress of the victim individually. Crisis theory is a model that provides the conceptual framework for crisis intervention with crime victims. In response to crises, individuals strive to maintain their equilibrium by using familiar coping mechanisms. Crisis intervention is time-limited and the goal is to reduce individual's feelings of distress, helplessness, and isolation; activate social resources; and support effective coping. This is accomplished through utilizing education, listening, validation, normalization, reassurance, acceptance, advocacy, and resource linkages. Immediately following the trauma, the crisis counselor's emphasis should be on self-regulation and on rebuilding. This means the reestablishment of a sense of security and predictability and active engagement in adaptive action.

While there is not one single model of crisis intervention (Jacobson, Trickler, & Mosley, 1986), there are generally agreed upon principles used to alleviate distress in victims and restore equilibrium. Crisis intervention involves three components: (1) the crisis and the perception of an unmanageable situation, (2) the individual or group in crisis, and (3) the helper or mental health worker who provides aid. Crisis intervention requires that the person experiencing a crisis receive timely and skillful support to help cope with his or her situation before future physical or emotional deterioration occurs. Roberts's (2005) seven-stage crisis intervention model can facilitate effective intervention with crime victims by emphasizing rapid assessment of the victim's problem and resources, collaborating on goal selection and attainment, finding alternative coping methods, developing a working alliance, and building up the client's strengths. This model has as its goals to (1) mitigate the impact of the event (lower tension), (2) facilitate normal recovery processes, and (3) restore to adaptive functioning.

Roberts's (1991, 2005) R-SSCIM includes the following stages:

1. Plan and conduct a thorough assessment (including lethality, dangerousness to self and/or others), and immediate psychosocial needs).

2. Make psychological contact, establish rapport, and rapidly establish the relationship (conveying genuine respect for the client, acceptance, reassurance, and a nonjudgmental attitude).

3. Examine the dimensions of the problem in order to define it (including the last straw or precipitating event).

4. Encourage an exploration of feelings and emotions.

5. Generate, explore, and assess past coping attempts.

6. Restore cognitive functioning through implementation of an action plan.

7. Follow up and leave the door open for booster sessions one, three, and/or six months later.

To fully utilize the seven steps, the crisis counselor must initially utilize active listening techniques to obtain a thorough assessment and develop rapport with the client. The clinician should assess potential suicidal or homicidal risk. The first hour may be spent on assessing the immediate crisis situation and surrounding circumstances. Accurate assessment of the precipitating event and the resulting crisis is tantamount to ensuring the victim's safety from a psychological and physical perspective. The victim may have suppressed some feelings, such as depression or anger, and recognition of these feelings will allow for reduction in tension caused by these emotions. Information is sought to identify strengths and coping skills of the victim, thus enabling an exploration of what the victim is feeling and how he or she may have successfully coped in the past. The minimum goal of crisis intervention is the individual's psychological resolution of the immediate crisis and restoration to pre-crime functioning. Planning and implementation of a therapeutic intervention does not

necessarily bring about major changes, but it is meant to restore the victim to their precrisis level of equilibrium.

The following is a vignette and description of the application of the seven stages in the R-SSCIM in the aftermath of a violent assault. First, it is important to be aware that stages one and two often take place simultaneously, and stages three and four sometimes overlap.

> John Smith is a 42-year-old male. He has worked as a schoolteacher for the past 23 years. He has been married to Maria for 17 years. He is the father of two children: James, age 15, and Brian, age 11.
>
> James and Brian were the victims of a robbery/simple assault six weeks ago. They were confronted by four young boys with guns while walking across the bridge on their way home. James was beaten on the head and face with the gun and was told he could be shot and robbed of his wallet. Brian had a gun held to his head for several minutes and was told his brother couldn't protect him and the next time would be worse. James is severely depressed and has extreme guilt regarding his perceived inability to protect his younger brother. James has been withdrawing from the family and isolating himself. He refuses to go anywhere. John takes his son to the crisis unit of the local community mental health center.

STAGE 1 of R-SSCIM—Rapidly Plan and Conduct a Crisis Assessment

Psychosocial assessment and determination of level of danger requires an immediate assessment of a victim-survivor's current situation. Successful early intervention is often based on the crisis counselor's ability to respond in a nonjudgmental and sensitive manner when completing an accurate assessment and while beginning to establish rapport. The therapeutic goal of the intervention during the initial crisis assessment is for the crisis worker to facilitate the restoration of equilibrium in favor of stability and well-being. The severely traumatized or profoundly depressed person will find it easy to find reasons for expressing intense anxiety, sadness, and fear, but may need help in identifying reasons for living and/or specific levels of fear.

- Assess lethality by asking his father if James is currently taking any medication.
- Ask James's father what specifically caused him to bring his son into the center now? Was there a triggering or precipitating incident?
- Obtain background information quickly from John and then speak to James alone.
- Assess the presence of suicidal thought or homicidal thoughts, substance abuse history, and preexisting mental disorders.
- Assess James's sense of helplessness and hopelessness. Ask about the frequency of thoughts about suicide, whether or not there is a specific plan for carrying it out.
- Investigate social support network and follow through with procedures to ensure James's safety (e.g., removal of medications or potentially dangerous items referred to in his plan).
- Listen for unexpected pieces of the client's story and reflect these parts back through mirroring of feelings and paraphrasing.
- Ask James how his distress has affected his thoughts of being a failure as a protective older brother.

STAGE 2 of R-SSCIM—Establish Rapport and a Therapeutic Relationship (Stages 1 and 2 Often Occur Simultaneously)

It is very important to introduce yourself and speak in a calm and neutral manner.

The crisis worker should do his or her best to make a psychological connection with the 15-year-old in a precrisis or acute crisis situation. Part of establishing rapport and putting the person at ease involves being nonjudgmental, listening actively, and demonstrating empathy.

- Establish a bridge, bond, or connection by asking James what sports or music he likes? "Are you playing in any sport now?" "Do you have a favorite team?" "Do you have a favorite recording artist?"

- Understand that many adolescents are impulsive and impatient, may have escape fantasies, and may be very sensitive and temperamental. As a result, don't lecture, preach, or moralize. Make concise statements, be caring, display keen interest, and do not make disparaging or insulting statements of any kind.

Stages three and four sometimes take place simultaneously.

STAGE 3 of R-SSCIM—Identify the Major Problem, Including Crisis Precipitants or Triggering Incidents

- Ask questions to determine the final straw or precipitating event that led James into his current situation;
  Focus on problem or problems, and prioritize and focus on the worst problem;
  Listen carefully for symptoms and clues of suicidal thoughts and intent.
- Make a direct inquiry about suicidal plans and nonverbal gestures or communication (e.g., diaries, poems, journals, school essays, paintings, or drawings).
- Since most adolescent suicides are impulsive and unplanned, it is important to determine whether or not the youth had easy access to a lethal weapon or drugs (including sleeping pills, methamphetamines, or barbiturates).

STAGE 4 of R-SSCIM—Deal With Feelings and Emotions and Provide Support

- Deal with the client's immediate feelings or fears.
- Allow client to tell his story and why he seems to be feeling so bad.
- Tune in and provide preliminary empathy to the impact of the assault.
- Use active listening skills (i.e., paraphrasing, reflection of feelings, summarizing, reassurance, compliments, advice giving, reframing, and probes).
- Normalize clients' experiences.
- Validate and identify her emotions.
- Examine past coping methods.
- Encourage ventilation of mental and physical feelings.

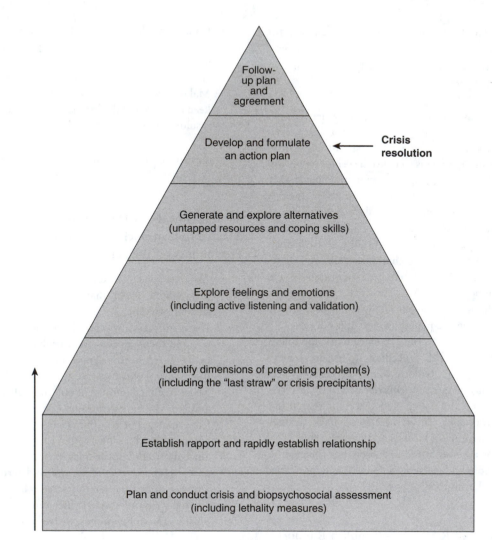

Figure 15.1   Roberts's Seven-Stage Crisis Intervention Model.
SOURCE: Copyright Albert R. Roberts, 1991. Reprinted by permission of the author.

STAGE 5 of R-SSCIM—Explore Possible Alternatives

First reestablish balance and homeostasis, also known as equilibrium:

- Ask James what has helped in the past: For example, what has he done to cope with earlier situations. By assessing inner resources, the discovery develops as a collaborative experience and looking at pros and cons of his perceived helpless and hopeless situation.

When the client is able to view the situation logically, his sense of hopelessness decreases.

- Integrate Solution-Based Therapy (e.g., full or partial Miracle question).
- Ask him about from his hobbies, birthday celebrations, sport successes, academic successes, and vacations.
- Mutually explore and suggest new coping options and alternatives.
- Jog the client's memories so he can verbalize the last time everything seemed to be going well, and he was in a good mood. Help the

client to find untapped resources. If appropriate, it may be helpful to mention that you have specialized in helping young people and have helped hundreds of other teens in crisis.

It is also important to provide client(s) with a specific phone number of a therapist who has extensive experience working with young crime victims and a plan to follow. The therapist needs to be someone who is willing and able to work with challenging and difficult adolescents in crisis. He or she also should have extensive clinical experience with crime victims so he or she can prepare James with an open-door return policy, if he needs a new appointment exactly one month or one year after the victimization.

STAGE 6 of R-SSCIM—Formulate an Action Plan

Victims must feel a sense of ownership in the action plan so that they can increase their level of autonomy and ensure that they are not dependent on other supportive persons or agency staff. Obtaining a commitment from the victim to follow through with the action plan and any referrals to community-based agencies and therapists can be maximized by using a mutual and collaborative process of intervention planning. Termination and closure of crisis intervention should begin soon after the client has achieved the goals of the action plan or has been referred to another social service or mental health center.

STAGE 7 of R-SSCIM—Followup with Phone Call, In-Person Appointment for Booster Session, or Home Visit

Let James know that he can call you, and give him your beeper number or cell phone pager. Let him know that the beeper is for an emergency. In addition, depending on the crisis worker's assessment at the exit interview session, it would be useful to schedule a follow-up with the therapist who James is being referred to, so that there is a team approach. Follow-up may include a booster session with the crisis worker scheduled for three days, one week, or 30 days later.

CRISIS INTERVENTION IN PRACTICE: TWO SUCCESSFUL MODELS

Begun in 1978 as Victim Service Agency, Safe Horizon now has more than 600 employees, most of whom are victim advocates and counselors in all five boroughs of New York City. The comprehensive array of programs developed by Safe Horizon includes a multitude of storefront crisis intervention offices, 24-hour crime victim and domestic violence hotlines, court-based domestic violence intake and intervention programs, police–social work teams, emergency shelters for battered women and their children, mental health counseling for all crime victims, and lock repairs, window replacements, and other concrete services to crime victims. Its licensed mental health professionals provide goal-focused individual counseling and trauma reduction and supportive group services for victims of violent crime, including domestic violence, sexual assault, incest, robbery, and homicide. At precincts and in courts and community-based offices, the agency offers crisis intervention and stress reduction and advocacy services to victims shortly after the crime is committed.

Counseling is also available in schools and shelters for children who witness crimes, including domestic violence, and a crisis response team has been established to respond to victims of natural and community disasters. At all sites, and in every setting where mental health services are offered, staff are available to address the practical needs of victims by, for example, helping them navigate the court system, obtain crime victim compensation, arrange for child care, or repair or replace locks.

The National Organization for Victim Assistance (NOVA), in Washington, D.C., has trained mental health counselors and social workers all over the country as part of their crisis response team training. NOVA's crisis response teams include trained mental health providers and victim advocates who work together with law enforcement, medical professionals, victim assistance staff, religious leaders, and others to provide assistance to communities in the aftermath of major crimes, community-wide disasters, and acts of terrorism. NOVA's crisis response teams were previously trained by Marlene Young, the first and longtime former executive director, and currently by Jeannette Atkins, who has more than 20 years' experience in victim advocacy and victim assistance in the state of Ohio (Roberts, 1991, 2005; Roberts & Roberts, 2005).

CONCLUSION

Due to the prevalence of violence and the importance of victim services, a growing number of program evaluations during the past few decades focused on the development of descriptive data regarding emotional, financial, and medical factors. There is now ample evidence to indicate the deleterious emotional and physical consequences of crime that can lead to feelings of depression, anxiety, PTSD, and fear of crime in victims. Because of these preliminary findings, research efforts must search for evidence-based research and outcome measures that will facilitate the victim's positive coping as well as crisis resolution. The concrete needs and psychosocial stresses confronting victims of crime are complex and often overwhelming. Social, cultural, and economic conditions have significant and measurable effects on violence in the United States. One result is a growing awareness of the demands for services desperately needed by victims of crime. Early intervention such as structured time-limited crisis intervention and multicomponent critical incident stress management for victims of crime discourage

feelings of helplessness and encourage feeling of confidence and hopefulness (Roberts & Everly, 2006). Information must be systematically collected regarding service providers' perspectives of victim's needs and compared and contrasted to victims' perspectives of their unique needs and situations and evaluate what is necessary for positive recovery. When these two components are looked at, holistically, comprehensive and productive resources and treatment can be provided.

REFERENCES

Atkeson, B., Calhoun, K., Resick, P., & Ellis, E. (1982). Victims of rape: Repeated assessment of depressive symptoms. *Journal of Consulting and Clinical Psychology, 90*, 1–13.

Breslau, N., Davis, G. C., Andreski, P., & Peterson, E. (1991). Traumatic events and posttraumatic stress disorder is an urban population of young adults. *Archives of General Psychiatry, 48*, 216–222.

Brewin, C. R., Andrews, B., & Rose, S. (2003). Diagnostic overlap between acute stress disorder and PTSD in victims of violent crime. *American Journal of Psychiatry, 160*(4), 783–785.

Freedy, J., Resick, H., Kilpatrick, D., Dansky, B., & Tidwell, R. (1994). The psychological adjustment of recent crime victims in the criminal justice system. *Journal of Interpersonal Violence, 9*, 450–468.

Gray, M. J., & Acierno, R. (2002). Symptom presentations of older adult crime victims: Description of a clinical sample. *Journal of Anxiety Disorders, 16*(3), 299–309.

Green, D. L., & Pomeroy, E. C. (in press). Crime victimization: Assessing differences between violent and non-violent experiences. *Victims and Offenders*.

Green, D. L., Streeter, C., & Pomeroy, E. (2005). A multivariate model of the stress and coping process. *Stress, Trauma and Crisis, 8*(1), 61–73.

Jacobson, G., Strickler, M., & Mosley, W. (1968). Generi and individual approaches to crisis intervention. *American Journal of Public Health, 58*, 338–343.

Kerlinger, F. (1986). *Foundation in behavioral research* (3rd ed.). Orlando, FL: Harcourt, Brace & Jovanovich.

Kilpatrick, D., Best, C., Veronen, L., Amick, A., Villeponteaux, L., & Ruff, G. (1995). Mental health correlates of victimization: A random community survey. *Journal of Consulting and Clinical Psychology, 53,* 866–873.

McCann, I. L., Sakheim, D. K., & Abrahamson, D. J. (1988). Trauma and victimization: A model of psychological adaptation. *Counseling Psychologist, 16,* 531–594.

National Organization for Victim Assistance (NOVA). (2001). *Crisis intervention.* Retrieved July 13, 2006, from www.trynova.org/victim info/readings/CrisisIntervention.pdf

Norris, F., Kaniasty, K., & Scheer, D. A. (1990). Use of mental health services among victims of crime: Frequency, correlates, and subsequent recovery. *Journal of Counseling and Clinical Psychology, 58,* 538–547.

Office for Victims of Crime. (2000). *The immediate crisis response.* Retrieved March 25, 2006, from www.ojp.usdoj.gov/ovc/publications/infores/respterrorism/chap2.html

Pico-Alfonso, M. A. (2005). Psychological intimate partner violence: The major predictor of PTSD in abused women. *Neuroscience Biobehavioral Research, 29*(1), 181–193.

Resnick, H. S., & Kilpatrick, D. G. (1994, Summer). Crime related PTSD: Emphasis on adult general population samples. *National Center for PTSD Research Quarterly, 5*(3), 1–6.

Roberts, A. R. (1991). *Contemporary perspectives on crisis intervention and prevention.* Englewood Cliffs, NJ: Prentice Hall.

Roberts, A. R. (2005). Bridging the past and present to the future of crisis intervention and crisis management. In A. R. Roberts (Ed.), *Crisis intervention handbook: Assessment, treatment and research* (3rd ed., pp. 3–33). New York: Oxford University Press.

Roberts, A. R., & Everly, G. S. (2006). A meta-analysis of 36 crisis intervention studies. *Brief Treatment and Crisis Intervention, 6*(1), 10–21.

Roberts, A. R., & Roberts, B. (2005). *Ending intimate abuse: Practical guidance and survival strategies.* New York: Oxford University Press.

Turner, F. (1996). *Social work treatment: Interlocking theoretical approaches.* New York: Free Press.

Wallace, H. (1998). *Victimology.* Needham Heights, MA: Allyn & Bacon.

Wohlfarth, T., Winkel, F. W., & Ven Den Brink, W. (2002). Identifying crime victims who are at risk for PTSD: Developing a practical referral instrument. *Acta Psychiatry Scandinavia, 105*(6), 951–964.

16

The Key Contributions of Family, Friends, and Neighbors

ROBERT C. DAVIS

When someone is victimized, they may have a variety of needs, ranging from serious and immediate issues such as healing injuries sustained in the commission of a violent crime to lesser issues such as needing someone to watch the kids while the victim goes down to the police station or courthouse. Meeting many victim needs takes specialized knowledge: providing civil legal assistance to help a domestic violence victim file for divorce or helping a victim fill out an application for monetary compensation from the state. For these kinds of needs, victims turn to social service programs. But for a variety of other needs, ranging from borrowing money to getting a broken door fixed to just needing someone to talk to, victims most frequently turn to family, friends, and neighbors.

In this chapter, we take a look at how these informal networks of support function. We examine the numbers of victims who get help from these informal sources and the kinds of victims most likely to get this kind of help. We discuss the kinds of help that are provided by informal sources and the extent to which that assistance affects the recovery process. Finally, we examine the helpers themselves—who they are and how providing aid to victims affects them emotionally and financially.

WHO GETS HELP FROM INFORMAL NETWORKS?

Service programs reach only a small proportion of persons victimized by crime. The first evidence of this came from a study of Milwaukee residents by Knudten, Meade, Knudten, and Doerner (1976), who found that few persons who reported being victims sought aid from service organizations. A few years later, a study of New York City robbery, assault, and burglary victims by Friedman, Bischoff, Davis, and Person (1982) reported that only 15% received aid from service organizations including welfare, the housing authority, the Social Security Administration, senior citizens' groups, or the state's crime victim compensation program. Less than 1% received assistance from the city's victim service program. Similarly, Davis and Henley (1990) reported that between 2% and 10% of persons who filed criminal complaints with the police sought help from New York City's victim program even when outreach letters were sent describing the services available.

A study by the British Home Office based on the British Crime Survey reached similar conclusions (Maguire & Kynch, 2000). Among victims who reported crimes to the police, 9% were assisted by victim support schemes (service programs). An additional 6% received help from other service organizations, including the housing department, social services, Citizen's Advice Bureau, or neighborhood watch. These figures were far lower for victims who did not report the crime (see Figure 16.1).

Even among victims of violence against women, studies have indicated that few receive help from victim programs. Studies have found that just 5% to 14% of rape victims receiving assistance from rape crisis centers (George, Winfield, & Blazer, 1992; Golding, Siegel, Sorenson, Burnam, & Stein, 1989; Ullman & Filipas, 2001). Kaukinen (2004)

reported that 5% of domestic violence victims from the National Violence Against Women Survey went to a social service agency.

However, while few victims receive help from social service agencies, many are assisted by family, friends, and neighbors. The estimates of the proportion of victims receiving aid from informal social networks are remarkably consistent. Maguire and Kynch's analysis of British Crime Survey data and Ullman and Filipas's study of rape victims both found that one in three victims had received help from their informal social networks. Davis, Lurigio, and Skogan (1999) reported that 40% of victims across samples in four cities had been assisted by families or friends. Kaukinen's (2004) analysis of the National Violence Against Women Survey revealed that 52% were assisted by family, friends, or neighbors.

A comprehensive study of victims of burglary, robbery, assault, and domestic violence in six sites by Brickman (2003) highlighted the importance of family and friends. The researchers found that family and friends helped victims resolve more than half of the needs they had as a result of the crime. In contrast, victim service programs only helped with resolving about 5% of victim needs.

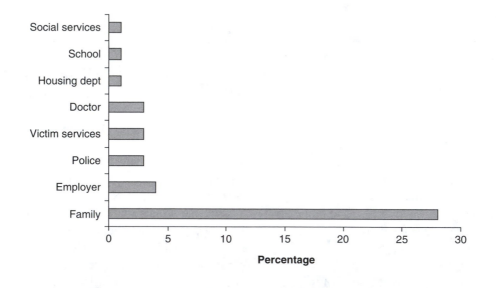

Figure 16.1   Sources of Victim Support

SOURCE: Maguire and Kynch (2000).

While there is good data on how many victims turn to informal social networks to ease the aftermath of crime, there is less information on which victims are most successful in getting help. There have been suggestions in the literature on help seeking that black women are reluctant to use professional social services, instead relying on extended family networks (e.g., Todd & Worrell, 2000). Riger, Raja, and Camacho (2002) noted that families of intimate partner violence victims in their largely black sample "often offered women housing and sometimes assumed custodial responsibilities while women sought to establish themselves educationally and financially" (p. 199). Kaukinen (2004) reported that white victims of intimate partner violence were more likely than blacks to use mental health and social services *as well as* more likely to receive support from their informal social networks.

The Friedman et al. (1982) study incorporated the most extensive analysis of which victims had best access assistance from informal social networks. They found that victims with the best developed support networks were those who were employed and/or had graduated high school. On the other hand, elderly victims had less well-developed support networks than younger victims. Friedman and colleagues also noted that less affluent victims are generally less successful getting assistance from other individuals or social service programs.

WHO IS LIKELY TO PROVIDE SUPPORT?

Contact with supporters usually occurs shortly after the incident. According to Friedman et al. (1982), 6 in 10 persons named by victims as supporters lent aid on the day of the crime, and 9 in 10 had assisted within two days. In the Friedman et al. study, 1 in 10 supporters was at the crime scene. Bystanders are, of course, the first persons that can lend assistance. However, at least since the infamous murder of Kitty Genovese in New York, social scientists have tried to explain the reasons why people may be unwilling to help others in crisis. Some victims in the Friedman et al. study reported being ignored by bystanders. A Queens couple, robbed as they walked in their neighborhood, complained that the street was alive with people after the incident, but no one stepped forward during it. One man began to get out of his car when he saw what was happening, but got back in. After the robber left, a college student ran over to ask how they were. Nonetheless, the couple felt that if people had stepped forward during the crime, the thief would have fled.

But for other victims in the Friedman et al. (1982) study, bystanders were the first persons to offer assistance (see text box). This kind of assistance from strangers often surprised victims and was therefore especially appreciated.

The story of a young, single victim of a chain-snatching in Queens

I was walking home with my groceries when this guy came out of nowhere and grabbed one of the gold chains around my neck. . . . A Spanish-speaking woman stopped and asked if I was all right. Then a Spanish-speaking man came and asked the woman what happened. She told him and he started to chase the robber. I started to walk down the street and an elderly woman who'd been sitting on a park bench came over and asked me if I was all right. I said, "Yes," and kept walking till I saw a police car and flagged it down. The police pulled over and then I became hysterical. They helped me and calmed me down. They were really concerned. Even when they dropped me off at my house they asked me if I was going to be all right alone.

Riger et al. (2002) in their study of predominantly black victims of intimate partner violence stressed the important role that families played in aiding victims. The Friedman et al. (1982) study also reported that many victims tend to turn for help to persons with whom they have well-established ties. The authors report that more than 6 in 10 individuals named as supporters by victims were persons they had known for five years or more; 4 in 10 supporters were family members.

Alternatively, Friedman et al. (1982) also noted that the robbery, assault, and burglary victims in their sample relied less heavily on individuals with whom they had strong ties than has been observed in some other studies of people in crisis. For example, nearly 6 in 10 of the supporters named by victims in the Friedman et al. sample were neighbors, and 4 in 10 supporters were not individuals included in victims' informal social networks. The authors suggest that reliance on persons with less well-established ties is necessary for victims because they experience an acute crisis, which forces them to rely on whoever is present at the time. In this respect, victimization differs from chronic crises such as illness, depression, divorce, death, or other changing life circumstances. Landlords and neighbors may be essential resources for burglary victims who need to get their broken door fixed or who need someone to watch their children while they file a report at the police station.

For many victim needs, persons who are proximate and immediately available may be the most useful supporters. Friedman et al. (1982) provide this example of help from neighbors:

> A 70-year-old Flushing man was robbed and beaten in his apartment and spent several days in a local hospital. While he was away, a woman across the hall cleaned his apartment. After being released from the hospital, the neighbor cooked meals for the victim and brought them to his apartment. Another neighbor checked on him periodically to make sure he had no problems. (p. 149)

WHAT KIND OF HELP DO INFORMAL SOCIAL NETWORKS PROVIDE?

Davis et al. (1999) found that more than two thirds of victims in their sample who needed emotional support or household logistical aid received help from family and friends, a far higher proportion than received these forms of help from victim assistance programs. Similarly, Friedman et al. (1982) reported that the most common forms of aid lent through informal support sources were emotional support, household logistical support, and long-term aid. Victims were unlikely to receive help from other individuals with financial assistance or lock repairs.

Similarly, the Brickman (2003) study found that family and friends were most relied on by victims when they needed someone to talk to about the crime and its effects—more than 8 in 10 victims who talked to someone reported that they talked with family or friends, and 7 in 10 relied on acquaintances to take them to the doctor. However, as needs became more technical, victims relied less on their informal social networks. Four in 10 victims relied on family and friends to fix broken locks, 1 in 4 relied on family and friends for information on avoiding revictimization, and just 1 in 10 relied on family and friends for help with getting a restraining order.

Friedman et al. (1982) noted that different kinds of people provided different types of support. For example, emotional support and long-term aid were more often received from relatives or friends—persons with whom victims had close ties—than from neighbors. Help with repairing locks or doors most often came from superintendents. Financial assistance was equally likely to come from relatives, friends, or neighbors (see Table 16.1).

There is another way that family and friends can help victims: that is by encouraging them to seek help from the police or service organizations. Ruback and Ivie (1988) noted that receiving help from individuals may lead more victims to seek help from

Table 16.1   Source of Support by Type of Help Given

	Emotional Support	Financial Support	Stay With Victim	Repairs	Practical Services	Long-Term Assistance
Relative	77%	15%	9%	5%	19%	51%
Friend	79%	14%	6%	4%	16%	49%
Neighbor	60%	11%	6%	5%	16%	40%
Superintendent	33%	17%	0%	58%	3%	27%

SOURCE: Friedman et al. (1982).

formal sources. They found that two in three sexual assault victims had talked to a family member or friend prior to informing the police about the incident.

Support from family and friends is perhaps most important for victims of domestic violence. Riger et al. (2002) observed that family members often provided a temporary help with taking care of victims' children. They also note long-term assistance, including assuming temporary custody of victims' children or taking in victims and their children after leaving a domestic violence shelter.

Of course, not all interactions that victims have with others after a crime is positive. For years, laboratory evidence has found that others tend to blame victims for their misfortune in order to maintain a belief in a just and predictable world (e.g., Krahe, 1988; Lerner, 1971; Lodewijkx, deKwaadsteniet, and Nijstad, 2005). Wortman and her colleagues (e.g., Dunkel-Schetter & Wortman, 1982; Wortman & Lehman, 1985; Wortman, Wolff, & Bonanno, 2004) suggested that other people are often uncertain how to act around victims of misfortune and that resulting feelings of discomfort may lead people to avoid victims altogether. Coates and Wortman (1980) further argued that people may have unrealistic expectations about how victims ought to be reacting to the crisis: When these expectations fail to be met, people may become frustrated and irritable with victims. In fact, Wortman and Lehman (1985)

suggested that those who care most about victims may be especially likely to engage in what they termed *inappropriate support*.

Davis and Brickman (1996) examined both supportive and unsupportive behaviors of others toward victims of either sexual or nonsexual assault. Supportive behaviors included emotional support, help with daily responsibilities, and encouraging victims to seek professional help. Unsupportive behaviors included withdrawal or hostility, blaming the victim, and egocentric actions. The study found no difference in the amount of supportive behavior received by victims of sexual and nonsexual assault. However, unsupportive behavior was significantly more often reported by victims of sexual assault than by victims of nonsexual assault. Further, sexual assault victims reported more unsupportive behavior coming from male family and friends than from female family and friends.

DOES HELP HELP?

A key question is the extent to which getting help from others facilitates victim readjustment. The question is both whether victims who get help from others are more successful at resolving their crime-related problems and whether victims who get help are better adjusted psychologically than victims who do not receive help or, worse, who are the subject of negative reactions from others.

The effect of getting help from others on victim recovery has been carefully researched for sexual assault victims, as we shall see in a moment. However, for victims of other crimes, the only research that has specifically addressed this issue is the Friedman et al. (1982) study. Friedman and colleagues did not find any difference in the number of crime-related problems that persisted either two weeks or four months after the crime as a function of the number of supporters that victims named. They did find, however, that victims who said they received all the help they needed from family and friends reported fewer problems persisting after four months compared to persons who reported themselves as less successful in getting help from others.

Friedman et al. (1982) did not find that the amount of help received by victims affected victims' emotional recovery from crime: Persons who received all the help they needed were indistinguishable in terms of mood four months after victimization from persons who were less successful in getting help. The researchers did find evidence, however, that social support affected how victims felt about other people. Victims who had few supporters or who didn't get all the help they needed were more likely to report a decrease in their belief that people are willing to help others in times of crises. Similarly, victims who did not get all the help they needed were more likely to report that relationships with others had gotten worse since the crime. One disillusioned assault victim, a man in his midtwenties, said, "It's hard to trust people. . . . Nobody would help me when I was held up. I screamed, asked people to help, but they didn't."

A study of San Diego victims of violent crime found some evidence for a beneficial effect of support from friends and family. Rienick, Mulmat, and Pennell (1997) report that violent crime victims who encountered supportive reactions from friends and family experienced fewer emotional problems a month after their victimization experience.

The sexual assault literature has not found strong evidence for a beneficial effect of social support (e.g., Norris & Feldman-Summers, 1981; Sales, Baum, & Shore, 1984). Davis, Brickman, and Baker (1991) argued that the behavior of others toward victims needs to be conceptualized as consisting of both supportive and unsupportive aspects, which exert independent effects upon victim adjustment. When analyzed separately, the researchers found that unsupportive behavior accounted for four times as much variance in victim adjustment as supportive behavior.

THE EXPERIENCE OF GIVING SUPPORT

As mentioned earlier, it is a natural human reaction to want to help people who have suffered misfortune. But, although people around the victim may want to help, they may also experience costs in doing so. Psychologists have suggested that victims threaten people's belief in a just and orderly world. Lerner (1971) was the first to popularize the idea that people have a need to believe that the world is a fair place where bad things do not happen to good people. Victims inadvertently challenge this belief and make others aware of their own fallibility.

There was evidence early on that people around the victim frequently experience heightened fear of crime as well as emotional distress (Knudten et al., 1976; Reactions to Crime Project, 1978). Conklin (1971) referred to this reaction as "secondary victimization." This theme was explored in depth in the Friedman et al. (1982) report. This study was the only one we are aware of that interviewed people who lent support to victims. The researchers found that nearly half of the supporters they interviewed reported feeling uncomfortable during the process of listening to the victim and lending a hand. The reasons for their distress varied.

For some, listening to the victim made them feel worried for the victim's safety. For many, the experience of lending support increased their own feelings of vulnerability. Friedman et al. report on such a case:

A mother witnessed an assault upon her 22-year-old son and subsequently testified in court. As a result of her testimony, she was threatened and her other two sons who lived with her were shot at. She said it was difficult listening to her son talk about the incident because it reminded her of the impact that crime had had on all of their lives. She said that none of them saw friends anymore because, "No one wants to be around people who are targets for shooting." (1982, p. 232)

Friedman et al. (1982) found that the experience of lending aid often resulted in heightened fear of crime. Roughly one in three supporters they interviewed said they were more suspicious of people, felt less safe in their home, or felt less safe in their neighborhood. Like victims, some supporters took added precautions: 6 in 10 reported being generally more cautious, while lesser percentages of supporters said they had installed new security hardware or curtailed trips out of their homes, especially at night. In an extreme case, one neighbor of a burglary victim reported that she had begun carrying a machete to the mailbox. As is true with victims, the increase in fear of crime among supporters usually abated over time. "It affects you for a few months," one supporter said.

Fear and precautions among supporters in the Friedman et al. (1982) study were strongly affected by the strength of ties between victim and supporter. Increased fear and precautions were more likely among supporters who were blood relations or intimate partners of the victim, and supporters who felt close to the victim (see Table 16.2). The mother of a victim said that she had never thought about being robbed before her

Table 16.2   Effect of Crime on Supporters by Strength of Ties to Victim

	Elevated Fear of Crime	*Took Precautions in Home*	*Took Precautions Outdoors*
Propinquity			
Live in same neighborhood	53%	73%	26%
Live in different neighborhood	34%	54%	2%
Relationship			
Intimate/Blood relative	47%	68%	14%
Less close relationship	33%	49%	13%
Emotional ties			
Close ties to victim	47%	69%	17%
Loose ties to victim	22%	39%	0%

SOURCE: Friedman et al. (1982).

daughter's apartment was burglarized. She added that because her daughter lived in a better area than she did, "It makes me think more." Supporters who had been victims themselves were especially sensitive to the dangers of crime.

Another cost in giving support is financial. The Friedman et al. (1982) study found that financial assistance was most often requested by low-income victims who were themselves poor. And low-income supporters were far more likely to report that providing such aid created financial problems for them. For example, one burglary victim's landlady called the police for the victim, had the victim's door repaired and locks changed, and accepted only half the rent for the next month. She did this in spite of the fact that helping the victim financially posed a major problem for her, because the rent money she received from tenants in the building was her only source of income.

Persons who help domestic violence victims place themselves in harm's way and may actually place their lives on the line. Riger et al. (2002) report that it is not uncommon for batterers to threaten family members who provide a place to stay or other help to the victims. In one of their cases, Riger and colleagues describe a batterer who followed the victim to her sister's house and "busted all the windows." Later he came looking for the victim at her aunt's house, breaking down the door with a shotgun (2002, p. 196).

One would expect that persons who lent support to victims of sexual assault might be especially vulnerable to feelings of distress. Davis, Taylor, and Bench (1995) tested this hypothesis by interviewing persons who had lent support to victims of sexual assault and victims of nonsexual assault. Surprisingly, they did not find greater distress among supporters of sexual assault victims. Further, contrary to Friedman et al.'s findings, they did not find that distress among supporters

was varied according to the distress level of the victim or the closeness of the relation between victim and offender. They did find, however, a strong effect of gender of supporter on their levels of distress: Female supporters reported higher levels of distress than male supporters. The difference in distress according to gender makes sense in light of the fact that women are far more likely to be victims of sexual assault than males.

Davis et al. (1995) found that distress suffered by persons who supported victims affected the kind of help they lent. They found that high levels of distress among supporters did not affect the amount of support they lent victims. Supporter distress was, however, associated with higher levels of *unsupportive* behavior, including egocentric behavior, emotional withdrawal, and blaming the victim.

In spite of the ill effects they often experienced, few supporters in the Friedman et al. study regretted that the victim turned to them for assistance. One in five supporters felt that they and the victims had been brought closer together by the experience, and all but a few did not wish that the victim had gone elsewhere for help.

CONCLUSION

Research studies have shown that victims need many different forms of assistance. Some needs can only be met by service programs: Victims filing claims for state compensation or domestic violence victims needing to gain child custody or alter the terms of visitation need help from trained professionals. But many needs are mundane. Victims may need a ride to the doctor, someone to watch the kids while they go to court, someone to watch their burglarized home while they get supplies to repair the door, or just a sympathetic ear to listen to their story. For these kinds of needs, family, friends, neighbors, and even strangers are often the closest source of assistance. In fact, virtually all victims report receiving some form of assistance from others.

Most persons who lend support are contacted within two days of the crime and are people the victim sees often and has known for a long time. Victims are most likely to receive emotional support and practical assistance from friends, family, and other members of their social networks. But neighbors—even those not well known to victims—often are the ones who stay with the victim or watch their home, and neighbors as well as landlords frequently lend financial assistance to victims.

The limited research on persons who lend support suggests that the effects of crime do not end with the victim, but are transmitted to others with whom the victim comes in contact. The closer the relationship between victim and supporter, the more likely supporters are to experience an increase in fear of crime and to take precautions themselves. Supporters of low-income victims most keenly feel the effects of lending money to victims for repairs or emergency expenses. Nonetheless, the overwhelming feeling among persons who lend a hand is that they feel good about doing so and are happy that they had the chance to be of assistance.

Victim service programs and individuals have complementary roles to play in helping victims to recover from the effects of crime. Family, friends, and neighbors are important resources that help victims with a variety of immediate and simple needs. Government should recognize the significance of social networks in the recovery process and work to enhance the effectiveness of this important resource. For example, government could train clergy and other key persons in understanding and responding to the needs of victims. Through an effective partnership of public and private efforts, victims can get the help they need to reassert control over their lives.

REFERENCES

Brickman, E. (2003). *Development of a national study of victim needs and assistance.* New York: Safe Horizon.

Coates, D., & Wortman, C. B. (1980). Depression maintenance and interpersonal control. In I. A. Baum, J. Singer, & Y. Epstein (Eds.), *Advances in environmental psychology* (Vol. 2, pp. 149–182). Hillsdale, NJ: Lawrence Erlbaum.

Conklin, J. E. (1971). Dimensions of community response to the crime problem. *Social Problems, 18,* 373–384.

Davis, R. C., & Brickman, E. (1996). Supportive and unsupportive aspects of the behavior of others toward victims of sexual and nonsexual assault. *Journal of Interpersonal Violence, 11,* 250–262.

Davis, R. C., Brickman, E., & Baker, T. (1991). Supportive and unsupportive responses of others to rape victims. *American Journal of Community Psychology, 19,* 443–451.

Davis, R. C., & Henley, M. (1990). *Victim service programs.* In A. Lurigio, W. Skogan, & R. Davis (Eds.), *Victims of crime: Problems, policies, and programs* (pp. 157–171). Newbury Park, CA: Sage.

Davis, R. C., Lurigio, A. J., & Skogan, W. G. (1999). Services for victims: A market research study. *International Journal of Victimology, 6,* 101–115.

Davis, R. C., Taylor, B., & Bench, S. (1995). Impact of sexual and nonsexual assault on secondary victims. *Violence and Victims, 10,* 73–84.

Dunkel-Schetter, C., & Wortman, C. B. (1982). The interpersonal dynamics of cancer: Problems in social relationships and their impact upon the patient. In H. S. Friedman & M. R. DiMatteo (Eds.), *Interpersonal issues in health care* (pp. 349–381). New York: Academic Press.

Friedman, K., Bischoff, H., Davis, R. C., & Person, A. (1982). *Victims and helpers: Reactions to crime.* Washington, DC: National Institute of Justice.

George, L. K., Winfield, I., & Blazer, D. G. (1992). Sociocultural factors in sexual assault: Comparison of two representative samples of women. *Journal of Social Issues, 48,* 105–125.

Golding, J. M., Siegel, J. M., Sorenson, S. B., Burnam, M. A., & Stein, J. A. (1989). Social support sources following sexual assault. *Journal of Community Psychology, 17,* 92–107.

Kaukinen, C. (2004). The help-seeking strategies of female violent crime victims: The direct and conditional effects of race and the victim-offender relationship. *Journal of Interpersonal Violence, 19,* 967–990.

Knudten, R. A., Meade, A., Knudten, M., & Doerner, W. (1976). *Victims and witnesses: The impact of crime and their experience with the criminal justice system.* Washington, DC: National Institute of Justice.

Krahe, B. (1988). Victim and observer characteristics as determinants of responsibility attributions to victims of rape. *Journal of Applied Social Psychology, 18,* 50–58.

Lerner, J. (1971). Observer's evaluation of a victim: Justice, guilt, and veridical perception. *Journal of Personality and Social Psychology, 22,* 127–135.

Lodewijkx, H. F. M., deKwaadsteniet, E. W., & Nijstad, B. A. (2005). That could be me (or not): Senseless violence and the role of deservingness, victim ethnicity, person identification, and position identification. *Journal of Applied Social Psychology, 35,* 1361–1383.

Maguire, M., & Kynch, J. (2000). Public perceptions and victims' experiences of victim support: Findings from the 1998 British crime survey (Home Office occasional paper). London: Home Office.

Norris, J., & Feldman-Summers, S. (1981). Factors related to the psychological impact of rape on the victim. *Journal of Abnormal Psychology, 90,* 562–567.

Reactions to Crime Project. (1978). *Responses to perceived fear and insecurity.* Evanston, IL: Northwestern University Center for Urban Affairs.

Rienick, C., Mulmat, D. H., & Pennell, S. (1997). *Meeting the needs of crime victims.* San Diego, CA: San Diego Association of Governments.

Riger, S., Raja, S., & Camacho, J. (2002). The radiating impact of intimate partner violence. *Journal of Interpersonal Violence, 17,* 184–205.

Ruback, R. B., & Ivie, D. L. (1988). Prior relationship, resistance, and injury in rapes: An analysis of crisis center records. *Violence and Victims, 3,* 99–111.

Sales, E., Baum, M., & Shore, B. (1984). Victim readjustment following assault. *Journal of Social Issues, 40,* 117–136.

Todd, J. L., & Worrell, J. (2000). Resilience in low-income, employed, African American women. *Psychology of Women Quarterly, 24,* 119–128.

Ullman, S. E., & Filipas, H. H. (2001). Correlates of formal and informal support seeking in sexual assault victims. *Journal of Interpersonal Violence, 16,* 1028–1047.

Wortman, C. B., & Lehman, D. (1985). Reactions to victims of life crisis: Support attempts that fail. In I. Sarason & B. Sarason (Eds.), *Social support: Theory, research, and application* (pp. 463–489). The Hague: Martinus Nijhoh.

Wortman, C. B., Wolff, K., & Bonanno, G. A. (2004). Loss of an intimate partner through death. In D. J. Mashek & A. P. Aron (Eds.), *Handbook of closeness and intimacy.* Mahwah, NJ: Lawrence Erlbaum.

17

Victim Participation in the Criminal Justice System

EDNA EREZ

JULIAN ROBERTS

According to the adversarial model of justice, a criminal trial entails a conflict between two theoretically equal adversaries, the state and the defendant, played out before an impartial adjudicator—the judge. The victim of the crime serves as the principal witness for the prosecution, and having served this function, has no further role to play. The victim is essentially a passive participant; she or he appears when called to testify and responds to examination in chief and cross-examination, if necessary. However, over the past 30 years, much has changed in the theory, policy, and practice of adversarial criminal justice. The role of the crime victim has been transformed from passive witness to active participant. While still lacking full "standing" as a party to the proceedings, victims nevertheless are consulted, informed, and participate more than ever before. To traditionalists, this evolution represents an unwelcome threat to core values central to the adversarial model. Victims' rights advocates hold a different perspective, viewing the new powers of the victim as evidence of progress toward an as yet unattained goal of full participation in the criminal process.

Until the 1970s crime victims were invisible to the general public and had little profile within the criminal justice system. The names of high-profile offenders were well recognized: Charles Manson, Peter Sutcliffe, Ted Bundy. Their victims, however, remained unknown. Public and media attention continues to focus on offenders and still overlooks their victims. However, this is no longer true for the criminal justice system. The governments of most Western nations have legislated many victim rights and created a wide range of services for the victims of crime. Victims have the right to receive information about the status of the case in which they are involved, and they also have the right to apply for financial and psychological assistance. More importantly, in many jurisdictions victims also enjoy participatory rights throughout the criminal process (Hall, 1991). Although most rights and benefits for victims have been generally accepted, the right to actively participate in the judicial process has proved controversial and continues to be the subject of heated debate.

Victim participatory rights apply throughout the criminal justice process, beginning with the arrest of a suspect and ending with the prisoner's release from prison. They pertain to hearings on bail or pretrial release of the offender, through plea agreements or sentencing, to posttrial relief or release hearings, including probation and commutation or pardon hearings. Victim participation is buttressed by laws that mandate victim notification, protection, and financial compensation in the event that they incur expenses in the course of participating. For instance, notification applies to the victim or victim's family, who should receive advance notice of proceedings where the victim has the right to attend and/or make a statement, as well as when hearings have been canceled and rescheduled. The right to protection from intimidation and harassment by the offender or the offender's family or associates may be extended to the victim's family members. The participation of victims whose victimization renders them particularly vulnerable to intimidation, such as domestic violence, is facilitated by rights that ensure police escorts to and from court, secure waiting areas separate from those of the accused and his/her family during court proceedings, and witness stands that are shielded from the direct view of the offender. This protection is particularly significant if the victim is a child, in which case many courts now allow videotaped testimony to be used to protect the child from the trauma of the courtroom and further exposure

to the accused. Other special circumstances allow for the closing of the courtroom to those who are not parties to the case and for the residence relocation of victims.

Victims' rights have also assumed a constitutional dimension in the United States. The Victims' Right Amendment is a proposed constitutional amendment that would enumerate various participatory rights for crime victims. These include notification of guaranteed admission to and the right to speak during the course of legal proceedings, including pretrial release, plea bargains, sentencing, and parole. The amendment also requires courts to consider victims' interests to ensure that trials occur without "unreasonable delays" and to consider the victim's safety when prisoners are considered for conditional release from prison. To be enacted, the proposed amendment requires a two-thirds vote in U.S. Congress (both the House and the Senate) as well as ratification by two thirds of all the states. To date, despite campaigns for its passage, including presidential endorsement in the last round, the proposed Victims' Rights Amendment has failed to gain the necessary number of states in support. The major argument against its passage has been that victim participation can be accomplished by enforcing existing laws found in state constitutional amendments or statutes.

This chapter surveys victim participatory rights and explores the continuing debate surrounding victims' claim to have a voice in criminal proceedings involving "their" offender. Exploring the issues and research on all stages of the system is beyond the scope of the chapter. Instead, after exploring some general issues and describing important participatory rights, we focus on the sentencing process. It is at sentencing that victims express greatest interest in participating and where victim input has generated the most opposition. We begin by describing the background from which victim participation emerged. Second, we summarize some important participatory reforms that have been adopted. Third, we consider some arguments for and against victim participation in sentencing. We pay particular attention to the victim impact statement (VIS). The VIS is in many respects the paradigm example of victim input, having been implemented in almost all common law jurisdictions. We then review future directions for victim participation in the judicial system, including attempts to inject restorative justice elements into an adversarial system that is fundamentally retributive in nature.

CRIME VICTIMS AND THE JUSTICE SYSTEM

The role of victims in a criminal prosecution has changed drastically over the centuries in common law countries—from an eye-for-an-eye system in which victims were expected to deal with their offenders directly, through a system in which the monarch assumed the duty of imposing punishment, to the present system in which the state prosecutes a defendant on behalf of the surrogate victim who is relegated to a role of (at best) lead witness (Zeigenhagen, 1977). For most victims, even their role as witness never materializes. As a result of attrition in the criminal process, most cases do not result in arrest, much less prosecution. Many crimes remain unreported to the police, and of those that are, a charge is laid in only a portion of incidents. Some charges are subsequently stayed or withdrawn by the prosecutor acting in the public interest or because there is no reasonable prospect of a conviction. In a large percentage of cases—estimates range as high as 90%—the offender enters a guilty plea, often following negotiations with the prosecutor. This obviates the need for a trial and the victim therefore has no opportunity to testify.[1] If the offender pleads guilty to a much less serious offense than the crime with which he was charged, victims may feel let down by the criminal process. The victim's principal role is as a backup—a threat waiting in the wings if plea bargaining breaks down.

Unlike continental legal systems (see Joutsen, 1994), the adversarial system accords victims no formal standing in the prosecution of their offenders, and until fairly recently, the crime victim provided no input into the treatment of "their" offender. Even today, in most states crime victims have no legal rights for input into the system that are guaranteed by remedies for nonenforcement, only courtesies to be extended or withheld at the discretion of the police or prosecutor. The result is a curious blend of independence and dependence, with the result that victims have little influence over whether or how the state chooses to proceed against their offenders. At the same time, the state is highly dependent on the cooperation of victims, without which a criminal prosecution is unlikely to succeed.

In the early 1970s victims began to exert more influence over decisions taken in the criminal justice system. This was largely due to an unexpected alliance of feminist scholars and advocates (advocating to improve the treatment of victims of rape and intimate partner violence) and law-and-order groups (lobbying to "get tough" on crime). As a result of their combined efforts, criminal justice procedures were adapted to make the justice system more sensitive to victims' needs and concerns. Efforts initially focused on responses to the economic and psychological problems that victims experienced as a result of the crime, leading to the creation of programs that addressed the psychological consequences of the crime (Erez, 1989). For instance, rape shield laws were enacted to limit the scope of defense efforts to introduce a victim's past sexual history in evidence at trial. In a similar way, domestic violence laws were enacted that are distinct from other laws against assault. Police departments began to offer specialized training regarding the investigation of crimes of sexual aggression and the needs of rape and domestic violence victims. These reforms were motivated both by a newfound compassion for victims and by a realization that the criminal justice system would benefit by treating victims with more sensitivity.

Victimization surveys at the time revealed that a large proportion of crimes were not reported to the police (Bureau of Justice Statistics, 1983), because, among other reasons, victimized citizens were apprehensive about how they would be treated by the justice system and whether they would be believed (Kidd & Chayet, 1984; Kilpatrick & Otto, 1987). Studies also showed that victims and witnesses were "uncooperative" with respect to prosecutorial efforts to bring offenders to justice because they were intimidated by the criminal justice system or were uninformed as to what was expected of them (Cannavele, 1975). Accordingly, victim-witness assistance units were established to respond to victims' desire for better treatment and information, as well as to address the state's need for cooperative witnesses. Today, such units form part of most Western criminal justice systems and provide a variety of services to crime victims from first contact with the police to the sentencing of the offender. Victims began to be notified when hearings were scheduled so that they would not be kept waiting in court unnecessarily. In many courthouses, separate waiting rooms were established for defense and state witnesses. In the past, victims and accused persons often came into close contact at the courthouse.

CLAIMS FOR PARTICIPATORY RIGHTS

Although these changes were welcome, crime victims demanded more than sympathy and support; they wanted to have a *voice* in the criminal justice system. A number of studies have found that while some victims prefer to stay out of the criminal justice system, many others wish to participate (e.g., Kelly, 1984; Shapland, Villmoare, & Duff, 1985). Moreover,

the need to accord victims participatory rights has been recognized by many national committees established to study victims in the criminal justice process, of which the following are examples:

- United States: the President's Task Force on Victims of Crime (1982)
- Canada: the report of the Standing Committee on Justice and Human Rights (1998)
- New Zealand: the Victim's Task Force (1987)
- England and Wales: Justice Committee on the role of the victim in criminal justice (1998)

The international community has also recognized the need to integrate victims into the criminal justice process. In 1985, the United Nations Seventh Congress on the Prevention of Crime and Treatment of the Offender adopted a declaration that required that victims be allowed to present their views and concerns at appropriate stages of the criminal justice process. As advocates pressed for victims' rights to participate in proceedings, their demands were met with considerable resistance. Victim participation threatened to disturb established routines at the courthouse, undermine the predictability of case outcomes and slow the processing of cases. Studies showed that prosecutors, defense attorneys, and judges operated as a "work group," sharing the mutual goal of disposing of cases as fast as time and justice would permit (Eisenstein & Jacob, 1977). It was feared that allowing victims to have some input would impair the efficiency of the work group and exacerbate the pressure of cases on the court's already overloaded docket.

EMERGENCE OF VICTIM PARTICIPATORY REFORMS

United States

In the midst of this debate, a new generation of participatory reforms emerged. Many of these reforms were prompted by the recommendation of the President's Task Force on Victims of Crime (1982) that the Sixth Amendment be amended to guarantee victims a right to be present and to be heard at all critical stages of a judicial proceeding. Most states in the United States adopted laws that address victims' right to be present in proceedings by excluding victims from sequestration requirements or otherwise accommodating their wish to participate. The 1991 Omnibus Crime Bill (Pub. L. No. 101–647) stated that victims have a right to "be present at all public court proceedings related to the offense." Title V, the Victims' Rights and Restitution Act of 1990, provides that victims in federal courts have rights to restitution; to be present "at all public court proceedings related to the offense" (unless the court determines that the victim's testimony would be affected by the testimony of other witnesses at trial); to confer with the U.S. attorney; and to be informed of the arrest, conviction, sentencing, imprisonment, parole, release, or death of the offender.

Many states in the United States have enacted victims' bills of rights, which vary in their scope from mandating that criminal justice officials show respect toward victims, to establishing a victim's right to be present and heard, to allowing victims to sit at the prosecutor's table during trial. In several states, victims' rights legislation is by specific statute, but a substantial number of states have adopted constitutional amendments to give victims' rights greater permanence and visibility. The majority of the states also allow for victim participation in sentencing and parole hearings. States also provide for victim participation in plea bargaining. For example, crime victims in Arizona have the right to be consulted with respect to any potential plea agreement. Furthermore, prosecutors are required to demonstrate that they have complied with victims' rights legislation (U.S. Department of Justice, 2002; see Verdun-Jones & Tijerino, 2004, for discussion).

However, the extent to which victims are allowed to participate in plea discussions varies widely, with no state providing victims with a veto over plea agreements.

Reforms addressing circumstances in which victims are afraid or reluctant to provide testimony or input into proceedings (such as domestic violence cases) were also adopted. These laws or statutory amendments require police to make arrests, regardless of whether the victim signs the complaint. Similarly, prosecutors are allowed to proceed with a case, even if the victim refuses to cooperate (known as a "no-drop" policy). Mandatory arrest laws and no-drop prosecutorial policies recognize that victims of domestic violence are especially vulnerable to retaliation for pressing charges and therefore remove this decision from victims. These mandatory charging and prosecuting policies create a potential conflict with the principal goal of victims' advocates: to give victims a say in decisions that affect their lives. Accordingly, some battered women's advocates and feminist scholars have criticized the mandatory element of these policies, arguing that they further disempower the crime victim.

Other Jurisdictions

Other jurisdictions have also adopted victims' rights legislation of various kinds, although not to the degree found in the United States. In Canada, victims have a statutory right to submit a victim impact statement at sentencing and to deliver the statement orally if they so desire (Roberts, 2003). Victims may also submit impact statements to parole board hearings. In Manitoba, according to the Victims' Rights Act, crime victims have the right to be consulted with respect to decisions taken at all stages of the criminal process, including whether the state appeals a conviction or a sentence. Some jurisdictions such as England and Wales have adopted "Victims' Charters," which are largely aspirational in nature, creating expectations that the system will conform to certain standards without actually conferring legal rights upon crime victims. Finally, the importance of victim participatory rights is apparent from Article 68 of the Rome Statute of the International Criminal Court. This provision recognizes the security interests and participatory rights of victims and witnesses.

Victim Impact Statements

Of all the participatory reforms, victim input into sentencing decisions, or victim impact statements (VIS), have attracted the most opposition. The remaining sections of this chapter focus on victims' right to submit a VIS—as the term is referred to in the United States and Canada—or victim personal statement (VPS), its counterpart in England and Wales.[2] We focus on VIS, as this reform represents a good example of a participatory mechanism, which on the evidence can be of considerable benefit to the victim and the court to which it is submitted. The VIS is a statement in which the victim describes the impact of the crime on his or her life, including physical, social, psychological, and financial harms. The VIS may be delivered at the sentencing hearing in writing, orally, or visually (in countries or jurisdictions that allow victim allocution or presentations through a video). VIS forms differ in content and form, ranging from simple checklists in some jurisdictions to lengthy descriptive statements in others (McLeod, 1988). Some permit considerable latitude in terms of the information that may be included; other forms restrict the victim to a much greater degree. In most jurisdictions, courts are directed to take the statement into account. For example, in Canada, a provision in the Criminal Code makes it mandatory for a court to consider the victim impact statement at sentencing.

THE DEBATE SURROUNDING VICTIM PARTICIPATION AT SENTENCING

Arguments for Victim Input

Advocates of victims' rights to participate in the criminal justice process have advanced a variety of arguments, some moral, some penological, and others practical in nature. Victim participation recognizes victims' wishes to be treated as a party to the proceeding and with dignity (Henderson, 1985). It reminds judges, juries, and prosecutors that behind the "state" stands an individual with an interest in how the case is resolved (Kelly, 1987). Some argue that sentencing outcomes will be more proportionate if victims provide accurate information about the impact of the crime (Erez, 1990) and that the criminal justice process will be more democratic and better reflect the community's response to crime (Rubel, 1986). Victim participation may also lead to increased victim satisfaction with the judicial process (Australian Law Reform Commission, 1988), and cooperation with the criminal justice system may thereby enhance the system's efficiency (McLeod, 1986). It may well also increase perceptions of the fairness of proceedings. Thus, when the court hears from offenders' family and friends, fairness dictates that the people who actually were injured should be allowed to speak (Sumner, 1987).

Victim participation may also promote psychological healing by helping victims to recover from the emotional trauma associated with their victimization and court experiences (Erez, 1990; Ranish & Shichor, 1985). In contrast, a criminal justice system that provides no opportunity for victims to participate may exacerbate the feelings of helplessness that often arise as a result of the crime (Kilpatrick & Otto, 1987, p. 19). Victim participation may also promote the rehabilitation of the offender, who upon hearing the victim's statement must confront the reality of the harm that he or she inflicted on the victim (Talbert, 1988). Later in the chapter we examine the validity of these claims.

Arguments Against Victim Input

The objections to victim participation at sentencing range from assumptions that vengeful justice will result to predictions that the system will grind to a halt as a result of the additional time needed to process cases if victims provide input (Erez, 1990, 1994). Some argue that allowing victims to participate will expose the court to precisely the public pressure from which it should properly be insulated (Rubel, 1986), or will result in substituting the victim's "subjective" approach for the allegedly "objective" one practiced by the court (Victorian Sentencing Committee, 1988). The legal profession, in particular, has found the prospect of allowing material that may be highly emotional in the courtroom unacceptable. Critics argue that a victim's input into sentencing is "irrelevant to any legitimate sentencing factor, lacks probative value in a system of public prosecution, and is likely to be highly prejudicial" (Hellerstein, 1989, p. 429).

Permission to deliver a VIS in person—exercising victim allocution right—has been regarded as particularly objectionable, as an oral version in a very serious crime may be very moving for the judge or jury, and this may increase sentence severity or promote sentencing disparity.[3] Critics argued that similar cases might end up being disposed of differently depending on whether a VIS is available and how persuasive the victim is (Grabosky, 1987, p. 147).[4] Legal professionals and scholars also argued that victim input violates the fundamental principles of the adversarial legal system, which, as previously noted, do not recognize the victim as a party to proceedings (Ashworth, 1993, 2002). Including victims would transform the trial between the state and the defendant into a tripartite court proceeding (state—victim—offender). Such practices, it was argued, belong only in so-called continental legal systems with adhesive prosecution or *partie civil* procedures, or to restorative justice schemes.[5]

Prosecutors sometimes object to victim input in sentencing because they fear that their control over cases will be undermined, with the consequence that court outcomes will become more unpredictable (Davis, Kunreuther, & Connick, 1984), and the system will be overburdened (Australian Law Reform Commission, 1988). Others argue that victim input is redundant or adds very little information that is not already available to the court, given that the criminal law already takes into account the harm done to the victim through its charging decisions and submissions from the prosecution at sentencing (Hellerstein, 1989; Paciocco, 1999). Moreover, as the law typically punishes offenders for harm that was foreseeable, critics argue that only effects on the "typical" victim should be considered (Victorian Sentencing Committee, 1988) and that the offender should not be held accountable for unforeseen consequences—for example, the effects of the crime on victims who turned out to be particularly vulnerable in ways unforeseen by the perpetrator (Ashworth, 1993).

It has also been argued that VIS may create unrealistic expectations in victims that are not or cannot be met (Fattah, 1986). For example, if a judge imposes a sentence that is at odds with the victim's wishes as expressed in a VIS, the victim may become resentful (Henderson, 1985). Although victims are not obliged to, they may feel compelled to submit a statement, and the process may be traumatic for victims who do not want offenders to know the extent of the harm they inflicted (Australian Law Reform Commission, 1988). Victims who do submit impact statements may feel as if they are responsible for the sentencing outcome and some may prefer not to assume this responsibility (Reeves & Mulley, 2000). In addition, it has been suggested that filling out a VIS raises the prospect in the victim's mind that his or her "submission" on sentencing will carry the same weight as any representations by the prosecution or defense counsel. When the court ignores a victim's sentence recommendation, the victim may feel that submitting a statement was in vain.

Other objections to victim input are based on ideological grounds. Opponents allege that any gain for victims constitutes a loss for defendants. They argue that victims have been exploited by a conservative "law-and-order" ideology, whose real goal is to get tough on offenders, not to help victims (Henderson, 1985), suggesting that the reform is just a euphemistic label to camouflage efforts to make sentencing harsher. The true intention behind the victim rights rhetoric, it has been suggested, is to mobilize hostility toward offenders or to demonstrate the leniency of the sentencing system. Critics depicted victims as merely "pawns" used in these politics of law and order. Because victims were portrayed as vindictive and motivated by a desire to maximize sentence severity, some scholars have attributed recent increases in punitiveness to the movement to grant victims participatory rights. A recurrent theme emerging in objections to victim input involves concern for defendants' rights.[6] The argument is advanced that victim input reflects a desire to strengthen the prosecution and therefore undermine the interests of defendants.[7]

The Context of the Debate and the Ensuing Research

Because the campaign to allow victim input into sentencing encountered such strong opposition from the legal profession, the justification for the reform was refashioned from its original purpose—advocating victim voice as a measure of healing (the expressive aim of VIS; see Roberts & Erez, 2004)—to emphasizing its potential to help judges impose sentences commensurate with the (intended) harm (the instrumental aim).[8] The time was ripe to connect and jointly address victim input and the quantum of sentences: In criminology, there was disenchantment with the idea of rehabilitation as the basis for punishment, and calls to replace it with "just deserts" philosophy were growing. According to just deserts principles, the punishment should be based on the offender's level of culpability and the extent of harm inflicted on the victim. Victim input, it was suggested, could be useful in this regard by providing full details on the extent of injury. In victimology, ample evidence accumulated on "secondary victimization" of crime victims—their wounds, frustration, and alienation from a justice system in which they had no voice, except as witnesses at trial. The framing of the VIS as a tool to help the court in meting out "justice" led to sometimes contradictory justifications for victim voice in sentencing, resulting in what has been described as "incoherence." It also redirected the discussion to questions such as whether the VIS fulfills its intended purpose, whether it meets the needs of the court, or what are its impacts on sentencing. More recent critics, however, claim that the goal of improving victim welfare, or the therapeutic benefits of having a voice—the original purpose of the VIS reform—is merely rhetoric, if not an illusion (Sanders et al., 2001).

RESEARCH FINDINGS ON THE EFFECTS OF VICTIM INPUT INTO SENTENCING

Research provides answers to some of the issues raised in the debate about victim input into sentencing. It suggests that (a) victim participation does not clog the criminal justice system by protracting the time taken to arrive at an adjudication, (b) victim participation does not necessarily result in harsher punishment of offenders, (c) victim participation has the potential to increase victim satisfaction with the judicial system, and (d) the implementation of victim input laws is still problematic, and many victims do not benefit from these reforms. First, however, we briefly discuss the levels of participation and the reasons that victims offer for wishing to provide impact evidence into sentencing.

Levels of Participation

In practice, many victim-related reforms never reach victims. Victims either are unaware of their rights to participate or elect not to exercise them (Erez & Tontodonato, 1990; Hillenbrand & Smith, 1989; Villmoore & Neto, 1987). Studies also reflect considerable confusion about the nature and purpose of VIS. Victims often do not know what VIS are or claim that they did not fill out such statements when, in fact, they did (Erez & Tontodonato, 1992; Erez, Roeger, & Morgan, 1994). This may be because victims are questioned by a seemingly endless array of people and may become confused about the purpose of particular interviews. Some jurisdictions have overcome this problem by having victims prepare their own VIS rather than merely provide the information to the investigating officer (the counterpart of probation or victim assistance officers in other countries).

One observation applicable to victim impact schemes in all common law jurisdictions is that only a minority of all victims participate by submitting a VIS. Based on research in England and Wales, Sanders et al. (2001) report a submission rate of 30%, while judges in surveys conducted in Canada reported seeing a VIS on average in 11% of cases proceeding for sentencing (Roberts & Edgar, 2006). The likelihood of an impact statement being submitted will depend greatly on the nature and seriousness of the crime as well as many other variables. Analysis of court files and surveys of criminal justice professionals such as prosecutors and judges confirm that most sentencing hearings take place without the benefit of an impact statement from the victim. There are a number of explanations for this state of affairs.

First, not all victims wish to submit a statement, or indeed to have any contact with the justice system. Some victims may be quite satisfied that the prosecutor will accurately describe the harm inflicted on the victim. Second, the justice system may fail in its duty to inform victims of their right to submit a statement. Third, issues such as plea bargaining may play a role. If the prosecution and defense agree to place a joint sentencing submission before the court, sentencing may take place before the system has had a chance to inform the victim. If this is the case, unless an impact statement was submitted early in the proceedings and filed for later use at the time of sentencing, the opportunity to provide input is lost. It is also clear that part of the low rate of participation arises from the fact that many victims of property crimes see little benefit or no need to submit an impact statement. This explains the fact that the submission rate is much lower for property crimes than crimes of violence.

The nature of the implementation of VIS schemes may also affect the participation rate. To the extent that victims learn of their right to submit a VIS only if the police or court officials tell them, victims' involvement depends on official support for such reforms. Criminal justice officials sometimes believe that VIS are redundant and contain no new information (Paciocco, 1999). Prosecutors may be reluctant to have the judge know the full impact of the crime for fear that it would jeopardize a negotiated plea (Corns, 1988) and may be skeptical about the extent to which judges consider victims' views (Davis & Smith, 1994; Erez et al., 1994). In addition, there may be practical problems in obtaining a VIS or an ideological resistance to giving victims a voice in criminal justice decisions, despite legislative authority to do so (e.g., Hellerstein, 1989; Victorian Sentencing Committee, 1988).

Reasons for Submitting a Victim Statement at Sentencing

Findings with respect to this issue vary across jurisdictions. Hoyle, Cape, Morgan, & Sanders (1998) found that the majority of the victims in their study in England and Wales explained that they had submitted a VIS for expressive reasons (i.e., to communicate a message of impact to the court). Slightly more than half cited an instrumental reason, namely the desire to influence the outcome of the sentencing hearing. In the survey of crime victims in South Australia, Erez et al. (1994) report that the main reason that victims cited for providing information for a VIS was to ensure that justice was done (cited by more than two thirds of the respondents). The most recent Canadian research found that victims were twice as likely to cite "want court to understand effect of crime" than "thought statement would affect sentence" as a reason for submitting a VIS (Prairie Research Associates, 2004). The other reasons cited included communicating the impact of the crime to the offender, and in order to discharge a civic duty. Clearly, there are many reasons why victims submit an impact statement. Indirect evidence also suggests that victims may be interested in participating for the purpose of "justice," even though it means reliving the experience of victimization. A study in Australia found that victims of serious crimes, in particular, were interested in receiving information concerning the case at all stages of the process (Gardner, 1990).

It is also apparent that the extent to which victims understand the purpose and function of a VIS varies considerably, and this level of understanding may affect submission rates. Some VIS forms may contribute to confusion

among victims. For example, one Canadian VIS guide states, "The Victim Impact Statement *may* be used during the sentencing hearing," and "the judge will decide whether or not to consider the victim impact statement when determining the sentence" (see Roberts, 2003). In fact, there is a statutory obligation on judges to consider the VIS at sentencing in that country. Not surprisingly, research has found that some participants were unclear as to whether judges are required to actually read the statements that they had prepared (Meredith & Paquette, 2001). In addition to holding misperceptions about the purpose of a VIS, many victims are simply confused about the nature of their input (e.g., Erez & Tontodonato, 1990). The fact that some victims want to influence sentencing is not unexpected; indeed it is a natural reaction, reflecting widespread public confusion over the role of the victim in the sentencing process and the nature of a criminal proceeding under the adversarial system. But victims may well accept the role currently assigned to them if it is explained thoroughly, with sensitivity, and by the relevant authorities.

The Effect of Victim Input on Criminal Justice Administration

Researchers have evaluated the effects of victim input in many ways, through the analysis of criminal justice statistics as well as surveys of criminal justice professionals such as prosecutors and judges. Research in jurisdictions that allow victim participation indicates that including victims in the criminal justice process does not cause delays or additional expense (Davis & Smith, 1994; Erez et al., 1994; Roberts & Edgar, 2006) and that very few court officials believe that victim input creates or exacerbates problems or slows down the proceedings (Hillenbrand & Smith, 1989). Court officials (prosecutors, defense attorneys, as well as judges) even in very busy jurisdictions generally view victim

Perceptions of the Judiciary

input positively (e.g., Henley, Davis, & Smith, 1994; Roberts & Edgar, 2006).

The views of judges are particularly relevant to the debate, as they are best placed to know whether victim impact statements contain probative or extraneous information. Surveys of the judiciary demonstrate that most judges see a benefit to receiving crime impact information directly from the victim by means of a victim impact statement. Although much of the information in VIS should already be reflected in evidence adduced at trial or prosecutorial submissions at sentencing, at times VIS may provide additional information useful to the judge when determining a sentence. According to surveys in Canada and Australia, most judges acknowledge that VIS contain information that is relevant to the purposes of sentencing (D'Avignon, 2001; Erez & Rogers, 1999; Roberts & Edgar, 2006). Studies of judges in the United States and Australia suggest that judges find VIS helpful for learning how victims are affected by crime (Davis & Smith, 1994). Judges in one study also indicated that without VIS they would have a less accurate idea of the true impact of the crime on the victim (Davis & Smith, 1994).

In most jurisdictions victims are discouraged from making specific sentencing recommendations in their VIS. Yet judges report that they do encounter sentence recommendations in VIS (Roberts & Edgar, 2006). The presence of sentence recommendations suggests that the form used, or the information conveyed to victims who submit a statement, may be at fault. If victims are encouraged to tell the court anything they wish, the victim may lose sight of the expressive, communicative function of the idea and see the statement in instrumental terms: to influence the court with respect to the sentence imposed. The justice system therefore needs to specify clearly the format, content, and exact use of a VIS. However, although judges report that they do sometimes read such recommendations, they appear to have little difficulty in setting the victim's views in this regard aside. Professional judges are trained to ignore testimony that has prejudicial but not probative value.[9]

In short, the most critical constituency at this stage of the criminal process—sentencing judges—perceive considerable utility in VIS. This is particularly true for crimes of violence, crimes in which property was stolen or damaged, or offenses in which the impact on the victim was disproportionate or unusual. Furthermore, judges in Australia reported that VIS not only educated them about the effects of crimes on victims but sometimes benefited the defendant—for example, when the information disclosed that the injury was not as severe as one might expect from the charge of conviction (Erez & Rogers, 1999).[10]

The VIS also creates an opportunity for the court to acknowledge the victim as the aggrieved party and to communicate state recognition of the harm sustained by the victim. If the victim is in court, the sentencing judge also has the opportunity to speak directly to the victim, validating his or her harm. Victims who hear their own words quoted in judges' sentencing remarks appreciate the validation and report being more satisfied with the justice system (Erez, 1990). As for the criticism that some victims use the opportunity to criticize or attack the defendant, judges who witness abuse of the right to communicate have the authority to intervene and stop the abusive communication, whether it is from the victim or from the defendant (Roberts & Erez, 2004). Judges are commonly aware of their power to acknowledge victims as the injured person, and that quoting the VIS in sentencing remarks enhances victims' sense of being recognized as victims. Judges appreciate the therapeutic value such recognition has, and many make use of it in court (Erez & Rogers, 1999; Roberts & Edgar, 2006).

Validity of VIS

Although defense lawyers occasionally express concern that victim statements are inaccurate, research indicates that, in fact, victim statements seldom include inflammatory or prejudicial material (Erez et al., 1994; Henley et al., 1994; Roberts & Edgar, 2006). On the rare occasions when this occurs, the prosecution can edit the statement to prevent the inflammatory phrases from coming to the attention of the court. Another erroneous criticism of the VIS is that victims often exaggerate the level of harm that they sustained. This appears to happen only rarely, and when it does, judges and prosecutors report that these exaggerations involve financial matters, not emotional or mental suffering (Erez & Rogers, 1999).

There is conflicting research as to whether impact statements improve the quality of justice by influencing restitution awards (Erez et al., 1994; Hillenbrand & Smith, 1989). Research has found that most judges and prosecutors believe it does. These findings are consistent with research in England suggesting that compensation is more likely to be ordered if it was mentioned in court proceedings (Shapland et al., 1985). Because prosecutors may be unaware of victims' preferences, or for various reasons may fail to convey them to the court, allowing victims to express their wishes directly by means of a VIS may be the only way to guarantee that the sentencing authority learns of their requests. Research in Australia, however, did not find any increase in the rate of restitution or compensation orders following the introduction of VIS because, unless offenders have means to pay, judges are precluded from imposing restitution or compensation orders (Erez et al., 1994).

The Impact of Victim
Input on Sentencing Practices

As noted, critics of VIS have claimed that the presence of these statements will tip the scales against the defendant, resulting in harsher sentencing patterns. Research largely refutes assumptions that victim participation results in harsher sentences for defendants. Studies suggest that sentences are determined predominantly on the basis of legal considerations such as the seriousness of the offense and the offender's criminal record (Davis & Smith, 1994; Erez & Tontodonato, 1990; Erez & Roeger, 1995). Victim participation either has no effect on sentence severity or cuts both ways in the sense that it sometimes results in a more lenient disposition. As a practical matter, VIS will have limited relevance in the U.S. federal system or in jurisdictions that employ a determinate sentencing scheme (Hellerstein, 1989). Judges and prosecutors in one study (Erez & Rogers, 1999) reported that VIS result in harsher sentences in some cases (e.g., when the intended harm was particularly serious or the crime was especially heinous) and in less severe sentences in other cases (e.g., when no harm occurred or when the harm was much less than would be expected). This may in part explain why aggregate studies (e.g., Erez & Tontodonato, 1990) do not find any effect of victims' participation on sentencing trends (Erez & Roeger, 1995).

With regard to victims' views on sentencing, a study of impact statements submitted in sexual assault cases found that the court was most likely to recognize the desires of the victim when they were consistent with the court's own view of the appropriate sentence. This study refutes the stereotype that all victims thirst for vengeance. It revealed that the court was *more* punitive than victims and was likely to ignore victims' desire for probation sentences over imprisonment (Walsh, 1986; see also Sherman & Strang, 2003). Moreover, once a prison sentence was imposed, the victim's opinion regarding sentencing did not significantly affect the length of term (Erez & Tontodonato, 1990). Other studies reaffirm that victim participation does not result in more severe sentences. One study that used an experimental design to examine the effect of VIS on sentences found that the use of VIS did not result in harsher sentences for offenders or increase the likelihood of incarceration as opposed to probation. Instead, the researchers concluded that the seriousness of the charge, rather than the harm described in the VIS, most affected the sentence imposed (Davis & Smith, 1994).

In contrast to victims' rights to file a written statement, one study of victims' right to speak, or allocate, in court found that it was victims' presence rather than their oral delivery that had an effect on the length of sentence. Typically, victims who attend court during sentencing tend to be involved in many phases of the trial process, thus providing a constant (and in our view, salutary) reminder to the judge that an individual and not the state is the principal injured party (Erez & Tontodonato, 1990). When a case proceeds to sentencing, the decision has already been made, so allocution is unlikely to affect the outcome. In this sense, the right to allocution is more symbolic than effective. By the time the victim comes to court, a well-prepared judge has already received the probation report, and there is little room for modification of the court's intended decision. An emotional appeal to the court by the victim cannot carry more weight than facts and sentencing precedent (Villmoare & Neto, 1987, p. 37). In contrast, because the written VIS is submitted *prior to* sentencing, it has a greater chance to influence sentencing, if at all (Erez & Tontodonato, 1990).

The Effect of VIS on Victims' Welfare and Satisfaction With the Justice System

Findings on the effect[11] of providing input into sentencing are inconsistent with respect to the issue of victim welfare and satisfaction and suggest, at best, modest effects. The lack of evidence on satisfaction, however, may simply reflect a problematic implementation of the law. One study found that filing VIS usually results in increased satisfaction with the outcome (Erez & Tontodonato, 1992), while a study of rape victims found that victim participation generally increases victims' satisfaction (Kelly, 1984). Another study that randomly assigned victims' cases to various treatments found that VIS had no effect on victims' feelings of involvement or satisfaction with the criminal justice process or its outcome (Davis & Smith, 1994). There was no effect of VIS on satisfaction levels. Similarly, studies of the VIS program in Canada and in Australia (Erez et al., 1994) revealed that victims who submit an impact statement are not necessarily more satisfied with the outcome or with the criminal justice system. The Australian study found that lack of evidence may be related to the problematic implementation of the law; many victims did not realize that the purpose of the interview they had was to gather input that would be provided to the judge. In some cases, filing VIS heightens victims' expectations that they will influence the outcome. When that does not happen, victims may be less satisfied than those who do not submit a statement (Erez et al., 1994). In contrast, a comparative study of victims in the continental criminal justice systems (which allow victims a party status and significant input into the proceedings) suggests that victims who participated as subsidiary prosecutors or acted as private prosecutors were more satisfied than victims who did not participate (Erez & Bienkowska, 1993). These differences suggest that in jurisdictions in which victims have more input into proceedings, levels of satisfaction are higher.

Research on victims' involvement in parole proceedings indicates that participation at this stage may enhance the image of the criminal justice system in the eyes of the crime victim. One study found that many victims who testified in parole hearings were dissatisfied with the criminal justice system's handling of their cases to that point because they had been excluded from earlier proceedings. These victims especially appreciated the opportunity to be heard by parole authorities (Parsonage, Bernat, & Helfgott, 1992).[12]

The effect of victim participation on victims' distress levels has not been systematically studied. Those few studies conducted were limited to rape victims, and their results are inconclusive (Lurigio & Resick, 1990). The only study that has examined the effect of VIS on victims' distress levels (Tontodonato & Erez, 1994) suggests that although distress is not directly influenced by filing a VIS, opportunities for such participation nonetheless may be important because they may affect whether a request for restitution is awarded (Erez & Tontodonato, 1990). Restitution, in turn, influences victims' perception of equity and their satisfaction with justice (Erez & Tontodonato, 1992; see also Boers & Sessar, 1991).

Research has identified three major factors that increase victims' overall satisfaction with the justice system and reduce their trauma. They include (a) procedural justice concerns such as whether the victim had the opportunity to be heard, and whether he or she was treated with respect and informed of key developments in their cases (see Wemmers, 1996); (b) the final decision of the court (e.g., whether the victims received financial compensation); and (c) whether there was an admission of guilt or request for forgiveness from the perpetrator (see Orth, 2002, 2003; Wemmers, 1996). These variables were found to be more predictive of victim satisfaction than the severity of punishment imposed. This research suggests that victims' interests or concerns relative to proceedings are not simply to generate a severe sentence but pertain to the court addressing a broad range of issues that are within its purview, issues that a well-implemented VIS program can facilitate. Finally, research with victims of violent crime in several countries has revealed that victims appreciate judicial recognition of the harm they sustained (Erez,

1999; Roberts & Edgar, 2006). Judicial acknowledgment may be expressed in a direct statement if the victim is present in court at sentencing, or it may be articulated in the reasons for sentence. Judges appear aware of the importance of this validation of the harm: a survey of the judiciary found that most reported acknowledging victim harm directly by addressing the victim in court or indirectly by citing victim impact in their reasons for sentencing (Roberts & Edgar, 2006).

RESTORATIVE JUSTICE, THERAPEUTIC JURISPRUDENCE, AND THE VIS

Victims have benefited greatly from the rise—worldwide—of interest in restorative justice (see Dignan, 2005, for discussion). This perspective offers an alternative to the conventional retributive model of criminal justice, and one that assigns a very prominent role to the victim. Victim rights and restorative justice are not interchangeable;[13] indeed, some scholars such as Zedner (2002) have questioned "whether, and how far, restorative justice is about serving the interests of victims" (p. 447). In our view, victims' rights and restorative justice are best viewed as related initiatives with overlapping interests. The importance of victim voice in proceedings on the one hand, and victims' role in the reentry of offenders[14] on the other, has been increasingly recognized in justice practices. This change is due in part to victim advocates' efforts on behalf of victims, and in part to research findings that challenge prevailing beliefs and myths about victims' interests, motives, and consequences of input into sentencing.

It is impossible to characterize all victims as vengeful, forgiving, or expressive. Some victims will be outraged by what they perceive as a lenient sentence. Others may seek a noncustodial sentence accompanied by compensation, whereas the court favors imprisoning the offender. And some victims will want nothing to do with the justice system, preferring to deal with the victimization experience in their own way and time. However, it is clear that many crime victims, particularly of serious offenses,[15] are eager to describe their victimization experiences. They want a voice to communicate a sense of the harm they sustained more than they wish to influence the sentence (Erez, 1999). In this context, the VIS can serve as a restorative justice element in adversarial proceedings, facilitating supervised communication between victims and offenders.

The idea that VIS can be recognized as injecting a restorative element into adversarial proceedings has precedence and support. The National Institute of Justice (NIJ) Web site lists the VIS as an example of restorative justice practices. It refers to it as "one of the most effective means to communicate the 'voice of the victim' throughout the criminal and juvenile justice systems," listing it together with restorative justice remedies or procedures such as restitution, sentencing circles, community service, family group conferencing, victim-offender mediation, victim impact panels, and victim impact classes. The therapeutic value of the VIS is similarly evident in official documents that state,

> It is significant for victims' healing that the judge acknowledge at the time of sentencing that victims have been injured, solicit specific information from victims on the crime's impact on their lives, and explain the terms of the offender's sentence. (U.S. Department of Justice, 1998, p. 108)

The inclusion of the VIS among restorative justice practices underscores its significance for improving victims' well-being. Beyond its symbolic value, the VIS is situated at the apex of the criminal justice process, when key courtroom participants determine the disposition of the case. As such, victim voice can trigger helpful reactions, and it can evoke appropriate emotions that serve therapeutic

ends. The emerging field of therapeutic jurisprudence,[16] which focuses on the law's impact on the emotional life and psychological well-being of the people its proceedings or remedies affect, has considered the VIS as an important reform that can promote the welfare of those engaged in it (see Wiebe, 1996; Herman, 2003).

The restricted opportunity for victim-offender exchanges in adversarial proceedings further highlights the importance of allowing and encouraging victims to deliver their statements in person. The victim is ideally placed to sensitize the offender to the consequences of the crime. Presentation of the VIS by the victim is preferable to having prosecutors convey impact information, as the offender would be able to relate to what a victim conveys more than to impact details presented by a legal professional who has the role of prosecuting the case. As most victims and offenders are laypersons rather than criminal justice professionals, and are often unfamiliar with its legal jargon, a direct appeal by the victim to the offender may be a more effective route to encourage offenders to accept responsibility.

Not all victims who are present in court during sentencing will wish to exercise the right to speak. Fear of public speaking, fear of the defendant, or just not feeling the need to express oneself may be some of the reasons for which victims would be reluctant to speak in open court. A sizeable proportion of victims nevertheless would wish to make use of this right and communicate with the defendant (see, e.g., Villmoare & Neto, 1987). Allowing victim-defendant communication at sentencing may serve as a step toward making the adversarial process more restorative in nature, thereby increasing defendants' awareness of the consequences of the crime on the victim. Research in various countries has shown that victims have an interest in communicating with the offender. A VIS delivered by the victim is more likely to induce a defendant to apologize and accept responsibility.

Victims may also feel empowered by their ability to confer or withhold forgiveness, and victims' aggressive feelings are likely to be attenuated following genuine requests for forgiveness (see Petrucci, 2002). When victims and offenders know each other, victims sometimes prefer (or request, in jurisdictions that permit victim statements at sentencing) a lenient sentence. Also in crimes involving strangers, where victims are more likely to express punitive sentiments, providing an occasion for victim-defendant exchanges benefits both: it increases victims' familiarity with the offender and the offender's circumstances, and it enhances offenders' understanding of the consequences of their acts. Victims may become more understanding if they hear the offender's story, particularly if it is preceded or accompanied by the expression of remorse, which a moving VIS may elicit (see Roberts & Erez, 2004, for discussion).

The VIS may well have therapeutic potential for defendants as well as their victims— for instance, by providing offenders with a concrete and unmediated picture of the harm their actions have caused, and an opportunity for apology following the VIS presentation. The option to formally submit a VIS should be considered as an occasion for communication between the victim and his or her violator and should become a vital legislated right. Victims who feel the need to express their harm should be afforded the option to submit a VIS, even in circumstances that may render the VIS "irrelevant" for sentencing purposes, such as a negotiated plea or a mandatory sentence.[17]

CONCLUSION

Victim participatory rights are now recognized as an important component of criminal justice proceedings. Reports from practitioners indicate that few administrative problems,

serious defense challenges, longer trials, or harsher sentences result from victim participation. Similarly, there is no evidence that incarceration levels in countries that allow victim input have increased due to victims' participation in proceedings. However, because victim participation in sentencing decisions challenges traditions and established patterns within the criminal courts, these rights often amount to lip service or encounter resistance in their implementation. Legislative reforms typically lack remedies for noncompliance. Victims' participation at times depends on the luck of the draw, or whether a victim encounters criminal justice personnel who support victims' rights (see Douglas, Laster, & Inglis, 1994; Kury, Kaiser, & Teske, 1994). Although legislatures were probably motivated to adopt victims' reforms as a way of ensuring victim cooperation, ultimately the decision of whether to allow or require victim participation largely rests on subjective moral judgments (Erez, 1994). Clearly, victims' participation is viewed skeptically by many in the legal community (e.g., Hall, 1991; Hellerstein, 1989) and the social science community (e.g., Davis & Smith, 1994; Sanders et al., 2001) because of fears that if only some victims avail themselves of these rights, the treatment of defendants in the criminal justice system will become more disparate.

There is a need for further research on the effect of victims' reforms. Even if such research confirmed that victims' rights pose no great danger to the system or to its defendants and resulted in recommendations to put "teeth" in such statutes (presumably by creating cases of actions against those who fail to notify victims of their rights, or to implement their rights in practice), such recommendations would probably never be adopted. Creating rights with remedies in the event that rights are violated would rupture the fragile alliance of victims' advocates, legislators, and prosecutors. As a result, victims are likely to remain where they are, hoping to work with sympathetic criminal justice personnel who will inform them of their rights and help ensure that these rights are respected.

Research has demonstrated that the right to participate in proceedings, including the right to be heard at various points in the criminal justice process, is important to many crime victims. Most victims are interested in participating in the justice process, and they want an opportunity to tell, in their own words, the way that the crime has affected them. Court procedures rarely provide victims with an occasion to construct a coherent and meaningful narrative (Herman, 2003). The VIS represents a means to provide victims with a voice at sentencing and allows them to express the impact of the crime on their lives. In adversarial legal systems, the VIS is the only tool by which victims can articulate their suffering, identify their concerns, and communicate the way their lives have been affected by the crime.

As legal cultures are transformed, and victims are increasingly perceived as a legitimate party in proceedings (see Cassell 1999; Pizzi, 1999), forms of victim input such as the VIS can become a routine practice of injecting restorative justice elements into adversarial justice systems. Ultimately, it is the underlying value system and ideology, not data, that will determine whether victims are meaningfully integrated into proceedings. The road to incorporating a victim voice in adversarial proceedings has not been smooth (see U.S. Department of Justice, 1998). Attempts to integrate victims outside the adversarial justice system through restorative justice schemes have worked for some victims but they have not served those who wish to remain within the protective structure of adversarial systems.

Perceptions of victims as "barbarians at the gates"[18] or arguments about alleged violation of "defendants' rights" should no longer be used in unsympathetic, if not hostile, adversarial legal cultures to deny victims the right to be heard and to participate.[19] A careful reading of research findings requires the position that victims do not belong in adversarial proceedings be reassessed, as should the notion that restorative justice practices and adversarial principles cannot coexist when it comes to integrating victim voice in sentencing (see Erez, 2004).

REFERENCES

Ashworth, A. (1993, July). Victim impact statements and sentencing. *Criminal Law Review*, 498–509.

Ashworth, A. (2000). Victims' rights, defendants' rights and criminal procedure. In A. Crawford & J. Goodey (Eds.), *Integrating a victim perspective in criminal justice: International debates* (pp. 185–204). Aldershot: Dartmouth.

Ashworth, A. (2002). Restorative rights and restorative justice. *British Journal of Criminology, 42*, 578–595.

Australian Law Reform Commission. (1988). *Sentencing*. Report No. 94. Canberra: Attorney General's Publication Service.

Boers, K., & Sessar, K. (1991). Do people really want punishment? On the relationship between acceptance of restitution, needs for punishment and fear of crime. In K. Sessar & H.-J. Kerner (Eds.), *Developments in crime and crime control research: German studies on victims, offenders and the public*. New York: Springer-Verlag.

Braithwaite, J. (2002). Restorative justice and therapeutic jurisprudence. *Criminal Law Bulletin, 38*, 244–262.

Bureau of Justice Statistics. (1983). *Reports to the nation on crime and justice*. Washington, DC: Institute for Law and Social Research.

Cannavele, F. (1975). *Witness cooperation*. New York: Lexington.

Cassell, P. G. (1999). Barbarians at the gates? A reply to the critics of the Victims' Rights Amendment. *Utah Law Review, 2*, 479–544.

Cole, M. (2003). *Perceptions of the use of victim impact statements in Canada: A survey of Crown Counsel in Ontario*. Unpublished master's thesis, University of Ottawa, Ottawa.

Corns, C. (1988). Offender and victims. In D. Biles (Ed.), *Current Australian trends in corrections* (pp. 204–216). Sydney: Federation Press.

D'Avignon, J. (2001). *Victim impact statements: A judicial perspective*. Winnipeg: University of Manitoba.

Davis, R., Kunreuther, F., & Connick, E. (1984). Expanding the victim role in the criminal court dispositional process: The results of an experiment. *Journal of Criminal Law and Criminology*, 75, 491–505.

Davis, R., & Smith, B. (1994). Victim impact statements and victim satisfaction: An unfulfilled promise? *Journal of Criminal Justice*, 22, 1–12.

Department of Justice Canada. (1990). *Victim impact statements in Canada, 7: Summary of the findings*. Ottawa: Department of Justice Canada, Research and Development Directorate.

Dignan, J. (2005). *Understanding victims and restorative justice*. Maidenhead: Open University Press.

Douglas, R., Laster, K., & Inglis, N. (1994). Victim of efficiency: Criminal justice reform in Australia. *International Review of Victimology*, 3, 95–110.

Edwards, I. (2001). Victim participation in sentencing: The problems of incoherence. *Howard Journal of Criminal Justice*, 40, 30–54.

Eisenstein, J., & Jacob, H. (1977). *Felonious justice: An organizational analysis of criminal courts*. Lanham, MD: University Press of America.

Erez, E. (1989). The impact of victimology on criminal justice policy. *Criminal Justice Policy Review*, 3, 236–256.

Erez, E. (1990). Victim participation in sentencing: Rhetoric and reality. *Journal of Criminal Justice*, 18, 19–31.

Erez, E. (1994). Victim participation in sentencing: And the debate goes on . . . *International Review of Victimology*, 3, 17–32.

Erez, E. (1999, July). Who is afraid of the big bad victim: Victim impact statements as victim empowerment and enhancement of justice. *Criminal Law Review*, 545–556.

Erez, E. (2004). Victim voice, impact statements and sentencing: Integrating restorative justice and therapeutic jurisprudence principles in adversarial proceedings. *Criminal Law Bulletin*, 40, 483–500.

Erez, E., & Bienkowska, E. (1993). Victim participation in proceedings and satisfaction with justice in the Continental systems: The case of Poland. *Journal of Criminal Justice*, 21, 47–60.

Erez, E., & Roeger, L. (1995). Crime impact vs. victim impact: Evaluation of victim impact statements in South Australia. *Criminology Australia*, 6, 3–8.

Erez, E., Roeger, L., & Morgan, F. (1994). Office of Crime Statistics, South Australian Attorney General's Department, *Victim impact statements in South Australia: An evaluation*. Adelaide: Office of Crime Statistics, South Australian Attorney General's Department.

Erez, E., & Rogers, L. (1999). Victim impact statements and sentencing outcomes and processes. *British Journal of Criminology*, 39, 216–239.

Erez, E., & Tontodonato, P. (1990). The effect of victim participation in sentencing on sentence outcome. *Criminology*, 28, 451–474.

Erez, E., & Tontodonato, P. (1992). Victim participation in sentencing and satisfaction with justice. *Justice Quarterly*, 9, 393–415.

Fattah, E. (1986). *From crime policy to victim policy*. New York: Macmillan.

Gardner, J. (1990). *Victims and criminal justice*. Adelaide: Office of Crime Statistics, Department of the Attorney General.

Grabosky, P. (1987). Victims in the criminal justice system. In G. Zdenkowski, C. Ronalds, & M. Richardson (Eds.), *The criminal injustice system* (Vol. 2, pp. 143–157). Sydney: Pluto Press.

Hagan, J. (1982). Victims before the law: A study of victims' involvement in the criminal justice process. *Journal of Criminal Law and Criminology*, 73, 317–329.

Hall, D. (1991). Victim voices in criminal court: The need for restraint. *American Criminal Law Review*, 28, 233–266.

Hellerstein, D. (1989). Victim impact statement: Reform or reprisal? *American Criminal Law Review*, 27, 391–430.

Henderson, L. (1985). The wrongs of victims' rights. *Stanford Law Review*, 27, 391–430.

Henley, M., Davis, R., & Smith, B. (1994). The reactions of prosecutors and judges to victim impact statements. *International Review of Victimology*, 3, 83–93.

Herman, J. (2003). The mental health of crime victims: Impact of legal intervention. *Journal of Traumatic Stress*, 16, 159–166.

Herman, S., & Wasserman, C. (2001). A role for victims in offender re-entry. *Crime and Delinquency*, 47, 428–445.

Hillenbrand, S., & Smith, B. (1989). *Victim rights legislation: An assessment of its impact on criminal justice practitioners and victims.* Washington, DC: American Bar Association.

Hoyle, C., Cape, C., Morgan, R., & Sanders, A. (1998). *Evaluation of the "one stop shop" and victim statement pilot projects.* London: Home Office Research Development and Statistics Directorate.

Joutsen, M. (1994). Victim participation in proceedings and sentencing in Europe. *International Review of Victimology, 3,* 57–67.

Justice Committee on the Role of the Victim in Criminal Justice. (1998). *Victims in criminal justice: Report of the Justice Committee on the Role of the Victim in Criminal Justice.* London: Justice.

Kelly, D. (1984). Victims' perceptions of criminal justice. *Pepperdine Law Review, 11,* 15–22.

Kelly, D. (1987). Victims. *Wayne Law Review, 34,* 69–86.

Kidd, R., & Chayet, E. (1984). Why victims fail to report: The psychology of criminal victimization. *Journal of Social Issues, 40,* 34–50.

Kilpatrick, D., & Otto, R. (1987). Constitutionally guaranteed participation in criminal justice proceedings for victims: Potential effects of psychological functioning. *Wayne Law Review, 34,* 7–28.

Kury, H., Kaiser, M., & Teske, R. (1994). The position of the victim in criminal procedure: Results of a German study. *International Review of Victimology, 3,* 69–81.

Lurigio, A., & Resick, P. (1990). Healing the psychological wounds of criminal victimization: Predicting postcrime distress and recovery. In A. Lurigio, W. Skogan, & R. Davis (Eds.), *Victims of crime: Problems, policies and programs* (pp. 50–68). Newbury Park, CA: Sage Publications.

McLeod, M. (1986). Victim participation at sentencing. *Criminal Law Bulletin, 22,* 501–517.

McLeod, M. (1988). *The authorization and implementation of victim impact statements.* Washington, DC: National Institute of Justice.

Meredith, C., & Paquette, C. (2001). *Report on victim impact statement focus groups.* Ottawa: Department of Justice Canada.

Myers, B., & Arbuthnot, J. (1999). The effects of victim impact evidence on the verdicts and sentencing judgments of mock jurors. *Journal of Offender Rehabilitation, 29,* 95–112.

Orth, U. (2002). Secondary victimization of crime victims by criminal proceedings. *Social Justice Research, 15,* 313–326.

Orth, U. (2003). Punishment goals of crime victims. *Law and Human Behavior, 27,* 173–186.

Paciocco, D. (1999). *Getting away with murder: The Canadian criminal justice system.* Toronto: Irwin Law.

Parsonage, W., Bernat, F., & Helfgott, J. (1992). Victim impact testimony and Pennsylvania's parole decision-making process: A pilot study. *Criminal Justice Policing Review, 6,* 187–206.

Petrucci, C. (2002). Apology in criminal justice setting: Evidence for including apology as an additional component in the legal system. *Behavioral Science and the Law, 20,* 337–362.

Pizzi, W. (1999). Victims' rights: Rethinking our "adversarial system." *Utah Law Review, 2,* 349–367.

Prairie Research Associates. (2004). *Multi-site survey of victims of crime and criminal justice professionals across Canada.* Ottawa: Department of Justice Canada.

President's Task Force on Victims of Crime. (1982). *Final report.* Washington, DC: Government Printing Office.

Ranish, D., & Shichor, D. (1985). The victim's role in the penal process: Recent developments in California. *Federal Probation, 49,* 50–57.

Reeves, H., & Mulley, K. (2000). The new status of victims in the UK: Opportunities and threats. In A. Crawford & J. Goodey (Eds.), *Integrating a victim perspective in criminal justice: International* debates (pp. 125–145). Aldershot: Dartmouth.

Report of the Standing Committee on Justice and Human Rights. (1998). *Victims' right: A voice, not a veto.* Ottawa: Standing Committee on Justice and Human Rights.

Roberts, J. V. (2003). Victim impact statements and the sentencing process: Enhancing communication in the courtroom. *Criminal Law Quarterly, 47,* 365–396.

Roberts, J. V., & Edgar, A. (2006). *Judicial perceptions of victim input at sentencing: Findings from surveys in Canada.* Ottawa: Department of Justice Canada.

Roberts, J. V., & Erez, E. (2004). Communication in sentencing: Exploring the expressive and the impact model of victim impact statements.

International Review of Victimology, 10, 223–244.

Rubel, H. (1986). Victim participation in sentencing proceedings. *Criminal Law Quarterly, 28,* 226–250.

Sanders, A. (2002). Victim participation in criminal justice and social exclusion. In C. Hoyle & R. Young (Eds.), *New visions of crime victims* (pp. 171–122). Oxford: Hart.

Sanders, A., Hoyle, C., Morgan, R., & Cape, E. (2001, May). Victim impact statements: Can't work, won't work. *Criminal Law Review,* 447–458.

Shapland, J., Villemore, J., & Duff, P. (1985). *Victims in the criminal justice system.* Aldershot: Gower.

Sherman, L., & Strang, H. (2003). Repairing the harm: Victims and restorative justice. *Utah Law Review, 15–42.*

Stolle, D., Winick, B. J., & Wexler, D. B. (2003). *Practicing therapeutic jurisprudence: Law as a helping profession.* Durham, NC: Carolina Academic Press.

Sumner, C. J. (1987). Victim participation in the criminal justice system. *Australia and New Zealand Journal of Criminology, 20,* 195–217.

Talbert, P. (1988). The relevance of victim impact statements to the criminal sentencing decision. *UCLA Law Review, 36,* 199–232.

Tontodonato, P., & Erez, E. (1994). Crime, punishment and victim distress. *International Review of Victimology, 3,* 33–55.

U.S. Department of Justice. (1998). *New directions from the field: Victims' rights and services for the 21st century.* Washington, DC: U.S. Department of Justice.

U.S. Department of Justice. (2002). *Victim input into plea agreements.* Washington, DC: Office of Victims of Crime.

Verdun-Jones, S., & Tijerino, A. (2004). Four models of victim involvement during plea negotiations: Bridging the gap between legal reforms and current legal practice. *Canadian Journal of Criminology and Criminal Justice, 46,* 471–500.

Victorian Sentencing Committee. (1988). *Sentencing: Report of the committee.* Melbourne: Attorney General's Department.

Villmoare, E., & Neto, V. (1987). *Victim appearances at sentencing hearings under the California Victims' Bill of Rights: Executive summary.* Washington, DC: U.S. Department of Justice.

Walsh, A. (1986). Placebo justice: Victim recommendations and offender sentences in sexual assault cases. *Journal of Criminal Law and Criminology, 77,* 1126–1171.

Wemmers, J. (1996). *Victims in the criminal justice system.* Amsterdam: Kugler.

Wiebe, R. (1996). The mental health implications of crime victims' rights. In D. Wexler & B. Winick (Eds.), *Law in a therapeutic key: Developments in therapeutic jurisprudence.* Durham, NC: Carolina Academic Press.

Zedner, L. (2002). Victims. In M. Maguire, R. Morgan, & R. Reiner (Eds.), *The Oxford handbook of criminology* (3rd ed., pp. 419–456). Oxford: Oxford University Press.

Zeigenhagen, E. (1977). *Victims, crime, and social control.* New York: Praeger.

NOTES

1. It is important to note that in some cases—particularly rape—it may be to the advantage of the victim to be spared the need to testify, which carries the likelihood of cross-examination. Indeed, this is one of the justifications for imposing a less severe sentence on offenders who plead guilty.

2. The difference between VIS and VPS is spurious. In this chapter we use the term VIS as a generic term to denote the impact materials victims submit at or for sentencing.

3. Practical concerns include the adverse impact that victim input or allocution may have on court resources and scheduling in an already overburdened judicial system. These and other themes reappear in the recent criticisms of the reform, suggesting that the phrase "victim input into sentencing" is a euphemism for increasing sentence severity, constituting exclusionary criminal justice politics that act to blur the overlap between offenders and victims (see Sanders, 2002).

4. Of course, although sentencing guidelines reduce this effect, it has always been true that defendants may receive varying sentences depending on how sympathetic, articulate, or persuasive they may be.

5. See Ashworth (2002), Sanders, Hoyle, Morgan, and Cape (2001), and Edwards (2001) for discussion.

6. See, for example, Ashworth (2000) and Edwards (2001). The argument about the violation of defendant rights may have some face value; one instinctively assumes that victims' and offenders' interests are in opposition to each other. However, there is little evidence showing that violations of defendants' rights have occurred in the VIS context, violations that the court could not prevent or, if having occurred, could not correct, as it often does with other violations of rights.

7. For further discussion, see Erez (1994) and Roberts (2003).

8. Edwards (2001) describes in detail the multiple rationales used by politicians and members of legislative bodies in the United States, England and Wales, as well as South Australia to convince relevant constituents to pass VIS legislation. Edwards argues that these multiple rationales result in incoherence and at times contradictory justifications that may create problems in implementing the ensuing reforms.

9. It may be harder for laypersons to lay aside an emotional appeal for a particular sentence. One study using simulated jurors found that subjects who heard victim impact evidence "imposed" harsher sentences (Myers & Arbuthnot, 1999). This may be an argument in favor of sentencing by judges rather than juries, but that is a story for another day.

10. Prosecutors in these studies, however, expressed skepticism about judges' interest in the impact of the crime on the victims, and whether they actually considered the VIS when sentencing (Davis & Smith, 1994; Erez & Rogers, 1999).

11. We use the term *effect*, but most of these studies are correlational in nature. Victims who submit a statement at sentencing may differ from those who decide not to participate. Differences in satisfaction levels may reflect previctimization differences in attitudes as much as the effects of submitting an impact statement.

12. Victim satisfaction also tends to increase when victims are informed about the factors that judges consider in determining sentences and know that their views are one of these considerations. Simply put, studies show that the more victims understand the sentencing process, the more satisfied they are with it (Department of Justice Canada, 1990; Erez et al., 1994; Gardner, 1990; Hagan, 1982).

13. Some victims' rights reflect a punitive, nonrestorative perspective. There is nothing restorative, for example, about the desire expressed by relatives of murder victims to witness the execution of the offender. Similarly, some restorative justice initiatives that result in a relatively mild outcome for the offender are vigorously opposed by victim rights' advocates.

14. See Herman and Wasserman (2001). Some critics have referred to the idea that victims play a role in offenders' reentry as "victims in the service of offenders" (see Ashworth, 2000).

15. Continental legal systems, such as the one used in Germany, which allow victims a role in the prosecution as adhesive prosecutor, restrict the application of this law to victims of serious crime.

16. See Stolle, Winick, and Wexler (2003). The commonality between restorative justice and therapeutic jurisprudence is explored in Braithwaite (2002).

17. See, for instance, Cole (2003) and Roberts and Edgar (2006).

18. See Cassell (1999).

19. Cassell (1999) concludes that the curriculum of law schools in the United States propagates this legal culture by the absence of any study materials related to victims' rights and interests.

18

Legal Rights for Crime Victims in the Criminal Justice System

SUSAN HOWLEY

CAROL DORRIS

HISTORICAL DEVELOPMENT

The adoption of legal rights for crime victims has been a fairly recent development in the United States criminal justice system. Crime victims' rights were not included in our nation's constitution or in the early criminal codes. This apparent omission can be explained by looking at our early justice system.

During colonial times, crime victims were integral to the criminal justice process. The victim could pay the sheriff to pursue and arrest the defendant, and then the victim hired the prosecutor. There was no need to provide separate rights for victims, because they were so closely involved in the pursuit of justice. In contrast, our founding fathers had great interest in the rights of criminal defendants, who had been powerless under the English system of jurisprudence.

Such a system of private prosecution was flawed, however, confining "justice" largely to those who could afford it. The criminal justice system therefore evolved into a system of public prosecution. The prosecutor represented the state. Crime victims, however, became increasingly marginalized, until they became merely witnesses.[1]

During the 1960s, a wave of social movements began to reconsider the status of various subgroups, such as racial minorities and women. The place of victims in a process directly tied to their interests also began to be reconsidered. The 1960s also saw the creation of the first crime victim compensation programs—state programs to reimburse victims for some of their out-of-pocket expenses relating to the crime.

Shortly thereafter, people began thinking about the rights of crime victims. The first victim impact statement was created in 1976, by Fresno County, California, probation officer James Rowland. The first statutory "bill of rights" for victims was adopted in Wisconsin in 1980, and the first victims' rights amendment to a state constitution was adopted in 1982 in California, along with significant statutory rights.

In 1982, President Ronald Reagan established a Presidential Task Force on Victims of Crime. That task force held a series of field hearings across the country, taking testimony from crime victims and criminal justice officials about the needs and interests of victims of crime. The task force released its *Final Report* in December of that year.[2] It included a series of recommendations to provide statutory and constitutional protection of the rights of crime victims. That report provided the impetus for a wave of reforms across the country, formalizing and expanding the rights of crime victims.

Today, every state and the federal government has a comprehensive set of statutory rights for victims, and 32 states have also amended their state constitutions to protect victims' rights. Victims' rights continue to expand in breadth and scope.[3] As the criminal justice system becomes more attuned to the interests of crime victims, victims' rights to be informed and to participate throughout the process are being further defined. These rights are generally viewed by criminal justice officials today as improving the quality of justice.[4]

WHO IS A VICTIM?

While every state provides crime victims' rights, they differ in the applicability of those rights, with varying definitions of "victim" and "crime." Every system provides rights for victims of violent felonies; the majority also extend rights to victims of violent misdemeanors; a little more than half also provide rights to victims of nonviolent felonies. Only about 40% provide any rights to victims of any crime.

In some states, all victims are entitled to certain rights, such as the right to be notified of their legal rights, while other rights, such as the right to confer with the prosecutor before a plea agreement is entered, are reserved for victims of violent felonies. In general, homicide survivors—or one designated survivor per family—have the same rights as other crime victims. The parent or guardian of a minor or incapacitated victim is generally afforded the rights of the victim, unless that person is accused of the offense.

In some states, people who have crimes committed against them while they are incarcerated have no rights as crime victims. In other states, such victims may have certain rights, such as the right to be informed or the right to submit a written impact statement, but not have other rights, such as the right to attend criminal justice proceedings relating to the case.

THE RIGHT TO NOTICE

A victim's right to notice takes one of two forms: the right to general information of interest to victims of crime and the right to be kept informed throughout the criminal justice process.

The right to notice is often called the fundamental victims' right. Unless a victim is informed of his or her legal rights, the victim cannot hope to exercise those rights. Unless a victim is notified of events and proceedings, the victim cannot exercise rights related to those events and proceedings. Information is also important to crime victims as they recover from crime. Their sense of safety and security is enhanced when they are kept informed of the status of the offender.[5] Further, as victims process the events of the crime, they have a need to know how the case is proceeding.

Victims often have a right to general information, such as information about the crime victim compensation program, referrals to local services such as rape crisis or domestic violence shelters, information about the steps involved in a criminal prosecution, contact information for an individual in the criminal justice system who can answer questions about the case, and information about their rights as crime victims.

Victims also have the right to case-specific information relating to criminal justice proceedings and the status of the offender. There are dozens of events and proceedings in the ordinary criminal justice process for which notice may be legally required by statute. These range from major proceedings, such as the trial, sentencing hearing, or parole board hearing, to such court proceedings as arraignment, grand jury proceedings, or probation revocation hearings. Some states give victims a right to notice of "all critical stages"[6] or "important criminal justice hearings."[7] Most, but not all, states also give victims the right to be informed when a proceeding is cancelled or rescheduled, saving them a trip to the courthouse with all the attendant stress and inconvenience.

Victims generally have a right to be notified of an offender's escape or postconviction release. Many states also give victims a right to be notified of any pretrial release, the transfer of a convicted defendant to a different facility, the death of an inmate while in custody, or other such matters.

The advent of automated notification systems has increased states' willingness to extend the right of notification to more victims. Such systems allow registered victims to call in at any time and, using a personal identification number (PIN), find the status of the offender. They also allow for victims to be automatically called in the event of a defendant's release, escape, or other event. As of 2005, 29 states either had statewide automated notification systems or used such systems for notice by their departments of corrections. Many local jurisdictions also use such systems to notify victims of criminal justice proceedings or releases from the local jail.

Victims who wish to be notified are generally required by law to request such information. Typically, victims are given a notification request form or card on which they indicate the proceedings and events of which they wish to be informed and provide an address and telephone number. Victims are also typically required to keep their contact information up-to-date with each agency from whom they wish to receive notice.

THE RIGHT TO BE PRESENT

Another basic right of crime victims is the right to attend criminal justice proceedings, such as pretrial hearings, the trial, sentencing, and parole hearings. This right is important to crime victims and their families who want to see justice at work. They may want to hear the information presented and the arguments made and to view for themselves the reactions of the judge, the jury, and the defendant.

Thirty-nine states give crime victims a right to attend criminal justice proceedings, including the trial. However, the majority of those states impose limitations on the right. These restrictions stem from concern that a victim's right to attend proceedings may conflict with the rights of the accused. Thus victims are often given a right to be present only "to the extent that it does not interfere with the constitutional or statutory rights of the accused"[8] or "consistent with the rules of evidence."[9]

The "rule on witnesses," generally Rule 615 of a state's rules of evidence, was crafted to limit the possibility that a witness will be influenced by hearing the testimony of other witnesses or the arguments of counsel. Thus, to ensure a fair trial, witnesses are excluded—sequestered—from the criminal trial except during their testimony. The rule does not apply to a defendant, who is exempted as a party to the case. The rule is often applied automatically—that is, witnesses are automatically excluded upon the request of either the prosecutor or defendant, without regard to the circumstances of the cases and whether such exclusion is truly necessary to protect the interests of the defendant.[10]

About a half-dozen states address the issue of the rule on witnesses by giving crime victims a right to be present only *after* they have testified.[11] One of those states—Washington—also provides that victims have a right to be scheduled to testify as early as possible to maximize their attendance at the trial.[12]

Several states have exempted crime victims from such routine sequestration under the rule on witnesses. However, many of these still permit a victim to be excluded if "necessary to protect the defendant's right to a fair trial"[13] or if the victim's right to be present would be "inconsistent with the constitutional and statutory rights of the accused,"[14] or similar language. Other states encourage courts to limit the application of sequestration rules. For example, Wisconsin's law states that an exclusion of the victim to preserve the defendant's right to a fair trial must be based on something more than the fact that the victim would be present during the testimony of other witnesses.[15] Florida's law provides that the court must determine the victim's presence to be prejudicial; the victim cannot be excluded merely because he or she is subpoenaed to testify.[16]

Some courts have upheld the victim's right to be present, even where there was no explicit exemption from the rule on witnesses. For instance, Wyoming's law gives victims a right to remain in the courtroom unless the court rules that good cause requires exclusion. In one case, the Wyoming Supreme Court found that the trial court, after hearing the arguments of counsel, had properly balanced the defendant's constitutional rights against the victim's statutory rights and did not err in permitting the victim to remain in the courtroom during the testimony of another victim. During trial arguments about whether the victim should be allowed to remain in the courtroom, the prosecution had noted that the victim had

made a lengthy pretrial statement, which had been provided to the defense.[17]

In addition to excluding a victim on the grounds that the victim will be called as a witness, defense counsel may argue that the mere presence of the victim in the courtroom can prejudice the jury and interfere with the defendant's right to a fair trial. However, courts have rejected this argument: "There is nothing inherently prejudicial in the presence of the victim. The fact that a defendant may not want the reminder of the crime to be a real presence, we do not see of itself, as an interference with the defendant's right to a fair trial."[18]

The ability of crime victims to remain present during criminal justice proceedings may be compromised simply by the stress of the event. To overcome this barrier, many of the statutes providing victims a right to attend proceedings include a right to have a support person present.[19]

THE RIGHT TO BE HEARD

Another principle right of crime victims is the right to be heard at various stages of the criminal justice process. The right basically takes two forms:

1. The right to consult with key criminal justice officials before certain decisions are made, such as the pretrial diversion of the defendant or a plea agreement

2. The right to address or submit a written statement to the court or other authority at various proceedings, including release proceedings or sentencing

Granting victims a right to be heard at points in the criminal process that impact their interests benefits both the victim and the criminal justice process. For the victim, an opportunity to be heard represents an acknowledgment that the victim was harmed by the crime and has an interest in the case. The right to be heard also provides victims an opportunity to make known any safety concerns or need for restitution, as well as the impact of the offense on their lives. Victim input also aids the criminal justice process, as it provides a means for decision makers to receive information about the dangerousness of the defendant, the concerns of the victim, and the extent of the harm caused by the crime.

The right of crime victims to be heard is not a right to control strategies or decisions made in the course of the criminal justice process; rather, it is the right to ensure that the victims' concerns are voiced at appropriate points in the process.

The Right to Consult With Officials Before Key Decisions Are Made

Many states require prosecutors to obtain the views of victims before entering a plea agreement, dismissing a case, or taking similar dispositive action. The California legislature provided an excellent summation of the significance of crime victim consultation when it amended its Victims' Bill of Rights to provide victims the right to advance notification of a plea agreement. The legislature included the following findings in the bill:

(a) Victims of crime and their families are not formally notified when criminal prosecutions are resolved before trial through "plea bargains."

(b) Victims of crime and their families have a right to know if a court intends to dispose of a prosecution through the method of plea bargaining.

(c) The lack of notification to victims and their families adds to a perception that they lack representation and participation in the criminal justice system.

(d) The right of victims of crime to notification can be compatible with the continuing vital need to protect a defendant's rights to due process.

(e) Nearly 90 percent of all felony cases in California are disposed of before trial through plea bargains.

(f) Therefore, it is the intent of the Legislature to require a district attorney's office to notify a victim of a violent felony . . . or in the event of a homicide, the victim's next of kin, of a pending pretrial disposition before a change of plea is entered before a judge. The district attorney's office shall also notify the victim of any felony of a pretrial disposition upon the victim's request. If it is not possible to notify the victim of the pretrial disposition before the change of plea is entered, the district attorney's office or the county probation department shall notify the victim as soon as possible.[20]

A majority of states provide victims with some level of consultation about a negotiated plea agreement. However, the extent of victim participation ranges from a right to be informed in advance, to a right to have the prosecutor obtain the views of the victim, to a right to confer, to a right to be consulted. Approximately half the states require the prosecutor to obtain the victim's views on a proposed plea agreement.

Many of these states provide the same right to consultation before certain other prosecutorial decisions are made, such as dismissing charges, declining to prosecute any charges, or seeking pretrial diversion.[21] In practice, such consultation takes place through mail and telephone contacts more often than in person.[22]

The Right to Address or Submit a Statement to the Court or Other Decision-Making Body

Crime victims may be given the right to address the court or submit a written statement at a number of stages. The first such stage is the pretrial release or bail hearing. About 10 states give victims the right to submit information at bail hearings, or at subsequent hearings to modify bail or pretrial release. Input from the victim at this stage can be vital in determining appropriate conditions to be imposed on such a release, particularly where the defendant poses a danger to the victim. However, extension of the victims' right to be heard at such an early stage has been limited by practical barriers. In some jurisdictions, defendants may be held only a few hours between arrest and the pretrial release hearing, making it very difficult to guarantee victims an opportunity to be notified and heard at this proceeding. A few states, such as Illinois, have attempted to get around this barrier by providing for written input from the victim or a representation by the prosecutor of the victim's concerns and the impact of the offense.[23]

A third of the states permit the victim to be heard, either orally or in writing, at plea entry proceedings.[24] In Missouri, for example, "prior to the acceptance of a plea bargain by the court, . . . the court shall allow the victim of such offense to submit a written statement or appear before the court personally or by counsel for the purpose of making a statement."[25] In some states, the court does not have authority to accept a plea agreement unless the prosecutor certifies that the victim has been informed of the plea agreement and the right to make a statement in court.[26]

At the sentencing stage, every state provides crime victims the right to be heard—in person or in writing—regarding the physical, psychological, and financial effects of the crime. Many of these states also permit victims to state their views on the appropriate sentence or their views about the defendant. In general, victim impact statements may be given by the victim, homicide survivors, or the parent or guardian of a minor victim. Many states also authorize statements by a representative or family member of a victim who is physically incapacitated; however, some limit such representatives' statements to cases where the incapacitation was the direct result of the crime. Several states also allow a judge to limit the number of victims who may make oral statements in a given case.

Victim impact evidence, at least at the sentencing level, can often be subjected to cross-examination and rebuttal. Some states have attempted to limit the potential for harassment by restricting any cross-examination. For example, New York requires the defendant to present written questions to the court, which the court may, if it chooses, put to the victim.[27] The defendant retains the right to present any evidence in rebuttal.

The use of victim impact statements has not been linked generally to increased sentences.[28] However, the right to make such a statement is considered "very important" by victims themselves.[29]

States also generally provide for victim input in the parole release decision. Nearly all states allow victims to present a written or oral statement to the parole board for consideration at the parole hearing. A few states, such as California, specifically authorize the use of audio or videotaped statements at the parole hearing. Fewer states extend the right to be heard to pardon or clemency proceedings.

THE RIGHT TO PROTECTION

Policymakers and criminal justice officials increasingly recognize the importance of crime victim safety. Prosecutors routinely cite witness intimidation as a barrier in their ability to secure convictions. Domestic violence advocates know that many victims believe they are safer returning to an abuser than trying to escape.

Approximately half the states give victims the right to be reasonably protected from the offender during the criminal justice process. Many of these states also require that victims be given information about the protection available to them or measures to take in the event of intimidation by the defendant. A majority of states provide at least one of these rights.

States are increasingly addressing victim safety at the pretrial release stage. Approximately one third of states allow a court to enter no contact orders as a condition of pretrial release when there is a danger of victim or witness intimidation. Colorado has gone farther. Under that state's law, there is a mandatory protection order issued against any person charged with a violation of the state's criminal code, which remains in effect from arraignment until final disposition. Such orders restrain the defendant from "harassing, molesting, intimidating, retaliating against, or tampering with any witness to or victim of the acts charged."[30] Similarly, Maryland law requires the court at the pretrial release stage to "consider including, as a condition of pretrial release for a defendant, reasonable protections for the safety of the alleged victim" and states that "if a victim has requested reasonable protections for safety, the court . . . shall consider including, as a condition of pretrial release, provisions regarding no contact with the alleged victim or the alleged victim's premises or place of employment."[31]

Nearly 40 states give victims the right to a separate and secure waiting area at court. Without such a designated space, victims have had to wait in close proximity to defense witnesses, creating an atmosphere that could be at a minimum uncomfortable and at worst threatening and intimidating. Many of these laws include a significant caveat, such as "subject to available resources," that keep them from being fully implemented.

THE RIGHT TO SPEEDY TRIAL

The criminal justice process is not always timely. An individual case can drag on for years, as the parties seek repeated delays and continuances. Meanwhile, the victim's life—and recovery—are put on hold.

To address this issue, approximately half the states give crime victims a right to a speedy disposition or speedy trial. In practice, this generally requires the court to consider the interests of the victim in ruling on a motion for continuance. For example, Utah's law states the following:

(1) In determining a date for any criminal trial or other important criminal or juvenile justice hearing, the court shall consider the interests of the victim of a crime to a speedy resolution of the charges under the same standards that govern a defendant's or minor's right to a speedy trial. . . .

(3) (a) In ruling on any motion by a defendant or minor to continue a previously established trial or other important criminal or juvenile justice hearing, the court shall inquire into the circumstances requiring the delay and consider the interests of the victim of a crime to a speedy disposition of the case.

(b) If a continuance is granted, the court shall enter in the record the specific reason for the continuance and the procedures that have been taken to avoid further delays.[32]

In many states, the law provides for accelerated disposition for cases involving child victims, elderly victims, or victims who are ill or disabled. For instance, Illinois law provides that

in prosecutions for violations of [listed kidnapping and sexual offenses] involving a victim or witness who is a minor under 18 years of age, the court shall, in ruling on any motion or other request for a delay or continuance of proceedings, consider and give weight to the adverse impact the delay or continuance may have on the well-being of a child or witness

and that "the court shall consider the age of the victim and the condition of the victim's health when ruling on a motion for a continuance."[33]

THE RIGHT TO RESTITUTION

"Restitution" is the act of restoring someone to a position they would have been in without the wrongdoing.[34] In the context of criminal cases, it generally refers to the defendant, acting under court order, paying back those who were harmed by the criminal acts. Courts may order a defendant to pay a crime victim for costs relating to physical injury, mental health counseling, lost wages, property lost or damaged, or other related costs. Courts may also order the defendant to reimburse others who had paid all or part of a victim's expenses, such as an insurance company or the state crime victim compensation program.

The payment of restitution is of great importance to victims of crime. Restitution for their financial harm can be a key factor in helping them rebuild their lives. It is also important as a tangible demonstration that the state, and the offender, recognize the harm suffered by the victim, and that amends will be made.

Restitution is also important to offenders. Courts have recognized that restitution is significant and rehabilitative because it "forces the defendant to confront, in concrete terms, the harm his or her actions have caused."[35] A recent study examining the connection between restitution and recidivism found that individuals who paid a higher percentage of their ordered restitution were less likely to commit a new crime.[36] Significantly, the payment of criminal fines did not have this effect, indicating that it is the act of reparation to the victim that is important.[37]

All states allow courts to order restitution to crime victims. In more than one third of those states, courts are required to order restitution, unless there are extraordinary or compelling circumstances why it should not be ordered. Of the 32 states with victims' rights amendments to their constitutions, 18 include a right to restitution from the offender. Many of the states that do not require courts to order restitution do require courts to state their reasons on the record if they fail to order restitution or order restitution for only part of the victim's financial losses.

More and more, the defendant's ability to pay is not taken into account in the court's decision whether to order restitution or in its determination of the amount ordered. Rather, the defendant's assets, earning capacity, and other financial obligations are considered when a payment schedule is set.

State law provides many avenues for enforcing restitution orders. Approaches that may be allowed in a particular state include automatically assigning a portion of a prisoner's wages to an unpaid restitution order, taking a percentage of an inmate's account to satisfy an order, seizing lottery winnings, capturing a state tax refund, reapplying the money originally posted as bail, and similar approaches. Some states allow for probation to be extended if a defendant has intentionally failed to pay restitution. In addition, most states provide that restitution orders will be converted to civil judgments, either immediately upon entry of the order or at the time the defendant's parole or probation period ends. The victim can then use such methods as garnishment of wages or attachment of assets to enforce the order.

Vermont has taken much of the burden of recovering restitution off crime victims. That state created a restitution fund, which is used to pay up to $10,000 of a victim's restitution order. The state then has the responsibility of collecting the restitution from the defendant.[38]

THE RIGHT TO PRIVACY/CONFIDENTIALITY

Privacy is a major issue for many crime victims. They may fear harassment or retaliation by the defendant or unwanted media attention, or they may not want their friends or family to know the details of the case.

Statutory protections of a victim's right to privacy take many forms. A number of states protect victims from having to testify about their home address or place of employment in open court. Many of these states limit this right to cases where the court finds that the victim has a "reasonable apprehension" of acts or threats of physical violence.[39] Other states provide a general protection but permit the court to waive that protection where the information is relevant evidence.[40]

Several states limit disclosure of victim identifying information in criminal justice records, including law enforcement reports or court files. For example, Alaska withholds documents relating to a crime from public inspection unless the victim's address and phone number have been deleted.[41] Alabama's law provides that confidential information in court records is not considered to be of public record.[42]

Many states provide that documents relating to a victim's claim for crime victim compensation,[43] or request for notice,[44] are to be kept confidential.

Along with general confidentiality provisions, states often have special provisions for certain classes of crime victims. These may apply to child victims,[45] elderly or vulnerable adult victims,[46] domestic violence victims,[47] or sexual assault victims.[48] In addition to these, more than 17 states have created address confidentiality programs for victims of domestic violence, dating violence, stalking, and sexual assault. These programs provide such victims an alternate official address; mail is then forwarded to a confidential address provided by the victim.[49]

THE RIGHT TO EMPLOYMENT PROTECTION

Crime victims' rights to participate in the criminal justice process are meaningless for victims who must risk their jobs to exercise them. As a result, states are passing laws to protect victims' employment status during the time they exercise their legal rights.

A majority of states have adopted laws protecting the employment of victims who participate in court-related activities. More than 30 states prohibit employers from discharging or penalizing an employee who must miss work as a consequence of responding to a subpoena. Some states provide employment protection when the victim attends hearings or consults with the prosecutor prior to the trial. A few states provide more expansive protection. For example, Arkansas and Delaware guarantee a victim's employment when the victim misses work to attend any criminal justice proceeding if such attendance is reasonably necessary to protect the victim's interests.[50] Pennsylvania guarantees a victim's employment if the victim attends court proceedings related to the offense, with no requirement that the victim show that his or her attendance is necessary to protect his or her interests or exercise his or her legal rights.[51]

A few states are extending employment protection to victims who miss work due to medical appointments, counseling sessions, or other activities related to the effects of the crime. These are generally limited to victims of domestic violence and, occasionally, sexual assault or stalking. In Maine, for example, an employer must grant reasonable and necessary leave for a victim of violence to attend court proceedings, receive medical treatment, or obtain necessary services to remedy a crisis caused by domestic violence, sexual assault, or stalking.[52] The law provides exceptions if the employee's absence would cause the employer undue hardship or if the employee does not communicate to the employer the request for leave in a reasonable amount of time under the circumstances.

Unlike most crime victims' rights, the violation of a victims' right to employment protection carries penalties. Criminal penalties against employers who violate employment protection laws, however, are minimal. Most states that provide criminal sanctions classify the violation as criminal contempt or a low-level misdemeanor, punishable by small fines or terms of imprisonment.[53] In addition to criminal penalties, about a third of the states that offer employment protection provide civil remedies to employees terminated or penalized in violation of employment protection laws. Employees typically have the option to sue for back wages and reinstatement. A few states allow victims to recover punitive damages or attorneys fees.[54]

VICTIMS' RIGHTS IN JUVENILE PROCEEDINGS

Crime victims have had far fewer rights in the juvenile justice system than they have in the criminal justice system, due largely to the traditionally closed and confidential nature of a system involving the disposition of minors. However, as the concept of crime victims' rights has become more thoroughly integrated into the criminal justice system, rights are being extended to the juvenile justice system— particularly in cases where the juvenile offense is equivalent to a felony. More than half of the states have a comprehensive set of rights for victims of serious juvenile offenses. Some of these states, such as Alabama, include victims of certain juvenile offenders in their general victims' bill of rights.[55] Others, such as Arizona and Michigan, set out a separate bill of rights for victims of serious juvenile offenders.[56]

For lesser offenses, crime victims' rights have not been as widely adopted. Crime victims rarely have the right to be kept informed throughout the juvenile justice process. They may have the right to file a written impact statement, but rarely have the right to make an oral statement at the disposition hearing of a juvenile. Those states that do provide victims' rights in less serious juvenile cases take the form of permissive, rather than mandatory, provisions. For example, Nevada, gives a judge discretion to allow a crime victim to attend a juvenile proceeding, but does not give victims a "right" to be present.[57]

Most states do allow a court to order a juvenile to pay restitution as part of the disposition. However, this is generally not a "right" of the victim, but within the discretion of the court. There is usually a cap on the amount of restitution that can be ordered.

VICTIMS' RIGHTS WHEN THE DEFENDANT IS MENTALLY ILL

Victims of offenders with mental illness who are transferred to the mental health system have fewer rights than the general crime victim population. This can occur when an offender is found incompetent to stand trial, not guilty by reason of insanity, or guilty but mentally ill. In the mental health setting, such offenders are perceived as patients rather than perpetrators, and consequently, their victims have been overlooked.

The interests of the victims, however, remain the same. Many want to be notified when offenders with mental illness are released or escape from confinement. They often want an opportunity to participate in proceedings that relate to the case. They may have suffered financial losses due to the crime.

A few states are beginning to mandate rights for victims of offenders with mental illness, incorporating provisions for notification, participation, and protection into their laws. Approximately half of the states have adopted provisions to notify victims when an offender with mental illness is released from a treatment facility. A few states have incorporated victim impact information provisions into their commitment or sentencing processes. Some states permit a victim to have input when changes in the offender's status are considered, or when the offender's mental health status is reviewed to determine whether he or she can be released. In general, victims cannot be awarded restitution from offenders with mental illness; because of their disability, such offenders are excused from any liability.

ENFORCING VICTIMS' RIGHTS

While every state provides legal rights to crime victims, few provide any recourse in the event those rights are violated. On the contrary, nearly every state provides that violation of a victim's rights does not create a cause of action for damages; many provide that a violation creates no cause of action whatsoever.

Several states have created a designated office or agency to receive, investigate, and attempt to resolve crime victim complaints. Such an office may take the form of an ombudsman, as in South Carolina; a committee, as in Colorado; or a state advocate, as in Connecticut. Experience in those states has shown that the majority of calls from crime victims are resolved by providing information or referrals. However, many go on to the formal complaint and investigation stages.

The ability to impose consequences on offending agencies or officials following a finding of a violation of rights varies between states but in general is very limited. Ombudsman-type offices are limited to investigating complaints and issuing reports. Colorado's Victims' Rights Subcommittee, after investigating and attempting to resolve any complaints regarding the provision of rights, may refer certain violations to the governor, who must ask the attorney general to bring an injunctive action.[58] In Wisconsin, the Victims' Rights Board is authorized to issue reprimands to offending officials, seek injunctive relief in the court, or bring civil actions to assess a civil forfeiture of up to $1,000.[59]

While it is important for victims to have an agency or official with whom they may register a complaint, many violations of victims' rights require immediate action. Therefore a number of states give crime victims limited legal standing to enforce their rights.[60] Arizona, Florida, Indiana, and Texas all give crime victims legal standing to assert their rights. In Alabama, Arizona, Florida, Mississippi, and Texas, the prosecutor also has standing to assert rights on the victim's behalf. Alaska and Connecticut give the state victim advocate the ability to advocate for the crime victim in the criminal case.

A few other states provide certain other limited remedies. Crime victims in Maryland are empowered by statute to file an application for leave to appeal to the state's court of special appeals any final order denying their basic rights.[61] A few states, including Louisiana and North Carolina, provide that victims may seek a writ of mandamus to enforce their rights.[62] In Utah, victims may bring an action for declaratory relief, petition for a writ of mandamus, or petition to file an amicus brief in a case affecting their rights.[63]

VICTIMS' RIGHTS AMENDMENTS

While all states provide legal rights for victims as part of their statutory codes, 32 states also guarantee rights for victims as part of their state constitutions.

The effort to obtain constitutional protection for crime victims' rights began in the early 1980s. In 1982, voters in California approved the first state crime victims' rights constitutional amendment. Called the Victims' Bill of Rights, it gave crime victims a right to restitution from offenders and contained other provisions related to public safety issues.[64]

That same year saw the release of the *Final Report of the President's Task Force on Victims of Crime*.[65] The report recommended that the Sixth Amendment of the U.S. Constitution, which protects the rights of criminal defendants to due process, be augmented to include the rights of crime victims. The proposed addition would read: "Likewise, the victim, in every criminal prosecution shall have the right to be present and to be heard at all critical stages of all judicial proceedings."[66]

Even though the task force made a number of recommendations for statutory protection of crime victims' rights, it believed constitutional protection of those rights was necessary. "The fundamental rights of innocent citizens cannot adequately be preserved by any less decisive action."[67]

Victim advocates have sought constitution protection for crime victims' rights for three reasons: permanence, strength, and enforceability. Constitutional protection provides a degree of permanence simply because the process to amend a state's constitution is arduous. Typically, a constitutional amendment must be passed by two thirds of the state legislature in two legislative sessions. The amendment is then put before the voters for their approval.

Constitutional protection increases the strength of a victims' rights provision. Because constitutional provisions take precedence over conflicting statutory provisions, providing constitutional protection for victims' rights makes them stronger. It appears that the process of enshrining crime victims' rights in state constitutions has, in fact, strengthened those rights. In considering victims' rights amendments, courts have observed that such amendments are strong expressions of public will. For example, the New Jersey Supreme Court pointed to the voters' expression of support for the victims' rights amendment in upholding one of the statutory rights that implemented it. "To hold the victim impact statute unconstitutional would require us to ignore the Victim's Rights Amendment and the will of the electorate that overwhelmingly approved the constitutional amendment. Over 1,200,000 citizens voted for the Victim's Rights Amendment while only 223,248 people voted against it."[68]

Constitutional protection for victims' rights also gives them an implied enforceability. Since the U.S. Supreme Court's ruling in 1803 in the case of *Marbury v. Madison,* it has been understood that "where a specific duty is assigned by law, and individual rights depend upon the performance of that duty, it seems equally clear, that the individual who considers himself injured, has a right to resort to the laws of his country for a remedy."[69]

Courts have not been uniform on the enforceability of victims' rights. A New Jersey court held that a state victims' rights amendment gave victims implied legal standing to oppose a petition by the media to open a juvenile proceeding regarding a sexual offense. "The judiciary . . . has an obligation to give effect to the voice of the sovereign voters expressed in the constitutional amendment process. Implicit in a determination that the amendment is self executing is the recognition that victims have standing to pursue their new constitutional rights."[70] However, South Carolina's Court of Appeals reached the opposite conclusion, stating that

> nothing in our Constitution or statutes provides the "victim" standing to appeal the trial court's order. Additionally, the rights granted by the South Carolina Constitution and statutes are enforceable by a writ of mandamus, rather than direct participation at the trial level.[71]

As of 2005, the states that have protected the rights of crime victims in their constitutions are Alabama, Alaska, Arizona, California, Colorado, Connecticut, Florida, Idaho, Illinois, Indiana, Kansas, Louisiana, Maryland, Michigan, Mississippi, Missouri, Nebraska, Nevada, New Jersey, New Mexico, North Carolina, Ohio, Oklahoma, Oregon, Rhode Island, South Carolina, Tennessee, Texas, Utah, Virginia, Washington, and Wisconsin. State victims' rights amendments have received strong approval from the voters as part of the ratification process, with an average voter approval rating of 78%.

Two basic forms of victims' rights amendments have emerged: a short, general statement of rights and a longer detailed list of victims' rights. Florida's assessment is an example of the short version:

> Victims of crime or their lawful representatives, including the next of kin of homicide victims, are entitled to the right to be informed, to be present, and to be heard when relevant, at all crucial stages of criminal

proceedings, to the extent that these rights do not interfere with the constitutional rights of the accused.[72]

Many other states, such as Arizona, Michigan, and Missouri, list a number of specific victims' rights within their amendments.[73] Most amendments state that the legislature has the power to define the terms and implement the rights. For instance, victims in Alaska and Illinois are guaranteed several listed constitutional rights "as provided by law."[74] Thus the legislature can limit the rights to certain stages or proceedings and can impose certain burdens on the victim, such as requiring the victim to file a request for notification before the right is awarded.

CRIME VICTIMS' RIGHTS: IMPLEMENTATION PROBLEMS AND RESEARCH PRIORITIES

Despite more than 25 years of progress creating crime victims' rights in our nation's laws, the reality for victims remains frustrating. Victims continue to report suffering through a system that seems to ignore their rights while bending over backward to honor the rights of the defendant. Victims report an inability to get information about cases, suffering through repeated case continuances, being denied an opportunity to be heard at sentencing, failing to receive an order of restitution, being unable to collect restitution, and so on.

The failure of crime victims to receive required notices has been documented in many studies. For instance, a recent study of law enforcement officers in Texas, who are required by law to notify crime victims of the victim compensation program, revealed that only 25% regularly informed victims of crime victim compensation.[75]

Similarly, when Florida recently audited the provision of victims' rights in that state, it found that victims were not always receiving the mandated notifications and services and that the agencies were not consistently documenting their own actions in providing notice and services. In particular, the audit found that criminal justice agencies were not consistently obtaining or documenting attempts to obtain complete victim notification cards from crime victims. In fact, two law enforcement agencies did not attempt to obtain completed cards as a matter of policy, and three agencies only prepared cards for cases involving domestic violence. In a sample of crime victims, 25% did not receive victims' rights information from first responders. In another 20%, there was no documentation regarding whether such information was provided.[76]

A survey of crime victims in Oregon also found that many were denied their legal rights. Approximately 30% reported that they were not afforded their right to be notified of pretrial and sentencing hearings and, if present, to be heard at those hearings or to be consulted about plea negotiations. Forty percent were not informed of parole hearings or permitted to appear and be heard at those hearings. Nearly 60% reported they were not provided prompt restitution from the convicted offender.[77]

Restitution remains especially problematic. Despite many strong laws and procedural reforms, many victims are not receiving the restitution ordered. The most recent public figures show uncollected criminal debt at the federal level to be more than $25 billion—70% of which is restitution owed to individuals and others harmed by defendants.[78] There has been no systematic tracking of unpaid restitution at the state level, but occasional reports show a similar failure.[79]

States would be better guided in their efforts with more targeted research. For example:

• When crime victims report that they were not informed of their rights or of available services, does this represent an actual failure to inform victims, or are victims unable to process or retain the information received due to the trauma of the crime or the crisis atmosphere? Is oral or written notification more effective?

• When victims have a right to a speedy trial, are their interests considered when a court rules on a motion for continuance? How frequently does this occur? Are the parties less likely to seek repeated continuances in a jurisdiction where victims have a right to a speedy trial?

• Why is it that many victims don't submit an oral or written impact statement? Do they not understand that they have the right, do they need assistance formulating their statement, or are they truly uninterested in submitting such a statement?

• How many victims are still excluded from courtrooms, and on what grounds?

• When victims have a right to be heard at proceedings (pretrial release proceedings, sentencing, probation revocation hearings), what do they actually say? What do they ask for? Are they interested in no contact orders, restitution, or long prison sentences?

• Is a victim's view of the appropriate punishment of the defendant impacted by the sensitivity and respect they receive from criminal justice officials? Is it impacted by the quality and nature of services they receive from victim service agencies?

• How many defendants are truly incapable of paying any restitution? If a defendant is ordered to pay an amount of restitution that is clearly beyond his or her ability to pay, does this have any impact on his or her likely recidivism?

The answers to these and similar questions would enlighten policymakers on the most effective way forward to ensure that victims' rights become a reality.

NOTES

1. For a discussion of the historical background of crime victims' rights, see Ken Eikenberry, "Victims of Crime/Victims of Justice," *Wayne Law Review* 34 (Fall 1987): 29.

2. President's Task Force on Victims of Crime, *Final Report* (Washington, DC: Government Printing Office, 1982).

3. Robert C. Davis, J. Nicole, and Caitlin Rabbitt, "Effects of State Victim Rights Legislation on Local Criminal Justice Systems," *Vera Institute of Justice* (December 2002): 29.

4. Ibid.

5. In a study of 1,300 crime victims across four states, victims rated the right to be informed of the arrest or release of the defendant as "very important." Dean G. Kilpatrick, David Beatty, and Susan Howley, *The Rights of Crime Victims—Does Legal Protection Make a Difference?* Research in Brief, National Institute of Justice (December 1998): 4.

6. Colo. Rev. Stat. § 24-4.1–302.5 (2005).

7. Utah Code § 77-38-3 (2006).

8. Kan. Const. Art. 15, § 15 (2005).

9. Miss. Code § 99-36-5 (2006).

10. Case law indicates that a defendant's right to a fair trial is not necessarily compromised by a crime victim's exercising the right to attend proceedings, even when the victim is a witness in the case. A "defendant must show more than the mere possibility that [the victim] conformed her testimony to that of the other witnesses," because the burden of proof is on the defendant to show he was denied a fair trial. *Utah v. Beltran-Felix,* 294 Utah Adv. Rep. 3, 12; 922 P.2d 30, 35 (Utah App. 1996).

11. Md. Crim. Proc. Code Ann. § 11-302 (2006); Mich. Comp. Laws § 780.761 (2006); Nev. Rev. Stat. § 171.204 (2006); S.D. Codified Laws § 19-14-29 (2006); Wash. Rev. Code § 7.69.030 (2006).

12. Wash. Rev. Code § 7.69.030 (2006).

13. Ark. Code Ann. § 16-90-1103 (2006).

14. N.H. Code § 21-M:8-k (2006).

15. Wis. Stat. § 906.15 (2006).

16. Fla. Stat. § 90.616 (2006).

17. *Gabriel v. Wyoming*, 925 P.2d 234, 236 (Wyo. 1996).

18. *People v. Ramer*, 17 Cal. App. 4th 672, 679; 21 Cal. Rptr. 2d 480 (1993; ordered not published).

19. As examples, see Ark. Code Ann. § 16-90-1103 (2006); Cal. Penal Code § 1102.6 (2006); 725 ILCS 120/4.5 (2006).

20. 1995 Cal. Adv. Legis. Serv. 411 (Deering).

21. As examples, see Ala. Code § 15-23-64 (2005); Ariz. Stat. § 13-4419 (2006); Fla. Stat. 960.001 (2005); Kan. Stat. § 22-3436 (2005); Mont. Code § 46-24-104 (2005).

22. Davis et al., "Effects of State Victim Rights," 13.

23. 725 ILCS 5/110-5 (2005).

24. For example, see Ariz. Const. art. II, § 2.1 (2006), and Ariz. Code § 13-4423 (2006); Colo. Rev. Stat. § 24-4.1-302.5 (2005); Conn. Gen. Stat. § 54-91C (2006); and Idaho Const. Art. I, § 22 (2006), and Idaho Code § 19–5306 (2006).

25. Mo. Rev. Stat. § 557.041 (2005).

26. See, for example, Ariz. Rev. Stat. § 13-4423 (2005).

27. N.Y. Crim. Proc. Law § 380.50 (2006). Such questioning is only allowed in cases where the victim's statement includes allegations about the crime not fully explored during the trial or materially varying from or contradicting trial evidence. If the court declines to ask the victim any of the submitted questions, it must state its reasons on the record.

28. For example, in a study of case files in two states before and after significant legislative expansion of victims' rights, there was no evidence that the adoption of victims' rights increased sentence lengths. Davis et al., "Effects of State Victim Rights," 28.

29. Kilpatrick et al., *Rights of Crime Victims,* 4.

30. Colo. Rev. Stat. § 18-1-1001 (2005).

31. Md. Code Crim. Proc. § 5-201 (2006).

32. Utah Code § 77-38-7 (2006).

33. 725 ILCS 5/114-4 (2005).

34. See *Black's Law Dictionary,* 5th ed. (St. Paul: West, 1979), 1180.

35. *People v. Moser,* 50 Cal. App. 4th 130, 135 (1996).

36. Cynthia Kempinen, *Payment of Restitution and Recidivism,* Research Bulletin 2, No. 2 (State College: Pennsylvania Commission on Sentencing, 2002).

37. Ibid.

38. 13 Vt. Stat. Ann. §§ 5362, 5362 (2005). In addition to monies collected as restitution from offenders, the restitution fund also receives 15% of any criminal fine imposed. 13 Vt. Stat. Ann. § 7282 (2005).

39. See Ala. Code § 15-23-69 (2005); Ind. Code § 35-37-4-12 (2006).

40. For example, see Minn. Stat. § 611A.035 (2005).

41. Alaska Stat. 12.61.110 (2006).

42. Ala. Code § 15.23.69 (2005).

43. For example, Wash. Rev. Code § 7.68.140 (2006).

44. For example, Iowa Code § 915.12 (2005).

45. R.I. Gen. Laws § 9-1-44 (2006).

46. For example, in the context of adult protective services records, see Alaska Stat. § 47.24.050 (2006); Conn. Gen. Stat. § 17b-452 (2006); Fla. Stat. § 415.107 (2006).

47. Del. Code Ann. Tit. 26 § 921 (2006).

48. Texas, for example, allows a victim of sexual assault to choose a pseudonym to be used instead of his or her name in all public files and records. Tex. Code Crim. Proc. Ann. Arts. 57.01–57.03 (2005).

49. Washington State provided the first such program. See Wash. Rev. Code Ann. §§ 40.24.010–40.24.900 (2006).

50. Ark. Code § 16-90-1105 (2006); Del. Code tit. 11 § 9409 (2006).

51. 18 Pa. Cons. Stat. Ann. § 4957 (2005).

52. Maine Rev. Stat. Ann. tit. 26, § 850 (2005).

53. For example, in Connecticut, an employer who violates the employment protection law is guilty of contempt and can be fined up to $500 or imprisoned for no more than 30 days. Conn. Gen. Stat. § 54-85b (2006).

54. For examples of punitive damages, see Alaska Stat. § 12.61.017(2006) and R.I. Gen. Laws § 12-28-10 (2006). For examples of states that allow victims to recover attorneys fees, see Ga. Code § 34-1-3 (2006) and N.D. Cent. Code § 27-09.1-17 (2006).

55. Ala. Code § 15-23-60 (2005).

56. Ariz. Rev. Stat. §§ 8-381–8-421 (2006); Mich. Comp. Laws §§ 780.781–780.802 (2006).

57. Nev. Rev. Stat. Ann. § 62D.010 (2006).

58. Colo. Rev. Stat. 24-4.1-303 (2005).

59. Wis. Stat. § 950.09 (2006).

60. Crime victims do not generally have legal standing in criminal actions, because they are not parties to the case, which is between the state and the defendant.

61. Md. Code Crim. Proc. § 11-103 (2006).

62. La. Rev. Stat. § 46:1844 (2006); N.C. Gen. Stat. 15A-840 (2006).

63. Utah Code § 77-38-11 (2006).

64. Calif. Const. Art. I, § 28 (2006).

65. President's Task Force on Victims of Crime, *Final Report*.

66. Ibid., 115.

67. Ibid.

68. *State v. Muhammad*, 145 N.J. 23, 678 A.2d 164 (1996). In Maryland, the state's highest court declined to permit an appeal of the victim's right to speak at sentencing, principally on the grounds that the appeal would be moot because it could not affect the finality of the sentence. However, the court did take the opportunity to provide important dicta on the victims' rights amendment. "Notwithstanding our affirmance of the judgment of the Court of Special Appeals, we wish to emphasize the significant duty of trial judges to respond to the will of the people as expressed in legislative acts and constitutional amendments." After setting out the text of the amendment, the court stated, "The mandate of the people is clear. In response to that mandate, trial judges must give appropriate consideration to the impact of crime upon the victims." *Cianos v. State*, 338 Md. 406, 659 A.2d 291, 295 (1995).

69. *Marbury v. Madison*, 5 U.S. (1 Cranch) 137, 163, 2 L. Ed. 60 (1803).

70. *State ex rel. K.P.*, *supra*, 311 N.J. Super. 123, 138; 709 A.2d 315 (Ch. Div. 1997), citing Richard E. Wegryn, "New Jersey Constitutional Amendment for Victims' Rights: Symbolic Victory?" *Rutgers Law Journal* 25 (1993): 183, 192–193.

71. *Reed v. Becka*, 333 S.C. 676, 511 S.E.2d 396, 399 (Ct. App. 1999).

72. Fla. Const. Art. I, § 16 (2006).

73. Ariz. Const. Art. II, § 2 (2006); Mich. Const. Art. I, § 24 (2006); Missouri Const. Art. I, § 32 (2005).

74. Alaska Const. Art. 1, § 12 (2006); Ill. Const. Art. 1, § 8.1 (2005).

75. Eric J. Fritsch, Tory J. Caeti, Peggy M. Tobolowsky, and Robert W. Taylor, "Police Referrals of Crime Victims to Compensation Sources: An Empirical Analysis of Attitudinal and Structural Impediments," *Police Quarterly* 7, no. 3 (September 2004): 372–393.

76. Auditor General, *The Provision of Victim Services Pursuant to Section 960.001, Florida Statutes: Operational Audit*, Report 02-044 (September 2001): 2.

77. Regional Research Institute for Human Services, Portland State University, *Oregon Crime Victims' Needs Assessment: Final Report*. Oregon Department of Justice (2002): 66.

78. United States General Accounting Office, *Criminal Debt: Actions Still Needed to Address Deficiencies in Justice's Collection Processes*, GAO-04-338 (March 2004): 2. This figure excludes restitution owed to federal agencies.

79. For example, a news account from Maryland found more than $66 million in crime victim restitution remained uncollected in 2002. Brian M. Schleter, *Millions in Restitution to Victims Go Unpaid, Capitol* (Annapolis, MD), March 30, 2003, p. A1.

19

Reaching Underserved Victim Populations

*Special Challenges Relating to Homeless Victims,
Rural Populations, Ethnic/Racial/Sexual Minorities,
and Victims With Disabilities*

BERNADETTE T. MUSCAT

JEFFREY A. WALSH

In the wake of the national crime victimization surveys of the 1960s, which revealed that crime victimization was much more prevalent than official reports suggested, greater attention to and recognition of victim's needs emerged. The latter part of the 20th century witnessed the advent of the victim's movement, which was largely an outgrowth of the general dissatisfaction in rising crime rates, rising recidivism rates, and newly emergent awareness of rape trauma, domestic violence, child abuse, and elder abuse, accompanied by the lack of attention and assistance provided to the victims of crime (Young, 1997).

Great strides were taken to alter attitudes regarding victimization, develop and expand services, and create policies and programs to better serve crime victims. After decades of struggle, the outcome is a more compassionate, service-oriented system that seeks to ensure and promote victims' rights. Despite all of the recent developments and accomplishments of the victims' movement, there remain victim populations that are underserved and in need of critical resources and services. These underserved populations are not unique in the types of victimizations that they experience, but they are unique in the challenges that they bring to the criminal justice, social service, and health care systems. Those who are classified as being "underserved" face a number of barriers in accessing services, including geographic isolation, mobility, language and communication, and citizenship status, to name but a few.

Underserved populations are also saddled by stereotypes and myths that are often untrue or exaggerated. Each misperception contributes to the lack of understanding of a particular victim group and enhances the "us versus them" mentality, posing barriers to service delivery. This chapter identifies several of these underserved and at-risk victim populations and the perils they face. For these vulnerable groups, and still others, more needs to be done.

THE HOMELESS IN AMERICA

Homelessness in America is certainly not a new social malady, but it is a growing concern, with public opinion regarding it as one of the most pressing social problems of the modern era (Honig & Filer, 1993; Schlay & Rossi, 1992). Optimistic predictions in the 1960s suggested that homelessness was declining and would eventually cease (Bogue, 1963). The homeless populations studied in the 1950s and 1960s, however, were different from today's homeless, and as such, concern for the homeless has persisted with the numbers growing and the outlook grim. In fact, throughout the 1980s and 1990s, the homeless population in the United States grew dramatically, although accuracy in accounting is widely debated because of inconsistent definitions of homelessness and methodological problems in measuring homelessness (National Coalition for the Homeless, 2005). For example, estimates over the last two decades have ranged from approximately 200,000 to 350,000 homeless (U.S. Census Bureau, 1991; U.S. Department of Housing and Urban Development, 1984) to estimates well in excess of 3 million (National Law Center on Homelessness and Poverty, 2004).

The poor have grown poorer, and a new homeless population has recently emerged. Historically, transient men comprised the vast majority of those occupying skid rows; but now they are joined by unsettling numbers of women, youth, and the mentally ill. This is compounded by the fact that the majority of women and children who are homeless are victims fleeing violent and abusive homes (Letiecq, Anderson, & Koblinsky, 1996; Zorza, 1991). In 2000, the United States Conference of Mayors found that 46% of cities surveyed identified domestic violence as a primary cause of homelessness.

With the creation of urban renewal programs, gentrification, and housing market shifts in prime urban areas in recent years, the nation's once undesirable and dilapidated skid rows have become ideal targets for revitalization and change. Many of the single-room occupancy hotels, which were once characteristic of skid rows, have been demolished to make room for more profitable real estate ventures, and the local homeless have been displaced throughout the cities (Rossi, 1989), making outreach and service delivery all the more difficult.

The increasing presence of America's homeless (men, women, and children) visibly residing on city streets has led to greater awareness and an increase in programs and services over the past two decades, which were developed to address their complex needs (Burt, Aron, Lee, & Valente, 2001). However, because the homeless are such a transient and mobile population, it makes it very difficult not only to find them but to provide food, shelter, clothing, and other needed services to them.

The specific causes of homelessness are varied; during the 1980s, two opposing explanatory paradigms emerged: structural- and individual-level causes. The structural causes focus on income inequality and poverty, reduced government support for the poor, and a lack of adequate affordable housing. The individual causes tend to focus on personal inadequacies such as substance abuse, mental illness, lack of education, and an inability to sustain meaningful relationships (Burt et al., 2001; Wright, 2000). Over the years, most people have come to recognize that it is the confluence of structural- and individual-level factors that result in homelessness. "The public came to understand the homeless as victims of social, psychological, and economic conditions beyond their control" (Fitzpatrick, La Gory, & Ritchey, 1993, p. 353).

A third emerging trend of homelessness stems from victimization and abuse within the home. In these circumstances, women and their children, or adolescents and teens who are primary victims themselves, are forced out of their homes, or they choose to flee the abuse. In communities where shelter programs are not available, or where they are beyond capacity, these groups live in cars, under bridges, or otherwise try to survive on the streets, inevitably placing themselves at increased risk of further victimization.

Until recently there has been very little research examining the extent to which the homeless are victims of crime and violence. Given what is known about the causes of homelessness, the transient lifestyle of the homeless, and their environmental exposure, research suggests that the homeless experience a greater likelihood of victimization, compared with the general population. A cursory news search reveals countless stories of assaults against the homeless. One of the most recent spate of attacks, captured on video and televised on news programs around the world, occurred Friday evening, January 13, 2006, in Fort Lauderdale, Florida, when at least two teenagers went on a sadistic rampage beating homeless men they encountered with baseball bats, hospitalizing at least two and killing one. Coverage of this story revealed a chilling reality: the brutality against the homeless for sport.

From an opportunity perspective, simply passing the days and nights on the street increases the chances of becoming a crime victim (Lee & Schreck, 2005). In 1999, there were 29 homeless persons killed in 11 cities across the United States and countless documented and undocumented assaults (Kelly, 2001). Fitzpatrick et al. (1993) found that homeless persons are approximately four times more likely than the general population to be victims of personal contact crimes, such as robbery and assault. Furthermore, 51% of homeless persons experienced violence compared with 29% of persons in the general population (Fitzpatrick et al., 1993). Homeless victims and homeless nonvictims also differ across several vulnerability characteristics. For example, homeless victims tend to have more substantial monthly incomes, making them more desirable targets. They suffer from mental illness and depression, rendering them more vulnerable to victimization (Fitzpatrick et al., 1993). This group is also more likely to have previously experienced child abuse, neglect, and domestic violence (Lee & Schreck, 2005; Wenzel, Leake, & Gelberg, 2001).

Typically, studies of homeless populations and the services offered to them have been directed at men, because they comprise the largest segment of the homeless population in the United States—nearly 70% (Kelly, 2001; Nunez & Fox, 1999). In recent decades, there has been a reduction in federal and state funding for the homeless, creating competition among service providers, politicizing the homeless issue, and taking much needed attention and energy away from the plight of the homeless. A general lack of coordinated efforts among community service agencies drew further attention away from the needs of the homeless. Many of the homeless are fearful of shelter living, especially in large urban settings, and resist seeking these services. They have been marginalized and are so far removed from mainstream society that they are either unaware of the availability of services or simply do not know how to access them. Others do not have the transportation needed to travel to service agencies (Friedman & Levine-Holdowsky, 1997).

In assessing the self-reported needs of the homeless, there are discrepancies between what needs the homeless perceive as critical, yet difficult to obtain, and what service providers are actually providing. For example, Acosta and Toro (2000) found food as the least difficult of 20 necessities to procure. However, other services such as housing, job training, education, and transportation were rated as very important and the most difficult to procure.

HOMELESS FEMALES AS VICTIMS

Despite men constituting the majority of the homeless population, the numbers of homeless women and youth are rapidly growing, and sufficient services and adequate service delivery mechanisms must be available to address their needs as well. The 1994 Violence Against Women Act "called for an increase in knowledge and control of violence against women, with special emphasis on the needs of traditionally underserved women" (Wenzel et al., 2001, p. 739). The needs of homeless female victims have been largely neglected, even though they experience higher rates of victimization than homeless male victims (Bassuk et al., 1996). This is particularly troubling, given that females with young children are the fastest growing homeless population in the United States (Letiecq et al., 1996). Women constitute the majority of heads of households in surveys of the occupants of homeless shelters (Nunez & Fox, 1999).

Wenzel et al. (2001) found that, compared with a 31% lifetime risk of violent victimization in a cross-section of females interviewed by telephone, one third of homeless women in their study experienced an act of major violence (being kicked, bitten, hit, beaten up, choked, burned, or threatened with a knife or gun) in the year prior to being interviewed. Moreover, 10% of homeless women reported being raped in the past *year* compared to a *lifetime* general population rate of 25% (Wenzel, Leake, & Gelberg, 2000). Similar to

homeless victims in general, women who had been assaulted in the past year were more likely to have earned an income via survival strategies, including panhandling and prostitution, making them more targets for victimization (Wenzel et al., 2001).

HOMELESS YOUTH AS VICTIMS

The number of runaway and homeless youth living on the streets of the nation's cities is suggestive of a sobering trend that has emerged over the last two decades. Many of these youth are fleeing intolerable abuse at the hands of a caregiver (Bao, Whitbeck, & Hoyt, 2000). Jencks (1994) states that as many as 70% of runaways are fleeing physical or sexual abuse at home. Unfortunately, while living on city streets is seen as a reprieve from the abuses at home, it presents its own life-threatening risks and opportunities for victimization (Hoyt, Ryan, & Cauce, 1999; Terrell, 1997).

Studies show that victimization rates of homeless youth are inordinately high, especially among young women (Tyler & Johnson, 2004). Furthermore, the more time youth spend living on the streets, the greater the likelihood that they will be assaulted (Hoyt et al., 1999). Youth who have been previous victims of assault are twice as likely to be victims of assault in the future (Hoyt et al., 1999). Terrell (1997) found that the victimization risk for adolescents differs significantly by gender and type of victimization. Adolescent males were more likely to be robbed, beaten up, threatened, or assaulted with a weapon, compared with adolescent females, who were four times more likely to be sexually assaulted. Compared with the general population of adolescents, drug use was substantially higher among homeless adolescents (Chen, Tyler, Whitbeck, & Hoyt, 2004). Substance abuse was also related to a significantly higher risk of victimization for male adolescents than it was for females (Hoyt et al., 1999).

BARRIERS TO REACHING UNDERSERVED HOMELESS VICTIM POPULATIONS

Reaching these homeless victim populations with effective services is paramount to reducing their numbers on the streets and meeting their needs as crime victims. However, the barriers are many and varied. A constellation of complex factors impedes their ability to receive much needed services. For example, violence screening and counseling services for the general female population have been adopted by the health care professionals through routine health care delivery. Given that the homeless have limited access to health care, this is not a promising avenue for detecting victimization (Wenzel et al., 2001). However, in locales where mobile health care units are used to go into areas heavily dominated by the homeless, medical services can be provided. In addition to basic health care provision, medical practitioners can screen for victimization and its associated health problems, mental health needs, and substance abuse. These mobile units have been used successfully for service provision, health care, and legal services to reach underserved, geographically isolated populations in the United States and throughout the world (U.S. Department of Justice, 1998). Specifically, health care units have been used with the homeless in urban centers with large homeless populations such as San Francisco and San Jose, California.

Many studies of homelessness advocate for the establishment of adequate shelters in which to begin the dissemination of social services. Shelters are viewed as the beginning of the line for community services (Friedman & Levine-Holdowsky, 1997). However, shelters often have rigid eligibility rules pertaining to age, gender, and screenings for histories of substance abuse, mental illness, and criminality that preclude some homeless persons from entering the shelter. Many shelters are also available to only one type of population. For example, a shelter for victims of domestic violence may be available only for females and male children under the age of 12. However, once the male child reaches 13 years old, he is considered a man and is not eligible to use these shelter services. The woman then has the difficult choice of having her 13-year-old male child live in a male-only shelter (typically designed for the homeless or for troubled youth), while she and perhaps the other eligible children live in a domestic violence shelter. Or she keeps the family united with no place for shelter.

Similarly, if a homeless woman has a dual diagnosis of victimization and substance abuse or victimization and mental illness, she is often not able to stay in a shelter for domestic violence. Conversely, if she stays in a shelter designed for the homeless, this setting typically does not provide the safety required for someone fleeing a violent home. An added problem is the lack of domestic violence shelters for male victims or for those in suburban and rural communities.

The opening of shelters may be a suitable first step for the adult homeless population, but research suggests that there are more than enough shelter beds available for homeless youth. In fact, a survey of youth shelters nationwide revealed that only 55% of youth shelter beds were occupied (Greene & Ringwalt, 1997). This finding does not suggest that there are more shelter beds than homeless youth; rather, it is likely attributable to homeless youth perceiving shelters as more dangerous than the streets. The rigid rules might also be reminiscent of rigid rules at home. Furthermore, youth may fear that shelters will contact their families, and reunification is often not desired when the departure from abusive and intolerable living conditions was intentional in the first place (Greene & Ringwalt, 1997; Terrell, 1997). Shelter beds need to become available for male children who are fleeing a violent home with a victimized parent. This type of program would allow for a safe environment for kids who cannot access domestic violence shelters and would address the unique circumstances that exist among homeless youth. There is a difference between an adolescent who is fleeing a home due to a primary victimization and a child who is a secondary victim leaving with a victimized parent. These shelters could assist with assessing for victimization and provide counseling for abuse witnessed in the home and subsequent post-traumatic stress.

As we previously stated, homeless females and youth are some of the most vulnerable victim populations in the United States today, and many barriers must be addressed before we can rest assured that the services they need are being provided. Intensive community outreach, the dissemination of information, and encouraging and securing shelter services are important first steps in overcoming these barriers. Finally, a reassessment of the real versus the perceived needs of the homeless is warranted to ensure the effective allocation and dissemination of finite resources.

RURAL CRIME VICTIMS

The definition of rural is not straightforward. In their review of 90 studies of rural crime, Weisheit, Falcone, and Wells (1996) found that 62% of the studies did not provide an operationalized definition of the term *rural* (Websdale & Johnson, 1998, p. 168). The most commonly employed operationalized definition used in social science research comes from the United States Census Bureau, which officially defines unincorporated areas with fewer than 2,500 residents as rural (Weisheit & Donnermeyer, 2000).

In thinking about crime and victimization, it is easy to understand why the focus of concern is on urban America, especially given the stereotype of rural America being an idyllic setting devoid of the troubles of city living. In 1998, urbanites represented 29% of the

population in the United States population, yet accounted for 38% of all violent and property crime victimization, whereas rural residents, representing 20% of the population, accounted for 15% of the violent and property crime victimization. The 47% suburbanite population accounted for the remainder (Bureau of Justice Statistics, 2000). These numbers tell us that rural America is not the battlefield for the war on crime. However, these numbers also tell us that all is not trouble free in rural America, and there most certainly are crimes and victimizations.

Victims of crime and violence in rural America have been largely neglected and underserved due to their geographic isolation and distance from metropolitan areas, where victim services are primarily located. Furthermore, barriers to service in rural areas are considerably different from those experienced by their urban counterparts. Arguably, no two rural victim populations are more impacted by the effects of geographic isolation and community insulation, and consequently more underserved, than victims of intimate partner violence and sexual assault. These two victim populations face similar barriers to services and are in desperate need of effective outreach and service options that can address their unique circumstances.

RURAL VICTIMS OF
INTIMATE PARTNER VIOLENCE

During the 1970s, public awareness of domestic violence greatly increased (Grama, 2000), with the women's movement and victim-support services spearheaded by feminists from the women's liberation movement (Karmen, 2004). Domestic violence and intimate partner violence, in particular, symbolized female oppression and institutional discrimination by men who controlled the criminal justice system. In recent decades, the prevalence and seriousness of intimate partner violence have been well documented (Websdale & Johnson,

1998). Today, intimate partner violence is probably the most studied victim-offender relationship (Karmen, 2004).

Unfortunately, as awareness has increased and progress has been made in the areas of prevalence (Tjaden & Thoennes, 1998), prevention (Websdale & Johnson, 1997), treatment (Davis & Smith, 1995), and the criminal justice system's response (Buzawa & Buzawa, 1996), the focus has been almost exclusively on urban areas (Websdale & Johnson, 1998). One class of victims has been nearly forgotten: rural victims of intimate partner violence (Grama, 2000). These victims have particular service needs. Their unique situation is driven by their isolation and geographic remoteness, which creates numerous barriers and significantly impedes the delivery of necessary services (Hilbert & Krishnan, 2000). Added barriers in rural areas stem from the population size; most people know everyone else in the community, which affords limited privacy for the victims. This poses a twofold problem, because victims often face issues of credibility and stigmatization. The victim may not be believed because others have different opinions of the offender and may articulate the impossibility that the offender would ever batter or rape. By the same token, the victim is reluctant to seek needed services because of the stigma of everyone knowing about the victimization.

Accurate accounting of victims of intimate partner violence has not been possible because of the victim's reluctance to report due to fear of reprisal and previous negative experiences with law enforcement (Fleury, Sullivan, Bybee, & Davidson, 1998). Tjaden and Thoennes (1998) found that as many as 25% of women are physically assaulted and/or raped by an intimate partner during their lifetime. Based on these estimates, approximately 1.5 million women are raped or physically assaulted by an intimate partner each year in the United States, representing an estimated 4.8 million intimate partner rapes and physical

assaults annually. However, it has been estimated that only 25% to 50% of all incidents of intimate partner abuse are reported to law enforcement each year (Fleury et al., 1998; National Center for Injury Prevention and Control, 2005).

Underreporting is more likely in rural areas, where victims are isolated and often unaware of available services or how to get the help they need. Despite profound urban and rural differences for other crimes, research suggests that self-reported intimate partner violence is as likely in rural areas as it is in urban areas, with few differences in the rates of abuse between the two (Websdale & Johnson, 1998). However, one difference is that rural women report more "hair pulling," "torture," and being "shot at" (Websdale & Johnson, 1998). A second difference found in rural areas is that neighbors there do not call the police for assistance. Often the distance between homes means that no one, except those in the home, can hear the abuse and call the police on the victim's behalf. Given a family member's reluctance to call the police on a loved one, there are fewer law enforcement interventions in rural than in other communities. When the police are called, the response time is delayed because fewer officers are available to respond; consecutive police calls for service are located far from one another; and multiple departments have jurisdiction over the same areas, which creates confusion about the responsibility for handling the call. By the time the police respond, the crisis has passed.

RURAL VICTIMS OF SEXUAL ASSAULT

Similar to the challenges faced in recording and reporting the incidence and prevalence of intimate partner violence in the United States, sexual assault is also difficult to quantify, with rape being one of the most underreported of all crimes. The National Opinion Research Center, conducting a victimization survey in 1967 on behalf of the President's Commission, found that nearly four times as many rapes occurred as were reported to the police (Doerner & Lab, 2005). This finding led to increased awareness and attention to sexual assault victims and their needs in an effort to reduce victimization rates and improve reporting practices. Widely varying rates of sexual assault have been reported among data sources. For example, "according to the Uniform Crime Reports, approximately .07% of women are sexually assaulted annually (FBI, 1999, p. 24), compared with .37% of the women, according to the National Crime Victimization Survey (BJS, 1997, p. viii)" (Ruback & Menard, 2001, p. 131). This disparity in rates becomes even more confounding when trying to understand urban and rural differences in sexual assault.

Studies relying on official (UCR) reports of sexual assault in rural areas are hindered by the fact that while 97% of police departments in metropolitan areas report their crime statistics to the FBI for inclusion in the UCR, only 89% of rural police departments participate (Ruback & Menard, 2001). The result is a further underrepresentation of the incidence of sexual assault in official data sources for rural victim populations. Contrary to many other studies, Ruback and Menard (2001) found that, in their study of rape crisis centers in Pennsylvania, rural counties reported higher rates of sexual victimization than urban counties. Despite having higher rates of sexual assault, reporting rates remain low in rural areas, which is largely attributable to the lack of anonymity there.

BARRIERS TO REACHING UNDERSERVED RURAL VICTIM POPULATIONS OF INTIMATE PARTNER VIOLENCE AND SEXUAL ASSAULT

Rural victims encounter many barriers that make service delivery particularly challenging.

Some of these more formidable barriers include geographic isolation and poor transportation, lack of anonymity, informal social controls, and a paucity of shelters and other services, several of which we discuss later (Grama, 2000; Grossman, Hinkley, Kawalski, & Margrave, 2005; Lewis, 2003; Logan, Walker, Cole, Ratliff, & Leukfeld, 2003).

Geographic isolation is quite possibly the most fundamental barrier facing rural victims, affecting nearly every aspect of providing and acquiring victim services (Grama, 2000). Rural victims are isolated, cut off from public transportation, medical services, social services, and even law enforcement. Some rural locations are so remote that telephone service may not exist and roads may not be navigable by typical use vehicles (Lewis, 2003; Ruback & Menard, 2001). Furthermore, rural victims may not have access to private transportation, because there is only one vehicle in the family, the abuser may leave in the vehicle after the violent incident, or the abuser may intentionally disable the vehicle in order to prevent the victim from leaving (Grama, 2000). The isolation may leave the victim trapped and helpless, increasing her feelings of fear and subordination. In addition, "many rural homes have police scanners, making any call to the police . . . public knowledge" (Grama, 2000, p. 178).

A dearth of available shelters and services is common in rural areas, with women in some locations forced to travel in excess of 100 miles to reach the nearest shelter, which is likely located in the more daunting larger metropolitan area (Grama, 2000). With services often unavailable in rural areas, rural victims frequently lack experience using them and feel uncomfortable making contact with or even simply calling a hotline (Lewis, 2003). Further complicating the absence of accessible local services is that making telephone calls to shelters and social service agencies in the surrounding larger cities often results in long distance telephone charges (Grama, 2000), which, unless the victim plans to leave immediately, will show up on the next phone bill, tipping off either an abuser or unsuspecting family that attempts have been made to seek social services.

Data on service needs for rural and urban victims of violence in Illinois found that rural victims overwhelmingly listed personal/emotional support and legal services as their two greatest needs, followed by shelter/emergency housing and transportation (Grossman et al., 2005). The need for additional personal/emotional services could be the direct result of the profound isolation of rural victims' experience. The need for legal services is likely due to a general lack of legal services in rural areas. Interestingly, white women listed this need as "greater," as compared with African American women. Grossman et al. (2005) suggested that this is likely a function of marital status, with white women more likely married and in need of legal assistance with issues related to divorce and child custody.

Rural communities are attempting to address these obstacles to services by providing transportation and cell phones to rural victims. The cell phones assist in keeping the victim connected to hotline services for crisis intervention, support, and transportation that will literally pick up the victim at her or his home and take him or her to the nearest shelter, social, or health care services. The difficulty with cell phones in rural communities is that many places still have sporadic or no service. In these circumstances, extending the coverage for toll-free hotlines has been helpful in allowing victims from throughout a state to contact any hotline for emergency services. The combined approach is used effectively in states such as Wyoming, which are considered highly rural and have only a limited number of programs in the entire state.

In conclusion, rural communities in the United States experience similar challenges in providing services to victims of intimate partner violence and sexual assault. These challenges stem largely from geographic isolation and community insulation, which not only inhibit these vulnerable victims from seeking services when offered but also create barriers to victim service delivery. Rural outreach and community involvement are necessary in efforts to empower rural victims, provide needed emotional support, and reduce their feelings of shame and helplessness.

ETHNIC MINORITIES AS VICTIMS

The United States has always taken pride in its rich racial and cultural diversity. Yet this diversity brings new cultures, traditions, beliefs, practices, and languages that mainstream America is not always prepared to meet or address. This poses a host of challenges on both sides, with misunderstandings, confusion, and the potential for heightened conflict and victimization.

In recent years, violent crime rates have declined among all racial and ethnic groups. However, the victimization experienced by ethnic and racial groups is higher than that for Whites. For example, according to the Bureau of Justice Statistics Web site, during 2004, Hispanics were victims of overall violence at a rate higher than non-Hispanics. Hispanics were also more likely to be victims of simple assault than non-Hispanics. Ethnic groups experienced higher levels of property crimes (204 per 1,000 Hispanic households, 191 per 1,000 Black households, and 157 per 1,000 White households). There were 44 burglary victimizations per 1,000 Black households, compared with just 28 burglaries per 1,000 White households. The disproportionate trend also applies to motor vehicle theft rates, with 19 vehicle thefts per 1,000 Hispanic households, 16 vehicle thefts per 1,000 Black households, and 8 thefts per 1,000 White households. From 1992 to 1996, Blacks were more likely than Whites to be victimized by a carjacking (6 versus 2 per

10,000, respectively). In a nine-year period (1992–2001), Native Americans experienced violent victimization at rates more than twice that of Blacks, 2.5 times that of Whites, and 4.5 times that of Asians.

Although any person can be a victim of any crime, there are distinct differences in how various ethnic minorities deal with victimizations, particularly those that happen in families. It is typically understood that there is a certain amount of shame, humiliation, and degradation associated with being a victim at the hands of a family member. Yet, for some ethnic groups, the shame and humiliation is intensified because it is perceived and internalized as a reflection on the honor of the family unit, the extended family, and in the case of some Asian cultures, on the family name that extends over thousands of years of ancestry. In contrast, because Native Americans have both a familial and a communal orientation, the shame and humiliation of victimization is experienced by the entire tribal community.

For different types of victimizations, there are delineated responses that are attributable to racial and ethic differences. For example, on the one hand, if the victimization is adult sexual assault, there is a different victim response than if the victim is a child. In the case of adult sexual assault, it is only a rape if the perpetrator is not married to the victim, because some cultures believe that a rape cannot occur in a marital context. On the other hand, in child sexual assault cases, if the child grows up in a culture in which virginity is a necessity for marriage, the reason for the lost virginity does not matter. In other words, the fact that the child may have been a victim of sexual assault is inconsequential—the end result is that the child is no longer a virgin. As such, she has brought shame to the family, she is considered impure, and she is not worthy of marriage and bearing children of her own. In these cultures, the victim response is intensified because she can be shunned as an outcast in her family and by her community.

As such, the victim often becomes suicidal, because she knows that according to her culture, she has a life with no future. There are other victimizations that are recognized in the United States, but are commonplace and not considered abusive in other cultures, such as verbal abuse, sexual harassment, isolation, and neglect, to name a few.

The target of victimization (e.g., children, women, men, or older adults) is another factor that is influenced by culture. For example, in the Asian community, male children are revered, but female children are not. As such, physical abuse against a female child might be condoned as acceptable to keep her in line, whereas it might be unthinkable to physically strike a male child. As a group, Native Americans view elders as possessing knowledge and power in the family and community. As such, an older adult is someone who is held in great esteem in this culture. This is not to say that any of these groups are immune from victimization, but their placement in that culture means two things: they are less likely to be the target of victimization, and when they are abused, they are less likely to come forward, because no one would believe that *they* could be abused.

The perpetrator of intrafamilial victimization is also influenced by culture. For example, in patriarchic societies such as Hispanic, Asian, and Asian Indian cultures, the female's responsibility is to keep other females in line. After a young woman is married, she is no longer a member of her family of origin. Instead, she is sold through a dowry system into her husband's family, and the females in the new family are responsible for ensuring that she does not upset her husband or bring shame to the family. In many cases, this includes berating, ignoring, isolating, and physically abusing her until she complies with the norms of her new family. In these settings, the husband may also be verbally or physically abusive.

BARRIERS TO SERVICE FOR ETHNIC MINORITIES

There are many nuances that contribute to the uniqueness of ethnicity and culture, which can pose barriers to service delivery. It is impossible to know each distinctive feature of every culture because the diversity in the United States is too great. For example, in Fresno, California, there are 76 different languages spoken in the Fresno Unified School District (Fresno Unified School District, 2004). It is impossible to know these 76 languages and the specific characteristics of each culture represented. However, it is imperative that victim service providers have a cultural awareness to be able to understand the impact that diversity plays on victimization.

Cultural awareness is the understanding of different cultures. It encompasses a wide range of issues including different races, religions, genders, ages, and physical disabilities, as well as gay, lesbian, and transgender issues (Almosaed, 2004). One or a combination of these poses a distinct challenge for the victim service provider. There are some guiding principles that can help service providers and practitioners in working with diverse populations.

It is important to understand that there is considerable heterogeneity within groups. For example, with Hispanics, there are differences among persons from Mexico, Argentina, Guatemala, and Spain. These groups cannot be lumped together with the expectation that they will all act and react in the same way. Instead, service providers must reach out to each victim as an individual and understand that there will be differences in victims' labeling of the abuse, disclosure, psychological functioning, intervention needs, and support systems (De Jong, Emmett, & Hervada, 1982; Sanders-Phillips, Moisan, Wadlington, Morgan, & English, 1995). After a victim is assessed along these lines, an effective intervention plan can be determined and implemented.

Next, it is important to be culturally sensitive as well to recognize and appreciate differences and diversity. One of the easiest ways to be culturally sensitive is to learn a person's name and its correct pronunciation. In doing so, the victim service provider is showing respect to the person and the family. Another option is to have available staff or volunteers who speak other languages and for whom English is not their primary language. Other options are to place different national flags around the office, to play music from different countries, or to have "welcome" written in different languages in a front lobby. Each of these shows an understanding and celebration of differences. Victims' thoughts, feelings, and beliefs should be validated in the context of their cultures (Dugan & Apel, 2003; Murdaugh, Hunt, Sowell, & Santana, 2004). Finally, it is essential to find out what is important to victims, to ask about how their victimization is viewed in the culture, and to help them accordingly, while continually validating their feelings.

SEXUAL MINORITIES AS VICTIMS

The acceptability of homosexual behavior has varied throughout history, from its acceptability in ancient Greece to its repudiation in Biblical interpretations. These sentiments are still held today. Certain sectors of society view homosexuality as an alternate lifestyle, whereas others think of homosexuality as unnatural, immoral, or evil. The debate continues to rage in the United States as some call for the acceptance of gay marriage while others speak vehemently against gay unions as the decay of the traditional marital contract. Homosexuality brings out intense emotions on both sides of the issue, which can erupt into violence against homosexuals (Balsam, Rothblum, & Beauchaine, 2005; Cochran, 2001; DiPlacido, 1998). The violence can be perpetrated by strangers or known assailants and be based on sexual orientation, perceived sexual orientation, disclosures of sexual orientation, or mannerisms and dress that do not conform to gender stereotypes (Balsam et al., 2005; Pilkington & D'Augelli, 1995).

In 1973, homosexuality was no longer declared a mental disorder by the American Psychiatric Association. The distinction of mental disorder was removed from the *Diagnostic and Statistical Manual (DSM–II)*, yet it was not until the early 1980s that the *DSM–III-R* classified homosexual behavior as an alternative sexual lifestyle rather than a deviant behavior. Over the past 25 years, we have come a long way in our recognition of homosexuality, resulting in the establishment of a strong community that advocates for policies and equal protections under the law for lesbian, gay, bisexual, transgendered, and queer and questioning (LGBTQ) persons.

Despite these advances, homosexuals continue to be the victims of hate crimes. Traditionally, these crimes have been under-reported, yet research on antigay victimization has found differences in the ways gays and lesbians are victimized. Gay men experience more extreme levels of violence than do gay women. The location of victimization also differs, with men being victimized in public and gay-identified locales, whereas females are more likely to be victimized in or near their primary residence. Race also plays a role: Black and Latina lesbians were more likely to be victimized by antigay violence than their White counterparts (Aurand, Addessa, & Bush, 1985; Comstock, 1989; Gross, Aurant, & Addessa, 1988; Kuehnle & Sullivan, 2003; LeBlanc, 1991).

Christopher et al. (1991) found that the history of insensitivity and discrimination by the police toward victims of racially motivated hate crimes has created reluctance in the LGBTQ community to report hate crimes. Several other studies have supported this conclusion (Berrill & Herek, 1992; Comstock, 1989; Finn & McNeil, 1997; Gross et al., 1988; Kuehnle & Sullivan, 2003). As such, there is still much that is unknown about

violence and victimization of the LGBTQ community, particularly in a family or partnership context.

Homosexual couples face many of the same problems as heterosexual couples. In terms of victimization, both experience verbal, physical, and sexual abuse as well as various types of neglect and controlling behaviors. The prevalence of violence in homosexual couples has yet to be accurately determined, because of the difficulty in defining homosexuality, the seriousness of the relationship (i.e., dating, cohabitating, marriage), and the type and severity of the violence (Balsam et al., 2005). During 1997, the National Coalition of Anti-Violence Programs (NCAVP) documented 3,327 cases of LGBTQ domestic violence victimization. Men reported 1,746 of the cases, compared with 1,581 incidents reported by women. In 2002, the NCAVP replicated the study by collecting data from 14 participating agencies across the United States and found 5,092 cases of domestic violence. The victims were men (52%), women (46%), and transgendered (4%). This represents an increase of 1,765 cases (65%) over the previous five-year period (Bieber, 2004).

Despite the lack of accurate information about homosexual battering, the elements of domestic violence are quite similar, with only a few distinctions. Although most couples regardless of sexual orientation note reluctance and difficulties in leaving a violent partner, homosexuals may face additional problems in disclosing the abuse. Some of these problems stem from the LGBTQ community, because the relationship is accepted and the coupling is viewed as legitimate. As a result, the victim may be unwilling to admit that the relationship is dysfunctional, let alone violent. The victim may be isolated from family and friends because of their sexual orientation, and they rely on the LGBTQ community for support and acceptance. This reliance makes it very difficult to acknowledge and admit violence. Furthermore, in this setting, the victim may not be in a singular friendship, but rather in a friendship facilitated by being part of a couple. This raises issues regarding the credibility of victims, and whether they will receive support or be shunned for having a violent relationship by their only support system. This is akin to the heterosexual couple who is unwilling to mention problems in their relationship to family members. Similarly, homosexual couples are unwilling to disclose violence in their relationships to other members in the LGBTQ community. The inability to disclose leaves the victim further isolated with nowhere to turn for support and gives the batterer a greater means of control (McPherson, 1990; Snow, 1992).

Victims in a homosexual relationship face another difficulty in seeking help if they have not told others about their sexual orientation. If family and friends do not know about the victim's homosexuality, then it is difficult to disclose abuse in a secretive relationship. Batterers often use the hidden nature of the relationship to their advantage in order to control the victims' behavior by threatening to "out" them if they leave the relationship. In these circumstances, the batterer will threaten to tell others that the victim is in a gay or lesbian relationship. The victim may be intensely fearful of the potential negative repercussions associated with others knowing about their sexual orientation. Thus the victim will suffer in silence, concealing the violence with no support system, no means of escape, and nowhere to turn for help (Williams & Robinson, 2004).

Another means of control that batterers use in homosexual relationships is to state that nobody will believe the victim's reports of the abuse. The batterer will remind the victim about homophobic attitudes, homosexual stereotypes, and heterosexual preferences. The batterer will play on the victim's fears that there is nowhere to turn and, more important, that no one will care about abuse in a nontraditional relationship. Moreover, victims may be reluctant to call the police because they have had previous unfavorable encounters with the criminal justice system and have experienced the homophobic attitudes that some police officers still harbor (Aiello & Capkin, 1984; Savin-Williams, 1994).

If the police are called, they may not be able to identify the primary aggressor, because both parties claim the role of victim and both are basically the same height and weight. Police officers, without proper training, may assume that the violence between two similar individuals is "not that bad" and fail to take appropriate action. As a result, the batterer may be empowered to manipulate and use fear tactics to keep the victim locked in a violent relationship in which he or she can be further controlled and abused. A male victim, regardless of sexual orientation, may be reluctant to contact the police for fear that the police will ridicule him for not being a "man" by taking care of the situation himself.

A final challenge for victims in a homosexual relationship occurs if either the victim or batterer has AIDS or is HIV-positive. On the one hand, if victims have AIDS or are HIV-positive, they may be having health problems associated with the illness, which may jeopardize their ability to seek services or leave the relationship. The victim may be economically dependent or depend on the batterer for health benefits. In either situation, the victim's livelihood, health, and life are dependent on staying with the batterer. On the other hand, if the batterer has AIDS or is HIV-positive, this may be used as another way to manipulate and control the victim into not reporting the abuse or leaving the relationship. The batterer may prey on the victim's conflicted feelings (e.g., if you really loved me, you wouldn't leave me when I need you most) to keep him or her in the relationship (Melling, 1984).

BARRIERS TO REACHING LGBTQ VICTIMS

Gay and lesbian victims face a variety of barriers in reaching out for assistance from the criminal justice and social services systems. Professionals in these systems might harbor homophobic attitudes and be reluctant to provide assistance for domestics in homosexual relationships. These attitudes further humiliate and isolate the victim (Ryan & Rivers, 2003; Williams & Robinson, 2004). In other situations, domestic violence laws pertain only to heterosexual couples. Currently, only 44 states have laws that specifically apply to both hetero- and homosexual couples. To compound the problem, victims may not be able to get a restraining or protective order against a violent partner of the same gender. The lack of legal protections can minimize the perceived severity of the situation and contribute to the victims' unwillingness to report the abuse. These are significant barriers for the victim who is seeking help and legal protections from the criminal justice system.

Another barrier faced by homosexual victims is the lack of services that are available in the community. There may be victim services agencies in the area, but the victim could believe that these are homophobic organizations or that they will not understand the severity of same-sex victimization. These fears can be alleviated with a symbol or poster of LGBTQ pride that is placed prominently in a front lobby area.

Specialized programs may be available in large cities, but many smaller cities do not have these services. Even in communities that have specialized programs, victims are reluctant to walk into these agencies for fear that someone will see and identify them as a homosexual. The stigmatization associated with seeking services may be too great and as a result the victim chooses to go without the needed services.

Another barrier faced by homosexual victims is the lack of a single shelter in any city in the United States specifically designated to meet the needs of victims of same-sex violence (Wallace, 2005). This problem is partially addressed for female victims because most shelters for battered women have devised assessment tools to differentiate between the primary aggressor and the victim in female-female battering. In these situations, the female victim has a safe place to go without fear that her female partner will also claim abuse, be admitted to the shelter, or have access to the victim.

The same is not true for male victims, because shelters for this population are available only for homeless males. In these environments, the shelter typically will provide a place to stay on a first-come, first-served basis. The assessment tools in these settings are usually for alcohol and drug use and aggressive behaviors. If the person is not identified as being a danger to himself or others, he is admitted. In many cases, the male aggressor is not a danger to anyone else except the male victim and may be admitted to the shelter. Hence, these are not safe environments for the male victim of a violent male partner. Further complicating the situation is the short-term housing limitation of a 24-hour period. These shelters are typically not designed to provide long-term or transitional housing. There are often no counseling services in such settings, and they are ill-equipped to deal with domestic violence.

VICTIMS WITH DISABILITIES

About 54 million Americans have one or more disabilities (Tyiska, 1998). According to the Americans with Disabilities Act of 1990 (ADA), enacted by Congress to protect the employment and accessibility rights of persons suffering from disabilities, a person with a disability is one who has a physical or mental impairment. Mental disabilities include mental or psychological disorders, such as mental retardation, organic brain syndrome, emotional or mental illness, and specific learning disorders. Physical disabilities include physiological disorders, disfigurement, or loss of the use of a body part or system. Individuals can have both mental and physical disabilities and multiple types of each (Americans with Disabilities Act, 2006).

The source of disabilities differs from those that are congenital (occurring at birth), adventitious (occurring after birth), or the consequence of victimization (Davis, 2004). In terms of the victimization, there are further subdivisions: some individuals are the victim of a one-time, sudden, and violent victimization rendering them temporarily or permanently impaired. In contrast, someone may be the victim of long-term chronic victimization that ultimately limits one's visual, auditory, or sensory abilities. And still others may be victimized while pregnant, contributing to the premature birth of a child who has not fully developed. Regardless of the source and duration of the abuse, the resulting disability will influence every aspect of their lives (Office for Victims of Crime, 2000).

People with disabilities can experience verbal, physical, and sexual abuse as well as various types of neglect and abandonment. The prevalence of the violence and response to the victimization are different for persons with disabilities. According to Melling (1984), 60% of those with a mental disability will become victims of a crime at some point in their life. For individuals with psychiatric disabilities, the rate of violent victimizations, including sexual assault, was two times greater than in the general population (Hidday, Swartz, Swanson, Borum, & Wagner, 1999). Among adults who are developmentally disabled, approximately 80% of the females and 32% of the males were victims of sexual assault (Johnson & Sigler, 2000). Women with disabilities are at a higher risk for abuse in general, and by multiple perpetrators for longer periods of time, than their able-bodied counterparts (Young, Nosek, Howland, Chanpong, & Rintala, 1997).

The repetition of victimization across the lifespan for individuals with a disability is astounding. According to Valenti-Heim and Schwartz (1995), 49% of those with developmental disabilities have been the victim of a sexual assault and will experience 10 or more abusive incidents in their lives. In many circumstances, the victim knows the perpetrator. One third of abusers are natural or foster family members and acquaintances, and 25% are caregivers or service providers (Sobsey, 1994). Victims with disabilities are reluctant to report the victimization, making these one of the most underreported types of victimization. Despite underreporting, the rates of victimization among this population are higher than among the general population (Office for Victims of Crime, 2002).

BARRIERS TO SERVICES FOR VICTIMS WITH DISABILITIES

There are a number of barriers to reporting victimization by those with a disability. The most prevalent barriers stem from difficulties in communicating with others (Worthington, 1984). Communication problems may be the result of mental or developmental limitations or speech impairments. Each pose challenges for the victim in articulating an event, expressing thoughts, and remembering details. This may be exacerbated by the proximity of the disclosure to the victimization and corresponding crisis reaction. A victim with a disability may already have difficulty communicating with others, but this is made all the more difficult if the victim is in crisis. Depending on the type of disability, the victim may not be able to organize the event chronologically and may not remember crucial details about the situation. If the police are called, it is imperative that they are patient interviewers and that they use a third-party interpreter to ease the communication. Patience is essential because any sign of impatience or agitation can further communication problems. Likewise, the victim may be inclined to alleviate the situation by saying what he or she believes the officer wants to hear, which may not reflect the truth (Office for Victims of Crime, 2000). If the victim uses American Sign Language (ASL) to communicate, the officer should bring in a third-party interpreter. This is particularly important if there is any suspicion that the victim's interpreter is also the abuser (Deaf Hope, 2006).

Another type of communication barrier occurs when the victim is dependent on others to report on his or her behalf. This is particularly problematic if the person is isolated or immobile. In either of these situations, the victim is completely dependent upon another person to identify the abuse, affirm that the abuse occurred, and believe that the abuse was serious enough to merit providing assistance or contacting the police. Regardless of ability, many victims are ashamed of the abuse and think that no one will believe them. Many self-blame and question what they did to bring the abuse on themselves. These feelings are exacerbated for victims with a disability due to the prevailing stereotypes that question why someone would victimize a person with a disability. As a result, the victim may not disclose the incident. The victim then becomes dependent on someone to see the abuse or someone who is trained to identify physical and behavioral patterns associated with abuse. If the victim is socially isolated or the abuse is occurring at the hands of the caregiver, the victim has no outlet for disclosure (Office for Victims of Crime, 2000, 2002).

A final communication barrier occurs with victims who have a disability and who are victims of a sexual assault. Many people with disabilities receive no formal sex education and know little about the differences between appropriate and inappropriate sexual behavior. The victim may not know that some types of touching are inappropriate. Or the perpetrator may be a caregiver who assists with basic hygiene and takes advantage of a perceived opportunity. Other times, the victim may have been told that he or she is a "special friend" and that this is how "special friends" share their love and affection. Regardless of the situation, the perpetrator is taking advantage of the victim through manipulation and coercion, which are the hallmarks of sexual assaults. To add to the gravity of the circumstance, traditionally, those with a disability were socialized to listen and obey without question. The combination of a lack of sex education and passive obedience can make it very difficult to identify victimization. This is particularly problematic if the caregiver is also the abuser, as the victim is dependent upon his or her abuser for safety and security (Elman, 2005).

Many victims with a disability are unable to seek services as the result of limited mobility. They may have difficulty walking, use a wheelchair, or be bedridden. Even if the person has limited mobility issues, she still may not be able to access services. Once at the service provider, services may be located on an upper level with limited or no accessibility. Regardless of the ADA that requires organizations to be accessible, many places are still not in compliance.

Another barrier presents when a disabled person needs shelter services. The services, specialized assistance, and equipment they need may be unavailable, and the victim chooses to leave. These problems were evidenced during Hurricane Katrina when more than 100,000 people with disabilities living in New Orleans had to be evacuated quickly. Many were forced to abandon wheelchairs, walkers, and other medical equipment. When they arrived at their new shelters, replacement items were scarce or unavailable (Collins, 2005).

The realization that victims with disabilities present unique challenges has been acknowledged by the criminal justice and social services systems (Office for Victims of Crime, 2002). One of the first challenges that both systems face in responding to victims with disabilities is that each disability requires an individualized response. For example, a victim who is developmentally disabled will have different needs than one who is hearing or visually impaired. Just as any victim has particular needs, those with a disability bring peculiar challenges to the criminal justice and social service systems. By strengthening ties with other sectors of the community, such as health care, faith-based, and educational organizations, each service provider can coordinate efforts, share expertise, and pool resources to assist victims with disabilities.

Another challenge faced by the criminal justice and social service systems is to understand that the victim with a disability has individual needs. For example, sometimes the victim with a disability will seek services and will have a guardian, social worker, or interpreter with him or her to provide assistance. In many cases, these other individuals are accustomed to helping and speaking on behalf of the victim. The tendency is for the victim service provider to interact with the other person and overlook the victim, which is problematic because it diminishes the victim's importance and disempowers the victim. Instead, the victim should be addressed directly. The helper person should not be removed from the setting, but specific ground rules about personal communication need to be established. In doing so, the victim service provider should focus on the victim by interacting with and directing all questions to her. It may be essential for the victims to interact with their interpreters, or they may feel more comfortable talking with their guardians or social workers. It is important for the victim service practitioner to look directly at the victim and be aware of body language and nonverbal cues and mannerisms. This may help the victim service provider to detect differences in what an interpreter is saying and how the victim is reacting. In looking at the victim, it is important not to stare, particularly if the person has a physical disability that can be seen. Instead, focus on the person as an individual and not on the disability.

The victim service provider should ask what the victim needs. For example, if the victim is having difficulty moving or navigating in a small area, ask the person if he needs assistance. The tendency might be to rush to provide assistance, but the victim should be asked first about the nature of the help they require before intervening. The corollary to this is to respect the victim's wishes. If he or she is struggling, but he or she does not want assistance, it is essential to respect his or her wishes. In another example, a victim may have a hearing impairment, and an interpreter is not present. Do not ask the victim to write down their account of the situation. This might be easier for you, but it is not easy for someone who has just been victimized to write. Her hands may be shaking, she may be nervous, she may not be able to write as fast as her mind is racing, she may not know how to write, or she simply might find it offensive to be asked to write down a horrible event. Instead, take the time and wait for an interpreter to arrive, ensuring that the victim is aware of what is going on, how long it will take for the person to arrive, and that she is comfortable and safe. In this circumstance, you are helping to accommodate and attend to the victim's needs.

Another area of need in addressing victims with disabilities is to prevent the victimization in the first place. Prevention takes several forms, including training for those who work or live with people with disabilities. This training should include identifying the physical and behavioral indicators of abuse, helping someone to report abuse, and employing anger management strategies to reduce the possibility of abusive behavior. At an organizational or institutional level, screening and criminal background checks must be done on persons who apply to work with people with disabilities. This precaution will help identify problematic individuals before they are hired. A buddy or mentoring system for new employees may also help to reduce possible victimizations.

Of equal importance is having account-ability and investigatory mechanisms in place to report institutional victimizations to man-agement and to employ serious sanctions when abuse has been confirmed. Individuals with a disability should be taught about dif-ferent types of abuse, self-defense techniques, abuse reporting protocols, and service provi-sion. A comprehensive approach will help prevent, identify, and report abuse among victims with a disability.

Finally, victim service practitioners must understand that people with disabilities have the same rights as any other victims. They have the same rights to access and participation in services, but often they are not afforded legitimacy or respect. Therefore victim service providers must ensure that all victims are treated equally and all their rights are protected. Equity occurs when victims are believed, when they are treated as individu-als, when stereotypes and myths are dis-pelled, when they are given equal access to services, and when they are active partici-pants in the process of seeking justice.

CONCLUSION

This chapter focused on several of the most vulnerable, underserved victim populations in the United States as well as different types of victimization experiences. It has shed much-needed light on the perils of being an "under-served victim" who is caught in a system of justice and services created to address the needs of only "mainstream" victims. As we discussed, underserved groups experience spe-cial circumstances and face numerous chal-lenges and barriers in seeking services to address their victimization needs. The majority of barriers stem from personal and geographic isolation, problems with reporting and com-munication, the stigmatization associated with the victimization, and a lack of knowledge on the part of the criminal justice and social ser-vice systems in working with these groups.

These systems need to learn about underserved populations and how to reach out to them.

For necessary advances and progress to be made, greater emphasis must be placed on reporting, intervening, and preventing victim-ization. For special victim populations, we must also increase awareness of their prob-lems and create more inclusive victim policies and services. More must be done to educate practitioners about underserved victim popu-lations by increasing cultural awareness and dispelling myths and stereotypes, which can help victims feel comfortable in reporting vic-timizations and seeking services. Finally, all victims should be treated with dignity and respect, and their rights must be vigorously protected.

REFERENCES

Acosta, O., & Toro, P. A. (2000). Let's ask the homeless people themselves: A needs assess-ment based on a probability sample of adults. *American Journal of Community Psychology, 28*(3), 343–365.

Aiello, D., & Capkin, L. (1984). Services for dis-abled victims: Elements and standards. *Response to violence in the family and sexual assault, 7*(5), 12.

Almosaed, N. (2004). Violence against women: A cross-cultural perspective. *Journal of Muslim Affairs, 24*(1), 67–88.

Americans With Disabilities Act. (2006). Retrieved February 2, 2006, from www.usdoj.gov/crt/ada/adahom1.htm

Aurand, S. K., Addessa, R., & Bush C. (1985). *Violence and discrimination against Philadelphia lesbian and gay people.* Philadelphia: Lesbian and Gay Task Force.

Balsam, K. F., Rothblum, E. D., & Beauchaine, T. P. (2005). Victimization over the life span: A com-parison of lesbian, gay, bisexual, and heterosex-ual siblings. *American Psychological Association, 73*(3), 477–487.

Bao, W., Whitbeck, L. B., & Hoyt, D. R. (2000). Abuse, support, and depression among home-less and runaway adolescents. *Journal of Health and Social Behavior, 41*(4), 408–420.

Bassuk, E. L., Weinreb, L. F., Buckner, J. C., Browne, A., Saloman, A., & Bassuk, S. (1996). The characteristics and needs of sheltered homeless and low-income housed mothers. *Journal of the American Medical Association, 276,* 640–646.

Berrill, K., & Herek, G. (1992). Primary and secondary victimization in anti-gay hate crimes: Official response and public policy. In G. Herek & K. Berrill (Eds.), *Hate crimes: Confronting violence against lesbians and gay men* (pp. 289–305). Newbury Park, CA: Sage Publications.

Bieber, E. (2004, September). Domestic violence: Are you being abused? *Lesbian News,* 48.

Bogue, D. J. (1963). *Skid row in American cities.* Chicago: University of Chicago Press.

Bureau of Justice Statistics. (1997). *Criminal victimization in the United States, 1994.* Washington, DC: U.S. Department of Justice.

Bureau of Justice Statistics. (2000). *Urban, suburban, and rural victimization, 1993–98* (NCJ 182031). Special Report. National Crime Victimization Survey. Washington, DC: U.S. Department of Justice, Office of Justice Programs.

Bureau of Justice Statistics. (2004). *Victim characteristics.* Retrieved January 25, 2006, from www.ojp.usdoj.gov/bjs/cvict_v.htm

Burt, M., Aron, L. Y., Lee, E. K., & Valente, J. (2001). *Helping America's homeless: Emergency shelters or affordable housing.* New York: Urban Institute Press.

Buzawa, E. S., & Buzawa, C. G. (1996). *Domestic violence: The criminal justice response* (2nd ed.). Thousand Oaks, CA: Sage Publications.

Chen, X., Tyler, K. A., Whitbeck, L. B., & Hoyt, D. R. (2004). Early sexual abuse, street adversity, and drug use among female homeless and runaway adolescents in the Midwest. *Journal of Drug Use, 4*(1), 1–22.

Christopher, W., Arquellas, J., Anderson, R., Barnes, W., Estrada, L., & Kantor, M. (1991). *Report of the independent commission on the Los Angeles Police Department.* Los Angeles: Diane.

Cochran, S. D. (2001). Emerging issues in research on lesbians' and gay men's mental health: Does sexual orientation really matter? *American Psychologist, 56,* 931–947.

Collins, M. C. (2005, September 3). California's disability community helping Katrina survivors with disabilities. California State Independent Living Council, Press release.

Comstock, G. (1989). Victims of anti-gay/lesbian violence. *Journal of Interpersonal Violence, 4,* 101–106.

Davis, L. A. (2004, April). Abuse of children with cognitive, intellectual & developmental disabilities. *Arc,* 1–2.

Davis, R. C., & Smith, B. (1995). Domestic violence reforms: Empty promises or fulfilled expectations. *Crime and Delinquency, 41,* 541–552.

Deaf Hope. (2006). *Hearing service providers.* Retrieved February 2, 2006, from www.deaf-hope.org/index.html

De Jong, A., Emmett, G., & Hervada, A. (1982). Sexual abuse of children: Sex, race, and age-dependent variations. *American Journal of Diseases in Children, 136,* 129–134.

DiPlacido, J. (1998). Minority stress among lesbians, gay men, and bisexuals: A consequence of heterosexism, homophobia, and stigmatization. In G. M. Herek (Ed.), *Stigma and sexual orientation: Understanding prejudice against lesbians, gay men, and bisexuals* (pp. 138–159). Thousand Oaks, CA: Sage Publications.

Doerner, W. G., & Lab, S. P. (2005). *Victimology* (4th ed.). Cincinnati, OH: Anderson.

Dugan, L., & Apel, R. (2003). An exploratory study of the violent victimization of women: Race/ethnicity and situational context. *Criminology, 41*(2), 959–979.

Elman, R. A. (2005). Confronting the sexual abuse of women with disabilities. *VAWnet.* National Resource Center on Domestic Violence. Retrieved September 26, 2006, from www.vawnet.org/SexualViolence/Research/VAWnetDocuments/AR_SVDisability.php

Federal Bureau of Investigation. (1999). *Crime in the United States: Uniform crime reports.* Washington, DC: Government Printing Office.

Finn, P., & McNeil, T. (1997). *Bias crime and the criminal justice response: A summary report* (Prepared for the National Criminal Justice Association). Cambridge, MA: Abt. Associates.

Fitzpatrick, K. M., La Gory, M. E., & Ritchey, F. J. (1993). Criminal victimization among the homeless. *Justice Quarterly, 10*(3), 353–368.

Fleury, R. E., Sullivan, C. M., Bybee, D. I., & Davidson, W. S. (1998). Why don't they just call the cops? Reasons for differential police contact among women with abusive partners. *Violence and Victims, 13*, 333–346.

Fresno Unified School District. (2004). *2004–2005 facts and figures.* Retrieved September 26, 2006, from www.fresno.k12.ca.us/facts.html

Friedman, B. D., & Levine-Holdowsky, M. (1997). Overcoming barriers to homeless delivery services: A community response. *Journal of Social Distress and the Homeless, 6*(1), 13–28.

Grama, J. L. (2000). Women forgotten: Difficulties faced by rural victims of domestic violence. *American Journal of Family Law, 14,* 173–189.

Greene, J. M., & Ringwalt, C. L. (1997). Shelters for runaway and homeless youths: Capacity and occupancy. *Child Welfare, 76*(4), 549–561.

Gross, L., Aurand, S., & Addessa, R. (1988). *Violence and discrimination against lesbian and gay people in Philadelphia and the Commonwealth of Pennsylvania.* Philadelphia: Philadelphia Gay and Lesbian Task Force.

Grossman, S. F., Hinkley, S., Kawalski, A., & Margrave, C. (2005). Rural versus urban victims of violence: The interplay of race and region. *Journal of Family Violence, 20*(2), 71–81.

Hidday, V. A., Swartz, M., Swanson, J., Borum, R., & Wagner, H. R. (1999). Criminal victimization of persons with severe mental illness. *Psychiatric Services, 50,* 62–68.

Hilbert, J. C., & Krishnan, S. P. (2000). Addressing barriers to community care of battered women in rural environments: Creating a policy of social inclusion. *Journal of Health and Social Policy, 12,* 41–52.

Honig, M., & Filer, R. K. (1993). Causes of intercity variation in homelessness. *American Economic Review, 83*(1), 248–255.

Hoyt, D. R., Ryan, K. D., & Cauce, A. M. (1999). Personal victimization in a high-risk environment: Homeless and runaway adolescents. *Journal of Research in Crime and Delinquency, 36*(4), 371–392.

Jencks, C. (1994). *The homeless.* Cambridge, MA: Harvard University Press.

Johnson, I., & Sigler, R. (2000). Forced sexual intercourse among intimates. *Journal of Interpersonal Violence, 15*(1), 95–108.

Karmen, A. (2004). *Crime victims: An introduction to victimology* (5th ed.). Belmont, CA: Thompson/Wadsworth Learning.

Kelly, R. J. (2001). Status report on the homeless. *Journal of Social Distress and the Homeless, 10*(3), 229–233.

Kuehnle, K., & Sullivan, A. (2003). Gay and lesbian victimization: Reporting factors in domestic and bias incidents. *Criminal Justice Behavior, 30*(1), 85–96.

LeBlanc, S. (1991). *8 in 10: A special report of victim recovery program of the Fenway Community Health Center.* Boston: Fenway Community Health Center.

Lee, B. A., & Schreck, C. J. (2005). Danger on the street: Marginality and victimization among homeless people. *American Behavioral Scientist, 48*(8), 1055–1081.

Letiecq, B. L., Anderson, E. A., & Koblinsky, S. A. (1996). Social support of homeless and permanently housed low-income mothers with young children. *Family Relations, 45,* 265–272.

Lewis, S. H. (2003, September). *Sexual assault in rural communities.* National Resource Center on Domestic Violence. Retrieved December 29, 2005, from www.vawnet.org/Sexual Violence/Research/VAWnetDocuments/AR_ RuralSA.php

Logan, T. K., Walker, R., Cole, J., Ratliff, S., & Leukfeld, C. (2003). Qualitative differences among rural and urban intimate violence victimization experiences and consequences: A pilot study. *Journal of Family Violence, 18*(2), 83–92.

McPherson, C. (1990). Bringing redress to abused disabled persons. *NOVA Network Information Bulletin,* 14. Washington, DC: NOVA.

Melling, L. (1984). Wife abuse in the deaf community. *Response to violence in the family and sexual assault, 7*(1), 1–2.

Murdaugh, C., Hunt, S., Sowell, R., & Santana, I. (2004). Domestic violence in Hispanics in the Southeastern United States: A survey and needs analysis. *Journal of Family Violence, 19*(2), 107–115.

National Center for Injury Prevention and Control. (2005). Intimate partner violence fact sheet. Retrieved September 25, 2006, from www.cdc .gov/ncipc/factsheet/ipvfacts.htm

National Coalition for the Homeless. (2005, June). *How many people experience homelessness* (NCH Fact Sheet #2). Washington, DC: Author.

National Law Center on Homelessness and Poverty. (2004, January). *Homelessness in the United States and the human right to housing.* Washington, DC: Author.

Nunez, R., & Fox, C. (1999). A snapshot of family homelessness across America. *Political Science Quarterly, 114*(2), 289–307.

Office for Victims of Crime. (2000). *Serving crime victims with disabilities: Meet us where we are* (videotape). Washington, DC: U.S. Department of Justice, Office for Victims of Crime.

Office for Victims of Crime. (2002). *First response to victims of crime who have a disability.* Washington, DC: U.S. Department of Justice, Office for Victims of Crime.

Pilkington, N. W., & D'Augelli, A. R. (1995). Victimization of lesbian, gay, and bisexual youth in community settings. *Journal of Community Psychology, 23,* 33–56.

Rossi, P. H. (1989). *Down and out in America: The origins of homelessness.* Chicago: University of Chicago Press.

Ruback, R. B., & Menard, K. S. (2001). Rural-urban differences in sexual victimization and reporting: Analyses using UCR and crisis center data. *Criminal Justice and Behavior, 28*(2), 131–155.

Ryan, C., & Rivers, I. (2003). Lesbian, gay, bisexual, and transgender youth: Victimization and its correlates in the U.S.A. and U.K. *Culture, Health, & Sexuality, 5*(2), 103–119.

Sanders-Phillips, K., Moisan, P. A., Wadlington, S., Morgan, S., & English, K. (1995). Ethnic differences in psychological functioning among black and Latino sexually abused girls. *Child Abuse and Neglect, 19*(6), 691–706.

Savin-Williams, R. C. (1994). Verbal and physical abuse as stressors in the lives of lesbian, gay male, and bisexual youths: Associations with school problems, running away, substance abuse, prostitution, and suicide. *Journal of Consulting and Clinical Psychology, 62*(2), 261.

Schlay, A. B., & Rossi, P. H. (1992). Social science research and contemporary studies of homelessness. *Annual Review of Sociology, 18,* 129–160.

Snow, K. (1992, June). The violence at home. *Advocate,* 60.

Sobsey, D. (1994). Violence and abuse in the lives of people with disabilities: The end of silent acceptance? Reprinted by Wisconsin Coalition Against Sexual Assault: *Information Fact Sheets.*

Terrell, N. E. (1997). Street life: Aggravated and sexual assaults among homeless and runaway adolescents. *Youth & Society, 28*(3), 267–290.

Tjaden, P., & Thoennes, N. (1998). *Prevalence, incidence and consequences of violence against women: Findings from National Violence Against Women Survey.* Washington, DC: U.S. Department of Justice, Office of Justice Programs, National Institute of Justice.

Tyiska, C. (1998). *Working with victims of crime and disabilities. Office for Victims of Crime Bulletin.* Washington, DC: U.S. Department of Justice, Office for Victims of Crime.

Tyler, K. A., & Johnson, K. A. (2004). Victims and offenders: Accounts of paybacks, invulnerability, and financial gain among homeless youth. *Deviant Behavior, 25,* 427–449.

U.S. Bureau of the Census. (1991). *Fact sheet for the 1990 decennial census: Counts of persons in shelters for the homeless and visible in street locations, April 12.* Washington, DC: U.S. Bureau of the Census.

United States Conference of Mayors. (2000). *A status report on hunger and homelessness in American cities.* Retrieved February 2, 2006, from www.usmayors.org

U.S. Department of Housing and Urban Development. (1984). *A report to the secretary on the homeless and emergency shelters.* Washington, DC: U.S. Department of Housing and Urban Development Office.

U.S. Department of Justice, Office for Victims of Crime. (1998). *New directions from the field: Victims' rights and services for the 21st century.* Washington, DC: U.S. Department of Justice, Office for Victims of Crime.

Valenti-Heim, D., & Schwartz, L. (1995). The sexual abuse interview for those with developmental disabilities. Reprinted by Wisconsin Coalition Against Sexual Assault: *Information Fact Sheets.*

Wallace, H. (2005). *Family violence: Legal, medical, and social perspectives* (4th ed.). Boston: Pearson.

Websdale, N. S., & Johnson, B. (1997). The policing of domestic violence in rural and urban areas: The voices of battered women in Kentucky. *Policing and Society, 6,* 297–317.

Websdale, N. S., & Johnson, B. (1998). An ethnos-statistical comparison of the forms and levels of women battering in urban and rural areas of Kentucky. *Criminal Justice Review, 23*(2), 161–196.

Weisheit, R. A., & Donnermeyer, J. F. (2000). Change and continuity in crime in rural America. In *The nature of crime: Continuity and change* (pp. 309–357). Washington, DC: U.S. Department of Justice, Justice Programs.

Weisheit, R. A., Falcone, D., & Wells, E. (1996). *Crime and policing in rural and small-town America.* Prospect Heights, IL: Waveland Press.

Wenzel, S. L., Leake, B. D., & Gelberg, L. (2000). Health of homeless women with recent experiences of rape. *Journal of General Internal Medicine, 15,* 265–268.

Wenzel, S. L., Leake, B. D., & Gelberg, L. (2001). Risk factors for major violence among homeless women. *Journal of Interpersonal Violence, 16*(8), 739–752.

Williams, M. L. & Robinson, A. L. (2004). Problems and prospects with policing the lesbian, gay, and bisexual community in Wales. *Policing & Society, 14*(3), 213–232.

Worthington, G. M. (1984, March/April). Sexual exploitation and abuse of people with disabilities. *Center for Women Policy Studies, 7–8.*

Wright, T. (2000). Resisting homelessness: Global, national, and local solutions. *Contemporary Sociology, 29*(1), 27–43.

Young, M. (1997). Victim rights and services: A modern saga. In R. C. Davis, A. J. Lurigio, & W. G. Skogan (Eds.), *Victims of crime* (2nd ed., pp. 194–210). Thousand Oaks, CA: Sage Publications.

Young, M. E., Nosek, M. A., Howland, C. A., Chanpong, G., & Rintala, D. H. (1997). Prevalence of abuse of women with physical disabilities. *Archives of Physical Medicine and Rehabilitation, 78,* 34–38.

Zorza, J. (1991). Woman battering: A major cause of homelessness. *Clearinghouse Review, 25*(4), 324–348.

Index

About the Editors

Rob Davis is Senior Research Analyst with the RAND Corporation. He has directed more than 30 projects on policing, domestic violence, victimization, crime prevention, and prosecution for federal and state governments and private foundations. His interests include victimization, victim experiences in the criminal justice system, repeat victimization, and police accountability. He has authored two books on crime prevention and is editor of four books on crime prevention and crime victims.

Susan Herman is Associate Professor in the Department of Criminal Justice and Sociology at Pace University. From 1997 to 2005, she served as the executive director of the National Center for Victims of Crime, the nation's leading resource and advocacy organization for crime victims. Previously, Herman served as director of community services at the Enterprise Foundation, director of the Domestic Violence Division of Victim Services (now Safe Horizon) in New York City, and special counsel to the police commissioner of New York City. Her principle interest is in developing the concept of parallel justice for victims of crime.

Arthur J. Lurigio, a psychologist, is Associate Dean for faculty in the College of Arts and Sciences and a professor of criminal justice and psychology at Loyola University Chicago, where he received tenure in 1993. He is also a member of the graduate faculty and director of the Center for the Advancement of Research, Training, and Education (CARTE) at Loyola University Chicago and a senior research advisor at Illinois Treatment Alternatives for Safe Communities (TASC). In 2003, Lurigio was named a faculty scholar, the highest honor bestowed on senior faculty at Loyola University Chicago. His research is primarily in the areas of offender drug abuse and dependence problems, mental disorders and crime, community corrections, police–community relations, criminal victimization, and victim services.

About the Contributors

Anna Alvazzi del Frate is a research officer at the United Nations Office on Drugs and Crime (UNODC) in Vienna, Austria. In her current position and previously with the United Nations Interregional Crime and Justice Research Institute (UNICRI), where she worked between 1990 and 2003, she acted as the UN coordinator for the International Crime Victim Survey (ICVS). She has developed victim surveys in many developing countries, in particular in Africa. Other major areas of research include crime prevention, crime statistics, corruption, transnational organized crime and illegal markets, comparative criminal justice systems, environmental crime, and gender-related issues.

Eve Buzawa is Professor and Chairperson of the Department of Criminal Justice and Criminology at the University of Massachusetts-Lowell. Her research interests and publications encompass a wide range of issues pertaining to policing, domestic violence, and violence against women. She has authored and edited numerous books and monographs, including her most recently published book, *Domestic Violence: The Criminal Justice Response* (2003). She is past president of the Society of Police and Criminal Psychology, past president of the Northeast Association of Criminal Justice Sciences, and past board member for the Academy of Criminal Justice Sciences.

Leah E. Daigle is Assistant Professor of justice studies in the Department of Political Science at Georgia Southern University. Her most recent research has centered on repeat sexual victimization of college women and the responses that women use during and after being sexually victimized. Her other research interests include the development and continuation of offending over time and gender differences in the antecedents to and consequences of criminal victimization and participation across the life course.

Debbie Deem, FBI victim specialist for Los Angeles, has worked with hundreds of victims of personal financial crime, including identity theft; cybercrimes; mass marketing crimes; and health care, real estate, and investment fraud, in addition to her work assisting victims of violent crimes. She has provided training and consultation for many years on issues related to victims of financial crime and restitution, including assisting in creating Office for Victims of Crime resource material for financial crime victims and identity theft. She is a coauthor of "Financial Crime," in the National Victim Assistance Academy Text (2002 edition), published by the Office for Victims of Crime.

Charles DiMaggio is Assistant Professor of clinical epidemiology at Columbia University's Mailman School of Public Health, where he is investigating the behavioral health effects of the terrorist attacks of September 11, 2001, as part of a Centers for Disease Control and Prevention Health

Protection Research Initiative grant. He served 12 years as chief physician assistant and director of research for the emergency department at Mt. Sinai School of Medicine at Elmhurst Hospital Center, New York, where he also coordinated the Advanced Trauma Life Support training program for physicians and served on the hospital's institutional review board. As a chief research scientist with the Nassau County Department of Health, he worked on a variety of projects including bioterrorism preparedness, syndromic surveillance, and health disparities.

Carol F. Dorris is the public policy senior staff attorney for the National Center for Victims of Crime in Washington, D.C., where she has been on staff since 1991. She provides legislative technical assistance across the country and conducts comprehensive research on pertinent victim-related legal issues for state and local jurisdictions. She also directs the VictimLaw project, the nation's first public access comprehensive victim rights legislative database. She is a graduate of Pennsylvania State University and the University of Georgia School of Law.

Edna Erez is Professor and head of the Criminal Justice department at the University of Illinois at Chicago. She has written more than 100 publications in criminology/victimology, addressing topics such as victim participation in justice, women in crime and justice, violence against women, electronic monitoring of domestic violence, immigrants as victims, and victims of terrorism. She is past editor of *Justice Quarterly* and is currently coeditor of the *International Review of Victimology* and associate editor of *Victims and Violence*.

Amy Farrell is Principal Research Scientist and Associate Director of the Institute on Race and Justice at Northeastern University. Her research focuses on disparate treatment of individuals within the criminal justice system, including race and gender differences in traffic enforcement practices, disparate prosecution and sentencing outcomes in state and federal criminal justice systems, and bias in crime reporting.

David Finkelhor is Director of Crimes Against Children Research Center, Codirector of the Family Research Laboratory, and Professor of sociology at the University of New Hampshire. He has been studying the problems of child victimization, child maltreatment, and family violence since 1977. He is well known for his conceptual and empirical work on the problem of child sexual abuse, reflected in publications such as *Sourcebook on Child Sexual Abuse* (1986) and *Nursery Crimes* (1988). He has also written about child homicide, missing and abducted children, children exposed to domestic and peer violence, and other forms of family violence. He is editor and author of 11 books and more than 150 journal articles and book chapters.

Bonnie S. Fisher is Professor in the Division of Criminal Justice at the University of Cincinnati. Her two current research projects examine predictors of reoccurring sexual victimization among college women, and the extent and effects of drug-facilitated sexual assault victimization and perpetration among college students. Her recent published work examined repeat victimization and its characteristics among college and older women and the effectiveness of self-protective actions in rape and other sexual victimization incidents among college women.

Deborah Fry is Research Director at the New York City Alliance Against Sexual Assault. At the Alliance, Deborah is currently working on four citywide research projects: a prevalence study of dating violence and exposure to child sexual abuse among New York City (NYC) youth; a community-needs assessment of undocumented immigrant women in NYC around sexual violence; mapping of acute care services for sexual assault survivors in NYC emergency departments; and a citywide survey of survivors and their experiences with service providers. In addition, Deborah also provides research technical assistance to NYC rape crisis programs.

Sandro Galea is Associate Professor of epidemiology at the University of Michigan School of Public Health. He was formerly associate director of the Center for Urban Epidemiologic Studies at the New York Academy of Medicine and assistant professor at the Columbia Mailman School of Public Health. Galea is primarily interested in the social and economic production of health, particularly mental health and behavior in urban settings. He has an abiding interest in the social and health consequences of collectively experienced traumatic events and has published extensively in these fields. His work includes basic epidemiologic research, theoretic development, and the application of innovative methods to epidemiologic problems.

Diane Green received her Ph.D. in social work from the University of Texas at Austin in 1999. She is currently Associate Professor and director of field placements, Department of Social Work, Florida Atlantic University, Boca Raton. She has five years' experience as a medical social worker and domestic violence advocate in Texas.

Pamela Guthrie is Research Analyst at the Vera Institute of Justice, where she has worked on studies of sexual revictimization and human trafficking. She is also a crisis counselor for sexual assault and domestic violence survivors and runs a group on relationship violence for teenage ex-prostitutes. Guthrie has an M.A. in psychology from the City University in New York and is pursuing her doctorate in clinical psychology at Long Island University.

Candace Heisler served as Assistant District Attorney for the city and county of San Francisco for more than 25 years. She served as Chairperson of the California District Attorney's Association Domestic Violence Committee. She has authored numerous articles on domestic violence and elder abuse and developed curriculum for judicial and law enforcement officials on these topics. She has conducted trainings and presented throughout the United States on elder abuse and domestic violence subjects. She is also an assistant adjunct professor of law at the University of California's Hastings College.

Susan Howley has worked at the National Center for Victims of Crime since 1991, serving as its director of public policy since 1999. She is one of the nation's foremost experts on crime victim legislation and regularly provides technical assistance to federal and state lawmakers and advocates. She has testified before state legislatures on bills designed to strengthen the rights of crime victims and has conducted numerous trainings on public policy at the national and local levels.

Jack McDevitt is Associate Dean for Research and Graduate Studies at the College of Criminal Justice at Northeastern University. Jack also directs the Institute on Race and Justice and the Center for Criminal Justice Policy Research. Jack is the coauthor of three books: *Hate Crimes: The Rising Tide of Bigotry and Bloodshed* (1993 with Jack Levin), *Hate Crime Revisited: American War on Those Who Are Different* (2002 with Jack Levin), and *Victimology* (2002 with Judy Sgarzi).

Bernadette T. Muscat has worked with victims of domestic violence by serving as a legal advocate and by providing counseling, education, and legal advocacy in shelter and court environments. She has worked with law enforcement agencies, victim service programs, and court programs in program and policy development, evaluation, research, and training to ensure effective administration of victim assistance. She has also worked with state coalitions to develop and implement victim-related polices. She has written and presented on a variety of topics related to victimology, family violence, female victimization, domestic violence, underserved victim populations, and campus-oriented crimes.

Lisa Nerenberg has been actively involved in the field of elder abuse prevention for more than 20 years. For 16 years, she directed the San Francisco Consortium for Elder Abuse Prevention. She has presented at hundreds of professional forums, testified before congressional committees, served on governmental advisory committees, and provided training and technical assistance to state and local programs. She has authored numerous articles, chapters, and publications, including a series of 18 technical assistance manuals for the National Center on Elder Abuse on topics ranging from coalition building to elder financial abuse.

Chris O'Sullivan has conducted studies of the social dynamics and prosecution of group sexual assault, served as consultant on two national studies of trafficking in persons, and was coprincipal investigator of a study of revictimization of sexual assault survivors. She has served as principal investigator or coprincipal investigator on 15 studies of domestic violence and sexual assault funded by the National Institute of Justice, the State Justice Institute, and other government agencies and foundations. Currently, she is working with the Center for Court Innovation and VCS of Rockland on research on batterer programs and domestic violence courts.

Albert Roberts has more than 30 years of full-time university teaching experience at the undergraduate and graduate levels in both criminal justice and social work and 18 years' administrative experience as department chairperson, program director, project director, and director of field placements. He has been a tenured professor of criminal justice and social work at Rutgers University since 1989. He also has more than 225 publications to his credit and he is Editor in Chief of the *Victims and Offenders* journal.

Julian Roberts is currently a member of the Centre of Criminology, University of Oxford. He is the editor of the *European Journal of Criminology,* and his research interests include sentencing, public opinion and criminal justice, and the role of the victim in the criminal process. Recent publications include *The Virtual Prison* (2005) and *Understanding Public Attitudes to Criminal Justice* (2005).

Danielle Rousseau is a Research Assistant with the Institute on Race and Justice. Prior to coming to Northeastern University, she worked as a therapist in both correctional and community settings.

Jessica Snowden is a doctoral candidate in the Clinical Psychology Program at Loyola University Chicago. She earned her master's degree in Clinical Psychology and is completing her master of jurisprudence degree in child and family law at Loyola's Law School. Snowden has taught courses in psychology and in law and personality, and she has provided services in a variety of treatment settings for adolescents with behavioral problems.

Nan Stein has been a Senior Research Scientist at the Center for Research on Women at Wellesley College since 1992, where she directs research projects on bullying, sexual harassment, and gender violence in elementary and secondary schools. She has coauthored four teacher's guides on sexual harassment, bullying, and gender violence as well as many book chapters, law review articles, and articles for academic journals and the educational press. She is author of *Classrooms and Courtrooms: Facing Sexual*

Harassment in K–12 Schools (1999). She has served as an expert witness in sexual harassment lawsuits and often provides commentary for the national press.

Martie Thompson is Research Associate Professor in the Department of Public Health Sciences and the director of research for the Center for Collaborative Research. Thompson received her Ph.D. in community psychology from Georgia State University. She received a National Research Service Award from the National Institute of Mental Health (NIMH) for postdoctoral training at Emory University School of Medicine and was an epidemic intelligence service officer at the Division of Violence Prevention at the Centers for Disease Control and Prevention. Her research has focused on risk factors and consequences of violent victimization.

Richard Titus received his Ph.D. in man–environment relations from Pennsylvania State University, his M.C.P. in urban planning and urban design, and his B. Arch. in architecture from the Massachusetts Institute of Technology. His research interests and publications have been in the areas of fraud victimization, burglary, situational crime prevention, victimology, and evaluation of victim services. In 1978–1979 he was Visiting Scholar, University of California at Berkeley, where his research explored the use of environmental displays and resident panels to conduct preconstruction security assessments in public housing.

Pat Tjaden has taught sociology and women's studies classes at various colleges and universities, including the University of North Carolina at Wilmington and the University of Canterbury in Christchurch, New Zealand. From 1987 to 2001, Tjaden was senior researcher at the Center for Policy Research in Denver, Colorado, where she conducted groundbreaking research on violence against women, including the first-ever national study of stalking in America. In recent years, she has worked with the United Nations Division for the Advancement of Women to develop international protocols for collecting data on violence against women.

Jeffrey A. Walsh is currently Assistant Professor of Criminal Justice Sciences. He teaches courses in research methods, juvenile justice, victimology, and criminological theory. He has worked with law enforcement agencies and with at-risk juvenile delinquent youth in clinical settings. He has research interests in a number of areas and has written and presented on topics including predatory crime, child–parent violence, parricide, underserved victim populations, motor vehicle theft, community correlates of crime, and the use of crime mapping and Geographic Information Systems (GIS).

Russell Wolff is a Senior Research Associate with the Institute on Race and Justice and Center for Criminal Justice Policy Research at Northeastern University. He is currently involved in several criminal justice practitioner/researcher partnerships working to reduce firearm and gang violence in Boston-area jurisdictions and in a national evaluation of police accountability and integrity initiatives.

Marlene A. Young is currently President of the International Organization for Victim Assistance. She received her PhD from Georgetown University and her JD from Wilamette University. She was a founding member of the National Organization for Victim Assistance, a former President of the Organization and its Executive Director for 25 years. She is the immediate past President of the World Society of Victimology.